The 28th North Ca

The 28th North Carolina Infantry

A Civil War History and Roster

FRANCES H. CASSTEVENS

McFarland & Company, Inc., Publishers
Jefferson, North Carolina, and London

The present work is a reprint of the library bound edition of
The 28th North Carolina Infantry: A Civil War History
and Roster, *first published in 2008 by McFarland.*

LIBRARY OF CONGRESS CATALOGUING-IN-PUBLICATION DATA

Casstevens, Frances Harding.
The 28th North Carolina Infantry :
a Civil War history and roster / Frances H. Casstevens.
p.   cm.
Includes bibliographical references and index.

ISBN 978-0-7864-7713-5
softcover : acid free paper

1. Confederate States of America. Army. North Carolina Infantry Regiment, 28th.
2. North Carolina — History — Civil War, 1861–1865 — Regimental histories.
3. United States — History — Civil War, 1861–1865 — Regimental histories.
4. Soldiers — North Carolina — Registers.
5. North Carolina — History — Civil War, 1861–1865 — Registers.
6. United States — History — Civil War, 1861–1865 — Registers.
7. United States — History — Civil War, 1861–1865 — Campaigns.
I. Title.
E573.528th .C37   2013   973.7'456 — dc22   2007041252

BRITISH LIBRARY CATALOGUING DATA ARE AVAILABLE

Front cover: 28th Regiment's Flag, capture #364, captured either at Petersburg,
April 1-2, or surrendered at Appomattox, April 3-9 (courtesy North Carolina
Museum of History); background canvas iStockphoto/Thinkstock

Manufactured in the United States of America

*McFarland & Company, Inc., Publishers
Box 611, Jefferson, North Carolina 28640
www.mcfarlandpub.com*

To my son Danny,
with my thanks for his diligent search for the letters
from Samuel and Greenberry Harding, my great-uncles,
both sergeants in Company I, 28th Regiment,
North Carolina Infantry, C.S.A.

To the memory of my son Tim (who died in 2003),
with eternal gratitude for his interest, support
and companionship on our many trips
to the battlefields of Virginia.

Acknowledgments

My sincere thanks to the members of the Harding family who cherished the past and saved all they could of their heritage. If not for that trait, I would not have the letters from Sam and Greenberry Harding written 1862–1864.

I am greatly indebted also to my cousins, Ruth Harding Lillie and Ailene Steelman, for the picture of Sam Harding. I appreciate Harvey Harding and Libby Harding Carter for sharing pictures and family documents.

Mike Cumbie and Greg Cheek, Confederate reenactors and history buffs, have helped in innumerable ways over the years by sharing their intimate knowledge of the war.

Special thanks to the North Carolina Department of Cultural Resources and the North Carolina Museum of History, Raleigh, North Carolina; Duke University, Durham, North Carolina; Auburn University Archives and Manuscript Department, Auburn, Alabama; and the Library of the University of North Carolina at Charlotte, North Carolina.

Michael Hardy, an author, teacher and reenactor, graciously shared some of the source material he found about the 28th. He deserves special recognition, both for past publications and future ones.

Cheryl L. Martin and her friend Gary D. Reeder have came to my aid and supplied out-of-print articles and the photographs of the Choplin boys.

I appreciate the Yadkin County Public Library for the resources they hold and for obtaining other documents through interlibrary loan.

And thanks to my daughter, Caren, who used her artistic talents to draw the maps.

Table of Contents

"28th Regiment, N.C.V."

Words by Lt. George B. Johnston, sung to the tune of *Dixie Land*. This song was sung while the 28th Regiment was camped near Wilmington in 1861, awaiting the arrival of their new colonel, James H. Lane. The chorus is sung after every verse.

Verse: Away down South in the Land of Cotton
Times of peace are not forgotten,
Look away, look away, look away, Dixie Land.
Though the clouds of war hang o'er,
We soon shall see its storm no more,
Look away, look away, look away, Dixie Land.

Chorus: Then shout "Hurrah for Dixie!"
Hurrah! Hurrah!
In Dixie Land we'll take our stand,
To live and die for Dixie;
Hurrah! Hurrah!
We'll live and die for Dixie!

Verse: 'Tis true their ships our ports blockade,
And cruel feet our soil invade;
But when the Twenty-Eighth gets there
The scamps will run in wild despair.
Look away, look away, look away, Dixie Land.

Verse: When "Norman" brings his boys to scurry
The Yankees better move in a hurry
The "Invincibles," if well equipped
And led by "Edwards," can't be whipped.
Look away, look away, look away, Dixie Land.

Verse: The Yankee rogues would better pack,
When the "Stanly Hunters" find their track.
When "Lowe" shall bid his "Farmers" fire
His foes will reap destruction dire.
Look away, look away, look away, Dixie Land.

Verse: As "Barringer" leads on his "Grays"
Full many a Yankee'll end his days.
When "Kinyoun" comes with his "Yadkin Boys,"

He'll put an end to the Yankees' joys.
Look away, look away, look away, Dixie Land.

Verse: And "Martin's Guards of Independence"
Have fame in store for their descendants.
And "Wright" with his "Cleveland Regulators,"
Will send dismay to Yankee traitors.
Look away, look away, look away, Dixie Land.

Verse: And "Speer" with his brilliant "Yadkin Stars,"
Will die in defense of the *Stars and Bars,*
While the "Stanly Guards," by "Moody" led,
Will be the Yankees' special dread.
Look away, look away, look away, Dixie Land.

Verse: The Twenty-Eighth is organized
With "Reeves" and "Lowe," both highly prized.
If "Lane" will only be their Colonel,
Then their glory'll be eternal.
Look away, look away, look away, Dixie Land.[1]

Words to this song were also brought home from the war by Isaac Columbus Poindexter, Sergeant, Company F, 28th Regiment, N.C. Infantry. This version was taken from "Song of the 28th NCT," online at http://hometown.aol.com/nct28th/song.html.

Introduction

In recent years, with revived interest in the Civil War, countless letters, diaries, and other documents have been unearthed and published. Each document provides another piece of the puzzle and helps us understand why the Northern states and the Southern states were fighting, often pitting brother against brother.

After writing several books on various men who were officers in both the Union Army and in the Confederate Army, I thought it was about time to write about some of the noncommissioned officers. What better place to start than with my own family?

For over 20 years I knew of the existence of some letters from my grandfather's brother, Samuel Speer Harding, a Confederate soldier who was killed in 1864. I kept asking my aunt to let me see them, and finally she located them. I was delighted as I read the letters and deciphered the fading handwriting.

After both my aunts died, my son Danny Casstevens was sorting through tons of books and papers (the Hardings tended to save everything), and he located several more letters from the Harding brothers. Because both of the Harding brothers were in Company I, 28th Regiment, North Carolina Troops, I incorporated their letters, among those written by others, into a history of the 28th Regiment. I was encouraged to do so by Greg Cheek, who was instrumental in forming a company of reenactors known as "Company I, 28th Regiment." The official formation of this company took place on August 13, 2006, 145 years after the original company was formed.

Although books and articles about many of the battles in which the 28th Regiment participated have been published, seldom is there mention of the 28th Regiment, North Carolina Infantry. Some of the battles, such as the engagement called "Hanover Court House," have received little attention. In 2006, Michael Hardy wrote a book entitled *The Battle of Hanover Court House,* in which he pointed out how little has been written about that battle, the first one in which the 28th Regiment was engaged. Hardy includes a 25-page appendix which lists both Confederate and Union casualties (killed, wounded, and captured) sustained on May 25, 1862.[1]

In the following work, for those not completely familiar with the hundreds of battles fought during the American Civil War, I have included a short, capsule summary of each battle, whose forces were involved and how many, the number of casualties, and the outcome as determined by the Civil War Sites Advisory Commission Report on the Nation's Civil War Battlefields, updated 1997. This brief summary is followed by the official reports found in the *Official Records of the War of the Rebellion* and in *North Carolina Troops, 1861–1865: A Roster.* Where available, the official reports have been supplemented by personal observances written by participants in the battles.

With any eyewitness accounts of an event, the official reports as well as individual accounts sometimes differ greatly. The commanders were at odds sometimes with who did what and who moved where, or over which regiment captured an enemy flag. They, the soldiers of more than a century ago, were only human, and thus subject to error, as we all are.

Please also keep in mind that numbers of men killed, wounded, and/or missing can vary from one report to another. Probably, casualties were even higher than reported.

Glossary of Military Terms

Abatis—a defensive line formed by felled trees with sharpened ends which are placed to face the enemy.

Arms—instruments or weapons of offense or defense.

Army—a large organized body of men armed for war; a unit capable of independent action, consisting usually of a headquarters, two or more corps, and artillery troops and trains.

Artillery—heavy, mounted guns, or cannons; that branch of an army involved with operating, aiming, and firing the heavy artillery.

Bivouac—an encampment for a short time, under temporary shelter or none at all.

Breastworks—A defensive works of moderate height, usually constructed quickly for protection from enemy attack. The breastworks can be made of a variety of materials: dirt, logs, brush, etc.

Brogans—shoes made of leather, often scarce in the South, worn by the foot soldier.

Caisson—a chest to hold ammunition; an ammunition wagon for mobile artillery.

Canister—a case for shot used at close range to be fired from a cannon.

Cannon—a generic term for all firearms larger than small arms (rifles, pistols). They are classified as guns, mortars, or howitzers according to the path of their projectiles. They can be smooth bored or rifled; breechloading or muzzleloading, made of iron, bronze, or steel. Widely employed were the Armstrong, Blakely, Brooke, Columbiad, Dahlgren, Napoleon, Parrott, Rodman, and Whitworth.

Carbine—a short, light rifle, used especially by cavalry.

Cartridge—a small paper tube which contained gunpower and a bullet.

Cavalry—a unit of the army which is mounted on horses. Sometimes they dismount and fight as infantry. Cavalry units, such as that of J.E.B. Stuart, were used to travel great distances in order gather information about the position of the enemy.

Commissary—the organized system for which armies are supplied with food and daily necessities; the department supplying equipment and provisions; an officer or officers who are in charge of distributing supplies, etc., to the military.

Conscription—a compulsory enrollment of men in military or naval service, a draft, imposed by governments during a time of war.

Corps—a subdivision of the military establishment, a large unit of an army comprising two divisions and auxiliary troops.

Detachment—a body of troops or part of the main body sent on a special mission.

Drill—act or exercise of training soldiers in the military art, as in the manual of arms.

Echelon—an arrangement of troops with the various units drawn up in parallel lines, but with each somewhat to the left or right of the one in the rear.

Enfield rifle—a muzzle-loading rifled musket which used .577 caliber bullets, manufactured in Middlesex, England, and imported and used during the Civil War, principally by Confederate troops.

Enfilade—raking gunfire in the direction of the entire length of a trench or line of troops.

Flank—the right or left of an army.

Forage—to scour the countryside in search of food, and sometimes taking it from farmers.

Grapeshot—a cluster of small iron balls used as a cannon charge.

Hardtack—a very hard biscuit made of flour, water, and sometimes salt.

Haversack—a canvas sack used to carry a soldier's food.

Howitzer—a short, light cannon used to deliver shells with a curved trajectory, which are angled at from 20 to 45 degrees, while having shells of lower muzzle velocities than those from guns.

Infantry—the majority of the army, soldiers trained, armed and equipped to fight on foot.

Kepi—a small cap or hat which was part of the standard uniform.

Knapsack—a pack carried by a soldier on his back to hold clothing and other personal items.

Maneuver—to perform movements in military or naval tactics for getting an advantage in an attack or in defense; to cause to execute tactical movements.

Mess—a group of persons who regularly eat together.

Musket—a smoothbored firearm, carried and used by the infantry.

Napoleon—a smoothbored, muzzleloading field piece; the 12-pounder was a basic piece of artillery. It had a caliber of 4.62 inches, and could fire grapeshot, shell, balls or canister effectively. Maximum range was 1,680 yards. This cannon reportedly inflected more injuries than all others combined.

Ordnance—military supplies, which includes all artillery with mounts, carriages, and ammunition, small arms, and machinery, and material for making or repairing these. Also refers to cannon and artillery.

Picket—a sentinel; a detached body of soldiers which guard the main body of troops from surprise attack.

Pontoon bridge—a bridge across a stream made by securing a number of boats (usually flat-bottomed) to support some sort of roadway so that troops, vehicles, etc., can cross over the stream.

Quartermaster—a commissioned officer whose duty is to provide quarters, clothing, transportation, forage, subsistence, etc., for troops.

Reconnaissance—An examination of a territory in order to gain information about enemy troops, the terrain, or other information regarding the opposition.

Reconnoiter—The act of examining or surveying for military purposes.

Redan—a work having two parapets forming a salient angle.

Rifle—a firearm with grooves inside the barrel that causes a projectile to spin and thus gives greater accuracy than a musket.

Salient—an outwardly protecting part of a trench system or line of defense.

Sap—an extension of a trench dug from within the trench itself; one dug from the attacker's line to a point beneath the enemy's works.

Sibley tent—a conical, light, easily-pitched tent invented by Henry Hopkins Sibley, with a single pole held up by a tripod. A fire could be made in the center of the tent.

Skirmishers—soldiers deployed ahead of the main body of troops to engage in small fights (skirmishes).

Slouch hat—a wide-brimmed hat sometimes worn instead of a kepi.

Spencer rifle—a breechloading, repeating rifled carbine patented in 1860 by Christopher M. Spencer.

Trench—a narrow ditch with the earth piled in front of it which soldiers use to protect them from enemy fire, and from which they could fire at the enemy (e.g., the trenches around Petersburg, Virginia).

Whitworth gun—a rifled cannon made in England of various calibers, used by the Confederacy. The cannon used solid shot principally. Those manufactured after 1863 were muzzleloaders.

Zouaves—some of the volunteer regiments in the Union Army who adopted the colorful dress similar to that of the Algerians, and noted for their dash and valor.

Chapter 1

Spring 1861: North Carolina
Leaves the Union

You can get no troops from North Carolina.
— Governor John Ellis[1]

The causes of the war fought in America from 1861 to 1865 are more numerous than the names by which that conflict is called. The reasons for the war have been explored in countless books and articles, so that complicated and unresolved subject will not be further explored in this work.

Southern States Secede

The slow-burning fuse of discontent in the nation was accelerated on November 5, 1860, with the election of Abraham Lincoln to the presidency of the United States. Lincoln's victory triggered the secession of states in the lower South.[2] South Carolina took the lead and seceded from the Union on December 20, 1860. In January of 1861, that state was followed by Mississippi, Florida, Alabama, Georgia, and Louisiana.[3]

Secession Convention Proposed, February 1861

North Carolina was not so quick to leave the Union. In January of 1861, the North Carolina General Assembly passed the Convention Act, which authorized the voters of the state to hold a convention to decide the question, and allowed them to elect 120 delegates to attend that convention. Of the 120 delegates elected on February 28, 1861, 42 were for secession, 28 were "conditional unionists," and 50 were "unconditional unionists." Out of the 86 counties that existed in North Carolina at the time, only 30 counties elected delegates who favored secession. Of those counties who elected delegates who were pro-secession, 22 had a slave population which exceeded the white population by 25 percent.

Overall, the people of North Carolina were opposed to secession, and they voted 47,322 to 46,672 against even calling a convention. Thus, a convention which might have been controlled by unionists never was held.[4] In Yadkin County, one of the counties of the Piedmont section of the state, the sentiment was 1,490 against to 34 for holding a convention to decide whether to remain in the Union or to secede.[5]

War Begins at Fort Sumter

A string of Federal forts ran along the east coast from Massachusetts to the Florida Keys. South Carolina again took the first steps toward war when it determined that Fort Sumter in

Charleston Harbor could not be allowed to remain under Federal control. The fort was bombarded and Major Anderson surrendered to the South Carolina forces. The capture of Fort Sumter was the spark that ignited a war that would last four years and devastate the South.

After the capture of Fort Sumter on April 12, 1861, by Confederate forces, President Lincoln called for troops to bring South Carolina in line. Those Southern states that had not already seceded were motivated to do so by his action. The Southern states would not fight against their sister state, South Carolina. Determined to protect themselves from an invasion by Lincoln's Union Army, they joined with South Carolina in forming the Confederate States of America.

North Carolina Unprepared for War

In 1860, North Carolina was just beginning to be industrialized. From 1850 to 1860, there was an increase in industries from 2,663 to 3,689. However, the majority of the population was engaged in profitable agricultural pursuits.[6] The total population in the state in 1860 was 992,622. Of that number, only 24,544 (2.5 percent) lived in the towns and cities. The majority of the people (968,068) lived on farms or in very small communities.[7]

The largest town and leading seaport and railroad terminal was Wilmington. It had a population in 1860 of 9,552. Fayetteville and Raleigh each had about 4,000 inhabitants, with Salisbury and Charlotte trailing with only about 2,000 each. Several other towns had about 1,000 people, while the majority of towns (25) had a population of less than 1,000.[8]

There was much Union sentiment in the state, and many people, whether slaveholders or not, did not wish to leave the Union. The Piedmont and Mountain sections of the state had few slaves, and many of the people, especially in those areas, did not wish to leave the Union. Others throughout the state did not want to see the state embroiled in war. The Friends (Quakers) were opposed to both slavery and war. Those people who wanted to leave the Union were called "secessionists," while those who favored remaining were called "unionists." Yet even the unionists in North Carolina were divided, while the secessionists were united and they prevailed in the movement to secede.[9]

Soon after Fort Sumter in Charleston Harbor was captured, North Carolina leaned more toward secession. John W. Ellis, governor of North Carolina, responded quickly to Lincoln's call for 75,000 troops to invade the South. On April 17, 1861, Ellis stated emphatically and in no uncertain terms, as he denied the President's request for troops:

> I regard the levy of troops made by the administration for the purpose of subjugating the States of the South as in violation of the Constitution and a gross usurpation of power. I can be no party to this wicked violation of the laws of the country, and to this war upon the liberties of a free people. You can get no troops from North Carolina.[10]

The governor saw Lincoln's action as an infringement on individual rights, an "invasion of the peaceful homes of the South," and a "violent subversion of the liberties of a free people...."[11]

Future governor Zebulon B. Vance recalled his own thoughts in April of 1861: "If we had to shed blood, I preferred to shed Northern rather than Southern blood. If we had to slay, I had rather slay strangers than my own kindred and neighbors." Vance believed at the time, whether it was right or wrong, "that communities and States should go together and face the horrors of war in a body — sharing a common fate, rather than endure the unspeakable calamities of internecine strife...."[12]

Governor Ellis ordered the seizure of the Federal forts Caswell and Johnston, the Federal arsenal at Fayetteville, and the United States mint at Charlotte. He called for 30,000 volunteers, and he summoned a special session of the legislature which authorized the election of delegates for a convention to decide on the secession question.[13]

North Carolina Secession Convention, May 20, 1861

Another general election was held across North Carolina to choose delegates to attend a state convention. Delegates were also elected from each county to attend the Provisional Congress of the Confederate States. From Yadkin County, R.C. Puryear was elected. Those delegates chosen to attend were listed in papers across the state.[14]

On May 20, 1861, a convention of 120 delegates approved an ordinance introduced by Burton Craig which stated that "the union now subsisting between the state of North Carolina and the other states, under the title of 'The United States of America,' is hereby dissolved, and that the state of North Carolina is in full possession and exercise of all those rights of sovereignty which belong and appertain to a free and independent state." That same day, the convention ratified the Provisional Constitution of the Confederate States of America.[15] North Carolina was now part of the Confederate States of America. The state convention also ordered that the flag of North Carolina should consist of a red field with a white star in the center. Two dates were to be inscribed in a semi-circular form above the star, "May 20, 1775," and below the star, "May 20th, 1861."[16] The first was the date of the Mecklenburg Declaration of Independence from England, and the second, the date of independence from the United States.

May 20, 1861, the day North Carolina entered the fight for "Southern Independence," was a fateful day which forever changed the course of history of the nation, the North and the South, and especially the state of North Carolina.

The war pitted 13 (actually 11) Southern states against 21 Northern "free states" and 8 western territories. The three border states (Kentucky, Maryland, and Missouri) were pro–Confederate slave states forced to remain in the union by Federal troops, which resulted in much internal conflict. Stars were included on the Confederate flag for the states of Kentucky and Missouri but they never actually joined the Confederacy.[17]

No matter what the period 1861–1865 is called, it was a bloody four years of death, destruction, and devastation. The most commonly used names for the war give some idea as to what some believed was caused of the war: *The Civil War* (used by Northerners and others for brevity); *the American Civil War*; *the War of the Rebellion* (part of the title of the *Official Records of the War of the Rebellion*); *the War between the Confederate States of America and the United States of America* (the official name used on documents during the War in Richmond, shortened to the following); *the War Between the States* (now preferred by many Southerners); *the War for States' Rights* (a name coined in the 20th Century, not used in the 1860s).

Other less commonly used terms, especially popular in the South, in the 20th and 21st centuries were: *War in Defense of Virginia*; *Mr. Lincoln's War*; *the War of Secession*; *the Lost Cause* (title of a book published in 1866); *the Late Unpleasantness*; and simply *the War*.

In the Northern states, another set of terms are used to describe the conflict: *War of the Insurrection*; *Slaveholder's War*; *Great Rebellion*; *War to Save the Union*.

Writers and historians continue to invent new terms to describe the war of 1861–1865: *The War of Southern Independence* (also popular with Southerners); *the War of Northern Aggression* (popularized by Neo-Confederates in the 1980s). Some terms that seldom appear in print or in conversation, but have been used occasionally, are: *War for Abolition*; *War of Southern Reaction*; *War to Prevent Southern Independence*.[18]

Likewise, there were names used to designate the different armies. The United States forces were called "the Union," "Federals," and "Yankees."[19] Sometimes they were referred to by Confederates as "Bluecoats" or "Yellow bellies."

Southern forces were commonly called "the Confederates, "the South," the "Rebels," and their home land was "Dixie." Individual soldiers were often referred to as "Billy Yank" (Yankee) or "Johnny Reb" (Confederate).

To complicate matters even further, most battles have at least two names—the one used by the Confederacy (usually from the closest town or community), and the one used by the Union (usually named after the nearest stream). For example, the battles at or near Manassas, Virginia, are called 1st Manassas and 2nd Manassas by Southerners, and 1st Bull Run and 2nd Bull Run by the North and the Union forces. A run was a small creek.

Chapter 2

The 28th Regiment, North Carolina Volunteer Infantry Is Formed

... Look Away, Dixie Land.[1]

The South Mobilizes for War

Once North Carolina joined the Confederacy, men of all ages were eager to show the Northern aggressors that the South could win a war, and win it in record time. These volunteers enlisted in companies which were soon joined together to form regiments.

The Company — Basic Unit of a Regiment

A company, the basic unit of the armies engaged in the Civil War, consisted of approximately 100 men commanded by a captain. At first, these companies were called by a local name, such as the "Yadkin Stars," or the "Surry Regulars." Those designations were soon dropped in favor of the letters A through K. The letter "J" was omitted because it was too similar to "I."

Ten companies made up a regiment. The regiment consisted of approximately 1,000 men and was commanded by a colonel. If a unit had fewer than 10 companies, it was called a "battalion" instead.

The 28th Regiment consisted of 10 companies:

Company A — Surry County, "Surry Regulars"
Company B — Gaston County, "The Gaston Invincibles"
Company C — Catawba County, "The Catawba Farmers"
Company D — Stanly County, "The Stanly Yankee Hunters"
Company E — Montgomery County, "The Montgomery Grays"
Company F — Yadkin County, "The Yadkin Boys"
Company G — Orange County, "Guards of Independence"
Company H — Cleveland County, "The Cleveland Regulators"
Company I — Yadkin County, "Yadkin Stars"
Company K — Stanly County, "The Stanly Guards."[2]

How Company F, 28th Regiment was formed is typical. According to Captain John Hendricks Kinyoun, who kept records in a small, 3 × 6 inch account book, Company F was formed on June 12, 1861, from men who lived in the East Bend area of Yadkin County. Three days later, the new company was "accepted by the Governor." On July 17, the company camped at East Bend. (That camp is believed to have been on the southeast side of the intersection of the Flint Hill

Company and 28th Regimental officers, from Walter Clark, ed., *Histories of the Several Regiments and Battalions from North Carolina in the Great War, 1861–1865, Written by Members of the Respective Commands.* 1. S.S. Bohannon, Capt., Co. I; 2. Thomas B. Lane, Asst. Surgeon; 3. James M. Crowell, Capt., Co. K; 4. Romulus S. Folger, Adjutant; 5. J.P. Little, 1st Lt. and Ensign, Co. C; 6. M.A. Throneburg, 1st Lt., Co. C; 7. M.M. Throneburg, 2nd Lt., Co. C (courtesy of the North Carolina Department of Archives and History).

Road and the Highway 67 Bypass, opposite the present East Bend Elementary School.) About two weeks later, on August 6, the company moved to Enon (a small community on Old Highway 421 near the Yadkin River where Conrad's Ferry once operated).[3]

The Brigade

The next unit was a brigade, usually composed of four regiments. The brigade usually numbered 4000–5000 men. The brigade was commanded by a brigadier general. Confederate brigades were usually named after their commanders (e.g., Branch's Brigade).

The Division

Two to five brigades made up a division. At its normal strength, a division contained about 12,000 men, headed by a major general. A Confederate division often had twice as many men as Union division.

The Corps

Three divisions made up a corps, which usually contained about 36,000 men. The corps was commanded by a major general in the Union Army, or a lieutenant general in the Confederate States Army.

The highest level of organization was an army. The Confederate armies usually were named after territories, such as the Army of Northern Virginia, commanded by General Robert E. Lee, while the Union armies were named after rivers, such as the Army of the Potomac.[4]

After four years of fighting, North Carolina could claim that her troops were *First at Bethel, Fartherest to the Front at Gettysburg and Chickamauga, and Last at Appomattox.* That distinction was earned at a terrible cost in the lives of the soldiers of the combined North Carolina Regiments and the citizens of North Carolina.

Camp Fisher, High Point

Company B, the Gaston Invincibles, was organized in August of 1861 at Dallas, the county seat. The soldiers then marched to Brevard Station to take the train to the training camp. Before the boys left, the ladies of Gaston County treated "The Invincibles" with a picnic at the train station, and the new recruits enjoyed a fine dinner at a Charlotte hotel along the way.[5]

While the men were at Camp Fisher, Captain John H. Kinyoun (Company F) made two trips to Raleigh on business concerning his company. One of those trips, he mentioned in his account book, was "about getting b[o]unty money for camp." His expense for that trip was $6.00. Kinyoun mentioned many items that were purchased for the new officers of his company at Camp Fisher: fish, tent, bathtub, candles, sausage, and salt.[6]

The new companies were placed in 28th Regiment, North Carolina Volunteer Infantry at Camp Fisher, near High Point, on September 21, 1861. At the time of its organization, the regiment contained about 900 men.[7] Shortly thereafter, the men held an election. They chose James Henry Lane, colonel; Thomas L. Lowe, Lt. Col., and Richard E. Reeves, Major. At the time of the election, Colonel Lane was a lieutenant colonel in the 1st North Carolina Volunteers, and Lowe and Reeves were captains of individual companies.[8]

"The Yadkin Boys" (soon to be designated as Company F) left Yadkin County and arrived on August 27 at Camp Fisher, near High Point. A month later, September 30, this company and others left for Wilmington. They arrived in the coastal city on October 2, 1861.[9]

In 1861, the excitement and the urge to enlist were at their peak among both young and old. James Howell, of Montgomery County, enlisted in Company E. He was 67 years old (born about 1794), the oldest man to enlist in the entire regiment. Howell was discharged in December of that year because he suffered with bronchitis and chronic diarrhea.[10]

On the other side of the coin, some were just as determined not to serve. Alexander Lanier, a resident of Gaston County, enlisted on July 30, 1861, at age 23. Two and a half months later, he was discharged for "cutting off three of his fingers." The records do not state whether this was deliberate or not, but self-mutilation was not uncommon to avoid military service.[11]

Brigadier General James Henry Lane (1833–1907)

At the time of his election, James H. Lane was serving as a lieutenant colonel of the First North Carolina Regiment. He was not from North Carolina, but was a native of Virginia.[12] Lane was promoted to lieutenant colonel of the 1st North Carolina Volunteers after D.H. Hill was promoted from colonel to brigadier general. Subsequently, Lane was then elected colonel of the 28th Regiment.[13] Captain George B. Johnston wrote Lane on September 21, 1861, to advise him that he had been elected unanimously as colonel of the regiment. Johnston told Lane that the officers of the 28th were "rather green" and that the lieutenant colonel and the major "possessed no extraordinary qualifications" but that a "first rate" colonel, such as Lane, was all that was needed to make the regiment the best in the service.[14]

James Henry Lane was a graduate of Virginia Military Institute (VMI) and the University of Virginia. At VMI, Lane studied under Thomas J. Jackson (later known as "Stonewall" Jackson). After graduation he taught mathematics and military tactics at VMI, and then at the North Carolina Military Academy in Charlotte, North Carolina, where he held the chair of philosophy. Lane was first commissioned a major in the 1st North Carolina Regiment in the spring of 1861. When the war began, he left his teaching post at Charlotte to become an instructor of tactics at a camp of instruction camp near Raleigh. Lane won fame for his part in repulsing the enemy at Big Bethel, Virginia, on June 10, 1861, the first land battle of the war.[15]

Lane was an excellent choice and he would provide quality leadership throughout the war. One Yadkin County soldier, John Thomas Conrad, of Company F, thought highly of Lane: "Colonel Lane is liked very much by all, both officers and privates. I think he is a perfect gentleman in the strictest sense of the word, he is strict, though not overbearing, and I think we made an excellent choice."[16] The men fondly called Lane "The Little General."

Wilmington, North Carolina

The 28th Regiment had been ordered to Wilmington because the state authorities feared the enemy would attack this important city.[17] On September 30, 1861, the regiment traveled by train to Wilmington and arrived there October 1.[18] (Kinyoun gave October 2 as the date they arrived.) The train on which the troops were transported was involved in an accident near Goldsborough (Goldsboro). Two trains were needed to carry the entire regiment. The first train, heavily loaded with troops, stalled on an incline, and the second train rear-ended it. Several of the soldiers were severely injured, including Major Richard E. Reeves of Company A.[19]

The Most Troublesome Regiment

John Thomas Conrad wrote home in October of 1861 that the men of his company had been given "some old flynt and steel muskets" in order to learn how to the maneuver their arms. Conrad hoped that the old muskets would soon be replaced by newer ones.[20]

Colonel Lane refused to accept antiquated arms and wrote a letter to the adjutant general of the state of North Carolina. Lane said it would be better to disband the regiment than to equip it with such "useless masses of wood and metal." Lane's letter was forwarded to the governor, who replied to Lane and chastised him for being "disrespectful" and acting in a manner "unbecoming an officer." To disband the regiment, wrote the governor, would bring "lasting reproach" to both the regiment and any officers who recommended such a move. For his efforts on their behalf, Lane was liked even more by the men in the regiment. However, because of this confrontation early in their history, in which they had stood up and demanded their "just dues," John Thomas Conrad believed that the state authorities had formed the opinion that the 28th Regiment was "most troublesome."[21]

Motivated by the recent burning of several bridges in Tennessee, on November 13, 1861, Brigadier General R.C. Gatlin, commander of the Department of North Carolina at that time, issued orders to Brigadier General Anderson which were designed to prevent the burning of bridges by the enemy. Anderson was ordered to send a detail consisting of an "officer, four non-commissioned officers, and forty privates" to guard the bridges along the Wilmington and Weldon Railroad, those bridges which spanned the Northeast, Neuse, and Roanoke rivers in eastern North Carolina. The plan was to station one noncommissioned officer and 10 men at each of those bridges to ensure that no damage was done to any of the bridges. The men were to be provided with "camp equipage and rations" for 8 days, and were to be relieved each week. Gatlin did not want any delay but ordered the guards to be sent on the train the next day, "if practicable, as no time should be lost" in securing the safety of those railroad bridges.[22]

Nicholas Biddle Gibbon, of Mecklenburg County, left a first-hand account of the early days of the 28th Regiment. He was appointed on September 3, 1861, as a drill master, having had some military experience by participating in the battle at Big Bethel Church in June of 1861. He was to receive $33 per month, and was told to report to Camp Fisher, at High Point, in Guilford County. On September 7, six of the companies that were to be part of the 28th Regiment arrived, and enough men to complete the regiment were expected soon.[23] Gibbon requested and received a short furlough, and he went to Charlotte to visit friends. He returned for duty on September 16, and was kept "busy drilling the raw companies who knew nothing of the science of war."[24]

The 28th was assigned to General Joseph R. Anderson, commander of the Cape Fear District. The regiment went into camp near the Atlantic & North Carolina Railroad, where they built barracks in which to live, and were drilled daily. Detachments were sent to guard the railroad bridges from Wilmington to Goldsboro and north to the Virginia line.[25]

Regiment and Company Officers

After Colonel Lane joined the regiment, he made several staff appointments. These commissioned officers are usually referred to as "field and staff." In addition to Lowe and Reeves, the field and staff consisted of: Duncan A. McRae, adjutant; First Lieutenant J. Pinkney Little, ensign; Milton A. Lowe, sergeant major; Captain George S. Thompson, assistant quartermaster; Edward Moore, quartermaster sergeant; W.A. Mauney, commissary sergeant; Robert Gibbon, surgeon; F.N. Luckey, assistant surgeon; John Abernathy, hospital steward; Gabriel Johnston, ordnance sergeant; and Oscar J. Brent, chaplain.[26] Nicholas Biddle Gibbon was appointed commissary, with the rank and pay of a captain.[27]

Each company had a captain, who was in command of the company, and several lieutenants who were commissioned officers. Noncommissioned officers included the sergeants, corporals, and privates. Most companies also had musicians (a drummer and/or fifer).[28]

Each regiment had its own flag. The battle flag was made of heavy cotton or wool in the shape of a red square with a blue St. Andrew's cross on which were placed 13 stars. Later, many Confederate regiments, including the 28th, painted the names of the battles in which they had

Some of the Company captains, from Walter Clark, ed., *Histories of the Several Regiments and Battalions from North Carolina in the Great War, 1861–1865, Written by Members of the Respective Commands.* 1. E.F. Lovell, Co. A; 2. R.D. Rhyne, Co. B; 3. T. James Linebarger, Co. C; 4. Moses I. Eudy, Co. D; 5. Thomas V. Apperson, Co. F; 6. E. Graham Morrow, Co. G; 7. Gold G. Holland, Co. H (courtesy of the North Carolina Department of Archives and History).

participated on their flags. These were called "battle honors." The flag helped identify friend from foe, and it was a great loss when a flag was captured.[29] Each regiment also had a flag bearer. If the original flag bearer fell in battle, another member of the regiment was duty bound to pick up the flag and carry it forward. The soldiers did everything they could to prevent their flag from touching the ground or from being captured.

Winter Quarters, 1861–1862

The 28th Regiment remained camped at Wilmington during the winter of 1861–1862.[30] Strict discipline was maintained in the regiment. The men were well drilled. They proudly displayed their skills, according to Colonel Lane, as the new volunteers marched down Wilmington's Second Street with a "steady tramp, the long line of their bayonets gleaming in the sun, and the firm bearing of the men indicative of determination and giving promise of gallant service when called upon."[31]

At first, the people of Wilmington were very hospitable to the soldiers, probably in appreciation of the many hours the men of the 28th Regiment spent guarding various bridges of the Wilmington & Weldon Railroad. Citizens from Wilmington visited the camp of the 28th Regiment, and their assessment was published in the *Wilmington Journal.* The visitors were "pleased to see that a complete town of neat wooden tenements has taken the place of the canvas village of the latter part of the summer and fall, affording convenient and comfortable quarters with chimneys...." The wooden buildings provided quarters for the men, for stores and supplies, and other purposes. Most of the wooden structures had been completed, except some of the officers' quarters, including the quarters of Colonel Lane.[32]

However, the people of the town of Wilmington shortly became unhappy with the presence of the regiment when some of its soldiers confiscated the produce in the town market for their own use. The citizens claimed that the food supplies should come from the counties that furnished the companies, because we "cannot feed us and them."[33] The soldiers also became dissatisfied and disappointed as well. Private John Thomas Conrad wrote his wife:

> If the Yankees knew as much about this place as I do, they would not have it, and the longer I stay here the less I think of this place, or rather the kind and generous citizens. I know there is no place in the State where the people think as little of a soldier as the people of this place do. There are no kind hearted ladies to visit our sick and suffering soldier and administer to his sufferings....[34]

The situation was not improved by the unhealthy climate of the coastal area. By October 28, 1861, the regiment numbered 970 men,[35] but by February 13, 1862, the number had decreased to 933 men.[36]

Captain John H. Kinyoun, who was also a doctor, recorded several deaths that occurred while the 28th Regiment was in winter quarters. He noted that J.M. Bran died December 29, 1861; A.J. Hauser, February 13, 1862; W.H. Apperson, February 19, 1862; H. Mitchel, February 25, 1862; and R. Rush, March 6, 1862. No cause of death was listed.[37] These and other deaths that occurred from disease are noted in the brief accounts of the men of the 28th Regiment (see Appendix IX).

First to Reorganize

Most of the soldiers in this regiment had enlisted for only a year, and the expiration of their term of service was fast approaching. To remedy the situation, an ordinance was passed by the North Carolina Convention in February of 1862 to encourage the soldiers to reenlist. The inducement was a furlough plus a bounty, and the right to reorganize their units by electing new officers.[38]

Regimental numbers soon increased to 1,250 men. About half of Company A reenlisted, and other companies followed their lead.[39] Colonel Lane was very proud that his 28th was "the first North Carolina regiment to reorganize." Lane noted that six companies had reorganized before they left Wilmington; the last four companies soon followed suit, and the reorganization was completed by April 12, 1862.[40]

Colonel Lane's comments about reenlistment were published in the *Raleigh Journal.* Although those who reenlisted were to receive a bonus in addition to the two months' back pay due them, plus a furlough to go home, when time came for their furloughs, the payroll had not been received from the quartermaster. Captain William M. Norman used $300 of his own money and then borrowed $400 more so that all could be paid in his Company A. With money in their pockets, and after transportation had been arranged, many of the men started for home on March 7.[41]

Elections

The men of the regiment elected their field officers. James H. Lane was again chosen colonel, and Thomas L. Lowe was elected lieutenant colonel. There was a lively contest for the position of major. After several ballots, Captain Samuel D. Lowe was elected.[42]

Discord among the soldiers of Company F led Captain John H. Kinyoun to leave the regiment. One group, led by Lieutenant Thomas Apperson and Private William Kelly, tried to discredit Kinyoun and prevent his reelection by claiming that a friend of Kinyoun's had accepted only those new recruits who would vote for Kinyoun to continue as captain. When Colonel Lane was informed of these charges, Kinyoun counteracted with an accusation that John Thomas Conrad was doing the same to admit new recruits who favored Apperson. Kinyoun resigned and declared: "I will not be Capt. with the division that there would be if Apperson and Kelly should be elected." He did not wish to be associated with either of the men in any situation if they were elected company officers.

Kinyoun expressed his feelings to his wife:

> The army is filled with some of the lowest demagoggs [*sic*] and they are seeking office and an honorable gentleman will not content with them and such low dishonorable scoundrels suit the majority of men as they promise them a great many privileges that are denied them as will be all the time.[43]

When the 1862 elections were over, a total of 44 officers from the 18th, 28th, and 37th regiments had been defeated. Four captains and 11 lieutenants were removed from office in the 28th Regiment.[44]

The 28th North Carolina and Its Position in the Confederate Army

A short history of the 28th Regiment, North Carolina Troops appears in Volume 8 of *North Carolina Troops, 1861–1865: A Roster.* The regiment became part of the Branch–Lane Brigade under A.P. Hill's Division, and thus part of Robert E. Lee's Army of Northern Virginia. Detailed battle reports and casualty numbers from the *Official Records of the War of the Rebellion* are quoted for some of the major battles in *North Carolina Troops, 1861–1865: A Roster.* Additional information about these conflicts and other activities of the 28th Regiment has been extracted in the following chapters from the letters and diaries of some of the individual soldiers of the regiment.

The 28th Regiment, North Carolina Troops, was placed in the District of Cape Fear Division, in the Department of North Carolina, from October 1861 until March 1862. The regiment was assigned in March 1862 to General Lawrence O'Bryan Branch's Brigade, of the North Carolina District of Pamlico. Organized at Kinston, this brigade contained five North Carolina regiments: the 7th, 18th, 28th, 33rd, and 37th.[45]

Brigadier General Lawrence O'Bryan Branch (1820–1862)

Lawrence O'Bryan Branch was from a wealthy North Carolina family. His uncle had been governor of the state. He attended the University of North Carolina and graduated from Princeton. Afterwards, he practiced law in Florida, then fought in the Seminole War. As a Democratic Congressman, Branch urged the South to beware of "immoderation," but later resigned his seat in Congress and was named quartermaster and postmaster general of the North Carolina troops. He was not satisfied with that job and wanted be involved in the actual fighting. He was appointed colonel of the 33rd Regiment, which later became part of the Branch Brigade.[46]

On November 16, 1861, Branch was appointed a brigadier general and given command of the forces around New Bern. As part of Thomas J. "Stonewall" Jackson's unit, Branch took part in the battles at Hanover Court House, Seven Days' Battles, Cedar Run, 2nd Bull Run, Fairfax Court House, Ox Hill, Harper's Ferry and Sharpsburg (Antietam) , where he was killed on September 17, 1862.[47]

From April 1862 through May 1862, the 28th was a part of Branch's Brigade, in the Department of North Carolina. That same month, the North Carolina troops were turned over to the Confederacy, and the regiment came within the jurisdiction of Branch's Brigade, Department of Northern Virginia. As part of A.P. Hill's Division, Branch's Brigade (including the 28th Regiment) became part of the 1st Corps, of the Army of Northern Virginia.[48]

While a part of A.P. Hill's Division the brigade would participate in some of the more famous battles of the war: Hanover Court House (Taliaferro's Mill), Mechanicsville, Gaines' Mill, Frayser's Farm, the Seven Days' Battles, 2nd Manassas, Sharpsburg, Fredericksburg, Chancellorsville, Wilderness, Spotsylvania Court House, 2nd Cold Harbor, Gettysburg, Petersburg, Reams' Station, and many engagements that are not as well known. At its peak, the 28th Regiment, North Carolina Troops consisted of over 1,200 men. After four years of war, fewer than 300 remained of the 28th to surrender at Appomattox Court House, April 9, 1865.[49]

This table identifies the position of the 28th Regiment throughout the war.

From	To	Brigade	Division	Corps	Army
Oct 1861	March 1862		District of Cape Fear		Dept. of North Carolina
March 1862	March 1862	Branch's	District of Pamlico		Dept of North Carolina
April 1862	May 1862	Branch's			Dept. of North Carolina
May 1862	May 1862	Branch's			Dept. of Northern Virginia
May 1862	June 1862	Branch's	A.P. Hill's		Army of Northern Virginia
June 1862	July 1862	Branch's	A.P. Hill's	1st	Army of Northern Virginia
July 1862	May 1863	Branch/Lane's	A.P. Hill's	2nd	Army of Northern Virginia
May 1863	April 1865	Lane's	Pender/Wilcox's	3rd	Army of Northern Virginia[50]

Major General Ambrose Powell Hill (1825–1865)

A.P. Hill, native of Culpeper County, Virginia, was a graduate of the United States Military Academy. He served in both the Mexican and Seminole Wars. On March 1, 1861, he resigned his commission to join the 13th Virginia Regiment with the rank of 1st Lieutenant Colonel. He was in the reserve unit at 1st Manassas. Hill was appointed brigadier general in February of 1862 and given a brigade. Promoted to Major General on May 26, 1862, Hill led his division at Mechanicsville, Gaines' Mill and Frayser's Farm. Hill called his division "The Light Division," because of its speed in marching. After Hill quarreled with Longstreet, his division was placed under the command of Thomas J. "Stonewall" Jackson. Hill succeeded the famous "Stonewall" when Jackson was mortally wounded at Chancellorsville. Promoted to lieutenant general in

Some Regimental and Company officers, from Walter Clark, ed., *Histories of the Several Regiments and Battalions from North Carolina in the Great War, 1861–1865, Written by Members of the Respective Commands*. 1. 1st Lt. Milton A. Lowe, Co. H; 2. 1st Sergt. P.A. Apperson, Co. F; 3. Commissary Sergt. W.A. Mauney; 4. Sgt. J.M. Grice, Co. C; 5. Pvt. L.C. Turner, Co. C, Sharpshooter; 6. Pvt. W.A. Martin, Co. C; 7. Hospital Steward John A. Abernethy (courtesy of the North Carolina Department of Archives and History).

May of 1863, Hill took command of the new 3rd Corps, which he commanded at Gettysburg and Wilderness. One historian did not believe that Hill lived up to expectations as a corps commander. Douglass S. Freeman attributed Hill's lack of success to either "ill health or a sense of larger, overburdening responsibility."[51]

Hill was easygoing with his men in camp or on the march, but he was a different man when the fighting began. High-strung and temperamental, he often sent his men into action with an aggressiveness that won him the respect of his enemies. With his reddish-brown beard and his red "battle shirt," Hill was an imposing figure on the battlefield, and he worked well with his brigade commanders and inspired confidence in his men.[52]

Freeman saw Hill as a "genial, approachable, and affectionate" man in private life, but as "restless and impetuous in action." Hill was absent on sick leave May 8–21, 1864, but he rejoined his corps for the battles at North Anna, 2nd Cold Harbor, and the Petersburg campaign. It was in the Petersburg campaign that Hill "rose to his greatest heights as a corps commander. He was absent due to sickness again in March of 1865, but returned to take charge of the final defense of Petersburg. In the very last days of the war, A.P. Hill was killed at Petersburg on April 2, 1865. Hill's widow was the sister of Brigadier General John Hunt Morgan, the daring cavalry officer.[53]

Chapter 3

Life in the Confederate Army

War is Hell!
— William Tecumseh Sherman[1]

Life of a Soldier According to Colonel James H. Lane

> We see nothing, hear nothing and know nothing, here, but to obey orders. A man has to be very patriotic, on good terms with his fellow soldiers, and on prodigiously good terms with himself, to see much enjoyment here; but so long as our country needs our services, we will be contented in her service wherever it may be.[2]

The war between the states pitted friend against friend, brother against brother, and father against son in a deadly conflict. Sentiment for either the North or the South was so intense that reconciliation was never achieved in some families.

Captain Nicholas Biddle Gibbon served as commissary for the 28th Regiment, North Carolina Infantry. One of his three brothers, Major General John Gibbon, chose to remain with the Union Army.[3] In the fall of 1864, Major John Gibbon wrote to Nicholas, his Confederate brother, that he had obtained permission from General Grant for them to meet under a flag of truce at Aiken's Landing. Nicholas replied, "It is not agreeable that I should meet you under the circumstances proposed in your note, although I have no doubt that I could obtain permission from General Lee if I desired it."[4]

Army Living Quarters

At the onset of the war, soldiers on both sides slept in canvas tents. A favorite shelter was the "Sibley" tent, invented by Henry H. Sibley, who later became a Confederate brigadier general. The Sibley tent was a large cone, 18 feet in diameter, and 12 feet tall. It was supported by a pole in its center, with a circular opening at the top for ventilation. A dozen men could fit inside comfortably, but usually about 20 men shared each tent.[5] A fire could be made in the center, and the men slept with their feet toward the fire. However, this comfortable tent was seldom used,[6] and the men usually slept in the smaller "dog" tents. A dog tent consisted of two parts that were buttoned together[7] and supported by two upright sticks or by a musket with its bayonet stuck in the ground. Other tents in use during this period were the "A" or wedge tent, and the wall tent which was used for officers' quarters and for hospitals.

Army regulations decreed that tents should be set up when the army was camped. The camp was laid out in a grid pattern of streets, with officers' quarters at the front of each street and enlisted men's quarters behind them. The position of each company and regiment was usually along the lines that would be drawn up for battle. Each company displayed its flag (or colors) outside a tent. Regulations even decreed where the mess (eating) tents were to be placed, as well as the medical tents or cabins, and the location of the baggage train in relation to the tents. This ideal situation, as regulations required, was often impossible due to the terrain.[8]

Initially, while the regiment was stationed near Wilmington in 1861, the men of the 28th Regiment slept in tents. These were useful to "keep the night air off of them, and some of them arranged theirs nicely," reported John Thomas Conrad (Company F).[9]

Improvements made to some quarters were described in a letter from Calvin Holcomb in March of 1862. He reported that a fight between Bob Gentry and Ellis Long "shook the floor." Holcomb's quarters, whether in a building or tent, possibly had a wooden floor.[10]

The 28th was moved by train to Virginia in 1862. They first camped at Howard Grove, about two miles from Richmond. John Thomas Conrad wrote to his wife that the men slept on the ground with nothing to cover them except "the blue canopy of heaven."[11] Sleeping on the ground without any sort of shelter would become more prevalent as the war continued.

In the spring of 1862, a soldier in Company A, 28th Regiment, James M. Collins of Surry County, wrote to his brother back home that "we have lay on the ground since we come to VA and sometimes we have a tent brake [a thicket or brushwood] to stretch over us and sometimes it

Sergeant Samuel Speer Harding, Company I, 28th Regiment, enlisted at age 23 on August 31, 1861.

is rainy and we have to scrooch up under two or three of the brakes." Battles often resulted in the loss of knapsacks and other equipment. Thus, after the fighting at Hanover Court House, Collins stated that the men of Company A had only about 12 blankets between them.[12]

When the 28th camped near Orange Court House in November of 1863, one soldier reported that they had "all built our little huts & have moved in them now & got chimneys built to them which makes them very comfortable."[13]

Clothing

Clothing in first year of the war for soldiers in the 28th Regiment was minimal, as described by Private Samuel Speer Harding. He had "one pare of pants and one shiret and one pare of drawers, one pare of shoes, and one pare of socks and one over coat" in addition to "one good blanket that I wouldn't take ten dollars for it." When Harding (Company I) received a coat from the army, he sent his brother Berry's coat back home, although he could have "sold it for seven dollars."[14]

After his promotion in 1862, Lieutenant John Thomas Conrad wrote home to request a red "sash" to wear with his sword. He preferred silk, if it could be obtained.[15]

In late fall of 1862, the men of the 28th Regiment received shoes from their quartermaster. They bought blankets from those captured by the Confederate cavalry near Harper's Ferry. John Thomas Conrad paid $10 for one of them. The folks back home in North Carolina supplied their men with as much clothing as they could. As winter approached, John Thomas Conrad's wife sent him "warm gloves, socks and [an] over coat."[16]

In January of 1863, Sam Harding's mother wrote that she had made him some pants and other things. He replied: "we have got plenty of clothing."[17] After a year of marching and fighting, the situation changed. By November of 1863, Greenberry Harding, who had joined his brother in Company I, 28th Regiment, wrote home that the "Brigade is nearly clothesless, lots of the boys are nearly naked & barefooted & there is not any of the boys that has socks & ... only those that has had them sent to them from home." Greenberry assured his parents that he was "doing very well about clothing & shoes & socks." This was during the time when "Major Thompson told the soldiers that there were 2,000 suits in Richmond for their brigade."[18]

When marching, the soldiers discarded much of their clothing and personal belongings to lighten their heavy load. John Thomas Conrad wrote to his wife that he had sent his trunk back to her by the railroad to High Point. He only kept two blankets and what clothing he could "conveniently carry in a Knap Sack"—two over shirts, one checked shirt, one pair of drawers, one pair of pants, and an overcoat. In May, he sent his flannel shirt home in his trunk.[19]

Army Rations and Other Foods

While we tend to think that our Confederate soldiers survived on "hardtack and army coffee," their meals usually consisted of more food, especially in the early part of the war and in summer months.

At the beginning of the war, the Confederate government adopted the official United States Army ration. This ration consisted of "one 16-ounce biscuit (hardtack, pilot bread, or crackers), or 22 ounces of bread or flour," plus 1¼ pound of fresh or salt meat or ¾ of a pound of bacon. Federal regulations authorized eight gallons of beans for each 100 men, 10 pounds of rice or hominy, 10 pounds of coffee, 15 pounds of sugar, four gallons of vinegar, and two pounds of salt.[20]

Shortly after the Yadkin County boys first left home in 1861, their relatives and neighbors sent the boys in Company F a great variety of edible items: bushels of beans, onions, and potatoes; fresh cucumbers, squash, apples, fresh beets and pickled beets, cabbage, peaches, fruit pies, milk, butter, home-baked loaves of bread, oven-light biscuits and sugar cakes; honey, sugar, jam and molasses; pickles, gallons of cider, whiskey and cordial; mutton, pork and chickens, and dry wood to use in cooking and for warmth.[21] The soldiers were sent all kinds of edible items by the folks at home, especially in the early days of the war, when the families in the South still had plenty to share.

Obtaining food to feed a large army was always a problem, but in 1861, the fare was not so bad. 1st Lieutenant John Thomas Conrad (Company F) wrote his wife that he had "a very hearty dinner of pork and coarse corn bread."[22]

Even by the summer of 1862, food for soldiers was not an insurmountable problem. Private William A. Tesh (Company I, 28th Regiment) wrote home that he and his fellow soldiers "got a plenty of Bacon Flour Peas salt candle," but he wanted his father to "be saving with your salt, because it is mighty high and scarce."[23]

However, the standard ration for the Confederate army was determined by the available supplies of food. Because of food shortages, Confederate authorities were forced to reduce the amount of food authorized in the standard ration.[24]

When they had money, soldiers sometimes bought food. John Thomas Conrad and Tom Apperson (both of Company F) went to the market in Wilmington and bought some "sausage and pork," and considered themselves "living pretty high." Conrad thought that the prices were high for soldiers, with pork selling for "15¢ per pound and sausage at 20 cts." He would not have minded paying the high prices so much, if he could get paid the back wages owed him.[25]

John Thomas Conrad was sent to Lynchburg in the fall of 1862 because of "intermittent fever." He recovered and even managed to gain some weight. The meals served in the private home in which he stayed included cabbage, tomatoes, corn, Irish potatoes, sweet potatoes, mutton, beef, and sometimes even fried chicken.[26]

Food from home continued to be hoped for and relished when it was received. John Thomas Conrad thanked his wife for the "butter, lard and cakes" she had sent him.[27] Samuel Speer Harding asked his father to bring some "dryed fruit, honey, and some butter and some sausage meat" when William Harding came from Yadkin County to visit his son at Camp Gregg.[28]

Whiskey was a commodity that was easily transported, did not spoil, and had a variety of uses, including but not limited to medicinal purposes. When John Thomas Conrad's keg of whiskey arrived at the train station, he did not especially need it, and was not in any hurry to retrieve it.[29] He had grown to like oysters, so abundant where he was stationed near the North Carolina coast, and he knew he would want them once he was home.[30]

After the battle of Fredericksburg in December of 1862, Artha Bray, Jr. wrote to his brother to send him "three gallons of Brandy, half gallon of Honey, and five pounds of butter boxed up ... and a pare [*sic*] of pants." He advised his brother to take the items to Dobson (Surry County, North Carolina), where they could be brought to him by one of the Normans, who would be bringing items to M.W. Norman.[31]

Once the North Carolina boys moved to Virginia, they foraged for food or sometimes purchased items. Two of the boys in Company F, 28th Regiment, bought a large hen for $1.50, and a turkey hen for $2.00. Another soldier bought a chicken, then sold it for $2.25. Some items were scarce. Butter, reported John Thomas Conrad, "can't be had at any price," although he had seen it advertised in a Richmond paper for $1.50 per pound. Conrad sent someone to Richmond to buy some "genuine Coffee" in May of 1862, priced at $1.50 a pound.[32]

By May 1862, from near Rapidan Station, Culpeper County, James Collins (Company A) wrote to tell his brother in Dobson, North Carolina, about the conditions in the Confederate army: "...we have been laying on the ground without tents one week today, and I don't know how much longer we will have to do...." The food was meager: "We live on crackers and Bacon meat 55 days ... it was pretty hard living and no coffee to drink...."[33] Coffee was one of those items that could not be obtained in the South, but in November of 1862, John Thomas Conrad enjoyed drinking some "Yankee Coffee" which had been captured at Sheperdstown.[34]

In the summer of 1862, soldiers could sometimes find a garden to supply them with vegetables. At one deserted home, the men of Company F found two very large "English Pea patches." The peas were gathered, cooked and eaten. These were the first vegetables that John Thomas Conrad had eaten that summer. They had "fried some meat to get the Grese [*sic*] then poured in water and then the peas...."[35]

In order to eat, the soldiers found that they had to do jobs ordinarily done by females or slaves. John Thomas Conrad wrote to his wife that she would probably enjoy seeing him "frying meat and making coffee." He had not yet attempted to make bread, he told her, but had left that task for "more experienced hands."[36] Conrad and his men enjoyed a treat for Christmas in 1862. They baked some "very nice green apple pies," and then made some out of dried fruit, which had cost $2 a gallon. They used "beef lard to shorten" their pie dough and bread, and to fry a steak. To complete the feast, Conrad had to contend with a cup of coffee made from "wheat and rye," because he had used all the coffee from home.[37] A couple of days later, Conrad made a pot of beef soup, to which he added an onion and black pepper for seasoning. He also noted that they only ate two meals a day.[38]

Schnitz pies were a favorite with the Yadkin boys. John Thomas Conrad wrote that a comrade was "stewing the fruit while I am writing." (Schnitz was made from sliced dried fruit, such as apples, and sometimes used with dumplings.) He looked forward to having a fine meal of "Cabbage Soup as we bought a few heads yesterday."[39]

By 1863, obtaining food was not easy. Private Caleb McCurdy wrote his brother from Richmond on February 17, 1863: "Since last Saturday & with the Exceptions of two potatoes I haven't bought nor Eat anything but Beef & Bred & it cost me two dollars & 10 cents per day." He tried to get rations from the Commissary Department, but was told that he could not. The officer in charge told McCurdy that he "was bound to take money in stid [stead] of Rations." The Commissary officer told him that "one man could not draw Rations when on Detached service," unless he could "draw from his Regt." McCurdy was informed that he was entitled to get $1.20 per day in money. Yet that was not enough, when pork was $1.20; beef, $7.00; bread, $.70 per loaf; molasses, $71 per gallon. McCurdy bemoaned his situation, "Such is the State of affairs in our Confederacy. They allow a soldier one half the money that it takes to board him...."[40]

The soldiers' fare improved at times but, at best, was usually never enough to satisfy a hungry soldier. In November of 1863, Greenberry Harding wrote to his parents that our "fair is tolerable good now. We get a plenty of good Beef & Bread & some time we get some few potatoes & turnips...."[41]

Daily Duties

The standard book of instruction for drill and other activities necessary in the infantry was written by Lieutenant General William James Hardee. A West Pointer, Hardee had served in the Mexican War as a major and was brevetted lieutenant colonel. While serving as United States Secretary of War, Jefferson Davis asked Hardee to work on an updated manual to be used with the new rifles. Thus, in 1855, Hardee's *Rifle and Light Infantry Tactics* was published. This manual was used by both sides during the war. As the new three-band, rifled percussion musket came into use, Hardee revised his manual, which was published in Mobile, Alabama, in 1861. Hardee was from Georgia and when the war began, he resigned and was appointed a lieutenant colonel, then was promoted to brigadier general of an Arkansas brigade.[42] Hardee's manual was revised and reprinted in 1862 for the North Carolina troops. Reprinted several more times, the manual is now referred to as the "1862 Hardee's" or the "Confederate Hardee's." It can be seen online at the Drill Network.[43] From just a quick look at this book, or others like it, it is apparent that soldiering was not easy. Much more was involved than just marching and performing complicated drill maneuvers.

In the early part of the war, while the regiment was stationed at Wilmington, four hours each day were allocated to drill. As time when on, and the men became competent in the drill routines, the amount of time spent in drilling was decreased. By late November, John Thomas Conrad wrote home that "The Col is drilling us only once a day now, though we have company drill every morning and battalion in the evening...."[44]

Conrad was proud of the way he and his men had learned the drills. He told his folks back home, "I wish you could see us drill, it is one of the most imposing and grand scenes ever you beheld, the guns and bayonets glittering in the sun and the whole battalion off at the same step in one solid column." Conrad believed that his regiment was improving so rapidly that in a short time they would be "able to compete with any regiment on a drill."[45]

In the spring of 1862, the daily routine for the soldier was to rise at 5 o'clock in the morning, wash, put on his clothes, and attend roll call. Even if a soldier did not want to get up that early, according to Conrad, "it is the law and we all must yield cheerful obedience." After the reorganization of the North Carolina troops, Conrad was promoted to 1st lieutenant.[46]

Other non-combat routine duties involved guarding roads and bridges. Samuel Speer Harding wrote home while he was stationed at Wilmington that he and six other privates had been sent to Weldon to guard the bridges, where they remained for nine days.[47]

Marching took some getting used to. Captain Nicholas Gibbon described how his feet were so "badly swollen and sore" that he could hardly put "one foot after the other." He was relieved when the troops stopped their march at a plantation after the fiasco at New Bern. There he had the chance to put his feet in a tub of cold water. After Gibbon had bathed his feet for nearly an hour, he felt much better, but the time spent taking care of his feet caused him to miss out on the food. He did get a "hot cake of cornbread." Gibbon saw a man eating "something like molasses out of a tumbler" and when he saw another "tumbler on the table" full of what he thought was molasses, he dipped his cornbread in it. He got a big surprise when he took a bite and found that the tumbler had been full of "soft soap." Captain Gibbon laughed with his companions at his error.[48]

When the 28th moved to Virginia, near the Chickahominy River, some of the Yankees and the Confederates "agreed not to shoot at each other while on picket," John Thomas Conrad thought that was a "good agreement as picket fighting can not benefit either party...."[49]

Paperwork

For the officers there was always paperwork — letters to write, and reports to be submitted. In his post as a sergeant, Greenberry Harding (Company I) kept a record of the men who were present in his company. His daughter, Flora Harding Robinson, sent a typed copy of that record to the Museum of the Confederacy in Richmond, Virginia. Unfortunately, the document contains very few dates.

Financial Opportunities

The boys in Company I were enterprising. When they received packages from home, some of them sold the items to make money. In February of 1862, Calvin M. Holcomb received some apples from his brother, who was still living in Yadkin Country, and immediately sold them. He wrote his brother: "if we had about five bushels we could make some money."[50]

While stationed near Wilmington, Samuel Speer Harding received a "keg of whiskey" from home. He sold several gallons, then wrote his father (who operated a still in the Big Woods near Huntsville) that if he had a whole barrel of whiskey, he could "sell the last bit of it at 50 cents a quart."[51]

Health and Hygiene

Cleanliness was not stressed in the 19th century because of the lack of knowledge of germs and viruses which caused many diseases. Much sickness could have been prevented if care had been taken to use clean eating utensils, drink clean, unpolluted water, and attend to bodily cleanliness. Soldiers on the march had few, if any, opportunities for hygiene, especially when they were more concerned with dodging bullets. Conditions deteriorated swiftly after a battle when the bloody ground was littered with the bodies of men and animals. Land and water soon became contaminated and provided a fertile field for bacteria and disease-causing agents.

Whenever the armies stopped and camped, there were usually women who followed them. Some of the women made their living taking in washing. John Thomas wrote home in the fall of 1861 that there was a "woman that lives just behind our tents about ten steps" who washed his clothes.[52]

Sickness and War-Related Injuries

The soldiers who were very sick or badly injured were sent to Richmond or to one of many other hospitals. Joseph H. Kinyoun, formerly a captain in Company F, 28th Regiment, applied for a medical position and was appointed assistant surgeon for the 66th North Carolina.[53] While still in Company F, Kinyoun began his record keeping by recording the heights of the men in his company (see Appendix IV). Later, as a surgeon, Kinyoun kept meticulous records in his "diary" in which he listed the patient's name, rank, regiment, company, complaint/diagnosis, date seen, and remarks. Kinyoun was called on to treat every kind of disease from syphilis and gonorrhea to diarrhea, rheumatism, and jaundice.[54]

The men of the 28th Regiment were mainly from the Piedmont section of North Carolina. They were not accustomed to the climate on the coast and its inherent diseases. Thus, while the regiment was stationed at Wilmington during the fall and winter months of 1861–1862, many of them became ill from malaria, yellow fever, and other tropical diseases. Measles, smallpox, and tuberculosis affected soldiers everywhere, and could be fatal. Measles and colds took their toll on the men, and probably made them susceptible to other diseases. (Appendix X will show just how many died of typhoid fever and other diseases.)

The Collins brothers, Hezekiah W. and James, wrote home from the camp of the 28th Regiment near Wilmington that their health was good, but "We cannot tell you [how] many is sick in our Regt. But several of the boys has got the measles and some has the chills."[55] Tom Scott and Berry Harding, both of Company I, were reported by their comrade William A. Tesh to have been sick with the measles while stationed at Kinston in April of 1862.[56] John Thomas Conrad wrote in November 1861 that 25 men in his company of approximately 100 were "not able to perform duty...."[57]

Although not acting in the capacity of the regiment's doctor, Captain John H. Kinyoun reported that there were 30 cases of measles in the regiment. Two weeks later, the situation worsened, and he wrote that the number who were sick had increased over the last few days. "The measles," wrote Kinyoun, "is playing with the health of our Regiment, some of the men are looking very badly." By the first of November, 20 members of Kinyoun's Company F were sick.

Captain Joseph H. Kinyoun, Company F, 28th Regiment (courtesy of Joseph K. Houts).

With colder weather came colds, pneumonia and pleurisy. There were also several cases of mumps in the regiment.[58]

On November 8, 1861, eight men in Company F had measles, but by this time, the disease had about run its course.[59] Because of all the illness, Colonel Lane had to occasionally suspend drill.[60]

Other diseases were more serious than measles and mumps. Samuel Speer Harding became ill while he was with a group sent to guard the bridges near Weldon. He wrote to his folks that the doctor had said he had "tifoid [typhoid] fever but as it happened it did not take much hold on me...." However, the young soldier had lost a lot of weight, and declared that he did not weight more than 120 pounds, having lost "at least 40 pounds."[61] Typhoid fever is an infectious disease caused by the typhoid bacillus that has contaminated the soldiers' food or drink. It can cause diarrhea and fever, and can be fatal.

Diarrhea was a common ailment among soldiers. James M. Collins (Company A) wrote that after the battle at Hanover Court House that he was well, "except the diarrhoea," which had bothered him for several days. The regiment as a whole "is not in as good health as it has been." Sometimes diarrhea was the result of poor diet, impure food, or polluted drinking water. Chronic diarrhea could weaken a soldier until he was unfit for duty and had to be hospitalized or sent home. Many died of "chronic diarrhoea."

Captain Nicholas Gibbon was bothered by the water in Virginia. Gibbon found that the water in the (Shenandoah?) valley was all "limestone which did not at all agree" with him. He claimed that was what affected his bowels for about three months from the time he was camped near Martinsburg until he left the valley. The result was that he was so reduced in weight and so weak he could hardly get on and off his horse. In a different location, with a change in the type of water and a better diet, his health rapidly improved.[62]

Wounds, amputations and other injuries often caused intense, unremitting pain. One soldier, John Smith, of Yadkin County, enlisted on January 6, 1862, at age 18. Two years later, February 5, 1864, he was dead from a "self-administered overdose of morphine."[63] Perhaps this soldier could not stand the pain from an injury or an amputation.

Sometimes when a soldier had been injured, he was given a furlough to go home to recuperate. From College Hospital at Lynchburg, Virginia, Calvin Holcomb wrote to his brother Bloom to tell him that "Bob Jenkins came by here last week on his way home on furlough. He is wound[ed] in the rite arm & hand this time."[64] The letter sounded like Jenkins had been wounded previously.

In May of 1862, John Thomas Conrad wrote from Gordonsville, Virginia, that he had been "right sick for the last two or three days with cold and sore throat," and although he had improved, he was still very weak. To cure his condition, he had taken "Blue Mass," a purgative.[65]

In the spring of 1862, Calvin Holcomb reported that James Brindle was "very sick" and Willie Pilcher was "bad off."[66] On April 12, 1862, Samuel Harding was promoted to sergeant, but on June 16, 1862, he was hospitalized in Chimborazo Hospital No. 2, Richmond, Virginia, for "continued fever," then was transferred on July 26 to Danville. Because of his illness, Sam missed the fighting at Mechanicsville, Gaines' Mill, Cold Harbor, Frayzer's Farm, Malvern Hill, and Gordonsville, Virginia, which occurred during the period from June 26 through July 29, 1862. He may not have rejoined his regiment until he reenlisted on August 13, 1862, for "2 years or the war."[67]

In August of 1862, 1st Lieutenant John Thomas Conrad was sick again, this time with "intermittent fever." He had become ill while camped near the Rappahannock River, and he was sent to a private home at the corner of Main and 12th Street in Lynchburg to recover. The policy of sending the sick home had been changed and he wrote that there was "no possible chance for a sick man to get a furlough now, else I would have come straight on home, when I was first taken sick." There were four or five other "boarders" who stayed in the same room with him.[68]

In the fall of 1862, Artha Bray was confined in the hospital at Danville with rheumatism and a bad case of "yellow jaundice." Smallpox was also prevalent among the troops.[69]

Many of the diseases that were fatal in the 19th century can be cured today with antibiotics. Private Caleb S. McCurdy, of Company K, 28th Regiment, died in General Hospital No. 24 in Richmond on November 25, 1863. A letter from T.M. Bellamy to McCurdy's widow informed her that he died of "Phthisis Pulmonalis," a term for pulmonary tuberculosis or consumption.[70] Many men were discharged because of this contagious lung disease.

Venereal Diseases

Soldiers on both sides were exposed to and contracted a variety of venereal diseases. Venereal diseases were more prevalent among the soldiers at the beginning and at the end of the war, and more frequent among soldiers stationed in or near cities.[71] The *Medical and Surgical History of the War of the Rebellion,* published in the 1880s, has a large section on venereal diseases. Among the Union soldiers, there were 73,382 cases of syphilis reported and 109,397 cases of gonorrhea, a rate of 82 cases per 1,000 men. It is likely that the same was true of the Confederate forces.[72]

Thousands of prostitutes gathered in the cities and around the camps of the armies. When the men were not drinking or gambling, they often enjoyed the horizontal refreshments that could be provided by these prostitutes and camp followers. It is estimated that about 8 percent of soldiers in the Union army were treated for some type of venereal disease. Many cases went unreported. These diseases were treated unsuccessfully by herbs and minerals, such as mercury, zinc sulfate, pokeweed and elderberries. Some of these treatments may have relieved the symptoms but did nothing to cure the disease.[73]

Concerns About Home and Family

Every soldier worried about the folks back home. Most families did not have slaves, so the wives, children and older relatives were left to manage the farm on their own. Many letters contained advice from the soldier to his wife or family about things to be done, or not done, while he was away. Artha Bray, Jr. (Company A, 28th Regiment), mentioned twice in a letter to his mother, Mary Whitaker Bray, that he did not want his "oxen to be worked at all." Instead, he wanted his oxen "to be well wintered." He told his mother that if she needed wood hauled, she should ask Jesse Stanley to use *his* oxen to do the work.[74]

Artha wrote to his brother, K.H. Bray, and asked that he "attend to the selling of Mother's Brandy and see that she gets a good price for it." He also directed his brother to purchase "me and mother a good two horse wagon." Looking ahead, he said, "If I ever return, I shall be obliged to repare old fences."[75]

Death and Burial

After battles that resulted in the deaths of thousands of soldiers, some of the bodies were buried in mass graves. Others lay on the field waiting for burial details to come and dig individual graves. Sometimes, a soldier was disinterred and taken home for burial.

When John Thomas Conrad learned of the death of Louis Kimbro (Lewis W. Kimbrough, a musician in the regimental band of the 33rd North Carolina Regiment, who had died of typhoid fever[76]), he wrote that he would "willingly bring the remains ... home," but he was uncertain where he and his troops were going. He believed it would be better if "Duke" (Dr. John H. Kinyoun) would come for the body.[77]

After Sergeant Sam Harding was killed at Reams' Station on August 25, 1864, a friend marked the place where he was buried and wrote to his parents about their son's death.[78] The father, William Harding, and his youngest son, Thomas Renny Harding, age 9, traveled to the battlefield in a wagon, recovered the body and brought it back to Yadkin County for burial.[79]

It is known that the remains of other soldiers were recovered and brought home for burial in a local church or family cemetery.[80] Sometimes the bodies were sent home in lead coffins. Other times they were encased in a canvas body bag or a woven body "basket." Two of the sons of Robert Alexander and Charlotte Martin Pettitt Poindexter were brought home and were buried by candlelight because the bodies were so decomposed. T.C.M. Poindexter, of Company F, 28th Regiment, died on July 10, 1862, from typhoid fever in a Richmond hospital. William George Poindexter died at Gettysburg on July 3, 1863. Since the two died a year apart, it is unlikely, but not impossible, that they were brought home at the same time.[81]

Entertainment

When the soldiers were not marching, fighting or drilling, they tried a variety of ways to keep themselves occupied. Playing card games, checkers or chess helped them while away the endless hours. Some spent their free time writing letters, others reading their Bibles, or cleaning their muskets.

Lieutenant John Thomas Conrad noted that the men of his brigade were going to hold a "Tournament," which he believed would be similar to the one some of the Virginia troops had already held. It may have been something like the medieval tournament, since Conrad described it as "very hard riding but then a man has the honor of crowning his lady-love or the prettiest one present if he takes the prize." He believed the tournament would do well as a bit of entertainment, but nothing more.[82]

Discipline

Discipline was important. Obedience to orders could make the difference between life and death. Those who disobeyed commands or deserted, if caught, were punished severely. According to John Thomas Conrad, Colonel J.H. Lane "ordered a fellow out of ranks yesterday evening, just for not keeping his hands down while on dress parade...." Conrad thought that was a "very slight offence," but he liked Colonel Lane because he was strict.[83]

Soldiers who were under arrest for various crimes, mostly desertion, were kept in a "poor house," one soldier wrote while he was stationed in Wilmington. Their place of confinement was called that because the prisoners were given only "pone bread and water."[84]

Calvin Holcomb wrote on March 10, 1862, that while he and his fellow soldiers were on dress parade, someone slipped into their company (Company I) and stole some money. The identity of the thief was unknown.[85] If the thief were caught, he would have been punished.

Letters from the Soldiers

The mail system worsened as the war continued. Soldiers were always anxious to get mail from home, and they feared the letters they sent would not reach their loved ones. Sometimes, letters from home never reached the soldiers, who desperately waited for news.

Writing paper became scarce, and in order to conserve paper, some of the men began writing on one page twice—first from left to right, then the paper was turned and the letter continued by writing across the first lines.[86]

While confined to a hospital in Lynchburg, Virginia, in the summer of 1864, Calvin Holcomb advised his brother Bloom to use the back side of his letter to let him know how his younger brother and the family were getting along. (Calvin was wounded at Chancellorsville in May 1863, but returned to duty. He was wounded in the foot near the Rappahannock River, and retired to the Invalid Corps on Jan. 28, 1864.[87]) He added, "I would send you a sheet to write on but I don't know whether you will get it or not."[88] Calvin's brother, Bloom Virgil Holcomb, enlisted on Feb. 28, 1863, in Company I, 28th. He was wounded near Gaines' Mill about July 28, 1864.[89]

Not only was it difficult for the Confederate soldier to send a letter home, but receiving mail was a problem. During the summer months, armies moved frequently. If a Confederate soldier was captured, he was not always allowed to receive mail by his Federal captors, although the policy regarding mail seemed to vary among the Yankee prisons. While a prisoner of war on Johnson's Island in Lake Erie, Captain William M. Norman (formerly a member of Company A, 28th Regiment) complained in January of 1865 that the "weather was very cold and there was but little communication between here and Sandusky." While he was distressed by news of the defeats of Hood, Hardee, and Breckenridge, the worst "of all I have to contend with is not hearing anything from my affectionate family."[90]

Private John Holcomb, of Company I, was captured and confined to Davids Island in New York Harbor. He was allowed to write home, and he advised his folks that if they wrote to him to "put a Confederate Stamp on and leave it open and it will come."[91]

Sometimes the soldiers relayed rumors about battles and casualties to those back home. James Collins (Company A) wrote that he had heard about a battle at "Yorke Tavern and yesday [sic] and the day before and up to 12 o'clock yesday they [Yankees] had kild thirty thousand of our men but we was still in possession of the Lands." He repeated that he had heard "Our strength is over one hundred thousand men there," but added, "I can't tell whether this report is true or not." Situated only 15 miles from the enemy, Collins had also heard that "they are coming on and if they come we will give them what they came for."[92]

Furloughs

Laura, the daughter of John Thomas Conrad, was ill, and he applied for and was granted a leave of absence of seven days to go home. However, his beloved daughter, nicknamed "Scrappie," died soon after his return. Little Laura, born in September of 1860, was only 15 months old at the time of her death.[93]

Photographs and Tardy Pay

Many of the soldiers had their photographs taken, usually Daguerreotypes or tintypes, to send to loved ones back home. They also cherished pictures sent to them by their wives and families. John Thomas Conrad promised his wife to have his "Type" taken when he returned from doing picket duty at Kinston, North Carolina. His wife had sent him a "Type" of herself, which she had forgotten to pack in his trunk the last time he was home.[94] Although Conrad had promised his wife to send her a picture of himself, he had neither the opportunity nor the funds to do so by the time he arrived in Virginia. He complained that he had not received his wages for the last two months, and was uncertain when he would get paid.[95]

While in the College Hospital at Lynchburg, Virginia, in 1864, Calvin Holcomb complained that he had not "drawn any money in a bout five months." Although he signed the "Pay Rolls every two months" he never received any money.[96] The problem of paying the soldiers increased as the war went on, and inflation devaluated what pay the soldiers did receive.

Battle Fatigue

Commissary Nicholas Biddle Gibbon, whose duty was to furnish the troops with food, noticed that after a hard day of fighting at Gaines' Mill in 1862, the soldiers were so exhausted they preferred "sleep and rest to the provisions I brought for them, and lay scattered about the ground in their blankets."[97]

The life of a soldier, whether Union or Confederate, was not one of glory, but a struggle each day to survive. Those young men who had marched so eagerly to war soon found that they faced death from every quarter. The individual service records of these soldiers provide a glimpse into their years fighting for the cause they believed in. Many were captured and imprisoned more than once, others were wounded multiple times, while others died of disease.

War is not glorious; as General William T. Sherman said, "War is Hell."

Chapter 4

January–May 1862: Wilmington to Hanover Court House

Col. Lane was as cool and composed as if we had been only on a battalion drill. My men never will show any more bravery than on that day.
— Captain W.H. Asbury Speer[1]

Under the command of Colonel James H. Lane, the 28th Regiment was assigned to the Department of Cape Fear through March of 1862.

During their time on the coast, Private Samuel S. Harding (Company I) reported that a large Federal fleet was sighted off Cape Hatteras. Although there were perhaps as many as 120 ships, Harding did not foresee any danger of being involved in a battle, no more so than "getting into one at home."[2] He was soon proved wrong. The Union soldiers that arrived on those ships would soon win a major victory at New Bern, and the 28th and other Confederate regiments would learn the shame of defeat.

First Assignment

On March 13, 1862, the 28th Regiment was transported by train from their camp to New Bern, which was under attack by the Federal forces of General Ambrose E. Burnside. However, the 28th arrived too late to take part in the engagement, but it did act as rear guard to cover the Confederate retreat to Kinston. Still, six men of the regiment were reported missing.[3]

New Bern, March 14, 1862

Forces Engaged: Expeditionary force and Foster's, Reno's, and Parke's Brigades (Union); 5 regiments, and militia (Confederate)

Principal Commanders: Brig. Gen. Ambrose E. Burnside (Union), Brig. Gen. Lawrence O'B. Branch (Confederate)

Estimated Casualties: 1,080 total

Results: Union victory

On March 11, Brigadier General Ambrose Burnside's men left Roanoke Island to rendezvous with Federal gunboats at Hatteras Inlet for an expedition against New Bern. On March 13, the Federal fleet sailed up the Neuse River, and Federal infantry landed on the south bank of the river. They approached the Confederate defenses of New Bern under the command of Brigadier General Lawrence Branch. On March 14, the Federal troops of John G. Foster, Jesse Reno, and John G. Parke attacked along the railroad. After four hours of fighting, the Union troops drove the Confederates out of their fortifications. The Federal soldiers captured nine forts and 41 big guns, and occupied New Bern, which they held until the end of the war.[4]

At the time of the move to New Bern, most of the men of the 28th had just reenlisted and had gone home on the promised 30-day furlough. The ranks were reduced to only 350 men. Colonel Lane was away in Richmond on leave, and the Sergeant and Adjutant were absent from camp, while Major Reeves was sick in bed. Lieutenant Colonel Lowe had to take charge.[5]

The reduced ranks of the 28th Regiment left Wilmington about 10 P.M. on March 10, and arrived in New Bern via Goldsboro about 8 A.M. on March 14. Commissary Nicholas Gibbon recalled that as the troops entered the town, they heard the "heavy rolling of artillery and were told by the men standing about that our men were doing good work and had repulsed the enemy several times." Anxious to join in the fighting, the new arrivals cheered and shouted.[6]

An account by Private W.F. Swaringen published years later in the *Confederate Veteran* tells a different story.

> Arriving there we got out of the freight cars, got forty rounds of cartridges, loaded our guns and got back into the cars. There was great confusion on the streets—horses hitched to vehicles running wild. Two or three men were all but frightened to death when the enemy's big shells were dropped about the city from gun boats. After crossing the long bridge a short distance, our train ran slowly and finally stopped. We could see numbers of soldiers, crippled, falling back to the rear.[7]

After only a short delay, the soldiers of the 28th Regiment moved over the railroad bridge to the battlefield. However, as soon as the train crossed the bridge, they were met by returning Confederate soldiers who told them that the Yankees had "taken possession of our trenches" and that the Confederate forces were in retreat. The men in the 28th did not want to believe that, because they were anxious to join in the fight, but they soon met "such quantities of men" that they could no longer doubt the facts. Gibbon wrote that "we could see whole Regts. crowding along the R. R. for some distance before us." The railroad cars had returned to Kinston. Confederate regiments were positioned in line of battle where the county road crossed the railroad, and had been ordered to "cover the retreat of the defeated Army." The 28th remained in place until the retreating soldiers passed and the enemy was in sight. The Yankee artillery fired at them, and fire from Union gunboats shelled the woods constantly. There was nothing for the 28th to do but follow the retreating army. The 28th was the last of the troops to cross the county bridge, which was then set on fire. The town of New Bern and the railroad bridge were also in flames. Enemy gunboats rained shells down on the town and the railroad cars which were loaded with women and children fleeing the battle scene.[8]

Those Confederates troops who fled across the bridge were portions of the 7th, 33rd, 37th, and 28th regiments, and stragglers from several other North Carolina regiments. Colonel Campbell, of the 7th Regiment, took command and marched the men around New Bern. Gibbon describes that march as "very tiresome on account of the bad condition of the road and the want of provisions for the Army." The men stopped once a day and "ate such provisions as we could get or whatever the kind citizens could provide for us...." Gibbon was especially grateful for the people and "especially the females [who] exerted themselves to provide for our tired and hungry men and then refused to receive any pay."[9]

William Groves Morris, of Company H, 37th North Carolina Regiment, wrote his wife that the 28th was not involved in the fight, but had been ordered to follow up the retreat. However, they came "very neare being surrounded by the Enemy, but all Luckilly Made their Escape."[10]

The flag of Company A, 28th Regiment ("Surry Regulators") was captured on March 14, 1862, by the 3rd New Jersey Regiment. This flag is in very poor condition, extremely soiled, and much of the material is missing, but it is being preserved by the North Carolina Museum of History, Raleigh, North Carolina.[11]

Defeat at New Bern

Three of the regiments at New Bern, and who were to be assigned to Branch's Brigade, had no battlefield experience. In fact, the 37th had only recently been given muskets, and they were not yet proficient in the quick and efficient use of their guns. The 18th and 28th were sent as reinforcements but arrived too late to take part in the action. In addition, with his inexperienced force of about 4,000, Branch faced greatly superior numbers of eight Union infantry regiments, two batteries of artillery, and a cavalry force.[12]

After the battle at New Bern, the North Carolina troops at Kinston were divided into two brigades. The first brigade was placed under General Robert Ransom. The second brigade was placed in a brigade under the command of General Lawrence O'Bryan Branch. Initially, this brigade was known as the Second North Carolina Brigade. This designation remained in effect until the Second Brigade was placed under the command of General A.P. Hill, where it was known as the Fourth Brigade of the Light Division. Orders were later issued which decreed that all brigades, divisions and corps should be called by the names of their commanders; hence those five North Carolina regiments became known as Branch's Brigade.[13]

On March 17, 1862, the 28th regiment, commanded by Colonel James H. Lane, was assigned to the new brigade commanded by General Lawrence O'B. Branch. This brigade was composed of the 18th, 25th, 28th, and 37th regiments, plus John N. Whitford's foot artillery battalion, Alexander C. Latham's and Samuel R. Bunting's batteries, and Peter G. Evan's cavalry unit.[14] While most brigades had only four regiments, the brigade of General Branch (and later under General Lane) contained five regiments. These five regiments remained together in the same brigade until the end of the war.

Branch had no military background, and his appointment to the command of the District of Pamlico,[15] reportedly, came through his political connections.[16] One North Carolina newspaper criticized the appointment of Branch over those officers who were older and more experienced. The paper described Branch as being "incapable of thorough company drill much less to manoeuver a battalion, a regiment, or a brigade."[17] Branch's lack of military training and experience would initially prove costly to the troops under his command, especially at Hanover Court House in Virginia. He learned quickly, and soon redeemed his reputation, but not until after the fighting at Hanover Court House.

28th Ordered to Virginia

Nicholas Gibbon recorded in his diary that the regiment returned to Kinston and remained two or three days before moving eight miles west to the railroad where they camped until the 1st of April. Then they were ordered back to Kinston and remained until the beginning of May, when they received orders to go to Richmond, Virginia.[18]

The 28th Regiment, which now consisted of 1,199 duty-ready men, was ordered to Virginia on May 2, 1862. They were armed with "old smooth-bore muskets" obtained from the Fayetteville arsenal. These muskets had been altered from flint to percussion, but were soon discarded for newer and more modern weapons "gathered on the bloody battlefields in that grand old State."[19]

The regiment arrived in Virginia on May 3 and the next morning they moved to Gordonsville. Here, they waited to receive orders from General Richard S. Ewell. Remembering his uncomfortable experience the last time he had to march for any distance, Captain Nicholas Gibbon bought a horse. This was the first horse he had owned while in the Confederate Army, but he had been entitled to one since October 1861, when he had been appointed assistant commissary of subsistence.[20]

On May 7, 1862, the regiment was ordered to move to the Rapidan River 18 miles north of

Gordonsville. They spent about a week there near the Orange & Alexandria Railroad. Capt. Gibbon believed the area was "one of the prettiest countries that ever was." Without seeing any action, the 28th was ordered back to Gordonsville, and the next day the entire brigade (General Lawrence O'B. Branch's brigade) marched to Madison Court House. The men were shuttled back and forth from Madison Court House to Gordonsville. When ordered back to Gordonsville, after marching only 9 miles, they received orders "to remain" where there were. As commissary, Gibbon spent the rest of the day (Sunday) trying to procure supplies, and he did obtain a good load of flour.[21] After all that marching, one soldier reported that his feet were so sore he had to stop at "Madison till the next day...."[22]

The regiment spent a couple of days marching west toward the Blue Ridge Mountains before being ordered back to Gordonsville. Part of Branch's Brigade left for Hanover Court House on the afternoon of May 21.[23]

Private Caleb Shive McCurdy (Company K), wrote to a friend on May 24, 1862, that in his camp in Hanover County, he had heard enemy cannons firing from below Richmond since about daybreak until about twelve o'clock. He assumed that there had been a fight. Later, he learned that the Yankees were within nine miles of Richmond, and near the railroad. Although his regiment had been called up that morning in "line of battle," the order was rescinded. Still, McCurdy expected to be involved in a fight soon.[24]

William A. Tesh, a private in Company I, wrote that the regiment had been ordered out "in a line of battle yesterday and had to stand their [sic] in the rain about 2 hours." They were told that there was about a thousand "Yankey cavalry in 1 ½ miles," but that the enemy cavalry had got "skerd [scared] and turned around and went back." Tesh believed the Yankees were wise in retreating, because the Confederates had "6 or 7 Regiments all ready." Most of the men of Tesh's regiment had never been in a battle, and the appearance of the enemy so near "made some of them look mighty skerry." Tesh told his father "it did not frighten me a bit," because, if it was God's will, there was no use "to be skeerd about it."[25]

The day before the battle, William A. Tesh answered his father's question about what kind of guns the men had been issued. William replied that most of them still had the "old United States muskets," but that two companies had Enfield "Rifels that will shoot 800 yards." Tesh foresaw the upcoming battle would be "one of the Bigest Fights at Richmond that ever was," and according to rumors circulating, it would be the "battle that would end the war."[26] The rumors were very wrong.

Hanover Court House (Slash Church, Lebanon Church, Taliaferro's Mill), May 26–27, 1862

Forces Engaged: Divisions

Principal Commanders: Brig. Gen. Fitz John Porter (Union), Brig. Gen. L. O'B. Branch (Confederate)

Estimated Casualties: 397 Union (355[27]); 930 Confederate (Porter's figures; 243 killed and wounded, excluding the 28th, per Branch)

Results: Union victory

Part of Porter's V Corp moved to protect the flank of McClellan's army that straddled the Chickahominy River. His objective was to cut the railroad and to clear Telegraph Road for Union reinforcements of Maj. Gen. Irvin McDowell coming from Fredericksburg. Confederates tried to stop the Federals, but were defeated south of Hanover Court House.[28]

Branch's Brigade was sent to join Jackson in the Shenandoah Valley, but was ordered to return to Gordonsville. The Confederate northern flank was in danger. Major General Irvin McDowell had 31,000 Federal soldiers at Fredericksburg. Confederates believed that McDowell

28th Regimental Officers, from Walter Clark, ed., *Histories of the Several Regiments and Battalions from North Carolina in the Great War, 1861–1865, Written by Members of the Respective Commands.* 1. Colonel James H. Lane; 2. Lt. Col. Samuel S. Lowe; 3. Lt. Col. W.H.A. Speer; 4. Robert Gibbon, Surgeon; 5. F. Milton Kennedy, Chaplain; 6. George S. Thompson, Quartermaster; 7. Capt. Nicholas Gibbon, Commissary (courtesy of the North Carolina Department of Archives and History).

would move southward to join with McClellan's army near Richmond. Johnston ordered Branch to guard the Virginia Central Railroad and to link up with the main Confederate force of 10,000 men under Brigadier General Joseph R. Anderson just south of Fredericksburg.[29]

Brigadier General Lawrence O'Bryan Branch reported on May 29, 1862, that he had been ordered to protect the railroad against destruction by the enemy. In order to "carry out the other views and wishes of General Johnston," Branch had moved his brigade to the mouth of the road leading to Ashland. This position gave him a route to retreat if he encountered a large enemy force.[30] Branch was inexperienced, and was unaware of the enemy's position and strength. He relied on reports from the local citizens, which were totally inaccurate.[31] To make the situation worse, Brigadier General Anderson had withdrawn to Richmond, leaving Branch and his men to make up the left flank of Johnston's army and to take part in the attack on McClellan's right as part of the Confederate offensive.[32]

General McClellan ordered his Federal troops under General Fitz John Porter of the V Corps to reconnoiter toward Hanover Court House, and drive the enemy out of the area. Porter had 15 regiments of infantry, three regiments of cavalry, and four batteries of artillery. Porter's men outnumbered Branch's by about 3:1.[33] Unaware of the strength of the enemy, Branch moved his brigade of about 4,000 men toward to Hanover Court House. Most of Branch's Brigade, both officers and men, had never been in a battle.[34] Some of the soldiers had enlisted only two months earlier. James W. Ashburn, a private in Company A, 28th Regiment, volunteered on March 18, 1862, at age 18. (Ashburn was one of those captured near Hanover Court House, May 27, 1862.[35])

Captain Nicholas Gibbon recorded in his diary that on the 25th of May, the 28th Regiment of Branch's Brigade marched two miles to a farm on the road to Richmond. When night came, they returned to their camp. On Monday, May 26, the Brigade marched down toward Richmond as far the fork in the road to Ashland. Here, they set up camp and spent a very "wet and disagreeable" night without tents or shelter except what could be made from brush.[36]

Taliaferro's Mill (Kinney's Farm)

On May 27, 1862, sporadic fighting took place east and south of Hanover Court House, the county seat of Hanover County. The courthouse lies south of the South Anna River and the Pamunkey River, near the Virginia Central Railroad. It is approximately 18 miles northeast of Richmond, and as the crow flies, probably even closer. The 28th Regiment was involved in fighting the enemy at Taliaferro's Mill, Dr. Kinney's farm, and in the fields and woods of the area.

General Branch had set up his headquarters at Slash Church, where he received the report that Federal troops were advancing toward Taliaferro's Mill (on Crump's Creek[37]), where two companies of the 37th Regiment had been on picket duty the previous night. Branch decided to send Colonel James Henry Lane and his 28th Regiment, with part of Latham's Battery, to that area to repel any Federal troops they encountered. Branch also dispatched the 45th Georgia to repair the railroad at Ashcake, and to watch for the approach of the enemy from that direction. The Georgia troops did not encounter any enemy forces, but the 28th did.[38]

Colonel Lane reported: "In obedience to your [General Branch's] orders, I proceeded to Taliaferro's Mill on the morning of the 27th of May with 890 of my regiment and a section of Latham's battery, commanded by Lieut. J.R. Potts."[39]

While Lane examined the area for a suitable position for his forces, he received news that the enemy was approaching from the direction of Hanover Court House. He turned his men and retraced his steps, and sent out a platoon of Company G as flankers, under Capt. George B. Johnston. These men went to the right, the supposedly in the direction of the enemy, and another group, under Lieut. E.G. Morrow, was sent to his left and front. Not until the 28th was almost out of the pine thicket in front of Dr. Kinney's house did they discover some of the enemy were not where they were expected. Lane ordered his regiment to halt and to face "by the rear rank, and wheeled to the right through the woods." They sent volleys of deadly fire into a portion of the 25th New York Regiment, as his men executed the movement. Out of the thicket, they saw another group of enemy soldiers in the road that passed Dr. Kinney's and continued toward Richmond. Federal troops had previously been concealed in the wheat field and behind the house immediately in front of Lane's men. The enemy's fire was promptly returned by the 28th.[40]

Colonel Lane then ordered his regiment to charge, and they "did it most gallantly, many of them, shouting, leaped the ditch and high fence inclosing the field of wheat, while the rest rushed into the yard and around the house." Although the Federal soldiers were armed with Springfield rifles, they were flushed out like game, and were forced to drop back into the wheat field under the barrage of the unerring marksmen of the 28th.[41]

Lane reported that his casualties in killed and wounded were "not less than 200." His men also captured a large number of prisoners, but only about 75 of the prisoners were able to be sent to the rear. These were placed with a small detachment of cavalry from the 4th Virginia Regiment, which was retiring from Taliaferro's mill.[42]

One diarist recorded that in the middle of the firing, Colonel Lane sat on his horse yelling "Charge on the scoundrels, boys!" Only when the 28th chased the Federals beyond the wheat field did Lane realize what he was up against. The Union troops that Lane's men had routed were only the skirmish line of an entire brigade supported by two heavy guns.[43]

According to a Captain Morris, a member of the 37th Regiment of Branch's Brigade, Colonel Lane's 28th Regiment was entirely "cut off and had to take care of itself." Morris stated that 28th had "Encountered the advanced Regt of the Enemy and killed some 80 or More & captured some 68 prisoners...." Because of their actions, Colonel Lane was very proud of his men. Lane had good reasons to be proud. His inexperienced men had met a superior force, and most of his men had managed to fight their way out.[44]

Lane described the situation in his report.

After the 28th had had swept the 25h New York Regiment from their path, and were crossing the wheat field themselves, they discovered they were in the "presence of a whole brigade, commanded by General [John H.] Martindale, about 400 yards distant from our extreme right...." The enemy opened a heavy fire on the 28th from two batteries which sat upon an eminence. The enemy's aim was off and the big guns fired too high. This gave Lane and his men time to reform in a field opposite Dr. Kinney's dwelling, perpendicular to their earlier position. As they were reforming, the flag-bearer was shot down, but one of his comrades seized the flag and carried it forward.[45]

At this point, Colonel Lane sent a message to Branch asking for reinforcements. He told Branch that they "had been cut off by an overwhelming force." Lane also sent a courier to Hanover Court House for help.[46]

After Lane's men had reformed, the hot, excited, and exhausted soldiers threw off their knapsacks, which had been made heavier than usual by the drenching rain of the previous night, and advanced a short distance before they were ordered to lie down. Some of Lane's heavy artillery moved from the road to take a more commanding position in rear of the dwelling house. Thus situated, the artillery was only about 600 to 700 yards from the enemy's guns. In their new position, Lane ordered his infantry to fire at the enemy, and forced the Federals to withdraw one of their artillery pieces. Lane remarked that Lieutenant John R. Potts and his men acted with "great gallantry and must have done considerable execution."[47]

Lane kept his men fighting for over three hours, still expecting to get reinforcements either from Branch or from Hanover Junction. Help did not come, and Lane learned from Captain W.J. Montgomery that the enemy was sending a large force through a wooded ravine on their right that would soon surround them.[48]

Montgomery was immediately ordered to follow the head of their line along a fence running parallel to the road, and the other companies of the regiment were ordered to follow after him. After extending their line in a new direction, Lane saw that fire from the enemy was continuing, and that they were sending out sharpshooters to move between Lane's infantry and his artillery up the hollow. In addition, Lane discovered that the Federal artillery had corrected their range and was "pouring a hot fire upon us." He could see that the enemy had a "strong infantry reserve in rear of their batteries," and he deemed it advisable to retire. Lane was unable to recall Captain Johnston from the left, and was forced to leave his dead and badly wounded on the field. They also left an "an old ambulance, a two-horse wagon, and our knapsacks." A 12-pound brass howitzer had to be abandoned, because one of the horses that pulled it was killed and three other horses badly wounded.[49]

Regrettably, Lane knew that he had left seven of his men dead and 15 wounded when he ordered the retreat across the field to the road while under enemy fire. During the retreat, many of his men fell from exhaustion along the roadside, and Lane reported that many of them were still missing. He was sure that in a few days the number of missing would be greatly reduced, since some had already found their way back. The men did well, considering they had spent the previous night in a drenching rain without tents or shelter. They had marched over a horribly muddy road with unusually heavy knapsacks, and had been deprived of food. Lane believed that they had "fought bravely and willingly for three hours in anticipation of being re-enforced," because they were in no condition to retreat.[50]

Captain Nicholas Gibbon saw the action differently. He said that the fighting he saw was over in less time than it took to write about it. He described how the Confederates drove the enemy through a wheat field and "cut them down by our destructive fire and taking sixty-eight prisoners." With only the two small pieces of artillery of Capt. Latham's company, the men of the 28th had opened fire on the enemy, and continued fighting for about 1½ hours. Gibbon noted that Colonel Lane sent the prisoners to the rear, and asked General Branch for reinforcements, "but none came." Soon Gibbon heard cannon fire from the direction where General Branch had remained with six regiments and part of the artillery. Gibbon first believed that Branch was attacking the enemy, but soon became apparent that a large force of Yankees was about to surround them. Colonel Lane saw what was about to happen and directed his men toward Hanover Court House.[51]

Captain William H. Asbury Speer, Company I, 28th Regiment, wrote a first-hand account of the fighting at Hanover Court House (Taliaferro's Mill), a battle in which he was captured. Speer's 28th regiment and the rest of brigade had camped about 5 miles away from the Hanover Court House on the night of May 26. It was a rainy night and, having no tents, the men suffered greatly. Speer recalled that they had slept in tents only one night in the last five weeks. Speer was ordered to send a detail from his company to assist Captain Latham with his battery. The 28th Regiment was then ordered into line of battle, but then were ordered to return back to the road leading to Hanover Court House. In obeying that order, Speer and his regiment passed the rest of the brigade.[52]

The road was so muddy it was almost impassable in places, and occasionally they had to walk along the banks. When they reached Dr. Kinny's house, which was 2 ½ miles from their camp, they halted in an old field. Ten men from each company went to Dr. Kinney's well to fill their canteens. Leaving Dr. Kinney's house, Speer and his men continued on the road to a mill on the Pamunkey River. They halted there on a hill and loaded their guns. The scouts then reported that the enemy was flanking them, but it was believed that it was two companies of their brigade on picket duty. Speer and his soldiers then returned along the road to Dr. Kinney's house. Captain G.B. Johnston of Company G and 20 of his men, acting as skirmishers, were moving along the right side of the road moving in a wooded area. Just as he and the rest moved by the old field at Dr. Kinney's, their left flank was fired upon by the 25th New York, who were in battle formation in Kinney's apple orchard. They were also attacked by the 5th Massachusetts on their left from a thicket of pines. Thus, Speer and his men suddenly found themselves in a crossfire. Orders were given for the men to turn about face, "by companies, half wheel through the woods," which was done by all except the companies of Captain Montgomery from Stanly County and Captain Apperson's Company F, who marched up the road to engage in battle.[53] (This maneuver of "halt-front-about-face by company right wheel-march" was also reported by Capt. Nicholas Gibbon.[54]) The other companies continued through the woods, where they were able to fire upon enemy skirmishers. The left of Speer's company fired a volley and wounded or killed 10 of the enemy. Shortly thereafter, a horse came running through the woods. At first it was believed to have been Colonel Lane's horse and it was feared that he had been killed or wounded.[55] It was learned that the horse belonged to Captain Nicholas Gibbon. Gibbon had been riding behind the companies when they were fired upon by the Yankees. His horse bolted at the sound of the musketry and ran through the roods. Gibbon lost his balance and was "dashed against a tree." He soon regained his composure and rejoined the men, but on foot.[56]

Speer's men came out of the woods and ran up the road, where they chased a retreating force of enemy troops. After crossing a plank fence and a wheat field, Speer's men were ordered to fall back to the woods along the road. They saw a regiment of the enemy coming up the road in their rear. From the woods, Speer's men began firing when the enemy was within 60 yards. They were able to kill many and drive the enemy back. Speer recalled that one of his men, Headspeth, was shot through the hand. Lieutenants Neal (or Simon) Bohannon and Frederick Long coolly marched in front of the company trying to keep the men "quiet & showing them how to aim & fire deliberately while in the woods" in the earlier part of the engagement. Speer saw the enemy's adjutant killed, "shot off his horse by one of Captain Linebarger's men."[57]

The men returned to the Kinney farm, where they were under enemy artillery fire. Captain G.B. Johnston and 20 of his Company G were ordered to ascertain the enemy's position and their number. As a result, Johnston and his men were captured.[58]

Speer saw a shell hit young Pleasant H. Roberts of Surry County, which fractured both his thighs and caused his death. He saw two more of Company A killed by shells. One shell took "off the top of one of their heads & cutting the other [in two]."[59]

Colonel Lane then ordered his men to leave the top of the hill and to lie down behind a fence. Then they were deployed along a fence to the right and to cross a branch below a spring. They crossed the branch and Captain Montgomery sent some of his men to ascertain the enemy's position. Major Samuel Lowe approached on his horse and ordered a retreat. The men trooped into the main road to Hanover Court House, where they had to pass "directly under the fire of the enemy's guns," and one man in Company H was killed.[60]

By the time Speer and 70 of his men reached the road, they were exhausted. Still, they had to move to avoid the Minié balls and artillery shells which were falling all around them. The Confederate artillery did not know the infantry was in retreat. Thus, Captain Stowe, who had remained at his post with the big guns, was captured.[61]

The Confederate artillery began firing and Colonel Lane saw the enemy raise a white flag. He ordered the firing stopped, and sent a man ahead carrying a white handkerchief on his gun. It was just a ploy, however, and the enemy resumed their deadly bombardment toward the McKinney property.[62]

Captain Speer reported that all the officers of the 28th acted "cooly & brave," especially Colonel Lane, who was "as cool and composed as if he had been only on a battalion drill." Speer commented that his men would never show any more bravery than on that day.

My Lieuts. were very cool & acted with as much bravery as old soldiers. Lieut. Long is deserving of much credit for his conduct. I cannot praise my men & officers as well as they deserve.[63]

During the retreat to Hanover Court House, many of the exhausted men fell by the way and were captured by the pursuing enemy. Although the Federals were being attacked in their rear by a Confederate brigade, they did not stop their pursuit of Speer and his men. When the Confederate cavalry and artillery came rushing down the road, Speer and his men took to the woods. They soon returned to the road and continued to the bridge at the river, with the enemy cavalry right behind them. Ahead, Speer could see the rest of the regiment across the river. He hoped that he and the 15 men who were with him could cross the river to reach them. The stream was "very deep and much wider" than he expected. He could swim across the river to safety, but he did not want to leave his men, some of whom could not swim. Thus, Speer and the others were forced to surrender to a group of about 60 Yankee cavalry. Now prisoners, Speer and his men were forced to march back to Hanover Court House, and then on to Dr. Kinney's house where the fighting had begun. His privates were marched to a stable and kept there under guard. Speer and other officers were taken to General Daniel Butterfield and questioned about the fight. He was also questioned by the Yankee general about Union sentiment in North Carolina.[64]

Speer summarized the part the 28th had in the battle. The 28th faced three enemy brigades: the 25th New York, the 44th New York, and the 5th Massachusetts, all of whom had been "badly hurt" by Confederate soldiers. Skirmishers from the 6th Pennsylvania had also been badly hurt in the fight.[65]

Although Speer had been captured, Captain Nicholas Gibbon, with the guidance of a Negro boy, reached the bridge over the Pamunkey River. He and several of the men following him heard the sound of horses coming down the hill, and they hid. As he Yankee officers dismounted, Gibbon led the men into the swamp. The men, including two lieutenants from Company B, agreed to follow Gibbon, and they moved further into the swamp where the cavalry could not penetrate. Gibbon and the men lay in the swamp all night, "cold and shivering." The next day they reached the road to Ashland and the forces under General Branch, except for the 28th, "which had been overpowered and compelled to retire with considerable loss." Gibbon reported to General Branch how he had escaped with about 70 men.[66] For his efforts, Gibbon was accused by General Branch of abandoning his regiment "while in action." Gibbon replied, "It's no such thing, sir."[67]

Many of the 28th Captured

When the fighting was over, Colonel Lane returned with only about half of his regiment. Four hundred could not be accounted for.[68]

Nicholas Gibbon reported that in the fighting at Hanover Court House his regiment (the 28th) "lost many good men as prisoners—our Major, Surgeon, Asst. Surgeon, 4 Captains, 4 Lieuts. and many men." The surgeon (probably W.R. Barham) was not content to remain a prisoner and he quietly "walked off without saying a word" before his Yankee captors had a chance to parole him.[69]

The captured Confederates were initially lined up in the road in front of Dr. Kinney's house. Then they were marched to General George McClellan's headquarters, 18 miles away. As they passed the battlefield, Captain W.H.A. Speer saw 50 of his Confederate comrades lying beside a large hole in which they were to be buried. He observed New York Zouaves pillaging the pockets of dead Confederates "to steal money, pocket knives, and other little tricks."[70]

The captives marched all day, and were given little time to rest. The road conditions along which they traveled were very bad, and in some places, wrote Captain Speer, they had to "wade in mud and water up to our boot tops...." He saw the mark the enemy invaders had left on the countryside: "fences thrown down burnt and crops turned out." There were, however, a few kindly individuals among the Federal troops. In the yard of a "fine residence," a Federal cavalry man took Captain Speer's canteen, filled it with water and returned it to him. He also offered Speer a "drink of good whiskey," which he also accepted. The Yankee cavalry soldier allowed Captain Speer to ride his horse from the house to the Federal camp, five miles away.[71] Once they arrived at the Union headquarters, the Yankees lined the road "to get a good look at the dirty rebels." Speer and his fellow prisoners were "gazed and stared at as if we had been live Devils and they were nearly as fearful of us." After they reached the Federal camp, the name, rank and regiment of each prisoner was recorded. On closer inspection, the Yankee soldiers seemed amazed that their captives were "human beings as same as themselves." After all the names were recorded, the prisoners were put into a "bull pen," and a double guard was set to watch them. The guards were not very friendly toward their prisoners.[72]

The hardships of the prisoners were just beginning They had had nothing to eat for 36 hours. They had slept in the rain without any tents the night before the battle, they had marched and fought all day, and had been captured. As prisoners, they were forced to march 18 miles, without anything to eat. When at last they were issued crackers and fresh beef, some of the men were so hungry they ate the beef raw.[73]

On the morning of May 29, another group of prisoners arrived from the 28th of Branch's Brigade. This brought the total number of prisoners to about 500, according to Captain Speer. They started marching toward White House Landing, 16 miles away on the Pamunkey River. After they had marched only part of that distance, they were put on a train to ride the rest of the distance. At White House Landing, the Confederate prisoners boarded a steamer and were taken to Fort Monroe.[74]

From Fort Monroe, the prisoners were dispatched to various prisons. Captured officers were sent to Fort Columbus, in New York Harbor; and privates were sent to Castle William.[75] Captain Speer and the other officers were eventually imprisoned on Johnson's Island in Lake Erie.[76]

At this point in the war, prisoners were being exchanged by both sides. Major General George B. McClellan wanted to obtain the release of Lieutenant Perkins, an aide-de-camp to Brigadier General Butterfield, who had been captured at Hanover Court House. McClellan offered to exchange Confederate prisoners Lieutenant Marens A. Throneburg [Thornburg] or Lieutenant Neil (Neal) Bohannon (both from the 28th North Carolina) for Perkins. However, before the exchange could take place, Throneburg and Bohannon had been sent to the "rear" and so passed out of McClellan's department. Throneburg was transported to Fort Columbus on the steamer *Star*. McClellan tried unsuccessfully to get Throneburg sent to City Point for the exchange.[77] In a subsequent communication to the Commander of the Army of Northern Virginia, McClellan did not know whether Throneburg had been sent to Fort Columbus or Fort Delaware.[78]

A member of the 37th Regiment summarized the Battle of Hanover Court House: "A sad but so far as the men, Company, & Regimental officers are concerned, a brilliant affair for North Carolinians. Of the Rest, the public must judge."[79]

The War Continues

Those men of the 28th Regiment who escaped capture eventually reached Taylorsville about sunset. For the next three days they attempted to rejoin the rest of the brigade, with "scarcely anything to eat."[80]

General Branch reported a total of 243 killed and wounded among his brigade at Hanover Court House, "excluding those in J.H. Lane's Twenty-eighty North Carolina."[81] Exact casualty figures for this engagement are controversial. Over 400 men were captured (possibly 500), including Captain William H. Asbury Speer.[82] Documents among Governor Clark's papers indicate that of the three regiments that bore the brunt of the fighting, the 37th Regiment had 29 killed, 76 wounded, and 132 missing; the 18th lost 38 killed, 88 wounded and 56 missing, and the 28th had 6 killed, 14 wounded, and 268 missing.[83] Branch's loss was counted as 72 killed and 191 wounded.[84] This figure is 20 more than initially reported.

The Federals suffered 355 casualties. Union General Porter claimed to have buried 200 Confederates and taken 730 Confederate prisoners.[85]

A count of the individuals listed in *North Carolina Troops, 1861–1865: A Roster,* Vol. 8, shows that 8 men were killed, 14 wounded, and 263 taken prisoner in the 28th Regiment alone on May 27, 1862, at or near Hanover Court House.[86] By June 26, 1862, the 28th regiment could muster only 480 men.[87]

Branch Blamed for the Defeat

Brigadier General Lawrence O'B. Branch had suffered a second defeat at Hanover Court House. Lieutenant John Thomas Conrad survived the fighting and several days afterwards wrote to tell his wife of his own "safe delivery." Conrad was thankful that five of his men — Flinn, Adams, Colvard, Martin and Shepperd — had escaped being captured by the Yankees. Conrad did not like General Branch, and neither did some of his fellow officers and private soldiers:

> I don't think there is an officer or private in the whole Brigade that thinks any thing of him [Branch] or that he is competent.... On the day of the battle there was two Brigades near us, one in three miles of us, the other in 5 miles, and both sent to Branch to know if he needed reinforcements and he sent them word that he did not, when he knew that there was a much larger force opposed to us than we had.[88]

Conrad blamed Branch for the defeat: "We could have easily whiped the Yankees if we had only been reinforced by another Brigade and why Branch let the 18th and 37th fight against 6,000 and the 28th against 5,000 and not ask for reinforcements when they were near us, is a mystery...."[89] Conrad soon learned of the location of some of the prisoners captured at Hanover Court House: "Neal [Bohannon] and Captain Speer are in Fort Columbus, New York, with the balance of our brigade officers."[90]

Other officers blamed General Branch for their defeat at Hanover Court House. William Groves Morris attributed the loss to bad management on Branch's part. He believed that Branch had been slack in accepting the unverified information obtained from a citizen that the enemy force was small. Branch had "believed it but No person else did." According to Morris, Branch did not utilize the forces that were under his command.[91]

An account was published in a Richmond newspaper by one of Branch's own men which blamed Branch for leaving three regiments to face a much larger enemy force without support, although he had the means to remedy the situation with four regiments and a battery of artillery he did not deploy. The writer criticized Branch for not being on the battlefield to direct his troops in person.[92] Branch corrected this deficiency and in subsequent battles, he was on the battlefield with his men. This practice probably led to his death at Sharpsburg.

Although Branch sent pickets composed of cavalry and two companies of infantry to Taliaferro's Mill, the pickets were not aware that the enemy they spotted was only part of the 6th Pennsylvania Cavalry. Branch, unaware of the size of the approaching Federal force, subsequently sent only the 28th North Carolina and a section of artillery to Taliferro's Mill. When Lane arrived at the mill, he could not find the pickets from the 37th North Carolina. There, he was told that the Federals were in his rear, between his regiment and the rest of Branch's Confederate forces. Lane tried to get back to Branch, but he encountered the 25th New York. His only recourse was to order his men to charge. He then had to reform and order his command to fall back because they were being attacked by Butterfield's brigade.[93]

Lane, unaware of the large numbers of Federal troops that were approaching, chose to stay and fight, rather than retreat to Hanover Court House. This resulted in the capture of a large number of his regiment.

Brigadier General Branch attributed his defeat at Hanover Court House to the fact that his men had been faced with an entire division of the enemy, and that a large part of General McClellan's force was near by.[94] When Branch wrote his report, he had not received a report of the engagement from Colonel Lane, and while he reported that he had lost 66 men killed and 177 wounded, he was unaware of the losses in the 28th and the large number that were taken prisoner.

Other factors played a part, including poor communication, inadequate knowledge of the movement of the enemy, inexperienced Confederate soldiers, and the failure of Branch to send reinforcements to aid the 28th.

Historian Douglas S. Freeman believed the affair at Hanover Court House was "in no sense discreditable to Branch."[95] The Confederates were, however, driven west to Ashland, but only after putting up a stiff fight.

Some of the blame may be attributed to General Joseph E. Johnston. The Confederate commander had ordered both Branch and Anderson to move closer to Richmond, and Branch was not only to act as a rear guard for Anderson, but he was supposed to guard the railroads in the area.[96]

However, General Robert E. Lee wrote to commend Branch and his men for their fight against superior numbers. He also expressed his approval of Branch's actions, and asked Branch to express his "hearty approval of their [the men's] conduct, and hope that on future occasions they will evince a like heroism and patriotic devotion."[97]

Branch believed the press had unjustly criticized him. He believed that his troops fought well and, if Porter had not received reinforcements, they might have been forced to retreat. Branch had intended to use the 33rd and the 12th North Carolina regiments to attack the enemy's right, but they failed to reach the field in time. Branch had held the 7th back as a rear guard and thus avoided capture. While Branch had sent to Brigadier General Charles W. Field for reinforcement, for some unknown reason they never arrived.[98]

Branch attempted to reverse opinions against him by writing an article to the *Wilmington Daily Journal*: "If there is not honor and justice enough left in the State to protect me whilst absent in the discharge of duties to the country, from such base and foul attacks, I will remain without defence until time and circumstances permit me to return."[99]

Regardless of the loss of many of the men of the 28th, Brigadier General Branch had shown progress in the way he handled the encounter. His main failure was one of communication and reconnaissance. He was misinformed as to the strength of the approaching army, and thus the men he sent out were vastly outnumbered, defeated, and many captured.[100]

In June of 1862, Branch's Brigade of A.P. Hill's Division became part of the 1st Corps, Army of Northern Virginia.

Chapter 5

June 25–July 1, 1862:
Seven Days' Battles

*...the incessant roar of musketry hissed with the loud boom
of the cannon.... I don't think any thing ever equaled it.*
—1st Lieutenant John Thomas Conrad[1]

After Hanover Court House

During the Peninsular Campaign, the Federal forces were commanded by General George McClellan. General Robert E. Lee assumed command of the Army of Northern Virginia on June 1, 1862, after General Joseph E. Johnston was wounded twice at Seven Pines. Initially, the battles planned and executed by General Lee were fought while the Confederate forces were at their zenith, and Lee's victories gave the Confederacy hope of winning the war. Although there were casualties during this period, they were nothing compared to the number of casualties that both sides would suffer in the Battle of Antietam (Sharpsburg, Maryland), on September 17, 1862, or at Gettysburg in 1863 (Appendix VII). As Lee's forces diminished, so did his ability to wage an offensive war or to win over his enemy.

The 28th Regiment made camp west of Richmond after the fighting at Hanover Court House until June 26, 1862, when they left camp and crossed the Chickahominy River. There they clashed with the right flank of McClelland's army near Mechanicsville. This was the opening conflict of a series of battles known as the Seven Days' Battles.

During June, while Confederate troops were massed to protect Richmond, the Federal forces began sending up balloons to determine the location of the Confederate troops. One soldier reported that fighting had been occurring below Richmond for three or four days, and that the "Yankeys have bin a sending up Balloons 8 or 10 times a day to see what our men is a doing."[2]

At this point in time, even before the Seven Days' Battles, Private William Tesh had doubts about the duration of the war. "Some times I think Peace will be made in a few months and then a gain I don't think it will be made in two or three years, But it will be made...."[3]

This series of battles was fought over a seven-day period around the Confederate capitol of Richmond, Virginia. The fighting began on June 25 and continued through July 1, 1862. Individually, these battles are named after the location in which the fighting took place, and most also have several other names, depending on which side was writing the reports:

1) Oak Grove (Henrico, King's School House, and The Orchards), June 25, 1862;
2) Mechanicsville (Ellison's Mills, Beaver Dam Creek), June 26, 1862;
3) Gaines' Mill (First Cold Harbor, Chickahominy), June 27–28, 1862;
4) Garnett's and Golding's Farms, June 27–28;
5) Savage's Station and Allen's Farm (Peach Orchard), June 29, 1862;

6) White Oak Swamp/Frayser's Farm (Glendale, Charles City, New Market Cross Roads, Nelson's Farm, or Turkey Bend), June 30, 1862; and

7) Malvern Hill (Crew's Farm), July 1, 1862.[4]

The classification found in Boatner's *Dictionary of the Civil War* disagrees with the listing of the Civil War Sites Advisory Commission Report on the Nation's Civil War Battlefields (CWSAC). The Commission does not include Garnett's and Golding's Farms (which was an engagement between McClellan and Magruder) in the major battles fought over the seven days.

During the Seven Days' Battles, the 28th Regiment, North Carolina Infantry was part of the Fourth Brigade (Branch's Brigade). That brigade was one of six in Major General A.P. Hill's Light Division.[5]

---

1. Oak Grove (Henrico, King's School House, The Orchards, French's Field), June 25, 1862

Forces Engaged: Corps

Principal Commanders: Maj. Gen. George B. McClellan (Union), Gen. Robert E. Lee (Confederate)

Estimated Casualties: 1,057 total (516 Union; 541 Confederate)

Results: Inconclusive (Union withdrew their lines).

On June 25, 1862, the first of the Seven Days' Battles took place as Major General George McClellan moved his lines along the Williamsburg Road in order to bring Richmond within the range of his heavy artillery. Union forces attacked over swampy ground, but the battle was stopped by darkness. McClellan was unable to stop the Confederate offensive which had already begun. The next day, Lee took the initiative and attacked McClellan at Beaver Dam

---

Early in June, Branch's Brigade was moved to a site about three miles north of Richmond on the Brook Turnpike. They remained there until June 25 when they were ordered to move near Half Sink in preparation for General Lee's planned attack on the Federal right at Mechanicsville. The division of General A.P. Hill (of which Branch's Brigade was a part), along with General Longstreet's division, were positioned to the northwest of the Meadow Bridge Road. Branch's men were on the left of A.P. Hill's line, with General Thomas J. ("Stonewall") Jackson's troops moving upon the left of Branch's line. Lee planned for A.P. Hill to advance on Mechanicsville and Jackson was to move forward on Hill's left. However, Lee's plan failed when Jackson did not reach his assigned position on time and Hill launched his attack with authorization from Lee. Colonel Lane went into this series of battles with 480 men, less than half the regular strength of a regiment. When Lane wrote up a report of the activities of his regiment beginning on June 25, 1862, he reported that he and his men, with the rest of Branch's Brigade, had marched up the Telegraph Road. They crossed the Chickahominy on the morning of the 26th, and advanced toward Meadow Bridge. He sent two companies to Mrs. Crenshaw's bridge to inform Lieutenant Colonel Robert F. Hoke, with a part of his regiment who were doing picket duty on the south side of the Chickahominy, that the way was clear. They then continued the march toward Mechanicsville. Lane reported that another one of his men was wounded on the way to Mechanicsville.[7]

Lane reported that the fighting had already begun when Branch's Brigade reached Mechanicsville. His regiment was ordered to support a battery which was firing from the works to the left of the road. One man was wounded that evening.[8] Branch received orders to move forward to support those already engaged in battle.[9]

2. Mechanicsville (Ellison's Mills, Beaver Dam Creek), June 26, 1862

Forces engaged: 31,987 total (15,631 Union; 16,356 Confederate)

Principal Commanders: Brig. Gen. Fitz John Porter (Union), General Robert E. Lee (Confederate)

Casualties: 1,700 total (400 Union; 1,300 Confederate)

Results: Union victory

The second of the Seven Days' Battles began when General Lee initiated an offensive move against McClellan's right flank on the north side of the Chickahominy River. A.P. Hill's division, reinforced by one of D.H. Hill's brigades, began a series of futile assaults against the Union V Corps, who were behind Beaver Dam Creek. The Confederates were driven back and suffered heavy casualties. Jackson's Shenandoah Valley divisions approached from the northeast and forced Union General Porter to withdraw to a position behind Gaines' Mill.[10]

Lane reported that he and his men slept upon the ground that night, and acted as a support group the next morning. When the enemy artillery fired upon them, another one of his men was wounded.[11]

During the night, the Federal forces fell back behind a defensive position at Gaines' Mill, and then retired to Cold Harbor.

The fighting at Gaines' Mill (also called 1st Cold Harbor and Chickahominy), occurred on the third day of the Seven Days' Battles during the Peninsular Campaign. After the failure of the Confederates at Mechanicsville, Lee pressed on toward Gaines' Mill where the Federals were entrenched in a new position. A.P. Hill attacked along Beaver Dam Creek early on the morning of June 27, and encountered only a small force, but by about 2 P.M., Hill faced the main Federal line along a strong defensive position along Boatswain's Swamp. Subsequent attacks by the brigades of Gregg, Branch, Pender, Anderson, Archer, and Field failed to get through the swamp to attack the main Federal positions. Lee ordered Hill to delay until Jackson could get into position, but Jackson was delayed. Longstreet was ordered to conduct a diversionary attack to relieve pressure on the Confederate right until Jackson could attack. When Jackson finally arrived, he held back his own division for fear they would encounter fire from other Confederate troops. Jackson was unaware that the attack of both A.P. Hill and Longstreet had been stopped await-

3. Gaines' Mill (1st Cold Harbor), June 27, 1862

Forces Engaged: 91,232 total (34,214 Federal; 57,018 Confederate)

Principal Commanders: Brig. Gen. Fitz John Porter (Union), Gen. Robert E. Lee (Confederate)

Total Casualties: estimated 15,500 total (6,800 Union: killed, 893, wounded, 3,107, missing/captured, 2,836; 8,700 Confederate, killed or wounded)[12]

Result: Confederate victory

On June 27, 1862, Lee renewed his attack against Porter's V Corps, which had established a strong defensive line behind Boatswain's Swamp north of the Chickahominy River. Porter's Federal soldiers held fast for the afternoon against disjointed Confederate attacks, and inflicted heavy casualties. At dusk the Confederates mounted a coordinated assault that broke Porter's line and drove the Union forces back toward the river. The Federals retreated across the river during the night. The defeat of the Union forces at Gaines' Mill convinced Union General McClellan to abandon his advance on Richmond, and he began a retreat to the James River. The Confederate victory at Gaines' Mill saved Richmond for the Confederacy in 1862.[13]

Vicinity of Cold Harbor, ruins of Gaines' Mill (Library of Congress, LC-DIG cwpb 00545).

ing his arrival. About an hour before dark, the Confederates finally began an attack all along their front line, and after severe fighting the Federals were driven back.[14]

From General R.E. Lee's perspective as he wrote in his report, A.P. Hill and his division arrived at Cold Harbor about 2 P.M. to encounter enemy forces. Hill then formed a line parallel to the road leading from there to the McGehee house. Lee noted that the "principal part of the Federal army" was situated north of the Chickahominy. It was Hill's division alone that met the enemy with the "impetuous courage for which that officer and his troops are distinguished." Although Lee knew that most of Hill's men had never been in a battle before, they still "were rallied and in turn repelled the advance of the enemy." The men of Hill's Division managed to hold their ground until the arrival of fresh troops enabled them to withdraw.[15]

General Hill noted that when his division arrived, Branch's Brigade was ordered to form on Gregg's right. Anderson's men formed on Branch's right, and Field to the right of Anderson, connected to Archer's men. Hill delayed giving the order to attack until about 2:30 P.M., when he could hear fire from General Longstreet's troops. Gregg, Branch, and Anderson's men became engaged in battle. "The incessant roar of musketry and deep thunder of artillery," according to Hill, "told that the whole force of the enemy were in my front." Pender's men were sent to relieve the men of Branch's Brigade, who were being "hard pressed."[16]

The position of the Federal soldiers made the task of Branch's Brigade extremely difficult. To reach the enemy, the regiments had to advance through a thickly wooded swamp, then climb up a slope. Instead of maneuvering and firing at once, the men of the brigade separated, with each fighting his own separate battle in the attempt to reach the Federal line.[17]

A.P. Hill declared, "These brave men had done all that any brave soldiers could do." After about two hours of fighting, the situation was reversed, and Hill's men found themselves being attacked by the enemy. Nevertheless, Hill's men "stubbornly, gallantly" held the ground. At about 7 P.M., Hill received orders to advance his whole line. This was done and the enemy was "swept from the field." The fighting continued until darkness and the exhaustion of the troops ended it.[18]

Colonel Lane reported on the movements of the 28th Regiment during the battle at Gaines' Mill. After it was determined that the enemy was in full retreat, Lane and his men were ordered to follow them. At the village of Cold Harbor, the 7th North Carolina Regiment and Lane's 28th regiment were ordered into the woods on the left of the road that led to the battlefield. The 7th went before the 28th. Just when Lane was about to form his regiment on its left, both artillery fire and fire from the guns of enemy infantry began, and one of the wings of the 7th Regiment gave way. Colonel Reuben P. Campbell, commanding officer of the 7th Regiment, ordered his men to fall back. There was large pond of water in the rear of the 28th, so Lane had to lead his regiment out of the woods by the left flank. There he met General Branch and was ordered back. Lane and his entire regiment then marched up the road and entered some woods. Colonel Charles C. Lee followed with his regiment, the 37th North Carolina, which he intended to post to the right of the 28th. However, the enemy fired upon them just as they were about to turn the angle of the road, and the men on his right were thrown into confusion. As a result, Companies A, D, H, and I to the left of the colors in Lane's 28th Regiment gave way, but Company D promptly reformed and came back into line, while the other three companies reformed and attached themselves for the remainder of the day to other regiments.[19]

According to Lane's report, during the fighting at Gaines' Mill, 13 men of the 28th Regiment were killed, and 78 wounded.[20]

Private G.B. ("Berry") Harding was one of those wounded near Gaines' Mill on June 27, but he recovered enough to return to duty and was involved in the fighting at Frayser's Farm on June 30, 1862.[21]

Alford N. Dull, a private in Company I, was killed near Gaines' Mill about June 27, 1862. Dull, a Yadkin County resident, had enlisted on March 8, 1862.[22] According to his close friend W.A. Tesh, Dull was "shot in the Head just above his left eye, and it came out on the Back part of his head." He was not killed instantly but he was not expected to live. Tesh, like many others who witnessed the death of friends and relatives, was saddened by the loss. He wrote that Dull's death "troubled me to my heart when he fell, for me and him was just like Brothers...."[23]

According to Tesh, three of his company, and 15 or 20 more in other companies, had been wounded. After the battle, Tesh picked up a "Yankey" sword and a knapsack. Unfortunately, he had to discard both the knapsack and the sword. Another in the company picked up "4 Razors," and still another soldier got a "Pistol worth Fifty dollars."

On June 30, 1862, from his camp near Richmond, Lieutenant John Thomas Conrad (Company F, 28th Regiment) wrote to his wife. He knew that she must have heard of the battles going on, and he sought to reassure her of his safety. "God has been again gracious in preserving my life from the balls of our enemies, and unto him I give thanks. I was struck in the side by a spent ball, which never broke the skin and was very painful at first, but I am well now with the exception of a soreness from a slight wound."

Lieutenant Conrad gives his account of the fighting that occurred at Gaines' Mill, the first battle at Cold Harbor:

> ...the great battle ... has been raging here since Thursday last, and by the assistance of Almighty God we have succeeded in driving the enemy before us from all of his strong positions. We left Camp (Branch's Brigade) on last Wednesday night and Thursday morning we crossed the river driving the Yankee Pickets before us. We did not meet the forces as soon as we expected, and did not get up to where they made a stand until late Thursday evening, and not in time to assist in the engagement with other of our forces who had crossed the river lower down. Thursday night

we slept on the battle field and early Friday morning the attack was renewed and the Yankees were soon driven from their fortifications, and fell back some 5 or 6 miles. Our brigade did not arrive on the field of battle until late in the evening (the sun was about 2 hours high) and we were marched in under a most terrific fire, and were compelled to fall back a short distance, but rallied and went at them again....[24]

Conrad tried to described the sounds of battle: "I cannot describe the incessant roar of musketry hissed with the loud boom of the cannon, and I don't think any thing ever equaled it." The engagement was a Confederate victory. Conrad believed they had taken 7,000 Yankee prisoners, and he hoped that, since the enemy was surrounded, they would either have to "surrender or else be cut to pieces."[25]

Conrad listed the many casualties in his Company F. Allen Womack was mortally wounded; H.C. Baker's leg had to be amputated, but the rest of the injuries to the men of Company F were minor "flesh wounds."[26] Overall, in the Seven Days' Battles, Conrad wrote home that the 28th

Robert Choplin, Company F, 28th Regiment, wounded at Gaines' Mill on June 27, 1862, died on August 3, 1862 of his wounds and disease (courtesy of Cheryl L. Martin).

Regiment had lost 19 men killed, 130 wounded, and 26 missing. In Company F alone, 2 were killed (T.R. Hicks and G.M. Danner), and 14 wounded. Of those, Conrad and Trulove were wounded slightly. Also slightly wounded were: Lee Cornelius, J.C. Brown, J.H. Poindexter, S.D. Creson, R.H. Hutchens, A.E. Head, and John Tacket. Those severely wounded were H.C. Baker, Robert Choplin, John T. Sprinkle and Allen Womack. Missing in action were Coston Kittle and Joseph Choplin.[27]

Conrad wrote that Colonel Lane was not with them because he was confined in camp "with the piles." He sincerely hoped that his colonel would recover soon because they had no officers present and "the regiment [was] being commanded by a Captain...."[28]

According to Conrad, the 28th Regiment had not had an easy time of it: "We have all had a hard, hard time, living nearly all the time on half rations and making some hard marches, but they [the soldiers] have all borne their sufferings manfully, flattering themselves that with the help of God we have gained a Great victory over our enemies."[29]

Another soldier, Noah Collins, recorded the scene of the battlefield:

> All the undergrowth of the very thick timbers were mowed in two ... at various heights, by the iron and leaden hailstorm which prevailed at that place on the evening of the 28th ... and the pools of blood being so very thickly scattered about that a person could scarcely set his feet clear of them....[30]

Collins noted in his diary: "...what a lamentable evil war is, nothing but the great power of God could ever lead a single mortal through such a scene as this."[31]

The history of the 28th Regiment does not mention the regiment's being involved at Garnett's and Golding's Farms or at Savage's Station (Allen's Farm/Peach Orchard), the fourth

Joseph Choplin, Company F, 28th Regiment, reported missing in action at Gaines' Mill, June 27, 1862 (courtesy of Cheryl L. Martin).

and fifth of the Seven Days' Battles, the latter of which was fought by the Confederate forces of Major General John Magruder and his Army of the Peninsula. Although Magruder was successful against McClellan's forces during the battles of Mechanicsville and Gaines's Mill, in subsequent action during the Seven Days' Battles, Magruder was "cautious and bumbling."[32]

Branch's Regiment got a break from fighting and spent most of the day searching for wounded and burying their dead who had fallen on the battlefield. That evening, the soldiers cooked two days' rations to carry with them as they resumed their pursuit of McClellan's army.[33]

After the battle at Savage's Station, the Army of the Potomac withdrew, and Major General McClellan concentrated his troops behind White Oak Swamp in an attempt to block the pursuit of Lee's Confederates. "Stonewall" Jackson's division and that of D.H. Hill reached the swamp at 11 A.M. to find the bridge destroyed and two Confederate divisions in defensive positions. Although Jackson could have crossed the swampy area by way of several fords, he chose to shell the Federals across the creek. Hampered by "poor staff work," Lee was unable to coordinate his efforts to stop McClellan's movements.[34]

6a. White Oak Swamp, June 30, 1862

Forces Engaged: Armies

Principal Commanders: Gen. William Franklin (Union), Gen. T.J. Jackson (Confederate)

Casualties: estimated 500 total

Results: Inconclusive

The Union rear guard under Major General William Franklin blocked General T.J. "Stonewall" Jackson's division at the White Oak Bridge crossing. An artillery duel raged, but the main battle was fought two miles further south at Glendale or Frayser's Farm.[35]

On June 30, Lee launched another attack against the Federals, who had retreated to an area protected by the mire of White Oak Swamp. The Confederates launched an assault in the afternoon, and were successful, but Lee was unable to follow up his victory.

Longstreet and Hill moved to a position opposite the Federal forces. They sent out their troops and waited for the sound of battle. However, Confederate generals Holmes and Huger failed to get their men into position, and T.J. Jackson could not move as planned. Jackson had made an attempt to cross the White Oak Swamp but remained on a hill and left the fighting to others. Lee then ordered Longstreet to attack the Federal troops to prevent McClellan from escaping without some casualties. This fighting began about 4 P.M. at Frayser's Farm.[36]

Lee ordered Longstreet and A.P. Hill to attack, even though this could not begin until 4:30 P.M., giving them little chance of success. Following some hand-to-hand fighting, many of the Federals were driven back. The battle ended about 9 P.M. because of darkness. Union Generals

---

6b. Frayser's Farm (Nelson's Farm, Glendale), June 30, 1862

Forces Engaged: Armies (Army of the Potomac, Army of Northern Virginia)

Principal Commanders: Maj. Gen. George G. McClellan (Union), Gen. Robert E. Lee (Confederate)

Estimated Casualties: approximately 6,500 total[37] (2,853 Federal; 3,615 Confederate[38])

Result: Inconclusive

This engagement saw the Confederate divisions of Huger, Longstreet, and A.P. Hill converge on the retreating Union Army near Glendale or Frayser's Farm. The attacks of Longstreet's and Hill's forces penetrated the Union defense near Willis Church. McCall's Union division was routed and McCall was captured. Counterattacks by Union generals Hooker's and Kearney's divisions sealed the break and saved their line of retreat along the Willis Church Road. Huger's advance stopped on the Charles City Road; "Stonewall" Jackson's divisions were delayed at White Oak Swamp. Confederate Major General T.H. Holmes tried to turn the Union left flank at Turkey Bridge but failed and was driven back by Federal gunboats on the James River. During the night McClellan established a strong position on Malvern Hill.[39]

Meade and Sumner were wounded, as well as Confederate generals J.R. Anderson, Pender, and Featherston. McClellan withdrew to Malvern Hill during the night.[40]

General A.P. Hill noted that once the firing became heavy, he was ordered to move forward with his division. With springing steps, Branch's Brigade pressed forward. After arriving at an open space, Branch and his men moved to support the troops in their front.[41]

Colonel Lane reported that in the fighting on Monday evening, June 30, 1862, his regiment was among the first to engage the enemy. The whole brigade advanced, and drove the Union soldiers before them, in spite of the ground. As Lane's regiment advanced, the men had to pass through some woods which contained a swampy area. There was also an open field, in which there stood a house with a yard and garden. This had been converted into a temporary breastwork by the enemy. Lane's men did not hesitate. He recalled: "All of my men behaved well in this action, notwithstanding they were exposed to a murderous fire of shell, grape, and small-arms...." He noted that his regiment lost 6 killed and 50 wounded.[42] Lane himself was wounded in the right cheek and had to withdraw from the field of battle.[43]

Private Hezekiah Collins described the victory at Frayser's Farm near Camden Court House on the 30th of June, 1862. He proudly reported to his folks at home that the 28th Regiment was "the first that commenced the fight." As advance guards of the 28th encountered the 25th New York Regiment, the 28th "fell upon them and gave them a decent whipping killing a great many of them and captured some 60 odd as prisoners." Collins reported that, in Company A, Cornelius Cain, William A. McGuffin, W.H. Cockerham, and [Frederick] Shouse were killed. Watson Holyfield, Fill Nixon, L.B. Alberty, and J.P. White were slightly wounded. R.S. Nance, James Tilly, and Azarah Marion were severely wounded, while Calvin Bray had a finger shot off. Two were missing—Silas Wood and William Blackwood. Collins reported that they had taken over 12,000 enemy prisoners, plus guns, wagons, mules and horses, and "All sorts of property too tedious to mention."[44]

At the battle at Frayser's Farm, Lee and his Confederates lost another opportunity to destroy McClellan and his Federal troops. The fighting only added to the casualty list and not much more.[45] However, according to General Lee's report, "At the close of the struggle, nearly the entire field remained in our possession, covered with the enemy's dead and wounded." Many prisoners had been taken, including a "General of division, as well as several batteries and thousands of small arms." He concluded that if other some of his other commanders had cooperated with Hill and Longstreet, the outcome would have "proved more disastrous to the enemy."[46]

7. Malvern Hill (Poindexter's Farm), July 1, 1862
Forces Engaged: Armies
Casualties: Estimated 8,569 total (3,214 Union; 5,355 Confederate[47])
Result: Union victory
In the last of the Seven Day's Battles, General Robert E. Lee launched a series of assaults at the Union position on Malvern Hill. The Confederates suffered more than 5,300 casualties without gaining any ground. Despite the victory, McClellan withdrew to the entrenchments at Harrison's Landing on the James River, where he had protection of Federal gunboats. This battle ended the Peninsular Campaign.[48]

General A.P. Hill learned that General Magruder needed help, and he sent in two of his brigades, those of Branch and Thomas (Anderson's). They were not actively engaged. However, his division was ordered into a line of battle near the scene of the fighting, and came under fire.[49]

The next day, July 1, 1862, Branch's men were ordered to support Lee's final attack on McClellan at Malvern Hill. The brigade remained in reserve and suffered only light casualties from long-range artillery bombardments.[50]

The Federal troops had taken up a formidable defensive position at Malvern Hill. Confederates approached by a frontal attack, and units of D.H. Hill's division suffered heavy casualties from Federal artillery. Branch's Brigade was not directly involved in the fighting, and its losses were minor. Thus ended the Seven Day's Battles. Lee had achieved his objective to save the Confederate capital at Richmond from being captured, and he had driven General George McClellan's Federal army back to their base at Harrison's Landing on the James River.[51]

Losses in the 28th Regiment at Malvern Hill were 6 killed and 50 wounded.[52]

Losses and Bravery

The 28th Regiment, North Carolina, entered the fighting on June 25 with 480 men. One historian stated that they lost 19 men killed and 130 wounded during the entire Seven Days' Battles.[53] During those battles, Branch's Brigade had a total of 839 casualties (110 killed, 701 wounded, 28 missing).[54]

Colonel James H. Lane called the attention of the brigade commander to the gallantry and bravery shown by the following men:

Capt. T. James Linebarger, Co. C;
Capt. D.A. Parker, Co. D;
1st Lt. N. Clark, Co. E;
1st Lt. E.G. Morrow, Co. G;
1st Lt. W.W. Cloninger, Co. B;
2nd Lt. J.W. Rundle, Co. D;
2nd Lt. George W. McCauley, Co. G;
2nd Lt. Robert D. Rhyne, Co. B.

He also commended Sergeant Major Milton A. Lowe for his actions on the battlefield on June 27 and 30. Lane noted that color bearer J.P. Little, of Company C, was wounded on the 27th, but returned to duty in a short while.[55] (J.P. Little rose from the rank of a private in Company C to become an ensign or 1st lieutenant, on the field and staff of the 28th Regiment. He was captured at Spotsylvania Court House on May 12, 1864, and confined at Point Lookout, Maryland, until transferred to Elmira, New York, on August 10, 1864. Little was released on June 16, 1865, after taking the Oath of Allegiance.[56])

According to Colonel Lane's report, the 28th Regiment was greatly weakened by the retreat from Hanover Court House, and by sickness. Yet, he knew the number of casualties, 150 killed and wounded out of 480 (including the ambulance corps), a third of those who went into battle, would testify to "how nobly" the 28th Regiment fought in "this great struggle for independence."[57]

In his report of the Seven Days' Battles, Brigadier General Branch stated that "it was a week of hard fighting and hard marching with my brigade...."[58]

After the Seven Days' Battles, General Lee reorganized his forces. A.P. Hill's division was assigned to Thomas J. "Stonewall" Jackson's command. This included Branch's Brigade, of which the 28th North Carolina Regiment was a part.[59] Hill's Light Division consisted of four brigades made up of regiments from Virginia, Georgia, South Carolina, and North Carolina.[60]

The Seven Days' Battles proved to be a series of lost opportunities. The problems of coordinating such a large force and getting them to attack as directed was a major one. The different divisions that had been gathered into the Army of Northern Virginia were not used to working together as a unit. These failings were paid for by the soldiers in the ranks.[61]

Throughout the period, Branch's Brigade usually fought on its own rather than with other units, and they were not involved in all the main actions. However, according to historian William Kelsey McDaid, at Gaines' Mill, Branch's men and the rest of the Light Division had attacked a strong Federal position "before any troops could come to their aid." Because of the dismal conditions of the terrain over Boatswain's Swamp, Branch had little control over the men as they pushed forward. At Frayser's Farm it was the same story: bad terrain and poor communications. The good news was that, even though there were no conclusive victories, McClellan's Army had been pushed back to the James River and was no longer an immediate threat to Richmond.[62]

List of Casualties in the Army of Northern Virginia
near Richmond from June 25–July 1, 1862
Branch's Brigade only[63]

Regiment	Killed	Wounded	Total
7th North Carolina Infantry	28	183	211
18th North Carolina Infantry	14	82	96
28th North Carolina Infantry	12	146	158
33rd North Carolina Infantry	8	43	51
37th North Carolina Infantry	11	114	125
Johnson's Battery	1	18	19
Total casualties	**74**	**586**	**660**

In another tabulation of losses for the period, June 25–July 1, 1862, Branch's Brigade sustained a total of 839 casualties. This figure includes those missing in action, which was not set out in the above table.[64]

It is clear from the above table that the 28th Regiment suffered heavy casualties. They were second in the number of wounded, and third in the number of men killed in Branch's Brigade. Colonel James H. Lane initially believed the 28th Regiment had lost 150 men (killed and wounded), but he later calculated the number to be 177. He lost one field officer, three captains, and some lieutenants. Lane believed his regiment was at a disadvantage due to sickness, "caused by the hardships we had to undergo in our retreat from Hanover Courthouse."[65]

A table in the *Official Records of the War of the Rebellion* gives more details of the casualties suffered by the Confederate Army during the Seven Days' Battles, June 25–July 1, 1862. This table is divided by corps, division, and brigades. It is further divided as to the specific battles in which those casualties occurred. It is beyond the scope of this book to list all of the casualties, other than to submit a grand total of losses in Lee's Army of Northern Virginia. By adding the totals for each unit, including infantry, artillery, and cavalry, the total number of casualties (killed, wounded and missing) was 16,107. This number covers the fighting at Mechanicsville, Gaines' Mill, Malvern Hill, Garnett's and Golding's Farms, Peach Orchard, Savage's Station, and Glendale.[66] While perhaps the number of casualties in the individual battles fought over the seven days was not large, altogether Lee's Army of Northern Virginia, as well as Branch's Brigade, sustained heavy casualties.

1st Lieutenant J.P. Little wrote in his history of Company C, 28th Regiment, that the overall Federal losses in men in these battles were over 20,000, while the Confederates sustained losses of 19,533 of their soldiers.[67]

Private William A. Tesh, of Company I, concluded after participating in three battles during one week:

> ...we whipt the Yankeys a bout right but we Lost a heap of men and taken a heap of Prisoners. I recon we taken a bout ten Thousand and Killed several Thousand and Taken a bout one Hundred and Twenty Five pieces Artillery from Them and Wagons and horses Guns and Ammunition Knap sacks Blankets and in fact every Thing they had.[68]

Even those men who survived were affected for days after the fighting. Robert A. White, a private in the 28th Regiment, noted a change in his comrades when he returned to his regiment after being on sick leave for four months. White noted that the soldiers "seemed a great deal more civil," and that many stopped such frivolous practices as card playing, dancing, and swearing. He saw some men reading Bibles who had never had one in their hands before.[69]

At the conclusion of the Seven Days' Battles, Brigadier General Branch addressed his troops, and complimented them on their performance:

> While making this bloody but brilliant record for your brigade, you have been, as soldiers of freedom should always be, modest, uncomplaining, and regardful of what is due to others. Your ranks have been thinned by the casualties of war, but be not discouraged. In a few days they will be filled by recruits, and yours will be the proud task of teaching them to maintain the reputation you have achieved.[70]

On July 20, 1862, Brigadier General Branch addressed the remaining members of his brigade. Although the brigade was seldom able to "turn out 3,000 men for duty," they had engaged in six pitched battles and several skirmishes, and had "lost 1,250 in killed and wounded." Not only privates had been lost, but Branch's Brigade had lost five colonels—two were killed in battle, two wounded, and one taken prisoner. For their efforts, the men had been authorized to inscribe on their battle flags the names of the battles in which they had participated. The 28th Regiment and the 7th Regiment were entitled to have inscribed on their flags the battles at New Berne, Slash Church, Mechanicsville, Gaines' Mill, Frazier's [sic] Farm, and Malvern Hill. Branch then ordered the quartermaster of the brigade to furnish newly-inscribed flags.[71]

Chapter 6

August 9–September 14, 1862: Cedar Mountain, Manassas Junction, 2nd Manassas, Ox Hill

Hill's men fought with rocks from a railroad cut. Many [Union] men were killed by having their skulls broken with rocks.
— J.P. Little, Company C, 28th Regiment Volunteers[1]

Cedar Mountain (Cedar Run, Slaughter's Mountain), August 9, 1862 (part of the 2nd Manassas/Bull Run Campaign)

Forces Engaged: 24,898 total (8,030 Union; 16,868 Confederate)

Commanders: Major General Nathaniel Banks (Union), Major General Thomas J. "Stonewall" Jackson (Confederate)

Casualties: 2,707 total (1,400 Union, 1,307 Confederate)

Results: Confederate victory

Major General John Pope had just been placed in command of the newly-organized Federal Army of Virginia. Confederate General Lee sent Major General T.J. Jackson with 14,000 men to Gordonsville, Virginia, in July; Jackson was reinforced by A.P. Hill's Division. Early in August, Pope moved his forces south to Culpeper County in a move to capture the railroad junction at Gordonsville. On August 9, Jackson engaged Banks' forces at Cedar Mountain. Although the Federals gained an advantage early on, a Confederate counterattack led by Hill won the day. This battle marked a turn in the fighting from the peninsula to northern Virginia.[2]

When General Robert E. Lee reorganized his army into only two commands—Thomas J. Jackson and James Longstreet—A.P. Hill's Division was assigned to Jackson. Jackson was ordered to move with two of his divisions to intercept the Federal army under General John Pope. Hill's Division (including Branch's Brigade) was ordered to join Jackson on July 27, while the remainder of the Confederate army stayed to watch McClellan at Harrison's Landing. On August 9, Jackson took the offensive at Cedar Mountain and attempted to destroy an isolated corps of Pope's army. However, Jackson was on the verge of being defeated when A.P. Hill's Division arrived to launch a devastating counterattack. After Branch was wounded, Colonel James H. Lane assumed temporary command. Lane submitted a report of the encounter:

> After a long, rapid, and weary march we reached the battle-field at Cedar Run on the afternoon of August 9, and took the position assigned us in the line of battle by General Branch in the woods to the left of the road leading to the Run, the right of the Thirty-seventh resting on the road, the Twenty-eighth, Thirty-third, Eighteenth, and Seventh being on its left. The Twenty-eighth ...

moved cheerfully and irresistibly forward and in perfect order through the woods upon the enemy, who had succeeded in flanking the First (Stonewall) Brigade, of General Jackson's division, which was rapidly giving way.[3]

The Federal infantry was soon driven from the woods into a field beyond, and the enemy's infantry and cavalry retreated in "great disorder from the scene of action." Lane reported that many prisoners were captured, and a large number of Federal soldiers deserted their colors and voluntarily surrendered. Lane was proud of his officers and men, who "behaved as well as could be desired, notwithstanding the disorderly manner in which some of the troops we were ordered to support fell back."[4]

General Lee's report on the fighting noted that the battle opened with "fierce fire of artillery," which continued for about two hours. Confederate Brigadier General Charles S. Winder was wounded during this time. The enemy's infantry advanced about 5 P.M. to attack General Jubal Early's front, while another enemy force moved on Early's right. Thomas' Brigade of A.P. Hill's Division arrived and the fight became more "animated." The main body of Federal infantry, under cover of the woods, moved to the left of Jackson's Division, where the troops were commanded by Brigadier General William Booth Taliaferro. The enemy fired into the flank and rear of Jackson's men. Campbell's Brigade gave way and left Taliaferro's flank exposed. They also gave way, as did those on the left of Early's line. The remainder of Early's brigade held their ground, and when the brigades of Winder and Branch of Hill's Division arrived, they advanced promptly to support Jackson's Division. After a bloody struggle, the enemy was repulsed. More reinforcements arrived from Pender's and Archer's brigades and the enemy was driven back, leaving their dead and wounded on the ground. It had already grown dark, but Jackson was determined to reach Culpeper Court House before morning, and Hill's Division led the advancing troops. However, once Jackson learned that the retreating enemy forces had been reinforced, he called a halt to the march.[5]

An account written by 1st Lieutenant J.P. Little, Company C, stated that after a "sharp fight," the Confederates defeated the enemy and drove them from the field. Little believed that Federal losses amounted to 1,800, while the Confederates lost 1,314.[6]

General Lee focused on the gains in this engagement and reported that 400 enemy prisoners were captured, including a brigadier general, and "5,300 small arms, 1 piece of artillery, several caissons, and 3 colors fell into our hands."[7]

Brigadier General Branch reported that the battle had resulted in a "complete rout of the enemy," and that after it was over, the men "slept on the ground they had so bravely won." Branch also reported that two of his staff officers, Captain F.T. Hawks and Lieutenant J.A. Bryan "conducted themselves gallantly."[8]

Out of all the units of Jackson's Division which were engaged at Cedar Mountain, 229 were killed, 1,047 wounded, for a total of 1,276 casualties. Branch's Brigade had 12 killed and 88 wounded. There were 394 casualties in Hill's Light Division. The 28th Regiment alone lost 3 killed, 26 wounded.[9]

The battle at Cedar Mountain (Cedar Run) was a great achievement for Branch's Brigade. His journal entries reflect his pride in the actions of his men who had managed to hold an unbroken line of battle. The five regiments in this brigade had shown that they were capable of working together, despite the chaos of battle.[10]

The men received further encouragement when General Thomas J. Jackson rode up from the rear and across the front line of the brigade. A man of few words, Jackson simply rode with his hat off, a silent tribute to the soldiers who had been so instrumental in the victory on August 9, 1862. This simple gesture won the hearts of the men,[11] and from that day until his death, the men of Branch's Brigade were prepared to follow "Old Jackson" wherever he led them.[12]

On August 11, General Nathaniel Banks asked for an armistice in order to bury the dead.

That night, before Pope's army could be reinforced, Jackson withdrew south of the Rapidan to Orange Court House. He left lighted campfires behind so that the Union general would believe the Confederates were still in position.[13]

After a three-day period of rest, Branch was ordered to march his brigade with Jackson's men to Clark's Mountain to participate in General Lee's plan to defeat Pope's Federal forces. Lee planned to have Longstreet's and Jackson's men attack Pope's right flank, while J.E.B. Stuart and his cavalry rode around Pope's left and blocked their retreat across the Rappahannock River. The plan was to trap and defeat Pope's Army of Virginia between two rivers. Lee's plan was thwarted when Stuart failed to comply with his orders. Pope learned of the plan and withdrew across the Rappahannock. With no enemy to confront, Branch's Brigade abandoned picket duty on Clark's Mountain and joined the rest of the Confederates as they pursued Pope across the Rapidan River at Somerville Ford. By August 22, Branch's Brigade reached Warrenton Springs near the Rappahannock, and were close enough to the enemy to be shelled from across the river by Federal artillery.[14]

General Lee wisely changed his tactics before all of the Union's Army of the Potomac could unite with Pope's Army of Virginia. With his usual brilliancy, Lee kept Longstreet in front of Pope while he sent three of Jackson's divisions around the Federal right flank through Thoroughfare Gap in the Bull Run Mountains to Manassas Junction.[15]

On the evening of August 24, Branch's Brigade joined the rest of Jackson's command camped near the village of Jefferson. Preparations for a night march were made. The men were told to leave their knapsacks behind and to carry three days' rations in their haversacks. However, the commissary failed to distribute the rations in time, and most of them began the long march without enough food.[16]

Manassas Junction (Kettle Run, Bull Run Bridge, Union Mills), August 26–27, 1862

Forces Engaged: Divisions (Brig. Gen. G.W. Taylor, Union; Maj. Gen. T.J. Jackson, Confederate)

Estimated casualties: 1,110 total

Results: Confederate victory

On the evening of August 26, Jackson's wing of the army struck the Orange & Alexandria Railroad at Bristoe Station, and before daybreak the next day, had marched to capture and destroy the massive Union supply depot at Manassas Junction. This surprise movement forced Union General Pope to abruptly retreat. That same day, Jackson routed a Union brigade near Union Mills (Bull Run Bridge), and inflicted heavy casualties. Confederate General Ewell's Division fought a brisk rear-guard action against Hooker's Division at Kettle Run, inflicting 600 casualties. Ewell succeeded in holding back the Union forces until dark. During the night of August 27–28, Jackson moved his division north to the site of the Manassas battle, where he positioned his troops in an unfinished railroad cut.[17]

After the battle at Cedar Mountain, Jackson's men withdrew to Gordonsville. When Federal troops arrived to reinforce Pope, Lee countered by withdrawing troops from Richmond to support Jackson.

Lee again did the unexpected. Facing an enemy that outnumbered him 75,000 to his 44,000, the Confederate commander split his forces, and sent half on a mission to cut Federal communications. The rest of the army would follow a day later. His success depended on speed, deception and the skill of his generals. He took advantage of the weak Federal leadership and knew that if he could get his army between the Union troops and Washington, panic would result.[18]

The Confederates began to march at 4 A.M. and kept up a steady pace without rest stops until they had crossed the Rappahannock at Hinson's Mill. They marched for 26 miles until they were within two miles of Salem. Jackson rode up and down the line all day and urged the men to close up ranks. Every soldier was "pressed to the utmost of his walking capacity," recalled a solder of the 7th Regiment. The only food that most of the men had was corn and apples snatched from the fields and orchards along the route. The march halted about 11 P.M., and the men fell exhausted along the side of the road.[19]

The march resumed the next day, again at 4 A.M., and continued through Thoroughfare Gap toward the Orange & Alexandria Railroad. That day's march ended about 10 P.M., after another 25 miles had been covered — one of the most remarkable feats of sustained marching during the entire war.[20]

Jackson and his army reached Manassas Junction on August 26. There, they destroyed Pope's supplies. Jackson then withdrew his force about five miles to Groveton and assumed a defensive position. Branch's Brigade was positioned on the left of the Confederate line along the unfinished railroad cut of a branch of the Manassas Gap Railroad. Pope now tried to find Jackson. Pope outnumbered Jackson's force three-to-one, but while Pope blundered about in search of Jackson's troops, Lee sent Longstreet's command to reinforce Jackson to even the odds a bit.[21]

Branch's Brigade reached the depot at Manassas Junction on the morning of August 27. The warehouses and freight cars were filled with tons of supplies and food. There were barrels of flour, pork and biscuits. The men expected to enjoy a feast. Unfortunately, a Federal brigade approached to take back control of Manassas Junction. They were met with resistance from Hill's Light Division, who gave their famous "Rebel" yell and returned the enemy fire. The enemy forces gave up the fight and chose to retreat across Bull Run.[22]

Once the Federal troops had been dispatched, the hungry Confederates returned to Manassas Junction to get crackers and bacon.[23] After the men ate their fill, and shoes and clothing had been distributed, Jackson ordered the rest to be burned. At midnight, the depot, warehouses, and two miles of freight cars filled with supplies went up in flames.

One soldier of the 28th Regiment got a surprise when he jumped over a bush from the railroad embankment and found he had also jumped over a Yankee who crouched on the ground.

Second Manassas (Second Bull Run, Groveton, Manassas Plains, Gainesville, Brawner's
    Farm), August 28–30, 1862

Forces Engaged: Armies

Commanders: Maj. Gen. John Pope (Union); General R. E. Lee and Maj. Gen. T.J.Jackson
    (Confederates)

Estimated Casualties: 22,180 total (13,830 Union; 8,350 Confederate)

Result: Confederate victory

In an attempt to draw Pope's army into battle, on August 28, Jackson ordered an attack on the Federals who were moving along the Warrenton Turnpike. The battle at Brawner's Farm lasted several hours, but ended in a stalemate. Pope believed he had Jackson trapped and sent the bulk of his forces against him. On August 29, Pope launched a series of assaults against Jackson's position in the railroad cut. The Federal attacks were repulsed, but with heavy casualties on both sides. On August 30, Pope renewed the attack, unaware that Longstreet had arrived with reinforcements. Confederate artillery devastated Union General Fitz John Porter's assault, and when a wing of 28,000 of Longstreet's men counterattacked, it was the largest simultaneous assault of the war. The Union left flank was crushed and the Federal troops withdrew back to Bull Run. Pope retreated to Centreville. The next day, Lee sent his army in pursuit. This was one of the most decisive battles fought in Northern Virginia.[24]

Stone bridge at Manassas, Virginia. Photograph by Frances H. Casstevens.

Another Confederate was surprised when, as he got down on all fours to get a drink of water from a stream, he spied a Yankee who had sought the safety of a culvert. The Yankee was an Irishman, and after he emerged from his hiding place, he slapped the Tar Heel on the back and laughingly said, "You got us badly this time. Come, let's take a drink." Although on opposite sides in the war, with a smile, both drank out of the same canteen.[25]

After leaving Manassas Junction, Jackson's men separated and each of his three divisions took a different road northward. A.P. Hill was ordered to march on Centreville; Ewell was to cross Bull Run and move along the north side of the creek; while Taliaferro was to move direct. All were to join up on Stony Ridge. This move began the night of August 27–28, and was completed the next day.[26]

The 28th Regiment was a part of Hill's Division which crossed over a stream called Bull Run. Here, the North Carolina troops awaited their enemy.

After crossing over the stone bridge that spanned Bull Run, the 28th was ordered into the woods on the right of the road. The action of the 28th Regiment and others was reported by Colonel J.H. Lane:

> As soon as the engagement was opened on our right General [James J.] Archer's brigade, which was in front, moved from the woods into the field up to and to the right of the battery, where it was halted. Our brigade also moved a short distance into the field in the same direction, when the enemy opened a left enfilade artillery fire upon us.[27]

General Branch then ordered Lane, and the 28th, to continue and advance to the rear of General Archer's troops. Thus, "the whole brigade, with no protection whatever, stood this artillery fire for several hours in the open field." Although the 28th was not actively engaged on August 28, that night the whole command was moved into the shelter of the woods and the railroad cut, where they "slept upon our arms."[28]

The railroad cut, with its high embankments, was an ideal defensive position. The Confederates concealed there could hold out against the Federals until Longstreet arrived with reinforcements. Hill's Light Division was deployed on the left of Jackson's line. Behind the railroad cut, the front line was composed of the brigades of Gregg, Thomas, and Field, while Branch, Pender and Archer formed another line behind those first three. Skirmishers were deployed and they encountered the enemy. The volume of fire indicate that the Union troops had entered a patch of woods in large numbers. Branch sent the 28th and the 33rd to drive the enemy out of the woods. Lane's men arrived on the scene to find Captain John M. Turner and skirmishers from the 7th Regiment had already driven the Federals back. Branch then ordered Lane to remain in position and support Gregg against any Union forces remaining in the woods along the railroad cut. Lane brought up three more companies.[29]

When the Federal troops received reinforcements, they threw their weight against Hill's Light Division in force. Gregg requested reinforcements, and Branch ordered the 37th to move forward. This regiment was soon engaged in heavy fighting, and their flank was exposed to deadly enemy fire.[30] Branch rode to the rear amidst a rain of shot and shell to bring up more troops. He found that Colonel Edward Haywood, commander of the 7th, had been wounded, so Branch ordered the 7th Regiment to follow him, and he led that regiment and the 18th to support Barbour and the 37th.[31] Quickly, Branch's regiments forced the enemy to flee in disorder across the railroad cut.[32]

On the second day of fighting, August 29, the 28th Regiment was not engaged until the other regiments of the brigade were nearly out of ammunition. Then, General Branch ordered the 28th to join him to cover his front. However, the order was not delivered correctly, and the regiment went into action to the left of the brigade of General Charles W. Fields. The 28th advanced "boldly into the woods, driving the enemy before it, although exposed to a left enfilade and direct fire, but fell back when it found itself alone in the woods and unsupported." The men rallied and advanced a second time, and the enemy "was not only driven beyond the cut, but entirely out of the woods." Lane stated: "Never have I witnessed greater bravery and desperation than was that day displayed by this brigade."[33]

It was a day of bitter fighting, much of it hand-to-hand combat. In between the fighting, Branch's men searched the ground for fallen cartridge boxes to replenish their meager supply of ammunition.[34]

A Federal attack about 4:30 in the afternoon was met by resistance from Hill's Light Division. Gregg's men gave way, but the men of Branch's Brigade stood in the line of battle with bayonets fixed. Hill ordered the reserves brought up and with the arrival of Jubal Early's brigade and two of Ewell's regiments, the Union troops withdrew in confusion. Jackson's line was restored.[35]

At the end of the day, the sound of cannon fire from the far right signaled the long-awaited arrival of Longstreet's reinforcements had come. The men slept soundly that night, confident that they had delivered a crushing blow to Pope's Federal soldiers. One soldier wrote home that "all would be well on the morrow."[36]

Although the 28th Regiment was not engaged in the fighting on the 29th, it held its position under a deadly barrage of heavy artillery fire from the enemy guns. Then, advancing, they followed the enemy until about 10 P.M., through a body of woods to a large hospital were many of the Federal wounded were being cared for.[37]

Junius Pinkney Little, a 1st lieutenant of Company C, 28th NC Regiment, recalled that at 2nd Manassas "Hill's men fought with rocks from a railroad cut. Many men were killed by having their skulls broken by rocks." Little estimated the Federal losses at 17,000, and the Confederate losses at 8,000, only half as many.[38]

Casualties sustained by the 28th Regiment at the battle of 2nd Manassas were slight: 5 men were killed and 45 wounded.[39] Lane reported brigade losses over the three days' battle at 30 killed, 185 wounded, and 1 missing.[40] Surgeon Lafayette Guild, C.S. Army director, reported the casualties sustained in August at Manassas Plains. He noted that in Branch's Brigade there were 194 casualties, which included 50 sustained by the 28th Regiment.[41]

Brigadier General Lawrence O'Bryan Branch demonstrated in the battles of August 1862 that he could be an effective commander. His movements along the battle line encouraged his men and inspired confidence in them. Branch was especially glad to know that at Manassas, he and his men had defeated some of Union general Burnside's IX Corps, the same troops who had defeated the North Carolinians at New Bern. Branch reminded his men, and shouted, "Burnside whipped us at New Bern, but we have whipped him this evening."[42] It is tragic that Branch would not live to see the South's greatest victory or its worst defeat.

About the second battle at Manassas, in his report, General Lee stated that when a large enemy force advanced on the left of Jackson's position, that portion of the line held by A.P. Hill's men, the enemy attack was "received by his troops with their accustomed steadiness, and the battle raged with great fury." Lee observed that the enemy forces were "repeatedly repulsed but again pressed on the attack with great fury."[43] General Jackson repeated statements made by General A.P. Hill that on August 29 "six separate and distinct assaults were thus met and repulsed by his division...."[44]

On August 31, the weary Confederate soldiers pulled back to the rear where they could get food. Along the way they saw the horrors of war — dead men and dead horses were lying everywhere, especially at the points of attack and repulse.[45]

When my son Tim and I visited the battlefields at Manassas, Virginia, we walked over the stone bridge that spanned Bull Run. We also saw the railroad cut where Lane's Brigade had waited for the enemy. It was a strange experience to stand in those same woods where my great-uncle participated in a Confederate victory.

Ox Hill (Chantilly), September 1, 1862

Forces Engaged: Divisions (Maj. Gen. Philip Kearney and Maj. Gen. Isaac Stevens, Union; Maj. Thomas J. "Stonewall" Jackson, Confederate)

Estimated Casualties: 2,100 total (1,300 Union; 800 Confederate)

Results: Inconclusive (strategic Confederate victory)

General Jackson hoped to cut off the retreat of the Union forces from Manassas. Beyond Chantilly Plantation, near Ox Hill, Jackson sent his divisions against two Union divisions. Confederate attacks were stopped by fierce fighting during a severe thunderstorm. Pope then ordered the retreat to Washington to resume, and Lee turned his attention toward Maryland, where he would soon be engaged in major battles at South Mountain and Sharpsburg (Antietam).[46]

Coming right after the Confederate victory at Manassas, the battle at Ox Hill on September 1, 1862, has had little attention by historians.

As the defeated Federal army retreated toward Washington, General R.E. Lee ordered Jackson to turn the Federal right flank. Advance elements of Jackson's force met the enemy at Ox Hill late on the afternoon of September 1, 1862. Branch's Brigade was ordered to advance in a "blinding rainstorm." and a battle ensued between Jackson's column and the Federal rear guard. The Federals managed to hold their position, but retired under cover of darkness. Colonel Lane reported the role of Branch's Brigade in this engagement:

> The pursuit [of the enemy] continued the whole of Sunday, and on Monday afternoon [September 1] about 4 o'clock we came up with the enemy again at Ox Hill, near Fairfax Court House, on

the Alexandria and Winchester turnpike, when the engagement was immediately opened. This brigade pressed eagerly forward through an open field and a piece of woods to the edge of another field, where we were for a short time exposed to the enemy's infantry fire without being able to return it.[47]

The Federals attempted to flank Branch's Brigade, and the 18th Regiment was detached from the center of the brigade to the right to stop the Federal move. The 18th was without support and came under deadly enemy fire, but as the enemy advanced through a field of corn, they sustained many casualties. Casualties would have been greater but most of the Confederates' guns misfired because of the heavy rain. When Branch learned that the rain had ruined their ammunition, he appealed to A.P. Hill to withdraw the brigade. Instead, Hill ordered Branch to hold his position "at the point of a bayonet."[48] The men obeyed without question.

The men of the 28th Regiment remained in position until dark, when the whole command fell back to a field behind the woods. Cold, wet, and hungry, the 28th was ordered back to the battlefield to do picket duty during the night and without any fires. This engagement was regarded by the brigade as one of their severest, especially when faced with the many explosive balls hurled at them by the enemy.[49]

Losses in the 28th Regiment alone were 14 killed, 92 wounded, and 2 missing.[50] Two of those known killed from the 28th Regiment were Private William A. Jolley, of Company H; and Private William Petitt, of Company F (see Appendix X of this book).

Captain Nicholas Gibbon recalled that the Confederate troops left Manassas and marched all night toward Fairfax Court House. At Ox Hill, which was nearby, the Confederates engaged the enemy in a fierce battle, and drove them from the field.[51]

In a letter to his wife, Brigadier General Branch expressed the hardships of the recent battles his men had endured:

> ...we have been almost constantly in the enemy's rear.... We have performed the most remarkable marches recorded in history. If we had not the actual experience it would not be credited that human nature could endure what we have endured. Fighting all day and marching all night — not for one day only, but for a whole week. The little sleep we have had has been generally on the battle field surrounded by the dead and wounded. Some of the soundest sleep I have ever had has been on the naked ground without cover and the rain pouring down in torrents. The only rations we have had for a week are fresh beef — our wagon trains can't keep up with us.[52]

Lee abandoned his pursuit of Pope's army and did not try to cut off the Federal retreat. Instead he turned his army north to cross into Maryland.[53]

Chapter 7

September–December 1862: Harpers Ferry, Sharpsburg and Fredericksburg

*...after a very rapid and fatiguing march, [we] recrossed the Potomac
and reached Sharpsburg in time to participate in the fight.*
— Brigadier General James H. Lane[1]

Harpers Ferry in 1862

Because the little town of Harpers Ferry was of such great military value, between 1861 and 1865 it changed hands eight times. It was a supply base for Union troops operating in the Shenandoah Valley, and it stood at the junction of the Chesapeake & Ohio Canal and the Baltimore & Ohio Railroad. It was also at the intersection of the Potomac River and the Shenandoah River, as well as the point where the states of (present-day) West Virginia, Maryland, and Virginia met. The Confederates had burned the Federal armory in 1861. The churches and mills had been turned into hospitals, and the civilian population had fled.[2]

When Union Colonel Dixon S. Miles took command of the garrison there in the spring of 1862, the town was in ruins. To defend the area, Colonel Miles had 14,000 men garrisoned at Harpers Ferry and Martinsburg at his command.[3]

Confederate control of Harpers Ferry was essential for Lee to maintain communications with his forces in the Shenandoah Valley. The town was now under Federal control, but Lee was determined to retake it.[4] In order to do so, Lee again did the unexpected, especially in the face of the superior numbers of the enemy — he split his army. Jackson was ordered to capture Harpers Ferry and then to rejoin Lee. Jackson and six divisions were to move south against Harpers Ferry, while Longstreet and three divisions were to march north to Hagerstown to await the troops sent to Harpers Ferry.[5]

For his plan to work, Lee counted on McClellan's hesitancy to act and that would give him time to reunite his Confederate forces. The plan was almost sabotaged by the loss of a copy of Lee's orders, the famous "Special Order No. 191." This order, wrapped around some cigars, was dropped. It was found and taken to McClellan. From this one order, the Union commander learned that Lee had divided his forces. But McClellan did not take action immediately. As always, McClellan moved slowly and cautiously, because he feared he might be heading into a trap set by the Confederates.[6]

After the resounding Confederate victory at Manassas, General Lee decided to carry the war to the North. The invasion, Lee hoped, would boost Confederate morale, and bring terror to the North. In addition, in untouched Maryland, the Confederates would be able to live off

Harpers Ferry, September 12–15, 1862

Forces Engaged: Corps

Principal Commanders: Col. Dixon S. Miles (Union), Maj. Gen. T.J. Jackson (Confederate)

Estimated Casualties: 12,922 total (44 killed, 173 wounded, 12,419 captured, Union; 39 killed, 247 wounded, Confederate)

Result: Confederate victory

After Lee invaded Maryland, he learned that the garrison at Harpers Ferry was controlled by Federal troops. By dividing his army into four columns, he sent three to surround Harpers Ferry. On September 15, after bombardment from Confederate artillery placed on the heights above the town of Harpers Ferry, the Union commander of the garrison surrendered his 13,000 troops. "Stonewall" Jackson quickly took possession of Harpers Ferry, then led his troops to join Lee at Sharpsburg. After paroling the Federal prisoners, A.P. Hill's Division followed Jackson to Sharpsburg, where they arrived in time to save Lee from defeat.[7]

Commanding Officers, Branch-Lane Brigade, from Walter Clark, ed., *Histories of the Several Regiments and Battalions from North Carolina in the Great War, 1861–1865, Written by Members of the Respective Commands.* 1. Brigadier General James H. Lane; 2. Brigadier General Lawrence O'Bryan Branch; 3. Brigadier John D. Barry; 4. Major E.J. Hale (courtesy of the North Carolina Department of Archives and History).

the land. Thus, the Confederate army spent only one day near Ox Hill before marching west toward Leesburg, where a ford on the Potomac gave easy access into Maryland.[8]

General T.J. Jackson was now in command of a corps which included A.P. Hill's Division. Also part of Jackson's corps was Branch's Brigade and the 28th Regiment. The corps crossed the Potomac River on September 4 in a move toward Harpers Ferry.[9]

Captain Nicholas Gibbon recalled that when the troops forded the Potomac, some of the men waded through the stream with their shoes and pants "hanging from their guns." Some rolled up their pants to their knees. Even the artillery crossed without trouble because the bed of the river was covered with round stones. Following them came the wagons and beef cattle, which were Gibbon's responsibility. When the army crossed a bridge over a canal in Maryland, one 4-horse wagon and an ambulance "ran off and some of the horses drowned.[10]

The first camp of the 28th North Carolina in the state of Maryland was at a point where the railroad from Frederick joined the Baltimore & Ohio Railroad. The troops remained there several days, before going through Frederick City, Williamsport, and Martinsburg to reach Harpers Ferry.[11]

On September 10, Jackson crossed the Potomac near Williamsport.[12] His forces marched through Martinsburg and reached Harpers Ferry on September 14. With the 7th Regiment in the lead, its skirmishers drove the enemy's sharpshooters from their positions high above the town. The rest of the brigade arrived about midnight.[13]

At Harpers Ferry, Hill's Division encountered Federal troops strongly entrenched on Bolivar Heights.[14] This high ridge extended from the Potomac to the Shenandoah River. Hill ordered the woods over which he intended to move his troops shelled before the advance began. He then moved his men down the Shenandoah when he discovered an "eminence crowning the extreme left of the enemy's line," which was devoid of all "earthworks," and consisted of abatis and fallen timber. The enemy, according to Hill, occupied the hill with a force of infantry but no artillery. Generals Branch and Gregg were ordered to continue to move their men along the river. Under cover of night, they would be able to move through the ravines as cover and then to take a stand on the plain to the left and behind the enemy's work.[15]

Generals Pender, Archer and Brokenbrough were ordered to reach the crest of Bolivar Heights, with Thomas as reserve. Pender was in charge of the maneuver, which was accomplished with only slight resistance. Brigadier General John C. Walker was ordered to bring up his artillery, which was done during the night. Generals Branch and Gregg attained their positions and by daybreak they were in the rear of the enemy's defensive line. At dawn, Walker's men opened fire on the enemy from about 1,000 yards. After about an hour of resistance, the enemy ceased firing and soon displayed the white flag of surrender.[16]

On September 15, after Major General Lafayette McLaw's and Walker's men were in position above the town, the Federal garrison at Harpers Ferry surrendered.[17] Brigadier General James H. Lane recalled there was a "short but rapid and well-directed fire from our batteries," and soon there after the Federal garrison had put up several white flags.[18] The surrender came after the Confederate artillery had been bombarding the Yankee position all day Saturday and Sunday. The Federal defenders surrendered to General A.P. Hill at about 9 o'clock A.M.[19] Unfortunately, shortly after the Union garrison raised the white flag, a Confederate shell exploded directly behind Colonel Miles, and he was mortally wounded. Brigadier General Julius White negotiated the final surrender terms with the Confederates.[20]

Captain William G. Morris of the 37th Regiment wrote home that at Harpers Ferry they captured "twelve thousand yankees" and all their arms and stores, including plenty of sugar, coffee, and "allmost any thing we could wish, clothing, etc."[21]

Lieutenant J.P. Little recalled that the Confederate forces had captured about 12,000 Federal soldiers, and "more arms and ammunition that we could get away with."[22] The number of troops captured is believed to be the largest single capture of Federal troops during the course of the war. In addition, Confederates seized 13,000 arms and 47 pieces of artillery.[23]

Brigadier General Lane reported that in his brigade, only four men were wounded.[24]

As soon as Harpers Ferry was secured, Lee ordered Jackson to move his troops towards Sharpsburg. Hill's Division was left at Harpers Ferry to receive the captured Federal troops while Jackson moved north to rejoin Lee and Longstreet at Sharpsburg, Maryland,[25] and a battle that would forever be known as the "bloodiest single day of the war."

Sharpsburg (Antietam), September 16–18, 1862

Forces Engaged: Armies

Principal Commanders: Maj. Gen. George B. McClellan (Union), Gen. Robert E. Lee (Confederate)

Estimated Casualties: 23,100

Results: Inconclusive

When McClellan's Union forces met Lee's Confederates at Sharpsburg, extremely heavy fighting occurred — the bloodiest single day of this or any previous American war. At dawn on September 17, Hooker's Union Corps launched a massive assault on Lee's left flank. Attacks and counterattacks raged across Miller's cornfield and around the Dunker Church. The Union assault against the Confederates in the Sunken Road finally pierced the Confederate line, but the Federals did not follow up their advantage. Late in the day, Burnside's Corps finally managed to cross the bridge over Antietam Creek. When A.P. Hill's Division arrived from Harpers Ferry, a counterattack was launched which drove Burnside back and saved the day for the Confederacy. Lee's forces were outnumbered 2 to 1, but by sending in his entire force, he halted the Federal offensive. Skirmishes continued throughout the next day, after which Lee ordered his Army of Northern Virginia to withdraw back across the Potomac River into the Shenandoah Valley.[26]

While at Harpers Ferry, at 6:30 A.M. on September 17, A.P. Hill received orders from General Lee to move to Sharpsburg. Only Thomas' Brigade was to be left at Harpers Ferry to remove all captured property. Hill's Division started out about 7:30 A.M. and reached Sharpsburg at about 2:30 P.M.[27]

Captain Nicholas Biddle Gibbon recalled that A.P. Hill's division, including the 28th Regiment, remained at Harpers Ferry a day and a night before they marched towards Shepherdstown. Here, they crossed the Potomac.[28]

Encouraged by A.P. Hill, the men of his Light Division started on the grueling 17-mile march to Sharpsburg on that hot September day. Much of the march was done in double-quick time, and the ranks were decimated by stragglers who could not keep up the pace.[29]

When Hill arrived at Sharpsburg, the battle between the opposing forces had been going on for some time. Hill reported to General Lee, and was directed to take a position on the right of the Confederate line. He quickly deployed his troops, with Pender and Brockenbrough on the extreme right facing the road which crossed Antietam Creek near its mouth. The men of Branch, Gregg, and Archer extended the line on the left to connect with the division of Major General David Rumph Jones.[30]

At Sharpsburg, Brigadier General Branch was killed instantly by "a minnie ball passing through his head."[31] He had been sitting on his horse and had just raised his field glasses to peruse the enemy when a bullet toppled him from his horse into the arms of a staff member, Major Joseph Engelhard.[32]

Colonel Lane took over command of the brigade, and it was he who subsequently reported on the activities of Branch's Brigade at Sharpsburg:

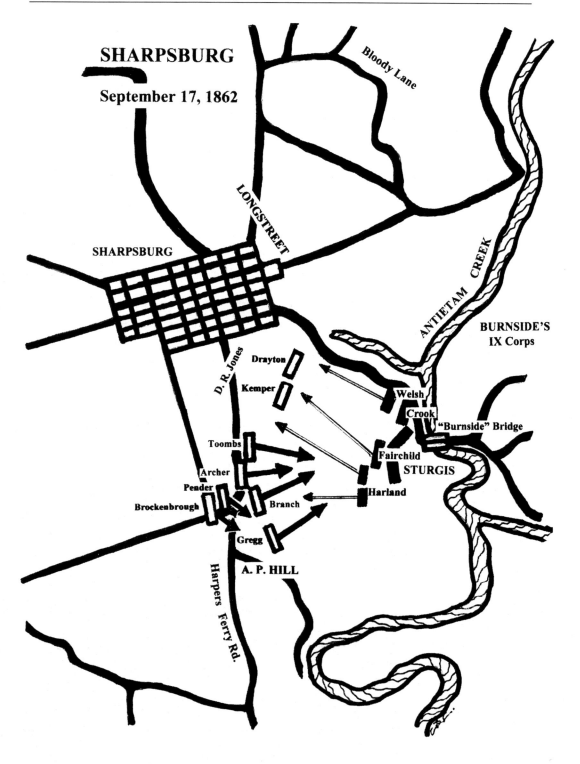

Map 1— Sharpsburg, Maryland, September 17, 1862 (Caren Casstevens, artist).

We left Harpers Ferry on September 17, and, after a very rapid and fatiguing march, recrossed the Potomac and reached Sharpsburg in time to participate in the fight. The entire brigade was ordered to the right, and, on reaching the field, the Twenty-eighth was detached by General A.P. Hill, in person, and sent on the road to the left leading to Sharpsburg to repel the enemy's skirmishers, who were advancing through a field of corn. The rest of the brigade moved nearly at right angles to our line, and on the enemy's flank. The Thirty-third, Seventh, and Thirty-seventh were the regiments principally engaged. They fought well, and assisted in driving back three separate and distinct columns of the enemy. The Eighteenth was not actively engaged. I was ordered, about sunset, to rejoin the brigade, and on doing so ascertained that General Branch had been killed. It was after sunset when I assumed command of the brigade.[33]

After Lane assumed command of the brigade, he found the 7th, 37th, and 33rd were positioned behind a stone fence. The 18th was sheltered in a hollow to the rear. He ordered the 28th to the left of the line. By mistake, the order was delivered to the 18th Regiment instead, which was posted on the left behind a rail fence. The 28th was on the left of the 7th in a gap caused by the withdrawal of the Georgia troops. Although annoyed by the enemy's sharpshooters, Lane and his new command managed to hold their position until ordered to fall back on the night of September 18. The next day, they crossed the river and along with the troops of Gregg and Archer, formed the rear guard.[34]

Captain William G. Morris wrote home that General D.H. Hill had been attacked by McClellan's and Pope's Federal forces at Sharpsburg. Branch's Brigade had been engaged in "a hard fight." From his position on the right wing, Morris could see that "We whiped them badly with little loss, but they [the enemy] held there [sic] own on the left pretty well." After the fighting ended, Morris told his wife that the Confederates fell back to the Virginia side. They were followed by the enemy, who believed them to be defeated. However, according to Morris, "Our Division was sent back & we had a fight, whipping them badly. Drove them across the River capturing 300 prisoners, Killing a great many of them."[35]

General A.P. Hill believed that his division had arrived in time to prevent the Confederates from being overrun. He noted that the "enemy had already advanced in three lines, had broken through Jones' division, captured McIntosh's battery, and were in the full tide of success." Upon the arrival of his men, they gave a "yell of defiance," and then Archer's men charged, recaptured McIntosh's guns, and drove the enemy "back pell-mell." Hill commended Branch and Gregg, who with their brigades of "old veterans, sternly held their ground," and poured heavy, destructive gunfire into the enemy. The Union troops were pushed back, and broke in confusion. Hill noted that at the time of the engagement at Sharpsburg, he had less than 2,000 men in the three brigades of his division. Yet, with the help of his "splendid batteries," they had driven Burnside's 15,000 men back.[36]

Casualties

Casualties at Sharpsburg (Antietam) were extremely heavy. According to historian Thomas L. Livermore, out of 75,316 Federal soldiers, 2,108 were killed, 9,549 wounded and 753 were missing, for a total of 12,410 casualties. Confederate forces, estimated at 51,844, lost 2,700 killed, 9,024 wounded, and about 2,000 missing, for total casualties of 13,724.[37]

Casualties in the five regiments of the Lane-Branch Brigade were: 20 killed, 79 wounded, and four missing, a total of 103. Of that number, the 28th Regiment had only two men wounded.[38]

James Henry Lane was officially promoted to brigadier general and given command of Branch's Brigade by General Robert E. Lee on November 6, 1862.[39] Lane would continue to command this brigade, now known as the Branch-Lane Brigade, at Fredericksburg, Chancellorsville, Gettysburg, the Wilderness and Petersburg.[40] He was fondly nicknamed "The Little General" by the men under his command.[41]

Shepherdstown (Boteler's Ford), September 19–20, 1862

Forces Engaged: Brigades

Principal Commanders: Maj. Gen. Fitz John Porter (Union); Brig. Gen. William Pendleton and Maj. Gen. A.P. Hill (Confederate)

Estimated casualties: 625 total

Results: Confederate victory

A detachment of Union general Porter's V Corps crossed the Potomac River at Boteler's Ford and attacked the Confederate rear guard commanded by Brigadier General Pendleton. The Federals captured four guns. On the morning of the 20th, Porter pushed part of his two divisions across the Potomac to establish a bridgehead. Hill's division counterattacked and hit the Federals as they were crossing. The 118th Pennsylvania (the "Corn Exchange" Regiment) was nearly wiped out. The Federals sustained 269 casualties, which discouraged any further pursuit. [42]

General Lee learned that McClellan had sent troops to the Virginia side of the Potomac River at Shepherdstown. He relayed the news to Jackson, and Jackson selected Hill's Light Division to drive the enemy back across the river.

Branch's Brigade, under the commander of Colonel Lane of the 28th, was one of three brigades which formed the rear guard while Lee's Army of Northern Virginia retired across the Potomac River. On September 20, Hill's division, including Branch's Brigade, moved to Shepherdstown and drove the Federal forces back across the Potomac. [43]

Hill's men left their camp at Martinsburg to march back toward the Potomac to prevent McClellan from pursuing Lee's Army of Northern Virginia. Hill did not hesitate but, by using a cornfield to conceal his men, he formed the Light Division into two lines of three brigades each and ordered them to move forward. Hill's men encountered only a small Federal force, and some of them had already begun to retreat back across the Potomac. However, the Federal artillery rained down "showers of grape and canister" on the advancing Confederates. [44] Brigadier General James J. Archer recalled that the men under his command at the time (the brigades of Field's, Lane's, and his own), advanced under the "heaviest artillery fire I have ever witnessed." "Too much praise," Archer said, "cannot be awarded to officers and men for their conduct." [45]

As Hill's Division came closer to the Federal line, Lane's Brigade moved forward with two other brigades to prevent the Federals from outflanking Pender's North Carolina troops on the far left. With a "yell" and "deadly fire," the Confederate attack sent a Union regiment fleeing, who made excellent targets for the North Carolina sharpshooters. In a short time, the area around the ford was littered with dead Union soldiers. [46] Casualties in the Branch-Lane Brigade amounted to three killed and 71 wounded. [47]

Lieutenant J.P. Little (Company C, 28th Regiment) remembered that, while crossing the Potomac at "Shepard's Town," the Confederate forces put up a fight and forced the enemy back across the river. The "surface of the Potomac was floating with dead bodies." Little believed that Federal losses were 3,000 to only 261 Confederate casualties. [48]

Lane complimented several men in the 18th and 7th Regiments for their bravery. He noted that Lieutenants W.W. Cloniger and G.W. McCauley of the 28th also deserved "special notice for their great bravery and faithfulness in the discharge of their duties." [49]

After destroying part of the Baltimore & Ohio Railroad, the division camped near Bunker Hill with the rest of Lee's Army. [50]

The actions of Hill's Division effectively blocked the Federal pursuit of Lee's Army of Northern Virginia. Subsequently, on November 7, 1862, President Abraham Lincoln relieved Major General George McClellan of command because he had failed to capture Lee's retreating forces.

Lincoln replaced McClellan with Major General Ambrose E. Burnside and placed him in command of the Union Army.[51]

In 1995, when my son Tim and I were on our way to visit the battlefield at Gettysburg, Pennsylvania, we stopped off at Sharpsburg. We drove down "the bloody lane," and saw the Dunkard Church. Fortunately for the Harding brothers (Sam and Greenberry), my great-uncles, A.P. Hill's forces did not arrive at Sharpsburg until 4:30 P.M. Hill's men entered the town on the south side near what has become known as "Burnside Bridge." There, Confederate forces under Georgia's Brigadier General Robert Toombs were entrenched on a high bluff above Antietam Creek, where they prevented the advance of Major General Burnside's 11,000 troops over the bridge for three hours.

After Sharpsburg

Captain Gibbon recalled that the brigade marched to near Martinsburg where they camped for several days. Here, some new recruits from North Carolina joined them. The regiment then moved to Bunker Hill, Virginia, on the road from Martinsburg to Winchester, where the brigade remained in camp at Winchester until the middle of October. They were then ordered to move to Hedgesville, a small village situated on the B & O Railroad, about 12 miles north of Martinsburg. The brigade destroyed the railroad and tried to live off the country, "which had been drained of nearly everything like commissary stores." Gibbon did, however, succeed in furnishing the men with flour, beef and salt "by riding constantly and empressing cattle and flour...."[52]

The Branch-Lane Brigade was then ordered to rejoin the division, which was engaged working on the railroad between Martinsburg and Harpers Ferry. The men returned to camp at Bunker Hill, then marched to Berryville, where they encamped about two miles north of the town. Winter came early, and in the first weeks of November, the men suffered through two snowstorms. The soldiers were badly in need of blankets and clothing. Many had no tents.[53]

After breaking camp at Bunker Hill, 1st Lieutenant Little wrote of the march up through the Shenandoah Valley. He saw destruction everywhere. They crossed the Shenandoah River near Winchester and made their way up a winding trail to the top of the mountains, a distance of about nine miles. Once they reached the top, the army stopped. Little looked around and was amazed by the cloud-capped mountains of the Blue Ridge Mountains. Poetically, he described the scene of "lofty peaks and smoky terits [turrets] in the very clouds of heaven and basking her towering spires in the dazzling sunlight of eternal day." Below, they could see the "blood stained valley" and the Shenandoah River. The once-peaceful river ran through a valley now "laid to waste and dessolation [sic]." Continuing their long march, the 28th Regiment arrived with others of the brigade at Fredericksburg in time for the battle.[54]

Captain Gibbon recalled that about November 12, 1862, he and the troops of the 28th Regiment and the rest of the Branch-Lane Brigade moved 8 miles north of Berryville to what was called "Camp Lee." From there, they moved on to Fredericksburg, Virginia.[55]

In retrospect, memories are not always accurate, and accounts by two different men recalling the same event will remember events differently, even in dates and place names. Thus, Colonel Lane's account (below) does not entirely agree with the account of Captain Nicholas Gibbon (above).

Colonel James H. Lane wrote in his history of the 28th that after the fighting at Sharpsburg and Shepherdstown, the regiment went into camp near "Castleman's Ferry, or Snicker's Gap, in Clark County, Virginia." They remained for some time doing picket duty "in snow storms and freezing weather." Then the 28th moved to Winchester where they remained with Jackson's Corps until the army moved to Fredericksburg on November 22.[56]

As cold weather set in, the Confederate Army issued clothing to the soldiers. William A. Tesh (Co. I, 28th Regiment) was issued an overcoat, one pair of pants, one shirt, a pair of drawers, plus a pair of shoes. The folks back home sent their boys whatever additional clothing they could. Tesh received socks and gloves and some tobacco from his folks. He was thankful for the needed gifts, but he wanted very badly to be home for Christmas. He would give "Fifty Dollars" for a 30-day furlough so that he could go home and get "something good to eat and a Dram." But unless a soldier was very sick or wounded, there was little chance of a furlough. All he could do was urge his parents to have a "good dinner at Christmas and think of me and eat some for me...."[57]

Casualties in the Branch-Lane Brigade from the battle at Cedar Mountain (Cedar Run) through Shepherdstown totaled 438 (79 killed, 352 wounded and 7 missing). The 28th Regiment suffered 126 casualties during that same time period (13 killed, 112 wounded, and 1 missing).[58]

In order to reach Fredericksburg, Virginia, the Branch-Lane Brigade marched along the road to Stanton and New Market, then they took the turnpike to Madison Court House. According to Captain Gibbon, the march lasted 12 days, including two days spent resting during that time. Early in December, the brigade reached an area near Hamilton's Crossing. Here they remained until they heard the "roar of Artillery" from the two opposing armies at Fredericksburg.[59]

Fredericksburg, VA, December 13, 1862

Forces Engaged: 172,504 total (100,007 Union; 72,497 Confederate)

Principal Commanders: Maj. Gen. Ambrose E. Burnside (Union), General Robert E. Lee (Confederate)

Estimated Casualties: 17,929 total (13,353 Union; 4,576 Confederate)

Result: Confederate victory

When General Ambrose Burnside took over command of the Army of the Potomac, he sent a corps to Fredericksburg. The rest of his army soon followed. Lee counteracted by entrenching his army on the heights above the town. On December 11, the Union soldiers built five platoon bridges across the Rappahannock and crossed the river on the 12th. On December 13, Burnside launched an attack against the entrenched Confederates on Prospect Hill and Marye's Heights. Meade's Division briefly penetrated Jackson's line but were driven back. Burnside finally called off the assault and retreated back across the river on December 15. This failure prompted Lincoln to replace Burnside with Major General Joseph Hooker in January of 1863.[60]

When General Robert E. Lee learned that the Federal forces under General Ambrose E. Burnside were moving down the Rappahannock River opposite Fredericksburg, the Confederate general ordered both Longstreet and Jackson to move their men to a position on the heights overlooking the town of Fredericksburg.[61]

Because of the heavy casualties suffered by the Federal forces, the battle for the town of Fredericksburg is outstanding among the many battles fought during the American Civil War. The Marye House and part of the stone wall at the base of Marye's Heights still stand. It was behind this wall and along the sunken road that Confederates rained down death on thousands of Union soldiers. The snow-covered ground was soon stained red with the blood of wounded, dying, and dead Federal soldiers on the hill that sloped down from Marye's Heights and the stone wall. Heavy fighting occurred some distance from Marye's Heights as well along the railroad tracks, where the 28th Regiment was engaged in battle.

The passage across the Rappahannock by the Grand Army of the Potomac at Fredericksburg at midnight, December 10, 1862. From a sketch by Henri Lovie, which appeared in *Frank Leslie's Illustrated Newspaper* on December 27, 1862 (Library of Congress, digital ID cph 3c19619).

A.P. Hill's men were east of and some distance away from Marye's Heights along the railroad, and just north of the Massaponax River.[62] On Saturday morning, according to Major General A.P. Hill's report, General T.J. "Stonewall" Jackson ordered Braxton's battery and two batteries from Taliaferro's division to be placed "in advance of the railroad." General Lane was ordered to support them with his brigade. When the fog lifted the morning of December 13, Lane and his men could see that they faced an enemy which was "in battle array on the low grounds between" them and the river. The Federals were spread out along A.P. Hill's whole front and even extended along the Confederate left toward the town. The enemy was "deployed in three lines," with reserves stationed behind the Port Royal Road. The enemy also had 10 full batteries engaged as they moved forward to attack the Confederate forces.[63]

Lane's five-regiment brigade (7th, 18th, 28th, 33rd and 37th North Carolina Regiments) faced the Federal forces of Gibbon's 88th Pennsylvania, 97th New York, 12th Massachusetts, 26th New York, 90th Pennsylvania, and the 136th Pennsylvania across the railroad tracks.[64] Lane's position in a woods facing an open field should have been secure. However, this site was undermined by an order given by A.P. Hill which directed Lane to position his brigade 150 yards in advance of the main line.[65] This decision left a gap through which the Federal forces almost penetrated the Confederate line. Lane had misgivings about the position, and he talked with other officers to alert them to the vulnerability of their position. He then talked with A.P. Hill but Hill assured Lane that Gregg would furnish adequate cover for his right.[66] No change in position was ordered, but the events the following day proved that Lane's concerns had been correct.

Lane wanted his men to remain concealed as long as possible, although Colonel Clark Avery of the 33rd sought his permission to advance to the top of a hill in anticipation of the enemy's attack.[67] In spite of Lane's orders, two soldiers from the 28th Regiment could not wait.

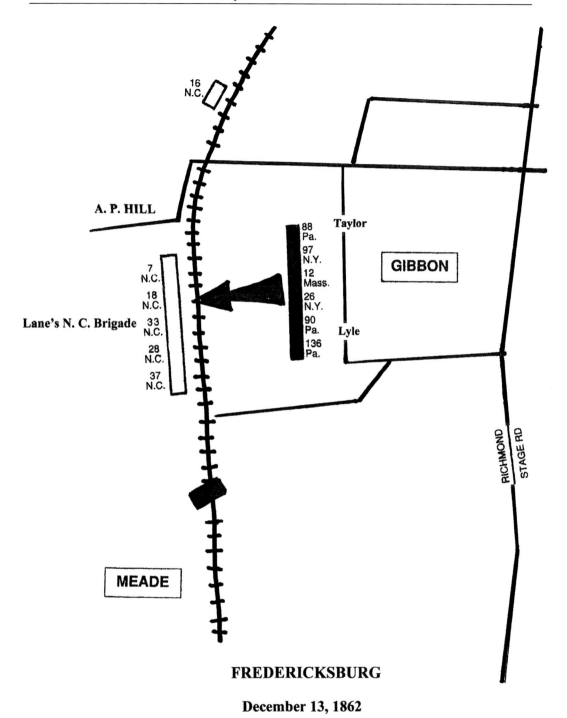

FREDERICKSBURG

December 13, 1862

Map 2 — Fredericksburg, Virginia, December 13, 1862 (Caren Casstevens, artist).

Captain Edward Lovell, of Company A, refused to lie down as the rest of the men were doing. Instead, he stood up on the railroad track and waved his cap, cheering his men, fully exposed to enemy gunfire. Another soldier, Private William A. Martin, "cooly sat on the [railroad] tracks and called to his comrads to watch the Yankee colors," then he proceeded to fire repeatedly at the enemy from rifles handed him by his fellow soldiers. Martin hit several of the Federal flag bearers. Both Lovell and Martin escaped being hit by enemy gunfire at this time.[68]

Brigadier General Lane reported the details of the actions of his brigade at Fredericksburg, in which the 28th and the 37th regiments played a major part. These two regiments had been positioned on "open, level ground in their front...." When the enemy was within 150 yards of Lane's line, Lane's men opened up with a terrific and deadly fire on the advancing Federals and repulsed "their first and second lines" and succeeded in checking the third.[69]

Lane's brigade was the first to come in contact with the enemy, and the encounter caused the Union boys to shift their attack to the right, in an attempt to penetrate the gap between Archer's men and Lane's. The attack was directly in front of Archer and when Walker's guns had been repulsed, the enemy took shelter along the railroad. Then they concentrated their efforts and attempted to turn Lane's line on the right.[70]

Lane reported that the 28th and 37th regiments "were subject not only to a direct, but to right and left oblique fires," from a portion of the enemy's force which was behind the hill nearest the 28th Regiment. As the right of his command "became engaged with such an overwhelming force," he dispatched Captain Hawks to General Maxey Gregg to request reinforcements. Lane also asked that if Gregg was unable to send men, then to apply to General Edward L. Thomas, or "anybody else whom he might see in command of troops, for assistance."[71] Yet Gregg did not send reinforcements. His troops spent the entire morning lying on the ground with their muskets stacked, which would seem to indicate that Gregg did not believe his men would be engaged by the enemy. However, when the fire from the 28th and the 37th caused the Federal troops to shift to their left, they came in contact with Gregg's men. Although the enemy had reached the right of his brigade, Gregg failed to see the danger. He rode in front of his men and knocked their muskets upward, shouting that they were firing on their friends. He could not have been more wrong, and that error cost him his life. He made a good target riding on his horse in front of his line, and was soon mortally wounded by the enemy. Thus, Gregg's men did not lend any support to Lane's Brigade.[72]

Lane noted that his entire command held their ground until the 28th and the 37th regiments had fired not only all "their own ammunition, but that of their own dead and wounded, which in some cases was handed them by their officers." After these regiments ceased firing, the Federal soldiers, in a "column doubled on the center, bore down in mass from behind the hill upon the left" of the 28th and the right of the 33rd. Their overwhelming force propelled them across the railroad. The 28th and the 37th, "being flanked right and left, fell back in an orderly manner," where they were resupplied with ammunition. The 33rd Regiment sent a well-directed volley of fire which checked the enemy for a time. Colonel Clark M. Avery ordered a charge, but, being "unsupported on his right," he had to countermand the order and withdrew his regiment into the woods, which were about 75 yards from the railroad.[73]

Historian William Kelsey McDaid noted that "most historians blame Hill" for the gap in the line between Archer and Lane's men. However, Branch Spalding, according to McDaid, believed that Jackson, rather than A.P. Hill, was responsible for the gap and that he was setting a trap for the advancing Federals.[74] This work will not delve further into who was to blame, or speculate on whether the gap was deliberate or simply an oversight.

This breach in the Confederate line could have been disastrous, but the men of Lane's Brigade, especially the 28th and 37th, without any reinforcements, managed to regain their positions along the railroad. Lane reported that his brigade spent the night of December 13

Building in Fredericksburg damaged in a skirmish on December 13, 1862.

"aligned along the track." An order to advance was countermanded and the men "rested on their arms until morning, when, having already been on duty upward of forty-eight hours, there was heavy skirmishing along my whole front," and a number of men were killed and wounded. On Monday, December 15, Lane's men formed a portion of a second line and occupied an "exposed position, but the men soon constructed temporary breastworks of logs, bush, and dirt, behind which they rested until Tuesday morning," when it was learned that the enemy had fled back across the Rappahannock.[75]

Casualties at Fredericksburg

The fighting at Fredericksburg on December 13, 1862, is remembered for the number of casualties suffered by the Federal soldiers as they attempted to climb toward Marye's Heights. Casualties at Fredericksburg were tremendous. Out of 106,000 Federal soldiers, 12,700 were killed or wounded. Confederates lost 5,300 out of 72,500 men engaged.[76]

A.P. Hill's Division suffered 231 men killed, 1,474 wounded, and 417 missing for a total of 2,122[77]— or 1,619, according to Dr. Guild. Whichever figure is correct, Hill's Division had more casualties than any other division in either the 1st or 2nd Corps.[78]

Losses in the 28th Regiment alone were 16 men killed and 49 wounded.[79] The losses of Hill's Division and Lane's Brigade can be attributed to their position along the railroad south of the town, which was southeast of Marye's Heights. William Norman (Company F, 28th Regiment) noted that at the front where the "last bold stand was made," the scene was a nightmare. Dead soldiers and officers "lie in heaps— some shot through the head, some through the heart, and in most every other portion of the body you can name; some with their brains dashed out against their comrades...."[80]

Private Artha Bray, Jr. (also of Company F) wrote his brother that Confederate losses in "killed and wounded was two thousand and five hundred. The enemy loss was ten thousand."[81] Bray greatly underestimated Confederate casualties (2,500 vs. 5,300), but he was more accurate in counting the enemy's losses (10,000 vs. 12,700).

Lieutenant J.P. Little, of Company C, later wrote in his regimental history that at Fredericksburg the Federals lost 12,321, and the Confederates lost 4,201.[82] His figures were more accurate than those of Private Bray.

As usual, there were discrepancies in the numbers of casualties reported. General R.E. Lee noted on April 16, 1863, that the "differences between the number of casualties appearing in Dr. Guild's return dated January 19, 1863, and the number given a month earlier on December 14, 1862, was due to the fact that the first report "was made while the army was in order of battle, and there was no time to obtain full information." He added that the number of "slightly wounded was ususually large," but that "no report was made of them until the enemy had retired."[83]

There was also heavy fighting below Marye's Heights. The town of Fredericksburg suffered greatly, and many of the homes and other buildings were burned. Lieutenant J.P. Little was moved by the plight of the citizens: "I shall never forget the scene of the women and children as they passed through our lines, some with babies in their arms. What became of them I never knew."[84]

Valor of Lane's Men

Brigadier General Lane did not forget the heroic actions of the men of the 28th and 37th regiments at Fredericksburg, and his report reflected their valor. They "fought like brave men, long and well." He was especially pleased with the new conscripts who had proved themselves "worthy accessions to a brigade which had borne itself well in all of the battles of the last eight months."[85]

There were acts of bravery and courage on both sides. Colonel Lane recalled that the 28th Regiment "held an advanced, open, unfortified position on the railroad, and fought with great coolness and gallantry, using all its ammunition, including that from the boxes of its dead and badly wounded." They held even though the "right flank of the brigade" had been turned by a large force of the enemy, and the enemy were pouring through a gap in the Confederate lines. Lane's 28th "repulsed two lines of battle in its front, before finally being forced to withdraw during a third attack.[86]

Major William H. Asbury Speer wrote to his mother a few days after the battle: "The great battle the other day ... was as horrible as you can imagine, but thank God I came through safe & I do trust that I will be saved through all."[87]

Captain Gold Holland, of Company H, escaped serious injury and death at Fredericksburg. After the fighting was over, Holland told General James H. Lane that he was "indebted to a biscuit" for his own life." Then, Holland reached into his haversack and pulled out a camp biscuit about the size of a saucer. It had been cooked without salt or shortening and was as hard as a rock (hence the name *hardtack*). Halfway imbedded in the biscuit was a Yankee bullet. The biscuit had caught and held the deadly bullet intended for Captain Holland.[88]

Captain Nicholas Gibbon wrote that his brigade took an "active part in the Fredericksburg fight" on December 13, 1862. He saw many "a brave man and officer [fall] to rise no more."[89]

Not only were there casualties among the soldiers, but where the artillery had been placed, there were dead horses, shattered caissons, and dismounted guns. William Norman described the horrifying scene of casualties among his own troops in vivid detail:

> The best of horses, the bravest of soldiers and officers, lie in piles. The poor horse has fallen under his gallant rider. The brave soldier or officer has fallen, with his musket clenched as if in the act of a brave charge, when he was struck with the messenger of death. The gallant officer with sword unsheathed and clenched, has fallen here, as if in the act of leading his brave command to victory or death, and lies, a lifeless corpse.[90]

Once the fighting ended, the care of the wounded and burying of the dead began. Captain William M. Norman (formerly of Company A, 28th Regiment) wrote in his memoirs a very graphic description. "The battlefield does not present a very agreeable sight immediately after a hard-fought battle." In order to be carried to a safe place in the rear, the wounded were placed on a "litter, which is made by fastening a piece of tent cloth or a blanket to two poles, about eight feet in length, which are parallel with each other." Litter bearers were selected with care. They had to have the "stoutest hearts and in every way disposed to do their duty...." These brave men often had to work in dangerous situations. Those designated as "litter bearers," usually two to four in number, picked up the litter by the ends of the poles and carried the wounded officer or soldier to the rear. This was done "amid the bursting shells and roaring missiles of death from a thousand pieces [while] the blood of the injured man often gushed in perfect torrents." Frequently, when arriving at their destination, the litter bearers found that the wounded man had died along the way, before they could reach the field hospital.[91]

The Field Hospital

During each battle, a field hospital was set up near the conflict. The surgeons worked very quickly dressing wounds, amputating limbs, and trying to stabilize the wounded until they could be transported out of the area to a regular hospital. The wounded sometimes covered acres of ground. Norman recalled: "This is one of the bloodiest sights that a man ever looked at!" The "groans and dying shrieks" of the wounded was a "din that is not easily forgotten." As the doctors worked, mounds of amputated limbs accumulated and piles of bloody clothing grew in height.[92]

The Aftermath

Once the fighting ended, Captain Gibbon noted that the Yankees retreated back across the river "under the cover of darkness." A.P. Hill's Division moved along the road toward Port Royal in attempt to block the enemy's crossing. After a 10-mile march, the Confederates stopped for the night. The next day they gave up the pursuit of the Federals, and went into winter camp.[93] The winter camp of the Army of Northern Virginia was near Moss Neck below Fredericksburg. The soldiers remained there until April 30, 1863.[94]

A month after the battle, Lieutenant John Thomas Conrad and several others from Company F, 28th Regiment, returned to the scene of the fighting at Fredericksburg. He wrote his wife: "We could not see much as it has been a month since the battle, except dead horses and half buried Yankees, pieces of shell, etc. and etc. We did not have time to go to Fredericksburg only going over the field in front of where we fought and on the right of our lines." He added a hopeful note: "We are much better prepared now to resist an attack than we were then, having thrown up breast works and [letter torn] from Port Royal to Fredericksburg, though the Yankees seem to be in strong force on the other side of the river." He expressed his concerns about Yankees having a large force at New Bern, North Carolina.[95]

About the fighting at Fredericksburg, Samuel Harding (Company I, 28th Regiment) wrote to his mother: "You have heard of the fight at Fredericksburg. We had a hard time there. I am glad [to] say that we have been Blessed so far, but I think that they ought to give a furlow for I have done a heap of hard marching and hard Fighting. I think that I deserve a furlow if any one in the Company does...." Harding replied to his mother's chiding that he "had forgotten" her, saying, "I never will forget you as long as I live but I have not written to you in a long time [because] we have been marching so much that I could not write to you nor any body else."[96]

To his father, Sam Harding wrote that they had received "marching orders for ten days," but he was not sure of his destination. Sam thought it possible the troops would return to North Carolina or maybe Tennessee. Sam stated that he had plenty of clothing, but in case his father should come to visit, he wanted him to bring some "dryed fruit, ... some honey, and some butter and some sausage meet...." In a footnote, Sam told his father that brother Berry was now a provost guard.[97] (See Appendix IX for complete transcript of letters.)

Repercussions

During the fighting on the third day at Gettysburg, the situation was reversed and it was the Federal army that held the high ground. As the Confederates launched their assault on the Federal line on July 3, 1863, across the Emmittsburg Road, they were shot down by the men in blue, the Union soldiers, who shouted: "Remember Fredericksburg."

Little houses used for winter quarters, March 1862, Manassas (Library of Congress, digital ID cwpb 01312).

Casualties of the Year 1862

Lane's Brigade suffered heavy casualties from their first battle on May 27 at Hanover Court House through December 13 at Fredericksburg. According to one official report the total number, including officers and men killed, wounded, and missing, was 2,286. That number is the equivalent to more than two entire regiments. The greatest number of casualties, 535, was at Fredericksburg; the second highest, 275, was at Hanover Court House (73 were killed and 202 were wounded). That number does not include those who were captured.[98]

Winter 1862–1863

The 28th Regiment spent the winter months camped only a mile from the Rappahannock River near Fredericksburg. The men did picket duty all winter, taking turns among the various regiments of the brigade. Captain Nicholas Gibbon recalled that the last four or five months of winter "were very severe" and it was made "more so on account of our army being so scantily supplies with tents and having no winter quarters." Those who had tents built "little chimneys to them," while others constructed "little pole huts and covered them with dirt," to make them more comfortable.[99]

The weather during the winter of 1862–1863 was marked by the snow, sleet and rain. When the roads became impassable, the men of Lane's Brigade were ordered to help in "corduroying" (laying down logs on) the roads. This work was done during and just after a heavy snowstorm. The snow had to be removed before the logs could be laid, and there were times that the men could not return to their quarters because of the distance. On such nights, their "suffering was intense," according to General James H. Lane.[100]

General Robert E. Lee's childhood home, Stratford Hall. Photograph by Frances H. Casstevens.

Fredericksburg and Vicinity Today

Tim and I enjoyed the trip to Fredericksburg very much. In addition to seeing the wall and the sunken road beneath Marye's Heights, it was only a short drive through undeveloped land, over several country roads, to the battlefields of Chancellorsville, Spotsylvania, and the Wilderness. From Fredericksburg, we drove several miles down the peninsula to visit the magnificent mansion, Stratford Hall, which was the childhood home of General Robert E. Lee. The house and grounds have been restored and are open to the public.

Chapter 8

May 1863: Chancellorsville, the South's Greatest Victory

Lane's boys were a bad, quarrelsome set of
fellows, and too fond of a fight altogether.
— Augustus C. Hamlin[1]

After a dull Christmas, in the following month, the men of the 28th Regiment had little to do but stand guard on picket duty. Often there was little space between Union and Confederate sentries. A Yankee soldier on picket duty shouted across the river to Confederate Private W.A. Tesh (Company I, 28th Regiment) that he believed if "old Abe" [Lincoln] and "old Jeff" [Davis] had to stand at "our posts," the war would soon be over.[2]

To break the monotony, troop reviews were held. This gave the men a chance to exhibit the skills they had learned in their many hours of drill training. Private Tesh wrote his parents that they had had "General Review" on January 6, 1863, and then General Hill was to have a general review. The day after that, they would be reviewed by General Robert E. Lee.[3]

In an almost unprecedented move, and although outnumbered two to one, Robert E. Lee

---

Chancellorsville, May 1–4, 1863

Forces Engaged: 154,734 total (97,382 Union; 57,352 Confederate)

Principal Commanders: Maj. Gen. Joseph Hooker (Union), General Robert E. Lee (Confederate)

Estimated Casualties: 24,000 total (14,000 Union; 10,000 Confederate)

Result: Confederate victory (Lee's greatest victory)

Major General Joseph Hooker and his V, IX and XII Corps were determined to turn the Confederate left flank. Federal forces crossed the Rappahannock and Rapidan Rivers above Fredericksburg, and concentrated their forces near Chancellorsville on April 30 and May 1. Lee split his forces and left part under Major General Jubal Early at Fredericksburg, then marched to Chancellorsville with the rest of his men. Meanwhile, Union troops under Hooker encountered resistance on the Orange Turnpike as they moved toward Fredericksburg. After Hooker learned the location of the larger Confederate force, he redirected his troops to concentrate on Chancellorsville. Lee took the initiative against Hooker's defensive position. On May 2, Jackson sent his troops around the Federal left flank. Fighting was sporadic throughout the day. At 5:20 P.M., Jackson launched an attack and crushed the Union XII Corps, but the Federals launched a counterattack, and fighting continued until dark. While making a night reconnaissance, Jackson was mortally wounded by his own men. J.E.B. Stuart took temporary command of Jackson's Corps. On May 3, with the help of their artillery, the Confederates attacked both wings of Hooker's army at Hazel Grove. The Federal line broke and Hooker withdrew. [4]

---

split his forces and moved part of them to meet Hooker at Chancellorsville. The move was successful, and Lee achieved his greatest victory at Chancellorsville, but that victory came at the cost of the life of Lieutenant General Thomas "Stonewall" Jackson.

During the Chancellorsville campaign, Brigadier General Lane's Brigade (the 4th Brigade) was still part of A.P. Hill's Light Division, and under the command of T.J. "Stonewall" Jackson.[5] At Chancellorsville, Jackson exhibited his military genius in a daring flank attack, but it was to be his last battle.

May 1, 1863

A.P. Hill's Light Division moved down the Orange Plank road toward Chancellorsville on May 1. Lane's Brigade was not involved in the fighting that day, but was formed in a line of battle near Chancellorsville late that evening.[6]

Lane's reported that his brigade moved from a position near Hamilton's Crossing south of Fredericksburg along a plank road towards Chancellorsville. There, he formed his men into a line of battle, and sent skirmishers forward to the right of the road.[7]

William H. Asbury Speer, now a Lieutenant Colonel on the field and staff of the 28th Regiment, wrote of the events after the battle was over.

> We stayed there [Fredericksburg] ... till day break (but did no fighting but was under the shells of the enemy Thursday) at which time we took up march for Chancellorsville. We were under the fire of the enemy all day Friday and fighting also Friday night. Saturday morning we left by day under Gen. Jackson and went around the enemy's flank, traveling 20 miles. Attacked them in their rear about two hours by sun and drove them four miles by dark — we continued to fight till 3 o'clock Sunday morning. We had a hard fight for two hours Saturday night from 1 o'clock till 3....[8]

May 2, 1863

Jackson's Corps was dispatched to turn the right flank of the Federal Army. After hard marching, Jackson reached a point about four miles west of Chancellorsville. As Jackson's men arrived, he deployed them in three lines for the attack.[9] On the morning of May 2, Lane reported that after an artillery fight on his right, his brigade marched to the plank road above Chancellorsville by Welford's Iron Forge.[10]

That same day, the men under Jackson's command made their way through the woods undetected by the enemy because of the dense undergrowth. The soldiers dutifully followed Jackson, their fearless commander. One soldier in Lane's Brigade recalled: "It was not ours to know, we were there 'to do or die,' but there is one thing we did know ... that old Jack [Jackson] was going round the bulls horns but unless the bull kept his tail switching very fast the old hero would have a grip on it before the sun went down."[11]

Hill's division was placed in the third line. Lane's Brigade (which included the 28th North Carolina), was in a column on the Orange Turnpike and was ordered to move forward along the turnpike as the men advanced toward the enemy. With about two hours of daylight left, the attack began about 5:15 P.M., and it caught the Federals by surprise. The Federal soldiers fell back in disorder toward Chancellorsville. The first two Confederate lines drove the enemy until they were forced to halt by the darkness of night. The third Confederate line was exposed to heavy artillery fire as it advanced. After the attack stalled, the men in the third line moved to the front to become the first line.[12]

Night Attack Planned

After Lane learned that the enemy was rapidly falling back, his men pushed forward with the artillery to beyond the third and second lines. At dark, Lane was ordered by A.P. Hill to send one regiment of skirmishers across the road to form a line of battle in the rear with the rest of the brigade. They were to push "vigorously forward," to make a night attack and capture the enemy's artillery. However, the Federals opened fire and the Confederate artillery responded. When the barrage was over, Lane sent the 33rd Regiment forward as skirmishers to form a line of battle, and he moved his other regiments into position.[13]

The Situation Before Jackson Was Shot

General Lane wrote in 1892 to Augustus C. Hamlin, of Bangor, Maine, a former Union soldier who was writing a history about the battle at Chancellorsville. Augustus was the nephew of Hannibal Hamlin, Lincoln's vice president.[14] Lane told Hamlin that when General Jackson moved unexpectedly and successfully upon the enemy's flank at Chancellorsville, Jackson's "front line was composed of Rodes' division, and his second line that of A.P. Hill's. That line was without McGowan's [South Carolina] brigade and Lane's [which was composed wholly of North Carolinians]." These two brigades moved by the flank along the plank road behind their artillery. About dark, Lane and the others reached the breastworks from which they had driven the enemy, then halted and remained standing in the road for some time. General Hill then ordered Lane to form "across the road," with two regiments on the right, two on the left, and one "thrown forward as a strong line of skirmishers for the purpose of making a night attack." However, as soon as the order was received, Confederate artillery opened fire and was returned by the Federal guns. Lane saw that it was futile to try to move forward under the "murderous enfilade fire," and he ordered his men to lie down. Lane sent a message to Hill and told him that if he wished him and his men to advance, Hill would have to stop the Confederate artillery fire. The bombardment only added to the dangers of moving troops in the dark. Once the artillery fire ceased, Lane began to form his men in a line. The 33rd Regiment under Colonel Avery was sent forward as skirmishers, the 7th and 37th Regiments were on the right of the plank road. The left of the 37th was resting on the road, and the 18th and 28th Regiments were on the left of the road, with the right of the 18th Regiment resting on the road. The woods in front of the men were filled with large oak trees, but little undergrowth. When he ordered his men forward, Lane cautioned them to keep "a bright look out," because their position was in front of everyone else, and he knew they would soon be ordered forward to make an attack at night. Once he had his men formed into a battle line, Lane rode back down the road to report to A.P. Hill. In the dark, he encountered General Jackson. Lane told Jackson that he was looking for Hill, but could not find him, and to save time, he asked Jackson for orders. "In an ernest tone & with a pushing gesture with his right hand in the direction of the enemy, Genl Jackson said 'Push right ahead Lane' & then rode forward." That was the last time Lane saw of General Jackson.[15]

The situation was tense at Chancellorsville that night. In the dark, the men could not tell friend from foe. Unknowingly, Lane's men had taken up a position formerly occupied by General Alpheus Williams' division of the Federal XII Corps. When Williams returned from a foray, he found Lane's men in his former position.[16] Lane's men were in a precarious position, isolated in dense woods, and very close to enemy troops.[17]

The situation became even more bizarre when General Williams, a Union officer, moved toward the 7th North Carolina Regiment under a flag of truce to investigate whether the men he faced were his own or Confederate. The officer stated that he was not there to surrender, and demanded that he be allowed to return to his command. Lane sent a courier to ask A.P. Hill what to do. The Union soldiers were worried because the officer they had sent under the white flag had not returned, and so they threatened to open fire. The nervous men of the 7th North Carolina were advised by General Hill to be prepared for gunfire from the Federals. It was all that Hill and the company officers could do to prevent their men from firing at anything and everything that moved in front of them.[18]

When another Federal soldier rode up to the line of the 37th and called for his General Williams, some of the men of the Lane's 37th Regiment began firing. Soon, there were gunshots all along the skirmish line. The shooting set off a chain reaction along the main line and shots were heard up the entire length of the brigade. The 37th found that they were in danger of being hit by their own men. In the confusion, the 37th did lose many men who were either hit or who ran toward the enemy lines trying to escape gunfire, only to be captured.[19]

Jackson Shot by His Own Troops

It continued to be a night of unexpected and tragic events. After "Stonewall" Jackson had ordered Lane to attack, Jackson, along with A.P. Hill and other staff officers, rode forward to reconnoiter for themselves the Federal positions around Chancellorsville. They passed through the main Confederate line without notice, and halted a short distance before they reached the skirmish line of the 37th. Upon hearing gunfire, Jackson turned back, but just as he and his group reached the line of the 18th North Carolina Regiment, firing on the right began again. This barrage caused Jackson to spur his horse and move rapidly in order to get back behind the brigade before the fighting worsened.[20]

Erroneously, the men of the 18th thought that the approaching horsemen were enemy cavalry. Captain Alfred Tolar, of the 18th, recalled that the night was calm, and they heard the "tramp of 30 horsemen advancing through a heavy forest at a rapid gate...."[21] Captain Thomas Purdle ordered his men to fix their bayonets and to load their muskets. When the horsemen were within 100 yards, Major John Barry, commander of the 18th Regiment, gave the order to fire. As they did so, several of the horsemen fell wounded from their horses. The horsemen shouted, "We are friends! Cease firing!" However, those words did not convince the men of the 18th, and Colonel Barry yelled back, "It's a lie!" He then ordered his men to "Pour it into them, boys!"[22] The mistake was finally discovered when Private Arthur S. Smith, of Company K, 18th Regiment, knocked one of the soldiers from his horse with the butt of his rifle and was close enough to see what kind of uniform he wore.[23] By that time Jackson had already been mortally wounded.

With the help of two aides, Jackson made his way back toward the rear, weak from pain and loss of blood. General Pender rode up and asked who had been wounded. Captain James P. Smith had been ordered by Jackson not to tell anyone of his injury, but Pender recognized Jackson. Pender told Jackson that the Confederate lines were so broken, it might be necessary to fall back. Jackson rallied, straightened up and said, "General Pender, you must hold on to the field; you must hold out to the last." That was the last order Jackson ever gave on the battlefield. Jackson was carried to the field hospital where Dr. Hunter McGuire administered chloroform to the wounded general, and proceeded to amputate his left arm. There were two wounds in his arm, the first was about 3 inches below the shoulder joint. That ball had divided the main artery and fractured the bone. The second bullet had entered the outside of Jackson's forearm, about an inch below the elbow, and had exited just about the wrist. These wounds clearly indicated amputation.[24]

After Jackson was carried away, A.P. Hill returned to the front line to get the attack organized. However, by this time, the Federal artillery was bombarding the Confederate front. Just as Hill passed Lane's line, he was wounded in the calf from a spent Minié ball or a shell fragment. According to one source, as Hill hobbled back, he was in a foul mood and berated some of the men of the 18th Regiment for "firing at noise." One member of the 18th yelled back, rebuking Hill's criticism. "Everybody knows the Yankee army can't run the Light Division," the

Top: House in which Thomas J. "Stonewall" Jackson died in May 1863 near Guinea Station. *Bottom:* Bed in which Jackson died. Both photographs by Frances H. Casstevens.

soldier explained, "and one little general needn't try it."[25] Hill continued to the rear where he turned over his command temporarily to J.E.B. Stuart.[26]

Colonel John D. Barry, commanding officer of the 18th Regiment, explained that "General A.P. Hill, Staff and couriers, were in the road in advance of them at the time, and to avoid the enemy's fire some of them dashed into the woods over the Eighteenth regiment, which fired into them, mistaking them in the dark for the enemy's cavalry."[27]

General Pender rode up and advised Lane not to advance, since General Jackson had been wounded, and he thought it was by soldiers under his (Lane's) command. After this devastating news, Lane did not advance, but went to the plank road, where he learned that A.P. Hill had also been wounded. Lane maintained that Colonel Barry did not know that Jackson and Hill had gone to the front. In the darkness, Barry could not distinguish friend from foe. Lane called Barry one of his "bravest and most accomplished officers," and that Colonel Barry always believed that both Jackson and Hill had been wounded by his command.[28] General A.P. Hill was with Jackson that night, but Lane believed Hill never blamed the 18th Regiment for Jackson's injury and "for firing under the circumstances...." Those who knew the talented young Colonel John D. Barry, then major of the 18th, remembered him as "one of those fearless, dashing officers who was especially cool under fire."[29]

Later, Lane sent a small group to check on the enemy's position, and they captured part of the 128th Pennsylvania Regiment. The captives were sent to the rear guard of John Young's 7th North Carolina Regiment, so the prisoners would not be fired upon by their own men. Young returned carrying a load of captured swords, which he gave to the various officers of his regiment.[30]

Heth Takes Charge

With both Jackson and Hill wounded, Brigadier General Henry Heth took command of Hill's Light Division so that the fighting could resume the next morning, May 2. Heth ordered Pender to move his brigade north along the plank road in line with Lane's Brigade. The 28th, 18th, and 33rd regiments moved south of the plank road to take a position on the right of the 7th of Lane's Brigade. All of Lane's Brigade was now south of the road and were positioned (from left to right) with the 37th, 7th, 33rd, 18th and 28th. The right wing of the 33rd served as a skirmish line.[31]

About midnight, Union General Sickles' III Corps, commanded by David Birney, launched an attack against Lane's right flank.[32] Between 12 and 1 o'clock that night, Lane reported that he could hear the enemy "marshaling their troops along our whole front," while their artillery rumbled up the road to Lane's right. Lane reported that Sickles' men rushed upon them with loud and prolonged cheering. Lane's men drove the enemy back on the left, but the fighting was heavier on the right — the main point of attack. The 18th, 28th and part of the 33rd drove the enemy back although the enemy had outflanked them and encountered the two right companies of the 28th. Another enemy attack about 30 minutes later was also repulsed. The 28th captured a staff officer and the colors of the 3rd Maine Volunteers.[33]

The Federal attack found Lane's right and overran it, but they did not exploit this position. The 28th North Carolina, on the far right flank, remained quiet until the Federals got within range of their line, cheering and shouting as they came, to be met with deadly fire from Lane's 28th.[34] Lane recalled that his were the only troops in line of battle to the right of the road, until after they had repulsed the enemy in the night attack.[35]

Heth later praised the men of Lane's Brigade for their "courage and zeal in repelling at least five times their number."[36]

After two days of fighting (May 1–2), Lee's Army of Northern Virginia had not achieved the total victory it sought. The two wings of the Confederate army were separated by the Federal troops, which were drawn up in a salient around Chancellorsville. It was clear that before they left this battlefield, the position of the forces must be captured before they could be reinforced by Hooker. That task fell to Hill's Light Division, now at the front of Jackson's corps. [37]

May 3, 1863

As stated by Colonel Samuel D. Lowe, the action began about 1 A.M. on the morning of May 3. The 28th encountered an enemy force which advanced upon their line with "loud and continuous cheers." Lowe's men quietly waited the charge, and held their fire until the Federal soldiers were within good range before sending a tremendous musketry fire upon the advancing column. The barrage caused the enemy to halt. The advance of the enemy was accompanied by a severe fire from a number of cannons, which came from their position toward C Chancellorsville.[38]

An hour later, all was quiet, and the 28th Regiment got the chance to rest until after daybreak. About sunrise on May 3 the enemy guns began to fire and killed some of Colonel Samuel D. Lowe's men.[39] Lane ordered the 28th to advance on the right, and they charged forward in the standard brigade line of battle. The men moved in a line nearly parallel to the plank road toward Chancellorsville.[40] The right flank of Lane's Brigade formed an angle with the left flank, and Lane ordered the regiments on the right to turn to the left so that the brigade line would be perpendicular to the plank road. In the midst of the turn, the men were stopped for some last-minute instructions. Captain Nicholson, of the 37th Regiment, told his men to: "Keep cool, men, and do your duty." Colonel William Barbour repeated Nicholson's instructions, and added: "Yes, men, do as Captain Nicholson tells you and let us die on this battle field or gain the victory."[41] Word passed all down the line of the impending attack and when the order, "forward," was given, the attack began.

When Lane's Brigade was within 300 yards of the Federal position, Colonel Lowe noted in his report: "we were met by such a storm of solid shot, grape and canister as I never before witnessed."[42] Federal forces facing the brigade were spread out in three lines behind log breastworks that were covered with brush. Behind those Union lines were the heavy artillery ready to support the Federal infantry. The Federal position seemed impenetrable, and to overtake it would result in many Confederate casualties.

The terrain did not favor the attacking force. In the woods and undergrowth, the right of Lane's Brigade overlapped part of McGowan's Brigade. The 28th Regiment on the far right was swallowed up as McGowan's Confederates advanced. All Lane could do was order the 28th to support McGowan's men, and so Lane's Brigade lost the services of 28th for the remainder of the day.[43]

At the breastworks, the Federals fell back under the onslaught of the 37th and 7th as they advanced giving the "Rebel yell." Lane's men jumped over the breastworks and captured several of the enemy. He ordered those on the breastworks to form a perpendicular line to the works and to fire into the enemy lines. This would provide cover and enable the other three regiments to rejoin the 37th and 7th.[44]

Lane's men had created a gap in the Federal line. There was heavy fighting between the opposing forces, and the enemy hurled grape and canister on Lane's men. Unable to advance, Lane's men lay on the ground and continued to fire at the enemy. They held onto their position for an hour and a half before finally being forced to retreat. The Federal forces then advanced though a gap between Archer and McGowan's brigades. McGowan was forced back, and Lane's right was exposed to enemy fire. Bombarded on two sides by both musket and cannon fire, the brigade could not maintain its position any longer. Lane's men fled back through Brockenbrough's brigade to the rear. During this retreat, the brigade suffered many casualties, and the flag of the 18th Regiment was captured when the flag bearer did not hear the order to pull back.[45]

When most of the brigade had pulled back to the rear, the 28th retreated only a short distance and reformed its line behind the abandoned Federal line. Lane ordered Colonel Lowe to assist wherever he could while Lane reformed the rest of the brigade at the rear. The 28th fought a separate battle for the remainder of the day. J.E.B. Stuart came up and ordered the 28th to charge again. The 28th advanced, but was not successful. Enemy fire from the right and lack of support forced the 28th to retreat to their former position behind the enemy works. While Lane was gathering the rest of his brigade, Stuart ordered the 28th forward again to support some of the Confederate batteries on the right.[46]

The situation changed suddenly when General Stuart came dashing along the line and ordered everyone to move forward for another charge. Thus, the whole Confederate line advanced and, according to Lowe, "fought with the most determined courage, the artillery and musketry mowing our men down, till suddenly the Yankees were discovered flanking my regiment on the right." Lowe had no choice but to withdraw to form for the second time behind the breastworks. Lowe then learned that Lane was forming the brigade on the plank road, but he was uncertain if he should send his men to join Lane. In the meantime, General Stuart ordered the line of the 28th forward, and the regiment again, for the third time, charged the enemy through a terrible artillery firing. They were led by Captain Edward F. Lovill, of Company A, to support Confederate batteries which were had occupied the position on the hill from which the enemy had been driven.[47]

In the chaos at Chancellorsville, the 28th Regiment of Lane's Brigade performed admirably. However, the rest of the regiments in the brigade were demoralized by being repulsed, and forced to retreat to the rear. They played no part in the action the rest of the day. Although the brigade had reformed behind the first line of Union breastworks, they refused do advance again in the face of the heavy Federal bombardment. There was even a fight between Brigadier General Robert Rodes and an officer of Lane's brigade over the failure of the men to advance. The situation was so perilous that the men of Brigadier General Stephen Dodson Ramseur's brigade were huddled 6 men deep along the breastworks, and refused repeatedly to attack the Federal lines.[48]

Brigadier General Lane was as upset as his men over their losses. When Major William Groves Morris approached where Lane was reforming his brigade, he found Lane with tears in his eyes. Lane told Morris, "Major, my brigade is cut all to pieces," and added that his brother, J. Rooker Lane, and "Colonel Avery, Lieutenant Campbell and others" had all been killed. Lane left Morris to reform the brigade, while he rode to the rear for a cup of coffee. He had had no food in 24 hours, and badly needed a stimulant. He returned in a few minutes, feeling much better.[49]

Gradually, the tide of battle turned as the Confederate artillery destroyed the Federal lines. Caught in a crossfire at Fairview, the Federal artillery abandoned their position and pulled out. The divided units of Lee's army came together at Chancellorsville in a resounding victory over the enemy.

By May 3, 1863, the Confederate forces of the Army of Northern Virginia occupied Chancellorsville, and the Federal troops had been driven back. Hill's division was ordered to entrench and occupy that position until Hooker's army re-crossed the Rappahannock. Lee then moved the army back to Fredericksburg.[50] After Hooker was driven across the river, the men of the 28th and other regiments of A.P. Hill's division returned to their old camp, according to Captain Gibbon.[51]

Casualties at Chancellorsville

At Chancellorsville, the Confederates, with 60,000 men, faced Hooker's force of 130,000, a greater than 2:1 ratio. The number of those killed or wounded was about the same on both sides: 1,649 killed and 9,106 wounded Confederates; 1,606 killed and 9,762 wounded Federal soldiers. The greatest difference was in the numbers of soldiers captured. The Confederates had only 1,708 men captured or missing, while the Federals lost 5,919 captured or missing.[52] As usual, casualty numbers vary.

Lane reported his casualties in his brigade at 909.[53] Among the officers, Lane lost 12 commissioned officers killed, 59 wounded, and 1 missing. Of the enlisted men, 149 were killed and 567 were wounded, plus 121 were missing or captured.[54] These losses, especially the officers, were a devastating blow to the brigade.

Another report of casualties at Chancellorsville lists the 28th Regiment with 12 men killed and 77 wounded.[55] Colonel Lowe initially reported that the 28th Regiment had lost 6 officers wounded, 14 men killed, and 84 men wounded.[56] This report was revised to 14 killed, 91 wounded, and 67 missing, for a total of 172.[57] This was about 12 percent of the total casualties sustained by the five regiments, slightly below the average of 181.8. The 37th had the most casualties with a total of 238.[58]

Chaplain Francis M. Kennedy of the 28th wrote in his diary, "We have gained another great victory, but 'Chancellorsville' is inscribed upon our banners with the blood of the best and bravest of the Confederacy."[59]

Lieutenant Colonel W.H.A. Speer was slightly wounded in the knee, which kept him out of the fight on Sunday. As an observer sitting astride his horse, he told his folks that it was "the bloodiest day of this war! We had 40,000 men engaged and the enemy 120,000.... The scene was awful. I cannot describe it to you as it was and will not try. Our men charged a battery of 28 pieces of cannon ½ miles 3 times before it was taken and it was charged many times by other Divisions, but our men at last drove them off at a great loss."[60]

Speer believed that Confederate casualties, either killed or wounded, amounted to at least 10,000. The enemy, he believed, had over 20,000 killed and wounded. In addition, the Confederates had taken approximately 10,000 Federal soldiers prisoner. He did not believe that any of the men in his old company (Company I, 28th Regiment) had been killed or wounded. The regiment "was lucky — we lost no officer in the field killed or any of the line officers." The regiment had lost 17 killed and 85 wounded of the non-commissioned officers and privates in the regiment.[61]

Speer was unaware of the actually toll of casualties to Lee's Army. Although a Confederate victory, it was at the cost of a heavy price in lives lost. At Chancellorsville, Lane's Brigade lost nearly ⅓ of its men, either killed or wounded. Thirteen of the field officers were killed or wounded.[62] Surgeon L. Guild said the casualties at Chancellorsville in Lane's Brigade alone were: 141 killed, and 598 wounded, for total casualties of 739.[63]

Death of Jackson

After General Thomas J. "Stonewall" Jackson's arm was amputated in a field hospital, he was transported 17 miles southeast of Chancellorsville to a safe house near Guinea Station. He died there of pneumonia eight days later on May 10, 1863.[64] The house in which he spent his last days is located a few miles south of Fredericksburg and is now a museum and open to the public.

The 18th Regiment, North Carolina Infantry, was never blamed for shooting Jackson. It was the wounded general's own fault. His desire to follow the retreating Federals overcame his better judgment, and nothing more could have been accomplished by him or his officers. Other factors — the denseness of the Wilderness, the darkness, and a flawed attack formation — according to McDaid, almost guaranteed that the assault would lose momentum as the two lead divisions became hopelessly mixed. These conditions worked against any prolonged pursuit of the enemy. Hill's Light division was strung out for miles along the route they had marched the previous day. It would have taken them many hours to reach a position from which they could launch an attack in sufficient numbers.[65]

McDaid believed that Jackson should have left the reconnaissance to his staff and reorganized his three divisions for battle the next day. At night, and in close proximity to the enemy, any movement would have alerted the soldiers and they would have fired almost automatically at the slightest sound.[66]

Prisoners and Flags Captured

On the plus side, the 18th Regiment captured an aide to Union General A.S. Williams. "A number of field and company officers as well as enlisted men were captured along our line," reported Brigadier General Lane.[67]

Captain Niven Clark, of Montgomery County, a member of Company E, 28th North Carolina, reported that he had captured some enemy soldiers and a flag on May 3, 1863. Clark captured several officers, the color sergeant, and the standard of the 3rd Maine Volunteers. The badly torn blue silk flag was turned over to Brigadier General Lane.[68] Lane gave the mutilated flag of the 3rd Maine to Charlotte Meade, a young lady who was living in Richmond, Virginia. She destroyed the flag when Richmond was evacuated. That lady later became Lane's wife.[69]

A Maine veteran and military historian, Augustus C. Hamlin, believed, as stated in a Federal regimental history, that "If Lane's Brigade had remained at home many New England regiments would have been happier." Hamlin described Lane's boys as "a bad, quarrelsome set of fellows, and too fond of a fight altogether."[70]

Brigadier General James H. Lane concluded that he had never seen men fight "more gallantly, and bear fatigue and hardship more cheerfully." He would always be proud of the "noble bearing" of his brigade at the Battle of Chancellorsville, "the bloodiest in which it has ever taken part ... with the Eighteenth and Twenty-eighth gallantly repulsed two night attacks made by vastly superior numbers...." However, like other battles, that "gallantry has cost it many noble sacrifices, and we are called upon to mourn the loss of some of our bravest spirits." Lane named some of his brave men individually:

> The fearless Purdie was killed while urging forward his men — the gentle, but gallant Hill, after the works had been taken — and Johnnie Young, a mere boy, not yet eighteen, but a brave and efficient captain, fell at the head of his company. Captain Kerr, and Lieutenants Campbell, Bolick, Emack, Weaver, Bouchelle, Babb, Callais and Regan, all fell in the discharge of their duties, as also did J. Rooker Lane of Company E, Fifth Virginia cavalry, who at the time was acting as my volunteer aid.[71]

In remembering that great battle, Lane praised his officers and the "behavior of his brigade." He credited Colonel Barbour, who "though wounded, was from time to time with his command, giving all the assistance he could." After the left wing of the 33rd was withdrawn, Major Mayhew and Lieutenant Colonel Cowan, who was wounded, "gallantly commanded the skirmishers in the night attack." Cowan was again wounded in the charge the next day and was believed captured by the enemy. Brigadier General Lane was also wounded during one of the night attacks. In the charge on Sunday morning Colonels Avery and Haywood, Lieutenant Colonels George and Ashcraft, and Major Davidson were wounded. Lane praised his field officers: Major Bartry, Captains Harris, Saunders, Brown and Nicholson for the help they had rendered.[72]

Nicholas Gibbon summed up the fighting at Chancellorsville as "one of the hardest fought battles of the war, where it [the Brigade] suffered a heavy loss in killed and wounded."[73] Colonel William Barbour, of the 37th North Carolina Regiment, stated in his report that Chancellorsville was "the bloodiest battle that I have ever witnessed."[74] Of course, these statements were made before the battle at Gettysburg that would occur within two months' time.

Colonel Samuel D. Lowe, in command of the 28th Regiment at Chancellorsville, complimented his officers, who had "behaved very gallantly. I cannot speak," said Lowe, "in too high terms of their bravery and activity during the whole of this hard fight. Not one of them misbehaved, so far as I could observe, but, on the contrary, all exerted themselves. The men proved themselves veterans."[75]

Major General William Dorsey Pender (1834–1863)

With the death of Jackson, Lee reorganized the Army of Northern Virginia into three corps under generals James Longstreet, Richard S. Ewell, and A.P. Hill. William Dorsey Pender was promoted to command what had been Hill's division, and Lane's Brigade came under Pender's command. Thus, the 28th Regiment was now a part of Lane's Brigade of Pender's Division, of Hill's 3rd Corps.[76]

William Dorsey Pender (1834–1863) graduated from the United States Military Academy in 1854. Before joining the Confederacy, he served in the United States Army on the frontier, fighting Indians. After resigning from the United States Army, he was commissioned as a Captain of Confederate States Army artillery. He transferred to the 6th North Carolina and fought in Whiting's Brigade on the Virginia Peninsula. Promoted to brigadier general on June 3, 1862, for his actions at Seven Pines, Pender commanded a brigade under A.P. Hill's division during the Seven Days' Battles, and fought under Jackson at 2nd Manassas, Antietam, Fredericksburg, and Chancellorsville. He was wounded three times at Chancellorsville but refused to leave the field. On May 27, 1863, when he was only 29 years old, Pender was promoted to Major General, and led his division, which included Lane's Brigade. Pender was highly regarded as an officer in the Confederate Army, and some even compared him to Thomas J. "Stonewall" Jackson.[77]

After Chancellorsville, Lane's Brigade returned to their winter quarters at Moss Neck near Fredericksburg. They remained there until they were needed for Lee's invasion of Pennsylvania.[78]

Chapter 9

July 1–3, 1863: Gettysburg,
a Devastating Defeat

*It is my opinion that no 15,000 men ever
arrayed for battle can take that position.*
— Major General James Longstreet[1]

Hill's Corps remained at Fredericksburg until the Federal troops evacuated their position across the river from the city. Then the corps was ordered to move north. On May 24, Hill's Corps crossed the Potomac at Shepherdstown (now in West Virginia), a few miles south of Sharpsburg, Maryland, and arrived at Fayetteville, Pennsylvania, on June 27. On June 29, they were ordered to move to Cashtown, about 12 miles southeast of Fayetteville. Lieutenant General James Longstreet was to follow, while Ewell's Corps was to rejoin the army at Cashtown or at Gettysburg, as circumstances decreed.[2]

Hill's men arrived at Cashtown on the evening of June 30 and, with Pender's division, decided to advance to the little town of Gettysburg, about 7 miles to the southeast.[3] While still at Cashtown, Hill sent one of his division commanders, Henry Heth, and his men on to Gettysburg. Heth was to seize a large supply of shoes reported to be in the town. This was not just a scouting force, but included a large body of troops, including Pender's (formerly Hill's) Divi-

---

Gettysburg, Pennsylvania, July 1–3, 1863

Forces Engaged: Armies, 158,343 total (83,289 Union; 75,054 Confederate)

Principal Commanders: Maj. Gen. George G. Meade (Union), Gen. Robert E. Lee (Confederate)

Estimated Casualties: 51,000 total (23,000 Union; 28,000 Confederate)

Result: Union victory

Robert E. Lee's Confederate forces had crossed into Pennsylvania and by July 1 had reached Gettysburg. Coming in from the west and north, on the first day of battle the Confederates drove the Union forces back through the streets of the town to Cemetery Hill. During the night, both sides received reinforcements. On July 2, Longstreet's and Hill's divisions attacked the Union left flank at the Peach Orchard, Wheatfield, Devil's Den, and the Round Tops, south of the town. Ewell's division attacked the Union right at Culp's Hill and east Cemetery Hill. By that evening, the Federals were in command of Little Round Top and had repulsed most of Ewell's men. On July 3, the Confederate infantry was driven from Culp's Hill. In the afternoon, after an ineffective artillery bombardment, Lee attacked the Union center on Cemetery Ridge across a broad, open field. The assault, known as Pickett's Charge (Pickett-Pettigrew), reached the Union line but was driven back with heavy casualties. On July 4, Lee withdrew toward Williamsport on the Potomac River. Lee's train of wounded stretched more than 14 miles, and Meade let him go without pursuit.[4]

sion. A.P Hill, now a corps commander, became suspicious and notified Lee and Ewell that he intended to advance the next morning to see "what was in my front." Hill believed that the main body of enemy troops was still miles away, and did not anticipate encountering any resistance.[5] He could not have been more wrong.

What followed was probably the most famous battle of the entire war, and one that stands out in the annals of warfare. Although the war continued for two more years, the fighting at Gettysburg was the turning point. Because of the huge numbers of men and officers lost, the Confederate Army never recovered is strength and its ability to win battles was greatly diminished.

During the 3-day battle at Gettysburg, the division of Major General William D. Pender consisted of four brigades plus artillery and artillery reserve. The First Brigade was composed of five regiments from South Carolina; the Second Brigade (Lane's) had five North Carolina Regiments, including the 28th. The Third Brigade was made up of four regiments from Georgia; while the Fourth Brigade (Scales' Brigade) was made up from five additional regiments from North Carolina.[6]

July 1, 1863

At daybreak on the morning of July 1, with Heth's men leading, the Army of Northern Virginia moved toward Gettysburg. They encountered a cavalry force under General John Buford and a battle ensued.

From Cashtown, Lane's Brigade, along with the rest of Pender's Division, marched eastward toward Gettysburg following the route Heth's Division had taken earlier. Pender's men had covered less than four miles when they heard the sound of artillery fire from the direction of Gettysburg. This was a sure sign that Heth's men had encountered opposition. When Pender's men were about three miles from Gettysburg, they caught up with Heth's men, who were engaged in battle with a force of Federal cavalry. The right line of Lane's Brigade touched the road, and Thomas's men were on Lane's left. The brigades of Scales and Perrin extended the line south of the road.[7]

McPherson's Ridge

On the first day of fighting, Lane's Brigade was ordered from the center of Hill's line to move to the right to protect the flank of the Confederate forces.[8]

Brigadier General James Jay Archer led his men (now a part of Heth's Division, Hill's Third Corps) in an attack on Federal forces west of the town in the first day's fighting. The first shot of the battle was fired by Archer's Brigade, and the first Confederate soldier who was felled by the enemy was a private in one of Archer's Tennessee regiments. The brigade occupied McPherson's woods, where they encountered Federal troops led by Major General John Fulton Reynolds. In the ensuing battle, Archer was wounded and he and most of his brigade were captured and imprisoned.[9]

General James H. Lane reported the action on that day:

> ... we moved from South Mountain, Pa., through Cashtown, in the direction of Gettysburg, and formed line of battle in rear of the left of Heth's division, about 3 miles from the latter place, to the left of the turnpike.[10]

The regiments of Lane's Brigade were positioned so that the right of the 7th Regiment was on the road. They marched nearly a mile in line of battle, then were ordered to the right side of the road where they formed on the extreme right of the Light Division (now under Pender).[11]

Lane and his men emerged from the woods and found that his line had passed General Archer's and that his "entire front was unmasked."[12]

Lane and his brigade then moved forward about a mile. The 7th Regiment had been detained a short time, and Colonel Barbour sent out 40 men, under Captain D.L. Hudson, to force back some of the enemy's dismounted cavalry, which had been firing on them.[13]

Unfortunately, the Federal cavalry soldiers were armed with Sharps carbines, a gun which could be loaded and fired quickly, up to as many as 10 rounds per minute. Overwhelmed with superior firepower, Lane had no choice but to turn his men toward the flank. Unnecessarily, Lane ordered his men to form a large, hollow square to face an enemy cavalry charge. This position left the men vulnerable and they made better targets for the enemy rifles.[14]

Lane's men moved across an open field until a body of enemy cavalry acting as infantry began to fire on them from the woods. Upon the arrival of by Pegram's battalion of artillery, Lane's men gave a yell, and rushed forward at a double-quick. The enemy retreated to Cemetery Hill."[15]

The Federals lost Major General John Fulton Reynolds, who was killed by a Confederate sharpshooter in McPherson's woods west of Gettysburg. A large statue of Reynolds has been erected there.[16]

The brigades of Thomas and Lane did not join with the forces of Heth and Pender in time to take part in the pursuit, but rejoined the rest of the division at Seminary Ridge, southwest of Cemetery Ridge. After six hours of fighting, General A.P. Hill was satisfied with the ground his men had gained that day. Since no orders had come from General Lee to continue that advance, Lane's Brigade and the rest of Pender's Division remained in position near the McMillan house on Seminary Ridge. They camped there for the night.[17]

General Heth was wounded on July 1 in the assault on Federal troops, and was out of the action for several days. He recovered in time to command the rear guard in the retreat from Gettysburg.[18]

Second Day of Battle — July 2, 1863

On the second day of fighting, only the 37th Regiment of Lane's Brigade was involved. The skirmishing skills of those men were praised by General Ewell.[19]

The Confederate line was spread out with Ewell on the left, Hill in the center, and Longstreet to the right of Hill's position. Longstreet and Ewell's men attacked along the left and right wings of the Federal army under the command of General George C. Meade. There was relatively little activity along the line where Lane's brigade was positioned. For the most part, Lane reported that "nothing of interest occurred in my command on the 2d."[20]

General Pender was slightly wounded during the fighting on July 2. He had been struck in the thigh by a shell fragment and did not seek medical attention. Back at Staunton, Virginia, a massive infection had spread, and Pender's leg had to be amputated. He did not survive the surgery, and the 29-year-old general died on July 18, 1863. His remains were buried at Tarboro, North Carolina.[21] Command of Lane's division was given General Isaac Trimble on July 3. Pender (Trimble's) division had been ordered to support Heth's division, now commanded by General James J. Pettigrew, after Heth was wounded on July 1.[22]

The Fateful Day — July 3, 1863

The assaulting force of Lee's Army on July 3 was made up from three corps. The only fresh troops were those of Major General George Pickett, who had been placed on the right of the assault line. Heth's division was brought up to join the brigades of Lane and Scales of Pender's Division to form the left wing. Since Pender had been wounded, Lane was in charge of the division, and Colonel Clark Avery was in command of Lane's Brigade.[23]

Lee planned a frontal attack on the enemy, who held the superior position on an elevation

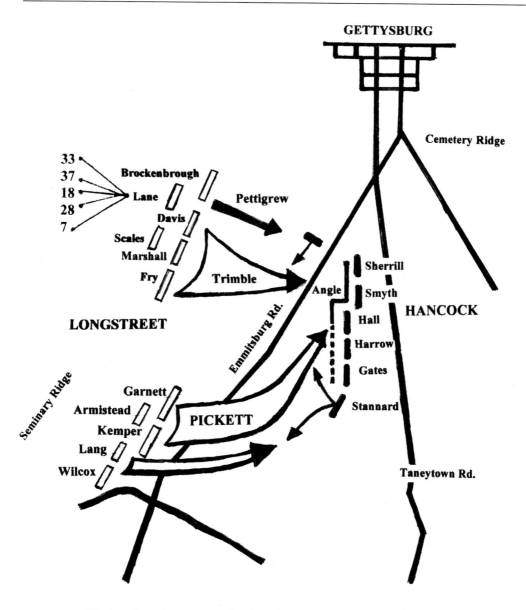

Map 3 — Gettysburg, Pennsylvania, July 3, 1863 (Caren Casstevens, artist).

known as Cemetery Ridge. The success of the Confederate assault depended on cooperation and communication, both of which failed. General Longstreet was opposed to the plan and reportedly told Lee: "It is my opinion that no 15,000 men ever arrayed for battle can take that position."[24] Unfortunately, Lee did not heed Longstreet's warning.

The position the Hill-Pender-Lane division had occupied on July 2 was taken over by General Isaac Trimble. Thus, on the third and final day at Gettysburg, Lane's Brigade was positioned on the extreme left of the line of battle from which would come the Pickett-Pettigrew charge.[25]

The battle took place across a valley split by the Emmittsburg Road. To the north lay the town of Gettysburg. On the east was Cemetery Ridge, an elevation which extended approximately two miles from the town to Round Top Hill. This was the position occupied by Meade's troops and his artillery. On the west was Seminary Ridge, where the Confederate troops and artillery were massed.[26]

About noon, Lane received orders from A.P. Hill to move to the right and to contact General Longstreet for further instructions. Longstreet subsequently ordered two brigades to move to the rear of Heth's (Pettigrew) division as a supporting line. The two brigades formed in some woods near Seminary Ridge with Scales behind the far right of Pettigrew's line and Avery (Lane's Brigade) to the left of Scales. Finally, all were ready to begin the attack by 1 P.M.[27]

Because Pender had been wounded on the second day of fighting, General Lee placed Major General Isaac Ridgeway Trimble in command of two brigades (Lane's and Scales's, now commanded by Lowrance) just about the time they were actually moving into position. As a result, the brigades of Lane and Lowrance were not placed in echelon (an arrangement of troops with units drawn up in parallel lines, but each somewhat to the left or right of the one in the rear). Instead they were not to the left and behind Pettigrew's exposed flank, as had been directed, but were more to the right and closer to Armistead's men.[28] Lane was aware of the faulty alignment, but he did not inform Trimble. Neither Longstreet nor Hill took steps to correct the misalignment, which could have weakened the planned assault. This was an example of the breakdown in communications that contributed to the Confederate defeat at Gettysburg.[29]

Trimble had just recently returned to duty, having been absent for some time because of a wound he received at 2nd Manassas.[30] Unaware of the faulty alignment of the troops on the left, he spent the last moments before the charge talking to the men. He told them not to begin firing until the enemy line was broken. He promised to advance with them to the farthest point.[31]

William G. Morris, an officer of the 37th Regiment, recalled in 1877 that Trimble had been suddenly placed in command of Lane's Division. Trimble addressed his command and told the men that the "Enemy was posted behind a stone fence on the crest of the hill & for us not to fire on them until we routed them from there [sic] position with the bayonets."[32]

After being bombarded by Confederate artillery for about an hour and a half, the Federal artillery stopped returning their fire, and were withdrawn. Even with all the thick smoke lingering in the air between the opposing forces, the silence of the Federal guns seemed to indicate that Lee's guns had done their job.[33] However, this was not the case and would prove disastrous to the advancing Confederates, who would face both musket and cannon fire as they advanced across the open field.

Lee's Confederates began their charge from behind the long row of 150 guns of the Confederate artillery. Their goal was across a mile-long open field, at the end of which they were to attack the center of the line of the Federal brigades of Webb and Smythe.

William G. Morris recalled that Lane's Brigade had charged in the following order: 7th, 37th, 18th, 28th, and 33rd. The 33rd was on the extreme left of the battle line. The enemy's position was "at least ¾ of a mile Distant over an opening with the exception of plank fences running in every direction." In front of Lane's Brigade was Davis' Brigade, which became engaged with the enemy, and exposed to a "terrible flanking fire both of artillery & infantry," and was forced to retreat. Morris recalled that Pettigrew's and Archer's men were next on their right and in front.[34]

Problems were immediately apparent as the assault began. Lee's heavy artillery had failed to soften the Federal line with artillery fire from across the broad field. The Confederate artillery fire had overshot the range, and had done little damage to the enemy or their big guns.

The field across which the Confederate soldiers had to cross was nearly a mile wide, and there was absolutely no shelter from the enfilade they faced from the Federal muskets and artillery. The left of the Confederate line was closer to the position of the Federal troops along the stone wall and the angle. The right of the line, from which Pickett's men came, was farther from the enemy, and they had a greater distance to cover.[35]

Confederate guns facing Cemetery Ridge. Photograph by Frances H. Casstevens.

In addition, on the left wing, Lane's line did not stretch far enough to provide for the four brigades in Pettigrew's line. Thus, when the charge began, two of Pettigrew's brigades (Brockenbrough and Davis) advanced with no line of reserve behind them. The number of men who began in this charge was greatly diminished, both of these brigades having already suffered heavy casualties in the first day of fighting at Gettysburg.[36]

After the assault began, a line of Confederate soldiers emerged from the woods to make their way across the field toward Cemetery Ridge. The Federal guns began to fire again and pounded the approaching Confederates, especially Pettigrew's forces. As Lee's men approached the enemy line, the Federal infantry joined the cannon in blasting away. Brockenbrough's men could go no further and fell back, and they were followed by Davis' Brigade on the right. Stragglers began drifting to the right into the line of Confederate General John McLeod Turner.[37]

Trimble reacted and sent the brigades of Lane and Scales forward to support Pettigrew. Scales' men went directly forward and took their place on the front line. Lane's Brigade split because of confusion over the orders. The 7th and part of the 37th moved to the right and overlapped Scales' left. The rest of the brigade took a position on the left of Pettigrew and now became the left flank of the attacking line. As Trimble's men merged with Pettigrew's, a cheer went up: "Three cheers," shouted one soldier, "for the Old North State." At that point, Trimble believed that the North Carolina troops were "going into the enemy's line."[38]

Lane's Brigade was in great danger from the enemy fire. The Federal artillery cut holes in their line in a ceaseless bombardment. One soldier recalled that the "Earth seemed to totter," and the air "was sulphury as the internal regions, while the wild hum of the deadly bullet sang shrilly around us."[39]

When the advancing Confederates reached the Emmitsburg Road they had to cross two fences, the first a rail fence one, the second a post fence. The rail fence that bordered the west-ern side of the road was easily dismantled, but the post fence on the east side could not be dis-mantled easily. Some soldiers climbed over the fence, while others sought shelter behind the fences as the enemy rained grapeshot, shell, and musket fire down upon them.[40] Casualties were great in Lane's 7th Regiment, and after every member of its color guard was either killed or wounded, the flag of the 7th was captured by the enemy.[41]

Leading his men as promised, Trimble was wounded in the leg as he tried to cross the fence. He dispatched a message to Lane to take command.[42] Trimble was captured by the enemy, and his wound resulted in the loss of his leg. Trimble was not released from prison until February of 1865.[43]

The rest of Lane's Brigade tried to reach the stone wall while firing on the enemy posi-tioned there. At first their efforts seemed successful: The Federal artillerymen fled, a color bearer led his regiment to the rear in retreat, and the Federal line wavered at that point. However, Lane's men were taking many hits from the left. He saw the danger, dismounted from his wounded horse, and ordered the men of the 37th, under the command of Colonel Avery, to face to the left to combat a force that was attempting to flank them. Avery refused and pointed out that Lane's men were alone and that most of those on the right were already in retreat. Lane saw that Avery was correct, and he ordered a retreat. He later declared: "My brigade, I know, was the last to leave the field, and it did so by my order."[44]

Trimble also saw that to continue the assault was suicidal. When an aide asked Trimble if they should rally the troops for another charge, Trimble looked to his right and saw nothing of Pickett's men except a few moving to the rear from the Emmittsburg Road. He then replied, "No, Charley [Grogan], the best thing these brave fellows can do, is to get out of this." Trim-ble agreed that Pickett's men were the closest to the enemy at the beginning of the charge, and "they did bear the brunt bravely, but they were not the only 'heroes of Gettysburg.'"[45] Trimble was referring to the soldiers from North Carolina, Lane's Brigade.

Brigadier General Lane was one of the few generals to survive that bloody battle, known as Pickett's Charge, and to report on that fatal assault. Major General George E. Pickett was not actually in command of the attack, nor did his troops make up the majority of those involved. The left wing of the assault was made up of Hill's Division, which had fallen to the command of Henry Heth. After Heth was wounded the division was commanded by Pettigrew. Therefore, the charge should more correctly be termed the "Pickett-Pettigrew Charge.'

Lane reported on the action of his brigade:

> ...I moved forward to the support of Pettigrew's right, through the woods in which our batteries were planted, and through an open field about a mile, in full view of the enemy's fortified posi-tion, and under a murderous artillery and infantry fire.
>
> As soon as Pettigrew's command gave back, [W.L.J.] Lowrance's brigade and my own, without ever having halted, took position on the left of the troops which were still contesting the ground with the enemy.[46]

As the fighting intensified, Lane's Brigade was ordered to march at the "double quick" and they soon became part of the first line forming on Pettigrew's left. At this time, the 7th Regi-ment was on the right of the brigade, and on Pettigrew's left. Orders were issued by Lane, but before they could be repeated by Morris, Trimble's men, who were between the 7th and 37th Regiments, were ordered to make "a bayonet charge." The result was that Lane's regiments became separated.[47]

Lane was very proud of the performance of his men in that charge. They had "never moved forward more handsomely." As ordered, the men held their fire until they were within good range of the enemy, "and then opened with telling effect, repeatedly driving the cannoneers from their pieces, completely silencing the guns in our immediate front, and breaking the line of infantry which was formed on the crest of the hill.[48]

Top: Looking across field where Pickett–Pettigrew's men charged. *Bottom:* The famous Stone Wall at the angle, the high water mark of the Confederacy. Both photographs by Frances H. Casstevens.

Lane reported that his men advanced to "within a few yards of the stone wall, exposed all the while to a heavy raking artillery fire from the right." Here, his line was exposed, and a column of the enemy's infantry came forward from that direction, and their gunfire "enfiladed my whole line." Under this deadly barrage, Lane was forced to withdraw his brigade, but not before those troops on his right (Pickett's and others) had already withdrawn. Lane's men "fell back as well as could be expected, reformed immediately in rear of the artillery ... and remained there until the following morning."[49]

About midway between the woods and the enemy's works, the land was slightly elevated on the right and the left, so that, according to Morris, "we could not see what was going on any great distance right or left." While the 37th Regiment was on low ground, it was not so exposed to the "flanking fire." The 37th and the 7th came to within a short distance of the turnpike road (Emittsburg Road), where they found the "enemy posted both in the road & behind the stone fence," about 40 paces away on the crest of Cemetery Ridge.[50]

Morris told Colonel W. Saunders that he "never saw Men act More Noble than did the 7th and right of the 37th & so far as I could see of the left of Pettigrew's men on my right." The men of Lane's Brigade almost reached the stone fence, the farthest point reached by any of the attacking Confederate troops.[51]

Those who survived the charge attempted to fall back to the shelter of the woods on Seminary Ridge. Even the retreat was plagued by fire from the enemy guns, and one soldier wrote that their loss in the retreat "was immense, as we were raked by a cross fire for a mile and a half by the guns of the enemy, without any protection whatever to shield us."[52]

Casualties of the Army of Northern Virginia, Gettysburg, July 1–3, 1863

The numbers of those killed, wounded or missing at Gettysburg are only approximate. The data were compiled by statements from Surgeon L. Guild, medical director of the Army, and reports from surviving brigade and other commanders.

Total Casualties for the Army of Northern Virginia at Gettysburg, July 1–3, 1863[53]

	Killed	Wounded	Captured or Missing	Total
First Army Corps	910	4,339	2,290	7,539
Second Army Corps	809	3,823	1,305	5,937
Third Army Corps (including Lane's)	837	4,407	1,491	6,735
Cavalry	36	140	64	240
Grand Total	2,592	12,709	5,150	20,451

Confederate and Union figures do not agree, especially as to the numbers captured. In the Adjutant General's office of the United States Army, there is a list of names of 12,227 wounded and non-wounded Confederates captured at Gettysburg from July 1–5.

Casualties — Third Army Corps, Pender's Division

As shown in the table above, total casualties of the Third Corps are listed at 6,735. Casualties in Pender's Division, the Third Corps of the Army of Northern Virginia at Gettysburg were: 262 killed, 1312 wounded, 116 missing, for a total of 1690.[54]

Casualties — Lane's Brigade

Casualties in Lane's Brigade of Pender's Division at Gettysburg were heavy. Over the course of the three days, Lane's Brigade lost 389 men (41 killed, and 348 wounded). The number of those captured or missing was not given in the *Official Records of the War of the Rebellion*.[55] However, William F. Fox does include them in his book on regimental losses. Out of 1,355 men present in Lane's Brigade, 41 were killed, 348 wounded, and 271 were missing. This total of 660 (48.7 percent), is nearly half of those in the brigade who went into the battle.[56]

Casualties — 28th Regiment

The 28th Regiment lost 12 men killed and 92 wounded, for a total of 104 casualties.[57] On the first day alone, according to a count made by Jim Pierce (North Carolina Division, Sons of Confederate Veterans, Historian & Genealogist), based on the information on the individual soldiers in *North Carolina Troops, 1861–1865: A Roster,* the 28th Regiment had 1 killed, 115 wounded, 14 captured and 3 missing in action.

The town of Gettysburg was the farthest point north reached by the Confederate Army. The foray, which had originally been planned as a diversionary tactic, as well as to obtain some much-needed shoes for the Confederate Army, turned into a three-day battle that decimated Lee's army. This was a defeat from which the South never recovered — too many men were killed, wounded, or captured. Ironically, this battle should never have taken place. Lack of communications left Lee in the dark as to the numbers of Federal troops he was about to face. One could go on and on about the mistakes, the lost chances, the advantages of one position over another, but what the Confederate soldiers lost here could not be replaced. According to a descendant of one of those men, out of the 346 men of the 28th Regiment who were engaged in the disastrous charge on July 3, only 104 made it back to the Confederate line.[58]

North Carolina Memorial at Gettysburg. Photograph by Frances H. Casstevens.

Flag Captured

Another blow to the 28th Regiment was the loss of their flag. Printed on this flag were the names of many major battles fought during the war: Manassas, Mechanicsville, Harpers Ferry, Frayser's Farm, Hanover Court House, Ox Hill, Cold Harbor, and Cedar Run (Cedar Mountain).[59] The flag of the 28th was one of 33 Confederate colors captured at Gettysburg on July 3, 1863.[60] Today, this flag is housed in the Museum of the Confederacy, Richmond, Virginia. The captured flag was one of the third Richmond Depot issue and was made of bunting. (Bunting, usually used for flags or patriotic decorations, could be made out of either a thin woolen material or a cotton material.) This flag was issued to Branch's North Carolina Brigade in December 1862. It is the typical "battle flag," with a red field crossed by a 5-inch St. Andrew's cross, edged in white, on which thirteen 3½ inch cotton stars are displayed. This flag was captured by Capt. Morris Brown, Jr., of the 126th New York Infantry, and is identified as capture number 66 by the United States War Department.[61] (See Chapter 15 for more about the regimental flags.)

Lieutenant Colonel W.H.A. Speer survived the bloody fighting at Gettysburg. He confided to his father:

> ...the tale is too awful to be told. Our grand army made its way into Pa. across the Blue Ridge at Gettysburg PA where we met the enemy on the 1st of July and had a battle on the 2nd and 3rd — the most terrific battles the world [has] ever seen or human being ever engaged in.[62]

According to Speer, the Confederates had 275 pieces of cannon, while the Yankees had over 500. Speer's 28th Regiment and Lane's Brigade were "in it all." They went into the fight on July

Statue dedicated to NC Troops at Gettysburg. Photograph by Frances H. Casstevens.

3 with 326 men with guns; the next day (July 4) he could only muster 100 men, a loss of two-thirds of his men. After a few slightly wounded soldiers rejoined the regiment and two or three stragglers were picked up, he counted 118 men left from a regiment that numbered over a thousand a few days before. Speer knew of 12 men killed, but 95 could not be accounted for. Those had either been killed or wounded and abandoned inside Yankee lines to be captured.[63]

The heights that had been reached on both ends by a flank movement of Lee's troops could not be held. Speer noted that the men of the 28th tried to break the Union line, but they had to fall back. He gave the North Carolina troops credit for doing "nearly all the fighting that day and have nearly been destroyed — none of the Regts. in our Brigade are as large as a good full company [125 men]." The magnitude of their losses was enormous. The new North Carolina regiments that had arrived with 1,200 men, were reduced to 200 to 300 men. Speer declared, "Our Division and Corps suffered worse than any other by much." He predicted that the three days of July 1863 would long be remembered by the people of North Carolina.[64]

Casualties in Speer's old company [Company I] were:

> Jones Holcomb, Jonas MaCokey were killed dead. A shell exploded in the line as we were charging, killing them both dead, wounding 3 others and knocking me down. Sgt. Cast and Buchanan supposed killed. Sgt. Hendricks wounded through the legs and in the hands of the enemy. John G. Holcomb — thigh and hand, left at our hospital in the Yankee hands. J.G. Danner mortal, since dead. E.H. Reece severe and [we] left D.C. Hall. _____ is across the lines. J.G. Reynolds in the Yankee lines wounded. Sgt. S. Bohanon slight, H.H. Snow severe. M. Carter severe, N.C. Dozier slight. Berry [Greenberry] Harding struck 3 times slight, C.V. Hutchens, S.N. Johnson both slight. All these are inside of our own lines. Capt. Apperson took in 24 men and only came [out] with 4 unhurt. Col. Lowe out. Marler in the Yankee hands. Capt. Lovell's company — every man in it was struck. Lovell wounded severe — S.T. Thompson wound very severely. [65]

Lieutenant Colonel Speer reported that he took 38 officers into battle at Gettysburg, and came out with only 17. He described the charge on July 3: "We charged a battery one mile off and pass[ed] over a very level piece of ground all the way with 70 pieces of cannon throwing all sorts of missiles into our ranks. We had two columns cut down and destroyed." [66]

Lee's army never again had the strength of numbers to defeat the Union forces. Gettysburg was the beginning of the end. In addition to the dead, wounded and captured, desertion increased after Gettysburg. Private C.J. McSwain of Company K deserted on August 26. He was caught, court-martialed, and executed by a firing squad at Liberty Mills, September 26, 1863.[67]

July 4, 1863

The defeated Confederates pulled back to Seminary Ridge and Oak Ridge. Lee ordered breastworks to be thrown up and rifle pits dug in case Meade attempted to follow their retreat.[68]

Even today, a visit to the battlefield at Gettysburg is overwhelming. To stand on the stone wall and look westward across the road toward Seminary Ridge, at the field across which the thousands of Confederates made that gallant, daring, but futile charge, is humbling. It is a sight that not only moves but breaks the heart of every Southerner, specially those who have ancestors who fought and died in that charge. Despite the overabundance of markers, statuary, and grand monuments placed by the states that participated, it is journey that everyone should take. To walk among the tombstones in the Evergreen Cemetery and see just how many Union soldiers died and were buried there (no Confederates are buried there) makes the horror more real. One can almost hear the sound of the battle everywhere on this hallowed ground. The tours, the visitors' center, and the Cyclorama provide the information and visualization needed to enable us to come away with a better understanding of what actually transpired here. It was the beginning of the end for Lee's Army of Northern Virginia and the Confederate States of America.

Falling Waters (Hagerstown, Williamsport), July 14, 1863

Forces Engaged: Divisions

Principal Commanders: Maj. Gen. George Meade (Union), Gen. Robert E. Lee (Confederate)

Estimated Casualties: 1,730 total

Results: Inconclusive

The retreat from Gettysburg began the night of July 4–5. Lee's Confederates left Gettysburg and moved southwest toward Hagerstown. The Union infantry followed the next day. On July 7, Confederate General Imoden stopped Union General Buford's cavalry from occupying Williamsport. However, Kilpatrick's cavalry drove two brigades of Confederate cavalry through Hagerstown before J.E.B. Stuart's cavalry arrived. When Lee's men reached the Potomac River, the water was up because of recent rains, and the pontoon bridge had been destroyed. Unable to cross, Lee's men dug in and waited for Meade's army. On July 12, Meade's forces reached the vicinity and encountered the Confederate line. A skirmish occurred on July 13. By then the level of the river had fallen enough to permit construction of a new bridge, and Lee's army crossed on the night of July 13. The next day (July 14), Kilpatrick's and Buford's cavalry attacked the rear guard of General Henry Heth, and took more than 500 prisoners. Confederate Brigadier General Pettigrew was mortally wounded. On July 16, Confederate forces of Fitzhugh Lee and J.R. Chambliss defended the Potomac River fords against the Union infantry. After several attacks, David McM. Gregg's cavalry (Union) withdrew.[69]

Both sides had suffered heavy losses at Gettysburg. After the fighting ended, on July 4 the wounded were picked up and the dead buried. That night, Lee's battered army began its retreat toward Hagerstown. Pender's division was now under the command of General Lane, who took charge after Trimble was wounded and captured. Lane moved his own brigade and that of Scales to the rear of Thomas and Perrin. They took up a position near the McMillan house. The seriously wounded were loaded into ambulances and the walking wounded followed the long wagon train along the Chambersburg Pike toward Cashtown. As the wagon train started on its way, Hill's Corps (including Lane's Division and the Lane Brigade) took the lead, while the rest of the army made their way along the Fairfield-Hagerstown Road in a steady rain.[70]

During the retreat, there was very little actual fighting, but there were several skirmishes. During one skirmish, 29 of Lane's pickets were captured by the enemy. The skirmish line was quickly reinforced.[71]

On July 12, the division was consolidated with the divisions of General Heth, who had returned to duty, and General Lane resumed command of his brigade. Heth's men acted as the rear guard when what was left of the Army of Northern Virginia recrossed the Potomac. General Lane reported on the retreat:

> The retreat from Hagerstown the night of the 13th was even worse than that from Gettysburg. My whole command was so exhausted that they all fell asleep as soon as they were halted — about a mile from the pontoon bridge at Falling Waters.[72]

According to Lane, just as they were about to resume their march, Heth's Division, which occupied the breastworks in the rear as a rear guard, was attacked by the enemy's cavalry. Lane immediately ordered his command to "fix bayonets," since most of their guns were unloaded, and they moved down the road after General Edward L. Thomas. Thomas was ordered to halt by General Heth, and he subsequently took a position in line of battle. This was to allow those brigades that were engaged to withdraw from the enemy. Lane sent out a strong line of skirmishers all along his whole front, under the command of Lieutenant James M. Crowell, of the 28th. Crowell was instructed not to fire until the enemy got close, then to fire, and to "fall back gradually when he saw the main line retiring toward the river." The 18th Regiment, under Colonel John D. Barry, was deployed to the right as skirmishers, while Colonel Clark M. Avery supervised the right wing. This allowed Lane to quickly determine the movements of the enemy. When other Confederate brigades withdrew, a large enemy force moved to Lane's right, and since Lane's left was also threatened, he "lost no time in falling back, which was done in excellent order."[73]

Lieutenant James M. Crowell, of Company K, 28th Regiment, in charge of the skirmish line, calmly shot every one of the pursuing enemy who got too close. He continued this until all of Lee's men had safely crossed the Potomac into Virginia.[74]

Little has been written about the fighting at Falling Waters. It has been overshadowed by the three-day battle at Gettysburg. The common story is that Lee's Confederates withdrew without being pursued by Meade's forces. However, this was not the case. They were pursued and some fighting did occur.

During the withdrawal from Gettysburg, Heth's division was attacked by the 1st and 3rd Federal cavalry (Buford's and Kilpatrick's). The Confederates lost two guns and about 500 stragglers. While Heth's actions at Falling Waters were viewed by the North as a "serious Confederate disaster," the Confederate side of the story is just the opposite. General Pettigrew, however, was wounded.[75] It is ironic that Pettigrew, who had survived Pickett's charge at Gettysburg, was mortally wounded in a minor incident 10 days later, and died July 17, 1863.[76]

Lane's Brigade was the last to cross the river at Falling Waters. Their skirmishers had been very efficient in keeping the Federals stalled to allow the main body of Lee's army cross the river. Heth assumed that Lane's whole brigade would be killed. In protecting the rear of the Army of Northern Virginia, Lane lost only 6 men wounded, and 38 missing, most of whom had been captured because they were too exhausted to follow across the river.[77]

The battles at Chancellorsville and Gettysburg took a heavy toll on Lane's Brigade. In both battles combined, the brigade sustained 1,640 casualties. [78]

Top: Confederate dead at Gettysburg, July 1863 (Library of Congress, digital ID cph 3c 17572). *Bottom:* Sidney Choplin, Co. F, 28th Regiment, killed at Gettysburg July 1–3, 1863 (courtesy of Cheryl L. Martin).

The name "Falling Waters" was added to the flag presented to the 28th Regiment in May 1864. This was one of 17 battles in which the regiment had participated up until that time.[79]

After what was left of Lee's Army returned to Virginia, the 28th North Carolina camped about a mile from the Orange Court House. Here the men rested and recovered from the long march and bitter defeat. Food was available, but it was expensive. Private William A. Tesh, camped there, wrote home that everything was "very high." Irish potatoes and beans were $12.00 per bushel. Molasses was $4.00 a quart. Crops in the area "looks splendid here, corn Looks as nice as I ever saw it and Wheat was splendid here for certain."[80] Food was a small consolation after Gettysburg.

Chapter 10

October–December 1863:
Bristoe Station to Mine Run

We have Seventy men in our Company for duty which is present.
— Sergeant Samuel Speer Harding, Company I,
28th Regiment, November 25, 1863[1]

Major General Cadmus M. Wilcox (1824–1890)

The promotion of Cadmus M. Wilcox was recommended to President Jefferson Davis by General Robert E. Lee. Brigadier General James H. Lane was passed over for the promotion, as was Edweard Thomas, a Georgia general.[2] Davis gave his approval and Wilcox was promoted and placed in charge of Pender's division. The 28th now became part of Lane's Brigade, Wilcox's Division (formerly Hill's Light Division), and Hill's Corps.[3] Wilcox was promoted to major general on August 13, 1863. He would command the division in the battles at the Wilderness, Spotsylvania, and others that occurred in the vicinity of Petersburg before he surrendered at Appomattox.[4]

Born in North Carolina, Cadmus M. Wilcox graduated from the United States Military Academy at West Point in 1846. He gained experience in artillery while serving in both the Mexican War and the Seminole War. Before he resigned in June of 1861, Wilcox taught tactics at West Point. He offered his services to the Confederacy and was commissioned a colonel in the 9th Alabama, and he led his regiment at 1st Manassas. Appointed a brigadier general in October 1861, he led a brigade on the peninsula, at 2nd Manassas, Fredericksburg, Chancellorsville and Gettysburg.[5]

Increases in Desertion

Morale among the Confederate military reached an all-time low after the defeat at Gettysburg. At the same time, Vicksburg on the Mississippi River was captured by U.S. Grant's forces. Desertion in the Army of Northern Virginia increased to the point where Lee had to take action. First, he issued an order on July 26 to the effect that all men who were absent without leave should return to their commands immediately.[6] To make his order more effective, Lee convinced President Jefferson Davis to declare an amnesty and a general pardon for all deserters who returned by August 31.[7] The amnesty extended to those who were currently accused or who were being punished in some form for desertion.[8] Lee also changed the policy regarding furloughs so that more men could go home on leave.[9]

The amnesty had just the opposite effect on the troops. Many soldiers took this opportunity to go home without approval, but planned to return before the end of August. Desertion rates were especially high among the troops from North Carolina.[10]

As a last resort, Lee now requested that the death penalty be placed in effect for desertion. This had an impact on Lane's Brigade. In the fall of 1863, 12 soldiers from Lane's Brigade were executed for desertion.[11] The division was ordered out to watch the execution of two soldiers from the 33rd Regiment — Allen Abosher and Esom Fugit. After being tied to stakes, with their hands behind their backs, the two condemned men were blindfolded and a detail of 24 soldiers fired at them from a distance of 15 feet. Both men died instantly. Each regiment was ordered to march by the bodies to see, according to Captain James S. Harris, "the terrible consequences of desertion." Chaplain Francis Kennedy wrote that the two men met their fate with "unflinching fortitude," but that it was "a very revolting sight."[12]

These executions did nothing to boost morale, nor did the execution of these two men stop the tide of desertion. A week later, seven more men were executed from the brigade. Four had deserted near Orange Court House and were caught after only a week. Three were from the 18th Regiment, and one, Charles McSwain, was from the 28th. Three men from the 37th were executed who had been convicted of misbehavior "in the presence of the enemy for deserting while the brigade was in line of battle at Fredericksburg, Chancellorsville and Gettysburg respectively." One of them had added to his crimes by attempting to influence his two nephews to desert.[13]

At the trial, some of the deserters blamed the North Carolina *Standard* and its stance that Jefferson Davis was a "tyrant" and that the Confederate cause was wrong. These men declared that they were only doing their duty by deserting.[14] Regardless of their reasons, the seven deserters were executed.

Executions for desertion continued, and the enforcement of the death penalty seemed to have an effect on the men, at least temporarily. However, the problem of desertion continued to increase until the end of the war, no matter what punishment the deserter faced if caught.

Dissension Within the Brigade

Colonel Clark Avery, commander of the 33rd Regiment, decided he wanted to withdraw his regiment from under Lane to form a new brigade with three other North Carolina regiments. Avery even went so far as to send a petition to North Carolina's Governor Zeb Vance. Avery had no complains about Lane, but he did think Lane had "slighted" the 33rd Regiment and not given it proper credit in some of his reports. An ulterior motive may have been that Avery thought if he were in a new brigade, he would have a better chance to advance his own career. Avery reasoned that since there were five regiments in Lane's Brigade, the loss of one would not noticeably diminish its strength, but put it more in line with other brigades which generally had only four regiments each.[15]

Wilcox opposed the move, as did General Lee, who noted that removing the 33rd would drop the brigade's strength from 2,398 to 1,900. Lee concluded that since the brigade was "composed entirely of North Carolina regiments, "he believed that any such move would be "disadvantageous.... I see no public benefit that would result from the changes within proposed; therefore cannot recommend them."[16] The 33rd Regiment remained in Lowe's Brigade.

Reorganization

After the devastating defeat at Gettysburg and the loss of many fine officers, by October of 1863, reorganization was necessary. The 28th remained in a division headed by Major General Cadmus Marcellus Wilcox (Hill's "Old Light Division"). Hill was now commander of the Third Corps. The division consisted of four brigades: Lane's North Carolina brigade, McGowan's South Carolina brigade, Thomas' Georgia brigade, and Scales' North Carolina brigade.[17]

The fighting was not over for the year 1863. There would be two more engagements before the men could settle down in their winter quarters. On October 14, 1863, Hill's men caught up with the enemy. The results of this chase were not what Lee had expected nor had wanted.

> Bristoe Station, October 14, 1863
> *Forces Engaged:* Corps
> *Principal Commanders:* Maj. Gen. G.K. Warren (Union), Lt. Gen. A.P. Hill (Confederate)
> *Estimated Casualties:* 1,980 total
> *Results:* Union victory
> On October 14, 1863, A.P. Hill's corps encountered two retreating Union Army corps at Bristoe Station. Hill attacked without proper reconnaissance. Federal soldiers of the II Corps situated behind the embankment of the Q&A Railroad inflicted heavy casualties on two brigades of Henry Heth's Division and captured a battery of Confederate artillery. Hill tried to reinforce his line but still could not budge the determined Federal defenders. The Bristoe offensive came to a halt after minor skirmishing near Manassas and Centreville. After this victory, the Federal forces withdrew to Centreville without further trouble. The Confederates then retired to the Rappahannock River, and they destroyed the Orange & Alexandria Railroad as they went. The events at Bristoe Station caused Lee to lose confidence in A.P. Hill. In anger, Lee simply ordered Hill to bury his dead, and would not discuss the battle further.[18]

General Lee learned that Meade had sent two of his corps to Tennessee to reinforce the Federal troops there. Lee wanted to strike at Meade's army one more time. With two Federal corps absent, Lee believed he could defeat his opposition. He planned to use Ewell's and Hill's corps to move across the Rapidan River to Culpeper and attack Meade's flank. Here, the Confederates could trap Meade's army between the Rapidan and the Rappahannock. However, Meade learned of the approaching Confederates and he sent his Army of the Potomac northward to the Orange and Alexandria Railroad. Meade's men burned all the railroad bridges as they passed.[19]

Lee did not give up his plan, so he ordered Ewell and Hill to swing to the left of Culpeper in hope that they could overcome the Federals and destroy a portion of Meade's army. Thus, Hill's Corps, including Lane's Brigade, circled around Sperryville and Waterloo to Warrenton. Although the weather was cooler, it proved to be a depressing march. The countryside had already been ravished. Houses, fences and trees had been cut down for use in military campfires. The country was barren of both animal and human life.[20]

The movement of Confederate troops caused Meade to move his Federal soldiers toward Centreville. On October 14, as the rear guard of Meade's army passed through Bristoe Station, it was attacked by Heth's Division.[21]

Without waiting to reconnoiter or for additional troops to arrive, A.P. Hill ordered an attack against a vastly superior force. Heavy casualties were sustained by two brigades of Heth's Division, while the Federals continued on their way. Wilcox's Division was formed in line of battle during the fighting at Bristoe Station but did not advance.[22] Fortunately, Lane's men and the 28th Regiment did not take part in Hill's disastrous attack. The brigade had moved under fire with the rest of the Light Division, but darkness fell before an attack could be launched.[23]

In the darkness, the Federal army continued to retreat. Lee notified the Confederate Secretary of War that the enemy had learned of his movements, and "withdrew so rapidly that we have not been able to come up with his main body," although there had been a number of encounters between the Federal cavalry and the Confederate cavalry of J.E.B. Stuart.[24]

Lee reported from Bristoe Station that the enemy was marching in "parallel lines" directly toward Washington, but that his army had been forced to make "considerable detours." Furthermore, it was impossible for his men to remain where they were because the country "was destitute of provisions for men or animals, and the railroad bridges on this side of the Rappahannock ... have been destroyed." He was, however, thankful that he had compelled the enemy "to fall back before us."[25] For numerous reasons, Lee did not order further pursuit of the enemy. The country was devoid of any food, and his men lacked overcoats, blankets, and even shoes.[26]

The action in October was described by Captain Nicholas Gibbon as a "grand flank movement" around the right flank of the enemy, which extended west of Culpeper Court House. Gibbon's division marched to Madison Court House through very "rough country" and entered the town of Warrenton from the west, where they camped. After the fight at Bristoe, the Confederate troops retired to the Rappahannock River.[27]

Loss of Colors

Major Thomas W. Baird, of the 82nd New York Infantry, reported that his men began firing at the 28th North Carolina Regiment as they crossed the railroad on the right of the Federals. The Confederate advance was stopped, and the "line thrown into confusion." Many in the front "threw down their arms and surrendered. Captain Thomas Culloen of Co. I, 82nd New York, captured the colors of the 28th North Carolina, by taking it from the hands of the bearer."[28]

In a slow retreat southwards, Lee's men finished tearing up the tracks of the Orange and Alexandria Railroad. After the tracks had been completely destroyed from Catlett's Station to Rappahannock Bridge, Lee's troops crossed the river and camped near Brandy Station to await the enemy.[29]

Casualties

Dr. L. Guild, the medical director of the Army of Northern Virginia, reported the Confederate casualties for the two-week period October 26 to November 8, 1863. Although Lane's Brigade was not involved in any major battles or skirmishes, Guild reported a total of 11 casualties in the brigade. The 28th Regiment had only one soldier wounded.[30]

This report covered the action at Kelly's Ford and the Rappahannock Bridge on November 7, 1863. During a rare night attack, Union forces under D.A. Russell (Corps I and VI) with Upton's 2nd Brigade and others (the 6th Maine and 5th Wisconsin) stormed the Confederate works and advanced to the head of the pontoon bridge. The 30th North Carolina had moved up to support the 2nd North Carolina and both regiments were captured, which resulted in the loss of 2,023 Confederates. Colonel A.C. Godwin held out for a short time before being captured along with 65 soldiers who had survived a bloody attack in which the Federal soldiers used bayonets.[31]

Because the Federals had captured two whole Confederate brigades, Lee was forced to order his army back across the Rapidan. Leaving camp on November 8, Lee's men retreated without opposition except with a brief encounter with a detachment of Federal cavalry. The 37th Regiment of Lane's Brigade was ambushed, and they lost one killed and ten wounded. The retreat continued through the cold and snow, and many stragglers fell by the way. The brigade crossed the Rapidan by wading through its icy waters to set up camp near Liberty Mills. Fence rails were gathered from the vicinity to make campfires.[32]

Major General Cadmus M. Wilcox reported on November 12, 1863, on the campaign which ended November 9. Losses in the Light Brigade were 3 killed, 12 wounded, 8 stragglers had not yet reported in, 3 deserted, for a total of 20 casualties. He noted that the "killed and wounded" were mainly from Lane's Brigade, "which was engaged with the enemy's cavalry and artillery" on November 8.[33]

Sergeant Samuel Speer Harding wrote to his father in November of 1863: "We have Seventy men in our Company [Company I, 28th Regiment] for duty which is present."[34] That number was about ¾ of the normal 100 men which made up a company.

After a few days, the Confederate forces moved to a camp near Brandy Station where they remained for three weeks. Suddenly, they were ordered to march at 1 A.M. By the next night, they were back at their old camp near Orange Court House. They remained in camp there until about December 1, when the Yankees began to move across the Rappahannock toward the Wilderness area east of the Orange Court House.[35] The result of these troop movements was the battle of Mine Run.

Mine Run, November 27–December 2, 1863

Forces Engaged: Armies, 114,069 total (69,643 Union, 44,426 Confederate)

Principal Commanders: Maj. Gen. George G. Meade (Union), Gen. Robert E. Lee (Confederate)

Estimated Casualties: 1,952 total (1,272 Union; 680 Confederate)

Results: Inconclusive

Several battles and skirmishes occurred during the Mine Run Campaign as the Union's General George Meade tried to march through the Wilderness to strike at the right flank of the Confederate army south of the Rapidan River. Confederate Major General Jubal A. Early, in command of Ewell's Corps, marched east on the Orange Turnpike to meet the advance of William French's III Corps near Payne's Farm. General Joseph Bradford Carr's 3rd Federal division attacked twice, while Johnson's Confederate division counterattacked. Confederates were scattered by heavy fire from Federal guns and the broken terrain. After dark, Lee withdrew to fortifications along Mine Run. The following day, the Union army closed in on the Confederate position. Although skirmishing was heavy, a major attack never occurred. Meade concluded that the Confederate line was too strong to attack, and he retired during the night of December 1–2.[36]

During the Bristoe Campaign of October and November, Union Major General Meade attempted to maneuver Lee and his Confederate forces out of their position on the Rapidan. Meade crossed the Rapidan at Germanna Ford with five corps, then turned west toward Orange Court House. Lee's cavalry detected the enemy's movement and Meade found Lee's Army of Northern Virginia strongly established along Mine Run. This position halted any further Federal advance.[37]

Orders were issued late on November 26 that the men of Lane's Brigade were to be given two days' rations of hard bread, and the men were to prepare to move forward. The brigade left camp at 2:30 A.M. in bitterly cold weather in ragged clothes, and without blankets or shoes. One member of the brigade, Chaplain Francis Kennedy, believed the suffering of the Confederates surpassed that endured by Washington's men at Valley Forge in the winter of 1777–78. The men marched 22 miles on November 27, and made camp in an old pine thicket.[38]

On November 28, the brigade reached Mine Run, a small stream that ran perpendicular to the enemy's line of advance. The men began to dig trenches in preparation for an enemy assault. In nearly blizzard conditions, the men had to lie in riflepits without fires because of the closeness of the enemy forces. It was so cold that men on picket duty had to be relieved every 30 minutes, and they came in almost too cold to talk.[39]

Lane's Brigade remained entrenched at Mine Run for three days awaiting an attack. Meade wisely decided not to attack such a well-fortified position, and he pulled his men out. On the morning of December 2, the defending Confederates awoke to find the enemy gone. The brigade was ordered to move down the Orange Plank Road in pursuit. They soon found that their enemy had crossed the Rapidan. Cold and weary, the men of the brigade returned to camp between Liberty Mills and Orange Court House where they remained the rest of the winter.[40]

According to William Tesh, the 28th was not involved in any fight. They left their winter quarters on November 27, to "run the Yankees across the river." Once that was accomplished, his regiment returned to their quarters on December 3. Tesh hoped they would remain in camp for the rest of the winter.[41]

Winter Quarters

Lane's Brigade set up their winter quarters in some woods that belonged to Dr. Newman. Here the brigade gained an enviable reputation for good order. Lane saw to it that the private property surrounding their camp was "respected," and the fences around the camp and picket lines were also maintained. When the brigade broke camp in the spring, Lane recalled that some of the citizens told him that "they had nothing to complain of except the great destruction of timber, which they knew was unavoidable," and "declared their fences were in better order than they had been for a long time...." The grateful citizens also extended a welcome for Lane's men to return if it was necessary to set up quarters in their neighborhood again.[42]

Meade withdrew without attacking and went into winter quarters near Culpeper. This ended the major operations until General U.S. Grant arrived and launched the Wilderness Campaign in May of 1864.[43]

Captain Nicholas Gibbon bragged that the Confederate army never had the "advantage of them [Federal troops] so completely [as] in [their] position at Mine Run...."[44]

An abstract of the field returns for the Army of Northern Virginia enumerating the troop strength as of December 10, 1863, showed that Lee's army was quickly dissolving.

Forces in the Army of Northern Virginia

	Officers Present for Duty	Men Present for Duty	Aggregate Present	Aggregate Present + Absent
General Headquarters*	40	325	633	790
2nd Army Corps (Ewell)	1,551	15,447	19,969	37,108
3rd Army Corps (A.P. Hill)	1,535	17,872	22,202	35, 061
Cavalry (Stuart)	614	7,481	9,381	17,239
Artillery Corps (Pendleton)	241	4,371	5,233	6,935
Total	3,984	45,596	57,418	97,033

(*General headquarters figures include provost guard, scouts, guides, and couriers.[45] These numbers are for the Army of Northern Virginia only, and do not include any of the other 23 Confederate operational organizations, either officially or unofficially classified as a Confederate army.)

Casualties sustained by Lane's Brigade during the campaigns of 1863 were substantial.

May 2–5, Chancellorsville, casualties totaled 909
July 1–3, Gettysburg — 660
July 13, Hagerstown — 29
July 14, Falling Waters — 42

The grand total of losses from May through July 15 was 1,640. Brigadier General Lane stated that at Chancellorsville, he lost ⅓ of the men in his command. The brigade losses sustained at Gettysburg and during the retreat totaled 731, "out of an effective total" of 1,355, which included ambulance corps and rear guard."[46] By the end of the summer of 1863, Lane's Brigade, which at one time had numbered over 4,000, now had lost more than a quarter of its men.

Winter 1863–1864

After Mine Run, the Confederate army went into winter quarters. The brigade, including the 28th North Carolina, returned to its previous camp at Liberty Mills on the Rapidan River above Fredericksburg. There they remained during the winter of 1863–64, and until May 4, 1864.[47]

Private William A. Tesh wrote from the winter camp near Orange Court House that the men had orders to build cabins. Tesh wrote home that he had one ready which he was going to share with Sam Harding, Sam's brother Berry Harding, and William Macy. The cabin was 12 feet square and had a "splendid chimney." Tesh's cabin had beds which were off the ground.[48]

Sergeant Sam Harding called those cabins "Little Shanties," in which he and the 70 men remaining in his company were housed. He reported that he was "in very good health at present," and that few of the men in his company were sick. Sam was distressed that he had not received any mail, and he expressed his desire to his mother to be home for Christmas, but he had no hope of a furlough for himself or his brother Berry.[49]

Greenberry Harding wrote a letter home the same day as his brother (November 25, 1863). "Berry" reported that there had been no movement of the army. The Confederate forces had set up winter quarters and had built "little huts," and they had added chimneys to them, "which makes them very comfortable." He reported that he could not complain of the food and that the men got plenty of "good Beef & Bread & some time we get some few potatoes & turnips."[50]

Greenberry described his daily activities while in winter quarters. He had celebrated his 21st birthday the day before (November 24), but he had to celebrate on picket duty in the rain, "a bad wet day for a birth day." Berry had once thought that when he became 21, he would be

"... free & aloud [allowed] to do as I please, but I have found out better now. Instead of being free I am bound down tighter than any slave is in Yadkin County." Sadly, Berry wrote that he had "always thought I was living a hard time when I was under you but I have found out that any one is the best of[f] when he is with his parents, & I wish I was with you all today...."[51]

A month later (December 20, 1863), a friend of the deceased Private Caleb S. McCurdy (formerly of Company K, 28th Regiment) wrote to J.M. McCurdy, a relative of Caleb's, that the enemy was reported to be in the vicinity of Culpeper Court House, where they had set up winter quarters. He did not fear an enemy advance because "the weather is getting very cold & usually wet."[52]

Reenlistment

In February of 1864, the men were asked to reenlist because the terms of enlistment of many of the men who had reenlisted at the reorganization in 1862 were about to expire. Confederate officials urged the men to rejoin "for the war."[53] The 28th North Carolina took the lead and was the first regiment of Lane's Brigade to reenlist. They did so because they believed the Cause was "a just and holy one." In order to express those feelings, they drafted a resolution to that effect.[54]

One soldier stated the men of the 28th Regiment might as well reenlist because "they will keep us in any how...."[55]

A ceremony was held in which the regiments who had reenlisted took part in a dress parade. Each company of each regiment was asked to step forward if they agreed to serve again. Those who did respond to the call of duty were given three cheers and a huge "Rebel yell" by the men of the 28th Regiment.[56] The names of those who did not reenlist or support a resolution were published in Richmond and Raleigh newspapers and listed as "revolters, deserters and base cowards."[57] Although some still refused to sign the resolution, eventually 100 percent of the 28th reenlisted.[58]

Chapter 11

Spring 1864: Wilderness, Spotsylvania Court House, Jericho Mills

In the bloody angle ... where blood flowed like water.
—1st Lieutenant J.P. Little[1]

Disloyalty at Home

The heavy casualties suffered at Gettysburg and the capture of Vicksburg, both occurring in the first week of July 1863, added to the growing dissatisfaction with the war. In the spring of 1863, the peace movement in North Carolina continued to grow. After Gettysburg, the Unionists and peace advocates started having open meetings, mostly in the Piedmont and mountain counties. Resolutions which were adopted at these meetings were published in William Holden's newspaper, the *Standard.* These resolutions, with their criticism of the Confederate government, demanded that state conventions be called to negotiate an "honorable peace." It was evident many people in North Carolina were tired of the war and wanted it to end.[2]

The North Carolina soldiers were left feeling that they had little support at home. Thus, on August 12, 1863, North Carolina troops held a "convention" at Orange Court House to show that the troops in the Confederate army were not in favor of the peace movement or the publicity it had been given in the *Standard.* Resolutions approved by the 28th, 33rd, and 37th Regiments of Lane's Brigade were published in an issue of the *Raleigh Register.*[3]

The resolution passed by the 28th Regiment made the sentiments of the soldiers clear:

> *Resolved,* That those who seek thus to bring the Commonwealth of North Carolina in conflict with the Government of the Confederate States, who thus create discord and disturbances at home and furnish our *detested foe* with further encouragement towards our further subjugation, and prevent our depleted ranks from being filled, as the law directs, are not only guilty of giving aid and comfort to our enemies, but are treating the North Carolina soldiers in the field with neither consideration nor justice.[4]

It was feared that if the peace movement continued to gain support, there could be civil war within the state. Many feared North Carolina would end up in the same condition as Maryland, Kentucky and Missouri,[5] states with divided loyalties and within whose borders there was constant and bloody warfare.

Loyalty of the 28th North Carolina

On January 30, 1864, a meeting was held among the men of Company C of the 28th Regiment, North Carolina Troops. The meeting was called to order by the chairman, Captain T.J. Linebarger, and Corporal G.A. Abernathy was appointed secretary. The purpose of the meeting revolved around the terms of service of any of those men who had enlisted in 1861 whose

114

three-year terms would be up in August. A resolution was drafted that expressed the sentiments of those present at the meeting:

> *Whereas,* the term of service for which we enlisted will expire in August next, and whereas the exigencies of the service demand of every soldier to remain at his post and to do battle for his country's rights;
>
> *Therefore, be it resolved by the officers and men of Company C, Twenty-eighth North Carolina Troops,* That we, believing our cause to be a holy and just one, do hereby pledge ourselves to reenlist for the war, and do further declare our intentions never to lay down our arms nor abandon the struggle till our Government shall be recognized, and soil freed from the invader, our liberties secured, and peace restored to our bleeding country.[6]

Another part of the resolution called for a "general convention" of the entire regiment to meet on February 1, 1864, and that Secretary Abernathy was to send a copy to Brigadier General Lane, and a copy to Lieutenant Colonel W.H.A. Speer. The company also requested that a copy of their resolutions be "published on parade" that afternoon.[7] Shortly thereafter, other regiments in the brigade held meetings and passed similar resolutions.[8]

The soldiers from North Carolina demonstrated their support of the Cause and the Confederacy at a time when many deserted from the army or dodged the draft, and the civilian population demonstrated Union sentiment in the state of North Carolina.

When the question arose as to whether the men would reenlist, Brigadier General Lane recorded the reaction of the companies in the 28th Regiment. They "stood unanimously by the colors, the captain was wild with enthusiasm, and jumping in front of it," he shouted, "Good for old Company A! Men, I love the very ground you stand on." The captain of Company K, not to be outdone, called, "Colonel, you forgot the Stanly Guards, but we are all here to a man." That motivated Captain Gold Holland, who got a big laugh by constantly singing out in his unique way, "Be firm, Company H," and they did stand firm behind the Confederate flag and for the Cause. Holland then shouted, "Colonel, old Cleveland is all right, let us give three cheers to the soldiers," and a great Rebel yell was given by all.[9]

Before the fighting resumed in 1864, the men amused themselves by holding a tournament, similar to those so popular in the Middle Ages. According to Lane, it was a "delightful day," and there was a large number of ladies present. Captain E.J. Hale, Jr. gave a speech to the 13 "knights" before the bugle sounded for them to begin. A band played at intervals, and "the riding was really fine. Each knight rode five times, and, to be perfectly successful had to cut off a head, take the ring, strike another head on the ground, and pierce still another on a pole" each time he rode. All of this had to be accomplished within a time frame of 10 seconds. The next event was firing a pistol at three targets, while riding a horse at full speed. The last part of the tournament involved the riders jumping their horses over rails set at different heights. At the end of the tournament, the "queen of love and beauty" was to have been crowned that night at Montpelier, along with her "four maids of honor." However, the queen's mother objected and that ceremony was discarded in favor of celebrating with dancing instead. The dancing lasted throughout the night, and it was daybreak before the "knights" started homeward.[10] This account was written with a heading of "Liberty Mills, Orange County, VA., April 22, 1864." The tournament most likely was held on April 21, 1864.

Third Year of War

In the spring of 1864, the Army of Northern Virginia was still commanded by General Robert E. Lee. His forces consisted of three corps of infantry, plus artillery and cavalry. The corps commanders were lieutenant generals James Longstreet, Richard S. Ewell, and A.P. Hill. Lieutenant General J.E.B. Stewart commanded the cavalry, and the artillery was distributed among several different commands.[11] While at one time the opposing armies were more evenly matched in numbers, after Gettysburg and in subsequent battles, Union forces usually outnumbered Confederates by nearly 2:1.

The Wilderness (Todd's Tavern, Brock Road, the Furnaces), May 5–7, 1864

Forces Engaged: 162,920 (101,895 Union, 61,025 Confederate)

Principal Commanders: Lt. Gen. U.S. Grant and Maj. Gen. George Meade (Union), General Robert E. Lee (Confederate)

Estimated Casualties: approximately 29,800 (18,400 Union, 11,400 Confederate)

Results: Inconclusive (Lee's Army of Northern Virginia failed to stop Grant's advance)

This was the first battle in Union Lieutenant General U.S. Grant's new offensive, the Overland Campaign. On the morning of May 5, 1864, the Union V Corps attacked Ewell's Corps on the Orange Turnpike. A.P. Hill's Corps encountered Getty's Division of the Union VI Corps and Hancock's II Corps on the Orange Plank Road. Fighting was fierce but inconclusive. Both sides tried to maneuver in the dense woods of the Wilderness. When darkness put a stop to the fighting, both sides moved reinforcements forward. At dawn on May 6, Hancock attacked along the Plank Road and drove Hill's Corps back. Longstreet's Corps arrived just in time to prevent the total collapse of the Confederate right flank. At noon, the Confederate flank attack in Hamilton's Thicket failed when General Longstreet was wounded by his own men. Burnside's Corps moved against the center of the Confederate line, but was repulsed. When the fighting ended, Grant did not withdraw as previous Union commands had done, but on May 7 his Federal troops advanced around the Confederate's left flank toward Spotsylvania Court House.[12]

The battle of the Wilderness was the first direct confrontation between Lieutenant General U.S. Grant and General Robert E. Lee. This first encounter became a contest to see who could control the junction of the Brock Road and the Orange Plank Road.

Ulysses S Grant (Library of Congress, LC-B8172 6371).

The terrain over which this battle occurred was an area of thick woods south of the Rapidan River. The few roads within the area were vital arteries for troop movement. Grant would have preferred a battlefield with more open ground, which would have allowed the Federal artillery to make a greater impact. Lee preferred advantages afforded by dense woods, something he had learned at Chancellorsville in 1863.[13] However, these same dense, dry woods would become a fiery inferno that would claim the lives of many wounded soldiers before they could be carried to safety.

The fighting began near the Wilderness Tavern on May 5, 1864, and continued for two days. During the course of the engagement, incoming troops faced a grim welcome when they encountered the skeletal remains which still littered the woods of soldiers who died there in May of 1863 during the battle for Chancellorsville.[14]

When General U.S. Grant moved into the area of the Wilderness, the 28th Regiment of Lane's Brigade was still camped at Liberty Mills. They were ordered to move eastward from Orange Court House along the Orange Plank Road.[15] After marching 18 miles they joined other brigades of Heth and Wilcox's divisions near New Verdiersville.[16]

After leaving camp, Lieutenant Colonel W.H.A. Speer reported that the 28th Regiment camped for the night of May 4 near the old Mine Run battlefield.[17]

May 5, 1864

The next morning, May 5, Lane's Brigade resumed their march down the Orange Plank Road. About 10 A.M., they encountered skirmishing in their front and to the right of the road. As they continued to march, skirmishing began on the left side of the road.[18]

Lane's Brigade was at the head of Wilcox's Division. They had moved about a mile through dense forests north of the Orange Plank Road before they came to a clearing. Wilcox sent McGowan's and Sales' men into the woods. After crossing a stream called Wilderness Run, Lane's men encountered Gordon's Brigade of Georgia troops. Lane and Edward L. Thomas then formed their brigades in a line of battle to drive a small body of enemy back.[19]

Lane ordered Lieutenant Colonel Speer to "deploy skirmishers on the left of the road" to protect the regiment. The 28th continued to move forward and came to a field near where the battle was being fought. Speer reported that the regiment "filed off to the left along a country road, through some fields, across a little stream into a piece of woods." There they halted and formed a line of battle with the 28th Regiment on the right of Lane's Brigade. They moved forward through the woods and captured some 150–200 prisoners.[20]

Meanwhile, back on the Plank Road, a column of Heth's Division encountered Federal cavalry near Parker's Store. At first, they managed to force the enemy back as they spread out in a line of battle across the Orange Plank Road.[21]

Wilcox received orders to bring his division back to the road as quickly as possible. There, the enemy had launched a heavy assault against Heth. The men began to turn back the way they had come. As they moved through a clearing, the men of Lane's Brigade got a good look at the long columns of Federal soldiers moving toward the Plank Road. The sound of fighting could be heard in the distance.[22]

Wilcox was ordered to move to the left and make contact with the right of Ewell's line, and the brigades of Lane and Thomas were moved further to the left to link up with Ewell. At about 4 P.M., the Federal II Corps assaulted Heth's line.[23] The fighting was so heavy that Heth had to call in his reserve brigade. Reinforcements from Scales' and McGowan's Brigades were sent to assist.[24]

As evening approached, General A.P. Hill found Lane and told him that part of Scales' Brigade had given way. Lane was to move his command forward to reestablish the line, and to bring his left in line with McGowan's right. Lane ordered his men forward, but with a word of caution not to fire into McGowan's men.[25]

The 7th Regiment of Lane's Brigade ran into problems as they reached the edge of the swamp. Lieutenant Colonel Davidson assumed the gunfire was coming from the enemy and was directed at McGowan's men. As they advanced carefully, they soon learned that there were no Confederate troops, McGowan's or any others, between them and the enemy. As they tried to make their way through the swamp, the enemy rained heavy fire into their ranks from only 50 to 75 yards away.[26]

Though the Confederate line was under attack on both ends, the 28th continued to advance from its position in the center. They succeeded in driving the enemy not only from the swamp but also from their entrenchments on the other side. The regiment was now 200 yards beyond the line of the 33rd on their left. Speer decided to advance no further than the entrenchments and to hold his position there. By this time, his men were out of ammunition, and had to take cartridge boxes from the dead in order to hold their position.[27]

When Brigadier General J.H. Lane wrote his report of the fighting in the Wilderness on

May 5, 1864, he described how the men of his brigade had marched to the left of the Plank Road to somewhere beyond Wilderness Run, near the home of a Mr. Tiening or Tuning. Together with Thomas' Brigade, Lane's regiments formed into a line of battle and advanced to drive the enemy from in front of General Scales. They continued to move forward, but were stopped when the enemy opened fire on the Confederate sharpshooters, under the command of Captain John G. Knox. The sharpshooters returned the enemy fire and charged. They captured 147 of the Union soldiers, including "eight commissioned officers." However, before they could become involved in the fighting, Lane's Brigade was ordered back to the Plank Road to support Heth's Division. There, they found the Division already engaged in battle. General Wilcox ordered Lane's Brigade to move to the right of Scales, who was engaged in fighting in the woods to the right of the road. As Lane's Brigade attempted to advance into the woods, they encountered fire from enemy sharpshooters. Lane ordered Colonel Barbour to send his 37th Regiment to the left, parallel to the road, to protect the flank of the brigade. The rest of Lane's Brigade were told by Major Palmer, of General A.P. Hill's staff, to halt in the rear of Scales' men. Lane was soon informed by Hill in person that part of Scales' Brigade had given way. Hill ordered Scales' Brigade to move forward and to reestablish their line. The left of Lane's line joined McGowan's line, and Lane cautioned the men of the 7th to take care not to fire into McGowan's ranks. Once the order to advance was given, Lane's Brigade moved forward with their "usual battle yell." However, the advance was slower than normal because they had to cross a swamp with dense undergrowth and fallen trees.[28]

When the 38th Regiment (of Scales' Brigade) got into position between the 18th and 28th Regiments, they were able to drive the enemy back and out of the swamp. The enemy made an attempt to flank Lane's men and move to the rear of the brigade. However, Colonel Barry pulled back two of his companies, and changed the entire front of his regiment to meet the advance of the enemy. The Federals pressed Barry's 18th Regiment hard on their right, and they retired at dark.[29]

Lieutenant Colonel Speer, commander of the 28th Regiment, termed the terrain an almost "impenetrable swamp of mud briars and bushes." However, he and his men drove the enemy back, out of the dense woods and thickets.[30]

The fighting was heavy as Lane's Brigade advanced toward the enemy, which was massed on some high ground beyond the swamp. There was a terrible enfilade against the enemy. When dark came, and under the cover of the dense smoke from the gunfire, the enemy sent a column toward the left flank of Lane's Brigade. When the enemy was within a few paces of the left of the 7th Regiment, the Union soldiers demanded that the men of the 7th surrender. This caused Lane's left flank to fall back in disorder. Lane took charge and ordered the rest of his brigade to the high ground in the rear of the swamp, a difficult task because of the terrain and the growing darkness.[31]

After heavy fighting, Lane's and Scales's brigades stopped a Federal move to turn the Confederate flank. Darkness ended the fighting.[32] Linked with the 33rd, Speer ordered his 28th to pull back slowly. Lane then ordered all of his brigade to fall back slowly, which they did in spite of the smoke, fading light, and swampy ground.[33]

Lane's brigade rested during the night in the rear of Scales' men and with part of Heth's Division behind them. The next morning, the enemy resumed their advance. Lane's Brigade had not been relieved by Anderson's Division, as promised, and he had to form his men in a line of battle perpendicular to the road. A large force of Federal soldiers pressed Scales's men to the left of the road and sent them running in disorder.[34]

Lane and his men had helped secure the right wing of the Army of Northern Virginia. Their advance through the swamp had put the brigade directly in the path of a Federal move to turn the Confederate right as ordered by Grant. Even facing the Federal corps of General Winfield

Scott Hancock, Lane's men had held on long enough to prevent Hancock from launching an attack that would have overrun the Confederate line.[35]

The brigade then reformed behind Scales' Brigade near a breastworks which ran on the right of the Orange Plank Road. When Lane reported to Wilcox the results of the day's fighting, he was told to leave his brigade where it was. Anderson was expected to arrive the next day to relieve the exhausted men.[36]

May 6, 1864

Fighting resumed the next morning about 5 A.M. when 13 Federal brigades struck the front and left flank of Hill's eight-brigade line. The sudden attack caused the entire Confederate line to fall back in disorder. Only the arrival of Longstreet's Corps to reinforce Hill prevented the collapse of the entire right wing of Lee's army. The Federals were driven back, and Hill's men reformed behind Longstreet. Hill's troops were dispatched to the vicinity of Chewing Plateau to bridge the gap between Longstreet and Ewell.[37]

Lieutenant Colonel W.H.A. Speer reported that on the morning of May 6, the 18th and 37th were in front of the 28th, and the 7th was between them and the front line where Scales' Brigade was in a line of battle. Scales' Brigade was suddenly attacked and it gave way. This caused a "stampede among the troops in the rear," and they fell back in a disorderly manner. However, Speer, with the help of his officers, reformed the 28th some distance from the Plank Road, and with the rest of the brigade moved to the left into a field where they had been the day before.[38]

The enemy forces also struck Lane's left, where there were two wings of the 33rd Regiment. The 33rd fought hard, but were forced back in disorder to reform at the rear. Afterwards, Lane's Brigade took a position to the left of the road, and that night joined with Ramseur's men of Ewell's Corps. Even though Lane's men had to retreat, he did not blame his "Brigade for anything it did on that occasion." He noted that the fight the previous day, and the subsequent actions of his brigade in many hard-fought battles, reinforced his belief that "brave men are sometimes forced to turn their backs to the foe." He declared that if any mistakes were made on May 5 or May 6, the blame should fall elsewhere.[39]

Lane was very proud of his entire regiment at Wilderness. They had performed with "cool and unflinching bravery" as both the "officers and men advanced against a largely superior force," which was constantly being reinforced. Lane reported: "Nobly did they perform their work, driving the enemy out of the swamp and forcing them to seek shelter behind their temporary breastworks...." Lane also noted that his brigade was the last of the Confederate units to "become engaged and, without hope of any assistance, [they] kept up this unequal contest," from 5 until 9 P.M., when he had to withdraw them to avoid being overrun by the enemy.[40]

Lane reported that his whole brigade (except the 37th which had been detached and was not actively engaged) fought with much gallantry. He commended the 28th Regiment because it had "advanced further than any other part of the Command and occupied for a time a portion of the enemy's entrenchments beyond the swamp." Although the soldiers of the 28th were "out of ammunition, the men supplied themselves from the boxes of the dead and wounded and held this position until dark, when they fell back and reformed on the right of the 33rd Regiment."[41]

Lane was especially proud of Colonel W.H.A. Speer, who had "proved himself a worthy commander of that gallant Regiment [28th] which occupied for a time a portion of the enemy's intrenchments beyond the swamp." Speer, in turn, praised Captain E.F. Lovill, of Company A, and his adjutant, R.S. Folger, for having acted "very gallantly throughout" the engagement.[42] Speer believed that each of his soldiers "seem to vie with his companions in arms in deeds of valor."[43]

Isaac Columbus Poindexter, Company F, 28th Regiment (courtesy of Richard Poindexter).

One of those captured at either the Wilderness or at Spotsylvania was Sergeant Isaac Columbus Poindexter, of Company F, 28th Regiment. He was taken to Point Lookout, Maryland, before being transferred to Elmira, New York, where he spent the winter of 1864–65. According to family tradition, those who survived at Elmira did so on a meager diet which sometimes included rats.[44]

Casualties at Wilderness

One Confederate soldier declared that after three days of fighting, they had been "led out of the Wilderness— not by Joshua of old, but by Gen. Robt. E. Lee," only to face an even deadlier conflict at Spotsylvania.[45] The fighting was so fierce and there was such confusion in the Wilderness Campaign that no accurate casualty figures have ever been compiled. It has been estimated that the Union lost 17,666 out of 118,000 men. The Confederates lost about 8,000 out of 61,000.[46]

The 28th Regiment had 88 men either killed or wounded.[47] In addition, a number of officers were killed, wounded or missing from among the five regiments that formed the brigade.[48] In Lane's brigade, a total of 43 men were killed, 229 wounded, and 143 missing or captured. The total casualties were 415.[49]

Brigadier General Lane noted that officers Lieutenant M.J. Eudy, Company D; Lieutenant E.S. Edwards, Company G; and Lieutenant A.W. Stone, Company E, from the 28th Regiment were all wounded. Lieutenant E. Hurley, of Company E, 28th Regiment, was reported missing.[50]

May 7, 1864

The fighting did not resume on May 7, so Confederate forces spent the day improving their fortifications. The men of Lane's Brigade used this time to cut down trees for abatis and to extend the entrenchments.[51]

Lane did not mention in his report that his brigade was near the woods that were burning. However, that same forest that gave cover to Confederates was soon ablaze from sparks from exploding shells. In the fire, many wounded soldiers were burned alive. The fires also spread to the Union's breastworks and both sides were shooting blindly through the flames and smoke.[52] The same thing had happened after the Battle of Chancellorsville the year before.[53]

Yet, letters from the soldiers do mention it. Sergeant Greenberry ("Berry") Harding, Company I, 28th Regiment, described the awful scene: "We made a charge up at the Wilderness & routed the Yankees & taken several prisoners. The [dead?] Yankees stunk so bad that we could hardly go over the Battle Field at Spotsylvania."[54]

Wilderness Today

The Wilderness, as it was called in 1864, is still a "wilderness." It is a quiet, desolate place, not unlike the woods of Yadkin County. There are no houses or billboards, and little traffic.

Driving through this now-serene area, one can sympathize with the wounded men who lay helpless in these woods as fire consumed them. It is not a pleasant way to die, and this battle is one that we do not like to think about, but the dead will not let it be forgotten.

Spotsylvania (Bloody Angle, Salient), May 8–21, 1864

Forces Engaged: 152,000 total (100,000 Union, 52,000 Confederate)

Principal Commanders: Lt. Gen. U.S. Grant, Maj. Gen. George G. Meade (Union), General Robert E. Lee (Confederate)

Estimated Casualties: 30,000 total (18,000 Union, 12,000 Confederate)

Results: Inconclusive (however, Grant continued his offensive)

After the Wilderness, Grant and Meade's advance toward Richmond was stalled at Spotsylvania Court house on May 8, as a series of battles over a two-week period ensued. The Union attack at the Bloody Angle at dawn on May 12–13 resulted in the capture of nearly a division of Lee's Army and almost cut the Confederate army in half. Confederates counterattacked and plugged the gap, but the fighting continued in full force for nearly 20 hours in what has been deemed the most ferociously sustained combat of the Civil War. On May 19, the Confederate attempt to turn the Union flank at Harris Farm failed, and they suffered many casualties. Union Generals John Sedgwick and James Clay Rice were killed, Confederate Generals Edward Johnson and George H. Stuart were captured, with Daniel and Perrin mortally wounded. Grant called off the fighting on May 21, but doggedly continued his march toward Richmond.[55]

Nothing seemed to stop Lieutenant General Grant, and he left the Wilderness only to march southeastward toward Spotsylvania Court House. Lee's Confederates marched through the night to beat the Federals to that important crossroads. By the morning of May 8, Hill's Corps had quickly built a strong defensive line. Temporarily under the command of General Jubal Early, Hill's men were placed on the right of the line with Ewell in the center and Longstreet on the left. Lane's Brigade was on the left of Hill's line and connected with Hill's (Early's) line with Ewell at a convex, U-shaped salient called the "Mule Shoe."[56]

May 8–9, 1864

In his report, Brigadier General James H. Lane noted that after leaving the Wilderness battlefield on the afternoon of May 8, 1863, the brigade marched "continuously and rapidly until 2 A.M. After a short rest, the march resumed at 6 A.M., and the brigade reached the courthouse at Spotsylvania.[57]

Lieutenant Colonel W.H.A. Speer reported the same troop movement, and on May 8, after they discovered the enemy moving to their right. Finally, the brigade stopped, made camp, and cooked rations before daylight. At noon, when Lane's men reached Spotsylvania, the brigade formed a line of battle. The right of the 28th joined the 18th and the left connected with Walker's Brigade.[58]

From their entrenchments on the left side of the Fredericksburg Road, Lane moved to the left to connect with Johnston's Brigade, and subsequently occupied Johnston's position. The night of May 9, Lane moved his men to support Ewell's command, but they were not needed, and so returned to their previous position. The right of Lane's Brigade rested at the "salient beyond the Brick Kiln."[59]

May 10, 1864

From Spotsylvania Court House, the regiments of Lane's Brigade moved frequently and occupied various points along the line to the left of the Plank Road. The men, according to

Brigadier General Lane, "worked with untiring energy, cutting down trees, making abattis [*sic*], and throwing up intrenchments."[60]

On May 10, Lane's Brigade moved along the line. Their left rested in an angle to the left of the Brick Kiln, and the brigade of General R.B. Johnston. The right flank of the 28th joined the 18th North Carolina. After spending the day on top of a hill, late in the evening, Speer's 28th Regiment rejoined Lane's Brigade. That night they returned to their old position and rested during the night.[61]

May 11, 1864

Speer reported that on May 11, the regiment moved to the left three different times, and entrenched. Later in the day, the men rested in an old line of breastworks that crossed a ravine.[62]

Lane did not like the position further to the left and, in order to get a better one, he shortened his line and connected it to Stuart's Brigade of Johnston's Division. He ordered all his regiments except the 37th Regiment to move forward out of the old line of works. The 28th Regiment was to the right of this line, and they moved close to Stuart's in a "double sap" (an extension of a trench from within a trench to the enemy's works) which had been constructed by Johnston's Pioneer Corps. The right was on some swampy or boggy ground.[63]

May 12, 1864

On May 12, according to Speer, his regiment was up and in the works early. To his left were General Steuart's men of Johnson's Division. General Lane rode up at daylight just as Johnson's Division was attacked, and he told Speer to hold his position.[64]

Early that same morning, the enemy penetrated the line of Johnston's front. Lane ordered the 28th Regiment to hold its position until he could ascertain the movement of the Federal troops. He then ordered Speer to move his 28th Regiment around the right flank to some old works, but before this could be accomplished, the enemy, hidden by a dense fog, struck the flank of the brigade and captured some prisoners from the 28th and 18th regiments. The 7th and 33rd withdrew in order, and the 18th and 28th "came up like brave men," according to Lane, although in some confusion, and formed on the left, Within the safety of the old works, the brigade met the enemy assault that followed.[65]

The Salient

Confederate General Johnson was attacked at dawn, and his lines were broken. Speer found that the enemy was in his front; and his troops on the left were scattering in utter confusion in every direction as the enemy stormed the works from both sides. Speer informed Lane what was happening, and he ordered Speer to move his regiment by the right flank. Speer returned to give the orders to his men and found that the enemy were already on both sides of his regiment, and 113 men had been captured.[66]

The Confederates held off the Federals in hand-to-hand combat, and a new line was formed across the base of the salient. After the original line was abandoned, the Federal attack stopped.[67]

Speer rallied what men he had left of the 28th and joined with Colonel Cowan's men in the works to the right on the top of a hill. He believed that the "stubborn fight made here by Lane's Brigade certainly saved the day," and he proudly reported that the men of his regiment did their part well.[68]

Subsequent action took place when the 28th Regiment moved in front of the works with General Mahone's men to take an enemy battery. A line of battle was formed with Lane's Brigade in front of some woods. The 28th was on the left of the brigade, and the 18th joined them on

Dead Confederate soldier, Spotsylvania, May 19, 1864 (Library of Congress, digital ID cph-3c04041).

the right. They moved by the right flank, halted, and moved forward again. Some of the men of the 28th were very close to the enemy's battery when General Lane ordered them to fall back. However, the 28th Regiment captured more prisoners than they had men engaged. Speer also noted that Lieutenants L.A. Todd, of Company I, and J.M. Starling, of Company F, "were captured with several [enemy] and then mistaken by our own men, capturing their captors." The men of the 28th Regiment, according to Speer, fought with "anything they could get hold of." His regiment regrouped at the works in front of the Spotsylvania Court House, and occupied the works, along with the 33rd and 37th North Carolina regiments. There, they drew their rations and settled down for the night, which, according to Speer, was "very desirable," after so "hard a day's work as we had done."[69]

Lane's men had moved forward and had driven the enemy's sharpshooters out of the woods. The Confederates attacked a Union battery of six guns and assaulted Burnside's column in flank and rear. Lane recorded, "Once men commenced yelling too soon and drew upon themselves a terrible fire of Canister" from four of the enemy's guns. They were also being fired upon by two other Federal batteries, and found themselves also in danger of being fired upon by their own guns. Lane's Brigade succeeded in capturing a six-gun battery but they could not retrieve the guns because there were no horses available and no road close by. They did manage to surprise

Burnside's column as it advanced to the salient. Some men of the brigade became "mixed up with the enemy & for a time there was fighting at close quarter."[70]

In his brigade history, Brigadier General James H. Lane noted that the brigade was situated on the left of the works at Spotsylvania Court House. Here they formed a new line and "piled the Yankees in front of it ... early on the morning of 12 May...." It was also this brigade (Lane's) who was chosen by General Lee to strike the flank of Burnside's Corps. The brigade crossed the works and captured between 300 and 400 prisoners, three flags, and a battery of six guns. General Lee acknowledged the capture of the flags, and his note, written on the battlefield, was read to the men by Brigadier General Lane. These brave men were also chosen to make a reconnaissance for General Lee in front of Spotsylvania Court House, although they had been fighting all day and fresher troops were available.[71]

Brigadier General Lane had high praise for the men under his command in repulsing this "terrible attack of the enemy." He believed that there were no other men who "could fight better nor officers behave more gallantly...." He noted that no matter what the danger, the officers would "pass along the line and cheer" the men in their "glorious work." Lane could not help brag a bit, and declared: "We justly claim for this Brigade alone the honor of not only successfully stemming but rolling back the tide of Federal victory which came surging furiously to our right."[72]

Lane noted that Colonel John D. Barry, of the 18th Regiment, and Colonel W.H.A. Speer, of the 28th Regiment, "behaved with great coolness in withdrawing their Commands while attacked in the morning" as did other regimental commanders and officers.[73]

In his history of Company C, 1st Lieutenant J.P. Little wrote that on May 12, 1864, the 28th Regiment was placed "where they fell into that historic bloody angle, where hand to hand conflicts ensued, and where blood flowed like water."[74]

Tim Casstevens at the Bloody Angle at Spotsylvania. Photograph by Frances H. Casstevens.

Sergeant "Berry" Harding wrote home from the battlefield at Spotsylvania, "I wish all the dead Yankees that has been killed in these fights was laid on the walk at Washington city for one day. That this war would end the next day [is] certain."[75]

Harding told his folks that the Yankees had withdrawn from Spotsylvania Court House. It was rumored that the Yankees were going down the opposite side of the South Fluanna River, "but as for myself, I cannot tell anything about where Grant is going to make his appearance next but I suppose he will appear before very long." Berry described the engagement at Spotsylvania as "very hard fighting," but claimed that the Yankees lost five to every Confederate killed or wounded. The number of prisoners taken was about equal on both sides, he believed. In the two charges made by his brigade:

> We had very good success both times. The first time we taken as many prisoners as they were men in our Brigade. It was a terrible mixed up affair. We was right in among the Yankee's lines. We [had] taken a batterie from the Yankees but did not keep it for the Yankees was aplundering us & we had to get out of their in double quick time.[76]

Harding concluded his letter by saying: "I think we have had very few men killed for the fighting that has been done [but] I am afraid the worst is to come yet."[77]

In retrospect, Captain Nicholas Gibbon wrote that after their "Army marched out of camp at Orange C. H. on the 3rd of May," the fighting began near the Wilderness, "and continued along the whole route from Rappahannock until we reached the south of Petersburg," on June 16.[78]

The 28th Regiment of Lane's Brigade fought in the battles at Chancellorsville in 1863, and at the Wilderness and Spotsylvania Court House in 1864. As a consequence, they suffered heavy casualties. For their sacrifices, the men of the 28th were complimented both by General A.P. Hill and Brigadier General Lane "for their bravery and good behavior." J.P. Little believed that there was "nothing in history to equal" the fighting in that 15-mile radius.[79] He declared: "Men gave their lives by the thousands and poured out their blood in torrents."

Casualties

1st Lieutenant J.P. Little believed that in the battles of Wilderness and Spotsylvania combined, "since passing the Rapidan," General U.S. Grant "had lost more than 40,000 men."[80]

Casualties in Lane's Brigade at Spotsylvania alone totaled 469.[81] On the plus side, Lane's Brigade, according to a statement by General Jubal Early, captured over 300 prisoners and three battle flags in an attack on the flank of the enemy.[82]

Losses in the 28th Regiment

One regiment of Lane's Brigade, the 28th, lost 8 men killed, 18 wounded, and 100 missing or captured, for a total of 126. These figures were the second highest among the five regiments in the brigade.[83]

Lane gave credit to the sharpshooters, under Captain W.T. Nicholson, who "did good service that day (May 12), and are deserving much praise." He bemoaned the loss of "the brave spirits that fell: his aide, Lieutenant Oscar Lane; Captain N. Clark, Company E, 28th Regiment; and four lieutenants and one captain from the 37th Regiment.[84]

Lieutenant Robert Dixon Ormand, of the 28th Regiment (Company B), was wounded on May 12. Missing were Captain S.S. Bohannon (Company I), Lieutenant H.C. Andrews (Company G), and Lieutenant P.H. Turner (Company K).[85] Captain Simon S. Bohannon was captured on May 12, 1864, and sent as a prisoner to Fort Delaware. He was later one of the "Immortal 600" sent to Morris Island in Charleston Harbor, South Carolina, in a failed attempt to exchange

Confederate officers for Union officers held in Charleston. Bohannon was released on June 16, 1865, and returned home to Yadkin County, where he married Jane Jenkins on September 14, 1865.[86]

Lane stated that "... none were more attentive to duty — none more upright in their conduct — none more gallant on the battle field."[87]

After the fighting on May 12, Lane's Brigade fell back and reformed. They occupied the works on the left of the road near Spotsylvania Court House, and held that position from May 12 to May 21, although they frequently moved to the left of the courthouse. They used that time to strengthen old defensive works and build new ones, and sometimes marched to support other troops. However, during those nine days, Lane stated that his brigade was "not actively engaged."[88]

Casualties Between Major Battles

The brigade had a total of seven casualties from enemy sharpshooters and artillery fire from May 13 to May 20, 1864. On May 21, the brigade moved to the right from the Spotsylvania Court House, then followed Scales' Brigade to a church some distance away. The 33rd, 28th, and 37th Regiments were ordered to form in a line of battle in the woods to the left of a small road. The 27th and 18th were formed in the rear for support. The regiments advanced through abatis, and managed to dislodge and drive back a line of enemy skirmishers. They held the enemy's line of breastworks until ordered back to the church. In this effort, Lieutenant E.S. Edwards, Company G, 28th Regiment, was killed. Edwards was regarded by Colonel W.H.A. Speer "as one of his best officers." In addition to the death of Edwards, two of the enlisted men were wounded. The brigade had a total of 18 casualties.[89]

Praise from General Lee

The efforts of Lane's Brigade and its sharpshooters did not go unnoticed by General Lee. He summoned Lane to his headquarters and said that he "had witnessed the gallantry of these brave men, as well as the cheerfulness with which they had endured the hardships of the day...." Lee expressed his "high appreciation of their services," and he was hesitant to send them forward again, but he needed them to make a reconnaissance on the road to Fredericksburg. Lane assured the old general that he was certain the men "would go wherever he wished them." Lee replied, "I will not send them unless they are willing to go." Then, Lane brought Captain W.T. Nicholson, who was in charge of the sharpshooters, forward and introduced him to General Lee. A short while later, the sharpshooters marched past General Lee, and as they did, they saluted him with cheers.[90]

It was now apparent to the men in the Army of Northern Virginia that with Grant in charge of the Federal army, they faced a different kind of general and that the nature of the war had changed. Captain T.J. Linebarger, of the 28th Regiment, remarked: "Grant is not like other Yankees." It was evident after the two battles that even "Half such a whipping," wrote the Catawba County soldier, "would have sent McClellan, Hooker, Burnside or Meade crossing to the other side of the Rappahannock, but Grant may join us again in battle at any moment."[91] Grant's determination to destroy Lee's forces, even if he had to sacrifice his own Federal army, soon became evident. After Spotsylvania, that was exactly what Lieutenant General U.S. Grant planned and what he did.

Frustrated at Spotsylvania, Grant continued his advance, and he planned another turning movement to the south. Union General Hancock's II Corps was to move, accompanied by a strong force of cavalry, along the Richmond, Fredericksburg, and Potomac Railroad to Hanover Junction. Grant hoped that Lee would attack Hancock's force, leaving the rest of the Union

Jericho Ford (Jericho Mills, Jericho Bridge, North Anna River, Hanover Junction), May 23–27, 1864

Forces Engaged: Armies

Principal Commanders: Lt. Gen. U.S. Grant and Maj. Gen. George Meade (Union), Gen. Robert E. Lee (Confederate)

Estimated casualties: 4,000 total

Results: Inconclusive

After the fighting ended in the Spotsylvania Court House area, Grant continued his Overland Offensive. He was brought to a standstill at the North Anna River by Lee's line. In order to attack, Grant had to divide his army into three parts. On May 23, 1864, one of A.P. Hill's divisions assaulted the Federal V Corp, which had crossed the river at Jericho Ford (Mill). The resulting fight was bloody. On May 24, the Union infantry was repulsed at Ox Ford, but were able to advance to near the Doswell House on the Confederate right. Lee hoped to strike an offensive blow, but he was ill, and he let the opportunity to defeat a portion of the Union army pass. Grant pulled both wings of his army back across the North Anna River, then moved downstream toward Richmond.[92]

forces free to attack Lee's men before he could entrench. If this strategy failed, it would at least motivate Lee to leave his position at Spotsylvania.[93]

May 21, 1864

According to the report submitted by Lieutenant Colonel W.H.A. Speer, the 28th Regiment and the rest of Lane's Brigade spent the next few days moving along the lines and strengthening their fortifications, although some sporadic shelling occurred. On May 21, the 28th moved to the right to take a position on the line formerly occupied by General Gordon's Brigade. Then they moved along the works to a church just south of the Spotsylvania Court House. They formed a line of battle and charged through some woods, where they succeeded in capturing the enemy's breastworks. Speer reported that in this charge, his men "acted well." However, he lost Lieutenant E.S. Edwards, of Company G, one of his best officers, and had several wounded. Afterwards, the 28th regiment emerged from the woods and moved down the road toward the Central Railroad above Hanover Junction.[94]

Leaving Spotsylvania Court House on the night of May 21, 1864, Lane's Brigade marched until about 2 A.M. They stopped to rest for about 2 hours, then resumed their march at 4 A.M. They bivouacked about noon the next day at Hewlett's Station on the Central Railroad.[95]

May 22–23, 1864

Grant moved his Federal forces eastward and fighting occurred at Jericho Ford (Mills) on May 23. Wilcox's division was engaged against the Federal V Corps as it crossed the North Anna River.[96]

About 6 P.M. on the morning of May 23, the brigade moved down the railroad to camp along the South Anna River near Anderson's Station.[97]

On the afternoon on May 23, Lane received orders to march up the railroad to form a line of battle. McGowan's troops were perpendicular to the road. The 7th Regiment was detached to guard the ford at the river. They continued to march up the road and sharpshooters were deployed in front of their old position. A line of battle was formed on McGowan's right, parallel to the railroad, and skirmishers were thrown forward to advance on the enemy at Jericho Ford.[98]

The advance force moved forward (from right to left) beginning with the 18th, 37th, 33rd, and lastly the 28th Regiment. They drove off the enemy's skirmishers, and advanced about 400 yards into the woods. There, they became engaged with the enemy's main line of battle, which was stretched out along a ridge. A portion of Lane's troops gave way. However, General Wilcox disregarded that fact and ordered Lane to push onward. By that time, Lane's Brigade was ahead of McGowan's. Subsequently, the 37th Regiment, according to Lane, "broke in a disgraceful manner and ran back." Lane then ordered his other three regiments back to the edge of the woods where the 37th was being rallied. Lane quickly reformed the line, as per Wilcox's orders, and again advanced into the woods. The 37th again broke and ran, in a "still more shameful and disgraceful manner." The other three regiments held their position and fought "very gallantly until ordered back." This they did in a "cool and orderly manner." Lane was especially proud of Lieutenant Colonel Cowan of the 33rd Regiment. Company B of the 33rd Regiment, under the command of Captain E. Price, marched "by the rear rank with arms shouldered as though it were a drill."[99]

The Role of the 28th Regiment

On May 23, the 28th Regiment resumed its march to near Anderson's Crossing, and marched on the left of the brigade. They moved to the river where they rested in the evening. The 28th then moved up the railroad with the brigade to form a line of battle, with General McGowan on the right of the 28th Regiment. The regiment moved forward to form a line parallel to the railroad to drive the enemy's pickets before attacking the enemy's main line in the woods. The 28th fought until dark and, according to W.H.A. Speer, "displayed its usual good conduct." They fell back with the brigade to the railroad, halted for a short while, then moved down the railroad to the Anderson house where they remained for the rest of the night.[100]

In his report, Lane wrote that the men reformed a second time an open field and advanced again to the woods. They threw out a line of skirmishers and managed to retrieve all the wounded and dead. Lane's Brigade was relieved that night by Davis' Brigade of Heth's Division. They then formed a line along the railroad and began fortifying, but before daylight they were ordered to move to Anderson's Station. There Lane's men stayed in the entrenchments until May 27.[101]

Casualties at Jericho Ford

The attack on May 23 at Jericho Ford (Mills) had resulted in many casualties to the division. Wilcox's division had 642 casualties.[102] During this fighting, the 28th Regiment lost 30 men killed and wounded.[103] Lane regretted that Lieutenant H.I. Costner, of Company B, 28th Regiment, had been killed. He noted that Costner was a "brave officer and conscientious in the discharge of all his duties." He also noted that Lieutenant John M. Cockhrane, of Company D, of the 37th Regiment, "behaved very handsomely," in spite of the display of cowardice by his company commander, Lieutenant A.I. Bost.[104]

At Jericho Ford, Lane's Brigade advanced farther than any other troops and held their position until relieved that night.[105]

General Lee rebuked A.P. Hill for not sending in all his men as "Jackson would have done."[106] Wilcox had not done much at Jericho Ford other than setting the brigades in motion. Somehow, the communication and teamwork that had been present in the Light Division were absent, and the opportunity to crush the Union troops was lost.

From May 24 through May 26, the 28th Regiment worked at constructing heavy breastworks while under fire from the enemy. On May 27, the Regiment moved by the Ashland Road and made camp east of Atlee's Station on the Virginia Central Railroad two miles from Mechanicsville.[107]

Pontoon bridge at Jericho Mills (Library of Congress, digital ID cwpb 01202).

The next morning their march resumed and by the afternoon they camped near Shady Grove Church. They remained there until May 29, when they were ordered back a short distance to bivouac at Atlee's. The morning of May 30, they formed a line of battle on the right of McGowan's men and entrenched near the railroad. On May 31, Lane and his men were ordered to Stowe's Farm on the Totopotomoy Creek near Pole Green Church, where they relieved Wofford's Brigade. All day long, Lane's Brigade was subjected to heavy artillery fire, and 20 men were killed or wounded. On June 1, they moved back and constructed a new line of works, and the next day they marched to Cold Harbor.[108]

Grant had withdrawn the night of May 26–27, toward Hanover Town where he crossed the Pamunkey and moved on to Totopotomoy Creek.[109]

Grant would soon face Lee's army again, this time at Cold Harbor.

Chapter 12

June–July 1864: 2nd Cold Harbor, Jerusalem Plank Road, Gravel Hill

Cold Harbor is ... the only battle I ever fought that I
would not fight over again under the circumstances.
— Lt. General U.S. Grant[1]

2nd Cold Harbor, June 1–12, 1864

Forces Engaged: 170,000 total (108,000 Union, 62,000 Confederate)

Principal Commanders: Lt. Gen. U.S. Grant, Maj. Gen. George Meade (Union), Gen. Robert E. Lee (Confederate)

Estimated Casualties: 14,500 total (12,000 Union, 2,500 Confederate)

Result: Confederate victory

The fighting began when General Phil Sheridan captured the crossroads at Old Cold Harbor. Having the advantage with their new repeating carbines and shallow entrenchments, Sheridan's cavalry repulsed several Confederate cavalry attacks. During the night, both sides dug in for a prolonged battle. Confederate reinforcements arrived from Richmond and from the Totopotomoy Creek position. By June 1, the Union VI and XVIII Corps had reached Cold Harbor and began to assault the Confederate works. Heavy fighting resumed on June 2 with both armies engaged in combat along a 5-mile front that extended from Bethesda Church to the Chickahominy River. On June 3, the II, VI, and VIII Federal Corps launched an attack from Bethesda Church to Cold Harbor, but were devastated along this line. Neither army would give way, but remained positioned opposite each other until June 12. Grant then launched an attack with his left flank, and continued to Windmill Point on the James River. The Union general changed his tactics and directed his forces to Petersburg. By June 14, the Federal II Corps had been ferried across the James River at Wilcox's Landing. On June 15, the remainder of the Federal army crossed the river over a 2,200-foot pontoon bridge.[2]

The next major battle after those at Wilderness and Spotsylvania was to be a second battle near the little village of Cold Harbor. A battle had occurred there before (June 26–28, 1862), which came to be called 1st Cold Harbor, or "Old" Cold Harbor. Although not really a town, just a crossroads, Cold Harbor did have a tavern, a well, a couple of houses, and a blacksmith shop.

When the second battle occurred in June of 1864, the battle lines were reversed from what they had been during the first fight. The crossroads at "Old" Cold Harbor was now in Union hands, and the major fighting took place several hundred yards south near a crossroads called "New" Cold Harbor.[3] This second battle, although fought over much of the same ground as the first battle, also included peripheral engagements at Gaines' Mill, Salem Church, and Hawes' Shop.[4]

Lee put every available man into the lines for the second battle at Cold Harbor. A Confederate deserter reported to Union Colonel George H. Sharp that in Richmond, all stores and shops, and even the governmental departments were closed, so that men could be spared for this battle.[5] Because Lee did not have men to replace those lost at Wilderness and Spotsylvania, he positioned his men behind entrenchments and fortifications whenever possible.[6]

The head of the Union forces, General U.S. Grant, ordered the Army of the Potomac and its various corps to move from the banks of the North Anna River on the night of May 26, 1864. General Lee responded quickly, and by the morning of May 27, he had set his forces in motion. On May 31, Union cavalry General Phil Sheridan had reached "Old" Cold Harbor which, as ordered by his commander George Gordon Meade, Sheridan was to "hold at all hazards." Grant planned to launch a two-pronged attack on the Confederate lines.[7]

Lane's Brigade, including the 28th North Carolina Regiment, moved to camp in the rear of General Heth's Division late in the day on May 29, 1864. The next day, the regiment formed into a line of battle, with the 18th North Carolina Regiment on the left of the 28th, and the 33rd North Carolina on its right. The men put up a strong line of works. On May 31, the 28th moved to the right, and took a position in the line of works on Stone's Farm. Here, the brigade of General Thomas was on their right. In this position the regiment came under heavy shelling from the enemy and lost five men. That night, the regiment moved back with the brigade to a second line of fortifications.[8]

June 1–3, 1864 — Cold Harbor

Heavy fighting between Grant and Lee's armies resumed on June 1. The next day, Hill's Divisions, commanded by Wilcox and Mahone, were ordered to move to the left in support of Anderson.[9]

Lieutenant Colonel W.H.A. Speer, commander of the 28th North Carolina Regiment, reported that he and his men spent June 1 behind their works resting, because they had worked all the previous night. On June 2, they marched to Gaines' Mill, and then moved by the right flank of General Breckinridge's Division to form a line of battle. They charged and took Turkey Ridge (Turkey Hill), where they again formed a line of battle, this time with the regiment's right extending to General Thomas' Brigade. Here the 28th threw up some strong defensive works.[10] The capture of Turkey Ridge completed a six-mile line of battle manned by Confederate forces which stretched from Pole Green Church to the swamps of the Chickahominy.[11]

The Confederate line began with Jubal Early's corps positioned on the northernmost end of the line near the old Church Road. Lieutenant General Richard H. Anderson's corps was in the center, and the corps of A.P. Hill was on the right. These three corps faced the five Federal corps of Warren, Smyth, Wright and Hancock, who were in a line running south from Bethesda Church, just west of "Old" Cold Harbor.[12]

On June 3, Grant launched another assault along the entire Confederate line. However, Wilcox's men, including Lane's Brigade, were not engaged in the fighting. They were positioned on the far right of the Confederate line near the Chickahominy.[13]

Historian Clement Eaton believed that the fighting at Cold Harbor was the "most violent fighting of the campaign." The charge ordered by Grant against the Confederate line resulted in a horrible slaughter. The Union forces sustained 55,000 casualties from "death, wounds, disease, and desertion."[14] Even General Grant commented in his memoirs: "Cold Harbor is, I think, the only battle I ever fought that I would not fight over again under the circumstances. I have always regretted that the last assault at Cold Harbor was ever made." Grant concluded that he had gained "no advantage" to compensate for the "heavy loss" his troops sustained. He admitted that "the advantages other than those of relative losses, were on the Confederate side." Cold Harbor demoralized Grant's men. They no longer were eager to fight when the odds were "one Confederate to five Yanks."[15]

Lieutenant Colonel Speer, of the 28th Regiment, reported that from June 3 through June 13, his regiment spent their time strengthening the works. During the period, he lost two men killed and five wounded by "enfilade shots."[16]

Over the next ten days, the two armies drew back into their entrenchments. Lane's Brigade returned to keeping only ⅓ of the men in the breastworks at any one time, while ⅔ were positioned in reserve at the rear. Federal artillery fire was still a danger, and shots killed an average of four men per day.[17]

Federal casualties for the 12-day period from June 1 to June 12, 1864 (which includes peripheral battles at Gaines' Mill, Salem Church, and Hawes' Shop), have been estimated at 1,844 killed, 9,077 wounded, and 1,816 missing, for a total of 12,737.[18]

During the period while the armies faced each other at Cold Harbor, Confederate morale was uplifted. Encouraged by the huge losses suffered by Grant's army, one member of the 28th Regiment wrote home that his regiment was "in fine spirits and confident of success and the ultimate defeat of Grant." Morale was also improved by an increase in rations that included summer vegetables such as peas, onions, Irish potatoes and rice added to the standard fare of bacon and cornmeal.[19]

Lee believed that the second battle at Cold Harbor had done much to elevate the spirits of the entire Confederacy and gave them hope that the South might succeed. However, that bat-

Burial crew picking up bones of the dead at Cold Harbor (Library of Congress, LC-B171 7926).

tle also demonstrated that the Southern troops would have to take a defensive stance. While Lee did succeed at Cold Harbor, this victory caused Grant to change his whole plan of operations, and he focused his attention on Petersburg. The siege of Petersburg would continue for almost an entire year before that city fell to the Federal forces.[20] Once Petersburg fell, the end of the war was not far behind.

(The photographs of the Choplin brothers who were in the 28th North Carolina Regiment are on display at the Cold Harbor visitors' center.)

June 13 — Riddle's Shop

The movements of the 28th Regiment after 2nd Cold Harbor were detailed by Lieutenant Colonel W.H.A. Speer. On June 13, 1864, the 28th crossed the Chickahominy at McClellan's Bridge. They continued to the Charles City Road and had gone some distance to form a line of battle at a right angle to the road to support General Scales' Brigade. They continued down the road and formed another line to support McGowan's Brigade, where they were positioned on the extreme right. Here, the men began fortifying. From their position, they moved forward in a charge for a mile and a half, and by dark had come to the enemy's line. The brigade commander ordered the men to halt and to move the right of the 28th regiment to protect the flank of the brigade. Later in the night, the 28th Regiment moved back and took a position near the Nelson house, where they remained throughout the next day (June 14).[21] This engagement, known as Riddle's Shop, was a minor Confederate victory. Lane's Brigade was not actively involved.

With McGowan and Scales in the front line, Lane and Thomas followed in the rear. The Light Division advanced toward some dismounted Federal cavalry holding Riddle's Shop. However, the sharpshooters in front of the division were so accurate that the main body of troops was not actively engaged. The enemy cavalry was driven away before darkness halted the action. Hill and Anderson's men began to entrench on either side of Riddle's Shop. The new line of entrenchments stretched from White Oak Swamp to Malvern Hill and effectively blocked all approaches to Richmond, south of the Chickahominy, from the east.[22]

June 15–21, 1864

From June 15 through June 17, the regiment moved to form new lines, then moved back to their former position at the Nelson house. From there, they marched toward Darbytown where they camped on the night of June 17.[23]

Petersburg, June 1864–April 1865

Lying south of the Appomattox River, Petersburg was a key element in the defense of Richmond. Men, food, and supplies were transported to Petersburg from other states by the three railroads that converged there. The defenses of Petersburg were almost impregnable. These consisted of a heavy line of redans (a work having two parapets which form a salient angle) connected by a line of rifle trenches. These defenses could accommodate 25,000 Confederate soldiers.[24]

After the defeat of his Federal forces at Cold Harbor, Grant concentrated his efforts on capturing Petersburg. He launched an offensive that began in June of 1864 and did not relent until April 1865.[25] Leaving an engagement at Riddle's Shop, Grant crossed the James River and began moving his Federal troops toward Petersburg. A.P. Hill's Confederates remained north of the James until ordered to move to Petersburg.[26]

Leaving Cold Harbor, General Lee arrived in Petersburg on the morning of June 18, 1864.

The troops of A.P. Hill's Corps arrived in the afternoon. From that time onward, a 10-month siege by Grant's forces took its toll on Union and Confederate soldiers alike. According to the National Park Service, the estimated casualties at Petersburg were approximately 42,000 Federal and 28,000 Confederate soldiers, either killed, wounded or captured.[27]

On the 18th of June, the 28th Regiment began its march to Petersburg. They crossed the James River at Drewry's Bluff and arrived at Petersburg about 6 P.M. This march, according to Lieutenant Colonel W.H.A. Speer, was "one of the hardest and most disagreeable marches" the regiment had ever made.[28] The men began the march without any breakfast. As the day wore on, the heat became almost unbearable, and the dust stirred by the marching army soon coated every inch of the soldiers. In addition, the march was undertaken at a fast pace, and the need for water grew with every mile. Men began dropping out of the ranks along the road, and the sound of artillery fire coming from Petersburg was the only incentive that kept the men going for those 22 miles.[29]

For months, fighting and skirmishing continued between the opposing forces in front of Petersburg, and all around Petersburg, both north and south of the James River. The 28th Regiment was involved in many of those battles. The importance of Petersburg is made evident when one considers that after the city was captured on April 2, 1865, the city of Richmond was evacuated, and Lee surrendered only a week later on April 9, 1865.

Once they reached Petersburg, the regiment passed through the city to the fortifications on the south and near the east side of the railroad. They rested overnight, then on June 19, took a position on the works. The left of the brigade joined General Mahone's right at the Wilcox Farm. The 28th remained in this position until June 21, when they moved to the right flank and marched down the road to assist some cavalry, in what is called the battle at Jerusalem Plank Road.[30]

Lane's Brigade was not assigned to duty in the trenches at Petersburg but, instead, was used as "flying infantry," or "foot Cavalry," under the command of Colonels John D. Barry and W.H.A. Speer.[31]

Jerusalem Plank Road (First Battle of Weldon Railroad), June 21–24, 1864

Forces Engaged: Corps

Principal Commanders: Lt. Gen. U.S. Grant, Maj. Gen. George Meade (Union), General Robert E. Lee (Confederate)

Estimated Casualties: 4,000 total

Results: Union gained ground

On June 23, the II Corps of the Union Army, supported by the IV Corps, attempted to cut the Petersburg-Weldon Railroad. Wilson's Federal cavalry division began destroying railroad tracks. On June 23, troops from A.P. Hill's Corps, led by Brigadier General William Mahone, counterattacked and forced the II Corps away from the railroad to the Jerusalem Plank Road. The Union forces were driven from their most advanced position, but they managed to extend their siege lines farther to the west.[32]

On June 22, Lane's Brigade was involved in the action on the Jerusalem Plank Road in a move to prevent the Federals from gaining a position along the Petersburg & Weldon Railroad.[33] The Jerusalem Plank Road ran south out of Petersburg between the Weldon Railroad and the Norfolk and Petersburg Railroad. Confederate troops from A.P. Hill's Corps were led by General William Mahone and General Cadmus Wilcox in a counterattack against the Federal II and VI corps. They drove the Federals away from the Weldon Railroad back toward the Jerusalem Plank Road.[34]

On June 22, the regiment moved again to the right and front to help in a flank movement against the enemy. Lieutenant Colonel Speer reported that after they had marched for some distance, the regiment halted, formed a line of battle, then moved forward through "as many natural difficulties" as he had ever seen. When the 28th encountered enemy skirmishers, they drove them back. In the process, the regiment captured 40 Union soldiers, while under heavy fire in which some members of the regiment were hit. The 28th moved out of the woods by the left flank, and reformed in a field which was under a heavy fire from the enemy. Then they moved to support General Wright's Brigade, until they were able to return to their former position that night.[35]

On June 26, 1864, Speer and the 28th Regiment were ordered to move by the left flank to the works to relieve some of General Finnegan's Brigade. In doing so, the regiment came under heavy fire. For their efforts, Speer praised the men of the 28th for the "manner in which it took its position in this very disagreeable and dangerous position." Here, Speer reported that the regiment held out until June 26 when the were relieved by one of McGowan's regiments.[36]

Casualties

During the three days from June 23–26, Speer reported that he had 7 men killed, and 16 wounded. One of those killed was Captain James M. Conkle, Company K, of the 28th. He was hit about 10 P.M. in the dark of night.[37]

During the month of June, Speer reported the loss of Captain T.O. Clark, of Company G, a "Christian and patriot"; Captain James M. Crowell, of Company K, "a colossus of genuine bravery"; Lieutenants Edwin S. Edwards, of Company G, and S.J. Cashman, of Company B, "both brave and gallant spirits...." In addition, Speer lost 32 enlisted men, with 121 wounded, and 132 missing (including 113 that had been captured on May 12). In his report filed July 19, 1864, Lieutenant Colonel Speer stated that he had "no field officers to assist me in the campaign."[38] Their ranks had been reduced to a critical point because of the casualties.

Speer was able to move his regiment to the rear of Lane's Brigade where the weary men were allowed to rest until July 1.[39]

The next day, the brigades of Lane and McGowan were sent north of the James River to relieve some of Heth's division which had been defending the trenches around Richmond when the rest of the troops had moved off to Petersburg. While there, the men were in a rather quiet sector. The two brigades had only to maintain a strong picket line and see to the strengthening of the defensive works.[40]

After marching all night, Lane's Brigade crossed the James River at Chaffin's Bluff on July 3. They then took up a position below the bluff on a farm near Four Mile Creek. Speer reported that his men had never "displayed more conspicuous gallantry than in this campaign, fighting, marching," which they endured without grumbling about the "fatigue and privations."[41]

As part of Grant's Petersburg campaign, the battle of Gravel Hill was a diversionary tactic to divert attention from Petersburg, where a tunnel was being dug under the Confederate trenches and fortifications. Hancock's Federal II Corps was to move secretly across the James River during the night of July 27 and move toward Chafin's Bluff. Sheridan was to cross the river behind him with cavalry divisions of Torbert and Gregg, and to add Kautz's cavalry division from the Army of the James. These forces were to lead a raid to Richmond and, if successful, enter the city. If not, their orders were to destroy the Virginia Central Railroad.[42]

Toward the end of July, Federal cavalry and infantry from Hancock's II Corps moved north of the James River in a threat to Richmond and to destroy two railroads running north from the city.[43] Lee met the threat by sending reinforcements to join Lane and McGowan, leaving the trenches of Petersburg undermanned and defended by only 3½ divisions. Hancock's men began to entrench near Deep Bottom, and Lee ordered his Confederates to drive the

Gravel Hill (Deep Bottom I, Darbytown, Strawberry Plains, New Market Road), July 27– 28, 1864

Forces Engaged: Corps

Principal Commanders: Maj. Gen. Winfield S. Hancock (Union), Maj. Gen. Charles Field (Confederate)

Estimated Casualties: 1,000 approximate total

Result: Confederate victory

Two divisions of Sheridan's Cavalry, commanded by Major General Winfield Scott Hancock, crossed to the north side of the James River at Deep Bottom, where they posed a threat to Richmond, the Confederate capital. Confederate forces were pulled from Petersburg in an effort to stop the Union troops. Although the Union forces made efforts to turn the Confederate position at New Market Heights and Fussell's Mill, these positions were abandoned when the Confederates reinforced their lines and counterattacked. During the night of July 28, the Federals retreated across the river. A Federal garrison was left to hold the bridgehead at Deep Bottom in order to continue the threat against Richmond.[44]

Federals back, and to capture the pontoon bridges that Hancock's men had used to cross the James River.[45]

Lane and McGowan's men were now under the command of Brigadier General James Conner, a South Carolina lawyer. He was in charge when these brigades fought at Riddle's Shop, Darby's Farm, Fussell's Mill, Petersburg, Jerusalem Plank Road, and Reams' Station. (Conner was wounded on October 13, 1864, in a skirmish at Cedar Creek, and his leg had to be amputated.[46])

Men from these two brigades were pulled from the defense of Petersburg to a point opposite Deep Bottom. They moved to the far left of the Confederate line in front of Richmond. Three companies of the 7th Regiment of Lane's Brigade were sent forward to look for enemy troops. They soon encountered enemy pickets, and returned their fire.[47]

When Conner received news that the enemy was at hand, he ordered the two brigades forward to engage the Federals. They advanced through a dense swamp to attack the Federal line and force them back beyond a cornfield. As the enemy retreated, the two Confederate brigades took shelter behind the slope of a hill just beyond the cornfield. The officers began trying to reform their men to continue to drive the Federals back.[48] The terrain presented problems and a gap developed between the two brigades. The men continued to move forward before the line could be adjusted, and some of Lane's men lost contact with others, while some overlapped the fronts of other units.[49] Thus, the men were not prepared to meet the Federal counterattack when it came. The Federals took advantage of the confusion and penetrated the gaps and flank of the brigade's right. Connor became aware of the problem, and ordered a withdrawal by the right flank. He wanted a new line of battle to be formed perpendicular to the old one. The attempts by the men to execute this order resulted in more confusion. The 33rd was left to face the enemy, while the 37th and the 28th fell back to the rear.[50] The 37th and 28th were being fired upon from the flank, and they were forced to retire in disorder back through the swamp and wood. The men became scattered and the retreat dissolved in to a disorderly rout that saw both brigades pushed back to the point from which they had originally begun to advance. The entire affair was a disaster. Lane's Brigade had 11 men killed, 49 wounded, and 77 missing for a total of 137 casualties.[51]

Lieutenant Colonel W.H.A. Speer, commander of the 28th Regiment, reported on the fighting that occurred on July 28. His regiment was between the 37th on the left and the 33rd or the right. The 37th moved forward with the brigade and encountered the enemy in a "very thick swamp but drove them out into a cornfield." In order to make their way through the swamp, the regiment had to split up, but reformed once they reached the cornfield. The soldiers of the 28th pressed the enemy through the cornfield. Speer noted that the right of his regiment moved along a fence. His right flank was under fire before he came out of the swamp. After the regiment traversed the cornfield, they came upon an open, untended field, where they were under heavy fire for about a fourth of a mile. They had driven the enemy to the top of a hill at the far end of the field, when the 28th suddenly encountered a heavy force of the enemy and were forced to retreat to a fence. However, Speer rallied some of his men and with others of the brigade, but was unable to hold his position. He saw that he was being flanked on his left, and had no support. He had no recourse but to order his men to fall back to a ridge and reform. He reported that he "never saw the men fight with more spirit and gallantry in my life." He commended the officers, who "did their part nobly," but also stated that if he had had proper support, he would not have been outflanked and had to withdraw. In this battle, two officers were missing from the 28th Regiment, one was killed, 14 wounded, and 23 were missing.[52]

Greenberry Harding, Company I, 28th Regiment, wounded at Gravel Hill on July 28, 1864, great-uncle of the author (courtesy Libby Harding Carter).

When Grant reached the scene, he saw that he had underestimated the strength of he Confederate forces. An envelopment of the Confederates' north flank was planned to shake cavalry loose for its raid. Foster's division was to make a demonstration to its front. However, before this could be done, Sheridan was attacked at 10 A.M. by Kershaw's division, and the Federal outposts were driven back. Sheridan's cavalry dismounted and, with their repeating carbines, drove Kershaw back. In the retreat, Sheridan captured 300 Confederates and two stands of colors. Gregg's division was one of those withdrawn to the New Market Road, and in a hot contest, he lost an artillery piece. On July 29, Hancock was ordered back to Petersburg. While this action had drawn the Confederates from Petersburg, they had met the threat quickly and had prevented a raid by Sheridan.[53]

Union casualties at Gravel Hill were reported at 334 killed and wounded, while total Confederate losses are unknown.

During the action at Gravel Hill on July 28, 1864, which involved 28th Regiment,[54] Greenberry ("Berry") Harding, of Company I, was wounded. He was discharged from the service because of disability, and returned home in December.[55] The injury he sustained at Gravel Hill might have saved his life. He was not with his brother Sam, who was killed at Reams' Station on August 25, 1864.

Below are some, but by no means all, of the men who were casualties at Gravel Hill from the 28th Regiment:

Captured:
Corporal William H. Blackwood, Company A;
Private David A. Bumgarner, Company C;
Private John W. Carden, Company G;

Private James Champion, Company H;
Private Franklin Cline, Company H;
Sergeant Milton A. Lowe, Company C.

Wounded and Captured:
Sergeant Joshua A. Little, Company C.

Wounded:
Private William Fraser, Company E;
Private William J. Hawkins, Company H;
Sergeant Bloom V. Holcomb, Company I;
Private Adley A. Holler, Company C.

Killed:
One of those killed was Private Henry A. Conrad, Company C.

See Appendix IX of this work and Jordan, *North Carolina Troops*, Vol. 8, for more names of individual casualties at Gravel Hill.

The idea for digging a tunnel under the Confederate lines at Petersburg came from Lieutenant Colonel Henry Pleasants, of the 48th Pennsylvania. Pleasants had been a mining engineer before the war and the men in his regiment were mostly former coal miners. Pleasants got approval from Burnside and Grant, his superior officers, and began work on June 25. The digging was completed by July 23, and the result was a well-made tunnel, which ran 511 feet to a point 20 feet under the Confederate battery in the salient. Two other tunnels, 75 feet long, ran under the trenches. The tunnel was five feet high, four and a half feet wide at the bottom, two feet wide at the top. A large amount of powder (320 kegs of black powder equaling 8,000 pounds) was placed in the tunnel and a fuse attached. Grant was never very optimistic about the project because its position was not favorable for tactical exploitation when the explosion occurred.[56]

Burnside's plan was to use black soldiers to move through the Confederate lines once the explosion had occurred. This was overruled by Meade, who knew there would be political repercussions, and he insisted that a white division would have to be used as the attacking force after the explosion. The commanders of Burnside's three divisions drew straws to see whose men would make the assault. Ledlie drew the short straw. Burnside failed to assure that there were passages through his parapets and abatis to make it easier for the attacking force to move forward. The explosion was set for 3:30 A.M. on July 30. However, the fuse failed to ignite the powder, and two Federal soldiers had to crawl back into the tunnel and relight the fuse. The explosion came at 4:45 A.M. It created a crater 170 feet long, 60 to 80 feet wide and 30 feet deep. In the initial blast, approximately 300 Confederates were killed or wounded. Ledlie's troops were slow to start their assault, and when they did attempt to cross over the crater, they were shot by Confederate artillery which had been moved into position. Behind Ledlie's men, Ferrero's colored troops were ordered forward, while both Ferrero and Ledlie crouched in a bombproof shelter for protection.[57]

Crater Casualties

Confederates sustained approximately 1,500 casualties. The assaulting Federal troops had 3,798 killed, wounded or captured.[58]

"The effort was a stupendous failure," stated Lieutenant General U.S. Grant, "and all due to inefficiency on the part of the corps commander and the incompetency of the division commander who was sent to lead the assault."[59] A court of inquiry headed by Hancock found Generals Burnside, Lidlie, Ferrero, and Wilcox and Colonel Z.R. Bliss responsible in varying degrees for the disaster.[60]

According to 1st Lt. J.P. Little, it "looked like a second Mount Vesuvius," into which the Federal troops (black and white) poured. What had seemed like a foolproof scheme to break the Confederate line turned out to be a disaster for the Union troops. Federal soldiers were "caught in their own death trap." Little noted that Confederate artillery was aimed at the crater and that the enemy within was "mowed down by the hundreds."[61]

However, Grant would not give up and he increased his activities north of the James and all along the Confederate defenses around Petersburg.

Lane's Brigade did as they were ordered and Lane noted in his history that his brigade fought with "its accustomed bravery" at Riddle's Shop, Gravel Hill, Fussell's Mill, and Petersburg.[62]

Chapter 13

August–October 1864: Chapin's Farm, Fussell's Mill, Reams' Station, Jones' Farm, Pegram's Farm

... the enemy was driven off in a desperate hand to hand struggle ...
in which clubs, muskets and bayonets were used freely.
—1st Lt. J.P. Little[1]

On August 3, 1864, Colonel John D. Barry was made a temporary brigadier general and ordered to take over the command of the Branch-Lane Brigade[2] until the return of Brigadier General James H. Lane. Lane had been wounded at 2nd Cold Harbor in June. After Lane's recovery, Barry returned to resume command of his 18th North Carolina regiment.[3]

Camp at Chafin's (Chapin's) Farm (Chaffin's Bluff), August 11, 1864

After the encounter at Gravel Hill, Lane's Brigade moved to Chaffin's Bluff, where they began extending the line of breastworks. The brigade was now under the command of Colonel William Barbour, of the 37th Regiment, the third temporary commander of the brigade since Lane had been wounded.[4]

On August 11, 1864, only two weeks before he was killed, Sergeant Samuel Speer Harding wrote to his mother from Chapin's Farm. He reported that Lieutenant Thomas and Private T.G. Scott had gone to Richmond to see his brother, Greenberry Harding, who was in a hospital there. "Berry" was doing very well, and was to be released in about 10 days. "Berry" had been wounded in the shoulder. A doctor attempted to get the ball out, but only got out a piece of bone. (Berry would carry that bullet with him to his grave.) Sam mentioned that he had also written letters to his father, his sister Ruth, and his brother Boone, but had received letters from none of them.[5]

Sam Harding wrote about the war as best he could, providing his parents with news that the Union's General Grant was extending his line on the Confederates' left along the Weldon Railroad. Some believed that Grant was reinforcing Sherman's forces at the Augusta Court House, and that Grant was also sending part of his forces into the Shenandoah Valley. Confederate General Longstreet was reported to have gone to the Valley with his corps, while General Ewell was going to keep "our brigade" near the "city guns on this side of the river." Sam believed that they would be at Petersburg as long as Grant remained. However, it was believed that Grant had about given up on capturing Petersburg, and would soon leave. He foresaw Grant's move to take Richmond: "It seems like Richmond is a hard road to travel...."[6]

In closing, Sam inquired about the Harding slaves, and asked his mother to tell them "I send howdy to them." Should he be wounded, Sam said he would get "some Friend to write."[7]

Having failed to break through the Confederate fortifications at Petersburg, Grant took another course of action and began assaulting both ends of the Confederate line. Lee had to spread his men further both north and south to meet the Federal threat. Grant moved two Federal corps and a unit of cavalry north of the James River in another attempt to outflank Lee's line between Fussell's Mill and White Oak Swamp.[8]

Fussell's Mill (Deep Bottom II, New Market Road, White's Tavern, Gravel Hill, Charles City Road), August 16, 1864

Forces Engaged: Corps

Principal Commanders: Maj. Gen. Winfield Scott Hancock (Union), Gen. Robert E. Lee and Maj. Gen. Charles Field (Confederate)

Estimated Casualties: 4,600 total

Results: Confederate victory

On the night of August 13–14, Union Corps II and X and Gregg's Cavalry division, commanded by Hancock, crossed the James River at Deep Bottom and posed a threat to Richmond. On August 14, the X Corp surrounded New Market Heights, and the II Corps extended the Federal line along Bailey's Creek. During the night, the X Corps shifted to the far right near Fussell's Mill. On August 16, Union assaults there were initially successful, but Confederate counterattacks drove the Federals out of the works they had captured. Heavy fighting continued throughout the day. Confederate General John Chambliss was killed during the Charles City Road fighting. The Federals returned to the south side of the James on August 20, and maintained their position at Deep Bottom.[9]

After being defeated on the Jerusalem Plank Road, Major General Winfield Scott Hancock, with other infantry and cavalry support, moved north across the James River to attack the Confederate fortifications southeast of Richmond near Fussell's Mill on August 16.[10] Undetected as they moved through in a dense forest about 10 A.M., the Federals got within 50 yards of the Confederate works before they launched their attack. The Confederates repelled the first assault but during a second try, Mahone's Georgia Brigade fled to the rear. This caused Lane's Brigade problems, and soon both the Georgians and the Carolina boys had moved to the rear in disorder. The Federals poured into the gap, confident that they were now on their way to Richmond.[11]

Under the direction of Colonel Barbour, the brigade was reformed on the Darbytown Road and together with McGowan's Brigade and Field's Division launched a counterattack. Barbour was wounded, but Adjutant General E.J. Hale took over and ordered the troops to move forward "at the double-quick." With a Rebel yell, the Confederates drove the Federals back. Hale called the attack "one of the most brilliant charges of the war," and it did gain them a large number of prisoners and needed supplies. Wilcox praised the two brigades of the Light Division as having "distinguished themselves highly." Hale reported that "all the army are complimenting us."[12]

After the Confederates counterattacked, part of the Union II Corps fled in panic. Hancock called off the advance on Richmond and Lieutenant General Grant permitted Hancock's forces to remain on the defense until August 20, when they returned to the south side of the James River.[13]

The encounter at Fussell's Mill was the first time the brigade had come up against black soldiers. These Union soldiers made up a high percentage of the captives. With their new uniforms and shiny shoes, it was evident that these new soldiers had probably been put into action with only brief training and no previous battle experience.[14]

Casualties

Casualties in Lane's Brigade at Fussell's Mill, August 16–18, 1864, totaled 89. Two officers and six men were killed, five officers and 49 men wounded, one officer and 26 men were missing or captured.[15]

One of those captured at Fussell's Mill was Private Thomas G. Hall (Co. F, 28th Regiment). Hall was taken prisoner about August 16, 1864, and sent to the Federal prison camp at Point Lookout, Maryland. He remained there until March 18, 1865, when he was paroled and exchanged.[16]

After their success at Fussell's Mill, Wilcox's Light Division followed the enemy and moved south of the James River to take a position along the Confederate right at Petersburg. The Federals, while blocked at Fussell's Mill, succeeded in capturing part of the Weldon Railroad below Petersburg on August 19.[17]

Although they were not involved in the first battle along the Weldon railroad, Wilcox's Light Division, including Lane's Brigade (and the 28th North Carolina), would soon be engaged in heavy fighting for control of the Weldon Railroad at Reams' Station.

Reams' Station, August 25, 1864

Forces Engaged: Corps

Principal Commanders: Maj. Gen. Winfield Scott Hancock (Union), Maj. Gen. Henry Heth (Confederate)

Estimated Casualties: 3,492 total

Results: Confederate victory

Preceded by Gregg's Federal cavalry division, on August 24 the Union II Corps moved south along the Weldon Railroad and tore up tracks as they went. On August 25, Heth launched a Confederate attack and captured the Union position at Reams' Station. The Union II Corps was shattered, and withdrew to establish a line near the Globe Tavern.[18]

The battle at Reams' Station on August 25, 1864, was a Confederate victory that seldom appears in print. The Confederate forces stopped Union general Hancock's II Corps from destroying the Petersburg-Weldon Railroad. If they had succeeded, it would have become difficult for General Lee to obtain supplies from North Carolina for his Army of Northern Virginia. Another rail line that ran from Petersburg to Norfolk was already blocked by Union forces. A third railroad was the Southside Railroad, which ran west out of Petersburg.[19]

The action at Reams' Station was precipitated by the advance of Major General Governor K. Warren's V Corps south. They moved along the Petersburg & Weldon Railroad about 3½ miles below Petersburg, where Warren's Federal troops had already demolished a long stretch of the railroad. The V Corps pulled up more railroad tracks, burned the ties, and heated the rails until they could be twisted to form a Maltese cross, the badge of V Corps.[20]

On August 21, Grant ordered Hancock's men to move to the railroad and to relieve Warren's Corps. Grant planned to have Hancock's II Corps continue the destruction of the railroad to Reams' Station (from four miles below Globe Tavern) then onward for four more miles south of Reams' Station.[21]

Hancock's men were worn out from the fighting north of the James River. He should have protested and told Grant, but he did not, and tried to obey Grant's orders. Hancock left General Gershom Mott's command at Petersburg, and sent Barlow's and Gibbon's men south from the besieged city. The tired Union soldiers moved southward after an all-night march from

Confederate fortifications around Petersburg (Library of Congress, LC-B8171 1071).

Deep Bottom. Many of them fell by the way from utter exhaustion. Those Federals that did reach the point where the railroad was being torn up, stacked their arms and, without rest, began to work at further destruction with levers, axes and crowbars. The troops of V Corps of the 1st Division worked for three days, and tore up tracks for a distance of three miles below Reams' Station.[22]

Early on August 24, Major General John Gibbon's division moved to the rear of Warren's Corps and occupied a horseshoe-shaped line of earthworks a short distance south of Reams' Station. These works had been constructed in late June by Meade's VI Corps, but were poorly planned and badly located. The line of Federal earthworks ran south about 700 yards, and with two parallel returns, each about 1,000 yards. These met at an acute angle which left the Federals exposed to fire from the Confederates. Gibbon tried to improve the defenses by constructing abatis and digging deep rifle pits inside the works.[23]

The night of August 24, an officer from a New Jersey regiment speculated on how soon an attack would come, confident that the Confederate troops would not allow them to continue their destruction of this vital railroad.[24] That officer was correct and the attack came with a fury the next day in the form of the North Carolina brigades commanded by Major General Cadmus Wilcox.

A.P. Hill sent seven of his Confederate brigades, including Lane's, from his corps south from their positions near Petersburg the night of August 24th. The troops took a roundabout way and moved down the Boydton Plank Road before turning eastwards. By morning on the 25th of August, they were only three miles from Hancock's position along the Weldon Railroad at Reams' Station.[25]

The First Assault

While the Confederates kept up a steady bombardment of the Federal works, Wilcox ordered his troops to strike and sent in the brigades of Lane and Scales, backed up by Anderson's Brigade. The fourth brigade of Wilcox's Division was sent south to support Wade Hampton's cavalry. At about 2 P.M., Wilcox gave the signal to attack, and he troops did so with "wild, weird yells," according to the Federals soldiers behind the earthworks.[26]

Initially, the Confederates failed in their attack and, according to historian Longacre, the "bulk of Lane's, Scales' and supporting troops scrambled back into the woods." However, Wilcox ordered a second attack about 3 P.M.[27]

The Second Assault

After a heavy artillery bombardment of Hancock's men, another attack was launched which was made up of North Carolina soldiers—the brigades of Lane, John R. Cook and William McRae. In front of Lane and Cook was a network of abatis constructed by the Federals.[28]

Major Samuel N. Stowe described the movements of the 28th Regiment, which was flanked by the 7th North Carolina Regiment on their left, and the 37th on their right. The brigade was halted and formed on the right of the Reams' Station road temporarily, then moved forward by the right flank a quarter of a mile. They halted after forming a line of battle to support other troops, which soon became engaged with the enemy. Some time later, other troops passed them to form on their right. The 28th was formed by moving to the left upon their line. Eventually, the entire line charged the enemy's works. The ground was difficult to pass over, and there were dense obstructions. As they approached the enemy works at an angle, the 28th was badly exposed to gunfire. For a short time, the 28th failed to advance as rapidly as other troops on the right. However, eventually the 28th was able to carry everything before them.[29]

There were heavy casualties on both sides of the earthworks. Over the next two hours, the Confederate sharpshooters kept up their fire. Some were even up in the trees, and from such an advantageous position they felled the enemy with much success.[30]

Major Stowe reported that at about 4:30 P.M., his regiment (the 28th), positioned on the right of the brigade, was ordered to join with the left of General Cook's men. Once that was done, the regiment formed into a line of assault, and the order to advance was given. The regiment moved forward and a portion of them entered the enemy's breastworks with the left wing of Cook's Brigade. They then pursued the enemy about ⅓ of a mile beyond the railroad to a battery. The advance was slow, but eventually the achieved what he believed was "to be the greatest victory of the war."[31]

The Union general Hancock saw that he was in a perilous position and he sent for reinforcements. Those reinforcements sent by Meade were ordered to go by the Jerusalem Plank Road, which doubled the distance and delayed their arrival. Meade did not send any troops from Warren's Corps, which was the nearest, for fear that the Confederate forces would be able to get between the forces of Hancock and Warren.[32]

The Third Assault

Lieutenant Colonel W.J. Pegram's artillery pounded the Union position, and a third assault was launched against the northwestern angle. About 5 o'clock, the Confederate guns stopped and the infantry rushed in. With Anderson's brigade on the flank, supported in the rear by Sanders and Weisiger, the Confederate forces of Cooke, MacRae, Lane, and Scales attacked with a determination that the earlier attacks had lacked. Under their combined assault, two sections of the Union line of Major General Nelson A. Miles' troops gave way, and five New York regiments fled in panic.[33]

Reportedly, Captain Gold Holland of the 28th North Carolina moved ahead of his company and was one of the first of his regiment to mount the enemy's works. Suddenly finding himself alone and facing the enemy, he bluffed the Yankees, and yelled, "Yanks, if you know what is best for you, you will make a blue streak toward sunset." Incredibly, the Union troops believed him and did what he asked. The commander of the 37th North Carolina, to the right of the 28th, reported how easily the prisoners were captured at this point. With few exceptions, the prisoners had only to be directed which way to go. Those Yankees who failed to make a "blue streak," threw themselves on the ground and surrendered.[34]

Captain Holland was a remarkable man and a lucky soldier. Before the war he had been a postmaster and a magistrate in Cleveland County, North Carolina. At 42, he was older than the age that conscripts were taken. Yet, he had volunteered and enlisted as a private in Company H. Promoted to captain in August of 1862, Holland soon won the admiration of his comrades. In addition to the standard knapsack, Holland sometimes carried a frying pan and a camp stool. He remained healthy throughout the war, and was never wounded. In the summer of 1864, he was suddenly placed in command of the regiment. As they advanced toward the enemy under heavy gunfire, Holland rushed to the front line with his sword in his right hand and his frying pan in his left, to shout at his men: "I command the Twenty-eighth North Carolina regiment — men, follow me." Without hesitation, his men obeyed his command.[35]

Some of Holland's exploits were also noted in the regimental history. After the battle of Fredericksburg in December of 1862, Captain Holland told General James H. Lane about his escape, and that he owed his life to a biscuit. Holland then pulled out a large camp biscuit from his haversack in which a Yankee bullet was half imbedded. Cooked without any salt or shortening, the biscuit was so hard that even a bullet could not penetrate it.[36]

In his *History of North Carolina*, Samuel A'Court Ashe described the battle at Reams' Station as "a brilliant feat of arms." Ashe tallied the spoils of war taken by the Confederates, which included 12 stands of colors, 9 guns, and 3,000 stands of arms. Ashe believed that the Union's General Hancock had lost between 600 and 700 killed, and had 2,150 taken prisoner.[37] A.P. Hill reported that his men had captured 3,100 small arms, nine cannon, and 12 colors from the Federal units.[38]

The Union II Corps tried to shift responsibility for the defeat away from themselves. They began circulating the story that the Confederates outnumbered Hancock's force by 2 or 3 to 1. Actually, the Union forces outnumbered the attacking Confederates about 1,000 to 2,000 men.[39]

With the four brigades of Major General Henry Heth, and those of Brigadier General John R. Cooke and William MacRae, plus men from Major General Mahone's division, commanded by Brigadier Generals J.C.C. Sanders and D.A. Weisiger, one historian has estimated that the Confederates had a force of about 13,000 men at Reams' Station. If this is true, the Confederates outnumbered the Union troops, who reportedly had only 6,000 infantry and 2,000 cavalry.[40] However, of the 6,500 men who left Petersburg under A.P. Hill , only 4,500 to 5,000 of them arrived at Reams' Station before the battle ended.[41]

The Federal defeat at Reams' Station tarnished the military record of Union General

Winfield Scott Hancock. His men had been surprised when a strong Confederate force attacked them, and a large number of Union soldiers did not put up much resistance before being captured.[42] The dashing Brigadier General John Hunt Morgan, the Confederate cavalry officer who had escaped prison by digging a tunnel out of the Ohio State Penitentiary, recalled hearing of a statement made by General Hancock when things were going badly for the Federal troops. In the midst of the battle, Hancock stood with his hand on a staff officer's shoulder and said: "Colonel, I do not care to die, but I pray to God I may never leave this field." This battle was the last time Hancock took an active part.[43]

The Union defeat can be attributed to a combination of factors. One of Hancock's staff officers wrote that by August of 1864 (before the second battle at Reams' Station), all three divisions of the Army of the Potomac were "worn out by excessive exertions ... their better officers and braver sergeants and men nearly all killed or in the hospital, regiments reduced to a captain's command, companies often to a corporal's guard...."[44] Hancock's assistant adjutant general stated said, "Reams' Station was but a nightmare and a hideous dream."[45] For some time after the battle, the men of Lane's Brigade joked among themselves that Grant would have to send Hancock back up North to recruit an entirely new command.[46]

A.P. Hill's Corps (including the 28th) played a major part in the victory at Reams' Station. Hill had again demonstrated the offensive power the Light Division had shown under "Stonewall" Jackson. While Hill had not always used good judgment, at Reams' Station he exhibited all of which he was capable, and it was probably his greatest victory.[47]

However, that victory was tempered by the loss of many good Confederate officers and their men.[48] Broken down by brigades, Lane's Brigade lost 12 killed, 97 wounded, and 6 missing. McGowan's Brigade lost 2 killed and 20 wounded, and Anderson's Brigade lost at least 2 killed and 27 wounded, but not over 50 casualties.[49]

Initially, Wilcox had stated that his entire loss in his division was 200, while McGowan's slight with only a total of 22. Lane's Brigade had the most casualties; Scales and Anderson had few. Later, Wilcox revised the number of casualties to tally over 300, which included 115 casualties in Lane's Brigade alone. Historian and author John Horn, in his book *The Destruction of the Weldon Railroad*, believed that Wilcox's tendency to revise his reports, sometimes years after their initial writing, left his credibility in question.[50] Horn cites the report of Major Samuel Stowe which gave casualties in the 28th North Carolina as 6 killed and 31 wounded.[51] Historian S.A. Ashe wrote that A.P. Hill only listed about 750 casualties, and most of those were from Lane's Brigade.[52] Those figures are slightly higher than Lee initially reported the day after the battle, as seen below.

General Robert E. Lee's official dispatch regarding the battle can be found in the diary entry of Catherine Devereaux Edmondston for August 29, 1864, published in *Journal of a Secesh Lady:*

Headquarters ANV, August 26, 1864

Hon. J. A. Seddon — Gen A P Hill attacked the enemy in his entrenchments at Reams' Station yesterday evening & on the second assault carried his whole entire line. Cooks & McRae's NC Brigades under Heth's & Lane's N C Brigade & Wilcox's Division under Connor with Pegram's Artillery composed the assaulting column. One line of breastworks was carried by the cavalry under Hampton with great gallantry which contributed largely to our success. Seven stands of colours, 2000 prisoners, & nine pieces of Artillery are in our possession. Loss of the enemy in killed & wounded is reported heavy, ours relatively small. Our profound gratitude is due to the Giver of all victories & our thanks to the brave men & officers engaged.

[Signed] R.E. Lee, General.[53]

Mrs. Edmondston received a note from her husband, Patrick Edmondston, about the fight at Reams' Station, and which was "ill omened news," in spite of "the blood shed at Reams' the Yankees still hold the R R at that point."[54]

A few days later, on September 6, 1864, Mrs. Edmondston wrote in her diary the official report of casualties at Reams' Station on September 25, 1864. General A.P. Hill's corrected report stated: "We captured 12 stands of colours, 9 pieces of Artillery, 10 caissons, 2150 prisoners, 3100 stands of arms, & 32 horses."[55] Hill's own losses in cavalry, artillery, and infantry were "720 men (seven hundred & twenty) killed, wounded & missing." Hill noted that the charge of the North Carolina troops on the breastworks "was magnificent, gallant almost beyond record even in this war of gallant deeds! Pegram turned the enemy's own guns on them with terrible effect," and fired "'second fuses' on the retreating mass doing great execution."[56]

Unsubstantiated rumors as well as actual facts about the battle appeared in a Petersburg newspaper on August 27. The paper noted that General Wade Hampton's cavalry had attacked a body of Yankee cavalry who were attempting to destroy the Weldon railroad about "four miles beyond Reams' station." Hampton's cavalry routed the Yankees and drove them back. About 5 o'clock A.P. Hill's Corps attacked and "after a severe fight of two hours captured the enemy works, about two thousand prisoners and nine pieces of artillery." The Petersburg press noted that the enemy "fought with more than his usual bravery," and that the Confederate troops were stopped in their advance at one point, and had to wait until support came up. Then they rallied and with "irresistible fury charged the enemy from his works," which the Confederates took over.[57]

The 28th North Carolina Regiment suffered many casualties among the men. Several of the officers were killed. Major Stowe believed the "sacrifice was truly fearful" with the loss of Colonel William H. Asbury Speer, who had been mortally wounded. There were other irreplaceable losses: Captain I.T. Smith of Company B, and five enlisted men were killed instantly. Six other officer were wounded, and 24 were badly injured in the battle.[58]

Colonel Speer died from his head wound either on August 27 or August 29, 1864.[59] In a letter to William Harding, Private Thomas G. Scott noted that Colonel Speer had been "shot though the head," and that his friend, Sergeant Samuel S. Harding, was dead. Scott was sorry to lose both "my Col. and Sergeant."[60]

Sergeant Harding, of Company I, 28th Regiment, was among those killed in the fighting along the Weldon Railroad at Reams' Station, on August 25, 1865.[61] Harding and Colonel W.H.A. Speer were distantly related, and both from Yadkin County. After the battle, Private T.G. Scott, also of the 28th Regiment, wrote to William Harding, Sam's father, to convey the sad news that his oldest son had been "shot through the hip." He promised to keep "Sammy's" things until William could come after them.[62] Had Sergeant Harding been gut shot, which was likely if shot in the hip, he could have lingered and endured a long and very painful death. Fortunately, Sam Harding did not survive very long after he was wounded.

Mr. Harding lived in Yadkin County, North Carolina, quite some distance from Petersburg. After receiving notification of Sam's death, his father and youngest son, 9-year-old Thomas Renny Harding, drove a wagon to Petersburg, Virginia, to retrieve his body. They returned with the remains and Samuel Harding was buried in the Speer-Harding Cemetery off Old Hwy. 421, about 3 miles east of Yadkinville.

George Washington Blakely (Company F, 28th Regiment) was

Tombstone for Sergeant Samuel Speer Harding in Yadkin County. Harding was killed at Reams' Station, August 25, 1864. Photograph by Frances H. Casstevens.

wounded at Reams' Station but survived, returned home to Yadkin County and lived until 1923. Having lost part of his hand, Blakely received a pension from North Carolina.[63]

While under the command of Brigadier General James Conner, Lane's Brigade was one of the three North Carolina brigades to assault Union General Hancock's troops in their entrenched position at Reams' Station. Their performance at Reams' Station motivated General Lee to write a letter to North Carolina Governor Vance about the gallantry of Cooke's, McRae's and Lane's brigades. He also told General Lane, when Lane rejoined his command just before the battle at Jones' Farm, that the gallantry of those three brigades "had placed not only North Carolina, but the whole Confederacy, under a debt of gratitude which could never be repaid."[64]

Lee mentioned that Lane's Brigade had advanced through a ticket of abatis made from trees, under the heavy fire from both musketry and artillery. They had captured the enemy's works with "a steady courage" that brought praise from corps and division commanders and the whole army.[65] To Governor Vance, Lee wrote, "I have frequently been called upon to mention the services of North Carolina soldiers in the army, but their gallantry and conduct were never more deserving of admiration than in the engagement at Reams' Station."[66]

Samuel A'Court Ashe cited a Major Stedman's observations: "Unshaken by the fall of Vicksburg and the disaster at Gettysburg, undismayed amidst the general gloom which was settling upon the fortunes of the South, these North Carolina regiments exhibited the same enthusiasm and valor which had marked their conduct upon every field where they stood for the honor, glory and renown of their State."[67]

When writing his history of Company C of the 28th, 1st Lieutenant Junius Pinkney Little was convinced that one of the "hardest fought battles in defense of Petersburg was on July [August] 25 1864 at Ream's and Malone's stations." Little stated that Heth's Division and Lane's Brigade had advanced under cover from the heavy guns of Pegram's battery, until they were "directly in front of the [enemy's] works." They then made a rush at the enemy which resulted in the capture of "the whole line — not however before the enemy had been driven off in a desperate hand to hand struggle in the works, in which clubs, muskets and bayonets were used freely." Little counted Confederate losses at 720, and Federal losses at 2,000.[68]

Brigadier General James H. Lane, having been absent for three months while recovering from the wound he received at Cold Harbor, rejoined his brigade to take command after the fight at Reams' Station.[69]

The regimental history of the 28th North Carolina does not give any casualty figures after the battles fought at Gravel Hill on July 28, 1864, through the end of the war.[70]

Reams' Station Today

Today, at the battlefield of Reams' Station about 200 yards of the original breastworks can be seen. The "angle" where the Confederates attacked their enemy still exists. The remains of the Oak Grove Church can be found in the woods, and the railroad bed is still in that same location.[71]

Grant, with superior forces, continued to launch dual attacks at Confederate positions. Again, he sent troops north of the James River to attack Lee's Confederate forces at Chaffin's Bluff, while also sending men against the Southside Railroad below Petersburg. Lee did not have enough men to meet attacks on two fronts, so he resorted to shuffling men from one position to another.[72]

Unless Grant's men could be driven back to the Weldon Railroad, they would have a great advantage. A.P. Hill came up with a plan. To accomplish his goal, he needed the brigades of Lane and McGowan and Heth's Division. While the two brigades approached the enemy at the Pegram Farm, MacRae and Archer withdrew during the night to join Heth's Division in a flank-

Jones' Farm (Pegram's Farm, Peeble's Farm, Poplar Springs Church), September 30–October 2, 1864

Forces Engaged: Corps

Principal Commanders: Maj. Gen. George G. Meade, Maj. Gen. John G. Parke, and Maj. Gen. G.K. Warren (Union), Lt. Gen. A.P. Hill (Confederate)

Estimated Casualties: 3,800 total

Results: Union victory

Grant extended his left flank to cut the Confederate communication lines southwest of Petersburg. Two divisions of the IX Corps and two division of the V Corps, plus Gregg's cavalry, took part in this encounter. On September 30, the Federal troops moved via Poplar Springs Church to the Vaughan Road. The initial Federal attack overran Fort Archer and flanked the Confederates from their line on Squirrel Level Road. Late in the afternoon, Confederate reinforcements arrived. On October 1, the Federals repulsed the Confederate counterattack of A.P. Hill. Reinforced by Mott's II Corps, the Federals resumed their advance on October 2, and captured Fort McRae. They extended their left flank to the vicinity of Peeble's and Pegram's farms. Afterwards, Meade suspended his offensive movement, and a new line was formed from the Federal works on the Weldon Railroad to Pegram's Farm.

ing maneuver. They moved down Squirrel Level Road against the end of the Federal salient. Lane and McGowan were to appear to make a move in front of the Federal works to distract their attention from Heth while he moved his command against the opposite flank.[73]

Having just sent troops to recapture Fort Harrison near Chaffin's Bluff, when Lee learned of an attack on the Southside Railroad, he pulled those troops back across the James River.

On the morning of September 30, Lane's Brigade was ordered to move to the north side of the James River to support Confederate troops who were engaged there. Lane's Brigade, with the rest of Wilcox's Division and that of Heth, moved to Confederate works just north of the Jones' Farm on the Church Road.[74]

Captain G.G. Holland, temporarily in command of the 28th Regiment, reported that on September 30, the 28th Regiment received orders to march from the vicinity of Petersburg along the Boydton Plank Road. After three miles they formed a line of battle in the existing works on the Jones' Farm, about 600 yards southwest of the Jones house. There was a small ravine between. Shortly after their arrival, the enemy skirmishers approached and the 28th and other regiments of the brigade moved forward across the ravine to form a line of battle.[75]

The Federals had already driven the Confederate cavalry pickets back when Wilcox arrived with his men. He ordered his sharpshooters to moved forward to cover the movement of the main body of troops. Major Thomas J. Wooten formed a skirmish line and advanced, but his line had not come within 200 yards of Jones' Farm when he encountered enemy troops. McGowan's sharpshooters assisted, and they were able to drive the enemy from the vicinity of the farmhouse. They even managed to capture several Federal prisoners.[76]

When Wooten encountered the Federal line of battle, he had to withdraw his sharpshooters. However, his actions had given Lane and McGowan time to move into a shallow ravine on both sides of the Church Road, with MacRae and Archer of Heth's Division supporting their rear. With everyone in position, they charged the Federal line.[77]

The brigades under Lane and McGowan succeeded in driving the Federal troops back and enveloped both of the enemy flanks. After a brief fight, the Federals broke and fled in confusion. The Confederates were able to confiscate much-needed oilcloths, blankets, knapsacks and other equipment abandoned by the fleeing enemy. Lane concluded in his report, "I never saw a richer battlefield."[78]

With the 37th on the right of the 28th, and the 7th on their left, the 28th was again ordered to move forward. They met the enemy near the Jones house and "drove them full well to Pegram's House," ¼ mile away (or one mile according to McDaid.[79]) During the engagement, Captain Lovill, who was commanding the regiment, was badly wounded, and Holland was asked to take command.[80]

This attack did not turn out as well as it should have. MacRae's Brigade rushed forward, rather than remain to support Lane's Brigade, and the two groups became so mixed up their officers lost control. The 18th made an attempt at the Federal position near the Pegram Farm, but with no support, their attack was repulsed.[81]

When night came, the 28th and others were ordered to fall back to the Jones house, where they slept. The next morning the 28th marched back to the Pegram house and formed into the same positions as they had held the day before. They constructed some temporary works and after a short time, the Confederate battery opened fire on the enemy. The sharpshooters charged and captured the works in Pegram's yard, then the brigade moved forward to occupy those works.[82]

Casualties

Casualties in the fighting at Jones' Farm amounted to 111 men. Lane had 1 officer and 8 men killed; 10 officers and 87 men wounded; and 5 men missing/captured.[83] However, Lane's Brigade captured nearly 500 prisoners, and a number of the enemy were killed or wounded.[84]

At day's end, the brigade was ordered to remove to the works at Petersburg. Captain Holland reported that the "Officers and men did their part nobly." The 28th Regiment had captured 28 prisoners, for which "receipts were given," and a large number of prisoners for which "no receipts were given." Holland noted that losses in the 28th Regiment were 2 men killed, 26 wounded, and 2 officers wounded.[85]

Lane complimented his aide, Lieutenant Everard B. Meade, and his brigade inspector, Captain E.T. Nicholson — "two accomplished officers and gentlemen" — who had been of great assistance, since Lane had not entirely recovered from his injury, and could not move "about rapidly."[86]

Colonel William Barbour was mortally wounded before the attack began on September 30. He died three days later. Colonel William Davidson of the 7th Regiment was dismissed from his command "for unsoldierly conduct in action." The specifics of this charge are not known, but previously he had been convicted of drunkenness while on duty, and this may have been the case in this instance.[87]

When darkness fell, Lane's Brigade moved back to the edge of the woods, on the Jones House side, where they slept on their arms that night.[88]

The Federals remained in the vicinity of the Pegram Farm. Although Lee's men had saved the Southside Railroad, Grant had managed to extend his lines, and Lee would also have to extend his lines to the right to prevent his flank from being turned.[89]

October 1, 1864

On the morning of October 1, 1864, Lane's Brigade left Jones' Farm and formed a line of battle in the woods they had occupied the previous evening. They prepared defensive works while they awaited Heth's signal that the attack on the left had begun.

Heth's artillery opened fire on the Federal position, and brigade sharpshooters advanced against the Federal fortifications alongside the Pegram Farm. The sharpshoots gained the fortifications and captured 200 prisoners. Lane estimated the enemy's dead at about 250, which would probably mean they had at least 1,750 wounded. The main body of his troops captured

500 prisoners. In the cellar of the Jones house, a "big-dog" (a high-ranking Federal officer), 60 privates and one officer were captured by one of his regiments.[90]

The main force moved forward behind the sharpshooters, in a hard rain while sustaining fire on their flank from the enemy.[91] Wooten's sharpshooters captured twice as many prisoners as they had men. Unfortunately, Brander's artillery turned their guns on them, believing them to be the enemy approaching. They fired several rounds before realizing their mistake. Some of the Yankee prisoners were wounded and a few killed, but the sharpshooters were not injured. General Wilcox came close to being killed by friendly fire at this time.[92]

Lane and McGowan had done their job, but Heth failed to make any headway along his line. Heth found the enemy in a well-fortified position across the Squirrel Level Road. He sent his brigades forward, but they failed to overrun the Federal position. By night, Hill admitted defeat and pulled back all of his brigades, and left the Federal troops in control of most of the ground they had gained west of the Weldon Railroad.[93]

Lane praised his brigade as having "behaved nobly in these two engagements [Jones' Farm, Pegram house], and again [having] proved themselves worthy of the high esteem of our Commanding General."[94]

Casualties

Casualties in Lane's Brigade at Pegram's Farm on October 1, 1864, totaled 12 (4 men killed, 8 men wounded).[95] Lane reported that during that his brigade had fought behind "breastworks only once, and then only for a short time." Instead, they had charged the "enemy's works four times," and they had been involved in several "flank movements." "I have just cause to be proud of my command," Lane said in October of 1864. " It [his brigade] has a splendid reputation in the army."[96]

Casualties, Summer–Fall of 1864

Total casualties in Lane's Brigade from May 5, 1864, at Wilderness to October 1, 1864, at Pegram's Farm were 1,618. One hundred twenty-one officers were killed or wounded, plus 1,497 men were killed or wounded. At least 589 were missing, which included 23 officers and 566 men.[97] As the war progressed and more of the officers of the 28th Regiment were either killed or wounded, it became more difficult to obtain reports and casualty lists.

The fighting at Pegram's Farm was the last major action involving the 28th Regiment. In mid–November, the regiment set up winter quarters behind the fortifications facing the Jones' Farm. The men built huts on each side of the road leading to the Jones house. The right side of their encampment stopped near the house of the widow Banks; the left extended beyond a small dam which had been built across a stream in front of the Confederate works.[98]

Chapter 14

Winter 1864–Spring 1865:
Petersburg to Appomattox

> *Lee surrendered the remnant of the grandest*
> *army of fighting men the world ever produced.*
> —1st Lieutenant J.P. Little[1]

Winter of 1864–1865

The winter of 1864–1865 brought hardships to the remainder of the Confederate Army. That winter was particularly cold and wet. Captain Nicholas Gibbon believed that the Confederate soldiers who endured that winter would always remember it.[2]

Much of the winter days were spent in constructing new or improving existing fortifications. The 28th was also saddled with the task of maintaining a strong picket line in front of their positions both day and night. The Federal picket lines were usually only a few hundred yards away. This danger, coupled with a very harsh winter, made picket duty a very unpleasant task, especially when the men lacked warm clothing, blankets and shoes. Because of these conditions, men were detailed for picket duty only every third or fourth day.[3]

Jarratt's Station Skirmish, December 8–9, 1864

On December 8, 1864, Lane's Brigade and the rest of Hill's Corps were ordered to move out of camp to Belfield to stop continued Federal attempts to destroy the Weldon Railroad south of Petersburg. The men marched through sleet and snow to a point just a few miles from Belfield before they learned that the Union forces had already left. Hill then attempted to cut off the enemy's retreat. His men intercepted some Federal cavalry at Jarratt's Station and, after a brief skirmish, the Confederates continued onward. However, most of the Federal troops were several hours ahead of them, and they were not successful in overtaking the enemy.[4]

The soldiers could not have had worse conditions in which to march. The weather turned bitterly cold. Snow began to fall, and then turned into freezing rain. A cold wind was blowing, and some of the thinly clad soldiers were almost barefoot. Lane described seeing two such soldiers with their toes exposed to the elements, because the upper portion of their shoes had separated from the soles. Lane talked to the men and learned that one was from east Florida and one from the middle of Florida. He told them he had once lived in west Florida. The pair hated the Virginia weather, and one asked Lane, "Mister, ain't Florida a great place? There the trees stay green all the time, and we have oranges and lemons, and figs and bananas, and it is the greatest country for taters you ever did see."[5] Lane probably agreed with them.

A North Carolina soldier in Lane's Brigade saw another Florida soldier who was barefoot walking over the frozen ground. The soldier with shoes looked at the Floridian and said, "Look here, mister, I don't know who you are, but I can't stand that." He then reached into his knapsack and pulled out a new pair of shoes, put them on, and gave his old shoes to the man who had none. After the exchange was made, the boys in the brigade cheered the kind-hearted "Tar Heel."[6]

By the time Lane and his troops reached the railroad, the Federals had already torn up 16 miles of track and left, and there was no enemy to fight. The return march to camp was even more arduous. The frozen ground made it hard for the soldiers to stand up and many kept slipping and falling down. That night when they stopped to camp, the men had to clear snow and ice from around the campfire in order make a place to sleep. The wet clothes and frozen blankets made the men even more miserable.[7]

Lane and Hill's men returned to camp at Hatcher's Run on December 13, 1864. The 28th Regiment saw no further action during the remainder of 1864.[8] Brigadier General Lane recalled that they returned to camp "as tired and stiff a set of beings as ever were seen." At their camp, they received another blow when they saw that all the chimneys that had been erected to warm their shelters had been "torn down and carried off." Again, the men were forced to camp outside around the campfire.[9]

Brigadier General Lane and Lieutenant Meade spent the winter living in two tents which had been joined together. The back tent was used for sleeping, and the front one, "which has a nice brick chimney," served as the sitting room. A plank floor was added, and the tent contained a "bedstead and blankets, two trunks and a clothes pole (suspended from the ridge pole)," which made an excellent ventilated wardrobe. "In the living quarters tent, Lane had added an "old camp-table, a few chairs, an old bent tin candle-stick, and inkstand and pens, tobacco and pipes," which sometimes created a "great deal of smoke." He would have preferred to have his quarters surrounded by a "wattled cedar fence to keep off the winds."[10]

Later, Lane wrote that a "mantle-piece" had been added to the chimney, the stables had been completed "just in time for the snow," and that the animals, including "Old Jim," were probably thankful. The "French bedstead" in Lane's sleeping tent had a mattress filled with "clean, fine straw, covered with an ample supply of blankets."[11]

Christmas that year was made a little more bearable when boxes arrived from home for the soldiers. But it was still a sad and depressing time. Alfred N. Profitt complained that Christmas was spent in the camp of the 28th Regiment with "no fun, nothing to drink, but little to eat." Even with items from home, rations were short, and two days of rations needed to be stretched to cover five to 6 days.[12]

It had been a year of almost continuous marching and fighting. Even though Lee's soldiers gave their all, Grant's Union troops were slowly wearing away at the Army of Northern Virginia and, inch by inch, gaining ground. The year had been a hard one, filled with more defeats than victories for Lee's men. From the fighting in the Wilderness in May to the last battle at Pegram's Farm, Lane's Brigade had suffered 1,618 casualties.[13]

Lee did not have enough manpower to take the offensive. He moved troops around in reaction to the offensive actions initiated by Grant. Whenever the Confederates had minor victories, these wins only stopped Grant temporarily, and all battles, whether victories or defeats, came with losses of men that the Confederacy could not replace.[14]

Draft Dodgers

Even when the Confederate government increased the age of military service to include all men from 17 through 50, not enough conscripts were brought into service to replace those who had been killed or wounded. Widespread draft dodging in North Carolina cut back on the number of conscripts, and made the lost soldiers difficult, if not impossible, to replace.[15] The draftees who were brought into military service were, according to James A. Graham, an officer in Hill's Corps, either "miserable cowards" or sympathizers with the peace movement in North Carolina.[16]

Losses from Desertion

The new conscripts were more of a liability than an asset. In the 18th Regiment, for example, of the 147 new recruits, 59 deserted between August 1864 and April 1865. Of the total number of desertions during that same period, 40 percent were new conscripts.[17]

Desertion in Lane's Brigade over a ten-day period in February of 1865 totaled 164 men, more than double the earlier peak reached in November of 1864.[18] Many of those who deserted were on picket duty, where it was easy to simply walk away unnoticed. In March of 1865, of the men on picket duty in Hill's Division, 18 deserted — 6 from Lane's Brigade, and 12 from Scales' Brigade.[19] Neither military officers nor Confederate authorities had any success in dealing with the problem of desertion.

On September 30, 1864, a report was issued from Wilcox's Division listing the number of men he could muster. At that time, the number "present effective for the field" totaled 4,955. Of that number, Lane's Brigade (one of the four that made up Wilcox's Division) could count 1,275 men present and ready for duty. Lane's Brigade was still composed of the 7th, 18th, 28th, 33rd, and 37th Regiments of North Carolina Infantry. The 28th was officially under the command of Major Samuel N. Stowe. Stowe had, however, retired to the Invalid Corps on July 8, 1864, because of "general debility," accompanied by a predisposition to "phthisis pulmonalis" (which usually meant consumption, and is called tuberculosis today).[20]

The Army of Northern Virginia was slipping away. A report issued on November 30, 1864, showed an effective number of 60,510 men present for duty out of a total 150,656 men. This figure covered the 1st, 2nd, and 3rd Corps, plus Anderson's Corps, and Hampton's Cavalry Corps, as well as those in the First Military District, Department of North Carolina and Southern Virginia (General Wise). Wilcox's Division (of Hill's 3rd Army Corps), had only 6,098 "effective present" for duty out of a total of 12,063 (both present and absent).[21]

Many of the soldiers were sick, tired and hungry. Sensing that the war was about over, they deserted and went home. One such soldier was William Henry Draughn, of Company A, 28th Regiment. Draughn had enlisted on March 18, 1864. He was present until he decided to go home, and was "arrested" on February 26, 1865. Two months later, the war was over, and he returned home to his wife and children. He later moved to Patrick County, Virginia.[22]

Siege of Petersburg

Captain Nicholas Gibbon recalled that there was almost "continual fighting" from the time the two armies were embroiled at Petersburg in June of 1864 until the trenches there were abandoned the night of April 2–3, 1865. He wrote in his memoirs that would never forget the "boom of the cannon and the crack of the sharpshooters rifles" which could be heard almost every minute of both day and night.[23]

Winter was not yet over when, early in February of 1865, Union General U.S. Grant moved his Federal troops to secure a position on the Boydton Plank Road at Hatcher's Run. Hill's Confederate troops attempted to prevent the enemy's advance. Wilcox's Division moved further to the right of the Confederate line to cover the extension of the Union lines.[24] Wilcox's Division consisted of four brigades: Lane's Brigade (commanded by Colonel John D. Barry), McGowan's Brigade (commanded by Brigadier General Samuel McGowan), Scales' Brigade (commanded by Brigadier General Alfred Moore Scales), and Thomas' Brigade (commanded by Brigadier General Edward L. Thomas).[25]

The beginning of the end to the fighting came when General Phil Sheridan moved his cavalry across the James River to Petersburg. This movement, which threatened the right flank of the Richmond-Petersburg defense, was stopped briefly on March 3, when Confederate forces under George E. Pickett drove Sheridan's cavalry back from Dinwiddie Court House. Pickett then moved to Five Forks and established a strong defensive position on the right of Lee's line.[26]

Fort Stedman, March 25, 1865

Forces Engaged: Corps

Principal Commanders: Maj. Gen. John G. Parke (Union), Gen. Robert E. Lee and Maj. Gen. John B. Gordon (Confederate)

Estimated Casualties: 3,850 total (950 Union, 2,900 Confederate)

Results: Union victory

In his last offensive action, General Robert E. Lee sent nearly half his army to try to break through Grant's position at Petersburg to threaten the Federal supply depot at City Point. Gordon launched a pre-dawn assault and overpowered the garrisons at Fort Stedman and Batteries X, XI, and XII. However, counterattacks by Major Generals Parke and Hartrantf stopped the breakthrough, and the Federals launched a heavy crossfire, which enabled them to cut off and capture more than 1,900 Confederates. During the day, part of the II and V Corps assaulted and then recaptured the entrenched picket lines in front of those forts.[27]

The Union army commander, U.S. Grant, put his plans to take Petersburg in motion when he sent the II and V Corps, along with Sheridan's cavalry, to outflank the right of Lee's line, and then to surround the Army of Northern Virginia.[28]

President Jefferson Davis insisted on directing the war. He ordered General R.E. Lee to take the offensive around Petersburg before the Federal forces could capture that city and move on to Richmond. Throughout the war, much time and effort had been put into protecting Richmond, the Confederate capital. While A.P. Hill, a corps commander, was absent because of sickness, General John Brown Gordon planned and led the assault on Fort Stedman. The plan involved the capture of a number of smaller forts behind Fort Stedman which, if taken, would allow the Confederates to fire on the Federal rear and allow the Confederate cavalry to get through.[29]

General Wilcox was also sick and Lane resumed command of his brigade and another brigade from the Light Division.[30] Gordon ordered Lane to remain in reserve along Lieutenant Run and to await further orders. Fortunately, Lane's men were not called on to participate.

The entire action was a disaster. At 4 A.M., the Confederates attacked and captured Fort Stedman. Gordon then sent three columns of 100 men each toward other nearby forts, but the assaulting force could not find them. A Federal counterattack from Hartranft's Division forced Gordon's men back into Fort Stedman. About 8 A.M., Lee gave the order to withdraw. However, by this time, the Federals were raining a heavy crossfire on the Confederates, and many chose to surrender rather than risk their lives trying to return to their positions at Petersburg.[31]

Casualties

Confederate loses were about 3,500, of whom nearly 2,000 were captured, while the Union troops lost only about 1,044.[32] Major General Meade continued the Federal assault later in the day. This additional fighting elevated the total casualties to between 4,400 and 5,000 Confederate losses, mostly men taken prisoner, compared to 2,080 Federal casualties.[33]

Returning to their old position, Lane found that the Federals had attacked that area while most of the Confederates had been engaged in the assault and capture of Fort Stedman. The entire Confederate skirmish line from Hatcher's Run to Lieutenant Run had been captured. Fighting ensued throughout the day, and the defenders of Petersburg eventually were able to reestablish their picket line, except for a small area in front of the left of Lane's line. This allowed enemy bombardment to hit the very area where Lane had his winter quarters.[34]

After Fort Stedman, Lane's Brigade returned to the trenches at Petersburg, and began skirmishing with the Federal forces. McGowan's Brigade, which had been positioned to the right of Lane's Brigade, was sent to assist in the attack at Dinwiddie Court House. Thus, with men removed from the trenches, those who remained were spread much too thin.[35]

On March 27, Lane was asked to dislodge the Federal troops on the hill in front of his line. The sharpshooters were to be used, but if they failed, Lane asked for two brigades of reinforcements. However, Major Wooten's sharpshooters did their job without casualties on their side. Lane expected the Union soldiers to counterattack, but they did not. Instead, they put a howitzer on the hill. Confederates shouted, "Yank, what are you doing there?" One Federal soldier replied, "Your Major Hooten [Wooten] is so fond of running up these hollows to break our line, we are putting a howitzer here to give him a warmer welcome the next time he comes."[36]

Battery Gregg and Hatcher's Run — April 1, 1865

On April 1, Phil Sheridan's Federal infantry cut the Confederate line at Five Forks between Pickett's men and Hatcher's Run, southwest of Petersburg. Pickett's troops were driven from the field with heavy casualties. The Federals took over 3,000 prisoners, and turned the Confederate right. This left a clear path to the rear of the defenses at Petersburg. The next day, the Federal forces launched an all-out attack on the Confederate line, and swept down the trenches at Petersburg.[37]

That same day, men from four of the regiments of Lane's Brigade were spaced from 6 to 10 paces along the works between Battery Gregg and Hatcher's Run. The regiments involved, from left to right, were: 28th, 37th, 18th, and 33rd. The men on the right of the 28th were near a "brown house in front of General [William] MacRae's winter quarters," and the left of the line of the 33rd was "on the branch at Mrs. Banks."[38]

The Federal forces began shelling Lane's line from several batteries about 9 o'clock at night, and the pickets in his front began firing at a quarter till 2 the next morning. McGowan's Brigade skirmishers, who were protecting the works, were driven back about 5 A.M. Lane's line was broken by a strong force of the enemy in a ravine in front of the right line of the 37th Regiment. The 28th were enfiladed on the left by the assaulting enemy that had broken the line to Lane's right, and they were forced to fall back to the plank road. The enemy soon took possession of that road, and the 28th Regiment had to fall back even further to Cox Road, where they began to skirmish with the enemy. The other regiments of Lane's Brigade engaged the enemy by McGowan's winter quarters and those occupied by his brigade, but were driven back. Lane's men "made a stand in the winter quarters" to the right regiment of Lane's command, but their line broke and part of them retreated along the works to the left. Others (the 18th Regiment under Colonel Robert H. Cowan) moved to the rear, where they made a stand on a hill near the home of Mrs. Banks. They could not hold their position, however, and were forced back to the plank road. There, they skirmished for some time before they, too, fell back to the Cox Road, where they had the support of a battery of artillery.[39]

Those on the left of Lane's command tried twice to resist the enemy and made a final stand in the Church Road leading to the Jones' house. They then fell back to Battery Gregg and another battery to its left, under Major Thomas J. Wooten. They were assisted by part of Thomas' brigade, and they were ordered by Major General Wilcox to charge the enemy. This action cleared the works as far as the branch where the 37th had rested the previous night. Colonel Cowan and his men rejoined them, and skirmishers were sent out to the left of the Church Road, perpendicular to the works. They could not hold that position and Lane's men were attacked by a "strong line of skirmishers, supported by two strong lines of battle." Some of Lane's Confederates moved back to Fort (Battery) Gregg, and the rest made a new line of works near the dam. Battery Gregg was then attacked by a large force, and it fell after the "most gallant and desperate defense." Lane's men had used their bayonets on many of the enemy as they tried to mount the Confederate-held parapet. After the loss of Fort Gregg, the rest of Lane's command along the new line was attacked both in front and flank. They were forced back to the old line of works which ran northwest from Battery 45. There they remained until Petersburg was evacuated. The 28th Regiment, under Captain T. James Linebarger, joined the rest of the brigade there.[40]

After the fall of Fort Gregg, the enemy began invading the inner line of defenses. Lane's Brigade was ordered to close to the right of the line. It was imperative that the Confederates hold the inner line until night so that they could withdraw across the only bridge left over the Appomattox River.[41] It had been mainly the men of Lane's Brigade who held out at Fort Gregg. Lane believed that "the stubborn defense of that little earthwork [was] one of the most brilliant events of the war."[42]

Lane's Brigade had been ordered to guard an area known as "Arthur's Swamp." During the winter months, this area had been guarded by McGowan's Infantry, but only a few days before the Federal assault on April 2, Lane's Brigade replaced McGowan's men. Facing the Federal forces, the 28th was positioned on the right of Lane's Brigade. The remainder of the North Carolina regiments in Lane's Brigade were also in place. The 37th was situated to the left of the 28th. Between them was a ravine through which ran one of the streams that fed Arthur's Swamp. To the left of the 37th, the 18th was placed, then to the left of that was the 33rd. Left of the 33rd was a brigade of Georgia troops under Brigadier General Edward L. Thomas. To the right of Lane's Brigade were two regiments of Brigadier General William McRae, the 11th and 52nd North Carolina, commanded by Colonel Eric Erson. It is estimated that at this time, Lane's four regiments numbered only about 1,100 men. The fifth regiment, the 7th North Carolina, had recently been sent to North Carolina to round up deserters and bring in conscripts to fill the ranks.[43]

The loss of Fort Stedman signaled the end for Lee and the Confederacy.

The Breakthrough at Petersburg, April 2, 1865

Forces engaged: Armies

Principal Commanders: Lt. Gen. U.S. Grant (Union), Gen. R. E. Lee (Confederate)

Estimated casualties: 6,400 total

Result: Union victory, Petersburg captured

After the Confederates were defeated at Five Forks on April 1, Union forces under Grant and Meade were ordered to launch a general assault against the lines at Petersburg on April 2. The Confederate defense at Fort Gregg prevented the Federals from entering the city that night. After dark, Lee had no choice but to order the evacuation of both Petersburg and Richmond. With the capture of Petersburg, one of Grant's major military objectives was finally achieved, and it was only a matter of days until the Union troops had taken what was left of Richmond. The end of the war was in sight.[44]

Dead soldier in trenches at Petersburg (Library of Congress, digital ID cwps 02556).

On April 2, 1865, 150 Federal guns began firing at the trenches and the city of Petersburg. One Confederate general recalled that there was a constant barrage of cannon, with "solid shot and shell whizzing through the air and bursting in every direction, at times equal in brilliancy to a vivid meteoric display."[45] The Federal infantry began their assault at 4:30 A.M. when it was barely daylight.[46]

When the Federal assault came, Lane's Brigade and other units of Hill's Corps were spread out in a defensive line from Battery 45 to Hatcher's Run. Four of the eight brigades from Heth and Wilcox's divisions had been sent beyond Hatcher's Run to meet Grant's flanking maneuver. There were not enough of those remaining to adequately man the defensive line at Petersburg and keep it from being overrun.[47]

Confederate pickets made a futile attempt to stop the advancing enemy troops and many were captured. The Confederate forces suffered many casualties, as whole regiments collapsed or were driven back. Keifer's Brigade of Federal troops concentrated on Arthur's Swamp, where the 28th North Carolina was stationed. Keifer sent the 6th Maryland through a narrow opening in the Confederate line. Soon, the 28th North Carolina was flanked and was forced to retreat to the Boydton Plank Road. Other regiments in Lane's Brigade retreated to Fort Gregg.[48]

The assault pushed through McGowan's skirmishers about 4:45 A.M., then advanced, hidden by a ravine, to break through Lane's front line between the 28th and the 37th regiments. The 28th was subjected to an enfilade fire from both sides and they were forced to fall back toward the Appomattox River to the plank road.[49]

Once the Confederate defensive line was breached, the Federal forces spread out in all directions. General Wilcox ordered the remnants of Lane's and Thomas' Brigades forward in a counterattack, and they did succeed in recapturing two cannon and in occupying part of the lost breastworks.[50] Lane and Thomas managed to gather about 600 men for the attack. Their efforts were successful because most of the Federal soldiers were moving around the Confederate flank. The Confederates captured a substantial portion of the line that had been lost earlier in the morning.[51]

The remnants of what had once been three brigades withdrew slowly to the inner line of defensive fortifications. Lane left about 50 men from his brigade in Fort Gregg under the command of Lieutenant George H. Snow, of the 37th Regiment. The 37th joined some of Harris' and Thomas' men, and a few artillerists who were trying to defend the little works. General Wilcox begged the men to hold on for two hours, long enough for Longstreet to bring up his troops.[52]

Lane and his staff quickly moved out of Fort Gregg while Lieutenant Snow's men remained to defend the fort.[53]

Chevaux-de-frise used as defense system at Petersburg (Library of Congress, cwp 02599).

Fort Gregg was attacked and captured by an immense force of Federal soldiers. The fighting was fierce, and Lane's men used their bayonets on the enemy as they mounted the parapets.[54] The Federal assault began about 10 A.M. Inside Fort Gregg, the men held their fire until the enemy was within 40 yards. Then they unleashed a volley that caused the first line of Federal soldiers to give way. The Federals attacked twice more, and were repulsed each time. However, during their fourth and fifth assaults, they made it to the ditch around the fort. The fighting for control of the parapet continued in a fierce struggle by both sides. Even after their ammunition was gone, the Confederates used bayonets, knives, clubbed muskets, and even rocks to defend the fort. Finally, the enemy took the parapet and poured fire into the small band of defenders. Hand-to-hand combat continued for half an hour before the Confederate defenders surrendered.[55]

The defenders inside Fort Gregg had done their job. They gave Lee time to bring reinforcements to man the inner line of defense around Petersburg. However, casualties were heavy. Of the 214 men who held Fort Gregg, 55 were killed, and 129 wounded. The Federals had sent 14,000 men to take the fort, and they lost 714 men in the attempt. Lieutenant General James Longstreet did sent troops to reinforce what was left of Hill's men. They formed a solid line from Battery 45 to the Appomattox River, which allowed the Confederates an avenue of retreat.[56] After General Lee decided to abandon the cities of Petersburg and Richmond, Longstreet organized an orderly withdrawal of all the Confederate forces at Petersburg during the late evening.[57]

The battle for Fort Gregg was the last major engagement for Lane's Brigade. The brigade had 662 men captured by the Federal soldiers. Debilitated by months of hard fighting, many of Lane's Brigade were wounded or killed in the encounters around Petersburg, and few were left to retreat.[58]

A. P. Hill Killed

Lieutenant General Ambrose P. Hill, a corps commander in Lee's Army of Northern Virginia, was killed during the night of April 2 while trying to reach his troops.[59] Hill was seen by two of his brigade officers, E.J. Hale and William McClaurin, as he rode his horse from his headquarters at Petersburg. Both men tried to warn Hill not to go any further and told him that enemy skirmishers had almost reached the Appomattox River. Hill ignored the warning and was determined to reach the right flank of his corps near Hatcher's Run. He and a single aide rode on, and a short time later, McClaurin heard gunfire from the direction in which Hill had gone. When Hill's horse returned riderless, the men know that their "gallant commander was off-duty forever." Hill had previously expressed a wish not to survive if Petersburg fell. Perhaps he exposed himself to enemy fire on purpose.[60]

Lieutenant General A.P. Hill, killed at Petersburg, April 2, 1865 (Library of Congress, cwpbh 00463).

The Retreat from Petersburg

As the 28th Regiment fell back slowly toward the Appomattox river, they were pursued by Federal soldiers. The brigade broke up into small groups, and continued to fight past the brigade's headquarters in the rear of the entrenchments. A mass of Federal troops moved to their left along the Boydton Plank Road to cut off those Confederates who were at Hatcher's Run. Another detachment of Federal troops moved eastward behind the Confederate works in an attempt to stop Lee's retreat from Petersburg. Lee's men now knew that Petersburg was lost. The only thing that was practical and possible was try to slow the enemy long enough for the Confederate forces to make an orderly withdrawal.[61]

Between 10 and 11 P.M. on the night of April 2, the dazed and exhausted remnant of a once-proud army crossed slowly to the north side of the Appomattox River. Along the way, they passed women and children who cried out in fear for their safety now that the Confederates were pulling out.[62]

With his flair for words, 1st Lieutenant J.P. Little movingly described the evacuation in his regimental history, not from an eyewitness perspective but from the stories told by others in his company. Little was in Elmira Prison at the time of the surrender, and was not released until June 16, 1865.[63] He described the final days: "As we passed out and looked back we saw that which added more to the horror, destruction — great clouds of smoke go up from the two great cities [Richmond and Petersburg] where men poured out their life's blood and perished by the tens of thousands." Their "fate was sealed, our cause lost." All that was left was to make their way to Appomattox Court House where General Lee "surrendered the remnant of the grandest army of fighting men the world ever produced."[64]

Amelia Court House, April 3, 1865

After evacuating Petersburg, the 28th Regiment and the rest of the troops that had been at Petersburg marched westward all night. Their goal was Amelia Court House, 36 miles from Petersburg, where Lee planned to gather all his forces and then unite them with General Joe Johnston in North Carolina. The ragged soldiers finally reached Amelia Court House on the 4th. Lee had hoped to have food there for the hungry men, but the food and ammunition that were to have been forwarded to Amelia Court House had not arrived. When detachments were sent out with wagons to scavenge food from the surrounding country, those wagons returned mostly empty — the country had already been depleted. Thus, a day was lost in the race to out-distance Grant's men.[65] That delay allowed the Federal troops to close in.

The numbers in the Light Division with refurbished with the arrival of Scales and McGowan's brigades. They formed a line of battle where they remained for most of the afternoon and evening.[66]

Jetersville (Amelia Springs), April 5, 1865

Forces Engaged: Divisions

Principal Commanders: Maj. Gen. George Crook (Union), Maj. Gen. Rosser and Maj. Gen. Fitzhugh Lee (Confederate)

Estimated Casualties: 250 total

Results: Inconclusive

This minor battle occurred when the Confederate cavalry of Fitzhugh Lee and Thomas Lafayette Rosser were attacked by George Crook's Union cavalry as they returned from burning the Confederate wagon train at Painesville. The fight began north of Amelia Springs and continued through and beyond Jetersville.[67]

On the morning of April 5, General Phil Sheridan sent out the Union cavalry brigade of H.E. Davies from Jetersville to determine the direction Lee and the remnant of his Confederate army were taking. At Paineville, about five miles from Jetersville, the 1st Pennsylvania Cavalry found the Confederate wagon train that was being escorted west by Martin W. Gary's cavalry. The Union cavalry charged through a swamp and captured a gun that was ready to fire at them. According to Davies, his Union cavalry routed the 400 wagon train guards, set fire to 200 vehicles, and captured 5 guns, 11 flags, and 320 white prisoners, and about as many Negro teamsters, plus over 400 horses and mules. It is also believed that General Robert E. Lee's headquarters records were destroyed when the wagon train was burned. The Confederate cavalry of Fitzhugh Lee and Gary retreated to Amelia Springs, and were pursued by Union soldiers. There, Davies was reinforced by a Union cavalry brigade of J.I. Gregg.[68]

The men of Lane's Brigade formed a line of battle between Amelia Court House and Jetersville. Sharpshooters from the 28th regiment under Major Wooten were active. They spent three days (April 5–7) formed in a line of battle to ward off the Federal cavalry. While the sharpshooters did most of the fighting, the entire body of troops had to remain on the alert in anticipation of an enemy attack.

On the night of April 6, Longstreet ordered a retreat toward Farmville, where the divisions of Heth and Wilcox, Mahone and Gordon crossed at High Bridge over the Appomattox River.

Farmville (Cumberland Church), April 7, 1865

Forces engaged: Corps

Principal Commanders: Maj. Gen. A.A. Humphreys (Union), Gen. Robert E. Lee (Confederate)

Estimated casualties: 910 total (655 Union; 255 Confederate)

Result: Confederate victory

At about 2 P.M. on April 7, the Union II Corps encountered Confederate forces entrenched on high ground near Cumberland Church. The Federals attacked twice but were repulsed. Darkness stopped the fighting.[69]

Lee's men were about to receive their first rations in five days at Farmville. However, before the distribution of the food could be completed, the brigade was ordered back to a "fortified hill to support" the Confederate cavalry, which was under attack.[70] Before they could reach the hill, the order was rescinded. Instead, they moved rapidly through Farmville, but not without the loss of men from enemy artillery fire while attempting to cross the river. In the afternoon, about a mile or two from Farmville, the men were ordered to form a line of battle as they faced the rear. Lane's sharpshooters were attacked by Federals.[71]

The night of April 7, Lane's men resumed their march. Straggling and desertion became a problem, as along the retreat, men dropped out from hunger and exhaustion. Wilcox issued a special order to gather the stragglers and "all such men as have fallen asleep by the camp-fires or by the wayside."[72]

For a day, it appeared that the Confederates had escaped their pursuers. The progress of the army was hindered by the muddy roads, and the wagons had great difficulty keeping up. Troop movement had been hastened by burning and leaving a large number of supply wagons at Farmville. Without the wagons, the troops could move at a steady pace. What was left of the Army of Northern Virginia, an advance guard under General John Gordon, and the rear guard under James Longstreet, continued westward in hope of finding sustenance.[73]

Appomattox Court House

The advance troops of Lee's army reached Appomattox Court House. Provisions for the Confederate army had been stored at Appomattox Station, three miles away. With the Federals coming closer from all sides, Lee attempted one last stand. While Longstreet protected the rear, Lee sent Gordon to attack the forces at Appomattox Station. If the enemy consisted only of cavalry, Gordon had a chance to get through and continue to North Carolina to meet Johnston. However, Lee advised that if the cavalry had infantry support, Gordon was not to engage in what would be a futile battle.[74]

Just before dawn on the morning of April 9, Lane's Brigade was ordered to fall in and march to the courthouse at Appomattox. They were two miles east of their destination when firing was heard in the distance as Gordan began his attack at Appomattox Station. At 10 A.M., the Light Division moved in the direction of the fighting to support Gordon. However, before they could reach Gordon and his men, Wilcox ordered two brigades to move southward to meet Federal troops from that direction. No sooner had the brigades started to move than the men were ordered to return. It was then that they weary soldiers were told to stack their arms because the Army of Northern Virginia had surrendered.[75]

In his report to President Jefferson Davis, General Robert E. Lee set out in detail the last days of the war leading up to his surrender at Appomattox Court House. It was a story of impossible roads, exhausted men, and lack of sleep and supplies. The Federal army outnumbered Lee's by 5 to 1. With every means of escape blocked, Lee saw no recourse but to surrender.[76]

General Lee Surrenders — April 9, 1865

Early on the morning of April 9, what was left of John B. Gordon's corps and Fitzhugh Lee's cavalry made a stand near Appomattox Court House. General Lee desperately needed to

222

Appomattox Court House, April 1865 (Library of Congress, HABS VA, 6-APPO, 6–2).

McLean House, at Appomattox Court House (Library of Congress, digital ID cwpb 01396).

reach Lynchburg where he could obtain supplies to feed his men. Initially, the Confederates gained ground against Phil Sheridan's Union cavalry. However, when the Union infantry arrived on the scene, Lee saw that it was hopeless. He requested a meeting with Lieutenant General U.S. Grant at the home of Wilbur McLean, where he surrendered himself and his men. Casualties amounted to about 700 in this last battle fought on Virginia soil.[77]

Lee's General Orders No. 9 announced the surrender to the Confederate president:

> After four years of arduous service, marked by unsurpassed courage and fortitude, the Army of Northern Virginia has been compelled to yield to overwhelming numbers and resources. I need not tell the brave survivors of so many hard-fought battles, who have remained steadfast to the last, that I have consented to the result from no distrust of them. But, feeling that valor and devotion could accomplish nothing that could compensate for the loss that must have attended the continuance of the contest, I determined to avoid the useless sacrifice of those whose past services have endeared them to their countrymen.[78]

Lee then listed the terms of surrender: "By the terms of the agreement officers and men can return to their homes and remain until exchanged." The old general never failed to appreciate the efforts of those who served under him, and he stated his appreciation: "With an increasing admiration of your constancy and devotion to your country, and a grateful remembrance of your kind and generous considerations for myself, I bid you all an affectionate farewell."[79]

On April 12, what was left of the Army of Northern Virginia, including the 28th Regiment of Lane's Brigade, marched between the two lines of Federal troops who stood on both sides of the road running west from Appomattox Court House. The Confederate soldiers stacked their

Hand press that printed paroles. Photograph by Frances H. Casstevens.

arms and surrendered their battle flags in an act of formal surrender. Lane's Brigade was at the rear of the column.[80]

From the evacuation of Petersburg to the surrender at Appomattox, the remnants of the Branch-Lane Brigade fought bravely by day and marched at night "without a murmur," according to Brigadier General James H. Lane. He recalled that when they reached Appomattox, and the brigade was told that General Lee had surrendered, both "officers and men burst into tears...." Some were heard to bitterly remark: "And have we endured all this for nothing?"[81]

The paroles given the Confederate soldiers who agreed to lay down their arms were printed on a little hand-turned press, which is now on display at Appomattox Court House.

Figures differ as to the number of Confederate soldiers who were paroled at Appomattox. A list compiled from the parole lists and published in *The Official Records of the War of the Rebellion* gives the total number of 28,231. That figures includes 2,781 officers and 25,450 enlisted men. Also included in this total were 1,466 listed as "miscellaneous troops, as well as General Robert E. Lee, his staff and escort and the staff corps (281 total)."[82]

Among Colonel James H. Lane's papers at Auburn University is a list of the brigade officers present on April 9, 1865:

James H. Lane	Brigadier General	
E.J. Hale, Jr.	Captain, Assistant Adjutant General	
E.B. Meade	1st Lieutenant, A.W.C. (Aide)	
E.W. Hearndon	Major, Quartermaster	
T.H. McCoy	Major, Commissary	
D.Y. Russell	Clerk, Brigade Headquarters	Co. I, 18th Regiment
A.R. Joyce	Courier	Co. I, 28th Regiment
I. Draughn	Courier	Co. A, 28th Regiment

Frank Ketner	Mail Boy	Co. I, 33rd Regiment
F.L. Alexander	Brigade Commanding Sergeant	Co. I, 18th Regiment
James Eure	Assist to Brigadier Commanding Sergeant	Co. E, 33rd Regiment[83]

Lane reportedly surrendered approximately 540 men, all that was left of a once-proud brigade.[84]

The regimental history of the 28th North Carolina ends with the surrender at Appomattox Court House. It states that by April 12, 1865, only 230 members of the 28th Regiment remained to be paroled there.[85] In R.A. Brock's list, published as *The Appomattox Roster,* the names of only 213 members of the 28th Regiment are given as follows:

Field & Staff officers, 28th North Carolina	3
Enlisted men and non-commissioned officers	
Company A	17 men
Company B	37
Company C	38
Company D	16
Company E	20
Company F	4
Company G	23
Company H	24
Company I	6
Company K	25
	Total 213[86]

Some refused to take the oath and walked away without receiving a parole. When Colonel Robert Cowan of the 33rd received the order to lead his command to formally surrender, he refused: "I won't surrender," Cowan said in anger. He turned to Major Weston and ordered him to take charge of the regiment. Then Cowan rode off and was never seen again by Weston.[87] One of those who survived the war and did surrender at Appomattox was 3rd Lieutenant Leander Alonzo Todd. He, like many others, walked home after the war, and died in 1870 at Dobson, Surry County, North Carolina.[88]

Appomattox Court House in the 21st Century

The McLean house has been reconstructed as it was in 1865 and is open to the public. The former courthouse is now a visitors' center, and there are several other structures visitors can explore.

Chapter 15

After Appomattox

...as brave as the bravest.[1]

—1st Lt. J.P. Little

Stoneman's Raid

The people of North Carolina feared that General William T. Sherman would turn his wrath on their state and wreak destruction as he had in Georgia the previous fall. Sherman did invade North Carolina but his passing was nothing like it had been in Georgia. Instead, another threat came across the Blue Ridge Mountains in the form of General George Stoneman and his cavalry force.

In the spring of 1865, the Piedmont and mountains had as yet suffered no major damage from invading armies. Stoneman's men changed that and wreaked havoc in several counties and towns from the Blue Ridge Mountains eastward as far as Stokes County just prior to the end of the war.

On April 10, 1865, Stoneman left Germanton with his second and third brigades under the command of Brigadier General Simeon Brown and Colonel John Miller. The Federal horsemen rode through Bethania, in Forsyth County, where they reportedly "ate everything they could find, and moved on to the Shallow Ford, on the Yadkin River...."[2]

Even after Lee had surrendered, the raid by Federal cavalry continued as they made their way from Forsyth County toward Salisbury. On April 11, on the bluff above the river, the local Home Guard awaited the arrival of the Yankee cavalry. They were taken by surprise about dawn and, reportedly, after putting up a weak resistance, fled "leaving behind a hundred new muskets." A musket has been found that is believed to have been left, shortly after the Yankees passed, by some slaves up from Cooleemee Plantation in Davie County. More recently an 1863 Colt pistol was found buried under 18 inches of soil.[3] It is inconceivable that any man or boy would abandon a new musket. Yet, some probably did throw down their guns and flee. The militia and Home Guard now consisted of only the very old and the very young who were incapable of stopping even a small force of Yankee cavalry.

Dr. William M. Phillips, who was 14 years old in 1865, remembered that the Home Guard dug ditches and set up breastworks along the west side of the river in Yadkin County at a point where they believed the Yankees would cross (probably at the Shallow Ford). However, Stoneman's men crossed a few miles below the breastworks in the vicinity of the Sarah Dalton or Joseph Bitting plantations, and then moved northward up the west bank of the river toward the Confederate breastworks. Phillips believed that when the Home Guard learned the Yankees had already crossed, they dispersed to their homes.[4]

After crossing the river and scattering the Home Guard, the Federal troops swept through the village of Huntsville and burned the Red Store. The Federal soldiers looted and burned surrounding plantations and took the stock of all the slaveholding plantation owners.[5] Then they moved on southward. When Stoneman reached Salisbury, the Confederate prison was empty, but his men did find a great stockpile of food and military stores at the Salisbury depot, which they burned, along with government buildings, stores, and factories.[6]

Discharged because of injuries, Greenberry Harding (formerly a sergeant in Company I, 28th Regiment), was at home in Yadkin County that spring. The Harding home was a large two-story log house which faced the Georgia Road (parallel to the present Wyo Road). "Berry," as the family called him, was in the field below the house plowing ground for the spring planting. One of his sisters came running and called him to come up to the house because two Yankees were there ransacking it. The former Confederate soldier did not hesitate but left the horse and plow and ran with his pistol in his hand. He fired the gun and killed one of the Yankees. He believed he wounded the other, but he could not be sure because that soldier "hightailed it" back across the river.[7] The two may have been from Stoneman's cavalry or deserters from other Federal regiments.

Surrender in North Carolina

On April 18, 1865, General Joseph E. Johnston signed an armistice with Union General William T. Sherman and surrendered his army on April 26. In spite of the orders given by President Jefferson Davis to continue the fighting, this effectively ended the war in the South. (Ironically, General Johnston died of pneumonia in 1891 after standing hatless in the rain while attending Sherman's funeral.[8])

The Last Battles

Although General Robert E. Lee surrendered at Appomattox Court House, it took some time for the news to reach all the units of both armies and the civilian population. Thus, there were several more battles fought after April 9, 1865.

In North Carolina, Union Colonel George W. Kirk moved his troops from Asheville to raid the little town of Franklin in Macon County.[9] A few days later, a small Confederate force of Thomas' Legion engaged a detachment of Federal cavalry in battle. The exact date of this fight varies between May 1 and May 10, 1865. Confederate Colonel J.R. Love is believed to have been involved. The Federal troops were probably part of Colonel C.G. Bartlett's command. This engagement was the last in North Carolina.[10]

A skirmish took place in Columbus, Georgia, on April 16. Federal forces under Brevet Major General James Harrison Wilson clashed with 3,000 Confederate troops under Major General Howell Cobb. The last person killed in the battle was Colonel C.A.L. Lamar, a member of Cobb's staff.[11]

While North Carolina holds the distinction of hosting the last "major" battle of the Civil war at Bentonville, Alabama claims the honor of being the "last combined-force" battle of the War. Here at Fort Blakeley on Mobile Bay from April 2–9, 1865, Union Major General E.R.S. Canby and his XIII and XVI Corps clashed with Confederate Brigadier General St. John R. Liddell and his 4,000 men. Casualties totaled 3,539 (639 Federal, 2,900 Confederate). [12]

Trans-Mississippi Fighting

Palmetto Ranch in Texas also claims to be the site of the last battle and a small marker has been erected there to commemorate that fact. Here on May 12–13, 1865, detachments from the 62nd U.S. Colored Infantry, the 2nd Texas Cavalry, and 34th Indiana Infantry clashed with detachments from Giddings' Confederate regiment, Anderson's battalion of cavalry, and other

Confederate units. The Federals had 118 casualties, but the number of Confederate losses is unknown.[13] Palmetto Ranch was a Confederate victory.

Trans-Mississippi Forces Surrender

M. Jeff Thompson, one of the last Southern commanders to hold out, formally surrendered on May 11, 1865, in Jacksonport, Arkansas.[14] This was a month after General Robert E. Lee surrendered at Appomattox. Lieutenant General Kirby Smith surrendered on June 2, 1865.[15] The last to give up was Brigadier General Stand Watie, who surrendered his Confederate Indians on June 23, 1865.[16]

The Very Last to Surrender

On the sea, the C.S.S. *Shenandoah* continued the war long after fighting had ceased on land. Commanded by Captain James Waddell, the Confederate cruiser, as it made its way to the Pacific Ocean around the Cape of Good Hope to Australia, continued to capture and destroy enemy vessels. Waddell did not learn of the collapse of the Confederacy until August of 1865. He surrendered his vessel in Liverpool, England.[17] Captain Waddell was from North Carolina.[18]

Confederate Prisoners-of-War Released

It was several months after Lee surrendered before the thousands of Confederate prisoners being held were released. Their release hinged on the prisoner taking the "Oath of Allegiance" to the United States. Many balked at doing so.

Henry J. Norman, of Company F, 28th Regiment, North Carolina Troops, was captured

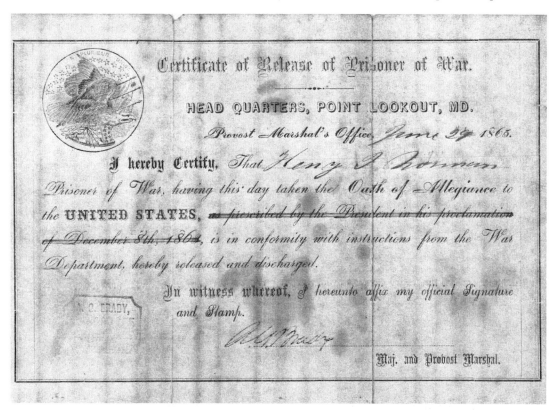

Release of Henry Norman, prisoner at Point Lookout, Maryland (courtesy of Mike Cumbie).

Oath of Allegiance (courtesy of Mike Cumbie).

near Petersburg, Virginia, on April 2, 1865. He was confined as a prisoner at Point Lookout, Maryland. He was not released until June 29, 1865, when he signed an Oath of Allegiance.[19]

Captain William M. Norman, of Company A, 28th Regiment, transferred to 2nd Company A, 2nd Regiment. He was captured at Kelly's Ford in November of 1863, and sent to Johnson's Island. Family tradition holds that when Norman was released from Johnson's Island in June of 1865, he was taken to the mainland but had to walk home, a distance of almost 500 miles by modern highways. It took him three months, and when he arrived he was so emaciated he was almost skeleton-like. He survived the war, but never fully recovered his health. His memoirs were later published.[20]

Some of the boys came home, but many never returned. Thousands died on the battlefields, in hospitals, or in prisons.

Of the five sons of George D. and Anna Long Holcomb, all of whom enlisted in Company I, 28th Regiment, only two returned safely (Bloom Virgil and Calvin Monroe Holcomb). Their brother, Daniel F. Holcomb, died in a Richmond hospital of smallpox. John T. Holcomb died in a Lynchburg hospital of "hepatitis acuta," and brother Jones Holcomb was killed at Gettysburg.[21]

Others returned minus limbs. Artha (Arthur) Bray, Jr. wrote home on July 14, 1862, from Richmond about some of the injuries he had seen. He saw R.S. Nance having his arm amputated "between his shoulder and his elbow." John N. Brinkley had his "thigh amputated about halfway between his hip and his knee." Bray saw another man's thigh amputated "close to his body." Bray wrote: "The scene is one that I never wish to see any more." Unfortunately, Bray did not get his wish. He was wounded and captured at Gettysburg, confined to Fort Delaware, and then Point Lookout, where he would have been among countless men minus one or more limbs.[22] Still others bore invisible injuries from the horrors of the war they had experienced.

The Final Accounting

Finally, the terrible war which began on April 12, 1861, in Charleston, South Carolina, was over. The fighting that had raged across the nation for four long years had ceased. It was a bloody war, a war that pitted brother against brother, and state against state. The cost of that conflict in property was enormous; the loss of lives was immeasurable.

The Cost to North Carolina in Manpower

Historians Hugh Lefler and Albert Ray Newsome believed that North Carolina's greatest contribution to the Confederacy "was manpower — the huge number of soldiers who bore the brunt of scores of battles." The state of North Carolina held only ⅑ of the population of the entire Confederacy, yet North Carolina furnished ⅙ to ⅐ of all the Confederate soldiers and sailors.[23]

The numbers are staggering. The 125,000 men furnished by North Carolina was larger than the entire voting population of the state. Of those, 111,000 were enlisted troops, all of whom except 19,000 were volunteers. The men were organized into 72 regiments. In addition, 10,000 reserves were organized into 8 regiments, plus there were 4,000 men in the Home Guard.[24] North Carolina furnished the Confederacy with 69 regiments and 4 battalions of infantry; 1 regiment and 5 battalions of cavalry; 2 battalions of heavy artillery; and 9 batteries of light artillery.[25]

North Carolina Casualties

Of those 125,000 men, 677 officers and 13,845 enlisted men were killed. North Carolina had 330 officers and 4,821 enlisted men who died from wounds. Disease took another 541 officers and 20,061 enlisted men. The total number of men who either died from wounds or disease or who were killed in battle during the four years of war thus was at least 40,275. That number was greater than from any other Confederate state.[26]

During the four years of the war, while approximately 23,000 soldiers from North Carolina deserted, some 8,000 of them returned to the service. The overall percentage of desertions among North Carolina troops was about 20 percent, similar to those from other states.[27]

The Achievements of the Branch-Lane Brigade

The Branch-Lane Brigade participated in practically all the campaigns in which the Army of Northern Virginia took part from the Seven Days' Battles to Appomattox. Although the brigade suffered many losses both to battlefield casualties and disease, it managed to remain a viable fighting unit until the end of the war. That those men did their part in battle was acknowledged by friend and foe alike.[28]

Complimentary letters from General Robert E. Lee were sent to the Branch-Lane Brigade for the battles at Slash Church and Kinney's Farm and Reams' Station, as well as for the capture of several flags at Spotsylvania Court House. These letters were published in the *Southern Historical Society Papers.*[29]

The gallantry of the brigade at Spotsylvania was described by a correspondent for a London newspaper when he wrote that "Lane's North Carolina veterans stopped the tide of Federal victory as it came surging to the right."[30] General Isaac Ridgeway Trimble admired the conduct of the Branch-Lane Brigade at Gettysburg.[31]

This brigade was the first to cross the Chickahominy River, and it cleared the way for the division to cross at Meadow Bridge. At Cedar Run, the brigade was the first of Hill's Division to begin the fight, and they repulsed the enemy's infantry and cavalry to restore General T.J. "Stonewall" Jackson's left flank.[32]

With the Rebel yell, the brigade chased Taylor's New Jersey Brigade of Pope's Army as they fled from Manassas Junction. The brigade was one of those who fought successfully at Ox Hill in a pouring rain. This same brave brigade scaled the cliffs above the Shenandoah River at midnight, and lay concealed in the woods on the left and rear at Bolivar Heights at Harpers Ferry.

From there these men marched to Sharpsburg just in time to help repel the new enemy reinforcements and save the right of Lee's army. After the fighting ended, Lane's Brigade was one of three brigades that formed the rear guard of the Army of Northern Virginia. Their efforts held off the enemy until every wagon and ambulance had safely crossed the Potomac.[33]

At Fredericksburg, the brigade fought hard and drove back two lines of battle after the enemy had penetrated an opening between General Archer and themselves. At Chancellorsville, this brigade was ordered to make a night attack in Jackson's famous flank movement. That attack was abandoned when Jackson and A.P. Hill were wounded by the 18th North Carolina who, in the dark, mistook them for the enemy. The Branch-Lane Brigade and Pender's men made up the front Confederate line that night. It was Lane's men who repulsed the Union's General Dan Sickle's midnight attack on the right.[34]

Lane's Brigade was never given proper credit for its part in Pickett's Charge on the third day of fighting at Gettysburg. The brigade was on the extreme left of the Pickett-Pettigrew charge. It was flanked by a large force of the enemy, but retired in order and reformed in the rear of the artillery, ready to repulse an enemy countercharge. This brigade was ordered to guard the rear of Lee's Army of Northern Virginia, as the defeated Confederates retreated across the Potomac via a pontoon bridge at Falling Waters. That task was so dangerous that General Henry Heth feared Lane's whole command would be killed, wounded or captured.[35]

Lane's men were the first to go into action at Wilderness on May 5, 1864. General Venable was so relieved to see them arrive that he went to tell General Lee, "...Lane has just gone in and will hold his ground until other troops arrive to-night." Lane's Brigade did just that, and even drove the enemy back some distance.[36]

The 28th Regiment

Counting both officers and men, the 28th Regiment furnished 1,893 soldiers to the Confederate cause. This number included all soldiers regardless of their term of enlistment or method of joining the 28th, whether enlisted, conscripted or transferred from other companies and regiments. A more detailed list of those men and what happened to them is shown below.

Total Who Served in the 28th Regiment	1,893	
Commissioned or enlisted (volunteers	1,851 (97.78%)	
Conscripts	14 (0.74%)	
Transferred into the 28th	28 (1.47%)	
Total	1,893	
Left the Regiment		
Killed or mortally wounded	251 (13.25%)	
Died as prisoners-of-war	71 (3.79%)	
Died of disease	342 (18.07%)	
Became disabled	130 (6.87%)	
Deserted	50 (2.64%)	
Discharged during the war	73 (3.86%)	
Transferred from the 28th	79 (4.17%)	
Total who left	996 (52.61%)[37]	-996
		897
In prison at end of the war, estimated	667? (35.24%)?	- 667 ?
Men Remaining on April 9, 1865,[38] **at Appomattox Court House**	230 (12.15%)	230

In 1867, the state of North Carolina began granting pensions to Confederate veterans who had been blinded or who had lost an arm or a leg. In 1885, the state granted pensions to all other disabled and indigent Confederate veterans or their widows. The applicant had to prove he was unable to work and was impoverished in order to qualify. More information may be obtained about pensioners from the North Carolina State Archives, Raleigh, North Carolina.[39]

What Became of the Commanders?

General Robert E. Lee, commander of the Army of Northern Virginia, took over the presidency of Washington College in Lexington, Virginia. Before his death in 1870, he turned the little college into one of the nation's finest institutions for higher learning. The school was later named Washington and Lee University in honor of the South's greatest general.[40]

Former General Robert E. Lee, C.S.A., now a civilian, president of Washington College (Library of Congress, cwpbh 03255).

Corps Commanders

Lieutenant General Thomas Jonathan "Stonewall" Jackson was given command of the II Corps of the Army of Northern Virginia. He led his men successfully at Fredericksburg and at Chancellorsville. He was accidentally shot by some of his own men on May 2, 1863, and died May 10 of pneumonia and complications after his arm was amputated.[41]

Lieutenant General Ambrose P. Hill, commander of Hill's Light Division, was in command at Mechanicsville, Gaines' Mill, and Frayser's Farm. He was promoted and took command of Jackson's II corps. When the Army of Northern Virginia was reorganized, he was elevated to commander of the III Corps, and he led them at Gettysburg and Wilderness. He returned after being sick to lead his corps at 2nd Cold Harbor. A.P. Hill was killed at Petersburg on April 2, 1865 (see Chapter XIV).[42]

Division Commanders

As a major general, A.P. Hill led his division until he was promoted to lead a corps (see above).

Major General William Dorsey Pender, who commanded a brigade under A.P. Hill during the Seven Days' Battles, was wounded three times at Chancellorsville. He briefly commanded the division at Gettysburg until he was badly wounded there on July 2, 1863. Pender died on July 18, after undergoing an amputation, because of wounds he received.[43]

Major General Cadmus M. Wilcox led a brigade at 2nd Bull Run, Fredericksburg, Chancellorsville and Gettysburg. After his promotion, he commanded a division at Wilderness, Spotsylvania, and in the fighting around Petersburg. He surrendered at Appomattox and was employed in various governmental posts after the war. He wrote and translated a number of books on military tactics and lectured in the United States army schools. He lived until 1890.[44]

Brigade Commanders

Brigadier General Lawrence O'Bryan Branch led his brigade at New Bern, Hanover Court House, the Seven Days' Battles, Cedar Run, 2nd Bull Run, Fairfax Courthouse, Ox Hill, and Harpers Ferry. Branch was killed leading his men at Sharpsburg on September 17, 1862.[45]

Brigadier General James Henry Lane assumed command of the brigade after the death of Branch. Lane continued to command the brigade through the war, and surrendered at Appomattox. He returned to teaching at Virginia Polytechnic Institute, then the Missouri School of Mines, and Alabama Polytechnic Institute (now Auburn University), Auburn, Alabama, where he was professor of civil engineering. He died in 1907.[46]

Colonel John Decatur Barry, of the 18th Regiment, was in command of Lane's Brigade at Petersburg. In a special order by General R.E. Lee, dated August 11, 1864, Barry was temporarily assigned the rank of brigadier general in order to take command of Lane's Brigade, Wilcox's Division, of the Third Corps.[47] Barry, a banker from New Hanover County, North Carolina, enlisted as a private at age 22 in Company I, 18th Regiment. He was elected captain of Company I on April 24, 1862. He was present until wounded at Frayser's Farm on June 30, 1862, but returned to duty.[48] Barry was promoted to major on November 11, 1862, then he was transferred to field and staff. He was promoted to colonel on May 27, 1863. Barry was wounded in the right hand by a sharpshooter while on a reconnoitering mission about July 2, 1864. He was out for six months, but returned to duty in January–February 1865. Barry survived the war and was paroled at Raleigh, North Carolina, on May 12, 1865.[49]

Regimental Commanders

As a Major, Lane took part in the Battle of Big Bethel on June 10, 1861. He was then asked to become colonel of the 28th Regiment. He was promoted to brigadier general and took over Branch's Brigade after Sharpsburg in September 1862.[50]

Colonel Samuel D. Lowe, took over the regiment after Lane was promoted. Lowe was captured at Hanover Court House, and was held as a prisoner of war at Fort Columbus, then on Johnson's Island. He returned to the regiment between September 1862 and January 1863. Lowe was wounded in the left thigh at Gettysburg and retired to the invalid corps on July 8, 1864.[51]

Colonel William H. Asbury Speer had previously served as a captain of Company I. He was captured at Hanover Court House, and imprisoned on Johnson's Island. When released he returned and was promoted to Lieutenant Colonel. Speer was wounded at Chancellorsville, but returned to duty. He was also wounded at Gettysburg. Promoted to full colonel on July 9, 1864, Speer was in charge of the 28th Regiment at Reams' Station, where he was wounded in the head on August 25, 1864, and died in a hospital a few days later.[52]

The last person to be classified as the commander of the 28th Regiment, North Carolina Troops, was Sergeant Major William Rufus Rankin. He was the highest ranking officer of three field and staff officers who surrendered at Appomattox.[53] Rankin had started out as a private in Company B, and was promoted to Sergeant Major in April of 1863. He transferred to field and staff, and was wounded at Gettysburg.[54]

Lane's Brigade Finally Recognized

Union veteran Augustus C. Hamlin, of Bangor, Maine, stated that justice has never been done to Lane's "brave fellows." Hamlin, who had highly praised Lane's Brigade in previous publications and speeches in the Northern states, promised to write a paper in the defense of the brigade for publication in the South. Lane was pleased and to help Hamlin, he wrote Colonel William G. Morris (formerly of Company E, 37th Regiment) in Gastonia to request his recollection of Chancellorsville. The *Charlotte Observer* believed it would be an "anomaly" to have a Northerner, at this late date, doing justice for the brigade, something which had been denied by Southern writers."[55]

Lane gladly furnished Augustus C. Hamlin with the information he requested for a book about the battle of Chancellorsville. The book, published in 1896, was titled *The Battle of Chan-*

cellorsville: The Attack of Stonewall Jackson and His Army upon the Right Flank of the Army of the Potomac at Chancellorsville, Virginia, on Sunday afternoon, May 2, 1863.[56]

In order to gather material for his book on Chancellorsville, Hamlin invited both Federal and Confederate officers to convene at Chancellorsville in the summer of 1894. Lane had a "delightful & interesting time," but, as he wrote Colonel Morris, "it seemed so strange — Yankees & Rebels fraternizing on such a bloody field & trying to get at the facts about that great battle."[57]

Captured Flags Returned

The physical evidence of the 28th Regiment North Carolina Troops has almost disappeared. Battlefields across Virginia contain the remains of many of those who died in battle, and various archives and repositories contain letters, diaries, and even photographs of some of the men who served in the 28th. The flags they carried are reminders of those hard-fought and bloody battles from North Carolina to Pennsylvania.

The flag of Company A, 28th Regiment ("Surry Regulators") was captured at New Bern in 1862. Its whereabouts is unknown.

28th Regiment's Flag, capture #134, captured at Spotsylvania, May 12, 1864 (courtesy of the North Carolina Museum of History).

28th Regiment's Flag, capture #149, captured near Richmond, July 28, 1864 (courtesy of the North Carolina Museum of History).

Four of the battle flags of the 28th Regiment, so revered by Southerners, still exist. The battle flag is a symbol of freedom for some and of oppression for others. It continues to evoke strong emotions even today whenever it is displayed.

The regimental flag of the 28th was captured at Gettysburg. It is now housed in the Museum of the Confederacy in Richmond, Virginia. This flag carries the names of only eight battles: Manassas, Cedar Run, Mechanicsville, Hanover, Harpers Ferry, Ox Hill, Cold Harbor, and Frazier's [Frayser's] Farm.[58]

According to the "Register of Captured Flags, 1861–1865," three other captured flags carried by the 28th Regiment, North Carolina Volunteer Infantry, were returned to the state on March 25, 1905.[59]

All Confederate flags captured by Union troops were given a "capture number." This, the

28th Regiment's Flag, capture #364, captured either at Petersburg, April 1–2, or surrendered at Appomattox, April 3–9 (courtesy of the North Carolina Museum of History).

first of these three flags captured from the 28th Regiment, designated Capture #134,[60] was taken at Spotsylvania Court House on May 12, 1864, by John M. Kindig of Company A, 63rd Pennsylvania Volunteers. Kindig received a Congressional Medal of Honor for its capture. The Congressional Medal of Honor was authorized by Resolution of Congress No. 43, approved July 12, 1862, and by an Act of Congress approved March 3, 1863. Numerous soldiers were so honored for capturing Confederate flags.[61]

The flag lost at Spotsylvania Court House was replaced by a flag which was captured just outside of Richmond on July 28, 1864, by Private Samuel L. Malleck, of Company I, 9th New York Cavalry. This regimental flag was designated by the United States War Department as capture #149.[62] It is believed to have been captured near the New Market Road.[63]

The flag designated by the War Department as capture # 364 is believed to have been captured either at Petersburg, Virginia, April 1–2, or sometime during the Appomattox Campaign, April 3–9, 1865. It may have been one of those surrendered at Appomattox Court House on April 9, 1865.[64] This flag had been given the regiment to replace the flag that was captured on July 28, 1864. This final flag carried by the 28th Regiment is unique in its appearance. A field of red is crisscrossed by a band of dark blue, on which are 13 white stars. A 1½" border of bunting surrounds the entire flag. In the center at the top between the cross of stars are the names of the battles in which the regiment participated: Hanover, Mechanicsville, Cold Harbor, Frazier's [*sic*] Farm, Malvern Hill. In the center at the bottom the names of the battles continue with: Wilderness, Chancellorsville, Gettysburg, Falling Waters. Words on the left side represent the battles at Cedar Run, Manassas Junction, Manassas Plains, and Ox Hill. On the right side are lettered the battles of Harpers Ferry, Shepherdstown, Fredericksburg, and Sharpsburg.[65]

The statement of 1st Lieutenant J.P. Little is both beautiful and tragic: "Our flag of the Confederacy is furled, and will live in song and story, though its folds are in the dust."[66]

Conclusion

It was the belief of 1st Lieutenant J.P. Little, of Company C, that the "war between the States was undoubtedly one of the most interesting events in the pages of modern history." Little knew from first-hand experience in battles and as a prisoner of war. He could relate many "thrilling narrations of battle scenes, daring adventures, narrow escapes and feats of personal prowess during the war...." His experiences, like many other veterans, made "indelible impressions upon the tablets of memory."[67]

From one who survived the war and participated in many of the battles fought by the 28th North Carolina, Little said it all when describing the part of his Company C, of the 28th Regiment:

> This company met their responsibilities and performed their duties faithfully and courageously; and on all occasions when the fire of the battles spread its deadly pall over the battlefield, they proved to be as brave as the bravest.[68]

The men of the 28th Regiment made the transition from raw, untrained farm boys to experienced soldiers. That transition was not easy and the battlefield victories were won with sweat and blood. The regiment had it moments of glory, but there were many more times of hardships, punctuated by grief over the death of commanders, relatives and comrades. Considering what the Confederate soldier endured through the four years of fighting, it is remarkable that any survived long enough to be present at the surrender.

The soldiers may have entered the army as young, idealistic, enthusiastic supporters of the Confederacy, but by 1865, they were all hardened by the realities of war and most welcomed peace. Those that endured and those that died on the battlefield deserve to be remembered.

One soldier who gave his life at Reams' Station (my great-uncle) has been immortalized in song. My son, Danny Casstevens, wrote, played and sang a song entitled "Reams' Station," which he has recorded on a CD. It is a beautiful but sad song, about the death of Danny's great-great-uncle, Samuel Speer Harding, and how his body was returned home to Yadkin County for burial in the family cemetery.[69]

Space will not permit full information about all the soldiers who fought in the 28th Regiment, North Carolina Infantry, but perhaps this work will help illuminate the lives and sacrifices of them all.

The author hopes that this book will fill a void and bestow the honor due those brave men of the 28th Regiment, as well as all who served the Confederacy. Their victories and their defeats are ours as well. It is our heritage, and something we must never forget.

Appendix I

Chronology of the 28th Regiment

The shifting of troops makes it difficult to pinpoint the exact location of the 28th in some of the battles. However, the 28th took part in or was present at the following places and battle sites, with the battles in which they participated appearing in italics.

September 21, 1861	28th Regiment organized at Camp Fisher, High Point, NC
Winter of 1861-62	Wilmington, NC
March 14, 1862	*New Bern, NC* 6 men reported missing
May 2, 1862	Board train at Kinston, NC for Virginia
May 26, 1862	*Hanover Court House, VA*
May 27, 1862	*Taliaferro's Mill* 400 men captured, total number killed/wounded unknown Capt. W. H. A. Speer captured
June 1862	Encamped along Brook Turnpike
June 25, 1862	Advanced to Meadow Bridge
June 25–July 1, 1862	*Seven Days' Battles*
June 26, 1862	*Mechanicsville, VA* 2 wounded
June 27, 1862	*1st Cold Harbor/Gaines Mill* 13 killed, 78 wounded
June 27–28, 1862	Garnett's and Golding's Farms
June 29, 1862	Savage Station, Allen's Farm (Peach Orchard)
June 30, 1862	*Frayser's Farm* 6 killed, 50 wounded
July 1, 1862	*Malvern Hill, VA* 19 killed, 130 wounded
July 29, 1862	Gordonsville, VA
August 9, 1862	*Cedar Mountain, VA (Cedar Run)* 3 killed, 26 wounded
August 24, 1862	Moved to Rappahannock River near Warrenton at White Sulphur Springs to destroy bridge
August 27, 1862	Manassas Junction
August 28, 1862	*2nd Manassas* 5 killed, 45 wounded
September 1, 1862	*Ox Hill, VA* near Fairfax Court House 14 killed 92 wounded, 2 missing
September 5, 1862	Crossed Potomac River into Maryland
September 14, 1862	*Bolivar Heights, Harper's Ferry*
September 17, 1862	*Sharpsburg, MD*
September 19, 1862	Back across Potomac

September 20, 1862   Shepardstown MD
                         Castleman's Ferry, Clarke Co., VA
                         Picket duty, snow, very cold weather

        (For casualties from Fredericksburg in 1862 to Petersburg in October 1864, see Appendix VII.)

November 22, 1862   Moved to Fredericksburg, VA
December 13, 1862   *Fredericksburg, VA*
Winter 1862-1863   Moss Neck, VA, below Fredericksburg
                         Picket duty on the Rappahannock River
May 2, 1863   *Chancellorsville*
                         12 killed, 77 wounded
May 4, 1863   Camped at Liberty Mills, VA
June 25, 1863   Crossed Potomac at Shephardstown
July 1, 1863   Moved from South Mountain, PA, to Cashtown
                         Fighting on the west of Gettysburg
July 2, 1863   *Gettysburg, PA*
July 3, 1863   *Pickett's Charge*
July 12, 1863   Hagerstown, MD
                         Falling Waters
                         Culpepper, VA
October 14, 1863   Bristoe Station, VA
October 1863   Tore up railroad tracks at Brandy Station
November 7, 1863   Crossed Rappahannock River
November 8, 1863   Culpepper, VA
                         Liberty Mills
November 27, 1863   *Mine Run*
Winter 1863-64   Encamped on Rapidan River at Liberty Mills
May 4, 1864   Left camp at Liberty Mills
May 5, 1864   *Orange Plank Road*
May 5–6, 1864   *Wilderness*
May 7, 1864   *Spotsylvania Court House* (Lane's Brigade at salient known as the "Mule Shoe")
May 21, 1864   Right of Spotsylvania Court House
May 31, 1864   Storr's Farm on Totopotomy Creek near Pole Green Church
May 23, 1864   *Jericho Mills*
June 1, 1864   *2nd Cold Harbor*
June 13, 1864   Riddle's Shop
June 22, 1864   *Jerusalem Plank Road*
June 23, 1864   Three miles southeast of Petersburg
June 28, 1864   *Gravel Hill*
August 16, 1864   *Fussell's Mill*
August 25, 1864   *Reams' Station, VA*
September 30, 1864   *Jones' Farm*
Winter 1864-65   South of Petersburg
                         Amelia Court house
                         Jetersville
April 9, 1865   Surrender at Appomattox Court House
                         (230 men out of 1,200 left to surrender arms.[1])

Appendix II

Engagements in Which Greenberry Harding Participated

From a list written on an envelope by Greenberry Harding, and found with other family papers in possession of Libby Harding Carter, Winston-Salem, N.C. Transcribed August 24, 2004, by Frances H. Casstevens, whose corrections are in brackets:

June [May 27] 62
Hanover Junction, Va
June
1   Chickahominy River
2   Frazier's Farm _____
3   Ga[i]nes Mill Aug
     2 days
Cavalry
Cedar Mt.   Malvern Hills
9th Aug   Ox Hill, Sept wounded In hand

63   Shepard Town
Gettysburg 2 days
Pickett's charge wounded
Two places Flesh wound
Hagers Town
Falling waters cavalry
Wilderness 2 days
Spotsylvania 3 days

Grapevine bridge
Cold Harbor
Petersburg 2 days

July 28
Gravel Hill near
Gaines Mill Seven miles
below Richmond
Wounded in Left shoulder
ball unextracted
Clavicle shattered

(On back side)
G. B. Harding, Co. I
28th Regt NC Troops
W. H. A. Speers, Cap.
James H. Lane, Col.
L. O'B. Branch, Brigadier Gen.
A. P. Hill Major General

Greenberry Harding (a.k.a. G.B. or "Berry") and the War

The experiences of Greenberry Harding while serving in Company I of the 28th North Carolina Regiment are typical of the experiences of hundreds, even thousands of soldiers, who took part in the War Between the States (the American Civil War).

In his post as a sergeant, Berry kept a record of the men in his company. His daughter, Flora Harding Robinson, sent a typed copy to the Museum of the Confederacy in Richmond, Virginia.

Greenberry noted the battles fought in Virginia in which he participated. Below is a chronological list of the major battles and the dates on which they occurred.

Hanover Court House — May 27, 1862
Gaines' Mill — June 27, 1862
Frayser's Farm — June 30, 1862
2nd Manassas — August 28–30, 1862
Ox Hill — September 1, 1862
Fredericksburg — December 13, 1862
Chancellorsville — May 1–4, 1863
Gettysburg, PA — July 1–3, 1863
Spotsylvania, the Wilderness — May 6 and May 8, 1864
Gravel Hill — July 28, 1864

Greenberry indicated that he was at Cedar Mountain and Malvern Hills, and that he was wounded in the hand at Ox Hill on August 9, 1862. He was wounded again in the fighting at Fredericksburg, Virginia, on December 13, 1862. He returned to duty and was promoted to sergeant in

March of 1863.[1] He was wounded at Gettysburg, Pennsylvania, July 1–3, 1863, and he said that he took part in Pickett's charge where he received two flesh wounds.

Greenberry was in Shepherdstown (now West Virginia) in the summer of 1863, and fought for two days at Gettysburg. He then marched to Hagerstown, and Falling Waters. He was in the fighting at the Wilderness for two days, and at Spotsylvania for 3 days. In addition, he was involved at Grapevine Bridge, Cold Harbor, and Petersburg. In July of 1864, he was involved in the fighting at Gravel Hill seven miles below Richmond. There he was wounded in the left shoulder and his clavicle shattered. The ball was never removed.[2] He was fortunate not to have developed gangrene.

After her father's death in 1931, Flora Harding Robinson, compiled a list of his military service. Greenberry "fought in 24 battles, wounded 4 times [in the] hand, ankle, shoulder and skin." He was wounded in the hand at Ox Hill, Fairfax County, Virginia, 12 miles from Washington, D.C. He was wounded in his shoulder at Gravel Hill while fighting with the Cavalry near Gaines Mill. He lay on the ground all night, and was then found by medics and carried to Druewy's Bluff, before being transferred to Camp Winder at Richmond.[3]

Appendix III

Field and Staff
and Company Officers
28th Regiment, North Carolina Infantry[1]

FIELD AND STAFF

Colonels
Lane, James Henry
Lowe, Samuel D.
Speer, William H. Asbury

Lieutenant Colonels
Lowe, Thomas L.
Barringer, William Davidson

Majors
Reeves, Richard E.
Montgomery, William James
Stowe, Samuel N.

Adjutants
McRae, Duncan A.
Folger, Romulus S.

Assistant Quartermasters
Thompson, George S.
Parker, Durant A.

**Assistant Commissary
of Subsistence**
Gibbon, Nicholas

Surgeons
Gibbon, Robert
McRee, James Fergus
Gaither, William Wiley

Assistant Surgeons
Cox, F.
Luckey, Francis N.
Barham, W. F.

Lane, Thomas B.
Mayo, M. Lewis

Chaplains
Brent, Oscar J.
Kennedy, F. Milton
Henkle, D. L.

Ensign
Little, Junius Pinkney, 1st Lieutenant

Sergeants Major
Lowe, Milton A.
Lowe, John F.
Smith, David B.
Rankin, William Rufus

Quartermaster Sergeants
Kelly, John C. (transferred from Company F, discharged because of "predisposition to disease of the lungs, accompanied with debility")
Moose, Edmund
Lowe, Tullius C.

Assistant Quartermaster Captain
Nicholas Gibbon

Commissary Sergeant
Mauney, William Andrew

Ordnance Sergeant
Johnston, Gabriel P.

Hospital Stewards
Abernathy, John A.
Barker, Larkin Jones

COMPANY OFFICERS

Company A "Surry Regulators"

Captains

Reeves, Richard E.
Norman, William M.
Lovell, Edward F.

Lieutenants

Dobson, Leander H., 3rd. Lieutenant
Dunnigan, A. C., 1st Lieutenant
Folger, Romulus S., 1st Lieutenant
Laffoon, Nathan D., 2nd Lieutenant
Nixon, F. M., 3rd Lieutenant
Norman, Matthew H., 2nd Lieutenant
Snow, James S., 3rd Lieutenant
Thompson, Elijah T., 1st Lieutenant

Company B "Gaston Invincibles"

Captains

Edwards, Thomas H.
Stowe, Samuel N.
Smith, Thomas T.
Rhyne, Robert D.

Lieutenants

Cloninger, Wiley W., 1st Lieutenant
Costner, Hiram J., 3rd Lieutenant

Company C "South Fork Farmers"

Captains

Lowe, Thomas L.
Lowe, Samuel D.
Linebarger, T. James

Lieutenants

Austin, E. Colman, 2nd Lieutenant
Cline, Ephraim Elcanah, 3rd Lieutenant
Gilbert, Jacob H., 1st Lieutenant
Kent, John, 1st Lieutenant
Kincaid, James, 2nd Lieutenant
Lowe, Milton A., 3rd Lieutenant
Throneburg, Marcus Augustus, 1st Lieutenant
Throneburg, Mathias Miller, 2nd Lieutenant
Williams, John Wesley, 2nd Lieutenant

Company D, "Stanly Yankee Hunters"

Captains

Montgomery, William James
Parker, Durant A.

Randle, John W.
Eudy, Moses J.

Lieutenants

Lowder, Lindsey, 3rd Lieutenant
Moose, Edmund, 1st Lieutenant
Parker, Howell A. 1st Lieutenant
Ramsey, Gilliam O., 2nd Lieutenant

Company E, "Montgomery Grays"

Captains

Barringer, William Davidson
Clark, Niven
Green, Thomas S.

Lieutenants

Ewing, James William, 1st Lieutenant
Hurley, Elias, 2nd Lieutenant
McRae, Duncan A, 3rd Lieutenant
McRae, James Lawrence, 3rd Lieutenant
Townsend, Solomon Richardson, 1st Lieutenant
Williams, Isaac, 2nd Lieutenant

Company F, "Yadkin Boys"

Captains

Kenyon [Kinyoun], John Hendricks
Apperson, Thomas V.

Lieutenants

Conrad, John T., 1st Lieutenant
Cornelius, John H., 3rd Lieutenant
Marler, William A., 2nd Lieutenant
Poindexter, John H., 2nd Lieutenant
Starling, James M., 3rd Lieutenant
Truelove, John George, 1st Lieutenant

Company G, "Guards of Independence"

Captains

Martin, William Joseph
Johnston, George Burgwyn
Morrow, Elijah Graham
McCauley, George W.

Lieutenants

Andrews, Henry Calvin, 2nd Lieutenant
Angerman, William H., 2nd Lieutenant
Edwards, Edwin S., 1st Lieutenant
Morrow, Daniel F., 1st Lieutenant

Oldham, William P., 3rd Lieutenant
Scott, Calvin, 3rd Lieutenant

Company H, *"Cleveland Regulators"*

Captains

Wright, William W.
Bridges, Isaac O.
Holland, Gold Griffin

Lieutenants

Abernathy, John A., 1st Lieutenant
Bridges, Burrel H., 3rd Lieutenant
Gilbert, William W., 1st Lieutenant
Green, Thomas Frank, 3rd Lieutenant
Lowe, Milton A., 1st Lieutenant
Rollins, Drury D., 2nd Lieutenant
Simmons, Stephen A., 3rd Lieutenant
Smith, David B., 2nd Lieutenant
Webb, Lorenzo Dow, 2nd Lieutenant

Company I, *"Yadkin Stars"*

Captains

Speer, William H. Asbury
Bohannon, Neal
Bohannon, Simon S.

Lieutenants

Folger, Romulus S., 2nd Lieutenant
Holcomb, Daniel F., 1st Lieutenant
Holcomb, John T., 3rd Lieutenant
Long, Frederick, 2nd Lieutenant
Snow, Jordan H., Jr., 1st Lieutenant
Thompson, Samuel Tunstall, 2nd Lieutenant
Todd, Leander A, 3rd Lieutenant

Company K, *"Stanly Guards"*

Captains

Moody, John A.
Crowell, James M.
Stone, Adam Whitmon

Lieutenants

Biles, Isaac T., 2nd Lieutenant
Bost, Daniel J., 2nd Lieutenant
Turner, Henry Clay, 2nd Lieutenant
Turner, Preston H., 1st Lieutenant

Height of the Soldiers
in Company F, 28th Regiment

(As Compiled by Dr. John H. Kinyoun)

Officers

Capt. John H. Kinyoun
1st Lieu. T. V. Apperson, 5'10"
2nd Lieu. John H. Poindexter
3rd Lieu. W. A. Marler, 5'5"
1st Serg. John C. Kelly, 5'10"
2nd Serg. G. D. Williams, 5'4"
3rd Serg. R. M. Logan (pro
    Tem), L. Choplin 6'1½"
4th Serg. Reps Martin, 5'8"
1st Corp. William H. Apper-
    son, 6'1"
2nd Corp. William D. Kelly,
    5'10" and 5'11"
3rd Corp. J. F. Fletcher, 6'
4th Corp. Joseph Choplin, 5'8"
Ensign T. C. M. Poindexter,
    6'1"
Drummer — Eugene Kittle, 5'5"
Fifer — Costin Kittle, 5'5"

Privates

B. F. Adams, 5'10"
T. V. Apperson, 5'10"
P. A. Apperson, 5'10"
William H. Apperson, 6'1"
J. W. Binkley, 5'8"
George Blakely, 6'
George W. Bovender, 5'9"
H. T. Brann, 5'6"
J. M. Brann, 5'6"

John F. Brown, 5'11"
J, K. P. Brown, 5'8"
Eugene Carter, 5'9"
J. A. Carter, 5'7½", 5'8"
Jos. Choplin, 5'8"
Robert Choplin, 5'10"
Sid Choplin, 6'2"
Wesley Choplin, ___
J. S. Colvard, 5'10"
T. E. Colvard, 5'10"
William M. Colvard, 5'6"
A. E. Cornelius, 5'9"
B. L. (S?) Cuzzens ___
Lemuel Cuzzens, 5'9"
Daniel Davis, 5'7"
Thomas W. Davis, ___
Lewis Donathan, 5'8"
William Donathan, 5'11"
Alex Fortner, 5'10"
J. W. Freeman, 5'7"
Frank Gough, 6'1"
William D. Hale, 5'5"
L. W. Hall, ___
B. C. Head, 5'6"
W. L. Head, 5'8"
T. R. Hicks, 5'7"
Richard Hunt, 5'10"
R. H. Hutchens, 5'10"
Samuel G. Hutchens, 5'6"
David W. Joyner, ___
J. L. (S?) Joyner, 5'10"
Timothy Joyner, 5'7"
J. M. Kirk, 5'8"

R. M. Logan, ___
J. F. Marler, 5'7"
A. Martin, ___
Gilbert Martin, ___
Nicholas Mikles, 5'10"
Hiram Mitchell, 6"
Milton Marrah, 5'9"
Abram Murphy, 5'10"
G. D. Myers, 5'11"
F. A. Myers, 6'2"
J. W. Nance, 5'11"
J. G. Nicholson, 6'1"
William Norman, 6'
J. R. Pierce, ___
I. C. Poindexter, 5'8"
A. T. Randleman, 5'11"
Robert Rash, 6'1"
R. M. Rash, 5'11"
J. M. Starling, 5'7"
William Spillman, 5'6", 5'7"
George Shepherd, 5'11"
George W. Shipwash, 6'
William H. Speas, 5'11"
John H. Speer, ___
L. H. Speer, 5'9"
John W. Tackett, 5'9"
Frank Taylor, ___
J. C. Truelove, ___
Thomas P. Webb, ___
G. D. Williams, 5'5"
Thomas H. Wooten, 5'8", 5'9"
A. Yarborough, ___

This list was compiled by Captain John Hendricks Kinyoun in a small, leather-bound notebook which consisted of 40 pages. The above is an alphabetical listing taken from two lists of officers, and privates. The first list consisted of 83 names, of which 66 were included in the second list of 75 names. An additional 17 names of privates on the first list were not included in the list which gave their heights. These were:

John R. Bovender
F. F. Brown

S. D. Cuzzins
John T. Conrad

John H. Cornelius
Jonathan Davis

Burrel Evans
Jesse F. Flinn
A. Y. Hauser
James N. Marler

T (R?) Pack
William Pettett
Ed Sawyers
James Sawyers

John Sawyers
A. M. Womack[1]

The average height for privates was 5'9½" and officers, 5'10".

Appendix V

Casualties in Lane's Brigade, May 5, 1864–October 1, 1864[1]

Battle	Killed Officers	Men	Wounded Officers	Men	Missing Officers	Men	Totals Officers	Men	Total
Wilderness, May 5–6	3	40	18	210	4	141	25	391	416
Spotsylvania C. H., May 12	5	39	14	106	14	293	33	438	471
Near Spotsylvania Court House, May 21	1	2	2	15	1	7	4	24	28
Jericho Ford, May 23		10	8	74		10	8	94	102
Storr's Farm, Totopotomoy Creek, May 31		2	2	18			2	21	23
Turkey Ridge, near Gaines Mill, June 3–12	1	2	3	27			4	29	33
Riddle's Shop, June 13				5		2		7	7
3 mi SE Petersburg, June 22		7	4	46		5	4	58	62
Petersburg, June 23–25, 1864	1	5		12			1	17	18
Gravel Hill, July 28	3	8	5	45	4	73	12	126	138
Fussell's Mill, Aug. 16–18	2	6	5	49	1	26	8	81	89
Ream's Station, Aug 25	?	10	15	82		6	17	98	115
Jones' Farm, Sept. 25	1	8	10	87		5	11	100	111
Pegram's Farm, Oct. 1		4		8				12	12
Grand Total	19	143	86	785	24	568	129	1496	1625

Appendix VI

Casualties Among Officers of the 28th Regiment, May–October 1864[1]

Wilderness, May 5–6

Killed: 0. *Wounded:* 1st. Lt. M. J. Eudy, Co. D; 1st Lt. E. S. Edwards, Co. G; 1st Lt. A. W. Stone, Co. K. *Missing:* 1st Lt. E. Hurless, Co. *Total:* 4

Spotsylvania C. H., May 12

Killed: Capt. N. Clark, Co. E. *Wounded:* 2nd Lt. R. D. Ormond, Co. B. *Missing:* Capt. S. S. Bohannon, Co. I; 2nd Lt. H. C. Andrews, Co. G; 2nd Lt. P. H. Turner, Co. K. *Total:* 5

Near Spotsylvania C.H., May 21

Killed: 1st Lt. E.S. Edwards, Co. G. *Wounded:* 0. *Missing:* 0. *Total:* 1

Jericho Ford, May 23

Killed: 0. *Wounded:* 1st Lt. R. D. Rhyne, Co. B.; 2nd Lt. H. J. Costner, Co. B. *Missing:* 0. *Total:* 2

Turkey Ridge, June 3–12

Killed: 0. *Wounded:* Brig. Gen. James H. Lane. *Missing:* 0. *Total:* 1

Riddle's Shop, June 13

Killed: 0. *Wounded:* 0. *Missing:* 0. *Total:* 0

Near Petersburg, June 22

Killed: 0. *Wounded:* 2nd Lt. J. G. Truelove, Co. F. *Missing:* 0. *Total:* 1

In front of Petersburg, June 23–25

Killed: Capt. J. M. Crowell, Co. K. *Wounded:* 0. *Missing:* 0. *Total:* 1

Gravel Hill, July 28

Killed: 0. *Wounded:* 0. *Missing:* 1st Lt. M. A. Lowe, Co. H; 2nd Lt. Isaac Williams, Co. E. *Total:* 2

Fussell's Mill, Aug 16–18

Killed: 0. *Wounded:* 0. *Missing:* 0. *Total:* 0

Ream's Station, Aug. 25

Killed: Capt. T. T. Smith, Co. B. *Wounded:* Col. W. H. A. Speer, 28th staff*; Capt. T. J. Linebarger, Co. C; Capt. T. S. Green, Co. E; Capt. G. W. McCauley, Co. G; 1st Lt. R. D. Rhyne, Co. B; 1st Lt. M. A. Thornburg, Co. C. *Missing:* 0. *Total:* 7

Jones' Farm, Sept. 30

Killed: 0. *Wounded:* Capt. E. F. Lovill, Co. A.; 1st Lt. M. A. Thornburg, Co. C; 2nd Lt. L. G. Truelove, Co. F. *Missing:* 0. *Total:* 3

Pegram's Farm, Oct. 1

Killed: 0. *Wounded:* 0. *Missing:* 0. *Total:* 0

Killed 4, Wounded 17, Missing 6 = Total 27

*Colonel W. H. A. Speer was mortally wounded and died a few days later. Sergeant Samuel Speer Harding, Company I, 28th, was killed by a shot through the hip.

Appendix VII

Casualties in the 28th Regiment, 1862–1864

Battle	Killed Officers	Men	Wounded Officers	Men	Missing Officers	Men	Totals Officers	Men	Total
Fredericksburg[1] 12/13/1862	?	16	?	49			?	65	65
Gettysburg[2] 7/3/1863	?	12	?	92			12	92	104
Wilderness[3] 5/5/1864		14	3	54	1	16	4	84	88
Spotsylvania[4] 5/12/1864	1	7	1	17	3	97	5	121	126
Near Spotsylvania 5/13–20/1864[5]		1		1				2	2
Spotsylvania[6] 5/21/1864	1			2			1	2	3
Jericho Ford[7] 5/23/1864	1	4	1	23		1	2	28	30
2nd Cold Harbor, etc.[8] 5/24–6/3/1864		1		6				7	7
Petersburg[9] 6/23/1864	1	7		16			1	23	24
Various battles[10] 5/5/–6/2/1864	4	32		121		132	4	285	289
Gravel Hill[11] 7/28/1864		1		14	2	23	2	28	30
Petersburg[12] 9/20–10/1/1864		2	2	26			2	28	30
Total	8	97	7	421	6	269	33	775	808

Appendix VIII

Officers and Men of the 28th Regiment Who Surrendered on April 9, 1865[1]

Allison, W. T., Pvt., Co. B
Almond, D., Pvt., Co. K
Angerman, W. H., 2nd Lt., Co. D
Anthony, H. G., Sgt., Co. A
Atwater, M., Pvt., Co. G
Austin, D. P., Pvt., Co. K
Baldwin, A. J., Pvt., Co. B
Ballard, W. M., Sgt., Co. E
Barbee, H., Pvt., Co. D
Barnett, C. M., Pvt., Co. H
Beaty, J. F., Pvt., Co. B
Bill, J. C., Pvt., Co. B
Bolch, J., Pvt., Co. C
Bolch, A., Corpl., Co. C
Bolch, H. A., Pvt., Co. H
Bolch, F., Pvt., Co. H
Bolch, F. H., Pvt., Co. C
Brannock, J., Pvt., Co. A
Bridgers, S. G. H., Pvt., Co. H
Bridgers, T. S., Pvt., Co. H
Brown, J., Pvt., Co. A
Bumbarner, A., Pvt., Co. C
Burlyson, A., Pvt., Co. D
Canady, J., Pvt. Co. G
Carpenter, M., Pvt., Co. B
Carpenter, A., Pvt., Co. D
Carpenter, C., Pvt., Co. B
Carson, R. W., Corpl., Co. B
Carter, J. C., Pvt., Co. C
Champion, D. O. P., Pvt., Co. H
Cheek, J. W., Pvt., Co. G
Chisholm, M., Pvt., Co. E
Clark, M. A., Pvt., Co. B
Clemmer, L. R., Pvt., Co. B
Coe, A., Pvt., Co. A
Conrad, S., Pvt., Co. C
Cook, L., Pvt., Co. C
Corkier, W., Pvt., Co. K

Crawford, J. A.., Sgt., Co. E
Crawford, S. A., Pvt., Co. G
Crayton, U., Corpl., Co. D
Davis, G. W., Pvt., Co. K
Dickson, W. H., Pvt., Co. F
Durham, J. S., Sgt., Co. G
Durham, W. P., Pvt., Co. G
Durham, F. R., Corpl., Co. G
Edwards, H. A., Sgt., Co. G
Eudy, J., Pvt., Co. K
Folger, R. S., Adjt., Field & Staff
Ford, L. H., Pvt., Co. B
Foster, T. M., Sgt., Co. B
Frada, A. J., Pvt., Co. C
Freeman, M. H., Pvt. Co. A
Fry, D. A., Pvt. Co. K
Furr, A., Pvt. Co. K
Gaither, W. W., Surgeon, Field & Staff
Gaston, R. W., Musician, Co. B
Gates, A. L., Pvt., Co. A
Gean, W. P., Pvt., Co. G
Gold, P. G., Corpl., Co. H
Green, J. M. J., Pvt., Co. H
Green, J. M. S., Pvt., Co. H
Green, T. F., 2nd Lt., Co. H
Green, Do. O., Pvt., Co. H
Green, R. H., Pvt., Co. H
Green, J. M., Sgt., Co. H
Grubs, L. E., Pvt., Co. F
Halton, R. J., Pvt., Co. E
Hambrick, J., Pvt., Co. H
Hathcock, Corpl., Co. K
Hawkins, J. R., Pvt., Co. H
Haynes, T. F., Pvt. Co. H
Hefner, G., Pvt., Co. C
Hefner, D., Pvt., Co. C
Hefner, S., Pvt., Co. C
Henkle, D. S., Chaplain, Field & Staff

Herman, J. N., Pvt., Co. C
Herman, D. M., Corpl., Co. C
Herman, T. J., Sgt., Co. C
Hicks, John, Pvt. Co. F
Hill, J. S., Pvt., Co. E
Hines, J. B., Pvt., Co. B
Hines, George, Corpl., Co. B
Holden, J. A., Sgt., Co. A
Holland, T. J., Sgt., Co. H
Holland, G. G., Capt., Co. H
Holler, A. D., Pvt., Co. C
Holt, B. A., Pvt., Co. K
Houston, J. M., Pvt., Co. C
Houston, J. F., Corpl., Co. C
Hovis, J. P., Prt., Co. B
Hunnucutt, S., Pvt., Co. C
Hutchins, I, Pvt., Co. H
Ingram, W. B., Pvt., Co. E
James, N. C., Pvt., Co. D
Johnston, J. P., Pvt., Co. G
Jolly, M. M., Sgt., Co. H
Key, A. J., Pvt. Co. A
Killian, C. E., Pvtg., Co. C
Kirk, W. A., Pvt., Co. K
Kiser, M., Pvt., Co. B
Lail, P. H., Pvt., Co. H
Leeper, F. W., Corpl., Co. B
Lewis, J. J., Pvt., Co. B
Liks, J. T., Pvt., Co. E
Linebarger, M. M., Pvt., Co. C
Linebarger, T. J., Capt., Co. C
Lisk, W. F., Musician, Co. E
Lloyd, L. J., Sgt., Co. G
Lovelace, J. L., Pvt., Co. H
Lovill, E.F., Capt., Co. A
Lowe, T. C., Q.M. Sgt., Field & Staff
Lynly, J. H., Corpl., Co. D
Magee, J. L., Pvt., Co. A
Marby, A. C., Pvt., Co. K

Marsh, Wm., Pvt., Co. A
Marten, James, Musician, Co. K
Martin, W. A., Pvt., Co. C
McCauley, J. T., Pvt., Co. E
McCraver, F. H., Pvt., Co. B
Miller, J. M., Pvt., Co. H
Milton, G., Pvt., Co. K
Moore, G. M., Sr., Pvt., Co. H
Moore, D. O. H. P., Pvt., Co. H
Morrow, D. F., 1st Lt., Co. G
Motley, Thomas, Pvt., Co. K
Nixon, W. P., Pvt., Co. A
Ormand, R. D., 2nd Lt., Co. B
Phillips, J., Pvt., Co. G
Plyer, E. A., Pvt., Co. D
Plyer, D. W., Corpl., Co. D
Plyler, H.D., Pvt., Co. D
Poe, S. A., Pvt., Co. G
Poe, R. P., Pvt., Co. G
Poindexter, P. H., Pvt., Co. G
Poovey, H. H., Pvt., Co. C
Poovey, J. A., Sr., Pvt., Co. C
Poovey, J. A., Jr., Pvt., Co. C
Poovey, T., Pvt., Co. C
Poovey, S., Pvt., Co. C
Poplin, D., Pvt., Co. K
Pruit, John, Pvt., Co. H
Pruit, J. C., Pvt. Co. H
Pruitt, J. A., Pvt., Co. D
Raider, W. P., Pvt., Co. C

Rankin, W. W., Pvt., Co. B
Rankin, W. R., Sgt. Maj., Field & Staff
Reece, E. H., Pvt., Co. H
Rhyne, A. M., Corpl., Co. B
Rhyne, A., Pvt., Co. B
Richin. M., Capt., Co. D
Robertson, H. H., Pvt., Co. G
Robinson, T. C., Pvt., Co. E
Ross, D. M., Sgt., Co. K
Ross, G. P., Pvt., Co. K
Rudisil, John, Pvt., Co. D
Sail, A., Pvt., Co. C
Sanders, T. L., Pvt., Co. B
Scott, Thomas G., Pvt., Co. H
Shields, J. C. D., Musician, Co., B
Shields, J. W., Pvt., Co. B
Shoe, R., Pvt. Co. K
Shurin, J., Pvt., Co. B
Sides, W. H., Pvt., Co. D
Smith, G. C., Pvt., Co. K
Smith, W. A., Pvt., Co. B
Spencer, S., Pvt., Co. C
Spencer, P. J., Pvt., Co. C
Starr, A., Pvt., Co. C
Stone, A. W., Capt., Co. K
Stone, R. B., Pvt., Co. B
Swaringen, W. V., Pvt., Co. K
Sykes, J. J., Pvt., Co. G
Talley, F. W., Sgt., Co. D

Thomas, J. F., Pvt., Co. B
Thomas, W. B. Pvt., Co. B
Thompson, S. T., 2nd Lt., Co. I
Thompson, T. H., Pvt., Co. G
Thornburg, M. M., 2nd Lt., Co. C
Thornburg, J. S., Pvt., Co. B
Todd, L. A., 2nd Lt., Co. I
Townsen, A. E., Pvt., Co. C
Turbyfield, J. S., Musician, Co. C
Turner, H. G., 2nd Lt., Co. K
Underwood, John, Pvt., Co. D
Vanhoy, A., Pvt. Co. K
Wagoner, J. W., Pvt., Co. H
Ward, J. R., Pvt., Co. G
White, W., Pvt., Co. A
White, R. A., 1st Lt., Co. B
Whitesides, W. E., Pvt., Co. B
Whitly, M., Pvt. Co. K
Williams, R. S., Pvt., Co. E
Williams, M. M., 2nd Lt., Co. C
Willis, M., Pvt., Co. B
Wilson, S. S., Pvt. Co. B
Workman, G. B., Pvt., Co. G
York, L. C., Pvt., Co. A
Yount, A. E., Pvt., Co. C

[Signed] T. J. Linebarger, Capt. Comdlg Regt.

Total Number = 199

Number of the 28th Regiment who Surrendered at Appomattox = 230 (includes 17 Officers, and 213 privates)[2]

Appendix IX

The Harding Family and Letters from the Battlefield

Samuel Speer Harding enlisted as a private at age 23 on August 31, 1861 for a period of one year. He became a member of the Yadkin County Company I, of the 28th North Carolina Infantry, and received a $50 bounty for enlistment. His monthly pay was $17. Sometime during the period August 13, through October 13, 1861, Sam was granted a 7-day furlough. This was probably before his regiment left for Wilmington on September 30. Sam was to spend the next few months in the Wilmington, North Carolina, area.[1]

His brother, Greenberry Harding, four years younger than Sam, enlisted at age 18 on March 8, 1862. He was wounded several times (three times at Gettysburg alone), but always returned to duty. He was promoted to sergeant in March of 1863. After being wounded at Gravel Hill on July 28, 1864, Greenberry was retired from service because of disability.[2] He returned to the family home near Huntsville to rebuilt his life and the fortunes of his family. He married and left many descendants.

The family of the Harding brothers was typical of many families that lived in the Piedmont section of North Carolina. They owned large tracts of land, and a few slaves.

Their parents, William Harding and his wife, Jane Elizabeth Speer, were married in 1838. Immediately, they began raising a family. Most of their children were born in a house that still stands just off Speer Bridge Road. Built in 1836, it is a typical two-story weather-boarded log house. In the 1850s, a two-story ell was added. The Harding family lived here until they sold out and traveled to Texas, intending to settle there.[3]

The Harding family returned from Texas in 1856 and settled nearer the town of Huntsville. This town grew up near the famous Shallow Ford of the Yadkin River. The town had churches, stores, blacksmith shop, a post office, a tavern and stage-coach stop, and a school. The streets of the town were 66 feet wide, and lots had been laid off and sold by Charles Hunt, the town's founder.[4] The village bordered the heavily-traveled Salem to Mulberry Fields Road.

At the Red Store in Huntsville, area residents could buy items that could not be grown or made at home. The extant store ledgers reveal a variety of purchases made by people from a wide area.

In 1860, William Harding was 52 years old, his wife, 45. He was listed as "farmer," and he owned real property valued at $4,500, and personal property valued at $11,567.[5] The Hardings were probably counted as part of the "upper class," because of the amount of land and slaves the family owned.

By the time the census was taken on July 24, 1860, five of the eight Harding children were listed as "attending school this year." Even the oldest son, Sam, age 21, who worked as a farm laborer, had attended school that year, as had Berry (age 17), Squire Boone (age 15), Alice Jane (age 10), and Joseph W. (age 5).

William Harding owned several slaves. His ancestors, including his grandparents, William and Obedience Harding, had owned slaves for generations. In 1790, grandfather William Harding, who had migrated to North Carolina from Virginia, was credited with owned 13 slaves, according to the census that year. When he died about 1795, his wife, Obedience Hutchens Harding, was dismissed from the Deep Creek Friends Church for owning the slaves she inherited at her husband's death.[6] Henceforth, the Harding family were either Baptists or Methodist, never again Quakers.

In 1860, the Harding family was prospering, and they worked and lived in the peaceful Yadkin River Valley. That peace and prosperity was soon shattered with the bombardment of Fort Sumter. Some of the experiences of the two sons in the Confederate Army can be gleaned from the following letters from Samuel Speer Harding and Greenberry Harding written 1862–1864, while both served in Company I, 28th Regiment, North Carolina Infantry, Confederate States Army.

1. Samuel Speer Harding to father, William Harding, Huntsville, Yadkin County, NC

Wilmington January 23, 1862
Dear Father   I find my self seated to drop you a few lines to inform you that I am better and I think that I will get well if nothing [else] dont happen. No than I think will altho though[t] is required for me to take leave of my self and I think I will certainly do that. I was glad to he[a]r from you all and to know that you was all well. The next week after N. Bohannon went home I went to Weldon me and six privates to guard the brigs [bridges?]. So we staid up there nine days and the last three days I was sick and I came back to Wilmington sick own Sunday and I have been very sick most of them. The Doctor said that I had tifoid [typhoid] fever but as it happened it did not take much hold on me he find. They broke it over me but you would not [know] me if you was to see me now. I dont think that I would way [weigh] more than 120 pounds. I think that I [have] falen off, at least 40 pound. I received my box, and it had my keg of whiskey, but Neal Bohanon had [his] own things on the express, but we had to pay own them. I had to pay four dollars own my box. I have sold several gallons, and if I had a barrel [of] whiskey, I could sell the last bit of it at 50 cent a quart. We have some nuse. We heard the other day that there was a large quantity of vessels at Cape Hatteras, some that they was a hundred 20 [120] vessels. They have been a fine vessels on the coast but dont think that they is any danger of getting at Wilmington to fite no more danger I dont believe than is getting into one at home. I received my shirt that you sent me and was glad to get trunk, a good thing as it was and we all got [our] own clothing. I got one pare of pants and one shiret and one pare of drawers, one pare of shoes, and one pare of socks and one over coat and drawed one good blanket that I wouldn't take ten dollars for it. You can tell Berry that I sent his coat home to him. I could of sold it for seven dollars, but I thou[ght] that I had better send it home. I am going to send you my blanket the first opportunity and want you [to] take good care of it for me. I don't want you to make me any more things for I have got as many things as I want to and I don't want you [to send] me any more. I sent by Neal, twenty-five dollars, to Pap and he said that he paid it to Pap but you never said any[thing] about getting it. You can tell all of them howdy for me. You may look for me when you see me a coming. I have no nuse of any information to write to you must excuse my handwriting and speling for I am quiet weak to day.

Samuel S. Harding

2. Samuel Speer Harding, in Virginia, to his mother, Jane Speer Harding,

Camp Gregg V. A.
January the 24 1863

Dear Mother.   It is with Pleasure that I seat my Self to drop you a few lines to let you know that me and Berry is both well at Present and in hope these few lines may find you all well when it comes to hand. we got a letter yesterday dated December 26 whitch was a month a go. We got one was wrote before that You said that I had forgotten your Poor old mother but I never will forget you as long as I live but I have not writen to you in a long time but we have ben marching so much that I could not write to you nor any body else I wrote to K. Long* when I was at Lynchburg, but I have not got any letter from noon of you. You may think hard of me for not writing to you, but I think hard of not getting no letters from me of late but I could not expect to get many when we was marching to much. I would like to see you all mity well but I do not no when I will get to come home.

they are furlowing to [2] men from every company ever twenty days then if two from our Company gone home I think that I will get to come the next time there is any to go I don't no whether there will be any more or not. I am a fraid they wont furlow any more. You have heard from the fight at *Fredericksburg.* we had a hard time there. I am glad [to] Say that we have ben Blesed so far, but I think that they out to give a furlow for I have done a heap of hard marching and hard Fighting I think that I deserve a furlow if any one in the Company does, but I could tell you now but I will bring my Letter to a close _____ have mor nus _____ something to you at that time. I remain your True Son until Death

S. S. Harding To his mother —

*his sister, Keziah Harding, wife of Dr. Thomas Long. Keziah died in 1863.

3. Samuel Speer Harding to father, William Harding, Huntsville, NC

Camp Gregg, VA
January 24, 1863

Dear Father,   Being at leasure this morning to drop you a few lines to let you know that we are both well at this time and in hope these few lines may find you all well. I wrote for you to come to see us but we heard that you had — — to come down to see us and we heard that you that you give out coming till you found out where we was for certain we heard that we was ordered two North Carolina we have been under marching orders for ten days but we do not know for certain whethere we will go or not. I think that we will go to North Carolina or two Tennessee we will write to you a gain before we leave I think that you hade better wait and see what we are a going two do we would be very glad to see you but we will let you know what to do. I think that maby I will get to come home between now and Spring I want you to come when you find out where we are for two come and see us. If we come toward Weldon it will be ___ nearer and it wount be any Trouble to you but I think you had better wait till you find out for certain _____ __ You wrote that Mother had maid some Pants and some other things but we have got plenty of clothing. So you need not to fetch any for us for we do not need them.

I want you to fetch us some dryed fruit if you do come and some honey, and some butter and some sausage meat, and several other things I have no more nus worth writing to you at Present.

I remain your true Son
S. S. Harding

Berry is Provost Guard and he told me to tell you that he was well and he would write to some of you in a few days. So no more at Present S. S. Harding

4. *Greenberry Harding to parents, William and Jane Harding*

Camp Near Orange Court House Virginia
November 25 1863 Co. I

Dear Father & Mother

It is with pleasure that I am seated to drop you a few lines to let you no that we are all well & doing as well as you could expect & I hope that these few lines may find you all Enjoying a reasonable portion of health. I have no very important news to communicate at this time. There is no movement with the army and as can be ascertained we have all built our little huts & have [moved?] in them now & got chimneys built to them which makes them very comfortable.

Our fair is tolerable good now. We get a plenty of good Beef & Bread & some time we get some few potatoes & turnips as to our fair I cannot complain. Our Duty on Picket is very hard we have to go every five days & guard a round the camp. Ever two days & drill twice aday when we are not on Picket or on guard. Our regt & the thirty seventh is under one guard line in camp & all the rest of the eight has moved out to theirselves & left us where the Brigade was camp at before they left Sun. Brigade is nearly clothesless lots of the boys are nearly naked & barefooted & there is not any of the boys that has socks & *hardly* Only those that has had them sent to them from home. Major Thompson says that there is two thousand suits at Richmond for our Brigade & that we will get them soon but as to myself I am a doing very well about clothing & shoes & socks. There is several men in the Guard House now for desertion. [I] think several will be shot from the charges that was brought up against them. George Shipwash of Co. F is hard suffering & has been ever since he was bought back under guard. There is several that has to wear a ball & chain for two months There is three out of our company that has to wear a ball & chain. James Chappel & L. M. Swaim & Issac Rose. There is one in our company is thought will be shot Elija Petty.

he was whiped at Yadkin for stealing leather. We heard here that Longstreet has won a great victory in the west & captured two thousand Prisoners & captured a lot of army equipage. It is to be hoped he will _____ at Knoxville this winter ____

Yesterday was my birthday & I was on Picket & had a bad wet day for a birth day. I hope against my birth day comes a gain I will be at home out of this terrible war I was twenty one years old yesterday. & I once thought when I became of age I would be free & aloud to do as I please but I have found out better now. instead of being free I am bound down tighter than any slave is in Yadkin County. I always thought I was living a hard time when I was under you but I have found out that any one is the best of[f] when he is with his parents & I wish I was with you all today & I could tell you of a heap of my ups & downs. Boone wrote in his letter that Thomas Brewbaker had threaten your life & his. I would not mind nothing he said nor pay any attention to his long tongue for you no how he always has his jah [jaw] arunning & besides that you never did no a barking dog to bite & that is the way with him. I must bring my letter to a close by saying take good care of your selves & write soon & give me all the news. Give my love to all the children & save a portion for your selves.

Your son, G. B. Harding

5. *Samuel S. Harding to father, William Harding (on back of Greenberry's letter)*

November the 25 1863

Dear Father

As Berry is writing to you I will drop you a few lines to let you know that I am in very good health at present and in hopes these few lines may find you in better health than you have been. I was sorry to hear that your health had ben bad since I left home. I was glad to hear that you was getting a long very well with your work we are in our Little Shanties know and are doing very well but I don't know how long we will get to stay hear But I think will get to stay a month or longer or mabe till Spring. I have no nuse of any importance Our Army is in very good health know. We have Seventy men in our Company know for duty whitch is present We have but fue [few] men sick in our company know. Colonel W. A. Speer is well and sends his best respect to you and the rest of the Family he is well and is doing well I think if I was in your Place I would write to Speer. I have not received one single letter from any of you since I left home. I will bring my few remarks to a close Saying write soon not more at Present only I remain

Your True Son until Death S. S. Harding.

Dear mother   I write you a few lines to let you know that I have not forgotten you. I am glad that you are get on as well. I have no nuse worth writing to you I would like to be at home at Christmas But there is no chance I am with hope Berry will get a furlow before long. I will close by sending my love to you and the children no more at present

S. S. Harding

6. Greenberry Harding to his brother, Squire Boone Harding

Hanover Junction, VA
Monday 23 of [May] 1864

Dear Brother Boon

As we have stoped hear at Hanover Junction I will drop you a few lines for the first time since the fight has been in opposition The Yankees with drew from Spottsylvania CH & we suppose they are going down on the opposite side of the South *Flu-vanna* river but as for myself I cannot tell any thing about where Grant is going to make his appearance next but I suppose he will appear before very long. We had some very hard fighting up at Spottsylva-nia but I think the Yanks lost five to our one in killed & wounded but I suppose they taken as many prisoners as we did as they done nearly all the charging. Our Brigade made two charges we had very good success both times. The first time we taken as many prisoners as they were men in our Brigade it was a terrible mixed up affair we was right in among the Yankee's lines we taken a bat-terie from the Yankees but did not keep it for the Yankees was *aplundering* us & we had to get out of their in double quick time . we made a charge up at the Wilderness & routed the Yankees & taken several prisoners The Yankees stunk so bad that we could hardly go over the Battle Field at Spottsylva-nia. I wish all the dead Yankees that has been killed in these fights was laid on the walk at Washington city for one day that this war would end the next day certain. I think we have had very few men killed for the fighting that has been done I am afraid the worst is to come yet give my love to all the family.

I remain your Brother G. B. Harding

P. S. Write soon if not sooner

(Note at top of page reads: Samuel is well & hearty as common.

7. Samuel Speer Harding to his mother, Jane Speer Harding (Berry has been wounded)

August 11, 1864
Chapin's Farm, VA

Mother

I once more embrace the First oportunity of dropping you a few lines to inform you that I am well and write these few lines may fined you and the rest of family well. Lieut Thomas & T. G. Scott was at Richmond and they went up to see Berry and they said he is doing well and is looking very well as They seemed to think that he would be able to go home in ten days. Berry said he would not go home

until he was stouter. He seemed to be well satisfied with his arm and good treatment he said that he is at the best hospital every was at an they was very good to him he said that the Doctor was going to cut the ball out Thursday. He got one peace of bone cut of his shoulder and it was a tolerable large peace. He will be certain to get a furlough as quick as he is able to come home. I know you all very sorry that he got wounded so bad but thank the Lord it was no worse I am sorry to think that he got wounded after going though so many hard fights. And though so many hard marches and so long but maby it tis all for the best. I have written to you Papa and to Ruth, Boon a line since I came back and have not received a single line from non(e) of you, Ruth all ways wants me to write and say how but I think if some of your have times to write.

I do want to hear from home so bad, and I want to hear from home whether any Body is coming after Berry. If it wont do any good for you to come after him, for the Doctor he wouldn't let him come till he got well and then he sould. Berry said the doctor was mity good to him. I would have wrote yesterday but I thought I would be certain to get a letter this morning. But I did not. I thought I would write this but I ain't going to write any more till I hear from home for this makes two letters for one since I came back that I have wrote home.

It seems to me like it has been three months since I seen any of you but taint one month. I haven't much newes.

We are under marching orders know but some of them said we was agoing to make another line of Brest works in front of these. It is reported that Grant is extending his line on his write (right) and on our left. It would be on the Weldon Railroad or near it. It tis reported that Grant [is] reinforcing Sherman at Augusta C. H. and some thinks that he is sending part of his forces to the Valley. Longstreet is gone to the Valley with his corps and General Ewel is going to keep our brigade and _____ him with city guns on this side of the river. I wish it would be so we have been on this side of the river for one month and better and I think we will be again hyar (here?) as long as Grant stays at Peters-burg. I think Grant has gave out takening Peters-burg. I think he aims to leave Petersburg before long. They say he has moved his siege peaces from there. He has nearly quit shelling the town. They are expecting a hard fight in the Valleys. I wish our men great success. Our men whip the Yankees in the west. The worst is _____ and I wish that they may whip them in the South. I am very sartain that we will keep them back here. We have got the best brest works here and some very large peaces of can-non. It looks like tis impossible for them to go this way to Richmond. It seems like Richmond is a hard road to travel for they have tryed several roads.

I heard that you had fine rains since I left. I am glad to hear that you had rain. I want you all to do the best you can and not see no more trouble than you an help __ have not be [been] on ____ about ____ ___.

I think I will write home if I should happen to get in a fight and get wounded I will write or get some Friend to write.

So I will close for this time so no more at present. Only I remain your true son.

I send howdy to all of the family and to you and tell the Black ones (slaves) that I send howdy to them.

I don't want you to think this is the best paper I can afford for it taint. Have plenty of nice paper. I had this sheet and I thought I would take this.

Write soon, yours
S. S. Harding, Serg.

8. Thomas G. Scott to William Harding, August 27, 1864, reporting death of Samuel Speer Harding at Reams Station, VA.

Petersburg, VA
August 27, 1864

Dear Willie, I sit myself to inform you of the late fighting. Your son Sammy was killed the twenty-fifth of this month. I am sorry to inform you of the fighting, but I felt hit was my duty to write to you about Sergeant S. S. Harding. I am sorry to tell you of his death. He was shot through the hip. He did not live long after he was shot. I did not get to see him after he was killed. I was gone out with one of our men that was wounded and I did not get back till after dark. On the way, we was forced to fall back from the battlefield. If I had of known that he was killed, I would [have] stayed there all night. But what I would of buried him, but I will tell you that I got all of his things. One of our company got through and give them to me. I have his knapsack and I got his pocket book.... I will tell you that Col. [William H. Asbury] Speer was shot through the head. He will die if he all ready ain't dead now. I was sorry to loose my Col. And Sergeant. I will keep Sammy's things till you come after them if I can, fur he was a good friend of mine.

T. G. Scott*

(*T. G. Scott later married Alice, Sam's sister, and they had one daughter, Cora).

Appendix X

Roster of the Troops of the 28th Regiment, North Carolina Infantry

The first attempt to identify those who served in the various regiments from North Carolina was made in 1882 by John W. Moore in a four-volume set entitled, *Roster of North Carolina Troops in the War Between the States*. An index to these books was compiled in 1958 from the card index in the North Carolina Department of Archives and History and placed on multi-volume rolls of microfilm. There are, however, errors on reels 8, 11–12, 14–15, and some of the names which were omitted from the alphabetical listing were inserted at the end.

Twenty years later, a history of the regiments, brigades and battalions from North Carolina was compiled Walter Clark, ed., in a five-volume set entitled, *Histories of the Several Regiments and Battalions from North Carolina in the Great War, 1861–1865, Written by Members of the Respective Commands*, published in 1901. These do not contain lists of individual soldiers but do have many photographs of the officers, and accounts written by participants.

The names and partial service records and other information about the individual soldiers who served in North Carolina units was published in by the North Carolina Division of Archives and History in *North Carolina Troops, 1861–1865: A Roster*, edited by Weymouth T. Jordan, Jr. Volume VIII contains the history and roster of the 28th Regiment, North Carolina Infantry.

More personal information about the men from Yadkin County who served in Company F and Company I of this regiment, and other regiments, can be found in my earlier work, *The Civil War and Yadkin County, North Carolina*, published in 1997 by McFarland & Company, Inc., Jefferson, North Carolina. That information will not be repeated here.

Detailed information about the men from Surry County who served in Company A of the 28th Regiment (and other regiments as well), can be found in Hester Jackson's book, *Surry County Soldiers in the Civil War*.

Pictures and information on some of the men from Company C can be found in an older work entitled, *The Catawba Soldier in the Civil War*, edited by George W. Hahn, and published in 1911.

In 1986, Virginia Greene DePriest published a book containing the names of the pensioners from Cleveland County in her book, *Cleveland and Rutherford Counties, N.C., Confederate Soldiers and Pension Rolls 1861–1865*.

A roster of the men in Company H of the 28th Regiment can be found online at http://freepages.genealogy.rootsweb.com/~judytalk/H28.htm.

All of the above have been consulted to compile the following roster. To make it easier to find a particular soldier, the names have been alphabetized for all 10 companies combined.

Each entry has the soldiers last and first names and, if given, his middle initial. That is followed by the letter of the Company (i.e., Co. I) and the highest rank achieved (i.e., Sergeant), even if reduced in rank at some point. Rank is followed by year of birth and death, if known, in parentheses (i.e., 1840–1862). County or place of enlistment is usually given, although in some instances that information was unknown.

In order to save space, much of the repetitive information has been abbreviated (see key).

Abbreviations Used

abt	About
AWOL	Absent without leave
B., b.	Born
Bur., bur	Buried
Ch.	Church
Co.	Company
CH	Court House
dau	Daughter
Dis	Discharged

DC . . . . District of Columbia
E., e. . . . . Enlisted
Exc, exc . . . . Exchange, exchanged
Ft. . . . . Fort
GA . . . . Georgia
m. . . . . Married
MD . . . . Maryland
NC . . . . North Carolina
NCT . . . . North Carolina Troops
OOA . . . . Oath of Allegiance
PA . . . . Pennsylvania
Pt. . . . . Point
POW . . . . Prisoner of war
Reg . . . . Regiment
SC . . . . South Carolina
trans . . . . Transferred
VA . . . . Virginia

Location of Battle Sites, Prisons, and Other Sites Mentioned Repetitively

Aiken's Landing, James River, VA
Amelia Court House, VA
Appomattox Court House, VA
Appomattox River, VA
Boulware's Wharf, James River, VA
Camp Fisher, near Salisbury, NC
Camp Gregg, VA
Camp Holmes, NC
Camp Stokes, near Greensboro, NC
Cedar Mountain, VA
Chancellorsville, VA
Charlotte, NC
Charlottesville, VA
Chester, PA
City Point, VA
Cold Harbor, VA
Cox's Wharf, James River, VA
Culpeper, VA
Danville, VA
Davids Island, New York Harbor, NY
Deep Bottom, VA
Elmira, NY
Falling Waters, MD
Farmville, VA
Fort Columbus, New York Harbor, NY
Fort Delaware, DE
Fort Monroe, VA
Fort Wood, Beloe's Island, New York Harbor, NY
Frayser's Farm, VA
Fredericksburg, VA
Fussell's Mill, VA
Gaines' Mill, VA
Gettysburg, PA
Goldsboro, NC
Gordonsville, VA
Gravel Hill, VA
Guinea Station, VA
Hanover Court House, VA
Hanover Station, VA
Hart's Island, New York Harbor, NY
Jericho Mills, VA

Johnson's Island, Lake Erie, OH
Jones' Farm, VA
Kinston, NC
Liberty Mills, VA
Lynchburg, VA
Malvern Hill, VA
Manassas, VA
Martinsburg, WVA
Mechanicsville, VA
Newport News, VA
Old Capitol Prison, Washington, DC
Ox Hill, VA
Petersburg, VA
Pickett's Farm, VA
Point Lookout, MD
Reams' Station, VA
Richmond, VA
Sharpsburg, MD
Shephardstown, WVA
Spotsylvania Court House, VA
Staunton, VA
Varina, VA
Venus Point, Savannah River, GA
Wilderness, VA
Wilmington, NC
Winchester, VA

The counties in which the soldiers lived who enlisted in the 28th Regiment (Alexander, Catawba, Cleveland, Forsyth, Gaston, Lincoln, Mecklenburg, Montgomery Orange, New Hanover, Randolph, Rutherford, Stanly, Surry, etc., are cited by name only. Thus, Yadkin County, North Carolina = Yadkin in the following roster.

19th Century Name for Disease   Modern name

diarrhoea . . . . diarrhea
febris typhoides . . . . typhoid fever
phthisis pulmonalis . . . . tuberculosis
consumption . . . . tuberculosis
phthisis (wasting or consumption of tissue) . . . . pulmonary tuberculosis
rubeola . . . . measles or rubella
smallpox . . . . smallpox

References Cited

HYC . . . Casstevens, Frances H., ed. *The Heritage of Yadkin County,* Vol. I
CWY . . . Casstevens, Frances H. *The Civil War and Yadkin County, North Carolina*
CSC . . . . Hahn, George W., ed. *The Catawba Soldier in the Civil War*
Hoots . . Hoots, Carl C., compl. *Cemeteries of Yadkin County, North Carolina*
SCS . . . . Jackson, Hester. *Surry County Soldiers in the Civil War*
NCT. . . . Jordan, Weymouth T. Jordan, Jr., and Manarin, Louis H., eds., *North Carolina Troops, 1861–1865: A Roster*

Roster and Service Record of the Officers
and Soldiers of the 28th Regiment, North Carolina Troops,
Confederate States Army, 1861–1865

ABERNATHY, Alonzo, Co. B, Private (1845–). A resident of Gaston, Alonzo e. in Wake 9/3/1863. Captured near Petersburg on 4/2/1865 and confined at Hart's Island until released 6/17/1865 after OOA (NCT 8, 126).

ABERNATHY, Ira, Co. H, Private (1826–1863). Lived and e. in Lincoln. 10/2/1862, age 36. Died in a Charlottesville hospital 1/16/1863 of typhoid fever (NCT 8, 197).

ABERNATHY, J. Henry, Co. C, Private. A resident of either Lincoln or Gaston counties, Abernathy e. 9/5/1861 at Camp Fisher. Captured at Hanover CH 5/27/1862; confined at Ft. Monroe then Ft. Columbus. Exc at Aiken's Landing, James River 8/5/1862. Captured near Petersburg 4/2/1865; confined at Harts Island until released 6/18/1865 after OOA (NCT 8, 140).

ABERNATHY, J.R., Co. B, Private (1824–). A Gaston resident, J. R. E. at age 39 on 9/3/1863, and trans to the C. S. Navy 4/3/1864 (NCT 8, 126).

ABERNATHY, J. Smith, Co. C, Private. B. in Catawba, he e. 3/14/1864. Died at Richmond 7/21/1864 of disease (NCT 8, 140).

ABERNATHY, John A., Co. H, 1st Lieutenant; Field & Staff, Hospital Steward (—10/8/1862). Lived in Gaston, e. in New Hanover in 1861, age 18, as a private in Co. H, 28th Reg. Promoted to hospital steward abt 12/28/1861, then trans to Field & Staff 28th Reg. Captured at Hanover CH abt 5/27/1862, and confined at Ft. Monroe, then at Ft. Delaware 6/9/1862 until exc abt 8/2/1862, elected 1st lieutenant of Co. H, trans from Field & Staff back to Co. H (NCT 8, 112, 196).

ABERNATHY, Miles L., Co. B, Private (1827–). Miles lived in Gaston but e. in Wake 4/30/1863. Captured near Petersburg 4/2/1865; confined on Hart's Island until released abt 6/18/1865 after OOA (NCT 8, 126).

ABERNATHY, S.M., Co. B, Private (1843–1864). B. and raised in Gaston S. M. E. there at age 19 on 3/29/1862. Wounded in right thigh at Wilderness 5/5/1864, and leg was amputated. Died in Charlottesville hospital 5/27/1864 of wound (NCT 8, 126).

ABERNATHY, Sidney M., Co. C, Private. Sidney e. in Catawba on 8/12/1863. Reported missing in action 5/1/1864 (NCT 8, 140).

ABERNATHY, William H., Co. C, Private. E. in Mecklenburg 3/5/1864. Reported missing in action 5/12/1864 (NCT 8, 140).

ABERNETHY, Gideon A., Co. C, Sergeant. Burke resident, e. in Catawba 8/13/1861 as a private. Promoted to corporal 9/1/1862. Reduced in rank 2/20/1863, then promoted to sergeant May 1863–Oct. 1864. Present through Feb. 1865 (NCT 8, 140).

ADAMS, Benjamin F., Co. F, Private (1841–). Lived, e. in Yadkin 6/18/1861, age 20. Captured near Gettysburg 7/1–5/1863; confined at Davids Island. Trans to City Pt. 9/16/1863 for exc. Captured near Pickett's Farm abt 7/21–22/1864. Confined at Pt. Lookout. Released 10/18/1864 after joining the U.S. Army, Co. D, 4th Reg U.S. Volunteer Infantry (NCT 8, 175).

ADAMS, Elam J., Co. F, Private (1842–) Lived, e. in Yadkin 3/4/1862, age 20. AWOL July–Dec 1862. Captured at Petersburg 4/2/1865; confined at Pt. Lookout until released 6/22/1865 after OOA (NCT 8, 175).

ADAMS, James B., Co. G, Private (1841–1862). Lived, e. in Orange 9/2/1861, age 19. Died near Chapel Hill, NC 1/16/1862 of disease (NCT 8, 185).

ADAMS, Walter, Co. G, Private (1839–1862). Lived, e. in Orange 9/2/1861; died of disease at Wilmington 1/1/1862 (NCT 8, 185).

ADKINS, Robert, Co. A, Private (1836–1862). Surry resident, e. in Forsyth. Reportedly was captured at Hanover CH in May of 1862; Federal Provost Records do not substantiate this claim. Hospitalized in Richmond on 7/2/1862 with a gunshot wound of back. Wounded at Second Manassas abt 8/28/1962; died at Middleburg. (NCT 8, 113; SCS 3).

AKARD, Morgan E., Co. D, Private. Lived in Alexander, e. at Camp Holmes 12/3/1864. Captured near Petersburg 4/2/1865; confined at Pt. Lookout, released 6/22/1865 after OOA (NCT 8, 154).

ALBERTY, Lemuel B., Co. A, Private (1841–1915). B. in Surry to Nathaniel and Rebecca Bray Alberty of Pigeon Roost Creek, e. 8/18/1862 and received $50-bounty. Present until he got pneumonia; given a 30-day furlough 8/23/1864. Captured in a Richmond hospital 4/3/1865. Confined in Richmond's Libby Prison, then trans to Newport News. Released on 6/3/1865. Lemuel m. in Surry Lucinda White, and had 6 children 1864–1876. Deacon of Center Primitive Baptist Ch., both are bur. at Liberty Primitive Baptist Ch. (NCT 8, 113; SCS 3).

ALDERMAN, Ira H., Co. F, Private (1835–). Lived in Alamance, e. in Forsyth 10/1/1862, age 26. Trans to the C. S. Navy 4/3/1864. NC pension records indicate he was wounded at Fredericksburg, Chancellorsville and Gettysburg (NCT 8, 175).

ALDRIDGE, William E., Co. K, Private. Lived in Stanly, e. at Liberty Mills 3/1/1864. Captured near Petersburg 4/2/1865; confined at Pt. Lookout. Released 6/23/1865 after OOA (NCT 8, 220).

ALLEN, Dawson B., Co. E, Sergeant (1834–). Lived, e. in Montgomery 3/10/1862 as a private. Wounded, captured at Gettysburg 7/1–4/1863. Hospitalized at Davids Island; paroled and trans to City Pt. 9/8/1863 for exchange. Promoted to sergeant Sep. 1863–Oct. 1864. Reduced in rank after 2/28/1865. Captured in Richmond hospital 4/3/1865. Trans to Newport News 4/23/1865. Released 6/16/1865 after OOA (NCT 8, 184–165).

ALLISON, James M., Co. H, Private (1844–). Lived, e. in Cleveland 8/22/1861, age 17. Wounded in arm at Gaines' Mill or Frayser's Farm 6/27–30/1862. Arm amputated. Dis 2/2/1864 (NCT 8, 197).

ALLISON, Jasper L., Co. B. Private (1838–). Lived, e. in Gaston 7/30/1861. Captured at Fredericksburg on 12/13/1862; exc on 12/17/1862. Present through Feb. 1865 (NCT 8, 126).

ALLISON, William T., Co. B, Private (1840–). Gaston farmer e., age 21, 7/30/1861. Captured at Hanover CH 5/27/1862; confined at Ft. Monroe, then Ft. Columbus. Paroled . Trans to Aiken's Landing for exchange 8/5/1862. Surrendered at Appomattox CH 4/9/1865 (NCT 8, 126).

ALMOND, Daniel, Co. K, 1st Sergeant (1838–1862). Lived, e. in Stanly 9/7/1861, age 23 as 1st sergeant. Wounded near Richmond 6/25–7/1/1862. Died in Richmond 7/25–28/1862 of wounds (NCT 8, 220).

ALMOND, David, Co. K, Private (1842–). Lived, e. in Stanly 3/15/1862, age 20. Promoted to corporal May–Dec. 1862. Captured at Fredericksburg 12/13/1862, exc abt 12/17/1862. Wounded at Chancellorsville 5/1–4/1863. Promoted to sergeant Nov.–Dec. 1864; rank reduced Jan.–Feb. 1865. Surrendered at Appomattox CH 4/9/1865 (NCT 8, 220–221).

ALMOND, Ervin, Co. D, Private (1841–) Lived in Stanly, e. in Guilford on 9/30/1861, age 30. Captured at Hanover CH 5/27/1862; confined at Ft. Monroe, then Ft. Columbus. Paroled and trans to Aiken's Landing for exchange on 8/5/1862. Captured at Gettysburg abt 7/3/1863; confined at Ft. Delaware; trans to Pt. Lookout 10/15–18/1863. Paroled there 2/18/1865; trans to Boulware's Wharf, James River on 2/20–21/1865 for exchange. Paroled at Charlotte, NC 5/11/1865 (NCT 8, 154).

ALMOND, Green, Co. K, Private (1838–). Lived, e. in Stanly, 9/7/1861, age 23. Wounded in right foot at Chancellorsville 5/3/1863. Trans to C. S. Navy 4/10/1864 (NCT 8, 221).

ALMOND, Harris, Co. K, Private (1845–1862). Lived, e. in Stanly 3/27/1862, age 17. Died in Richmond 8/20/1862 of fever (NCT 8, 221).

ALMOND, Nathan, Co. K, Private (1835–1864). Lived, e. in Stanly 3/15/1862, age 27. Died 8/27/1864 of disease (NCT 8, 221).

ANDREWS, Cyrus P., Co. E, Private (1843–1862). Lived in Montgomery, e. 8/1/1861, age 18. Killed at Gaines' Mill 6/27/1862 "while gallantly charging the enemy" (NCT 8, 165).

ANDREWS, Henry Calvin, Co. G, 2nd Lieutenant (1825–). Lived and e. in Orange 9/2/1861, age 36, as a sergeant; promoted to 1st sergeant May 1862. Captured at Hanover CH 5/27/1862; confined at Ft. Monroe, then Ft. Columbus. Exc at Aiken's Landing 8/5/162. Appointed 2nd lieutenant 4/18/1863. Captured near Spotsylvania CH abt 5/12/1864; confined at Ft. Delaware. Trans to Hilton Head, SC 8/20/1864 and confined at Ft. Pulaski, GA 10/20/1864. Trans to Charleston, SC, paroled 12/15/1864. Absent-sick 12/15/1865. Retired to Invalid Corps 2/24/1865 (NCT 8, 185).

ANDREWS, John C., Co. G, Private (1843–). Orange bricklayer, e. there 12/20/1861, age 18. Wounded at Chancellorsville 5/2–3/1863. Deserted 12/3/1863. Returned and captured near Spotsylvania CH May 1864. Confined at Pt. Lookout until released 5/30/1864

after joining Co. I, 1st Reg, U.S. Volunteer Infantry. Deserted from the Union army 8/1/1864 and returned to Co. G. Present through Feb 1865 (NCT 8, 186).

ANDREWS, N.K., Co. E, Private (1837–) Lived and e. in Montgomery 3/1/1862. Died in a hospital at or near Mount Jackson, VA 12/18/1862 of chronic diarrhea (NCT 8, 165).

ANDREWS, Seth, Co. E, Private. Lived in Montgomery, e. in Wake 2/10/1864. Captured near Petersburg 4/2/1865; confined at Pt. Lookout until released 6/22/165 after OOA (NCT 8, 165).

ANDREWS, Thomas S., Co. E, Private (1841–1862). Lived and e. in Montgomery, 3/1/1862. Died at Gordonsville 9/30/1862. (NCT 8, 165).

ANGERMAN, William H., Co. G, 2nd Lieutenant. Previously a private in Co. F, 12th Reg NCT, he trans to this company 3/4/1863 as a private. Appointed sergeant major of 33rd Reg NCT 11/1/1864; then trans back to Co. G, and appointed 2nd lieutenant 1/28/1865. Surrendered at Appomattox CH 4/9/1865 (NCT 8, 185).

ANTHONY, Henry Gray, Co. A, Sergeant (1842–1919). Lived and e. in Surry 5/4/1861, age 19. Wounded in May 1864. Promoted to sergeant. Surrendered 4/9/1865 at Appomattox. Son of Thomas F. and Serena Mosley Anthony, of Little Richmond area, Surry, he m. Nancy Emiline Roberts, and had six children. In 1901, while living at Rusk, Surry, he applied for a Confederate pension in which he stated he was shot in the hip on 5/16/1864. Bur. in Roberts-Anthony Family Cem., Surry (NCT 8, 113; SCS 5).

ANTHONY, Martin Columbus, Co. A, Private (1850–1936). Date and place of enlistment not stated. The son of Thomas F. And Serena Mosley Anthony, and a brother to Henry Gray Anthony, 7/1/1929 at age 81, Martin applied for a Confederate pension as a veteran of Co. A, 28th Reg., but records do not substantiate. He may have entered the war in 1865 when he was 15. Martin m. Susan E. Axum, dau. of Israel and Jeannette Nicholson Axon. Bur. in the Axum Family Cemetery near Little Richmond, Surry (NCT 8, 113; SCS 5).

APPERSON, John Alvis, Co. F, Musician (1845–). Lived in Yadkin, e. 2/1/1863 as a private. Promoted to musician before 1/1/1865. Present through Feb. 1865 (NCT 8, 175).

APPERSON, Peter Alexander, Co. F, 1st Sergeant (1841–1935). Lived in Yadkin, Peter e. 6/18/1861, age 20 as a private. Promoted to sergeant Jan.–June 1862. Wounded near Richmond 6/25–7/1/1862. Wounded in finger and/or back at Ox Hill. Promoted to 1st sergeant 12/1/1862. Wounded in the right shoulder and captured at Gettysburg 7/1–4/1863. Hospitalized at Davids Island. Paroled and trans to City Pt. On 9/16/1863 for exchange. Absent-sick Sept.–Dec. 1864. Captured near Petersburg 4/2/1865; confined at Pt. Lookout until released 6/22/1865 after OOA. Peter and wife both bur. Macedonia Ch. Cem., East Bend, NC (NCT 8, 175; HYC, 267).

APPERSON, Thomas V., Co. F, Captain (1838–). Lived and e. in Yadkin, appointed 1st lieutenant 6/18/861. Elected captain 4/12/164. Wounded in left leg and captured at Hanover CH 5/27/1862. Hospitalized at Portsmouth Grove, RI 7/7/1862. Trans to Ft. Monroe 9/17/1862. Paroled and trans to Aiken's Landing abt 9/23/1862 for exchange on 11/10162. Resigned 1/26/1865 due to ill health, and "to serve in the cavalry" (NCT 8, 174).

APPERSON, William H, Co. F, Ordnance Sergeant (1826–1862). Lived and e. in Yadkin, 6/18/1861, age 35, as corporal; promoted to ordnance sergeant 10/9/1861. Hospitalized at Wilmington abt 2/15/1862 with typhoid fever, and died 2/19–20/1862 (NCT 8, 175).

ARMSTRONG, Daniel M., Co. B, Private. E. at Liberty Mills 4/9/1864. Present through Feb. 1865 (NCT 8, 126).

ARMSTRONG, J.L., Co. B, Private (1844–1862). A Gaston farmer, e. at age 18 on 3/29/1862. Died of an unknown disease at Sulphur Springs, VA 7/27/1862 (NCT 8, 126).

ARMSTRONG, James, Co. B, Private (1838–1862). Lived and e. in Gaston where he e. at age 24 on 3/29/1862. Died at Rapidan, VA on 5/4/1862 (NCT 8, 126).

ARMSTRONG, Joseph, Co. H, Private (1827–). Lived and e. in Lincoln 10/28/1862, age 35. Deserted from Richmond hospital June 1863 (NCT 8, 197).

ARMSTRONG, Merideth T., Co. I, Private (1821–). Lived and e. in Yadkin 8/13/1861, age 40 Captured at Hanover CH 5/27/1862; confined at F t. Columbus. Trans to Aiken's Landing for exchange 8/5/1862. Wounded in thigh at 2nd Manassas 8/27–30/1862. Dis. abt 11/21/1862, overage per Conscription Act (NCT 8, 207).

ARY, George W., Co. D, Private (1830–). George lived in Rowan, e. in Stanly, age 32, 3/15/1862. Hospitalized in Richmond 4/27/1863 with gunshot wound. Absent on detached service April 1863–Feb. 1865. NC pension records state he was wounded in left hand and left leg in Virginia, date unknown (NCT 8, 154).

ARY, Henry, Co. A, Private (1842–). Lived and e. in Stanly 3/15/1862, age 20. Absent-wounded Sept.–Oct. 1864. Retired to Invalid Corps 12/28/1864 due to disability. Paroled at Salisbury, NC 5/24/1865 (NCT 8, 154).

ASBURY, Sidney M., Co. C, Private (1845–) Lincoln resident, e. in Catawba, age 18, on 8/12/1863. Wounded and captured near Spotsylvania CH abt 5/12/1864; confined at Pt. Lookout; trans to Elmira 8/8/1864. Released from Elmira 6/19/1865 after OOA (NCT 8, 140).

ASBURY, William H., Co. C, Private. Catawba resident e. in Mecklenburg 3/5/1864. Captured near Spotsylvania CH abt 5/12/1864; confined at Pt. Lookout; trans to Elmira 8/8/1864. Released from Elmira 6/27/1865 after OOA (NCT 8, 140).

ASHBURN, James W., Co. A, Private (1843–1916). James Ashburn, the son of John and Levisy Whitaker Ashburn, of near Siloam, volunteered on 3/181862, age 18. Captured at Hanover CH 5/27/1862. Sent to Ft. Columbus; exc at Aiken's Landing 8/5/1862. Wounded at Petersburg 9/20/1864, and captured there on 4/2/1865. Released 6/19/1865 after OOA. James m. in

1866 Martha A. Flinchum, and they had 5 children. Pension application lists his name as "James L" Ashburn." His widow applied for a pension 7/2/1917. Bur. in the family cemetery at Siloam, Surry County, NC (NCT 8, 113; SCS 6–7).

ASHBURN, John L., Co. A, Private. (1843–aft 1916). Lived near Dobson, Surry, e. 3/18/1862 at age 18, 5' 6" tall with a florid complexion. Dis. 10/2/1862 due to hemorrhage from his lungs. In 1916, age 75, he applied to enter a home for disabled veterans (NCT 8, 113; SCS 7). Probably same man as ASHBURN, John, Private, who e. at age 18 on 3/18/1862. Dis. 10/2/1862 due to "phthisis pulmonalis," of lungs, and hemorrhaging (NCT 8, 114).

ASHLY, Burgess H., Co. I, Private (1821–). Lived and e. in Yadkin 8/13/1861, age 40. Deserted 6/18/1863. Returned 12/13/1864. Deserted again 1/11/1865 (NCT 8, 207).

ATKINSON, Charles H., Co. A, Sergeant. (1843–) B. in Caswell to John E. and Elizabeth Ingram Atkinson, who had moved to Siloam in 1856 to farm, he e. in first from Surry on 5/4/1861 as a private. Promoted to sergeant 10/5/1861. Rank reduced 4/9/1862. Captured at Hanover CH 5/27/1862; confined at Ft. Columbus. Exc at Aiken's Landing on 8/5/1862. Promoted to sergeant March 1863–Oct. 1864. Wounded at Chancellorsville May 1863. Deserted abt 2/23/1865. He m. Virginia Leed, and had a son (NCT 8, 114, SCC 10–11).

ATWATER, Matthew, Co. G, Private. E. in Orange 10/19/1864. Surrendered at Appomattox CH 4/9/1865 (NCT 8, 186).

ATWATER, Wesley, Co. G, Private (1821–). Lived and e. in Orange 10/19/1864. Captured near Petersburg 4/2/1865; hospitalized at Baltimore 4/22/1865, to recover from "febris remittens." Trans to Ft. McHenry 5/9/1865; released there 6/9/1865 after OOA (NCT 8, 186).

ATWOOD, George W., Co. I, Corporal (1843–1862). Lived, e. in Yadkin 8/13/1861, age 18, a private. Promoted to corporal 4/12/1862. Killed at Gaines' Mill 6/27/1862 (NCT 8, 207).

ATWOOD, Jesse C., Co. I, Private (1843–1864). Lived and e. in Yadkin 3/8/1862, age 19. Died in Richmond hospital 3/6/1864 of typhoid fever (NCT 8, 207).

AUSTEN, W.C., Co. D, Private. Paroled at Grenada, MS abt 5/22/1865 (NCT 8, 154).

AUSTIN, Dallas P., Co. K, Private. E. at Liberty Mills 2/1/1864. Surrendered at Appomattox CH 4/9/1865 (NCT 8, 221).

AUSTIN, E. Coleman, Co. C, 2nd Lieutenant (18__–1863). Catawba resident e. 8/13/1861 as a sergeant. Rank reduced Jan.–Feb. 1862. Promoted to corporal 2/27/1862. Captured at Hanover CH 5/27/1862; confined at Ft. Monroe. Exc at Aiken's Landing 8/5/1862. Appointed 2nd lieutenant 11/17/1862. Killed at Gettysburg 7/3/1863, "a good officer" (NCT 8, 139).

AUSTIN, Samuel D., Co. K, Private (1833–1864). Lived, e. in Stanly 9/7/1861, age 28. Captured at Fredericksburg 12/13/1862; exc. 12/17/1862. Captured at Spotsylvania CH 5/12/1864; confined at Pt. Lookout;

trans to Elmira 8/8/1864. Died there 12/11/1864 of pneumonia (NCT 8, 221).

AXUM, Samuel J., Co. A, Private (1836–1862). Son of Andrew Axum and Elizabeth Weldon Axom, he farmed before he e. 3/18/1862, age 26. Captured at Hanover CH 5/27/1862; confined at Ft. Columbus. Exc at Aiken's Landing 8/5/1862. Died "at home" in Surry on 12/12/1862. He m. in Surry in 1857 Phoebe Nicholson (NCT 8, 114; SCS 12).

BAITY, Pleasant H., Co. I, Private (1843–1928). Lived and e. in Yadkin 3/8/1862, age 18. Wounded at Gettysburg 7/1–3/1862. Present through Feb. 1865. Bur. Courtney Bapt. Ch. Yadkin County, NC (NCT 8, 207' CWY 185).

BAITY, William W., Co. I, Private (1841–1862). Lived and e. in Yadkin 8/13/1861. Died at Winchester abt 12/8/1862 of "fever" (NCT 8, 207–208, CWY 186).

BAKER, H.C., Co. F, Private (1845–). B. and lived in Yadkin, a student before he e. as a substitute 4/12/1862, age 17. Wounded in right leg at Gaines' Mill 6/27/1862, leg amputated. Dis. 2/19/1863 (NCT 8, 175).

BALDEN, Andrew J., Co. B, Private. Gaston resident, e. at Liberty Mills on 3/5/1864. Wounded in left shoulder at Reams' Station on 8/25/1864. Surrendered at Appomattox CH 4/9/1865 (NCT 8, 126).

BALLARD, George M., Co. E, Private (1828–). B. and e. in Montgomery 8/1/1861, age 33. Mustered in as a corporal; reduced in rank Jan.–Feb. 1862. Dis. 4/14/162 due to "piles" (hemorrhoids) and general debility (NCT 8, 165).

BALLARD, James H., Co. E, Private (1835–1863). Lived and e. in Montgomery 8/1/1861, age 26. Captured at Hanover CH 5/27/1862; confined at Ft. Monroe, then at Ft. Columbus. Paroled and trans to Aiken's Landing for exchange 8/5/1862. Wounded in the ankle and captured at Gettysburg 7/1–3/1863. Hospitalized at Gettysburg, then at Chester abt 7/6/1863. Died in hospital at Chester 9/20/1863 of "pyaemia" (NCT 8, 165).

BALLARD, Miles M., Co. E, Private (1840–1865). Lived and e. in Montgomery 8/1/1861, age 21. Captured at Hanover CH 5/27/1862; confined at Ft. Monroe, then at Ft. Columbus. Paroled and trans to Aiken's Landing for exchange 8/5/1862. Captured near Petersburg 4/2/1865; confined at Pt. Lookout. Trans to Washington, DC 7/24/1865. Died in a hospital there 7/28/1865 of chronic diarrhea and scurvy (NCT 8, 165).

BALLARD, William M., Co. E, Sergeant (1824–). Lived and e. in Montgomery 3/1/1862, age 38, as a private, promoted to sergeant Nov. 1862–May 1864. Surrendered at Appomattox CH 4/9/1865. NC pension records indicated he was wounded in the neck near Richmond 5/1/1864 (NCT 8, 165).

BARBEE, Aaron, Co. D, Private (1841–). B., lived in Stanly, e. 7/29/1861, age 20. Wounded in wrist at Gaines' Mill, 6/27/1862. Surrendered at Appomattox CH 4/9/1865 (NCT 8, 154).

BARBEE, Hiram, Co. D, Private (1843–). Resident of Stanly, e. 3/15/1862, age 19. Surrendered at Appomattox CH, 4/9/1865 (NCT 8, 154).

BARBEE, James C., Co. D, Private (1842–1862). Lived, e. in Stanly 7/29/1861, age 19. Captured at Hanover CH 5/27/1862; confined at Ft. Monroe then Ft. Columbus. Died there 6/7/1862 of typhoid fever (NCT 8, 154).

BARGER, Allen, Co. C, Private (1840–). Lived and e. in Catawba 3/15/1862, at age 22. Captured at Hanover CH 5/27/1862; confined at Ft. Monroe, then Ft. Columbus. Exc at Aiken's Landing 8/5/1862. Trans to C. S. Navy 4/3/1864 (NCT 8, 140).

BARGER, David, Co. C, and Co. H, Private (1843–) E. 8/4/1862 in Co. H as a corporal, but was reduced in rank Jan.–Feb. 1865. Trans to Co. C of the 28th Reg. Wounded in left thigh at Petersburg, date unspecified. Captured before 4/4/1865. Hospitalized at Ft. Monroe. Released 7/20/1865 after OOA. Federal provost records lists age as 22 in 1865 (NCT 8, 140, 197).

BARGER, Gilbert A., Co. C, Private. Lived and e. in Catawba 5/6/1864. Captured at Petersburg 4/2/1865; confined at Ft. Delaware until released 6/19/1865 after OOA (NCT 8, 140).

BARGER, Josiah W., Co. C, Private. Lived and e. in Catawba 3/15/1862. Captured at Hanover CH 5/27/1862; confined at Ft. Monroe, then Ft. Columbus. Exc at Aiken's Landing 8/5/1862. Died at Guinea Station 5/29/1863 of disease (NCT 8, 141).

BARGER, Marcus, Co. C, Private (1837–) Lived and e. in Catawba 3/15/1862, age 25. Captured at Hanover CH 5/27/1862; confined at Ft. Monroe, then Ft. Columbus. Exc at Aiken's Landing 8/5/1862. Captured at Petersburg 4/2/1865; confined at Ft. Delaware until released 6/19/1865 after OOA (NCT 8, 141).

BARGER, Moses, Co. C, Private. Catawba resident e. at Camp Fisher on 9/9/1861. Died in a Charlottesville, hospital abt 5/21/1862 of typhoid fever (NCT 8, 141).

BARGER, Noah, Co. C, Private (1840–). Lived and e. in Catawba 3/15/1862, age 22. Paroled at Farmville 4/11–21/1865 (NCT 8, 141).

BARHAM, W.R., Field & Staff, Assistant Surgeon. Appointed in April 1862, he served only a short time with the 28th Reg. Newspapers reported he was captured at Hanover CH abt 5/27/1862 as he tended the wounded. Although Federal Provost Marshal records to not indicate he was captured, in the diary of Nicholas B. Gibbon mentioned that Barham escaped from before being paroled (NCT 8, 111, Gibbon Diary 15).

BARKER, Larkin Jones, Co. A, Private, Field & Staff, Hospital Steward. Yadkin resident, e. in Company I, 28th Reg. at age 18 on 8/13/1861, as sergeant; promoted to Hospital Steward March 1863–October 1864. Trans to Field & Staff November 1864–Feb. 1865. Surrendered with Reg at Appomattox CH 4/9/1864 (NCT 8, 112, 208).

BARNETT, Crawford M., Co. H, Private (1841–). Lived and e. in Cleveland 8/22/1861, age 20. Present until he surrendered at Appomattox CH 4/9/1865 (NCT 8, 197).

BARNETT, William T., Co. H, Private (1830–). Lived and e. in Cleveland 8/22/1861, age 31. Wounded in shoulder at Gettysburg 7/1–3/1863. Absent-wounded or absent-sick through Feb 1865 (NCT 8, 197).

BARRINGER, William Davidson, Co. E, Field & Staff, Lt. Colonel. Montgomery resident, appointed Capt. 8/1/1861. Promoted to Major 10/18/1862; trans to Field Staff. Promoted to Lt. Col. 11/1/1862. Captured at Fredericksburg 12/13/1862. Exc abt 12/17/1862. Resigned 3/2/1863 due to "predisposition of inflammation of mucous membrane" (NCT Vol. 8, 110, 164).

BASS, Alexander W., Co. E, Private (1823–). Lived in Union, e. in Wake 3/4/1863, age 40. Captured at Gettysburg 7/3/1863; confined at Ft. Delaware; trans to Pt. Lookout 10/15–18/1863. Paroled and trans to Aiken's Landing 9/18/1864 for exchange. Hospitalized at Richmond 9/22/1864 with chronic diarrhea. Furloughed for 60 days 10/4/1864 (NCT 8, 165).

BEAN, Alford Monroe, Co. F, Private (1833–). Lived in Yadkin, e. at Camp Gregg 2/18/1863. Deserted 6/5/163. NC pension records state he was wounded in May 1863 (NCT 8, 175).

BEAN, H.T., Co. F, Private ? NC pension records indicate he served in this company (NCT 8, 175).

BEAN, Wiley J., Co. F, Private (1840–1865). Lived in Yadkin, e. 2/18/1863 at Camp Gregg, age 23. Deserted 6/5/1863. Captured in Richmond hospital 4/3/1865; trans to Newport News 4/23/1865. Died there 5/8/1865 or 6/24/1865 of chronic diarrhea (NCT 8, 175).

BEAN, William, Co. E, Private. A resident of Randolph. Captured at Petersburg 4/3/1865; confined at Hart's Island until released abt 6/19/1865 after OOA (NCT 8, 165).

BEARD, W.S., Co. B, Private (1842–1863). Gaston resident, e. at age 20 on 3/29/1862. Captured at Fredericksburg 12/13/1862; confined in Old Capitol Prison, where he died abt 4/10/1863 of typhoid fever (NCT 8, 126).

BEATY, Andrew, Co. B, Corporal (1834–). Lived and e. in Gaston 7/30/1861, age 27, as a private. Promoted to corporal 2/27/1862. Wounded in left arm at Gaines' Mill, 6/27/1862. Arm amputated. Dis. 7/22/2862 (NCT 8, 126).

BEATY, James F., Co. B, Private (1843–). Gaston farmer, e. at age 18 in Gaston on 7/30/1861. Captured at Fredericksburg 12/13/1862; paroled abt 12/17/1862. Surrendered at Appomattox CH 4/19/1865 (NCT 8, 127).

BEATY, Jonathan P., Co. B, Private (1819–1864). Lived in Gaston, e. in Wake on 9/4/1863 at age 44. Captured near Spotsylvania CH on 5/12/1864, and confined at Pt. Lookout, trans to Elmira, on 8/8/1864, and died there 11/26/1864 of "scorbutus." (NCT 8, 127).

BEATY, R.M., Co. B, Private (1843–1862). B. and raised, and e. in Gaston, age 18, on 7/30/1861. Captured at Hanover CH 5/27/1862; confined at Ft. Monroe., then Ft. Columbus, NY. Exc. Killed at Fredericksburg on 12/13/1862 (NCT 8, 127).

BEGGARLY, Jerry, Co. I, Private (1834–). A saddler, b. in Surry, lived, e. in Yadkin, 8/13/1861, age 27. Dis. 10/17/1861 due to "scrotal hernia of both sides" (NCT 8, 208).

BELL, Benjamin F., Co. K, Private (1841–). Lived, e. in Stanly 9/7/1861, age 20. Present and surrendered at Appomattox CH 4/9/1865 (NCT 8, 221).

BELL, Joseph C., Co. B, Private. E. at Liberty Mills on 2/16/1864. Surrendered at Appomattox CH on 4/9/1865 (NCT 8, 127).

BELL, Lorense M., Co. B, Private (1843–). Gaston farmer, e. there, age 18, 7/30/1862. Wounded in left hand at Frayser's Farm on 6/30/1862. Left arm amputated below the elbow. Dis. 11/25/1863 (NCT 8, 127).

BELL, William B., Co. H, Private. E. in Edgecomb 9/1/1863. Died in Charlottesville hospital 1/14/1864 of chronic diarrhea (NCT 8, 197).

BELTON, James R., Co. A, Private. E. at age 34 on 5/4/1861. Captured at Spotsylvania CH 5/12/1864; confined at Pt. Lookout; trans to Elmira on 8/12/1864, where he died 3/11/1865 of "pleurisy." Bur. in grave #1869, Woodlawn National Cemetery, Elmira. Survived by wife Susannah Forkner and 5 children (NCT 8, 114; SCS 16).

BENGE, John, Co. I, Private (1841–). B. in Surry, lived and e. in Yadkin 8/13/1861. Dis. 5/1/1862 due to "epilepsy" (NCT 8, 208).

BENGE, Nathan, Co. I, Private (1843–1865). Lived and e. in Yadkin 8/13/1861, age 18. Captured at Spotsylvania CH 5/12/1864; confined at Pt. Lookout, trans to Elmira on 8/8/1864. Paroled and trans to Venus Pt. 11/15/1864 for exchange. Died "at home" 1/5/1865 (NCT 8, 208).

BENNETT, Alexander, Co. E, Private (1837–1864). Lived in Union, e. in Wake 10/2/1862, age 25. Wounded at Chancellorsville 5/2–3/1863. Captured at Spotsylvania CH 5/12/1864. Confined at Pt. Lookout where he died 6/6/1864 (NCT 8, 165).

BENNETT, William T., Co. A, Corporal (1835–1861). B. in Virginia, Bennett farmed in the Dobson District of Surry, where he e. as a corporal. Died on June 16, 1861, one of two of volunteers who died at training camp in Garysburg (NCT 8, 114; SCS 16).

BENSON, John W., Co. A, Private (1834–) Surry resident, e. 3/18/1862, age 28. Hospitalized at Richmond 1/19/1863 due to gunshot wound in the loins. Wounded again at Gettysburg in the left leg and right side, and captured. Sent to a Chester hospital then to Pt. Lookout on 10/4/1863. Trans on March 6, 1864, City Pt., for exchange. On detached service September–October 1864. Captured near Petersburg on 4/2/1865. Confined at Ft. Delaware, and not released until 7/19/1865 after OOA. Benson m. Lucinda J. Scott in 1853. They farmed in the Haystack community of Surry, and had 3 children. He may have died before 1870 (NCT 8, 114; SCS 17).

BEST, A.J., Co. B, Private (1834–). Gaston farmer, e. there at age 28 on 3/29/1862. Dis. 3/28/1864 due to loss of a hand from a gunshot wound (NCT 8, 127).

BILES, Isaac T., Co. K, 2nd Lieutenant (1840–). Lived, e. in Stanly, age 21, and appointed 2nd lieutenant 9/7/1861. Wounded at Chancellorsville 5/2–3/1863. Wounded in right foot at Gettysburg 7/3/1863. Resigned 12/10–/1863 due to disability (NCT 8, 220).

BILES, William A.C., Co. K, Corporal (1635–). Lived, e. in Stanly 9/7/1861, age 26. Promoted to corporal May–Dec 1862. Wounded in head and side, captured at Gettysburg 7/2–3/1863. Hospitalized there; transferred to Baltimore hospital 10/1/1863. Trans to

Pt. Lookout 1/10/1864. Paroled and trans to City Pt 3/20/1864 for exc. Absent-wounded until 12/21/1864, when he retired to Invalid Corps (NCT 8, 221).

BINKLEY, John W., Co. F. Private (1836–). Lived and e. in Yadkin 6/18/1861, age 25. Captured near Petersburg 4/2/1865; confined at Pt. Lookout until released 6/23/1865 after OOA (NCT 8, 175).

BIRD, Colin, Co. E, Private (1826–). A blacksmith, b. and e. in Montgomery 8/1/1861, age 35. Dis. 12/9/1861 due to "phthisis" (NCT 8, 165).

BIRD, Robert H., Co. E, Private (1842–1864). Montgomery resident, e. 8/1/1861, age 19. Wounded at Gaines' Mill abt 6/27/1862. Wounded in the arm and captured at Spotsylvania CH 5/12/1864. Hospitalized at Washington, DC and died 5/30/1864 of his wound (NCT 8, 165).

BISHOP, John, Co. G, Private (1820–). Lived and e. in Orange 9/2/1861, age 41. Captured at Hanover CH 5/27/1862; confined at Ft. Monroe, then Ft. Columbus. Paroled and trans to Aiken's Landing for exchange 8/5/1862. Captured at Fredericksburg 12/13/1862, exc 12/17/1862. Captured near Petersburg 4/2/1865; confined at Pt. Lookout until released 6/23/1865 after OOA (NCT 8, 186).

BLACK, Robert S., Co. K, Private (1838–). Lived in Cabarrus, e. in Stanly 3/12/1862, age 24. Present through Feb. 1865 (NCT 8, 221).

BLACKWELDER, Alexander, Co. D, Private (1837–1862). Lived and e. in Stanly 7/29/1861, age 24. Killed at Frayser's Farm 6/30/1862 (NCT 8, 154).

BLACKWOOD, Julius T., Co. A, Private (1842–1924). Surry resident, e. at age 16. Captured at Hanover CH, abt 5/27/1862; confined at Ft. Columbus. Trans to Aiken's Landing on 8/5/1862. Hospitalized the next month at Charlottesville, with a gunshot wound. Captured at Gettysburg on 7/3/1863. Confined as a prisoner at Ft. Delaware, then Pt. Lookout. Remained until paroled 2/18/1865; trans to Boulware's Wharf 2/20–21/1865 for exc. At age 74, lived at Elkin, NC, and applied for a pension and stated that he had been wounded in the mouth and hand at Manassas. His widow also applied for a pension 1/22/1925 (NCT 8, 114; SCS 17).

BLACKWOOD, William H., Co. A, Corporal (1845–after 1901). Blackwood, age 17, lived at Rockford, Surry, with his parents, Nathaniel H. and Mary Blackwood. He and his brother Julius T. joined the same day 3/18/1862. Promoted to corporal 4/9/1862. Captured at Frayser's Farm 6/30/1862; confined at Ft. Columbus, then Ft. Delaware on 7/9/1862; Exc 8/5/1865 at Aiken's Landing. Hospitalized 9/18/1862 at Charlottesville with gunshot wound. Wounded at Gettysburg in left thigh and captured. Hospitalized at Chester; paroled and trans to City Pt. for exchange 9/23/1863. Captured at Gravel Hill 7/28/1864. Confined at Pt. Lookout, then trans to Elmira 8/8/1864. Released on 6/16/1865 after OOA. At age 56, while living at Stony Knoll in Surry, applied for a pension on 6/5/1901 (NCT 8, 114; SCS 17).

BLAKELY, Eli Y., Co. F, Private. Lived in Yadkin, e. 11/1/1863. AWOL Nov.–Dec. 1864. Captured near Petersburg 4/2/1865; confined at Hart's Island until released 6/17/1865 after OOA (NCT 8, 175).

BLAKELY, George Washington, Co. F, Private (1839–1923). Son of Temple and Jane Stewart Blakely, e. 6/18/1861, age 22. Retired 2/18/1865. NC Pension records indicate he was wounded at Reams' Station. He lost part of his hand; returned to Yadkin. m. Sarah S. Matthews and had several children (NCT 8, 175; HYC, 276; Hoots, 276).

BLALOCK, Henry, Co. D, Private. Stanly resident e. at Camp Stokes 10/31/1864. Captured near Petersburg 4/2/1865; confined at Pt. Lookout until released 6/23/1865 after OOA (NCT 8, 154).

BLALOCK, J.B., Co. B, Private (1835–). B. in York District, SC, lived in Cleveland. E., age 26, at Camp Fisher on 9/18/1861. Wounded in the right arm at Cedar Mt. 8/9/1862; arm amputated. Dis. 10/5/1862 (NCT 8, 127).

BLANTON, Edward M., Co. H, Private (1814–). B. in Rutherford, lived and e. in Cleveland 8/11/1861, age 47. Dis. 6/19/1862 due to "advanced age & debility" (NCT 8, 197).

BLANTON, Francis A., Co. H, Private (1840–1862). Lived in Cleveland, e. 3/17/1862, age 32. Captured at Hanover CH 5/27/1862; confined at Ft. Monroe, then Ft. Columbus. Paroled and trans to Aiken's Landing for exchange on 8/5/1862. Died in Petersburg hospital abt 8/6/1862 (NCT 8, 197).

BLANTON, Frank B., Co. H, Private? NC pension records indicate he served in this company (NCT 8, 197).

BLANTON, George W., Co. H, Private (1843–1862). Lived in Cleveland, e. 8/22/1861, age 18. Died near Richmond 8/2/1862 of disease (NCT 8, 197).

BLANTON, John, Co. H, Private (1827–1862). Lived and e. in Cleveland 3/17/1862 there, age 35. Died in field hospital near Richmond 8/1/1862 of wounds (NCT 8, 197).

BLANTON, Josiah S., Co. H, Private. Previously served in Co. C, 15th Reg NCT; trans to Co. H 3/28/1864. Captured near Wilderness abt 5/6/1864; confined at Pt. Lookout. Trans to Elmira 8/15/1864, paroled and trans to Venous Pt. On 11/15/1864 for exchange. Absent-sick through Feb. 1865 (NCT 8, 197).

BLANTON, Thomas J., Co. H, Private (1812–1864). B. in Cleveland, e. 8/22/1861, age 49 as a sergeant. Rank reduced Jan.–Apr 1862. Captured at Hanover CH 5/27/1862; confined at Ft. Monroe then Ft. Columbus. Paroled and trans to Aiken's Landing for exchange 8/5/1862. Killed at Wilderness 5/6/1864 (NCT 8, 197).

BLANTON, William, Co. H, Private (1804–). B. in Rutherford, lived in Cleveland, e. 3/17/1862, age 58. Dis. 6/19/1862 due to "advanced age and want of physical ability to do duty" (NCT 8, 197).

BLANTON, William T., Co. H, Private (1839–1862). A resident of SC, he e.. 8/22/1861 in Cleveland, age 22. Hospitalized at Richmond 6/23/1862 with diarrhea and typhoid fever. Died 6/30/1862 after he "drank cold water to great excess" (NCT 8, 197).

BLEDSOE, Terrell B., Co. A, Musician (1823–aft 1868). Surry farmer, worked for L. W. Bray in the Dobson District, e. at age 38 on 5/4/1861, as a musician (fifer). Discharged on 5/1/1862 because he was over-age. In 1868 he m. Martha M. Poindexter Bray, the widow of William A. Bray who was killed at Gettysburg (NCT 8, 114; SCS 18).

BOBBITT, Andrew J., Co. A, Private (1834–). Grayson County, VA, resident, e. in Surry at 5/8/1861, age 27. Wounded at Gettysburg on 7/1–3/1863. Wounded again near Petersburg in left arm on 4/2/1865; hospitalized in Richmond. Captured in the hospital on 4/3/1865, and trans to Pt. Lookout 5/2/1865. Released 6/26/1865 after OOA (NCT 8, 114).

BOHANNON, Neal, Co. I, Captain (1830–1862). Lived and e. in Yadkin resident e. 8/13/1861, age 31, as a sergeant. Promoted to 1st sergeant 10/8/1861; to 1st lieutenant 4/12/1862. Captured at Hanover CH 5/27/1862; confined at Ft. Monroe, then Ft. Columbus. Exc.. Promoted to captain 11/1/1862. Died "in Virginia" abt 6/20/1863 of typhoid fever, "a brave and good officer" (NCT 8, 207).

BOHANNON, Simon S., Co. I, Captain (1835–1910). Lived and e. in Yadkin . 8/13/1861, age 26, as a sergeant. Promoted to 2nd lieutenant 4/12/1862; to 1st lieutenant 11/1/1862, and to captain 6/20/1863. Wounded at Gettysburg 7/1–3/1863. Captured at Spotsylvania CH 5/12/1864; confined at Ft. Delaware. Trans SC, he was held hostage, one of the "Immortal 600," on Morris Island before being trans to Hilton Head Island. The survivors were returned to Ft. Delaware 3/12/1865. Released 6/16/1865 after OOA. Bur. Boonville Bapt. Ch. Cem, Boonville NC (NCT 8, 207).

BOLCH, Aaron, Co. C, Corporal. Lived and e. in Catawba resident 8/13/1861 as a private. Captured at Hanover CH 5/27/1862; confined at Ft. Monroe, then Ft. Columbus. Exc at Aiken's Landing 8/5/1862. Wounded and captured at Gettysburg 7/3–5/1863. Hospitalized at Davids Island. Paroled and trans to City Pt. on 9/27/1863 for exchange. Promoted to corporal 12/1/1864. Surrendered at Appomattox CH 4/9/1865 (NCT 8, 141).

BOLCH, Abel, Co. C, Private. Lived and e. in Catawba on 3/15/1862. Wounded at Gaines' Mill 6/27/1862. Captured near Petersburg 4/2/1865; confined at Harts Island. Released 6/18/1865 after OOA (NCT 8, 141).

BOLCH, Emanuel, Co. C, Private. Lived and e. in Catawba on 3/15/1862. Died in Lexington hospital 8/15–17/1862 of "febris typhoides" (NCT 8, 141).

BOLCH, Franklin, Co. H, Private E. at Camp Vance 2/24/1864. Surrendered at Appomattox CH 4/9/1865 (NCT 8, 197).

BOLCH, Henry C., Co. C, Private (1848–). E. in Catawba 1/21/1865. Wounded in left leg and captured near Petersburg 4/2/1865. Hospitalized at Ft. Monroe. Released abt 7/13/1865 after OOA. Federal hospital records give his age at 17 in 1865 (NCT 8, 141).

BOLCH, Jordan, Co. C, Private. E. in Catawba 4/14/1864. Surrendered at Appomattox CH 4/9/1865 (NCT 8, 141).

BOLCH, Logan, Co. C, Private. (18__–1863) Lived and e. in Catawba 3/14/1863. Wounded and captured at Gettysburg 7/2–3/1863. Hospitalized at Chester where he died 9/30/1863 of "exhaustion." His widow stated in her pension application that he had e. as a nurse, "but could not endure that and he then was put into regular service" (NCT 8, 141).

BOLCH, Marcus, Co. C, Private. Lived and e. in Catawba 8/13/1861. Wounded at 2nd Manassas 8/28–30, 1862. Wounded at Chancellorsville 5/2–3/1863. Surrendered at Appomattox CH 4/9/1865 (NCT 8, 141).

BOLCH, Nathan A., Co. H, Private (1847–). E. 2/24/1864 in Catawba, age 18. Present through Feb. 1865 (NCT 8, 197).

BOLCH, Philip, Co. H, Private (18__–1864). B. in Catawba, e. 9/22/1863 at Camp Vance. Died in Richmond hospital abt 10/26/1864 of gunshot wound (NCT 8, 197).

BOLCH, Philip H., Co. C, Private. E. on 1/21/1865. Surrendered at Appomattox CH 4/9/1865 (NCT 8, 141).

BOLCH, William, Co. C, Private. Catawba resident, he e. 3/15/1862. Died at Farmville 7/15/1862 of "diarrhoea" (NCT 8, 141).

BOLCH, William H., Co, H, Private. Previously served in Co. E, McRae's Battalion, NC Cavalry. Trans to Co. H, 28th Reg June 1864. Present through Feb. 1865 (NCT 8, 197).

BOLICK, David, Co. D, Private. Lived in Catawba, e. at Camp Stokes 10/28/1864. Hospitalized in Richmond 4/2/1865 with a wound; captured there 4/3/1865. Trans to Newport News 4/23/1865; released there 6/30/1865 after OOA (NCT 8, 154).

BOLINGER, Levi A., Co. H, Private. E. at Camp Vance 3/1/1864. Captured near Pickett's Farm abt 7/21/1864; confined at Pt. Lookout. Paroled and trans to Boulware's Wharf for exchange 3/15/1864 (NCT 8, 198).

BOLTON, Atlas, Co. D, Private (1839–1862). Lived in Stanly, e. 7/29/1861, age 22. Died in Richmond abt 8/1/1862 of disease (NCT 8, 154).

BOLTON, Calvin C., Co. D, Private (1834–1864). Lived and e. in Stanly 3/15/1862, age 28. Listed as a deserter 9/14/1863. Captured at Spotsylvania CH 5/12/1864; confined at Pt. Lookout until trans to Elmira 8/8/1864. Died at Elmira 9/30/1864 of pneumonia (NCT 8, 154).

BOLTON, Terrell, Co. D, Private (1836–). Lived and e. in Stanly 7/29/1861, age 25. Wounded in left leg and captured at Wilderness abt 5/6/1864; confined at Old Capitol Prison. Trans to Elmira 10/25/1864. Paroled 2/9/1865; sent to Boulware's Wharf 2/20–21/1865 for exchange (NCT 8, 154).

BOST, Daniel J., Co. K, 2nd Lieutenant (1833–1864). B., lived in Cabarrus, e. In Lenoir 4/26/1862, age 29. Wounded at Ox Hill 9/1/1862. Promoted to sergeant Jan. 1863–June 1864; to 2nd lieutenant 7/1/1864. Died in Richmond hospital 9/5/1864 of wounds (NCT 8, 220).

BOST, James H., Co. K, Private. Lived in Cabarrus, e. At Liberty Mills 2/1/1862. Died in camp at Liberty Mills 4/23/1862 of "typhoid fever" (NCT 8, 221).

BOST, William A., Co. K, Corporal (1843–). Lived in Cabarrus, e. in New Hanover 2/4/1862, age 19. Promoted to corporal Jan. 1863–Oct.1864. Captured near Petersburg 4/2/1865; confined at Hart's Island until released 6/18/1865, after OOA (NCT 8, 221).

BOVENDER, General Green, Co. F, Private (1832–1863). The son of John ("Jackie") Bovender I, and Rachel Brown, he lived and e. in Yadkin County 3/31/1862, age 30. Wounded at Chancellorsville 5/2–3/1863 and died at Richmond 5/5/1863 of wounds. He married on 5/12/1858, in Yadkin, Nancy J. Colvard Vestal (NCT 8, 175; HYC 277).

BOVENDER, George W., Co. F, Private (1824–1862). Son of John ("Jackie") Bovender and Rachel Brown, he lived and e. in Yadkin 6/18/1861, age 37. George m. Rachel Lyons and had 12 children 1846–1862. He died "at home" abt 6/27/1862 (NCT 8, 175, HYC 277, 278).

BOVENDER, John R., Co. F, Private (1843–aft 1900). Son of Andrew Jackson and Anna Vestal Bovender, Yadkin, he e. there 6/18/1861, age 16. Deserted 9/13/1862. Wounded in right thigh near Amelia CH 4/5/1865. Reported in Danville hospital 4/6/1865. John m. Frances Reece 1/31/1866 in Yadkin, had several children (NCT 8, 175–176, 1850 Surry Census).

BOWEN, James D., Co. H, Private (1842–). B., lived and e. in Cleveland 3/17/1862, age 20. Dis. 7/21/1862 due to an inability to perform the "duties of a soldier" NCT 8, 198).

BOWENS, Elias P., Co. H, Private. E. 3/17/1862 in Cleveland ; present through April 1862 (NCT 8, 198).

BOWMAN, Calvin M., Co. C, Private (1844–1864). B. and e. in Catawba, age 18, on 3/15/1862. Captured at Spotsylvania CH 5/12/1864; confined at Pt. Lookout, trans to Elmira 8/8/1864. Paroled 10/11/1864 and sent to Venus Pt. on 11/15/1864 for exchange. Died at home 11/22/1864 of disease (NCT 8, 141).

BOYD, William, Co. B, Private (1837–1862). Lived and e. in Gaston, age 25, on 7/30/1862. Died at Wilmington 4/2/1862 of typhoid fever (NCT 8, 127).

BOYSWORTH, Jonathan, Co. K, Private (1844–1861). B., e. in Stanly 9/7/1861, age 17. Died in Wilmington hospital abt 12/7/1861 of typhoid fever and/or measles (NCT 8, 221).

BRACHLEY, William, Co. I, Private. (1834–) Place and date of enlistment not reported. Deserted to the enemy 1/15/1865. Took OOA at Beverly, WV 4/9/1865, age 21 per Federal provost marshal records (NCT 8, 208).

BRADDY, James, Co. H, Private (1826–1862). Lived in Rutherford, e. 8/22/1861 in Cleveland, age 35. Died Richmond hospital 7/23/1862 of disease (NCT 8, 198).

BRAN, Henry T., Co. F., Corporal (1843–). Lived and e. in Yadkin 6/18/1861, age 18, as a private. Promoted to corporal 11/1/1864. Captured near Petersburg 4/2/1865; confined at Pt. Lookout until released 6/23/1865 after OOA (NCT 8 176).

BRAN, John M., Co. F, Private (1839–1861). Lived and e. in Yadkin 6/18/1861. Died in Wilmington hospital 12/29/1861 (NCT 8, 176).

BRANNOCK, James, Co. A, Musician (1838–). Surry resident e., age 23, 5/4/1861 as a musician (drummer). Rank reduced May–Oct. 1862. With regiment at the surrender 4/9/1865 Brannock m. a cousin, Susan Brannock, and had several children (NCT 8, 114; SCS 19–20).

BRAY, Arthur (Artha), Jr., Co. A, Private (1836–1867). Son of Artha and Mary Whitaker Bray, who farmed near Dobson, Artha, Jr. was a school teacher before he volunteered for service on 5/4/1861. Wounded and captured at Gettysburg on 7/3/1863. Confined at Ft. Delaware then trans to Pt. Lookout in mid October 1863. Paroled abt 11/1/1864; trans to Venus Pt. on 11/15/1864 for exchange. He only lived 2 more years after the war. Family believed his death resulted from his wounds. Letters written by Artha Bray, Jr., were reproduced in *Surry County Soldiers in the Civil War* (NCT 8, 114–115; SCS 20).

BRAY, Calvin T., Co. A, Private (1841–) Son of Leban and Martha Smith Bray of the Dobson District of Surry, Calvin mustered in as a musician on 5/4/1861; rank reduced before 11/1/1861. Listed as deserter on 5/12/1862. Hospitalized in Richmond 7/2/1862 with a wound to his hand. Deserted again 4/4/1863. He m. Mary Reed, 1860, Surry (NCT 8, 115; SCS 210–21).

BRAY, Edward W., Co. A, Private (1837–1863?). A farmer, Dobson District, Surry, e. age 24, 5/4/1861. Captured at Hanover CH on 5/27/1862; confined first at Ft. Monroe, then at Ft. Columbus. Exc at Aiken's Landing on 8/5/1862. Wounded at Chancellorsville 5/2–3/186. Listed as a deserter on 7/25/1863, but he may have died or was captured. He m. Martha E. Alberty, 1851, Surry (NCT 8, 115; SCS 21).

BRAY, Lewis W., Co, A, Private. (1818–). Lived in Dobson District, Surry, e. at age 43; dis by July 1861, due to disability. May later have served Co. C, 5th Reg Senior Reserves (NCT 8, 115; SCS 21).

BRENT, Oscar J., Field & Staff, Chaplain. Guilford resident, appointed chaplain of the 28th 10/18/1861. Resigned 7/21/1862 due to "ill health" (NCT 8, 111).

BREWBAKER, Alexander, Co. I, Private (1841–). Lived at Huntsville in Yadkin, the son of Isaac and Elizabeth Dixon Brewbaker, e. there 3/8/1862, age 21. Deserted 4/5/1863. Family tradition holds that Alexander came home to see his sweetheart, Miss Mary Chapman, and was killed as a deserter by the Home Guard, sometime before 10/2/1864. Death confirmed in an 1864 letter (NCT 8, 208; CWY 190).

BREWBAKER, Washington, Co. I, Private (1828–). Lived at Huntsville in Yadkin, e. 3/8/1862, age 34. Deserted 8/5/1862. He married twice — Martha Stipe, then Susan Hill (NCT 8, 208; CWY 191).

BREWER, Eli H., Co. E, Private (1831–1863). Lived and e. n Montgomery 8/1/1861, age 30. Killed at Chancellorsville 5/3/1863 (NCT 8, 165).

BREWER, Oliver C., Co. E, Private (1844–). Lived and e. in Montgomery 3/4/1863, age 19. Wounded and captured at Gettysburg 7/3–5/1863. Hospitalized at Chester. Paroled and trans to City Pt. 9/23/1863 for exchange. Captured near Pickett's Farm 7/21/1864; confined at Pt. Lookout MD 7/28/1864. Released 6/24/1865 after OOA (NCT 8, 165–166).

BRIDGES, Burrell H., Co. H, 3rd Lieutenant (1843–). Lived and e. in Cleveland 8/22/1861, age 18, as a private. Promoted to sergeant Jan.–Apr. 1862; appointed 3rd lieutenant 4/7/1862. Resigned 10/3/1862 due to disability. May have later served as 1st sergeant, Co. D, 55th Reg NCT (NCT 8, 196).

BRIDGES, Isaac O., Co. H, Captain (1831–). Lived

and e. in Cleveland, age 30. Appointed 3rd lieutenant 8/22/1861; promoted to captain 4/7/1862. Resigned 7/23/1862 due to "chronic ulceration of the throat & mouth..." (NCT 8, 196).

BRIDGES, James W., Co. H, Private (1840–1862). Cleveland resident, e. 3/17/1862, age 22. Died in Branch's Brigade hospital 7/11/1862 (NCT 8, 198).

BRIDGES, John, Co. H, Private (1813–). B., lived and e. in Cleveland 8/22/1861, age 48. Dis. 6/19/1862 due to "debility and advanced age" (NCT 8, 198).

BRIDGES, Preston, Co. H, Private (1844–). Cleveland resident, e. 8/22/1861, age 17. Captured at Hanover CH 5/27/1862; confined at Ft. Monroe, then Ft. Columbus. Paroled and trans to Aiken's Landing for exchange 8/5/1862. Wounded in buttock at Chancellorsville 5/2–3/1863. Captured at Petersburg 4/3/1865; confined at Hart's Island until released 6/18/1865 after OOA (NCT 8, 198).

BRIDGES, Samuel G. H., Co. H, Private (1845–). Lived and e. in Cleveland 2/20/1863, age 18. Wounded and captured at Gettysburg 7/1–5/1863. Hospitalized at Chester 7/19/1863. Paroled and trans to City Pt. On 8/20/1863 for exchange. Surrendered at Appomattox CH 4/9/1863 (NCT 8, 198).

BRIDGES, Thomas S., Co. H, Private (1841–). Lived and e. in Cleveland 8/22/1861 there at age 20. Dis. 6/23/1862 due to "chronic rheumatism" age 21. Reenlisted in Co. H 10/1/1864. Surrendered at Appomattox CH 4/9/1865 (NCT 8, 198).

BRIDGES, Thomas Wallace, Co. H, Sergeant (1843–). Born and e. in Cleveland 8/22/1861, age 18, as a private. Promoted to sergeant May–Oct. 1862. Wounded in left arm at Chancellorsville 5/3/1863. Arm amputated. Dis. 2/22/1864 due to disability (NCT 8, 198).

BRINDLE, James Free, Co. I, Sergeant (1838–). Son of William and Nancy Brindle (Brendle), he lived and e. in Yadkin 8/13/1861, age 23, as a private. Promoted to corporal 6/11/1862, then sergeant Mar 1863–Oct 1864. Captured near Petersburg 4/2/1865; confined at Ft. Delaware until released 6/19/1865 after OOA (NCT 8, 208, CWY 191).

BRINDLE, Mark, Co. I, Private (1843–). Son of John and Elizabeth Huff Brindle, he lived and e. in Yadkin 8/13/1861, age 18. Wounded in arm, thigh and finger at 2nd Manassas. Returned. Captured near Petersburg 4/2/1865; confined at Hart's Island until released 6/18/1865 after OOA. Moved to Iowa and m. Mary Francis Faris, then Sarah Clemons (NCT 8, 208, HYC 289; CWY 191).

BRINKLEY, John H., Co. A, Corporal (1838–1862). Lived and e. in Surry 5/10/1861, age 23, as a private. Promoted to corporal May–July 1862. Hospitalized in Richmond on 7/2/1862 with a gunshot wound to his left knee. Leg amputated 7/12/1862. Died in the hospital on 8/4/1862 (NCT 8, 115; SCS 23).

BROCKWELL, Benjamin, Co. G, Private (1826–). Lived and e. in Orange 3/5/1862, age 36. Captured at Fredericksburg 12/13/1862; exchanged 12/17/1862. Captured at Spotsylvania CH 5/12/1864; confined at Pt. Lookout, trans to Elmira 8/8/1864. Released there 6/19/1865 after OOA (NCT 8, 186).

BROCKWELL, James I., Co. G, Private (1840–) Lived and e. in Orange 12/20/1861, age 21. Present through Feb. 1865 (NCT 8, 186).

BROCKWELL, John B., Co. G, Private (1839–). Previously served in Co. D, 1st Reg NC Infantry. E. in Co. G 12/20/1861, age 22. Deserted to the enemy abt 3/8/1865; confined at Washington until released abt 3/10/1865, after OOA (NCT 8, 186).

BROCKWELL, Joseph Joshua, Co. G, Private (1835–). Lived and e. in Orange 12/20/1861, age 26. Present through Feb. 1865 (NCT 8, 186).

BROCKWELL, William B., Co. G, Private (1824–1864). Lived and e. in Orange 3/5/1862, age 38. Captured at Hanover CH 5/27/1862; confined at Ft. Monroe, then Ft. Columbus. Paroled and trans to Aiken's Landing for exchange 8/5/1862. Killed at Wilderness 5/6/1864 (NCT 8, 186).

BROWN, Azariah, Co. F, Private (1841–). Lived in Rockingham, e. 3/25/1862 in Yadkin, age 21. Captured near Gettysburg 7/3–5/1863; confined at Ft. Delaware. Released after OOA and joining the U.S. Army, Co. G, 1st Reg Connecticut Cavalry (NCT 8, 176).

BROWN, Barnabas, Co. A, Private (1839–1862). Lived and e. in Surry, age 23, 3/18/1862. Captured at Hanover CH on 5/27/1862. Confined in Ft. Delaware, until Exc at Aiken's Landing on 8/5/1862. Died in a hospital at Mt. Jackson, VA 11/7/1862 of chronic diarrhea (NCT 8, 115; SCS 24).

BROWN, James, Co., A, Private. Lied and e. in 5/4/1861, at age 18. Hospitalized in Richmond on 7/2/1862, with a gunshot wound of left shoulder. Wounded in the shoulder at the Battle of Second Manassas abt 8/28/1862. Deserted 9/21/1862 from a Danville hospital. Surrender at Appomattox, 4/9/1865. James m. Elizabeth Collins in 1865, and had at least 2 children (NCT 8, 115; SCS 24).

BROWN, James K.P., Co. F, Sergeant (1845–) A Yadkin farmer, e. there 6/18/1861, age 16, as a private. Promoted to corporal 5/11/1863; promoted to sergeant before 11/1/1864. Captured near Petersburg 4/2/1865; confined at Pt. Lookout until released 6/23/1865 after OOA (NCT 8, 176).

BROWN, James M., Co. E, Private (1838–1862). Lived and e. in Montgomery 3/10/1862, age 40, as a substitute. AWOL 8/16/1862–12/1/1862. Captured near Petersburg 4/2/1865; confined at Pt. Lookout until released 6/23/1865 after OOA (NCT 8, 166).

BROWN, Jesse F., Co. F, Private (1843–1862). Lived and e. in Yadkin. 6/18/1861, age 18. Died in Richmond hospital 8/8/1862 of typhoid fever and "parotitis" (NCT 8, 176).

BROWN, John C., Co. F, Sergeant (1833–1863). B., lived and e. in Yadkin 4/4/1862, age 29, as a private; promoted to sergeant 5/1/1862. Captured between Aug.–Sept. 1862. Received at Aiken's Landing 9/27/1862 for exchange on 11/10/1862. Captured at Gettysburg 7/3/1863; confined at Ft. Delaware. Trans to Pt. Lookout 10/15–18/1863. Hospitalized there 11/17/1863 and died of smallpox 11/25/1863 (NCT 8, 176).

BROWN, Robert W., Co. I, Private (1842–1862). Son of Jacob and Elizabeth Calloway Brown, he lived and e. in Yadkin 8/13/1861, age 19. Wounded in right shoulder at Frayser's Farm; died in Richmond hospital from wound 8/13/1862 (NCT 8, 208, CWY 193).

BROWN, Squire, Co. F, Private (1837–1863). B., lived and e. in Yadkin 4/27/1862, age 25. AWOL Nov.–Dec. 1863. Died near Camp Gregg /15/1863 (NCT 8, 176).

BRYANT, Stephen H., Co. I, Private (1839–). Lived and e. in Yadkin 3/8/1862, age 23. Wounded at 2nd Manassas 8/27–30/1862. Trans to Co. A, 44th Reg NCT Mar.–Dec. 1863. Son of Hugh and Jane Patterson Bryant, Stephen married Deborah Farrington (NCT 8, 208; NCT 10, 401).

BUCHANNON, William, Co. I, Private (1839–) Lived and e. in Yadkin 8/13/1861, age 22. Captured at Hanover CH 5/27/1862; confined at Ft. Monroe, then ft. Columbus. Paroled and trans to Aiken's Landing for exchange 8/5/1862. Returned. AWOL 10/31/186. Returned, reported missing at Gettysburg 7/1–3/1863 (NCT 8, 208).

BULLIN, Edmund, Co., A, Private (1843–aft 1889). One of the five sons of William and Sally Holyfield Bullin who e. in the Confederate Army (Edmund, George, James, Jesse, and Joel.) A resident of Rockford, Edmund e. Surry, age 26, 5/4/1861. Present Jan.–Feb. 1863, when he was sick and in a hospital. Edmund m. in Surry Martha Snow, and had two daus before 1861. He m. second to Martha Hunter in 1889. (NCT 8, 115; SCS 25).

BULLIN, George, Co. A, Private (1844–aft 1868). George, the son of William and Sally Holyfield Bullin, lived and e. in Surry 1/18/1864. Captured near Petersburg 4/2/1865, and confined at Ft. Delaware. Released 6/19/1865 after OOA (NCT 8, 115; SCS 25).

BULLIN, Joel, Co. A, Private (1841–1862). Also a son of William and Sally Bullin, Joel e., age 20, 5/10/1861. Died in Wilmington 3/1/1862 (NCT 8, 115; SCS 26).

BULLIN, John A., Co. D, Private (1832–1862). Lived and e. in Stanly 7/29/1861, age 29. Killed at Hanover CH 5/27/1862 (NCT 8, 154).

BUMGARNER, Allen J., Co. C, Private. Lived and e. in Catawba 8/13/1861. Captured at Hanover CH 5/27/1862; confined at Ft. Monroe, then Ft. Columbus. Trans to Aiken's Landing for exchange 8/5/1862. Surrendered at Appomattox CH 4/9/1865 (NCT 8, 141).

BUMGARNER, David A., Co. C, Private. Lived and e. in Catawba resident 3/15/1862. Captured at Hanover CH 5/27/1862; confined at Ft. Monroe, then Ft. Columbus. Trans to Aiken's Landing for exchange 8/5/1862. Wounded at Chancellorsville 5/1–3/1863. Wounded in the back and captured at Gravel Hill 7/28/1864; confined at Pt. Lookout. Paroled and trans to Boulware's Wharf 3/18/1865 for exchange (NCT 8, 141–142).

BUMGARNER, Sidney A., Co. C, Private (18__–1862). Lived and e. in Catawba 8/13/1861. Died at Richmond 8/1/1862 (NCT 8, 142).

BUNDY, Henry, Co. I, Private (1838–). Lived and e. in Yadkin 8/13/1861, age 23. Captured at Hanover CH 5/27/1862; confined at Ft. Monroe, then Ft. Columbus. Paroled and trans to Aiken's Landing for exchange 8/5/1862. Captured at Gettysburg 7/3/1863; confined at Ft. Delaware, trans to Pt. Lookout 10/15–18/1863. Released there 1/25/1864 after joining U.S. Army. He had m. In Yadkin Sarah Nichols in 1856 (NCT 8, 208, CWY 194).

BUNDY, Nathan, Co. I, Private (1841–). Lived and e. in Yadkin. 3/8/1862. Captured at Hanover CH 5/27/1862; confined at Ft. Monroe, then Ft. Columbus. Paroled and trans to Aiken's Landing for exchange 8/5/1862. AWOL before 11/1/1862. Listed as deserter 10/1/1863 (NCT 8, 208).

BURGESS, Ambrose C., Co. H, Private (1841–1863). Lived and e. in Cleveland 3/17/1862, age 21. Captured at Hanover CH 5/27/1862; confined at Ft. Monroe, then Ft. Columbus. Paroled and trans to Aiken's Landing for exchange 8/5/1862. Killed at Chancellorsville 5/3/1863 (NCT 8, 198).

BURGESS, Edward T., Co. I, Private? (1816–1892). NC pension records indicate he served in this company. Edward m. Nancy A. Windsor in 1850, in Surry and had 5 children. He is bur. At Zion Bapt. Ch., Iredell County, NC (NCT 8, 208; CWY 194).

BURLEYSON, Adam, Co. D, Private. E, at Camp Holmes on 10/15/1864. Surrendered at Appomattox CH 4/9/1865 (NCT 8, 154).

BURLEYSON, Eben, Co. K, Private (1840–). Lived, e. in Stanly 3/15/1862, age 22. Captured near Petersburg 4/2/1865; confined at Pt Lookout; released 6/23/1865 after OOA (NCT 8, 221).

BURLEYSON, John W., Co. D, Private (1839–). Lived and e. in Stanly 7/29/1861 there, age 22. Captured at Waterloo, VA 9/8/1863; confined at Old Capitol Prison, Washington, DC until released abt 9/26/1863 after OOA (NCT 8, 154–155).

BURNS, John, Co. I, Private. E. 8/13/1861 in Yadkin. Present through Dec. 1861. (NCT 8, 208).

BURRIS, Adam C., Co. K. Private (1845–). Lived, e. in Stanly 9/7/1861, age 16. Wounded at Chancellorsville 5/2–3/1863. Wounded in right thigh and captured at Gettysburg 7/1–3/1863. Hospitalized at Gettysburg, then at Baltimore. Trans to City Pt. On 8/20/1863 for exc. Wounded in right shoulder near Bethesda Church, VA abt 5/31/1864. On duty as ambulance driver Nov.–Dec. 1864, and was with "ambulance train" Jan.–Feb. 1865 (NCT 8, 221).

BURRIS, Lee H., Co. A, Private (1841–). E., age 21, 5/4/1861. Captured at Hanover CH 5/27/1862; confined at Ft. Monroe, then Ft. Columbus. Trans to Aiken's Landing 7/12/1862 for exchange 8/5/1862. Deserted that same month but returned to duty 2/28/1863. Captured again at Wilderness 56/6/1864 and confined at Pt. Lookout, until released on 5/28/1864 after joining the U.S. Army, Company I, 1st Regiment, U.S. Volunteer Infantry (NCT 8, 115).

BURRIS, Levi P., Co. K, Private (1841–). Lived, e. in Stanly 9/7/1861, age 20. Wounded in left leg, captured at Gettysburg. Trans to Davids Island 7/17–24/1863. Trans to Fort Wood abt 10/15/1863, then to Pt. Lookout abt 1/8/1864. Paroled and trans to City Pt 3/6/1864 for exc. Absent on furlough through Feb. 1865 (NCT 8, 221).

BUTNER, C.T., Co. D, Private. Hospitalized at

Richmond 3/31/1865 with gunshot wound of left side. Captured while in hospital 4/3/1865; paroled 5/19/1865 (NCT 8, 155).

BYARS, Elias, Co. H, Private (1832–1864). B. and lived in Cleveland, e. 3/17/1862, age 30. Killed at Spotsylvania CH 5/12/1864 (NCT 8, 198).

CAGLE, Benjamin, Co. K, Private (1832–). B., lived, and e. in Cabarrus 9/7/1861, age 29. Dis 2/3/1862 due to "loss of hearing" (NCT 8, 221).

CAIN, Cornelius, o. A, 1st Sergeant (1842–1862). Son of David and Deborah Cain, of the Mt. Airy District, Surry, he was b. in Virginia, e. in Surry, age 19, 5/4/1861, as corporal; reduced in ranks on 10/3/1861. Promoted to 1st sergeant at the reorganization in April 1862. Killed at Frayser's Farm, 6/30/1862. His father filed a claim for back pay owed his son in the amount of $68, 96 (NCT 8, 115; SCS 30).

CALAWAY (Calloway), Charles M., Co. I, Private (1843–). E. 12/20/1863 at Liberty Mills. Captured at Petersburg 4/2/1865; confined at Ft. Delaware until released 6/7/1865 after OOA (NCT 8, 208; see 1850 Surry Census)

CALLAIS, James M., Co. E, Private (1838–1862). Lived and e. in Montgomery 8/1/1861, age 23. Died at Gordonsville 10/1/1862 (NCT 8, 166).

CALLAIS, Josiah, Co. E, Private (1839–1863). Lived and e. in Montgomery 8/1/1861, age 22. Wounded and captured at Gettysburg 7/1–2/1863. Died there 7/25/1863 of his wounds (NCT 8, 166).

CALLAIS, William, Co. E, Private (1840–1863). Lived and e. in Montgomery 8/1/1861, age 21. Hospitalized at Wilmington 8/16/1862 with a "puncture" wound. Died at Hanover Junction abt 5/4/1863 of "pneumonia" (NCT 8, 166).

CALLAWAY, Alfred S., Co. D, Private (1827–1863). Stanly resident, e. 7/19/1861, age 34. Died in Lynchburg hospital 2/15/1863 or 4/7/1863 of disease (NCT 8, 155).

CALVARD— see COLVARD.

CAMPBELL, Adolphus L., Co. C, Private (18__ –1863). Catawba resident, e. 8/13/1861. Wounded at Chancellorsville 5/2–3/1863. Wounded in the left shoulder and captured at Gettysburg, 7/1–3/1863. Hospitalized at Gettysburg where he died 7/15–18/1863 of his wounds (NCT 8, 142).

CAMPBELL, William A., Co. C, Private (1860–). Catawba farmer, e., age 21, 8/13/1861. Dis. 12/23/1861 due to a "scrotal hernia of the right side" (NCT 8, 142).

CANLEY, J.W., Co. B, Private (1839–1862). E., age 22, 7/30/1861 in Gaston Died in Danville hospital 8/22–22/1862 of chronic diarrhea (NCT 8, 127).

CANUP, Daniel, Co. D, Private (1843–1862). Lived and e. in Stanly 3/15/1862, age 19. Died in Richmond 7/15/1862 of disease (NCT 8, 155).

CANUP, David, Co. D, Private (1825–1861). Lived e. in Stanly 7/29/1861, age 36. Died 9/20/1861 of disease (NCT 8, 155).

CARDEN, John W., Co. G. Private. E. in Orange 3/1/1864. Captured at Gravel Hill 7/28/1864; confined at Pt. Lookout. Trans to Elmira 8/8/1864 and died there 10/1/19864 of "chronic dysentery' (NCT 8, 186).

CARKIER, Wiley, Co. K, Private (1841–). Lived in Cabarrus, e. in Stanly 9/7/1861, age 20. Present until he surrendered at Appomattox CH 4/9/1865 (NCT 8, 221).

CARKIER, William M., Co. K, Private (1838–). B. in Stanly, lived in Cabarrus, e. in Stanly 9/7/1861, age 23. Wounded in right arm, captured at Gettysburg 7/1–3/1863. Hospitalized at Chester. Trans to City Pt. 8/17/1863 for exc./ Present Sept.–Dec. 1864; retired to Invalid Corps 12/21/1864 (NCT 8, 221).

CARLTON, Sandford B., Co. 1, Private (1841–). Lived and e. in Yadkin 8/13/1861, age 19. Captured at Hanover CH 5/27/1862; confined at Ft. Monroe, then Ft. Columbus. Paroled and trans to Aiken's Landing for exchange 8/5/1862. Wounded at Chancellorsville 5/1–3/1863. Absent-sick Sept.–Oct. 1864. AWOL 11/15/1864 — Feb. 1865. He was the son of Bloom and Elizabeth Carlton (NCT 8, 208–209, CWY 195).

CARMODY, J. T., Co. G, Private. Surrendered at Appomattox CH 4/9/1865 (NCT 8, 186).186).

CARPENTER, Allen, Co. D, Private (1842–). Lived and e. in Stanly 7/29/1861, age 19. Surrendered at Appomattox CH 4/9/1865 (NCT 8, 155).

CARPENTER, Caleb, Co. B, Private (1840–). Lived in Gaston, e. in Lenoir, age 20, 3/19/1862. Captured at Fredericksburg on 12/13/1862, but paroled on 12/17/1862. Wounded at Chancellorsville 5/2–3/1863. Surrendered at Appomattox CH 4/9/1865 (NCT 8, 127).

CARPENTER, Churchwell, Co. D, Private (1844–1863). Lived and e. in Stanly 7/29/1861, at age 17. Killed at Gettysburg 7/3/1863 (NCT 8, 155).

CARPENTER, F.T., Co. B, Private (1841–1863). Lived and e. in Gaston, age 20, 7/30/1861. Wounded in shoulder at Cedar Mt. 8/9/1862. Captured at Fredericksburg 12/1862. Paroled abt 12/17/1862. Wounded and captured at Gettysburg 7/1–5/1863. Died at Gettysburg 7/18/1863 of wounds (NCT 8, 127).

CARPENTER, John C., Co. B, Private (1843–). Lived and e. in Gaston, age 18, on 7/30/1861. Captured at Hanover CH 5/27/1862; confined at Ft. Monroe, then Ft. Columbus. Paroled, trans to Aiken's Landing, and Exc 8/5/1862. Wounded and captured at Fredericksburg 12/13/1862. Paroled 12/17/1862. Captured near Petersburg 4/2/1865; confined on Hart's Island. Released 6/17/1865 after OOA (NCT 8, 127).

CARPENTER, John T., Co. B, Sergeant (1840–). Gaston resident, e., age 21, 7/30/1861 as a private. Captured at Hanover CH 5/27/1862; confined at Ft. Monroe, then Ft. Columbus. Trans to Aiken's Landing for exc on 8/5/1862. Promoted corpora Feb. 1863; promoted to sergeant Mar. 1863–Oct. 1864. Wounded in left leg near Petersburg 4/2/1865. Captured by enemy, and paroled at Farmville 4/11–21/1865. NC pension records indicate he was wounded in the leg in 1864 (NCT 8, 127).

CARPENTER, Marcus, Co. B, Private. Gaston resident e. at Liberty Mills on 2/5/1864. Captured at Dinwiddie CH on 4/5/1865 Confined at Pt. Lookout, until released 6/24/1865 after OOA (NCT 8, 127).

CARPENTER, Michael, Co. B, Private (1846–). E. at Liberty Mills, age 18, on 5/1/1864. Surrendered at

Appomattox CH 4/9/1965. NC pension records indicate he was wounded on 4/2/1865 (NCT 8, 128).

CARPENTER, Robert W., Co. D, Private. Stanly resident, e. 3/1/1864 at Liberty Mills. Died in Lynchburg hospital 5/18/1864 of chronic diarrhea (NCT 8, 155).

CARPENTER, William H., Co. B, Private (1843–1864). Lived and e. in Gaston 7/30/1861 at age 18. Captured at Hanover CH , 5/27/1862, and confined at Ft. Monroe, then Ft. Columbus. Trans to Aiken's Landing and exc 8/5/1862. Wounded at Gettysburg 7/1–3/1863. Wounded in the chest; hospitalized at Gordonsville. Died there on 5/23/1864 of his wounds (NCT 8, 128).

CARROLL, T.L., Co. B, Private (1840–1862). Gaston Farmer, e. 8/5/1861, age 21. Died in a Lynchburg hospital 7/24/1862 of chronic diarrhea, and/or wounds (NCT 8, 128).

CARSON, John B., Co. B, 1st Sergeant (1835–). Lived and e. in Gaston 7 /30/1861, age 26. Mustered in as corporal; reduced in rank 2/28/1862. Captured at Hanover CH 5/27/1862; confined at Ft. Monroe, then Ft. Columbus. Paroled, trans to Aiken's Landing for exchange 8/5/1862. Promoted to 1st sergeant 12/18/1862. Wounded in left arm at Chancellorsville 5/3/1863; arm amputated. Dis. ½/1864 (NCT 8, 128).

CARSON, Rufus Watson, Co. B, Corporal (1843–). B. in Lincoln, lived in Gaston, e. at Bunker Hill on 10/5/1862, at age 19, as a private. Wounded in head, shoulder and right arm at Fredericksburg 12/13/1862. Promoted to corporal 10/1/1864. Surrendered at Appomattox CH 4/9/1865 (NCT 8, 128).

CARTER, Eugene, Co. F, Private (1844–). Lived and e. in Yadkin 6/18/1861, age 17. Dis. 9/21/1861 due to disability (NCT 8, 176).

CARTER, James W., Co. C, Private. Catawba resident, e. 3/14/1864. Wounded in Virginia in May 1864. Captured at Petersburg 4/2/1865. Confined at Ft. Delaware, until released 6/19/1865 after OOA (NCT 8, 142).

CARTER, Joshua C, Co. C, Private (1835–). Lived in Catawba, e. 8/13/1861. Wounded at Chancellorsville 5/2–3/1863. Present through 11/17/1864 on detail as a teamster most of that time. Surrendered at Appomattox CH 4/9/1865 (NCT 8, 142).

CARTER, John A., Co. F, Private (1840–). B. and e. in Yadkin 6/18/1861, age 21. Dis. 1/12/1862. Later served in Co. A, 54th Reg NCT (NCT 8, 186).

CARTER, Josiah L., Co. D, Sergeant (1825–1861). Stanly resident, e. 7/29/1861 as a sergeant. "Murdered at Wilmington," NC abt 12/21/1861 (NCT 8, 155).

CARTER, Miles, Co. I, Private. Lived in Yadkin, e. at Liberty Mills 2/29/1864. Captured at Petersburg 4/2/1865; confined at Ft. Delaware until released 6/19/1865 after OOA (NCT 8, 209).

CARTER, William M., Co. I, Private (1840–1864). Previously served in Co. B, 28th Reg NCT, e. 10/16/1861. Wounded at Mechanicsville 6/26/1862. AWOL July–Aug 1862 and Oct–Dec 1862. Returned and trans to Co. I, 28th Reg 3/29/1863. Wounded and captured at Gettysburg 7/3/1863; confined at Ft. Delaware. Trans to Pt. Lookout 10/15–18/1863; died there 8/24/1864 (NCT 8, 209, NCT 10, 22).

CARTRIGHT, Thomas D., Co. I, Private (1821–1879). E. at Camp Vance 11/4/1863. On detail as a shoemaker at Richmond from 1/8/1864–Feb.1865. Captured in Richmond hospital 4/3/1865; paroled 5/3/1865. Bur. Cartwright Fam. Cem., Yadkin County, NC (NCT 8, 209; CWY 196).

CASEY, Daniel C., Co. I, Sergeant (1841–). Son of Henry W. and Sarah Ann Windsor Casey, Daniel lived and e. in Yadkin 8/13/1861, age 20 as private. Promoted to sergeant 4/12/1862 Wounded in shoulder at 2nd Manassas 8/27–30/1862. Captured at Chancellorsville 5/3/1863. Paroled and trans to City Pt. 5/13/1863 for exchange. Captured at Gettysburg 7/1–3/1863; confined at Ft. Delaware. Trans to Pt. Lookout 10/115–18/1863, until released 1/25/1864 after OOA, and joining the U.S. Army (NCT 8, 209, CWY 197).

CATES, Dennis M., Co. G, Private (1839–). Lived and e. in Orange 12/20/1861, age 22. Captured at Hanover CH 5/27/1862; confined at Ft. Columbus. Paroled and trans to Aiken's Landing for exchange 8/5/1862. Captured at Fredericksburg 12/13/1862; exc abt 12/17/1862. Captured at Spotsylvania CH 5/12/1864; confined at Pt. Lookout, trans to Elmira on 8/10/1864. Released there 6/19/1865, after OOA (NCT 8, 186).

CATES, Enoch C., Co. G, Private (1842–1864). Lived and e. in Orange 9/2/1861, age 19. Killed at Wilderness 5/5/1864 (NCT 8, 186).

CATES, John M., Co. G, Private (1843–1862). Lived and e. in Orange 9/2/1862. Died at Wilmington 1/29/1862 of disease (NCT 8, 186).

CATES, Richard L., Co. G, Private (1842–). Lived and e. in Orange 9/2/1861, age 19. Wounded at Gaines' Mill 6/27/1862. Captured at Falling Waters 7/14/1863; confined at Pt. Lookout. Paroled and trans to Cox's Wharf 2/20–21/1865 for exchange (NCT 8, 186).

CAVE, John, Co. A, Private (1830–). Surry farmer, e. 5/18/1861. Dis. 12/16/1861 for "general debility caused from anemia." (N. C. Pension records indicate he was wounded in an unspecified battle in 1864.) He reenlisted in Wake 8/17/1862 at age 32. Wounded in leg at Wilderness 5/5/1864. Surrendered at Appomattox CH 4/9/1865. Son of Thomas and Elizabeth Beamer Cave, Dobson District, Surry. (NCT 8, 115; SCS 32).

CENTER (or **SENTER**), Wilson, Co. A, Private (1837–1863) Son of John Center and Hallin (Helen?) Stanley Center, Dobson District, Surry, e. on 3/18/1862 at age 25. Died at Gettysburg 7/1–3/1863 (NCT 8, 115; SCS 32).

CHAMPION, David O. P., Co. H, Private (1837–). Lived and e. in Cleveland 8/22/1861, age 24. Present until he surrendered at Appomattox CH 4/9/1865 (NCT 8, 198).

CHAMPION, James, Co. H, Private (1845–). Lived and e. in Cleveland 3/17/1862. Wounded at Fredericksburg 12/13/1862. Wounded n right leg and captured at Gravel Hill 7/28/1864. Confined at various hospitals until confined at Old Capitol Prison 9/7/1864. Trans to Ft. Delaware 9/19/1864; paroled and trans to City Pt. for exc 2/27/1865. Furloughed for 60 days 3/9/1865 (NCT 8, 198).

CHAMPION, James M., Co. H, Private (1840–1862). Lived and e. in Cleveland 8/22/1861, age 21.

Wounded at Gaines' Mill 6/27/1862. Hospitalized at Richmond where he died 7/18/1862 of wounds (NCT 8, 198).

CHAMPION, John G., Co. H, Private (1843, 1862). Lived and e. in Cleveland 8/22/1861, age 18. Died near Gordonsville abt 12/10/1862. Cause unknown (NCT 8, 198).

CHANCEY, J.H., Co. E, Private (1841–1862). Lived and e. in Montgomery 3/6/1862, age 21. Died at Richmond 7/13/1862 of disease (NCT 8, 166).

CHANCEY, L.N., Co. E, Private (1839–1862). Lived and e. in Montgomery 3/6/1862, age 23. Killed at Gaines' Mill 6/27/1862 (NCT 8, 166).

CHANCEY, W.H., Co. E, Private (1842–1862). Lived and e. in Montgomery 3/6/1862, age 20. Died in a Richmond hospital 8/26–27/1862 of continued fever (NCT 8, 166).

CHANDLER, Andrew J., Co. A, Private (1835–1863). Lived and e. in Surry, age 27, 3/18/1862. Killed at Gettysburg on 7/3/1863 (NCT 8, 115; SCS 33).

CHANDLER, John, Co. A, Private (1831–) B. in Patrick County, VA in 1860, lived in the Stuart's Creek District, Surry, NC. E. 3/18/1862, age 31. Dis. 4/15/1863 due to chronic rheumatism and contraction of his left leg (NCT 8, 115; SCS 33).

CHAPEL, Lewis J., Co. I, Private (1837–). B. and e. in Yadkin 8/13/1861, age 24. Trans to Co. B, 38th Reg NCT 1/10/1862. Deserted 8/6/1862 (NCT 8, 209, NCT 10, 23).

CHAPPEL (Chappell), Calvin J., Co. I, Private (1837–). Lived and e. in Yadkin 10/20/1862, age 29 (?). Deserted 10/29/1862. May be the same as Calvin J. Chappel, who e. at Camp Gregg, 2/28/1863, age 26. AWOL Oct. 1864–Feb. 1865. NC pension records indicate he was wounded near Chancellorsville 5/4/1863. May have served previously in Co. G, 44th Reg NCT (NCT 8, 209, NCT 10, 457, CWY 198–199).

CHAPPEL, William, Co. I, Private. Lived in Yadkin, e. at Camp Holmes 11/14/1862. Captured near Pickett's Farm abt 7/21/1864; confined at Pt. Lookout 7/28/1864 until released 5/13/1865 after OOA (NCT 8, 209).

CHAPPELL, J.C., Co. I, Private (1845–). Lived and e. in Yadkin 2/28/1863. Deserted 6/18/1863 (NCT 8, 209).

CHAPPELL, James R., Co. I, Private (1831–). Lived and e. in Yadkin 8/13/1861. Wounded in both thighs and both hips and captured at Wilderness abt 5/6/1864 (NCT 8, 209)

CHAUNCY, David E.D., Co. E, Private (1829–). David lived in Montgomery where he e. 8/1/1861, age 32. Present through 8/11/1863 (NCT 8, 166).

CHAUNCY, Martin A., Co. E, Private (1839–). Lived and e. in Montgomery 8/1/1861. Wounded in hand at Frayser's Farm 6/30/1862. Absent-wounded through Oct. 1862. Hospitalized at Richmond 6/21/;1863 with chronic diarrhea; trans to another Richmond hospital abt 8/15/1863 (NCT 8, 166).

CHAVERS, Samuel, Co. G, Private (1840–). Lived and e. in Orange 9/2/1861, age 21. Captured at Fredericksburg 12/13/1862; exc 12/17/1862. Dis. Jan. 1863 because he was of "mixed blood." A "faithful soldier,"

he fought almost every battle from Hanover CH to Fredericksburg (NCT 8, 186–187).

CHEEK, Jesse H., Co. G, Private (1844–1863). Lived and e. in Orange 12/18/1862, age 18. Wounded at Gettysburg 7/1–3/1863, died 7/16/1863 (NCT 8, 187).

CHEEK, John W., Co. G, Private (1847–). Lived and e. in Orange 2/1/1865, age 18. Surrendered at Appomattox CH 4/9/1865 (NCT 8, 187).

CHEEK, Julius M., Co. G, Private (1838–). Lived and e. in Orange 9/2/1861, age 23, as a private. Promoted to corporal Mar.–Apr 1862. Captured at Hanover CH 5/27/1862; confined at Ft. Monroe, then Ft. Columbus. Paroled and trans to Aiken's Landing for exchange 8/5/1862. Wounded in the shoulder and captured at Fredericksburg 12/13/1862; exc 12/17/1862. Trans to Co. I, 6th Reg NCT 3/18/1863 (NCT 8, 167).

CHEEK, Ruffin, Co. G., Private (1816–). Lived and e. in Orange 9/2/1861, age 45. Captured at Fredericksburg 12/13/1862; exc 12/17/1862. Dis. 9/6/1864, overage (NCT 8, 187).

CHEEK, William J. A., Co. G, Private (1843–). Lived and e. in Orange 9/2/1861, age 18. Captured at Hanover CH 5/27/1862; confined at Ft. Monroe, then Ft. Columbus. Paroled and trans to Aiken's Landing for exchange 8/5/1862. Captured at Spotsylvania CH 5/12/1864; confined at Pt. Lookout; trans to Elmira 8/8/1864. Released there 6/19/1865 after OOA (NCT 187).

CHILDERS, Franklin A., Co. C, Private (18__ –1862). Resident of Lincoln, e. at Camp Fisher 8/26/1861. Died at Wilmington 3/4/1862 of disease (NCT 8, 142).

CHILDERS, James F., Co. I, Private (1838–). Born in Surry, lived and e. in Yadkin 8/13/1861. Dis. 12/14/1861 due to "varicocele" (NCT 8, 209).

CHILDRESS, Hiram, Co. A, Private (1842–). A Surry farmer, age 18/1862 at age 20. Dis. 7/7/1862 due to "anemia & dropsy of the lower extremities...." Son of Stephen and Margaret Childress, tenant farmers in the Hotel (Elkin) District, Surry (NCT 8, 115; SCS 34).

CHILDRESS, John, Co. A, Private. (1842–1864). Lived with his widowed mother, Kittery, Dobson District, Surry, e. 5/10/1861, at age 19. Captured at Hanover CH 5/27/1862, and confined at Ft. Monroe, then Ft. Columbus. Trans to Aiken's Landing on 7/12/1862 for exchange on 8/5/1862. Wounded at Gettysburg 7/1–3/1863. Killed at Wilderness, 5/5/1864 (NCT 8, 116; SCS 34).

CHILDRESS, Stephen, Co. A, Private (1813–). Stephen was m. and the father of several children when he e. at age 49, 3/18/1862. Went home on furlough abt 10/11/1862 and did not return (NCT 8, 116; SCS 34).

CHILDRESS, William H., Co. I, Private (1842–). Lived and e. in Yadkin 8/13/1861. Captured at Hanover CH 5/27/1862; confined at Ft. Monroe, then Ft. Columbus. Trans to Aiken's Landing for exchange 8/5/1862. Wounded at Gettysburg 7/1–3/1863. Captured near Petersburg 4/2/1865; confined at Ft. Delaware until released 6/19/1865 after OOA (NCT 8, 209).

CHISHOLM, Moses, Co. E, Private. E. in Wake 3/28/1864. Surrendered at Appomattox CH 4/9/1865.

CHISHOLM, William J., Co. E, Corporal. Previously served in Co. F, 44th Reg, NCT. Joined this company March–Aug 1862 "without a transfer." Mustered in as private; promoted to corporal Nov. 1862–July 1864. Paroled at Farmville 4/11–21, 1865 (NCT 8, 166).

CHOPLIN, Joseph, Co. F, Sergeant (1838–). Lived and e. in Yadkin 6/18/1861, age 23. Mustered in as corporal, promoted to sergeant 4/12/1862. Missing in action at Gaines' Mill 6/27/1862 (NCT 8, 176).

CHOPLIN, Robert, Co. F, Private (1843–1862). Lived and e. in Yadkin 6/18/1861, age 18. Wounded at Gaines' Mill 6/27/1862. Died at Richmond abt 8/3/1862 of wounds and/or disease (NCT 8, 176).

CHOPLIN, Sidney, Co. F, Private (1837–). Born in Franklin, lived and e. in Yadkin . 8/18/1861, age 24. Killed at Gettysburg 7/1–3/1863 (NCT 8, 176).

CHOPLIN, Wesley, Co. F, Private (1840–). Lived and e. in Yadkin 6/18/1861. Wounded in left elbow at Ox Hill 9/1/1862. Absent-wounded through Dec.1862. Detailed as hospital guard 10/17/1863. Paroled at Greensboro, NC 5/3/1865 (NCT 8, 176).

CLARK, B.Y., Co. E, Private. Paroled at Greensboro, NC abt 5/5/1865 (NCT 8, 166).

CLARK, Niven, Co. E, Captain (1835–1864). Montgomery resident, e. 81/1861, age 26 as a 1st sergeant. Appointed 3rd lieutenant 11/9/1861. Promoted to 1st lieutenant 2/28/1862 or 4 4/9 1862. Wounded near Richmond abt 6/29/1862. Promoted to captain 10/18/1862. Killed at Spotsylvania CH 5/12/1864 (NCT 8, 164).

CLARK, William, Co. G, Private (1839–). An Orange shoemaker, e. there 9/2/1861, age 22. Dis. 11/14/1862 due to "chronic rheumatism" (NCT 8, 187).

CLARKE, James R., Co. G, Private (1830–). A blacksmith, b. in Chatham, lived and e. in Orange 9/2/1861, age 31. Dis. 10/9/1861 due to "scrotal hernia of the right side..." (NCT 8, 187).

CLARKE, Milan A., Co. B, Private. E. at Liberty Mills 3/15/1864. Present at the surrender at Appomattox CH, 4/9/1865 (NCT 8, 128).

CLAYTON, James F., Co. D, Private (1840–1862). Lived and e. in Stanly 7/29/1861, age 21. Killed at Frayser's Farm 6/30/1862, "one of the best soldiers" (NCT 8, 155).

CLEMMER, E.J., Co. B, Private (1837–1863). Lived and e. in Gaston 7/3/1861, age 24. Wounded in thigh at Chancellorsville 5/1–3/1863. Hospitalized in Richmond; died on 9/25/1863 of erysipelas from fracture of thigh (NCT 8, 128).

CLEMMER, G.A., Co. B, Private (1840–1862). Gaston resident e. 7/30/1861, age 21. Killed at Fredericksburg 12/13/1862 (NCT 8, 128).

CLEMMER, John L., Co. B, 1st Sergeant (1843–). Lived and e. in Gaston, age 18, 7/30/1861, as a private. Promoted to 1st sergeant 10/1/1864. Captured near Petersburg 4/2/1865, and confined at Pt. Lookout until released 6/24/1865 after OOA (NCT 8, 128).

CLEMMER, Leander R., Co. B, Private (1843–). E. in Gaston, age 18, on 7/30/1861. Surrendered at Appomattox CH 4/9/1865 (NCT 8, 128).

CLINE, Adolphus, Co. C, Private. Lived and e. in Catawba 4/6/1864. Captured in a Richmond hospital

4/3/1865; trans to Newport News 4/23/1865. Released 6/30/1865 after OOA (NCT 8, 142).

CLINE, Alfred J., Co. C, Private (1843–). Lived and e. in Catawba 8/13/1861 there, age 18. Captured in Richmond 4/3/1865; trans to Newport News on 4/24/1865. Released, date unspecified. Paroled at Greensboro 5/2/1865 (NCT 8, 142).

CLINE, Ambrose, Co. C, Private (1839–1864). Lived and e. in Catawba 3/14/1863, age 24. Died near Richmond 6/6/1864 of wounds (NCT 8, 142).

CLINE, Ephraim Elcanah, Co. C, 3rd Lieutenant. Lived and e. in Catawba, and appointed 3rd lieutenant 8/13/1861. Defeated for reelection 2/17/1862. Later served as sergeant of Co. E, 57th NC Reg. (NCT 8, 139).

CLINE, Franklin, Co. H, Private (1818–). Lived at "Hickory Station," e. 10/9/1863 at Camp Holmes. Captured at Gravel Hill 7/28/1864; confined at Pt. Lookout, then at Elmira 8/8/1864. Released there 5/29/1865 after OOA (NCT 8, 198).

CLINE, J. Timothy, Co. C, Private. Lived and e. in Catawba 4/12/1864. Captured near Petersburg 4/2/1865. Confined at Ft. Delaware; released 6/19/1865 after OOA (NCT 8, 142).

CLINE, John L.H., Co. C, Private (1845–1864). Catawba resident, e., age 18, 2/18/1863. Deserted 6/5/1863, but Captured at Spotsylvania CH 5/12/1864; confined at Pt. Lookout, where he died 6/19/1864 (NCT 8, 142).

CLINE, Maxwell A., Co. C, Private (1842–). Lived and e. in Catawba 8/13/1861, age 19. Deserted 6/5/1863. Captured at Spotsylvania CH 5/12/1864; confined at Pt. Lookout, then trans to Elmira 8/8/1864. Released 5/19/1865 after OOA (NCT 8, 142).

CLINE, Monroe J., Co. C, Private. Lived and e. in Catawba 8/13/1861. Captured at Hanover CH 5/27/1862; confined at Ft. Monroe, then Ft. Columbus. Trans to Aiken's Landing for exchange 8/5/1862. Captured at Winchester abt 12/2/1862. Paroled 12/4/1862. Died in Petersburg hospital 12/27/1862 of typhoid fever (NCT 8, 141).

CLINE, Noah, Co. H, Private (18__–1864). B. in Catawba, e. 2/24/1864 at Camp Vance. Wounded in left knee at Fussell's Mill 8/16/1864. Left leg amputated. Hospitalized at Richmond and died there 10/11–12/1864 of wounds (NCT 8, 198–199).

CLIPPARD, John, Co. C, Private (1835–). A Catawba farmer before he e. there on 3/15/1862, age 27. Wounded in the jaw at Wilderness 5/5/1864. Retired to Invalid Corps 12/28/1864 due to disability (NCT 8, 142).

CLONINGER, D.R., Co. B, Private (1814–). A Gaston farmer e. on 3/29/1862, age 48. Captured at Fredericksburg on 12/13.1862; paroled abt 12/17/1862. Dis. 12/31/1863 due to chronic rheumatism and "infirmness of advanced age" (NCT 8, 128).

CLONINGER, James S., Co. B, Private (1841–). Lived in Gaston, e. in New Hanover, age 21, on 3/14/1862. Captured at Hanover CH 5/27/1862; confined at Ft. Monroe then Ft. Columbus. Paroled and trans to Aiken's Landing and exc 8/5/1862. Captured at Fredericksburg 12/13/1862. Paroled abt

12/17/1862. Promoted to corporal March–July 1863. Wounded in right elbow and captured at Gettysburg 7/1–5/1863. Hospitalized first at Gettysburg then Davids Island. Paroled and trans to City Pt., for exchange 9/16/1863. Rank reduced. Retired to Invalid Corps 5/2/1864 due to disability (NCT 8, 128).

CLONINGER, L.A., Co. B, Private (1844–1864). E., age 18, in Gaston 3/29/1862, killed at Reams' Station 8/25/1864 (NCT 8, 128).

CLONINGER, M.H., Co. F, Private. Captured near Petersburg 4/2/1865; confined at Pt. Lookout 4/6/1865. Released 6/3/1865 after OOA (NCT 8, 176).

CLONINGER, Sidney, Co. B, Sergeant (1828–1863). B. in Gaston, e., age 34, 3/29/1862, as a private. Captured at Hanover CH on 5/27/1862; confined at Ft. Monroe, then Ft. Columbus. Paroled and trans to Aiken's Landing and exc on 8/5/1862. Promoted to sergeant 11/5/1862. Wounded at Fredericksburg 12/13/1862. Hospitalized at Richmond where he died 1/9/1863 of his wound (NCT 8, 129).

CLONINGER, Valentine, Co. B., Private. E. 2/25/1864 at Liberty Mills. Hospitalized at Richmond on 5/25/1864 with rubeola. Absent-sick through Feb. 1865 (NCT 8, 129).

CLONINGER, Wiley W., Co. B, 1st Lieutenant (–1862). Lived and e. in Gaston on 7/30/1861. Mustered in as 1st sergeant; elected 1st lieutenant 2/27/1862. Wounded at Fredericksburg, 12/13/1864. Died in field hospital there on 12/14/1862 of wounds. Described as "a brave officer" (NCT 8, 125).

COBB, Jesse, Co. H, Private (1845–1862). Lived and e. in Cleveland 3/17/1862, age 17. Died in Lynchburg hospital 5/20/1864 of "pneumonia" (NCT 8, 199).

COBB, Thompson, Co. H, Private (1843–). Lived and e. in Cleveland 8/22/1861, age 18. Captured at Hanover CH 5/27/1862; confined at Ft. Monroe, then Ft. Columbus. Paroled and trans to Aiken's Landing for exchange 8/5/1862. Captured on unknown date but paroled 5/24/1863. Hospitalized at Richmond abt 6/12/1863 with gunshot wound. Absent-sick April 1864–Feb. 1865 (NCT 8, 199).

COCKERHAM, Columbus C., Co. A, Private (1835–1908). E. in Surry, age 25, 5/4/1861. Dis. 5/12/1862 after providing Jonathan Gentry as his substitute. Son of Joseph M. and Martha Marshall Cockerham of the Dobson District, Surry. After he returned home he m. Nancy Frances Bryan and had 5 children. Died 2/4/1908 and was bur. at Rocky Ford Bapt Ch. near Devotion (NCT 8, 116; SCS 36).

COCKERHAM, David, Co. I, Corporal (1831–). Lived and e. in Yadkin 8/13/1861, age 30 as private. Promoted to corporal Mar. 1863–Oct.1864. Captured at New Bern 3/14/1862; confined at Ft. Columbus. Trans to Aiken's Landing for exchange 8/5/1862. Captured near Petersburg 4/2/1865; confined at Pt. Lookout, until released 6/24/1865 after OOA (NCT 8, 209).

COCKERHAM, Jesse Woodson, Co. A, Sergeant (1832–1863). Son of Hughs and Nancy Roberts Cockerham, who farmed in the Dobson District, Surry, e. as a private 5/4/1861; promoted to corporal 11/4/1861. Captured at Hanover CH 5/27/1862; sent to Ft. Monroe, then to Ft. Columbus. Trans 7/12/1862 to Aiken's

Landing for exchange 8/5/1862. Promoted to sergeant Nov.–Feb. 1863. Killed at Gettysburg 7/3/1863 in the Pickett-Pettigrew charge on Cemetery Ridge (NCT 8, 116; SCS 38).

COCKERHAM, John, Co. A, Private (1845–1864). A brother to Jesse W. Cockerham, and the son of Hughs and Nancy Cockerham, John e. ,age 19, 3/18/1864. Captured at Spotsylvania CH, and confined first at Pt. Lookout, then trans to Elmira on 8/8/1864, where he died on 9/22/1864 of "chronic diarrhea." Bur. in Grave #475 of 8 at Woodlawn National Cem., Elmira (NCT 8, 116; SCS 39).

COCKERHAM, William Horton, Co. A, Private (1842–1862). The son of Joseph M. and Martha S. Marshall Cockerham, who farmed in the Devotion section of Surry, he e. on 5/4/1861. Killed 6/3/1862 at Frayser's farm (NCT 8, 116; SCS 41).

COCKERHAM, William M., Co., A, Private (1835–1915). The son of Hughs and Nancy Roberts Cockerham of the Dobson District of Surry, William e/ 5/4/1861. Wounded near Chancellorsville 5/3/1863. Captured at the Wilderness abt 5/12/1864; confined at Pt. Lookout, then in the Elmira prison 8/12/1864. Paroled there 3/14/1865; trans to Boulware's Wharf, James River, for exchange 3/18–21/1865. In 1867, William m. Nancy Emmaline Willey, and had 10 children. Bur. in the Mulberry Primitive Baptist Ch., Surry, NC (NCT 8, 116; SCS 41).

COCKLEREESE, Julius, Co. A, Private. B. in Orange, NC to Solomon and Olive Cocklereese, he grew up in the Dobson District of Surry; e. 5/4/1861 and left for training. Dis. 11/201861 due to bronchitis. He m. Martha A. Sopshire in Surry in 1861 (NCT 8, 116; SCS 42).

COE, Arnold, Co A, Private (1840–aft 1870). Surry farmer, he e., age 22, 3/18/1862. He was the son of William and Rachel Holyfield Coe, of Rockford District, Surry. AWOL Jan.–Feb. 1863, but at the surrender 4/9/1865 at Appomattox. NC pension application indicated he was wounded in right leg below the knee at Spotsylvania CH on 5/14/1864. Arnold and his wife, Columbia, had 3 children by 1870 (NCT 8, 116; SCS 42).

COGGIN, Daniel H., Co. E, Corporal (1841–). B. and e. in Montgomery. 8/1/1861, age 20, as corporal. Dis. 10/15/1862 due to "organic disease of heart" (NCT 8, 166).

COLE, Jesse W., Co. G, Private (1841–). Lived and e. in Orange 9/2/1861, age 20. Wounded in left leg at Gaines' Mill 6/27/1862; leg amputated. Retired to Invalid Corps 5/19/1864 (NCT 8, 187).

COLE, William Compton, Co. G, Private (1843–). B. in Chatham, lived and e. in Orange 12/20/1861, age 18. Dis. 3/21/1864 due to "chronic diarrhoea and general debility" (NCT 8, 187).

COLEY, Levi, Co. D, Private (1826–1864). Lived and e. in Stanly 7/29/1861, age 35. Hospitalized in Richmond 5/25/1864 with a gunshot wound of right leg. Died in Richmond hospital 6/2–3/1864 of wounds and kidney disease (NCT 8, 155).

COLEY, James F., Co. K, Private. Lived in Stanly, e. At Liberty Mills 4/22/1864. Captured near Petersburg 4/2/1865; confined at Pt. Lookout. Released 6/24/1865 after OOA (NCT 8, 222).

COLEY, Jesse M., Co. K, Private (1838–). Lived in Cabarrus, e. in Stanly 9/7/1861, age 23. Captured at Hanover CH 5/27/1862. Trans to Aiken's Landing for exchange 8/5/1862. Wounded in leg at Chancellorsville 5/2–3/1863. Wounded, captured at Spotsylvania CH 5/12/1864; confined at Pt. Lookout. Trans to Elmira 7/8/1864; released there 5/29/1865 after OOA (NCT 8, 222).

COLEY, John M., Co. K, Private (1746–1864). B., lived, e. in Stanly 3/12/1863, age 17. Died abt 6/6/1864 (NCT 8, 222).

COLEY, William M, Co. K, Private (1832–). Lived in Cabarrus or Stanly, e. in Stanly 9/7/1861, age 29. Captured near Petersburg 4/2/1865; confined at Pt. Lookout. Released 6/24/1865 after OOA. Roll of Honor indicates he served as "musician" for regiment (NCT 8, 222).

COLLINS, Hezekiah W., Co. A, Private (1837–1896). Lived and e. in Surry, age 27, 5/4/1861. His letters revealed he was at Wilmington with the 28th in Nov. 1861, and in the fighting near Hanover CH in May of 1862. He was present at the surrender at Appomattox CH 4/9/1865. He was the son of Anthony and Nancy Franklin Collins, of Rockford. By his first wife, Mary J. Hardy Collins, he had 7 children. He m. 2nd in 1889 a woman named Sarah, who applied for a widow's pension in 1901(NCT 8, 116; SCS 43).

COLLINS, James M., Co. A, Private (1839–). Surry resident, e., age 22, on 5/4/1861. Absent-wounded Sept.–Oct. 1864. Retired to the Invalid Corps on 1/11/1865 due to disability. James and Hezekiah Collins were brothers, both sons of Anthony Collins. James m. Christina Johnson in 1867. By 1880, James and his family of 7 children lived at Westfield (NCT 8, 116; SCS 43).

COLVARD (Calvard), Benjamin, Co. F, Private (1843–) B. and e. in Yadkin, age 19, 4/1/1862. Wounded in forearm and captured at Hanover CH, 5/27/1862; confined at Ft. Monroe, then Ft. Columbus. Exc at Aiken's Landing 11/10/1862. AWOL through Dec. 1862. Returned to duty; disc. 1/;3/1864 due to wounds received at Hanover CH (NCT 8, 176).

COLVARD, John S., Co. F, Private (1839–). Lived and e. in Yadkin 6/18/1861, age 22. Deserted 6/3/1863. Joined the enemy abt 7/31/1864, and took the OOA at Louisville, KY 8/10/1864 (NCT 8, 176).

COLVARD, Thomas E., Co. F, Private (1835–). Lived, farmed and e. in Yadkin on 6/18/1861, age 26. Hospitalized in Richmond 12/15/1862 with gunshot wound of forefinger. Trans to Danville hospital 1/8/1863. Deserted from hospital 3/24/1863, and went over to the enemy. Confined at Knoxville, TN 7/31/1864. Took the OOA at Louisville, KY 8/10/1864 (NCT 8, 176–177).

COLVARD, William, Co. F, Private (1837). Lived and e. in Yadkin 6/18/1861, age 24. Deserted 6/5/1863. Went over to the enemy; confined at Knoxville TN 7/31/1864. Took OOA at Louisville, KY 8/10/1864 (NCT 8, 177).

COMER, James Q., Co. I, Corporal (1829–1897).

Lived and e. in Yadkin 8/13/1861, age 32 as private. Promoted to corporal 10/30/1861. Captured at Hanover CH 5/27/1862; confined at Ft. Monroe, then Ft. Columbus. Trans to Aiken's Landing for exchange 8/5/1862. Rank reduced. AWOL Jan.–Feb. 1863. Present Sept.–Dec. 1864. Deserted 1/11/1865. James was a minister. He and wife, Lucinda are buried at Flat Rock Bapt. Ch., Yadkin County, NC (NCT 8, 209, CWY 201).

CONNELL, Sidney J., Co. C, Private (1840–). B. in Lincoln where he farmed, e. at Camp Fisher on 8/26/1861, age 21. Wounded at 2nd Manassas, 8/28–30/1862. Wounded again at Gettysburg 7/1–3/1863. Surrendered at Appomattox CH, 4/9/1865 (NCT 8, 152).

CONNER, Y.L., Co. B, Private. Hospitalized at Richmond on 4/2/1865, and captured while in hospital there on 4/3/1865. Trans to custody of Federal Provost Marshal 4/14/1865 (NCT 8, 129).

CONRAD, Henry A., Co. C, Private (1845–1864). Lived and e. in Catawba on 8/15/1861, age 16. Killed at Gravel Hill 7/28/1864 (NCT 8, 142).

CONRAD, James D., Co. F, Private (1845–1863). Lived and e/ in Yadkin 7/1/1863. Wounded and captured at Gettysburg 7/1–3/1863; died there 9/16/1863 of wounds (NCT 8, 177).

CONRAD, John T., Co. F, 1st Lieutenant (1837–1913). Lived and e. in Yadkin 8/10/1861 at Camp Enon as a private. Promoted to 2nd lieutenant 9/5/1861. Elected 1st lieutenant 4/12/1862. Furloughed home and "remained overtime." Dropped from the rolls abt 4/27/1862 (NCT 8, 174; CWY 202–203; O'Daniel and Patton, *Kinfolk of Jacob Conrad*, 166–174).

COOK, Abel, Co. C, Musician (1821–). Catawba resident e. at Camp Fisher 9/9/1861. Mustered in as private, promoted to musician Jan.–Apr. 1862. Wounded in left hip at Wilderness 5/5/1864. Absent-wounded through Feb. 1865. Confederate hospital records give his age at 39 in 1862 (NCT 8, 142).

COOK, Alvin, Co. I, Private (1841–). E. at Camp Holmes 10/14/1862. AWOL 10/20/1862, returned 12/1/1863. Trans to Co. I, 28th Reg NCT 10/1/1864. Present through Feb. 1865 (NCT 10, 458, NCT 8, 209).

COOK, J.R., Co. E, Private (1841–1862). Lived and e. in Montgomery 3/1/1862, age 21. Died at Lynchburg abt 8/12/1862 of disease (NCT 8, 166).

COOK, Lawson Obediah, Co. C, Private (1830–). Lived and e. in Catawba 3/15/1862 there, age 32. Wounded at Gettysburg 7/1–3/1863. Surrendered at Appomattox CH 4/9/1865 (NCT 8, 143).

COOK, Lewis, Co. E, Private (1834–). Lived and e. in Montgomery 8/1/1861, age 27. Wounded at Chancellorsville 5/2–3/1863. Wounded at Wilderness 5/5/1864. Paroled at Troy, NC 5/22/1865 (NCT 8, 166).

COOK, Nathaniel L., Co. E, Private (1838–1863). Lived, e. in Montgomery 8/1/1861, age 23. Hospitalized in Richmond 6/29/1862 with gunshot wound of head. Wounded in left arm and captured at Gettysburg 7/1–3/1863. Died in hospital there 9/1/1863 of wounds (NCT 8, 166).

COOK, William, Co. E, Private (1842–1862). Lived and e. in Montgomery 8/1/1861, age 19. Died at Wilmington 2/22/1862 (NCT 8, 166).

COOPER, Noah, Co. K, Sergeant (1831–1862). Lived in Cabarrus, e. in Stanly 9/7/1861, age 30. Promoted to sergeant 12/2/1861. Died in Staunton hospital 12/16/1862 of typhoid fever (NCT 8, 222).

COPELAND, Drury H., Co. A, Private (1828–1862). E. at age 35 on 5/4/1861; died at Wilmington abt 1/5/1862. Son of Freeman and Elizabeth Copeland, of Surry (NCT 8, 116; SCS 46).

COPELAND, James Madison, Co. A, Private (1838–1862). A medical student, the son of Jesse and Elizabeth Forkner Copeland of Copeland, Surry, James e. 5/4/1861. Died of disease 5/19/1862 at Kinston, NC (NCT 8, 116; SCS 46).

CORNELIUS, Alvius E., Co. F, Private (1841–). B. in Forsyth, he lived and e. in Yadkin 6/18/1861, age 20. Wounded in ankle and/or right knee at Cedar Mt. 8/9/1862. Absent-wounded through Dec. 1862. Dis. 8/22/1863 due to wounds (NCT 8, 177).

CORNELIUS, John H., Co. F, 3rd Lieutenant (1838–). Lived and e. in Yadkin at Camp Enon on 8/10/1861, age 23, as a private. Promoted to corporal 10/10/1861. Appointed 3rd lieutenant 4/12/1862. Wounded in the right thigh and captured at Hanover CH 5/27/1862. Hospitalized at New York City. Trans to Ft. Delaware 8/23/1862. Paroled and trans to Aiken's Landing 10/2/1862 for exchange 11/10/1862. Resigned 3/29/1863 due to wounds received at Hanover CH (NCT 8, 174).

CORNELIUS, L.M., Co. F, 1st Sergeant (1839–1862). Lived in Yadkin, e. in New Hanover, age 23, 3/13/1862, as private; promoted to 1st sergeant 4/12/1862. Died in Staunton hospital 11/25/1862 of typhoid fever (NCT 8, 177).

COSTNER, Hiram J., Co. B, 3rd Lieutenant (1839–864). Lived and e. in Gaston, age 22, on 7/30/1861 as a private. Captured at Hanover CH 5/27/1862; confined at Ft. Monroe, then Ft. Columbus. Paroled. Trans to Aiken's Landing for exchange 8/5/1862. Promoted to 1st lieutenant 12/18/1862. Wounded at Jericho Mills 5/23/1864; died of wounds 5/25/1864 (NCT 8, 125).

COSTNER, John H., Co. B, Private (1840–). Lived and e. in Gaston 7/30/1861, age 21. Wounded in left leg and captured at Spotsylvania CH 5/12/1864. Hospitalized in Washington, DC, then trans to prison at Elmira on 8/28/1864. Paroled from Elmira on 10/11/1864 and trans to Venus Pt. for exchange 11/15/1864 (NCT 8, 129).

COSTNER, Jonas L, Co. B, Private (1843–). Lived and e. in Gaston 7/30/1861, age 18. Captured at Hanover CH on 5/27/1862; confined at Ft. Monroe, then Ft. Columbus. Paroled and trans to Aiken's Landing for exchange 8/5/1862. Captured in Richmond hospital on 4/3/1865, and confined at Newport News 4/24/1865. Released 6/27/1865 after OOA (NCT 8, 129).

COX, F., Field & Staff, Assistant Surgeon. Appointed assistant surgeon on 9/21/1861, but served only a "short time" (NCT 8, 111).

COX, John M., Co. H, Private. E. at Camp Vance 10/16/1863. Captured near Gravel Hill abt 7/28/1864; confined at Pt. Lookout; trans to Elmira 8/12/1864.

Died there abt 9/5/1864 of chronic diarrhea (NCT 8, 199).

CRABTREE, Dallas, Co. G, Private (1847–). Lived and e. in Orange Feb. 1863, age 16. Captured at Spotsylvania CH 5/12/1864; confined at Pt. Lookout. Paroled and trans to Boulware's Wharf on 3/19/1865 for exchange (NCT 8, 187).

CRABTREE, John, Co. G, Private (1844–). Lived and e. in Orange 3/5/1862. Deserted Aug.–Sept. 1862 (NCT 8, 187).

CRABTREE, Norwood, Co. G, Private (1821–). Lived and e. in Orange 9/2/1861, age 40. Dis. 2/7/1863 due to "dropsy." May have later served in Captain Mark Durham's Company, 3rd Battalion, Senior Reserves (NCT 8, 187).

CRABTREE, Simpson, Co. G, Private (1825–). Lived and e. in Orange 9/2/1861, age 36. Captured at Hanover CH abt 5/27/1862; confined at Ft. Monroe, then Ft. Columbus. Paroled and trans to Aiken's Landing for exchange 8/5/1862. Dis. Feb. 1863 after providing a substitute (NCT 8, 187).

CRABTREE, William E., Co. G, Private (1838–1863). B. in Granville, lived and e. in Orange 9/2;/1861, age 23. Captured at Captured at Hanover CH abt 5/27/1862; confined at Ft. Monroe, then Ft. Columbus. Paroled and trans to Aiken's Landing for exchange 8/5/1862. Killed at Gettysburg 7/3/1863 (NCT 8, 187).

CRAIGE, James F., Co. G, Private (1836–). Lived and e. in Orange 9/2/1861, age 25. Captured at Hanover CH 5/27/1862; confined at Ft. Monroe, then Ft. Columbus. Paroled and trans to Aiken's Landing for exchange 8/5/1862. Captured at Spotsylvania CH 5/12/1864; confined at Pt. Lookout; trans to Elmira 8/8/1864. Released there 7/3/1865 after OOA (NCT 8, 187).

CRANFORD, Joshua A., Co. E, 1st Sergeant (1834–). Lived and e. in Montgomery 8/1/1861, age 27, as private. Promoted to 1st sergeant 11/1862–July 1864. Captured near Pickett's Farm abt 7/21/1864; confined at Pt. Lookout 7/28/1864. Paroled and trans to Venus Pt. 11/15/1864 for exchange. Surrendered at Appomattox CH, 4/9/1865 (NCT 8, 166).

CRAWFORD, Addison, Co. G, Private (1843–1864). Lived and e. in Orange 9/2/1861, age 18. Captured at Fredericksburg 12/13/1862; exc 12/17/1862. Killed at Wilderness 5/5/1864 (NCT 8, 188).

CRAWFORD, Henry C., Co. G, Corporal (1843–). Lived and e. in Orange 12/20/1861, age 18, as a private. Captured at Hanover CH abt 5/28/1862; confined at Ft. Monroe, then Ft. Columbus. Exc. Captured at Fredericksburg 12/13/1862; exc 12/17/1862. Wounded in left side at Chancellorsville 5/2–3/1863. Promoted to corporal 9/1/1863. Captured at Wilderness 5/12/1864; confined at Pt. Lookout. Trans to Elmira 8/8/1864, and released there 6/30/1865, after OOA (NCT 8, 188).

CRAWFORD, Robert Alvis, Co. G, Private. Lived and e. in Orange 2/13/1864. Wounded in left shoulder at Jones' Farm 9/30/1864. Retired 2/22/1865 due to disability from wounds (NCT 8, 188).

CRAWFORD, Samuel N., Co. G, Private (1833–).

Lived and e. in Orange 9/2/1861. Wounded at Gettysburg 7/1–3/1863. Present through Feb. 1865. Surrendered at Appomattox CH 4/9/1865 (NCT 8, 188).

CRAYTON, John A., Co. D, Corporal (1833–1863). Lived and e. in Stanly 7/29/1861, age 28. Mustered in as corporal; rank reduced Jan.–Apr. 1862. Killed at Chancellorsville 5/3/1863. "A medal was presented to his friends for his bravery" (NCT 8, 155).

CRAYTON, Uriah, Co. D, Corporal (1839–). Lived and e. 7/29/1861 in Stanly at age 22, as a private. Promoted to corporal 8/15/1863. Surrendered at Appomattox CH 4/9/1865. NC pension records indicate he was wounded in an unspecified battle (NCT 8, 155).

CRAYTON, William, Co. D, Private (1828–1862). Lived and e. in Stanly 7/29/1861. Died in Richmond hospital 6/24/1862 of disease (NCT 8, 155).

CRENSHAW, J.B., Co. B, Private (1843–1863). Lived and e. in Gaston. 7/30/1861, age 18. Wounded in right thigh and captured at Gettysburg 7/1–2/1863. Died in Gettysburg hospital on 7/4/1864 (NCT 8, 129).

CRESON, Samuel D., Co. F, Corporal (1838–). Yadkin resident, e. at Camp Fisher, age 23, 9/18/1861 as a private. Promoted to corporal Jan.–June 1862. Wounded at Gettysburg 7/1–3/1863. Deserted to enemy 9/10/1863. Took OOA at Knoxville, TN 10/5/1864 (NCT 8, 177).

CROWELL, David D., Co. D, Private (1837–1862). Stanly resident, e. 7/29/1861, age 24. Killed at Gaines' Mill 6/27/1862, "a good soldier" (NCT 8, 155).

CROWELL, Doctor F., Co. D, Private (1840–1862). Stanly resident, e. 7/29/1861, age 21. Died in hospital at Brook Church, VA, 7/26/1862 of disease (NCT 8, 155).

CROWELL, James, Co. D, Private (1827–). B. in Stanly, he was a farmer before he e. 7/29/1861. Dis. 5/1/1862, because the company had "more than the maximum number [of men] allowed by law" (NCT 8, 155).

CROWELL, James, Co. K, Private (1827–). Lived in Cabarrus, e. in Stanly 3/2/1863, age 36. Captured at Spotsylvania CH 5/12/1864; confined at Pt. Lookout. Trans to Elmira 8/8/1864. Released 5/29/1865 after OOA (NCT 8, 222).

CROWELL, James M., Co. K, Captain (1831–1864). Lived and e. in Stanly 9/7/1861, age 31, and appointed 1st lieutenant. Wounded at 2nd Manassas 8/28–30/1862. Promoted to captain 7/8/1863. Killed near Petersburg 6/24/1864 (NCT 8, 220).

CROWELL, John M., Co. D, Private (1843–) Stanly resident, e. 3/15/1862, at age 19. Captured at Hanover CH 5/27/1862; confined at Ft. Monroe, then Ft. Columbus. Trans to Aiken's Landing 7/12/1862, for exchange 8/5/1862. Captured at Petersburg 4/2/1865. Confined at Pt. Lookout until released 6/24/1865, upon taking the OOA (NCT 8, 155).

CROWELL, John T., Co. D, Private (1837–1863). Lived in Stanly, e. 3/15/1862, age 25. Captured at Hanover CH 5/27/1862; confined at Ft. Monroe, then Ft. Columbus. Trans to Aiken's Landing 7/12/1862, for exchange 8/5/1862. Died in Richmond hospital 5/28/1863 or 6/2/1863 of disease (NCT 8, 155).

CROWELL, William Franklin, Co. K, Private

(1827–). B. in Stanly, lived in Cabarrus, e. in Stanly 3/2/1863, age 36. Wounded in right leg, captured at Gettysburg 7/1–5/1863. Hospitalized at Davids Island. Trans to City Pt. 9/16/1863 for exc. Retired from service 2/11/1865, disabled from wound. Paroled at Salisbury 5/16/1865 (NCT 8, 222).

CROSELL, William H., Co. D, Private (1839–) Stanly resident, e. 7/29/1861, age 22. Hospitalized in Richmond 4/2/1865 with unspecified wound, and captured there 4/3/1865. Trans to Newport News 4/23/1865; released 6/30/1865 after OOA (NCT 8, 155).

CRUSE, William A., Co. D, Private (1843–). Stanly resident and farmer, e. 7/29/1861, age 18. Captured near Petersburg 4/2/1865; confined at Pt. Lookout until released 6/24/1865 after OOA. (NCT 8, 155–156).

CRUSOR, V.O., Co. B, Private? Died in Richmond hospital 7/6/1864 (NCT 8, 129).

CUNNINGHAM, Nicholas F., Co. A, Private (1827–bef/ 1867). Son of William Cunningham, Nicholas farmed in the Dobson District of Surry, before he e., age 33, on 5/4/1861. Present until February 1863. May have died in service. He m. Christina Crissman in 1854 in Surry, and had 2 children. She m. James Emory Burrus in 1867, Surry (NCT 8, 116; SCS 51).

CUNNINGHAM, Shadrach M., Co. A, Private (1838–) Lived and e. in Surry, age 23, on 5/4/1861. Captured near Wilderness abt 5/12/1864, and confined at Pt. Lookout, MY. Trans to Elmira 8/8/1864; paroled on 3/2/1865 and exc. Hospitalized at Richmond, 3/6/1865, and was given a 30-day furlough 3–8–1865 (NCT 8, 116; SCS 51).

CUNNINGHAM, William F., Co. A, Private. (1840–) B. to Richard and Elizabeth Franklin Cunningham in Surry, William e. 5/4/1861 at Dobson, Surry. Wounded in the right shoulder at Chancellorsville 5/1–3/1863. AWOL 5/1/1864, but was back by 10/11/1864. Captured on 4/2/1865 near Petersburg; confined at Ft. Delaware. Took the OOA on 6/19/1865 and released (NCT 8, 116; SCS 51).

CUZZENS, Bloom S., Co. F, Private (1836–). Lived and e. in Yadkin 6/11/1861, age 25. Deserted abt 6/30/1862 (NCT 8, 177).

CUZZENS, Lemuel, Co. F, Private (1839–1862). Lived and e. in Yadkin. 6/18/1861, age 22. Died in Richmond hospital 6/18/1862 of typhoid fever (NCT 8, 177).

DAILY, John H., Co. H, Sergeant (1831–). Lived and e. in Cleveland 8/22/1861, age 30, as sergeant. Rank reduced May–Oct. 1862. Captured at Spotsylvania CH 5/12/1864; confined at Pt. Lookout, then trans to Elmira 8/8/1864. Paroled and trans to Boulware's Wharf 2/20–21/1865 for exchange (NCT 8, 199).

DANIEL, Lucien, Co. G, Private (1841–1864). B., lived and e. in Orange. 9/2/1861, age 20. Killed at Wilderness 5/6/1864 (NCT 8, 188).

DANNER, G.M., Co. F, Private. E. in Yadkin where he lived 4/24/1862. Killed at Gaines' Mill 6/27/1862 (NCT 8, 177).

DANNER, Joshua G., Co. I, Private (1843–1863). Lived and e. in Yadkin. 3/8/1862. Wounded at Gettysburg 7/3/1863; died 7/4/1863 (NCT 8, 210).

DAVIS, Albert Cartwright, Co. B, Private; Co K, (1833–). Lived and e. in Gaston 3/29/1862, age 29. Captured at Hanover CH on 5/;27/1862; confined at Ft. Monroe, then Ft. Columbus. Paroled and trans to Aiken's Landing for exchange on 8/5/1862. Wounded at Fussell's Mill abt 8/18/1864. Absent-sick through Feb. 1865 (NCT 8, 129).

DAVIS, Daniel, Co. F, Private (1835–1862). Lived and e. in Yadkin. 6/18/1861. Killed at Hanover CH 5/27/1862 (NCT 8, 177).

DAVIS, David D., Co. D, Private, Co. K, Private (1843–). Lived in Stanly or Cabarrus as a farmer before he e. 7/29/1861 in Stanly, age 18. Trans to Co. K, 28th Reg in Feb 1862. Wounded in left leg and captured at Gettysburg 7/3/1863. Leg amputated. Confined at various Federal hospitals. Paroled at Pt. Lookout and trans to City Pt. 3/20/1864 for exchange. Absent-wounded through Feb. 1865 (NCT 8, 155–156, 222).

DAVIS, Drury Kersey, Co. A, Private (1830–1861) Surry resident, e. at age 31 on 5/4/1861. Died in Wilmington of disease on 12/29/1861; body was returned to Dobson for burial in the family cemetery at Hope Valley just north of Dobson. Drury, the son of Jonathan Davis and Patience Kersey, m. in 1854, Surry, Jane Snow, and had 3 children by 1860 (NCT 8, 116; SCS 52).

DAVIS, George W., Co. D, Private; Co. K, Private (1841–). Lived in Stanly or Cabarrus, e. 7/29/1861, age 20. Trans to Co. K, 28th Reg in Feb. 1862. Captured at Spotsylvania CH 5/12/1864; confined at Pt. Lookout. Trans to Elmira 8/15/1864, then to Pt. Lookout 10/11/1864. Paroled and sent to Venus Pt. 11/15/1864 for exchange. Surrendered at Appomattox CH 4/9/1865 (NCT 8, 156, 222).

DAVIS, Henry, Co. D, Private (1844–1862). Stanly resident, e. 3/15/1862, age 18. Died in Lynchburg hospital abt 6/9/1862 of typhoid fever (NCT 8, 156).

DAVIS, James, Co. B, Private (1817–). B. in Rutherford, lived and e. in Gaston 3/29/1862, age 45. Wounded at Gaines' Mill 6/27/1862. Dis. 9/29/1862 due to "cicatrices" of left army, thigh, and part of leg, the "effects of scrofula causing lameness." He later served in Co. E, 5th Regiment, NC Senior Reserves (NCT 8, 129).

DAVIS, James W., Co. D, Private (1843–). Lived and e. in Stanly. 3/15/1862, age 19. Hospitalized in Richmond 7/2/1862 with gunshot wound of left thigh. Wounded in right leg and captured at Gettysburg 7/1–4/1863. Hospitalized there then trans to Davids Island. Trans to City Pt. on 9/8/1863 for exchange. Captured at Petersburg 4/3/1865; confined at Hart's Island until released 6/19/1865 after OOA (NCT 8, 156).

DAVIS, Jesse, Co. F, Private. Lived and e. in Yadkin 11/5/1863. Captured in a Richmond hospital 4/3/1865; trans to Newport News 4/23/1865. Released 6/2/1865 after OOA (NCT 8, 177).

DAVIS, O.W., Co. B, Private (1831–). A Gaston carpenter, e. at Camp Fisher 9/18/1861, age 30. Dis. 7/20/1863 because "consolidation of whole of right lung and perfect aphonia, with general debility... (NCT 8, 129).

DAVIS, Robert, Co. E, Private (1821–). B. and e. in Montgomery 8/1/1861, age 40. Dis. 12/23/1861 due to "inguinal hernia" (NCT 8, 166).

DAVIS, Samuel B., Co. G, Private (1828–). Lived and e. in Orange 1/1/1863, age 35. AWOL Aug.–Oct. 1864. Returned. Captured near Petersburg 4/2/1865; confined at Pt. Lookout. Released 6/12/1865 after OOA (NCT 8, 188).

DAVIS, Samuel L., Co. I, Private (1837–1897). B., lived in Mecklenburg, e. in Yadkin 9/3/1861, age 23. Dis. 2/3/1862 due to "chronic rheumatism of the lower extremities." Bur. Center Meth. Ch., Yadkin County, NC (NCT 8, 210; CWY 208).

DAVIS, Thomas W., Co. F, Private (1826–). B. in Surry (Yadkin) where he was as a farmer. E. 6/18/1861. Dis. 11/17/1861 due to "ulcer upon the sole of the foot which has been in a state of ulceration for the last five month and interferes with the use of his foot" (NCT 8, 177).

DAVIS, William A., Co. I, Private. Yadkin resident (?), e. at Camp Holmes 8/20/1862. Not listed on rolls until Sept.–Oct. 1864. Present through Feb. 1865 (NCT 8, 210).

DAVIS, William J., Co. A, Private (1831–1864). B. in Rockingham, lived and e. in Surry, age 20, 5/4/1861. Killed in skirmish at Deep Bottom 7/27/1864 (NCT 8, 116–117).

DEAL, Junius, Co. C, Private (1744–1862). Catawba resident, e. 8/13/1861, age 17. Wounded at 2nd Manassas 8/28–30/1862; died at Middleburg, VA 8/31/1862 from wounds (NCT 8, 143).

DEAL, Levi, Co. C, Private. Catawba resident, e. 3/9/1863. Wounded at Chancellorsville 5/3/1863. Died in a Richmond hospital 6/10/1863 of typhoid fever and/or double pneumonia (NCT 8, 143).

DeBERRY, Benjamin, Co. E, Private (1842–1862). Lived and e. in Montgomery 8/1/1861, age 19. Died at Wilmington Jan. 1862 (NCT 8, 166).

DeBERRY, David D., Co. E, Private (1844–) E. at Liberty Mills 2/22/1864, age 20. Captured near Spotsylvania CH abt 5/10/1864; confined at Pt. Lookout until trans to Elmira 7/8/1864. Paroled on 10/11/1864 and trans to Venus Pt. 11/15/1864 for exchange (NCT 8, 166–167).

DeBERRY, John, Co. E, Private (1841–1862). Lived and e. in Montgomery 8/1/1861, age 20. Died in a Richmond hospital 7/30/1862 of disease (NCT 8, 167).

DeBERRY, John M., Co. D, Corporal (1844–1862). Lived and e. in Stanly 7/29/1861, age 17, as private. Promoted to musician after 10/31/1861, to corporal 12/5/1861. Died in hospital at Huguenot Springs, VA or at Lynchburg 9/1–3/1862 of typhoid fever (NCT 8, 156).

DICKENSON, Isaac D., Co. I, Private (1838–). Lived and e. in Yadkin 8/13/1861, age 23. Captured at Hanover CH 5/2/1862; confined at Ft. Monroe, then Ft. Columbus. Paroled and trans to Aiken's Landing for exchange 8/5/1862. Wounded at Chancellorsville 5/2–3/1863. Detailed to Richmond as a shoemaker Feb. 1864; absent on detail through Feb. 1865 (NCT 8, 210).

DICKERSON, David A., Co. I, Private (1839–1865). Lived and e. in Yadkin 3/8/1862, age 23. Captured on unspecified date. Paroled and trans to Aiken's Landing for exchange on 9/21/1862. Hospitalized at Richmond 1/10/1865 with diarrhea; died 1/24/1865 (NCT 8, 210).

DICKSON (Dixon), Henry, Co. I, Private. E. at Petersburg 9/22/1864. AWOL 12/15/1864 (NCT 8, 210).

DICKSON, J.R., Co. B, Private (1843–). Gaston resident, e. 7/30/1861, age 18. Captured at Fredericksburg 12/13/1862; paroled abt 12/17/1862. Deserted Aug. 1863 (NCT 8, 129).

DICKSON, W.H., Co. E, Private. Surrendered at Appomattox CH 4/9/1865 (NCT 8, 167).

DIXON, William S., Co. F, Private (1844–). Yadkin resident, e. in Alamance 10/1/1862, age 18. Wounded at Gettysburg 7/1–3/1863. Present through Feb. 1865 (NCT 8, 177).

DOBBINS, Daniel, Co. H, Private (1822–) Lived in Cleveland where he e. 8/22/1861, age 39. Dis. 11/2 or 11/21/1862 (NCT 8, 199).

DOBBINS, Dilliard P., Co. H, Private (1841–). Lived and e. in Cleveland 8/22/1861 there, age 39. Wounded near Shepherdstown 9/20/1862. Captured in Richmond hospital 4/3/1865; trans to Newport News 4/23/1865. Released there 6/30/1865 after OOA (NCT 8, 199).

DOBBINS, James, Co. I, Private (1842–1863). Lived and e. in Yadkin 9/20/1862, age 20. Died in Richmond hospital 5/27/1863 of "fever" (NCT 8, 210).

DOBBINS, Levi, Co. I, Private (1842–). B., lived and e. in Yadkin 3/8/1862, age 20. Captured near Winchester abt 12/2–3/1862. Paroled 12/4/1862. Dis. 5/1/1863 due to gunshot wounds of left arm and right hip. He was son of Joel and Sarah Dobbins (NCT 8, 210; CWY 210).

DOBBINS, Milas, Co. I, Private (1842–). Lived and e. in Yadkin 8/13/1861, age 19. Captured at Hanover CH 5/27/1862; confined at Ft. Monroe, then Ft. Columbus. Paroled and trans to Aiken's Landing for exchange 8/5/1862. Deserted Oct. 1862 (NCT 8, 210).

DOBBINS, William, Co. I, Private (1843–). Lived and e. in Yadkin 3/8/1862, age 19. Captured near Pickett's Farm abt 7/21/1864; confined at Pt. Lookout. Paroled and trans to Boulware's Wharf on 3/16/1865 for exchange (NCT 8, 210).

DOBSON, Leander H., Co. A, 3rd Lieutenant (1817–). Surry resident, e. 5/4/1861, age 44 as 3rd lieutenant, remained with Co. until defeated for reelection. Son of Atty. William Polk Dobson and Mary Hughes Dobson of Rockford, Leander was Deputy Clerk of Court for Surry before the war (NCT 8, 113; SCS 56).

DOLEHITE, John C., Co. G, Private (1840–1863). Lived and e. in Orange 9/2/1861, age 21. Captured at Fredericksburg 12/1/3862; exc abt 12/17/1862. Killed at Chancellorsville 5/3/1863 (NCT 8, 188).

DONATHAN, John, Co. F, Private (1845–). Lived in Yadkin or Surry, e. in Yadkin 4/1/1862, age 17. Wounded in left hand at Wilderness 5/5/1864. Hospitalized in Richmond 10/2/1864 with gunshot wound to left side. Captured in hospital 4/3/1865; confined at Newport News 4/24/1865. Released 6/16/1865 after OOA (NCT 8, 177).

DONATHAN, Lewis, Co. F, Private (1843–1862). B., lived and e. in Yadkin 6/18/1861, age 18. Wounded at Cedar Mt. 8/9/1862; died in Staunton hospital 9/3/1862 of wounds (NCT 8, 177).

DONATHAN, William, Co. F, Private (1811–1862). Lived and e. in Yadkin 6/18/1861, age 50. Wounded in the knee and feet at Ox Hill 9/1/1862. Hospitalized at Charlottesville where he died 9/26/1862 of "erysipelas" (NCT 8, 177).

DOUGLAS, Anderson, Co. F, Private (1848–1919). Lived and e. in Yadkin 10/27/1863. Wounded in right arm at Reams' Station 8/25/1864; arm amputated. Absent-wounded through Feb. 1865. B. Yadkinville, NC Town Cem. (NCT 8, 177; CWY 211).

DOZIER, Nathan C., Co. I, Private (1843–). Lived in Yadkin, the son of Dr. Nathan Bright Dozier and Olive Vestal Dozier, e. in New Hanover, 10/1/1861, age 18. Captured, but paroled and trans to Aiken's Landing for exchange 9/21/1862. Wounded at Gettysburg 7/1–3/1863. Wounded in right foot at Jericho Mills 5/23/1864. Absent-wounded through Oct.1864. Retired to Invalid Corps 2/18/1865 due to disability. (NCT 8, 210, CWY 211).

DOZIER, Smith W., Co. I, Corporal (1842–). B., lived and e. in Yadkin 8/13/1861, age 19, as private. Captured at Hanover CH 5/27/1862; confined at Ft. Monroe, then Ft. Columbus. Paroled and trans to Aiken's Landing for exchange 8/5/1862. Promoted to corporal 8/29/1862. Trans to C. S. Navy 4/3/1864 (NCT 8, 210).

DRAKE, Jefferson, Co. K, Private (1814–). Lived in Cabarrus, b. and e. in Stanly, 9/7/1861, age 47. Dis. 3/6/1862 due to "old age and a shortened leg from an old fracture of the thigh bone" (NCT 8, 222).

DRAPER, Jesse, Co. I, Private (1838–1862). Lived and e. in Yadkin 8/13/1861, age 23. Died in Richmond hospital 7/4/1862 of "typhoid fever" (NCT 8, 210).

DRAUGHN, C., Co. A, Private. Surrender at Appomattox CH 4/9/1865 (NCT 8, 117; SCS 57).

DRAUGHN, Isaac, Co. A, Private (1831–aft 1893). Surry farmer, e., age 20, 5/4/1861. Present through Feb. 1865. The Mt. Airy *The Yadkin Valley News* reported 10/5/1893 that Isaac Draughn was living in Monticello, KY (NCT 8, 117; SCS 57).

DRAUGHN, John, Co. A, Private (1847–1864) B. in Surry to Ashley and Lucinda Whitaker Draughn, of Siloam, he e. age 17. Died at Wilderness 5/5/1864 (NCT 8, 117; SCS 57).

DRAUGHN, William Henry, Co. A, Private (1838–1914). B. in Surry to John and Hannah Marion Draughn of the Dobson area, William was a blacksmith before he e. at age 24 on 3/18/1862. Present until "arrested" 2/16/1865. Family tradition holds that during the war, if William was close by, he would come home to see if the family was all right and if they had food. He m. in 1858 Emma Zetta McHone. In 1870 the couple were living at Eldora. After 1880, they lived the Patrick County, VA, and had 8 children. Draughn is bur. in the Red Bank Primitive Baptist Ch. cem. Claudeville, VA (NCT 8, 117; SCS 57, and Esther D. Johnson).

DRUM, David J., Co. C, Private. B., lived and e. in

Catawba 8/13/1861. Wounded in the finger at 2nd Manassas, abt 8/27/1862. Wounded at Gettysburg 7/1–3/1863. Wounded in right leg at Reams' Station 8/25/1864. Leg amputated; retired from the service 2/3/1865 (NCT 8, 143).

DRUM, Joseph M., Co. C, Private (18__–1862). Catawba resident, e. 3/15/1862. Wounded at Gaines' Mill 6/27/1862. Killed 8/29/1862 at 2nd Manassas, "a most gallant soldier" (NCT 8, 143).

DULL, Alford N., Co. I, Private (1838–1862). Lived and e. in Yadkin 3/8/1862, age 24. Killed near Gaines' Mill abt 6/27/1862 (NCT 8, 210).

DUNN, James T., Co. E, Private. Previously served in Co. E, 1st Reg NC Junior Reserves. Trans to Co. E 1/20/1865. Deserted 2/22/1865 (NCT 8, 167).

DUNN, William A., Co. E, Private (1842–1862). A resident of Montgomery, e. 3/10/1862, age 20. Died in Gordonsville hospital 5/9/1862 of "pneumonia" (NCT 8, 167).

DUNN, William J., Co. E, Sergeant (1837–1862). Montgomery resident, e. 8/1/1861, age 24, as a private. Promoted to sergeant 9/20/1862. Died in "the valley of Virginia" 11/1/1862 (NCT 8, 167).

DUNN, William J., Jr., Co. E, Private. E. in Montgomery 3/1/1862. No further record (NCT 8, 167).

DUNNIGAN, A. C., Co. A, 1st Lieutenant. E. in Surry, and was appointed 1st lieutenant on May 4, 1861. Resigned on 7/6/1861 (NCT 8, 113).

DURHAM, Asher S., Co. G, Private (1840–). Lived and e. in Orange 5/14/1862. Wounded at Chancellorsville 5/1–3/1863 (NCT 8, 188).

DURHAM, Bryant, Co. G, Private (1840–). Lived and e. in Orange 5/5/1862 as a substitute. Captured at Fredericksburg 12/1/3862; exc abt 12/17/1862. Wounded at Chancellorsville 5/2/1863. Present through Feb. 1865 (NCT 8, 188).

DURHAM, Franklin R., Co. G, Corporal. E. in Orange 10/31/1864 as a private; promoted to corporal 1/1/1865. Surrendered at Appomattox CH 4/9/1865 (NCT 8, 188).

DURHAM, James G., Co. G, Private (1842–). Lived and e. in Orange 9/2/1861, age 19. Captured at Spotsylvania CH 5/12/1864; confined at Pt. Lookout. Paroled and trans to Cox's Wharf 2/14–15/1865 for exchange (NCT 8, 188).

DURHAM, James S., Co. G, 1st Sergeant (1842–). Lived and e. in Orange 9/2/1861, age 19, as a private. Captured at Fredericksburg 12/13/1862; exc abt 12/17/1862. Promoted to corporal March 1863; to 1st sergeant 9/1/1863. Hospitalized at Richmond 5/8/1864 with gunshot wound of right knee. Returned and, surrendered at Appomattox CH 4/9/1865 (NCT 8, 188).

DURHAM, John S., Co. G, Private. Lived and e. in Orange 3/14/1862. Wounded at Chancellorsville 5/2–3/1863. Captured at Spotsylvania CH 5/12/1864; confined at Elmira until released 6/23/1865 after OOA (NCT, 188).

DURHAM, Joseph H., Co. G, Private (1833–). Lived and e. in Orange 9/2/1861, age 28, as corporal. Rank reduced abt 4/9/1862. Captured at Hanover CH 5/27/1862; confined at Ft. Monroe. Trans to Aiken's Landing 7/12/1862 for exchange on 8/5/1862. Wounded in

left thigh and right arm and captured at Gettysburg 7/1–4/1863. Hospitalized at Davids Island. Trans to Ft. Monroe 1/5/1864. Hospitalized at Pt. Lookout 1/10/1864. Paroled and trans to City Pt. 8/30/1864 for exchange. Retired to Invalid Corps 11/17/1864 due to disability (NCT 8, 188).

DURHAM, Robert A, Co. G, Corporal (1842–). Lived and e. in Orange 12/20/1861, age 19, as a private. Captured at Hanover CH 5/27/1862; confined at Ft. Monroe, then Ft. Columbus. Paroled and trans to Aiken's Landing for exchange 8/5/1862. Promoted to corporal 8/6/1863. Captured at Spotsylvania CH 5/12/1864; confined at Pt. Lookout, trans to Elmira. Released there 6/19/1865 after OOA (NCT 8, 188–189).

DURHAM, Sidney C., Co. G, Private. Lived and e. in Orange 3/24/1864. Captured at Hatcher's Run 4/2/1865; confined at Pt. Lookout until released 6/26/1865 after OOA (NCT 8, 189).

DURHAM, Thomas Maleus, Co. G, Private (1839–). Lived and e. in Orange 9/2/1861, age 22. Captured at Hanover CH abt 5/27/1862; confined at Ft. Monroe, then Ft. Columbus. Trans to Aiken's Landing for exchange on 8/5/1862. Captured at Spotsylvania CH 5/12/1864; confined at Pt. Lookout, trans to Elmira 8/8/1864. Released 6/27/1865 after OOA (NCT 8, 189).

DURHAM, William J., Co. G, Private (1839–1864). B., lived, e. in Orange 3/5/1862, age 23. Wounded at Fussell's Mill 8/16/1864. Hospitalized in Richmond where he died abt 9/6/1864 of wounds (NCT 8, 189).

DURHAM, William P., Co. G, Private (1839–) Lived and e. in Orange 9/2/1861, age 22. Captured at Spotsylvania CH 5/12/1864; confined at Pt. Lookout. Paroled and trans to Varina 9/22/1864 for exchange. Surrendered at Appomattox CH 4/9/1865 (NCT 8, 189).

EARNHARDT, George R., Co. K, Private (1844–1862). Lived, e. in Stanly 9/7/1861, age 17. Died in Goldsboro hospital 3/24/1862 of typhoid fever (NCT 8, 222).

EASLEY, James M., Co. D, Sergeant (1842–1863). Lived and e. in Stanly 7/29/1861. Mustered in as private, promoted to sergeant 8/1/1862. Killed at Gettysburg 7/3/1863 (NCT 8, 156).

ECKARD, Cyrus, Co. C, Private (1838–1862). Catawba resident, e. 8/13/1861. Captured at Hanover CH on 5/27/1862; confined at Ft. Monroe, then Ft. Columbus. Died at Ft. Columbus 6/22/1862 of typhoid fever (NCT 8, 143).

ECKARD, Rufus, Co. C, Sergeant (1835–1862). Lived and e. in Catawba 8/13/1861 as a corporal. Promoted to sergeant 2/27/1862. Captured at Hanover CH 5/27/1862; confined at Ft. Monroe, then Ft. Columbus. Exc.. Killed at Fredericksburg 12/13/1862 (NCT 8, 143).

EDR[I]DGTER, C.A., Co. I, Private. Captured in Richmond hospital 4/3/1865, remained until 5/28/1865. No further information (NCT 8, 177).

EDWARDS, Adolphus D., Co. C, Private (1843–). Lincoln resident, e. at Camp Fisher on 5/27/1862, at age 18. Captured at Hanover CH 5/27/1862; confined at Ft. Monroe, then Ft. Columbus. Paroled and trans to Aiken's Landing for exchange 8/5/1862. Wounded in left leg at Jericho Mills 5/23/1864; leg amputated. Absent-wounded through Feb. 1865 (NCT 8, 143).

EDWARDS, Daniel, Co. A, Private (1826–1863?). Lived at Westfield, Surry, e. at age 36 on 3/18/1862. Captured at Hanover CH on 5/27/1862; confined at Ft. Monroe then at Ft. Columbus. Paroled and trans to Aiken's Landing, James River, on 7/12/1862, and exc 8/5/1862. Absent-sick most of the time through Feb. 1863., and died on an unspecified date. He m. Lockey Bullen in 1844 and they had two daus. (NCT 8, 116; SCS 61).

EDWARDS, Edwin S., Co. G, 1st Lieutenant (1838–1864). Lived and e. in Orange 9/2/1861, age 23 as a sergeant. Captured near Hanover CH abt 5/27/1862; confined at Ft. Monroe, then Ft. Columbus. Paroled and trans to Aiken's Landing for exchange 8/5/1862. Appointed 2nd lieutenant 1/13/1863; to 1st lieutenant 7/19/1863. Killed at Spotsylvania CH 5/21/1864 (NCT 8, 185).

EDWARDS, Henry A., Co. G, Sergeant (1844–). Lived and e. in Orange 6/1/1862, age 18, as a private. Wounded in the left shoulder at Malvern Hill 7/1/1862. Promoted to sergeant Nov. 1862–June 1864. Surrendered at Appomattox CH 4/9/1865 (NCT 8, 189).

EDWARDS, Samuel A., Co. G, Private (1840–1864). B. and lived in Orange where he e. 3/5/1862, age 22, as a substitute. Captured at Spotsylvania CH 5/12/1864; confined at Pt. Lookout, trans to Elmira 8/10/1864; died 9/25/1865 of "chronic diarrhoea" (NCT 8, 189).

EDWARDS, Thomas H., Co. B, Captain. E. in Gaston; appointed captain to rank from 7/30/1862. Present until defeated for reelection at the reorganization 2/27/1862 (NCT 8, 125).

EDWARDS, William D.F., Co. G, Sergeant (1841–1864). Lived and e. in Orange 9/2/1861, age 20, as a private. Promoted to corporal 3/1/1862. Captured at Hanover CH abt 5/27/1862; confined at Ft. Monroe, then Ft. Columbus. Trans to Aiken's Landing for exchange on 8/5/1862. Captured at Fredericksburg 12/13/1862; exc abt 12/17/1862. Promoted to sergeant March 1863. Wounded and captured at Gettysburg; hospitalized at Chester. Paroled and trans to City Pt. 8/20/1863 for exchange. Killed near Petersburg abt 6/23/1864 (NCT 8, 189).

EFORD, Daniel R.A., Co. K, Private. Lived and e. in Stanly 11/29/1864. Captured at Amelia CH abt 4/5/1865; confined at Pt. Lookout. Released 6/12/1865 after OOA (NCT 8, 222).

ELLER, Henry P., Co. I, Private (1843–). B., lived and e. in Yadkin 8/13/1861, age 18. Captured at Hanover CH abt 5/27/1862; confined at Ft. Monroe, then Ft. Columbus. Trans to Aiken's Landing for exchange on 8/5/1862. Captured near Gettysburg 7/3/1863; confined at Ft. Delaware. Trans to Pt. Lookout 10/15–18/1862; released 1/25/1864 after OOA and joining the U.S. Army, Co. G, 1st Reg U.S. Volunteer Infantry (NCT 8, 210–211).

ELLIOTT, William A., Co. K, Private (1829–). Lived and e. in Stanly 9/7/1861, age 32. Present through Feb. 1865 (NCT 8, 222).

ELLIS, Henderson, Co. A, Private (1821–) The son of James and Lucretia Ellis , Ellis farmed near Rockford when he was conscripted into the army 11/1/1864. Captured on 4/2/1865 near Petersburg; confined at Ft. Delaware, and released after OOA on 6/19/1865. He m. first Mary Venable, had 3 children; 2nd Alcy Gentry (NCT 8, 116; SCS 61–62).

ELLISON, James M., Co. H, Private. Lived and e. in Cleveland 8/22/1861. Wounded in right arm near Frayser's Farm 6/30/1862; disabled, dis. 2/12/1864 (NCT 8, 199).

EPPS, Caswell G., Co. D, Private (1829–). Lived and e. in Stanly 3/15/1862, age 33. Captured near Petersburg 7/29/1864; confined at Pt. Lookout; trans to Elmira 8/8/1864. Released from Elmira 7/3/1865 after OOA (NCT 8, 156).

EUDY, David W., Co. K, Private (1839–). B., lived, e. in Stanly 9/7/1861, age 22. Wounded, captured at Gettysburg 7/3/1863. Hospitalized at Gettysburg. Trans to City Pt. On 8/20/1863 for exc. Dis. 1/18/1864, disabled from wound (NCT 8, 223).

EUDY, Henry H., Co. D, Private. Previously served in Co. G, 1st Reg NC Junior Reserves. Trans to Co. D. 10/15/1964. Captured near Petersburg 4/2/1865; confined at Pt. Lookout until released 6/12/1865 after OOA (NCT 8, 156).

EUDY, Jacob, Co. K, Private. E. in Stanly 10/31/1864. Surrendered at Appomattox CH 4/9/1865 (NCT 8, 222).

EUDY, Jacob W., Co. K, Private (1825–). Lived in Cabarrus, e. in Stanly 3/13/1862, age 27. Company records indicate he trans to Co. H, 8th Reg NCT 11/9/1864. Records of Co. H do not agree (NCT 8, 222).

EUDY, John C., Co. K, Private (1842–). Lived and e. in Stanly 9/7/1861, age 18. Captured near Petersburg 4/2/1865; confined at Pt. Lookout. Released 6/12/1865 after OOA (NCT 8, 222–223).

EUDY, Moses J., Co. D, Captain (1836–). Stanly resident, e. on 7/29/1861, age 25, as a corporal. Promoted to sergeant in Feb. 1863. Appointed 2nd lieutenant 8/1/163, then to captain 9/27/1863. Hospitalized at Charlottesville 5/12/1864 with gunshot wound in left foot. Captured near Petersburg 4/2/1865; confined at Old Capitol Prison. Trans to Johnson's Island, OH 4/9/1865. Released there 6/18/1865 after OOA (NCT 8, 153).

EUDY, William, Co. K, Private (1838–1862). B., lived, e. in Stanly 9/7/1861, age 23. Captured at Hanover CH 5/27/1862; confined at Ft. Monroe, then Ft. Columbus. Trans to Aiken's Landing for exchange 8/5/1862. Died in Petersburg hospital abt 8/16/1862 from diarrhea (NCT 8, 223).

EUDY, William R., Co. K, Private (1837–1862). Lived and e. in Stanly 3/14/1862, age 25. Died in Richmond hospital 7/13/1862 from typhoid fever (NCT 8, 223).

EVANS, Iredell C., Co. I, Private (1843–). Lived and e. in Yadkin 8/13/1861, age 18. Present through Feb. 1865 (NCT 8, 211).

EVANS, J.C., Co. I, Private. Lived in Catawba, e. 8/13/1861 per pension record (or July 1863, company records). Captured near Petersburg 7/30/1864; confined at Pt. Lookout; trans to Elmira 8/8/1864. Released 5/9/1865 after OOA (NCT 8, 211).

EVERAGE, Joseph, Co. I, Private (1834–). Lived and e. in Yadkin 8/13/1861, age 27. Captured at Hanover CH 5/27/1862; confined at Ft. Monroe, then Ft. Columbus. Trans to Aiken's Landing for exchange 8/5/1862. Wounded at Chancellorsville 5/2–3/1973. Deserted 7/15/19863. Hospitalized at Richmond 5/18/1864 with gunshot wound of right leg. Present through Feb. 1865. Hospitalized at Richmond 3/10/1865 with gunshot wound of right leg. Captured in hospital 4/3/1865; trans to Newport News 4/23/1865; released 6/30/1865 after OOA (NCT 8, 211).

EWING, James William, Co. E, 1st Lieutenant (1834–). Montgomery resident, appointed 1st lieutenant 8/1/1861. Defeated for re-election 2/28/1862. Elected 2nd lieutenant 9/5/1862. Promoted to 1st lieutenant 10/18/1862. Wounded in left leg at Fredericksburg 12/13/1862. Resigned 8/27/1863 due to atrophy of left leg, "a gallant officer" (NCT 8, 164).

FALLS, John James, Co. B, Corporal (1839–1863). Lived in Cleveland, e. at Camp Fisher on 9/18/1861, age 22, as private. Captured at Hanover CH 5/27/1861; confined at Ft. Monroe, then Ft. Columbus. Paroled and sent to Aiken's Landing, for exchange on 8/5/1862. Promoted to corporal Nov.–Dec. 1862. Captured at Fredericksburg 12/13/1862; paroled 12/17/1862. Wounded at Chancellorsville abt 5/3/1863. Died of wounds. (NCT 8, 129).

FARMER, John A., Co. K, Private (1840–1862). Lived and e. in Stanly 9/7/1861, age 21. Killed at Fredericksburg 12/13/1862 (NCT 8, 223).

FARMER, Leon R., Co. K, Private (1845–). Lived and e. in Stanly 9/7/1861, age 16. Captured at Hanover CH 5/27/1862; confined at Ft. Monroe, then Ft. Columbus. Trans to Aiken's Landing for exc 8/5/1862. Returned. Absent-sick 5/1/1864–Feb. 1865 (NCT 8, 223).

FARR, Ephriam, Co. D, Private (1840–). Lived and e. in Stanly 7/29/1861, age 21. Dis. 9/21/1861, reason not reported (NCT 8, 156).

FARRAR, Nathaniel P., Co. B, Private (1827–) Lived and e. in Gaston 7/30/1861, at age 34. Captured near Petersburg 4/2/1865; confined at Pt. Lookout until released 6/26/1865 after OOA (NCT 8, 129).

FARRINGTON, Nathan H., Co. I, Private (1840–). Son of William S. and Keturah Haynes Farrington, he lived and e. in Yadkin 3/8/1862, age 22. Dis. 7/18/1862 due to "scrotal hernia of the left side." Moved to Denton County, TX(NCT 8, 211, CWY 213, HYC 361).

FARRIS, Enoch H., Co. I, Private (1843–1864). B., lived and e. in Yadkin 8/13/1861, age 18. Captured at Hanover CH 5/27/1862; confined at Ft. Wood. Paroled and trans to Aiken's Landing for exchange 11/10/1862. Hospitalized in Danville 1/1/1863 with gunshot wound. Killed near Wilderness 5/5/1864 (NCT 8, 211).

FARRIS, Joseph, Co. I, Private (1842–). Lived and e. in Yadkin 8/13/1861. Wounded at Sharpsburg 9/17/1862. Died of wounds (NCT 8, 211).

FARRIS, Preston T., Co. I, Private (1845–). Lived in Yadkin, e. 9/8/1863 at Liberty Mills, age 18. Captured at Spotsylvania CH 5/12/1864; confined at Point Look-

out. Trans to Elmira 8/10/1864, released 7/11/1865 after OOA (NCT 8, 211).

FARRIS, William D., Co. I, Sergeant (1829–1862). Lived and e. in Yadkin 8/13/1861, age 33, as corporal. Promoted to sergeant after 12/31/1861. Killed at Gaines' Mill abt 6/27/1862 (NCT 8, 211).

FAUCETTE, R.C.P., Co. G, Private (1831–1863). Lived and e. in Orange 3/5/1862, age 21. Died near Lynchburg abt 1/18–22/1863 of disease (NCT 8, 189).

FESPERMAN, John E., Co. K, Private (1826–). Lived and e. in Stanly 9/7/1861, age 35. Wounded in left thigh at Cold Harbor 5/31/1864. Retired to Invalid Corps 12/24/1864 due to injury (NCT 8, 223).

FINK, Moses, Co. D, Private (1831–1862). Lived and e. in Stanly 7/29/1861, age 30. Wounded at Malvern Hill, 7/1/1862; died at Richmond 7/1/1862 from wounds (NCT 8, 156).

FISHER, Charles T., Co. D, Private (1845–) Lived and e. in Stanly e. 3/15/1862, age 17. Hospitalized at Richmond 3/28/1865 for gunshot to leg. Captured in the hospital there on 4/3/1865. Released abt 6/21/1865 after OOA (NCT 8, 156).

FISHER, George, Co. C, Private. Lived and e. in Catawba 3/15/1862. Present through April 1862 (NCT 8, 143).

FITE, J.C., Co. B, Private (1845–1863). Gaston resident, e. on 2/18/1863, age 18. Died in Richmond hospital 6/22/1863 of "febris typhoid' (NCT 8, 129).

FLEMING, James Henderson, Co. B, Private? NC pension records indicate he served in this company (NCT 8, 129).

FLEMING, John W, Co. F, Private ? NC pension records indicate he served in this company (NCT, 177).

FLETCHER, John F., Co. F, Corporal (1843–). B. in Yadkin, a shoemaker before he e. 6/18/1861, age 18, as corporal; dis. 3/12/1862 due to "inguinal hernia of left side" (NCT 8, 177).

FLINN, Jesse F., Co. F, Private (1840–). Lived in Yadkin, e. there at Camp Enon 6/18/1861. Deserted 4/4/1863 (NCT 8, 178).

FLINN, William C., Co. F, Private (1840–) Lived and e. in Yadkin 4/27/1862, age 22. Dis. 7/21/1862 due to "chronic cough accompanied with great debility" (NCT 8, 178).

FLOWERS, Noah T., Co. C, Sergeant (18__–1862). Lived and e. in Catawba 8/13/1861 as a corporal. Promoted to sergeant 2/27/1862. Hospitalized at Richmond 6/11/1862 with "paralysis [and] typhoid fever." Died in hospital in Richmond abt 6/25/1862 (NCT 8, 143).

FLOYD, John A., Co. B, Private (1841–). Lived in Gaston, e. 7/30/1861, age 20. Captured at Hanover CH 5/27/1862, and confined at Ft. Monroe, then Ft. Columbus. Paroled and exc at Aiken's Landing 8/5/1862. Wounded in the fight foot and captured at Gettysburg 7/1–3/1863. Hospitalized at Gettysburg then Baltimore, Confined at Pt. Lookout, 4/25/1864. Paroled abt 11/1/1864 and sent to Venus Pt. for exchange on 11/15/1864. No further information (NCT 8, 130).

FOLGER, Romulus S., Co. F, Private; Co. I, 2nd Lieutenant; Field & Staff, Adjutant (1st Lieutenant)

(1841–). Surry resident, e., age 20, 5/4/1861 in Co. F. Promoted to 1st Sgt. before 9/3/1861; elected 1st Lt. 9/3/1861. Resigned 4/9/1862. Appointed Adjutant (2nd Lt.) 1/7/1863 of Co. I and trans to Field & Staff. Promoted to Adjutant (1st Lt.); remained with Reg until the surrender at Appomattox 4/9/1865 (NCT 8, , 110–111, 113).

FORD, John N., Co. B, Private (1821–). Gaston resident, e. there 7/30/1861. Captured near Petersburg 4/2/1865, confined at Pt. Lookout, released 6/26/1865 after OOA (NCT 8, 130).

FORD, Lauson H., Co. B, Private (1838–). Lived in Gaston, e. at Camp Fisher 9/18/1861, age 23. Captured at Hanover CH 5/27/1862, confined at Ft. Monroe; trans to Aiken's Landing for exc 8/5/1862. Surrendered at Appomattox CH 4/9/1865 (NCT 8, 130).

FORREST, Samuel P., Co. K, Corporal (1841–1863). Lived and e. in Stanly 9/7/1861, age 20. Promoted to corporal Jan.–Apr.. 1862. Wounded in right arm, captured at Gettysburg 7/1–2/1863. Hospitalized at Gettysburg where he died abt 9/17/1863 of wound (NCT 8, 223).

FORREST, Thomas Y., Co. K, Private (1840–1861). Lived and e. in Stanly 9/7/1861, age 21. Died in Wilmington hospital 12/23/1864 of "fever" (NCT 8, 223).

FORTNER, Alexander, Co. F, Private (1840–1863). Lived and e. In Yadkin 6/18/1861. Hospitalized at Charlottesville 9/12/1862 with gunshot wound. Killed at Gettysburg 7/3/1863 (NCT 8, 178).

FOSTER, Tilmon M., Co. B, Sergeant (1841–). Lived in Gaston, e. on 7/30/1861, age 20, as a private. Promoted to corporal on 2/27/1862. Wounded in the arm at Cedar Mt. on 8/9/1862. Wounded again at Chancellorsville 5/1–3/1863. Wounded and captured at Gettysburg July 1863. Confined at Davids Island 7/17–24/1863. Paroled and sent to City Pt. for exc 9/16/1863. Promoted to sergeant Sept. 1863–Oct. 1864. Surrendered at Appomattox CH 4/9/1865 (NCT 8, 130).

FOULKS, John M., Co. D, Private (1843–1862). Lived in Stanly where he e. 7/29/1861, age 18. Killed at Cedar Mt. 8/9/1862, "a good soldier" (NCT 8, 156).

FOWLER, John, Co. A, Private (1834–1862). This a Surry resident, e. at age 18 on 3/18/1862. Died in a Kinston, NC hospital on 5/6/1862 of disease (NCT 8, 116).

FOY, Jesse S., Co. B, Private (1829–). B., lived, e. in Gaston, age 32, on 7/30/1861. Captured at Hanover CH 5/27/1862; confined at Ft. Monroe, then Ft. Columbus. Paroled and sent to Aiken's Landing for exc 8/5/1862. Captured near Petersburg 4/2/1865. Confined at Pt. Lookout until released 6/26/1865 after OOA (NCT 8, 130).

FRADY, Andrew J., Co. C, Private. Lived and e. in Catawba 8/13/1861. Surrendered at Appomattox CH 4/9/1865 (NCT 8, 143).

FRASER, John H., Co. E, Sergeant (1842–). Lived and e. in Montgomery 8/1/1861, age 19 as a private. Promoted to sergeant Nov. 1862–May 1864. Reported missing in action at Spotsylvania CH 5/12/1864 (NCT 8, 167).

FRASER, William T., Co. E, Private. E. in Wake 2/10/1864. Wounded at Gravel Hill 7/28/1864. Present through Feb. 1865 (NCT 8, 167).

FRASIER, Leander, Co. I, Private (1839–1862). Lived and e. in Yadkin 8/13/1861, age 22. Died in Richmond hospital abt 12/20/1862 of "pneumonia typhoides" (NCT 8, 211).

FRAYLEY, Alex A., Co. D, Private. E. 2/1/1865 in Stanly. Present through Feb. 1865 (NCT 8, 156).

FREEMAN, Jesse, Co. I, Private (1839–). Lived and e. in Yadkin 8/13/1861, age 22, Deserted 9/21/1861 (NCT 8, 211).

FREEMAN, John W., Co. F, Private (1844–1862). Lived and e. in Yadkin 6/18/1861, age 17. Died in Richmond hospital 9/5/1862 of typhoid fever (NCT 8, 178).

FREEMAN, Mark H., Co. A, Private (1832–). Surry resident, e. 5/4/1861, age 29. Wounded in right side in Virginia on 6/28/1864. Surrendered at Appomattox CH, 4/9/1865. Son of Elisha and Mary Kellehan (Callahan) Freeman of Bundy's District (NCT 8, 116; SCS 65).

FREEMAN, Richard C., Co. G, Private (1839–). Lived in Franklin, e. 9/12/1861, in Orange, age 22. Dis. 9/3/1862 due to back injury and "stricture of the urethra" (NCT 8, 189).

FRICK, C.J., Co. D, Private (1844–1862). Lived in Stanly, e. 3/15/1862, age 18. Killed at Frayser's Farm 6/30/1862 (NCT 8, 156).

FRIDAY, Andrew S., Co. B, Private (1841–). Lived and e. in Gaston 7/30/1861, age 20. Captured at Hanover CH on 5/27/1862, and confined at Ft. Monroe, then Ft. Columbus. Exc 8/5/1862. Captured at Fredericksburg 12/13/1862. Paroled abt 12/17/1862. Wounded in thigh near Petersburg abt 6/21/1864. Deserted to the enemy abt 1/20/1865. Confined at City Pt. until released abt 1/23/1865 after OOA (NCT 8, 130).

FRIDAY, J.H., Co. B, Private. (1843–1862). Lived and e. in Gaston, age 19, on 3/29/1862. Died at Richmond on 6/17/1862 of an unknown disease (NCT 8, 130).

FRONENBARGER, D.A., Co. B, Private (1843–1862). B. and lived in Gaston, where he e. on 7/30/1861, age 18. Captured at Hanover CH on 5/27/1862, and confined at Ft. Monroe, then Ft. Columbus until paroled and sent to Aiken's Landing for exchange on 8/5/1862. Killed at Fredericksburg 12/13/1862 by a "gunshot through the head" (NCT 8, 130).

FRY, David A., Co. K, Private. E. at Liberty Mills 3/15/1864. Wounded at Spotsylvania CH 5/12/1864. Surrendered at Appomattox CH 4/9/1865 (NCT 223).

FRY, Ephraim N., Co. C, Private (1824–). B., lived and e. in Catawba at age 37 on 8/13/1861. Wounded in forehead at Gettysburg 7/1–3/1863. Retired on 2/8/1865 due to "ulceration of the tibia causing extension & incurable ulcers of the legs" (NCT 8, 143).

FRY, Jacob A., Co. C, Private. Catawba resident, e. at Camp Fisher 9/2/1862. Captured at Gettysburg 7/1–3/1863; confined at Ft. Delaware, trans to Pt. Lookout, MY 10/15–18/1863. Paroled 2/18/1863 and trans to Boulware's Wharf on 2/20–21/1865 for exchange. NC pension records indicate he was wounded Sept. 1862 (NCT 8, 143).

FULBRIGHT, John, Co. C, Private. Lived and e. in Catawba 3/14/1863. Died in a Richmond hospital

1/3/1864 of "febris typhoides" or "orchitis" (NCT 8, 143).

FULKS, James, Co. D, Private. E. at Camp Stokes 10/31/1864. Captured near Petersburg 4/2/1865; confined at Pt. Lookout until released 6/26/1865 after OOA (NCT 8 156).

FURR, Aaron, Co. K, Private. E. at Liberty Mills 2/10/1864. Captured near Petersburg 4/2/1865; confined at Pt. Lookout until released 6/26/1865 after OOA (NCT 8, 223).

FURR, Allen M., Co. D, Private (1845–1862). Lived and e. in Stanly 7/29/1861, age 16. Killed at Fredericksburg 12/13/1862 (NCT 8, 156).

FURR, Crittenton, Co. K, Sergeant (1840–). Lived and e. in Stanly 9/7/1861, age 21. Wounded near Richmond 6/25–7/1/1862. Promoted to sergeant Jan.–July 1863. Captured at Spotsylvania CH 5/12/1864; confined at Pt. Lookout, trans to Elmira 8/10/1864. Released there 5/29/1865 after OOA (NCT 8, 223).

FURR, Farrenton, Co. K, Private (1835–). B. in Cabarrus, lived and e. in Stanly 9/7/1861, age 26. Wounded in side and right arm at Cedar Mt. 9/9/1862. Dis. 4/18/1863 due to wounds (NCT 8, 223).

FURR, James Chesley, Co. K, Private. Lived in Cabarrus, e. in Stanly 10/31/1864. Captured near Petersburg 4/2/1865; confined at Pt. Lookout, and released 6/26/1865 after OOA (NCT 8, 223).

FURR, Lauson Alex, Co. K, Private (1834–1864). Lived and e. in Stanly 3/17/1862, age 28. Captured at Hanover CH 5/27/1862; confined at Ft. Monroe, then Ft. Columbus. Trans to Aiken's Landing for exc 8/5/1862. Wounded at Chancellorsville 5/2–3/1863. Captured at Spotsylvania CH 5/12/1864; confined at Pt. Lookout. Trans to Elmira 8/10/1864, and died there 12/6/1864 of pneumonia (NCT 8, 223).

FURR, Rufus, Co. K, Private (1837–1862). Lived and e. in Stanly 9/7/1861. Died at Richmond 7/16/1862 of typhoid fever (NCT 8, 223).

FURR, Wilson M., Co. D, Private (1834–). Lived and e. in Stanly 3/15/1862, age 28. Wounded in head and captured at Wilderness 5/6/1864. Hospitalized in Washington, DC, then confined at Old Capitol Prison 9/7/1864. Trans to Ft. Delaware, 9/19/1864; released 6/19/1865 after OOA (NCT 8, 156).

GABRIEL A. Alonzo, Co. C, Sergeant (1844–). Lived and e. in Catawba 3/15/1862 at age 18. Captured at Hanover CH 5/27/1862; confined at Ft. Monroe and Ft. Columbus. Paroled and trans to Aiken's Landing for exchange 8/5/1862. Promoted to sergeant 1/1/1863. Trans to Co K, 23rd NC Reg 3/21/1863 (NCT 8, 143–144).

GADD, Jesse, Co. E, Private (1805–1862). Lived and e. in Montgomery 8/1/1861, age 56. Died at Wilmington 1/10/1862 or 1/21/1862 (NCT 8, 167).

GADD, William, Co. E, Private (1826–). Lived and e. in Montgomery 8/1/1861, age 35. Wounded at Gettysburg 7/1–3/1863. Hospitalized at Petersburg 6/25/1864 with gunshot wound. Deserted to the enemy abt 2/10/1865. Confined at Washington, DC. Released abt 2/16/1865 after OOA (NCT 8, 167).

GAITHER, William Wiley, Field & Staff, Surgeon. Previously surgeon of the 26th Reg. trans to this Reg

and appointed surgeon to the 28th on 11/4/1864, to rank from 9/2/1864. Present through Feb. 1865 (NCT 8, 111).

GAMBLE, Franklin W., Co. B, Private (1844–1862). Lived and e. in Gaston 3/29/1862, at age 18. Captured at Hanover CH 5/27/1862, and confined at Ft. Monroe, then Ft. Columbus. Paroled and sent to Aiken's Landing for exchange 8/5/1862. Died in Richmond hospital on 9/2/1862 of "pneumonia typhoid"(NCT 8, 130).

GAMBLE, W.A., Co. B, Private (1840–1862). Gaston resident e. at age 22 on 3/29/1862. Killed at Hanover CH 5/27/1862 (NCT 8, 130).

GARDNER, William G., Co. E, Private (1842–1862). Montgomery resident, e. 8/1/1861. Died in a Richmond hospital 7/11/1862 of typhoid fever (NCT 8, 167).

GASTON, Ross Marcius, Co. B, Private (1846–) Lived and e. in Gaston 7/30/1861, age 15, as a musician, but was reduced in rank before 12/31/1864. Surrendered at Appomattox CH 4/9/1865 (NCT 8, 130).

GATES, Albert L., Co. A, Private (1834–). Lived and e. in Surry, age 27, 5/4/1861. Present at the surrender at Appomattox on 4/9/1865 (NCT 8, 117).

GATES, Martin C., Co. H, Private (1835–). Lived and e. in Surry, age 18 on 2/28/1863. Wounded at Chancellorsville 5/2–3/1863 (NCT 8, 117).

GATES, Solomon G., Co. A, Private (1845–1864) Surry farmer, e. 5/4/1861, age 18. Wounded and captured at Gettysburg 7/3–4/1863; confined at Ft. McHenry, then Ft. Delaware. Trans to Pt. Lookout abt 10/18/163; died there on 1/16/1864 (NCT 8, 117).

GEAN, William P., Co. G, Private (1836–). Lived and e. in Orange 9/2/1861, age 25. Present through Feb. 1865 (NCT 8, 189).

GENTRY, Francis Lee, Co. I, 28, Private; Co. G, 44th Private (1840–1917). E. at Camp Holmes 11/28/1862, age 25, in Co. G, 44th Reg NCT. Deserted 6/9/1863. NC pension records indicate he served in Co. I. The sun of William and Lucy Myers Gentry, he is bur. at Flat Rock Bapt. Ch., Yadkin County, NC (NCT 8, 111; NCT 10, 459; CWY 216).

GENTRY, Jonathan, Co. A, Private. Surry resident, e. on 5/19/1863 as substitute for Columbus C. Cockerham. Deserted before 11/1/1862. Returned. Captured near Petersburg on 4/2/1865 and confined at Hart's Island, until released on 6/19–20/1865 after OOA (NCT 8, 117).

GENTRY, Robert W., Co. I, Private (1835–). Lived and e. in Yadkin 8/13/1861. Present through Feb 1863. He may be the same person as William R. Gentry (NCT 8, 211).

GENTRY, Wiley B., Co. A, Private (1838–). B. and e. in Surry 5/4/1861, age 23. Dis. 4/23/1862 due to "intermittent and chronic rheumatism," that caused contraction of one leg. The son of Calvin and Polly Hodges Gentry, of the Dobson District, Surry, Wiley m. in Surry in 1870 Catherine Lyons. By 1880 they had 3 children (NCT 8, 117; SCS 70).

GENTRY, William R., Co. I, Private (1835–). Lived and e. in Yadkin 8/13/1861, age 26, as sergeant. Rank reduced Nov. 1861–Oct 1862. AWOL 9/27–1864–Feb. 1865 (NCT 8, 211).

GIBBON, Nicholas Biddle, Field & Staff, Captain. Lived in Mecklenburg, appointed Assistant Commissary of Subsistence on 10/18/1861. Resigned abt 9/17/1863 (NCT 8, 111). Gibbon's account of his time in service is at the University of North Carolina-Charlotte NCT 8, 111).

GIBBON, Robert, Field & Staff, Surgeon. Lived in Mecklenburg (he may be a brother of Nicholas Gibbon), Robert e. in New Hanover; appointed regimental surgeon abt 9/25/1861; appointed Senior Surgeon of Brig. Gen. James H. Lane's Brigade abt 1/29/1864 (NCT 8, 111).

GIBSON, James T., Co. E, Private (1835–). B. in Richmond County, e. in New Hanover 1/28/1862, age 27. Present through Feb. 1865 (NCT 8, 167).

GILBERT, Jacob H., Co. C, 1st Lieutenant. Lived and e. in Catawba; appointed 2nd lieutenant 8/13/1861. Promoted to 1st lieutenant 9/27/1861. Defeated for reelection 2/27/1862. Later served as 2nd lieutenant, Co. E, 57th NC Reg. (NCT 8, 139).

GILBERT, Stephen, Co. K, Private (1845–1862). Lived and e. in Stanly 9/7/1861. Died Jan. 1862. Place and cause of death not reported (NCT 8, 223).

GILBERT, William W., Co. H, 1st Lieutenant (1838). Lived, e. in Cleveland at age 23. Appointed 1st lieutenant 8/22/1861. Dismissed from service by general court martial in April 1862. Reason for court martial not reported (NCT 8, 196).

GILLASPIE, Jonathan R., Co. K, Private (1834–1862). Lived, e. in Rutherford 3/17/1862, age 28. Died at Charlottesville 5/14/1862 of pneumonia (NCT 8, 199).

GILLESPIE, James B., Co. H, Corporal (1840–). B., lived in Cleveland, e. in Rutherford 3/17/1862, age 22, as private. Promoted to corporal 11/5/1863. Hospitalized at Richmond 5/28/1864 with gunshot wound. Present or accounted for through Feb. 20, 1865 (NCT 8, 199).

GILLESPIE, John M., Co. H, Private (1841–). Lived, e. in Cleveland 3/17/1862, age 21. Wounded near Ox Hill 9/1/1862. Wounded in left wrist on 12/12/1864. Absent-wounded through Feb. 1865 (NCT 8, 199).

GILLESPIE, William D., Co. H, Private (1836–1862). Lived, e. in Cleveland 8/22/1861, age 25. Died at Richmond 7/17/1862 of typhoid fever (NCT 8, 199).

GLOSSCOE, Colvin W., Co. A, Private (1843–1862). B. in Virginia, lived, e. in Surry age 19 on 3/18/1862. Captured at Hanover CH abt 5/28/1862. Paroled and trans to Aiken's Landing where he arrived 6/26/1862 for exchange on 8/5/1862. Died in a Richmond hospital abt 10/1/1862 of "phthisis pulmonalis," the name for tuberculosis or consumption at that time (NCT 8, 117; SCS 72).

GOINS, Philip P., Co. C, Private (1844–). Lived, e. in Catawba 8/13/1861, age 17. Captured at Hanover CH on 5/27/1862; confined at Ft. Monroe, then Ft. Columbus. Trans to Aiken's Landing for exchange on 8/5/1862. Wounded at Charlottesville 5/1–2/1863. Wounded in right hand at Jones' Farm 9/30/1864. Captured near Petersburg 4/2/1865; confined at Ft. Delaware, until released 6/191865 after OOA. NC pension records indicate he was wounded at Fredericksburg and Wilderness (NCT 8, 144).

GOLD, Perry G., Co. H, Sergeant (1841–). Lived e. in Cleveland 8/22/1861, age 20, as a private. Promoted to sergeant May–June 1862; rank reduced 7/7/1862. Promoted to corporal Nov. 1862–Oct. 1864. Surrendered at Appomattox CH 4/9/1865 (NCT 8, 199).

GOLDEN, Thomas, Co. A, Private (1828–1862). E. at age 33 on 5/4/1861. Died in a Richmond hospital 8/9/1862 of chronic diarrhea. Thomas, a farmer, was the son of Richard and Charlotte Cave Golden of the Dobson District. He m. in Surry in 1848 Azina Butcher. They had 5 children by 1860 (NCT 8, 117; SCS 73).

GOODSON, James, Co. C, Private (1844–1862). Lived, e. in Catawba 8/13/1861, at age 17. Wounded in the shoulder at Frayser's Farm 6/30/1862. Died in a Richmond hospital 6/1/1864 of wounds (NCT 8, 144).

GOUGH, Martin Franklin, Co. F, Private (1844–) Lived, e. in Yadkin 6/18/1861. Wounded at Gettysburg 7/1–3/1863. Present through Feb. 1865 (NCT 8, 178).

GRABS, Lewis E., Co. F, Private. E. in Stokes 12/19/1864. Surrendered at Appomattox CH 4/9/1865 (NCT 8, 178).

GREEN, David O., Co. H, Private (1837–). Lived in Cleveland, e. in New Hanover 10.6/1861, age 24. Captured at Hanover CH 5/27/1862; confined at Ft. Monroe, then Ft. Columbus. Paroled and trans to Aiken's Landing for exchange 8/5/1862. Wounded at Chancellorsville 5/2–3/1863. Surrendered at Appomattox CH 4/9/1865 (NCT 8, 199).

GREEN, Edmond, Co. H, Private (1841–1863). Lived, e. in Cleveland 8/22/1861, age 20. Captured at Hanover CH 5/27/1862; confined at Ft. Monroe, then Ft. Columbus. Paroled and trans to Aiken's Landing for exchange 8/5/1862. Died at Camp Gregg 2/1/1863, cause unknown (NCT 8, 199).

GREEN, Ewell, Co. H, Private (1835–). B., lived, e. in Cleveland 8/22/1861, age 26. Dis. 12/26/1861 due to "typhoid fever and acute rheumatism" (NCT 8, 199).

GREEN, George M., Co. H, Private (1843–1863). Lived, e. in Cleveland 8/22/1861, age 18. Killed at Gettysburg 7/3/1863 (NCT 8, 200).

GREEN, James M., Sr., Co. H., Private (1840–). Lived, e. in Cleveland 8/22/1861, age 21. Surrendered at Appomattox CH 4/9/1865 (NCT 8, 200).

GREEN, James M., Co. H, Sergeant (1827–). Lived, e. in Cleveland 8/22/1861, age 34, as corporal. Promoted to sergeant before 11/1/1861. Rank reduced Jan.–Apr. 1862. Promoted to corporal May–Oct 1862; to sergeant Nov. 1862–June 1863. Surrendered at Appomattox CH 4/9/1865 (NCT 8, 200).

GREEN, James Moore, Jr., Co. H, Sergeant(1844–). Lived, e. in Cleveland 4/22/1861, age 18, as a private. Captured at Hanover CH 5/27/1862; confined at Ft. Monroe, then Ft. Columbus. Paroled and trans to Aiken's Landing for exchange 8/5/1862. Promoted to sergeant Nov. 1862–June 1863. Rank reduced June–Oct. 1864. Surrendered at Appomattox CH 4/9/1865 (NCT 8, 200).

GREEN, Joel, Co. E, Private (18_–1865). Green e. in Wake 11/5/1864. Captured near Petersburg 4/2/1865; confined at Pt. Lookout and died 5/31/1865 of consumption (NCT 8, 167.)

GREEN, John L., Co. H, Private (1844–). Lived, e. in Cleveland 8/22/1861, age 17. Wounded in leg at Gettysburg. Absent-wounded through Oct. 1864. Detailed for light duty at Richmond Feb. 1865. Surrendered at Appomattox CH 4/9/1865 (NCT 8, 200).

GREEN, Miles, Co. F, Private. Captured at Hanover CH abt 5/27/1862; confined at Ft. Monroe, then Ft. Columbus. Paroled and trans to Aiken's Landing for exchange 8/5/1862. Deserted but was apprehended abt 8/29/1862 (NCT 8, 178).

GREEN, Reuben H., Co. H, Private. E. at Camp Holmes 9/25/1864. Surrendered at Appomattox CH 4/9/1865 (NCT 8, 200).

GREEN, Robert E., Co. E, Private (1845–1862). Lived in Montgomery, e. 3/10/1862, age 17. Died in Charlottesville hospital abt 5/21/1862 of "typhoid pneumonia" (NCT 8, 167).

GREEN, Thomas Frank, Co. H, 3rd Lieutenant. Previously served in Co. E, 12th Reg NCT. Trans to Co. H, 28th as a private 4/2/1863. Elected 3rd lieutenant 12/20/1863. Surrendered at Appomattox CH 4/9/1865 (NCT 8, 196).

GREEN, Thomas S., Co. E, Captain (1841–). Lived, e. in Montgomery 8/1/1861, age 20, as a private. Promoted to sergeant 11/9/1861; appointed 3rd lieutenant 10/7/1862, 2nd lieutenant 10/18/1862. Wounded at Chancellorsville 5/2–3/1863. Promoted to captain 5/12/1864. Wounded in left thigh at Reams' Station 8/25/1864. Absent-wounded until 1/9/1865 Resigned due to disability from wound (NCT 8, 164).

GREEN, William, Jr., Co. H. Private (1842–). B. lived, e. in Cleveland 3/17/1862, age 20. Dis. 9/28/1862 due to "tubercular phthisis" (NCT 8, 200).

GREEN, William H., (1829–1862). Lived, e. in Cleveland 8/22/1861, age 32. Died at Wilmington abt 2/2/1862 (NCT 8, 200).

GREEN, William T., Co. E, Private (1841–). Lived, e. in Montgomery 8/1/1861, age 20. Captured at 2nd Manassas 8/28–30/1862. Paroled and trans to Aiken's Landing and exc 9/21/1862. Deserted in Feb. 1865. Surrendered at Appomattox CH 4/9/1865. NC pension records indicate he was wounded 9/10/1863 (NCT 8, 167).

GREENE, William E., Co. D, Private (1827–). Stanly resident, e. at Camp Gregg 4/7/1863, age 36. Captured in a Richmond hospital 4/3/1865; confined at Pt. Lookout until released 6/26/1865 after OOA (NCT 8, 156).

GRICE, Henry Lee, Co. C, Private (1845–1864). Lived, e. in Catawba 8/12/1863, age 18. Killed at Reams' Station 8/5/1864 (NCT 8, 144).

GRICE, James M., Co. C, Sergeant. Lived in Catawba, e. at Camp Fisher 9/2/1861 as a private. Captured at Hanover CH 5/27/1862; confined at Ft. Monroe, then Ft. Columbus. Paroled and trans to Aiken's Landing for exchange 8/5/1862. Wounded at Fredericksburg abt 12/13/1862. Wounded at Chancellorsville 5/1–3/1863. Promoted to sergeant May 1863–Oct. 1864. Wounded at Gettysburg 7/1–3/1863. Present through Feb. 1865 (NCT 8, 144).

GRICE, John Littleberry, Co. B, Private (1836–). Lived, e. in Gaston, age 25, on 7/30/1861. Captured at

Hanover CH on 5/27/1862. Confined at Ft. Monroe and then Ft. Columbus. Exc.. Wounded at Chancellorsville 5/2–3/1863. Wounded in the left hip at Spotsylvania CH 5/12/1864. Captured near Petersburg 4/2/1865; confined at Pt. Lookout, until released 6/27/1865 after OOA (NCT 8, 130).

GRIFFIN, James H., Co. A, Private (1830–) B. in Franklin, lived, e. in Surry, age 31, 5/13/1861. Dis. 1/7/1862 due to "chronic rheumatism" (NCT 8, 116; SCS 77).

GRIGG, William A., Co. A, Private (1838–1862). E. at age 23 on 5/13/1861. Captured at Hanover CH on 5/27/1862; confined at Ft. Monroe, then Ft. Columbus. Paroled and trans to Aiken's Landing for exc 8/5/1862. Died in Petersburg hospital 8/13/1862 of "typhoid febris" (NCT 8, 117).

GRINDSTAFF, Jacob, Co. K, Private? NC pension records indicate he served in this company (NCT 8, 223).

GROSS, William E., Co. I, Private (18__–1864). E. abt 2/14/1862. Died in Richmond hospital 6/29/1864 of "rubeola" (NCT 8, 211).

GROVES, Caleb C., Co. B, Private. Lived in Gaston, Caleb e. at Liberty Mills on 3/5/1864. Captured near Petersburg on 4/2/1865; confined at Pt. Lookout until released 6/27/1865 after OOA (NCT 8, 130–131).

GROVES, James L., Co. B, Private (1840–) B., lived, e. in Gaston 7/30/1861, at age 21, James was captured at Hanover CH on 5/27/1862. Confined at Ft. Monroe then Ft. Columbus, he was paroled and sent to Aiken's Landing and exc 8/5/1862. Deserted on 5/28/1864. Deserted on 528/1864. Captured near Petersburg on 4/2/1865. Confined at Pt. Lookout until released on 6/27/1865 after OOA (NCT 8, 131).

HAGER, Simon, Co. C, Private. Lincoln resident, e. at Camp Fisher 9/5/1861. Died at Brook Church, VA 7/8/1862 of typhoid fever (NCT 8, 144).

HAGLER, McA., Co. K, Private. E. at Liberty Mills 3/29/1864. Hospitalized at Charlotte 11/1/1864 with gunshot wound of right knee. Absent on furlough through Feb. 1865 (NCT 8, 224).

HAITHCOCK, E. W., Co. E, Private ? NC pension records indicate he served in this company (NCT 8, 167).

HALE, William D., Co. F, Private (1840–1865). Lived, e. in Yadkin 6/18/1861, age 21. Absent-wounded Nov.–Dec. 1862. Wounded again in the chest at Chancellorsville 5/2–3/1863. Captured near Pickett's Farm abt.7/21/1864; confined at Pt. Lookout. Trans to Venus Pt. for exchange 11/15/1864.(Captured at Savannah 12/21/1864. Died in Federal hospital at Savannah 1/25/1865 of "debility" (NCT 8, 178).

HALL, B.L., Co. E, Private. B. and lived in Montgomery, e. at Camp Gregg 2/1/1863. Killed at Wilderness 5/6/1864 (NCT 8, 167).

HALL, Daniel C., Co. I, Private (1843–1911). Lived and e. in Yadkin 3/8/1862, age 18. Wounded and captured at Gettysburg 7/1–5/1863. Hospitalized at Davids Island abt 7/17/1863. Paroled and trans to City Pt. 9/8/1863 for exchange. Bur. Boonville Bapt. Ch. Cem, Boonville, NC (NCT 8, 211; CWY 218).

HALL, Elisha, Co. E, Corporal (1835–). Lived, e. in

Montgomery resident 8/1/1861, age 26. Mustered in as corporal. Captured at Hanover CH 5/27/1862; confined at Ft. Monroe, then Ft. Columbus. Paroled and trans to Aiken's Landing for exchange 8/5/1862. Rank reduced Nov.–1862–Oct. 1864. Wounded at Chancellorsville 5/2–3/1863. Deserted 8/15/1863. Wounded abt 5/6/1864 at Wilderness. AWOL 11/11/1865 through Feb. 1865 (NCT 8, 167).

HALL, James Sanford, Co. F, Private (1840–). E. in Yadkin 4/27/1864, age 24. Captured near Deep Bottom Aug. 1864; confined at Pt. Lookout until paroled and trans to Venus Pt. 11/15/1864 for exchange. Absent-sick through Feb. 1865 (NCT 8, 178).

HALL, John W., Co. E, Private (1838–). Lived, e. in Montgomery 8/1/1861. Captured at Hanover CH 5/27/1862; confined at Ft. Monroe, the Ft. Columbus. Paroled and trans to Aiken's Landing for exchange 8/5/1862. AWOL Oct. 1864–Feb. 1865 (NCT 8, 167–168).

HALL, Lewis W., Co. F, Private; Co. I, Private (1840–1909). Served in Co. G, 18th Reg NCT. Lived in Yadkin where he e. in Co. F, 28th Reg 6/18/1861, age 21. Deserted abt _/1862. Trans to Co. I, 28th Reg abt 9/1/1864. Present through Feb. 1865. Bur. Friendship Bapt. Ch., Yadkin County, NC (NCT 8, 178, 211; CWY 218).

HALL, Richmond, Co. I, Private; Co. G, 44th, Private E. 9/20/1863 at Camp Holmes. Deserted, returned 9/9/1864. Trans to Co. G, 44th Reg NCT abt 10/1/1864 (NCT 8, 211–212).

HALL, Thomas, Co. F, Private. E. in Yadkin 9/28/1862. Deserted 5/4/1864 (NCT 8, 178).

HALL, Thomas G., Co. F, Private (1828–1899) Lived near Siloam, e. in Yadkin 4/27/1864. Captured near Fussell's Mill abt 8/16/1864; confined at Pt. Lookout. Paroled and trans to Boulware's Wharf on 3/18/1865 for exchange. He m. Biddie Nading Hauser, and had one son. House still standing and being restored. Bur. Friendship Bapt. Ch., Yadkin County, NC (NCT 8, 178, CWY 218).

HALTON, Reubin J., Co. E, Private. Reubin previously served in Co. E, 1st Reg NC Junior Reserves. Trans to Co. E, 28th Reg 1/20/1865. Surrendered at Appomattox CH 4/9/1865 (NCT 8, 168).

HAMILTON, J.T., Co. B, Private (1840–1862). Lived in Gaston, e. at Camp Fisher 8/12/1861, at age 21. Died at Wilmington on 3/14/1862 of typhoid fever (NCT 8, 131).

HAMRICK, A.V., Co. H, Private (1828–1861). Lived in Cleveland where he e. 8/22/1861, age 23. Died at Wilmington NC 11/8/1861, cause not reported (NCT 8, 200).

HAMRICK, Alfred W., Co. H, Private (1843–). Lived, e. in Cleveland 8/27/1861, age 18. Wounded at 2nd Manassas 8/28/1862. Captured near Petersburg 4/2/1865; confined at Ft. Delaware until released 6/19/1865 after OOA (NCT 8, 200).

HAMRICK, Andre J., Co. H, Private (1831–1863). Lived, e. in Cleveland 3/17/1862, age 21. Died at Liberty abt 3/17/1863 from "typhoid fever" (NCT 8, 200).

HAMRICK, Asa, Co. H., Corporal (1840–1864). Lived, e. in Cleveland 8/22/1861, age 21, as a private.

Promoted to corporal 4/7/1862. Captured at Hanover CH 5/27/1862; confined at Ft. Monroe, then Ft. Columbus. Paroled and trans to Aiken's Landing for exchange 8/5/1862 Wounded in left thigh and captured at Spotsylvania CH 5/12/1864. Leg amputated. Hospitalized and died at Washington, DC 6/13/1864 of "exhaustion" (NCT 8, 200).

HAMRICK, James Bryson, Co. H, Private. E. 3/1/1864 in Cleveland. Wounded and captured at Fussell's Mill abt 8/16/1864; confined at Pt. Lookout. Paroled and trans to City Pt. For exchange 11/15/1864. Absent-sick through Feb. 1865 (NCT 8, 200).

HAMRICK, James M. Co. H, Private (1833–). Lived, e. in Cleveland 8/22/1861, age 28. Trans to Co. E, 12th Reg NCT 4/4/1863 (NCT 8, 200).

HAMRICK, Jonathan, Co. H, Private (1822–). Born, lived, e. in Cleveland 3/17/1862, age 40. Present through Feb. 1865 (NCT 8, 200).

HAMRICK, M.N., Co. H, Private. NC pension records indicate he served in this company (NCT 8, 200).

HAMRICK, Oliver A., Co. H, Private (1842–). Lived, e. in Cleveland 8/22/1861, age 19. Left the company and enlisted in Co. D, 55th Reg NCT before 7/1/1863 (NCT 8, 200).

HAMRICK, Price, Co. H, Private (1839–). Lived, e. in Cleveland 3/17/1862, age 23. Wounded at Spotsylvania CH 5/12/1864. Absent-wounded through Feb. 1865. Paroled at Charlotte, NC 5/1/1865 (NCT 8, 200–201).

HAND, Samuel Jasper, Co. B, Private (1841–). Lived in Gaston, e. at Camp Fisher on 9/18/1861 at age 20. Hospitalized at Charlottesville on 9/23/1862 with a gunshot wound to right arm; arm amputated. Absent-wounded until July 5, 1864; retired to Invalid Corps (NCT 8, 131).

HANEY, John Allen, Co. E, Private (1837–). Lived in Union, e. in Wake 10/2/1862, age 25. Present until 8/5/1864, then listed as AWOL. NC pension records indicate he was wounded at Petersburg, 7/7/1864 (NCT 8 168).

HARDIN, Almon S., Co. H, Private (1845–). B., lived, e. in Cleveland 8/22/1861, age 16. Dis. 6/19/1862 due to "debility & anemia following a protracted attack of typhoid fever" (NCT 8, 201).

HARDIN, Clayton, Co. H, Private. Served in Co. E, 12th Reg NCT; trans 4/24/1863 to Co. H, 28th Reg. Company records do not support this (NCT 8, 201).

HARDIN, Elijah, Co. H, Private (1843–1862). Lived in Cleveland where he e. 8/22/1861, age 18. Died in Lynchburg hospital abt 8/22/1862 of "febris typhoides" and/or phthisis pulmonalis" (NCT 8, 201).

HARDIN, Jesse, Co. H., Private (1818–). Lived, e. in Cleveland 8/22/1861, age 43. Dis. 9/5/1863. May have served in Co. H, 4th Regiment, NC Senior Reserves (NCT 8, 201).

HARDIN, Orville, S., Co. H, Corporal (1842–1864). B., lived, e. in Cleveland 8/22/1861, age 19, as a private. Promoted to corporal 4/7/1862, rank reduced. Killed at Spotsylvania CH 5/12/1864 (NCT 8, 201).

HARDING, Greenberry ("G.B." or "Berry") Patterson, Co. I, Sergeant (1842–1931). Lived, e. in Yadkin 3/8/1862, age 18, as private. Wounded at Gaines' Mill abt 6/27/1862. Wounded at Fredericksburg 12/13/1862. Promoted to sergeant March 1863–Oct 1864. Wounded three times at Gettysburg 7/1–3/1863. Wounded at Gravel Hill 7/28/1864. Retired from service 12/28/1864 due to disability. Son of William and Jane Elizabeth Speer Harding, married Elizabeth Jane Steelman; brother to Samuel Speer Harding. Berry moved to Farmington, Davie County, NC. Bur. Farmington Meth. Ch. (NCT 8, 212, CWY 219; HYC 384).

HARDING, Samuel Speer, Co. I, Sergeant (1838–1864). Lived, e. in Yadkin 8/31/1861, age 23, as private. Promoted to sergeant 4/12/1862. Reenlisted 8/13/1862 for "2 years or the war." Killed at Reams' Station 8/25/1864. His father, William Harding, traveled to Petersburg and brought his body home for burial in the Speer-Harding Fam. Cem, near Yadkinville, NC (NCT 8, 212, CWY 219; HYC 384).

HARDY, Charles, Co. A, Private. Surry resident, e. 1/18/1864. Captured near Petersburg 4/2/1865; confined at Ft. Delaware until released 6/19/1865 after OOA. Afterwards, Charles farmed near Siloam, and was a tobacco trader. He m. in Stokes Eliza Jane Vernon and had 8 children (NCT 8, 117; SCS 80).

HARDY, John H., Jr., Co A, Private (1833–). A "tobacco rowler (roller?)," the son of John and Kate Hardy, John lived in Rockford, Surry, before he e. 5/4/1861 at age 18. Wounded at Chancellorsville 5/2–3/1863. Wounded in leg at Gettysburg 7/1/1863. Captured, sent to Davids Island hospital, then to Ft. Wood. Trans to Pt. Lookout, paroled on 5/3/1864, and sent to City Pt. for exchange 6/6/1864. Retired 2/4/1865, because wound caused in "extensive loss of bone" and "atrophy of the muscles" (NCT 8, 117–118; SCS 80).

HARE, James E., Co. A, Private (1833–). Surry farmer, e. at age 19 on 3/18/1862. Wounded abt 8/21/1862. Trans to Co. A, 2nd Reg. South Carolina Artillery. Roll of Honor indicates he was wounded near the Rappahannock River, in Virginia, 10/24/1862 (NCT 8, 118; SCS 80).

HARKEY, Martin A., Co. K, Private. (1838–). Lived and e. in Stanly 3/15/1862, age 24. Hospitalized at Richmond 5/27/1864 with gunshot wound of left thigh. Returned. Hospitalized again at Richmond 7/28/1864 with gunshot wounds of arm and right shoulder. Furloughed from hospital 3/31/1865. Widow's pension application stated that he died on an unspecified date of wounds received in June 1864 (NCT 8, 224).

HARKEY, Solomon, Co. K, Private (1828–1863). Lived and e. in Stanly 3/27/1862, age 34. Captured at Gettysburg 7/3/1863; confined at Ft. Delaware. Hospitalized at Chester with scurvy and died there 9/20/1863 (NCT 8, 224).

HARKEY, Wilson, Co. K, Private (1841–1863). Lived and e. in Stanly 9/7/1861, age 20. Hospitalized at Charlottesville 8/11/1862 with gunshot wound. Died at Hanover Junction 6/10/1863 of fever (NCT 8, 224).

HARPER, James N., Co. E, Private (1835–). Lived, e. in Montgomery 8/1/1861, age 26. Captured at Spotsylvania CH 5/12/1862; confined at Pt. Lookout, then Elmira on 8/10/1864. Released from Elmira 6/19/1865 after OOA (NCT 8, 168).

HARPER, Thomas A., Co. I, Private ? Records of United Daughters of the Confederacy indicate he was killed at Reams' Station 8/25/1864. No further information (NCT 8, 212).

HARRELL, John H., Co. H, Private (1818–). B. in Rutherford, lived and e. in Cleveland 3/17/1862, age 44. Trans to Co. B, 34th Reg NCT 11/18/1864 (NCT 8, 201).

HARRIS, Alfred L., Co. A, Private. Surry farmer, e. 5/4/1861, age 3. Dis. 7/7/1862 due to disability from pneumonia (NCT 8, 118; SCS 80–81).

HARRIS, Eli, Co. E, Private (1839–). B., lived, e. in Montgomery 8/1/1861, age 32. Wounded in left thigh at Gaines' Mill 6/27/1862. Dis. 2/12/1863 due to disability. Paroled at Troy, NC 5/23/1865 (NCT 8, 168).

HARRIS, Eli T., Co. E, Private (1844–1862). Lived, e. in Montgomery 3/10/1862, age 18. Died in Charlottesville hospital 6/9/1862 of "pneumonia" (NCT 8, 168).

HARRIS, John, Co. A, Private (1832–1863). B. in Pitt, lived and e. in Surry 3/18/1862, age 39. Captured at Hanover CH 5/27/1862 and confined first at Ft. Monroe, then Ft. Columbus. Died in a Richmond hospital on 1/27/1863. (NCT 8, 118; SCS 81).

HARRIS, Lemuel B., Co. A, Private. Lived, e. in Surry 5/4/1861, age 21. Deserted 8/1/1862. Son of Joel and Sarah Norman Harris, of Union Hill, Lemuel m. in Surry in 1865 Annie Melissa Callaway, and had 6 children (NCT 8, 118; SCS 81).

HARRIS, Thomas A, Co. D, 1st Sergeant (1832–). Lived, e. in Stanly 7/29/1861, age 29, as corporal. Promoted to sergeant Jan.–April 1862; to 1st sergeant Jan. 1863–Oct. 1864. Present through 3/17/1865 (NCT 8, 156).

HARRIS, Wiley O., Co. B, Private (1831–). Lived, e. in Gaston, age 30, 8/6/1861. Captured near Hanover CH abt 5/28–31/1862; confined at Ft. Delaware. Exc at Aiken's Landing 8/5/1862. Hospitalized at Richmond 5/25/1864 with gunshot wound of right leg. Captured in Richmond hospital 4/3/1865; confined at Newport News 4/23/1864; released on 6/30/1865 after OOA (NCT 8, 131).

HARVIL, John W., Co. D, Private (1821–). B. in Moore, lived, e. in Stanly 7/29/1861, at age 40. Dis. 3/5/1862 due to hearing loss that made it "impossible for him to hear the commands" (NCT 8, 156).

HARVILL, John, Co. I, Private (1827–1864). B., lived, e. in Yadkin. 3/8/1862, age 35. Deserted 4/5/1863. Returned. Wounded in thigh near Petersburg abt 8/22/1864. Died of wounds (NCT 8, 212).

HARWELL, Watson A., Co. C, Private (18__–1863) Lived, e. in Catawba 3/14/1863. Mortally wounded, he was left to die on the field at Gettysburg 7/3/1863 (NCT 8, 144).

HARWOOD, Howell, Co. K, Private (1842–). Lived and e. in Stanly 3/15/1862, age 20. Present through Feb. 1865 (NCT 8, 224).

HARWOOD, Redding, Co. K, Private (18__–1864). E. in Stanly 11/17/1863. Captured at Spotsylvania CH 5/12/1864; confined at Pt. Lookout, and died there

6/2/1864. Widow's pension application indicates he was wounded at Spotsylvania 5/12/1864 (NCT 8, 224).

HARWOOD, Wesley, Co. K, Private (1840–1864). B., lived and e. in Stanly 3/15/1862, age 22. Died in Richmond hospital 9/21–22/1864 of intermittent fever (NCT 8, 224).

HASS, John A., Co. C, Private (1840–). Lived, e. in Catawba 8/15/1861, age 21. Wounded in the right shoulder at Chancellorsville 5/1–3/1863. Retired to Invalid Corps 4/8/1864 due to disability (NCT 8, 144).

HASS, Sidney, Co. C, Private (1846–) Catawba farmer, e. at Richmond 2/6/1864, age 18. Wounded in the arm; arm amputated. Absent-sick through Feb. 1865 (NCT 8, 144).

HASTEN, John C., Co. E, Private (18__–1863). E. in Wake 10/2/1862. Wounded in thigh and captured at Gettysburg where he died 7/7/1863 of wounds (NCT 8, 168).

HASTY, W. F., Co. E, Private (1832–). Lived, e. in Union 10/2/1862. Deserted 6/5/1863. Captured at Culpeper 8/3/1863; confined at Old Capitol Prison until released 9/24/1863 after OOA (NCT 8, 168).

HATHCOCK, Edney W., Co. K, Private (1844–). Lived and e. in Stanly 9/7/1861, age 17. Captured at Wilderness 5/12/1864; confined at Pt. Lookout. Trans to Elmira 2/9/1865, then to Boulware's Wharf for exc. 2/20/1865 (NCT 8, 224).

HATHCOCK, George W., Co. K, Musician (1835–1863). Lived and e. in Stanly 9/7/1861, age 26. Promoted to musician Mar.–Apr.. 1862. Captured at Hanover CH 5/27/1862; confined at Ft. Monroe, then Ft. Columbus. Trans to Aiken's Landing for exchange 8/5/1862. Died at Salisbury 9/3/1863 of "fever" and/or "chronic diarrhoea" (NCT 8, 224).

HATHCOCK, Green L., Co. K, Musician. E. ib Stanly 3/15/1862 as a musician. Present through Feb. 1865 (NCT 8, 224).

HATHCOCK, Uriah F., Co. K, Corporal (1842–). Lived and e. in Stanly 3/15/1862, age 20. Wounded in shoulder at Cedar Mt.. Promoted to corporal Jan. 1863–Oct. 1864. Surrendered at Appomattox CH 4/9/1865 (NCT 8, 224).

HATLEY, Daniel A., Co. K, Private (1844–1863). Lived and e. in Stanly 9/7/1861, age 17. Wounded near Richmond. Wounded in thigh and captured at Gettysburg 7/1–33/1863. Leg amputated. Died in Gettysburg hospital 7/24/1864 of wounds (NCT 8, 224).

HATLEY, Edmund, Co. K, Private (1826–1862). Lived and e. in Stanly 9/7/1861, age 35. Died in camp near Brook Church 6/19/1862 of disease (NCT 8, 224).

HATLEY, Hastings M., Co. K, Private (1828–1862). Lived and e. in Stanly 9/7/1861, age 33. Died in Richmond hospital abt 5/3/1062 of pneumonia (NCT 8, 224).

HATLEY, John, Co. D, Private. Stanly resident, e. at Camp Stokes 10/31/1864. Captured near Petersburg 4/2/1865; confined at Pt. Lookout until released 6/17/1865 after OOA (NCT 8, 157).

HATLEY, John, Co. K, Private (1822–). Lived and e. in Stanly 9/7/1861, age 39. Captured at Hanover CH 5/27/1862; confined at Ft. Monroe, then Ft. Columbus. Trans to Aiken's Landing for exc on 8/5/1862. Dis abt 9/23/1862, overage (NCT 8, 224).

HATLEY, John M., Co. D, Private (1832–1863). Lived in Stanly, e. in Guilford 9/18/1861, age 29. Killed at Gettysburg 7/3/1863 (NCT 8, 157).

HATLY, J.F., Co. K, Private. E. 1/3/1865. Present through Feb. 1865 (NCT 8, 224).

HAUN, Newton D., Co. C, Private. Lived, e. in Catawba 3/15/1862. Reported missing; believed killed or captured at Gettysburg 7/3/1863. Federal provost marshal records indicate he may have been paroled at Morganton, NC 5/16/1865 (NCT 8, 144).

HAUSER, Andrew J., Co. F, Private (1829–1862). Lived in Forsyth, e. at Camp Enon in Yadkin 8/20/1861, age 22. Died "at home" abt 2/12/1862 of disease (NCT 8, 178; *Salem People's Press*, 2/21/1862).

HAUSER, N.V., Co. F, Private. B. in Forsyth, e. in Wake 4/27/1864. Died In Richmond hospital abt 8/7/1864 (NCT 8, 178).

HAWKINS, Charles H., Co. H, Musician (1840–1862). Lived, e. in Cleveland 8/22/1861, age 21, as a musician (drummer). Died at Wilmington 1/19/1862 (NCT 8, 201).

HAWKINS, George M., Co. H, Private (1826–), B., lived, e. in Cleveland 8/22/1861, age 35. Dis. 7/25/1862 due to "advanced age & physical inability to do duty" (NCT 8, 201).

HAWKINS, John E., Co. H, Private (1842–1862). B., lived, e. in Cleveland 8/22/1861, age 19. Dis. 7/25/1862. Died in camp near Richmond 7 /29/1862 (NCT 8, 201).

HAWKINS, John R., Co. H, Private (1849–). E. in Cleveland 2/15/1864, age 19. Surrendered at Appomattox CH 4/9/1865 (NCT 8, 201).

HAWKINS, Lewis J., Co. H, Private (1838–1861). Lived, e. in Cleveland 8/22/1861, age 23. Died at Wilmington 12/29/1861 of disease (NCT 8, 201).

HAWKINS, Ransom N., Co. H, Sergeant (1838–). Lived, e. in Cleveland 8/22/1861, age 23, as a private. Promoted to corporal 11/15/1862, then to sergeant 12/20/1862. Hospitalized at Danville abt 4/4/1865 with gunshot wound of left hand. Paroled at Charlotte, NC 5/3/1865 (NCT 8, 201).

HAWKINS, Samuel C., Co. H, Private (1840–1862). Lived, e. in Cleveland 8/22/1861, age 21 as a musician (fifer). Rank reduced Jan.–Apr.. 1862. Wounded at Cedar Mt. 8/9/1862 and hospitalized at Staunton and died 8/20/1862 of wounds (NCT 8, 201).

HAWKINS, William D., Co. H, Private (1837–1863). Lived, e. in Cleveland 8/22/1861, age 24. Killed at Chancellorsville 5/3/1863 (NCT 8, 201).

HAWKINS, William J., Co. H, Private (1834–). B., lived, e. in Cleveland 8/22/1861, age 27. Wounded in neck and right shoulder at Gravel Hill 7/28/1864. Retired from service 1/18/1865, disabled from wounds (NCT 8, 201).

HAWKINS, Willis R., Co. B, Private (1834–). Lived, e. in Gaston 7/30/1861, age 27. Captured at Fredericksburg on 12/13/1862; paroled abt 12/17/1862. Captured at Gettysburg 7/1–3/1863. Confined at Davids Island; paroled and trans to City Pt. for exchange on 9/16/1863. Absent on detached service 4/4/1864. Furloughed on 4/28/1864. Absent on furlough through Feb. 1865 (NCT 8, 131).

HAWKS, Dickerson, Co. A, Private (1839–). Lived, e. in Surry 3/18/1862, age 23. Paroled at Lynchburg 4/13/1865. Son of Harding and Matilda Puckett Hawks of Carroll County, VA who moved to Surry. In 1860 he was tenant farmer living with his wife and 3 children in the Stuart's Creek District, Surry (NCT 8, 118; SCS 84).

HAWKS, William, Jr., Co. A, Private (1831–). Surry resident, the brother of Dickerson Hawks, e. in Carroll County, VA, age 21, on 3/18/1862. Died in a Richmond hospital on 9/1/1862 of "febris typhoides" (NCT 8, 118; SCS 85).

HAYES, Richard T., Co. G, Private (1841–). B., lived, e. in Orange 9/2/1861, age 20. Captured near Hanover CH 5/27/1862; confined at Ft. Monroe, then Ft. Columbus. Paroled and trans to Aiken's Landing for exchange on 8/5/1862. Dis. 4/16/1863 due to "loss of hearing following an attack of sickness" (NCT 8, 189).

HAYNES, Anderson H., Co. I, Private (1838–). Lived, e. in Yadkin 8/13/1861, age 23. Captured at Hanover CH 5/27/1862; confined at Ft. Monroe, then Ft. Columbus. Paroled and trans to Aiken's Landing for exchange 8/5/1862. Hospitalized at Richmond 5/18/1864 with gunshot wound of left arm. AWOL Nov. 1864–Feb. 1865. He m. Nancy Chamberlain 1/28/1864 in Yadkin (NCT 8, 212; CWY 221).

HAYNES, George W., Co. I, Private. E. at Camp Holmes 2/7/1864. Company records indicate he was captured 5/12/1864; Federal records do not substantiate this (NCT 8, 212).

HAYNES, Thomas F., Co. I, Private (1836–). Lived, e. in Yadkin 8/13/1861, age 25. Present until he surrendered at Appomattox CH 4/9/1865 (NCT 8, 212).

HAYNES, William M., Co. F, Private. E. in Stokes 10/19/1864. Present through Feb. 1865 (NCT 8, 178).

HAYWOOD, Wilson, Co. E, Private (1830–1862). Lived, e. in Montgomery 8/1/1861, age 31. Died at Wilmington 1/5/1862 or 1/14/1862 (NCT 8, 168).

HEAD, A.E., Co. F, Private (1837–). Lived, e. in Yadkin 3/25/1862, age 25. Wounded in shoulder at Ox Hill 9/1/1862; hospitalized in Danville. Deserted from hospital 10/16/1862. Returned to duty, but deserted again 7/19/1863 (NCT 8, 178).

HEAD, Benjamin, Co. F, Private (1835–1862). B., lived, e. in Yadkin 6/18/1861, age 26. Died "at home" 12/7/1862 of disease (NCT 8, 178).

HEAD, Wiley L., Co. F, Private (1841–1863). Lived, e. in Yadkin 6/18/1861, age 20. Died at Hanover Junction 5/5/1863 of fever (NCT 8, 178).

HEARN, Nehemiah, Co. K, Private ? NC pension records indicate he served in this company (NCT 8, 224).

HEARNE, Whitman F., Co. K, Private (1837–). Lived and e. in Stanly 7/8/1862, age 25. Captured near Petersburg 4/2/1865; confined at Hart's Island. Trans to Davids Island 7/1/1865, and released 7/11/1865 after OOA (NCT 8, 224).

HEFNER, David, Co. C, Private (1828–) Catawba resident, e. 8/13/1861, age 33. Shot four times (including once in the left side) and captured at Gettysburg 7/1–3/1863. Hospitalized at Davids Island; paroled and trans to City Pt. 9/27/1863 for exchange. Surrendered at Appomattox CH 4/9/1865 (NCT 8, 144).

HEFNER, George, Co. C, Private (1833–) Catawba resident, e. 3/15/1862, age 29. Surrendered at Appomattox CH 4/9/1865 (NCT 8, 144).

HEFNER, Levi, Co. C, Private (1840–) Catawba resident, e. on 8/13/1861, age 21. Wounded at Ox Hill 9/1/1862. Wounded at Fredericksburg 12/13/1862. Captured at Spotsylvania CH 5/12/1864; confined at Pt. Lookout until trans to Elmira on 8/10/1864. Released 7/7/1865 after OOA (NCT 8, 144).

HEFNER, Marcus, Co. C, Private (1843–1863). Lived, e. in Catawba 8/13/1861, age 18. Captured at Hanover CH 5/27/1862; confined at Ft. Monroe, then Ft. Columbus. Trans to Aiken's Landing for exchange on 8/5/1862. Killed at Chancellorsville 5/3/1863 (NCT 8, 144).

HEFNER, Serenus, Co. C, Private (1841–). Lived and e. in Catawba 8/13/1861, age 20. Captured at Hanover CH 5/27/1862; confined at Ft. Monroe, then Ft. Columbus. Trans to Aiken's Landing for exchange on 8/5/1862. Wounded in the left foot at Jones' Farm 9/30/1864. Surrendered at Appomattox CH 4/9/1865 (NCT 8, 144–145).

HEFNER, Wilson W., Co. C, Private (1845–). Lived in Catawba, e. 3/15/1862, age 17. Captured at Hanover CH 5/27/1862; confined at Ft. Monroe, then Ft. Columbus. Trans to Aiken's Landing for exchange on 8/5/1862. Wounded at Chancellorsville 5/1–3/1863. Present through Feb. 1865 (NCT 8, 145).

HELTON, Drayton, Co. H, Private (1840–). B. in Rutherford, lived in Cleveland, was a shoemaker. E. 3/17/1862, age 22. Dis. 10/25/1862 due to "hypertrophy of heart" (NCT 8, 201).

HENDERSON, Jehu S., Co. E, Private (1844–1863). Lived, e. in Montgomery 3/4/1862. Died at Guinea Station 6/8/1863 (NCT 8, 168).

HENDERSON, Joel, Co. E, Private (1843–). Lived, e. in Montgomery 8/1/1861, age 18. Trans to Co. K, 34th Reg NCT 3/12/1864 in exchange for Private Calvin Macon (NCT 8, 268).

HENDRICKS, Cleophus Dioclecian, Co. I, 1st Sergeant (1831–1899). Son of Henry and Anna Jenkins Ross Hendricks, Cleophus lived, e. in Yadkin 8/13/1861 as a musician, age 30. Rank reduced Jan.–Oct. 1862. Captured at Hanover CH 5/27/1862; confined at Ft. Monroe, then Ft. Columbus. Paroled and trans to Aiken's Landing for exchange 8/5/1862. Promoted to sergeant Nov. 1862–Feb. 1863; then 1st sergeant March 1863–Oct. 1864. Wounded in the leg and captured at Gettysburg 7/3–5/1863. Hospitalized at Gettysburg then at Chester. Trans to Pt. Lookout 10/2/1863. Paroled and trans to City Pt. On 3/6/1864 for exchange. Retired to Invalid Corps 9/19/1864 due to disability. He m. Elizabeth Gentry in 1854. Returned to Boonville where he was the postmaster 1872–1891, and 1894–1898. Bur. Boonville Bapt. Ch. Cem, Boonville, NC (NCT 8, 212, CWY 222).

HENKLE, D. L., Field & Staff, Assistant Chaplain. Appointed on 12/30/1864, Henkle remained with the Reg. on 4/9/1865 at Appomattox CH (NCT 8, 111).

HERMAN, Abel, Co. C, Private. B., lived, e. in Catawba 8/13/1861. Wounded at Chancellorsville 5/2–3/1863. Captured at Falling Waters 7/14/1863. Confined at Old Capitol Prison, Washington, DC, he was trans to Pt. Lookout 8/8/1863. Trans to Elmira on 8/16/1864; died there on 9/12/1864 of "chronic diarrhoea" (NCT 8, 145).

HERMAN, D. Alexander, Co. C, Private. Lived, e. in Catawba resident 3/15/1862. Died in Gordonsville hospital 5/27/1862 of typhoid fever (NCT 8, 145).

HERMAN, Daniel J., Co. C, Private. Lived, e. in Catawba 5/6/1864. Captured at Petersburg 4/3/1865; confined at Hart's Island, where he died 6/15/1865 of typhoid fever (NCT 8, 145).

HERMAN, Daniel M., Co. C, Corporal (1837–). Lived, e. in Catawba 8/13/1861 as a private. Captured at Hanover CH 5/27/1862; confined at Ft. Monroe, then Ft. Columbus. Trans to Aiken's Landing for exchange 8/5/1862. Wounded at Chancellorsville 5/1–3/1863. Promoted to corporal 12/1/1864. Surrendered at Appomattox CH 4/9/1865 (NCT 8, 145).

HERMAN, Darious L., Co. H, Private. Records of Co. E, McRae's Battalion NC Cavalry indicate he trans to Co. H, 28th Reg in June 1864. Co. H records do not agree (NCT 8, 201).

HERMAN, George Daniel, Co. C, Corporal (1839–1864). Lived, e. in Catawba 8/13/1861 at age 22 as a private. Wounded at 2nd Manassas 8/28–30/1862. Promoted to corporal 9/1/1863. Killed at Wilderness 5/5/1864 (NCT 8, 145).

HERMAN, James Noah, Co. C, Private. E. in Catawba County 8/6/1864. Present through Feb. 1865 (NCT 8, 145).

HERMAN, Joseph, Co. C, Private. B., lived, e. in Catawba 3/24/1864. Died "at home" 8/27/1864 of disease (NCT 8, 145).

HERMAN, Phanuel J., Co. C, Sergeant (1838–). B., lived, e. in Catawba 8/13/1861, age 23 as a private. Captured at Hanover CH 5/27/1862; confined at Ft. Monroe, then Ft. Columbus. Paroled and trans to Aiken's Landing for exchange 8/5/1862. Promoted to corporal 3/25/1863. Wounded and captured at Gettysburg 7/1–4/1863; hospitalized at Davids Island 7/17–24/1863. Paroled and trans to City Pt. 9/8/1863 for exchange. Promoted to sergeant abt 9/9/1863. Surrendered at Appomattox CH 4/9/1865 (NCT 8, 145).

HERMAN, Rufus D., Co. C, Private (1844–). Catawba resident e. 8/13/1861, age 17. Captured at Gravel Hill 7/28/1864; confined at Pt. Lookout, then trans to Elmira 8/8/1864. Released on 7/3/1865 after OOA. Roll of Honor indicates he was wounded and captured in an unspecified battle (NCT 8, 145).

HERMAN, William Henry, Co. C, Private. Catawba resident e. on 3/15/1862; died in a Richmond hospital 7/8/1862 of chronic "diarrhoea" (NCT 8, 145).

HERMON, J.S., Co. C, Private. Surrendered at Appomattox CH 4/9/1865 (NCT 8, 145).

HERREN, Darlin, Co. D, Private (1834–1864). Lived in Catawba, e. in Stanly were he lived on 7/29/1861, age 27. Hospitalized in Richmond 7/2/1862 with gunshot wound of the right forefinger. Died "at home" 8/15/1864 (NCT 8, 157).

HERRIN, Eli R., Co. K, Sergeant (1838–). B., lived and e. in Stanly 9/7/1861, age 23, as sergeant. Wounded in leg near Richmond June 1862, leg amputated. Dis. 8/15/1862, because of disability (NCT 8, 225).

HESTER, Jeremiah M., Co. E, Private (1842–). Lived in Montgomery or Forsyth. E. in Montgomery 8/1/1861, age 19. Wounded at Chancellorsville 5/2–3/1863. Detailed for light duty at Staunton 3/18/1864. Absent on detail through Feb. 1865. Captured and confined at Wheeling, WVA abt 3/12/1865. Released abt 3/13/1865 after OOA (NCT 8, 168).

HESTER, Stephen, Co. E, Private (1841–1864). Lived in Union, e. in Wake 10/2/1862, age 21. Captured at Spotsylvania CH 5/12/1864; confined at Pt. Lookout, then Elmira 8/10/1864. Died there 9/20/1864 of "pneumonia" (NCT 8, 168).

HIATT, George W., Co. A, Private (1831–). Surry resident e., age 21, 3/18/1862. Captured near Hanover CH; confined at Ft. Monroe, then Ft. Delaware. Paroled and trans to Aiken's Landing 6/9/1862 for exchange 8/5/1862. Captured at Deep Bottom 7/10/1864. Federal Provost Records do not substantiate this. Son of Martin and Rebecca Hiatt of Ararat, his widow, Virginia, applied for a pension (NCT 8, 118; SCS 87).

HICKS, Benjamin P. G., Co. H, Private (1828–). Lived, e. in Cleveland 3/17/1862, age 34. Absent-sick Feb. 1864–Feb. 1865. Captured in Richmond hospital 4/3/1865; trans to Newport News and released 6/16/1865 after OOA (NCT 8, 201).

HICKS, Daniel, Co. F, Private (1836–). Lived, e. in Forsyth 3/17/1862, age 26. Captured near Pickett's Farm abt. 7/21/1864; confined at Ft. Lookout. Exc abt 9/30/1864. Absent-sick through Feb. 1865 (NCT 8, 178).

HICKS, David, Co. H, Private (1832–1863). Lived, e. in Cleveland 10/2/1862, age 30. Died in Richmond hospital 6/4–5/1863 of typhoid fever (NCT 8, 201).

HICKS, Levi, Co. H, Private (1834–1863). Lived, e. in Cleveland 10/2/1862. Died in Richmond hospital abt 6/5/1863 of typhoid fever (NCT 8, 201–202).

HICKS, John H., Co. F, Private (1837–). Lived, e. in Forsyth 3/17/1862, age 25. Wounded at Gettysburg 7/1–3/1863. Wounded in right leg at Wilderness May 1864. Surrendered at Appomattox CH 4/9/1865 (NCT 8, 178).

HICKS, Jonathan, Co. F, Private (1826–) Lived in Forsyth, e. 3/17/1862, age 36. Captured at Hanover CH abt 5/17/1862; confined at Ft. Monroe, then Ft. Columbus. Paroled and trans to Aiken's Landing for exchange on 8/5/1862. AWOL through Dec. 1862. Returned. Absent-wounded Sep.–Dec. 1864. AWOL 12/14/1864–Feb 1865. Returned. Captured near Petersburg 4/2/1865; confined at Pt. Lookout until released 6/27/1865 after OOA (NCT 8, 178–179).

HICKS, Thomas R., Co. F, Private (1842–1862). Lived, e. in Yadkin 6/18/1861, age 19. Killed at Gaines' Mill 6/17/1862 (NCT 8, 179)./

HIGHT, Charnal, Co. E, Private. Lived in Montgomery, e. in Wake 11/19/1864. Captured at Appomattox River 4/3/1865; confined at Hart's Island until released 6/20/1865 after OOA (NCT 8, 168).

HIGHT, Samuel, Co. E, Private (1839–). Lived, e. in Montgomery 8/1/1861, age 22. Hospitalized at Richmond 7/1/1862 after being "brused by bomb." Retired to Invalid Corps 11/23/1864 due to disability (NCT 8, 168).

HILL, Harrison H., Co. I, Private. B. in Surry, e. 8/13/1861 in Yadkin, age 16. Dis. 11/18/1862 because he was underage (NCT 8, 212)

HILL, Jesse Lee, Co. E, Private (1839–). Lived, e. in Montgomery 8/1/1861, age 22. Surrendered at Appomattox CH 4/9/1865 (NCT 8, 168).

HILL, Jonathan F., Co. H, Corporal (1842–1862). Lived, e. in Cleveland 8/22/1861, age 19, as a corporal; rank reduced May–July 1862. Died in Richmond hospital 7/8/1862 of typhoid fever (NCT 8, 202).

HILL, Lorenzo H., Co. A, Private (1842–1864). Lived, e. in Surry, age 20, 3/18/1862. AWOL from 10/1/1862 until Jan. 1863. Hospitalized in Richmond 5/25/1864 with a gunshot wound to the right hand. Died in a Richmond hospital on 8/25/1864 (NCT 8, 118; SCS 88).

HILLIARD, Silas, Co. D, Private (1838–1862). Lived, e. in Stanly 3/15/1862, age 24. Captured at Hanover CH 5/27/1862; confined at Ft. Monroe, then Ft. Columbus. Paroled and trans to Aiken's Landing for exchange 8/5/1862. Died in Staunton (or Winchester) hospital 11/30/1862 of pneumonia (NCT 8, 127).

HINES, George, Co. B, Corporal (1837–). B. in Gaston, e. at Camp Fisher 9/18/1861, at age 24, as a private. Wounded in the head, he was captured at Gettysburg 7/3–5/1863. Blinded in the right eye from wound, hospitalized at Davids Island, NY Harbor until paroled and trans to City Pt. 8/28/1863 for exc. Wounded in the arm at Spotsylvania CH 5/12/1864 Promoted to corporal 2/1/1865, and surrendered at Appomattox CH 4/9/1865 (NCT 8, 131).

HINES, John B., Co. B, Private. E. at Liberty Mills on 1/19/1864. Surrendered at Appomattox CH on 4/9/1865 (NCT 8, 131).

HINSHAW, James, Co. I, Private. E. 3/1/1864 at Liberty Mills. Paroled at Burkesville Junction 4/14–17/1865 (NCT 8, 212).

HINSHAW, William A., Co. D, Private. E. at Camp Holmes 10/16/1864. Paroled at Burkesville Junction 4/14–17/1865 (NCT 8, 157).

HINSON, Alfred, Co. K, Private (1836–1863). Lived and e. in Stanly 9/7/1861, age 25. Captured on unspecified date. Trans to Aiken's Landing for exchange on 9/21/1862. Wounded at Chancellorsville 5/2–3/1863. Died near Guinea Station 6/6/1863 of typhoid fever (NCT 8, 225).

HINSON, George, Co. D, Private (1836–1862). Lived, in e. in Stanly resident 7/29/1861, age 25. Died at Middleburg 9/12/1862 from wounds (NCT 8, 157).

HINSON, John, Co. K, Private (1834–1862). Lived and e. in Stanly 3/24/1862, age 28. Died in Richmond hospital 7/27/1862 of typhoid fever (NCT 8, 225).

HINSON, Joseph M., Co. K, Private (1828–). Lived and e. in Stanly 9/7/1861, age 33. Wounded at Gettysburg 7/1–3/1863. Captured near Petersburg 4/2/1865; confined at Pt. Lookout until released 6/14/1865 after OOA (NCT 8, 225).

HINSON, Noah L., Co. D, Private (1837–). Lived, e. in Stanly 7/19/1861, age 24. Absent on detail as shoemaker or nurse through Feb. 1865 (NCT 8, 157).

HINSON, Robert, Co. K, Private (1845–1863). Lived and e. in Stanly 3/2/1863, age 18. Died in Richmond hospital 6/8/1863 of typhoid fever (NCT 8, 225).

HINSON, William, Co. K, Private (1834–). Lived and e. in Stanly 3/10/1862, age 28. Wounded and captured at Spotsylvania CH 5/12/1864. Died, date and place not reported (NCT 8, 225).

HOBSON, David Francis, Co. I, Corporal (1840–). Lived, e. in Yadkin 9/3/1861, as private. Promoted to corporal Mar. 1863–July 1864. Wounded near Chancellorsville abt 5/1–4/1863. Present through Feb. 1865. Son of David Hobson, Jr., and Matilda Lakey Hobson; m. Aggie Pauline Williams (NCT 8, 212; CWY 223; HYC 407).

HOBSON, Jesse F., Co. I, Private (1834–1911). Lived in Yadkin, son of David Hobson, Jr. and Matilda Lakey, he e. 10/8/1863. Present through Feb. 1865. His brothers, John Ellet and David Frances served in came company. He is buried at Forbush Bapt. Ch. cem, Yadkin County, NC (NCT 8, 212; CWY 223).

HOBSON, John E., Co. I, Private (1837–1901). Lived, e. in Yadkin 9/3/1861, age 24. Retired to Invalid Corps 13/7/1864 due to disability. He m. Mary Jane Brown and resumed his life as a farmer/merchant. Bur. Forbush Bapt. Ch. cem. Yadkin County, NC (NCT 8, 212, CWY 223–224).

HODGES, Henry, Co. A, Private (1845–1864). Lived, e. in Surry, age 17, 3/18/1862. Hospitalized in Richmond on 5/4/1864 with gunshot wound to left shoulder, died there 5/30/1864 from wounds. Son of Pleasant and Matilda Cuningham Hodges, of Dobson area (NCT 8, 118; SCS 89).

HODGES, James R., Co. A, Private (1830–). Lived in Surry, e., age 31, 5/4/1861. Wounded in the head at Cedar Mt. 8/9/1862. AWOL through Feb. 1865 (NCT 8, 118; SCS 90).

HODGES, Joel W., Co. A, Private (1841–). Surry resident, e., age 21, 3/18/1862. Present through 6/17/1864 (NCT 8, 118).

HODGES, Pleasant, Jr., Co., A, Private (1840–). Son of Pleasant and Matilda Cuningham Hodges, of Dobson, Surry, e. at age 21 on 5/4/1861. Wounded at Cedar Mountain on 8/9/1862. Deserted from hospital before 11/1/1862. Returned Captured near Petersburg on 4/1/1865. Confined at Ft. Delaware until released on 6/19/1865 after OOA. Pleasant m. Mary Moody in 1864 in Surry. Census of 1880 lists Mary as a widow (NCT 8, 118; SCS 90–91).

HODGES, Tyre, Co. A, Private (1825–). Surry resident e. 5/5/1861, age 36. Captured near Petersburg 4/2/1865; confined at Ft. Delaware until released on 6/19/1865 after OOA. Tyre was the son of Drury and Mahala Gillespie Hodges, of Fisher River near Dobson, NC (NCT 8, 118; SCS 91).

HOFFMAN, John Cephas, Co. B, Sergeant (1841–). B., lived, e. in Gaston 8/6/1861, age 20. Captured at Hanover CH on 5/17/1862; confined at Ft. Monroe, then Ft. Columbus. Paroled and sent to Aiken's Landing for exchange 8/5/1862. Captured at Fredericksburg 12/13/1862. Paroled 12/17/1862. Promoted to corporal March 1863–Oct. 1864. Wounded in right leg at Wilderness abt 5/5/1864. Promoted to sergeant 2/1/1865. Present through Feb. 1865. NC pension records indicate he was wounded at Chancellorsville in 1863 (NCT 8, 131).

HOFFMAN, John H., Co. B, Private (1840–). Lived, e. in Gaston, age 21, 7/30/1861. Wounded at 2nd Manassas 8/28–30, 1862. Absent-wounded through Oct. 1862. Detailed as guard at Hanover Junction Jan.–Feb. 1863. Present through Feb. 1865 (NCT 8, 131).

HOFFMAN, Thomas F., Co. B, Private (1842–1864). Lived, e. in Gaston 7/30/1861, age 19. Captured at Fredericksburg 12/13/1862; paroled 12/17/1862. Killed 5/5/1864 at Wilderness (NCT 8, 131).

HOLCOMB, Bloom Virgil, Co. I, Sergeant (1845–). Son of Col. George and Anna Long Holcomb, lived, e. 2/28/1863 in Yadkin, age 18, as private. Wounded near Gravel Hill abt 7/28/1864. Promoted to sergeant 11/21/1864. Captured near Petersburg 4/2/1865; confined at Ft. Delaware until released 6/19/1865 after OOA. He m. Beckie Kirkman in 1872 (NCT 8, 212; CWY 224; HYC 414).

HOLCOMB, Calvin M., Co. I, Private (1841–1918). Son of Col. George and Anna Long Holcomb, he lived, e. 8/13/1861, in Yadkin at age 20. Absent-wounded May–Oct 1862. Wounded at Chancellorsville abt 5/1–4/1863. Promoted to sergeant Jan. 1865. Retired to Invalid Corps 1/28/1865. Roll of Honor indicates he was wounded in the foot "near the Rappahannock" River, no date given. Calvin returned to Yadkin and in 1870 m. Elizabeth Casstevens; 2nd Ella Long. Dr. Calvin Holcomb practiced medicine in Yadkin (NCT 8, 212–213; CWY 224)

HOLCOMB, Daniel F., Co. I, 1st Lieutenant (1836–1863). Lived, e. in Yadkin 8/13/1861, age 25. Appointed 1st lieutenant 8/13/1861. Defeated for reelection, continued to serve as a private in Co. I. Died in Richmond hospital 12/8/1863 of smallpox (NCT 8, 207, 213).

HOLCOMB, James, Co. I, Private. Lived, e. in Yadkin 11/14/1863 at Camp Holmes. Captured near Petersburg 4/2/1865; confined at Ft. Delaware until released 6/19/8165 after OOA (NCT 8, 213).

HOLCOMB, John T., Co. I, 3rd Lieutenant (1838–1864). B., lived, e. in Yadkin 8/13/1861. Elected 3rd lieutenant, defeated for reelection 4/12/18621. Continued to serve in company as a private. Captured at Gettysburg 7/1–5/1863; confined at Davids Island. Paroled and trans to City Pt. On 9/16/1863 for exchange. Died in Lynchburg hospital 4/29/1864 of "hepatitis acuta" Son of George and Anna Long Holcomb. (NCT 8, 207, 213, CWY 225).

HOLCOMB, Jones, Co. I, Private (1842–1863). Lived, e. in Yadkin 8/13/1861, age 19. Killed at Gettysburg 7/3/1863 (NCT 8, 213).

HOLCOMB, Leander, Co. I, Private (1838–). Lived, e. in Yadkin 8/13/1861, age 23. Deserted 6/18/1863. Returned and trans to Co. G, 44th Reg NCT (NCT 8, 213).

HOLCOMB, William M., Co. I, Private (1842–1918). Lived, e. in Yadkin 11/14/1863 at Camp Holmes. Captured at Richmond 4/3/1865; confined at Newport News 4/24/1865; released 6/30/1865 after OOA. NC pension records indicate he was wounded in the battle of "Horse Shoe" in 1863. He and wife Julia are bur.

in Swan Creek Bapt. Ch., near Jonesville, NC (NCT 8, 213; CWY 226).

HOLDER, James H., Co. A, Private (1844–). Lived, e. in Surry 3/18/1862, age 18. Present through April 1862, but deserted from hospital. Reportedly died "at home" (NCT 8, 118; SCS 92). See HOLDER, James M., below.

HOLDER, James M. (Matt), Co. A, Private (1844–). Son of Davis M. And Sarah Holder of Stewart's Creek, in Surry, e. 3/18/1862, age 18. Wounded at Cedar Mt. 8/9/1862. Hospitalized in Danville, and he left on 9/22/1862. He m. Celia Cockerman, then Mary Alice Sams (NCT 8, 118; SCS 92). Note: James H. and James M. Holder could be the same person.

HOLDER, Jesse A., Co. A, Sergeant (1844–). Son of John and Susan Hughes Holder, of Stewart's Creek area of Surry, e. at age 18 on 3/18/1862. Promoted to corporal on 9/1/1864, then to sergeant abt 2/28/1865. Surrendered at Appomattox 4/9/1865. NC pension records indicate he was wounded at Fredericksburg 10/3/1863 (NCT 8, 118–119; SCS 92).

HOLLAND, Gold Griffin, Co. H, Captain (1820–). Lived, e. in Cleveland 3/17/1862 as a private. Appointed 1st lieutenant 4/7/1862. Surrendered at Appomattox 4/9/1865 (NCT 8, 195).

HOLLAND, James C., Co. H, Sergeant (1842–1864). Lived, e. in Cleveland. 8/22/1861, age 19. Promoted to corporal Jan.–July 1863. Wounded at Gettysburg 7/1–3/1863. Promoted to sergeant. Hospitalized at Richmond 5/24/1864 with gunshot wound of left thigh, died there 6/18/1864 of wounds (NCT 8, 202).

HOLLAND, Jerome W., Co. H, Private (1833–1863). Lived, e. in Cleveland 10/2/1862. Hospitalized at Richmond 12/15/1862 with gunshot wound of middle finger, right hand. Died "at home" 1/11/1863, cause not reported (NCT 8, 202).

HOLLAND, Phineas A., Co. H, Private (1843–). Lived, e. in Cleveland 8/22/1861, age 18. "Fell out" near Orange CH 8/13/1862. Returned, and captured near Jericho Mills abt 5/24/1864. Confined at Pt. Lookout; trans to Elmira 7/8/1864. Trans back to Pt. Lookout, paroled and trans to Varina for exchange 9/22/1864. Absent-sick through Feb. 1865 (NCT 8, 202).

HOLLAND, Thomas J., Co. H, 1st Sergeant (1843–). Lived, e. in Cleveland 8/22/1861, age 18, as a private. Promoted to sergeant 2/8/1862; reduced in rank before 5/1/1862. Wounded near Mechanicsville abt 6/27/1862. Promoted to 1st sergeant May 1863. Surrendered at Appomattox 4/9/1865 (NCT 8, 202).

HOLLER, Adley D., Co. C, Private. Previously served in 1st Co. G, 6th Reg SC Infantry; transferred to Co. C 3/30/1864. Wounded at Gravel Hill 7/28/1864. Surrendered 4/9/1865 at Appomattox CH (NCT 8, 145).

HOLLER, J.C., Co. H, Private (18__–1864). Previously served in Co. E, McRae's Battalion, NC Cavalry. Trans to Co. H, 28th Reg June 1864. Killed at Fussell's Mill 8/16/1864 (NCT 8, 202).

HOLLER, Lemuel, Co. C, Private. Lived, e. in Catawba 3/15/1862. Captured at Hanover CH 5/27/1862; confined at Ft. Monroe, then Ft. Columbus. Paroled and trans to Aiken's Landing for exchange

8/5/1862. Wounded and captured at Gettysburg 7/1–5/1863. Hospitalized at Davids Island until paroled and trans to City Pt. on 9/16/1863 for exchange. Present through Feb. 1865 (NCT 8, 145).

HOLT, Alexander, Co. K, Private ? NC pension records indicate he served in this company (NCT 8, 225).

HOLT, Benjamin A., Co. K, Private (1828–). Lived and e. in Stanly 9/7/1861, age 33 as a corporal. Rank reduced Jan.–Apr.. 1862. Hospitalized at Richmond 5/18/1864 with gunshot wound of head. Returned, and surrendered at Appomattox CH 4/9/1865 (NCT 8, 225).

HOLT, David, Co. K, Private (1836–1863). Lived and e. in Stanly 9/7/1861, age 25. Killed at Gettysburg 7/3/1863 (NCT 8, 225).

HOLT, John A., Co. K, Private (1829–). Lived and e. in Stanly 2/26/1863, age 34. Captured near Petersburg 4/2/1865; confined at Pt. Lookout until released 6/27/1865 after OOA (NCT 8, 225).

HOLTON, William B., Co. G, Corporal (1843–1862). Lived, e. in Orange 9/2/1861, age 18, as a corporal. Killed at Fredericksburg 12/13/1862 (NCT 8, 189).

HOLYFIELD, Byrd, Co. A, 1st Sergeant (1837–1862). B. at Rockford, Surry, to Hardin and Paulina Butcher Holyfield, e. 5/5/1861, as private. Promoted to 1st sergeant 9/23/1861. Died at Wilmington 1/11/1862 (NCT 8, 119; SCS 93).

HOLYFIELD, Columbus, Co. A, Sergeant (1836–). B. at Rockford, Surry, to Hardin and Paulina Butcher of Rockford, Columbus joined his brother, Byrd, and e. 5/4/1861. Promoted on 4/10/1862 to sergeant. AWOL from 5/26/1864–1/9/1864; reduced in rank. Columbus m. in Surry to Carry Ann Snow, and by the 1880 census had 6 children (NCT 8, 119; SCS 93).

HOLYFIELD, Hardin, Jr. Co. A, Private (1850–) Son of Hardin Holyfield, Sr., and wife, Pauline Butcher. No military record exists for him, but his pension record states he was a member of Co. A. He probably joined this company because his brothers were already in it. Hardin, Jr. m. Amelia Walker in 1876, and had several children (NCT 8, 119; SCS 93).

HOLYFIELD, Watson B., Co. A, 1st Sergeant. Another son of Hardin and Paulina Holyfield, Watson e. in Surry on 5/4/186, as a private. Wounded in right elbow at Gaines' Mill on 6/27/1862. Promoted to 1st sergeant on 9/21/1861. Wounded again in the back and right hand at the Wilderness on 5/5/1864. Wounded again 8/25/1864 in the right shoulder. Retired from service abt 2/22/1865 due to shoulder wound which made his arm "useless." Watson was 5' 11" tall, with blue eyes, fair complexion and light hair. Family tradition holds that he was wounded 9 times (NCT 8, 119; SCS 94).

HOOTS, J. Co. A, Private. Hoots died in a Richmond hospital on 8/7/1864 of disease. No further information (NCT 8, 119).

HOOVER, W. V., Co. F, Private. Died in Farmville hospital 8/7/1864 of typhoid fever (NCT 8, 179).

HOPKINS, James F., Co. D, Private (1833–1862). Stanly resident, e. there 7/29/1861, age 28. Died at Staunton 7/3/1862 of "gastro enteritis" (NCT 8, 157).

HOPKINS, James F., Jr., Co. D, Private (1837–1862). Stanly resident, e. there 7/29/1861, age 24. Died in Winchester hospital abt 11/22/1862 of smallpox (NCT 8, 157).

HOPKINS, John F., Co. D, Private (1825–1864). Stanly resident, e. there 7/29/1861, age 36. Captured at Hanover CH 5/27/1862; confined at Ft. Monroe, then Ft. Columbus. Paroled and trans to Aiken's Landing for exchange 8/5/1862. Wounded at Reams' Station 8/25/1864. Hospitalized in Petersburg; died there 10/2/1864 of his wounds (NCT 8, 157).

HOPKINS, Thomas, Co. C, Private (1812–). A miner, he lived and e. in Stanly at age 49, 9/10/1861. Dis. 4/30/1863 because he was overage (NCT 8, 157).

HOPPER, H., Co. H, Private. Date and place of enlistment not reported. Surrendered at Appomattox CH 4/9/1865 (NCT 8, 202).

HOPPER, John A., Co. H, Private. E. at Camp Stokes 10/4/1864. Deserted 2/22/1865 (NCT 8, 202).

HOPPER, Lansford M., Co. H, Private. Lived, and e. in Cleveland 9/22/1863. Trans to Co. I, 34th Reg NCT 11/18/1864 (NCT 8, 202).

HORTON, William P., Co. H, Private (1840–1862). Lived in SC, e. in Cleveland 8/22/1861, age 21. Died at Wilmington NC 2/4/1862 (NCT 8, 202).

HOUSTON, Jacob F., Co. C, Corporal (1837–). Lived and e. in Catawba 3/15/1862, age 25, as a private. Wounded at Shepherdstown 9/20/1862. Wounded at Gettysburg 7/1–3/1863. Promoted to corporal 12/1/1864. Surrendered at Appomattox CH 4/9/1865 (NCT 8, 145–146).

HOUSTON, John M., Co. C, Private (1843–). Lived and e. in Catawba 8/13/1861 at age 18. Captured at Hanover CH 5/17/1862; paroled, trans to Aiken's Landing on 7/12/1862 for exchange on 8/5/1862. Surrendered at Appomattox CH 4/9/1865 (NCT 8, 146).

HOUSTON, Martin L, Co. C, Private (1839–1862). Lived and e. in Catawba. 8/13/1861, age 22. Wounded in the leg at Gaines' Mill 6/27/1862. Hospitalized at Richmond; died 7/17/1862 of his wounds (NCT 8, 146).

HOVIS, G.F., Co. B, Private (1833–1862). Lived and e. in Gaston 7/30/1861, age 28. He died at Wilmington on 1/14/1862 (NCT 8, 131).

HOVIS, James P., Co. B, Private (1845–). Lived in Gaston, e. in Wake, age 18. on 9/3/1863. Surrendered at Appomattox CH 4/9/1865 (NCT 8, 131).

HOVIS, Martin Van Buren, Co. B, Private (1840–). Lived and e. Gaston on 8/6/1861, age 21. Captured at Fredericksburg, 12/13/1862; paroled abt 12/17/1862. Captured near Petersburg 4/2/1865. Confined at Pt. Lookout. Released on 6/27/1865 after OOA (NCT 8, 132).

HOWARD, Franklin W., Co. C, Private (1839–). Lived and e. in Catawba 1/1/1864. Surrendered at Appomattox CH 4/9/1865 (NCT 8, 146).

HOWARD, George W., Co. G, Private (1842–). Lived, e. in Orange 3/5/1862, age 20, as a substitute. Captured at Fredericksburg 12/13/1862; exc abt 12/17/1862. Surrendered 4/9/1865 (NCT 8, 189).

HOWARD, James H., Co. G, Private (1843–1863). Lived and e. in Orange 9/2/1861, age 18. Died at Camp Gregg 3/22/1863 (NCT 8, 189–190).

HOWARD, Samuel, Co. G, Private (1843–1862). Lived, e. in Orange. 12/20/1861, age 18. Died at Richmond 6/22/1862 of typhoid fever (NCT 8, 190).

HOWARD, Thomas W., Co. G, Private (1826–1863). Lived, e. in Orange. 9/2/1861, age 35. Wounded in thigh and captured at Gettysburg 7/1–3/1863. Leg amputated. Died in hospital there 7/19/1863 of wounds (NCT 8, 190).

HOWELL, James, Co. E, Private (1794–). B., lived, and e. in Montgomery 8/1/1861, at age 67. Dis. 12/18/1862 due to "Bronchitis and chronic diarrhoea" (NCT 8, 168).

HOWELL, James M., Co. D, Private (1842–). Lived, e. in Stanly 3/1/1862, age 20. Hospitalized in Richmond 6/30/1862 with two fingers amputated. Company records state he was captured 7/3/1863, not substantiated by Federal provost marshal records (NCT 8, 157).

HOWELL, John A., Co. K, Private (1839–1862). Lived and e. in Stanly 9/7/1861, age 22. Died at Wilmington 1/1/1862, cause not reported (NCT 8, 225).

HOWELL, John T., Co. K, Private (1839–1863). Lived and e. in Stanly 9/7/1861, age 22. Wounded in pelvis and captured at Gettysburg 7/3/1863. Died in Chester hospital 7/28/1863 of "exhaustion" (NCT 8, 225).

HUDSON, Henry H., Co. E, Private (1841–1862). Lived, e. in Montgomery 8/1/1861, age 20. Died in Richmond hospital 10/25/1862 from disease (NCT 8, 168).

HUDSON, John D., Co. E, Private (1843–). Lived, e. in Montgomery 3/1/1862. Captured at Burkeville, VA 4/3/1865; confined at Pt. Lookout until released 6/27/1865 after OOA. NC pension records indicate he was wounded 7/20/1862 (NCT 8, 168).

HUDSON, Martin C., Co. A, Private. E. in Surry 3/18/1862. Present through February 1865; absent much of the time due to illness. 1870 Surry census lists him as a shoemaker, with wife, Mary, age 18. She later applied for a widow's pension (NCT 8, 119; SCS 96).

HUDSPETH, Dirit D., Co. I, Private (1819–1861). Lived in Yadkin where he e. 8/13/1861, age 42. Died at Wilmington abt 10/31/1861 of "fever" (NCT 8, 213).

HUDSPETH, James, Co. I, Private (1837–1862). Lived, e. in Yadkin 8/13/1861. Captured at Hanover CH 5/27/1862; confined at Ft. Monroe, then Ft. Columbus. Paroled, trans to Aiken's Landing for exchange 8/5/1862. Died at home 9/6/1862 of disease (NCT 8, 213).

HUDSPETH, L.C., Co. I, Private (1840–1863). Lived in Yadkin, e. there 3/8/1862, age 22. Died in Richmond hospital abt 1/5/1863 of typhoid fever (NCT 8, 213).

HUFFMAN, Daniel W., Co. C, Private (1843–). Lived, e. in Catawba 8/13/1861, age 18. Wounded in chest at 2nd Manassas 8/27–30/1862. Captured at Spotsylvania 5/12/1864; confined at Pt. Lookout. Trans to Elmira 8/10/1864; released 6/19/1865 after OOA (NCT 8, 146).

HUFFMAN, Elijah, Co. C, Private (1834–1862). Lived, e. in Catawba 3/15/1862, age 28. Captured at Hanover CH 5/27/1862; confined at Ft. Monroe, then Ft. Columbus. Trans to Aiken's Landing for exchange 8/5/1862. Died at home 12/10/1862 of disease (NCT 8, 146).

HUFFMAN, Elijah J., Co. C, Private (18__–1863). Lived, e. in Catawba 3/15/1862. Captured at Hanover CH 5/27/1862; confined at Ft. Monroe, then Ft. Columbus. Trans to Aiken's Landing, exc 8/5/1862. Died at Camp Gregg 6/6/1863 of typhoid pneumonia (NCT 8, 146).

HUFFMAN, George F., Co. C, Private. Lived, e. in Catawba 8/24/1864. Hospitalized at Farmville 4/9/1865 with a gunshot wound. Died in hospital 4/25/1864 of wounds (NCT 8, 146).

HUFFMAN, Jeremiah, Co. C, Private (1835–1863). Lived, e. in Catawba 8/13/1861, age 26. Wounded in the hip at Gaines' Mill 6/27/1862. "Left at Gettysburg, sick" 7/3/1863, and was captured. Died in Gettysburg hospital on 10/20/1863 of "febris typhoides" (NCT 8, 146).

HUFFMAN, John F., Co. C, Private (1841–1862). Catawba resident, e. 8/13/1861, age 20. Wounded severely at Gaines' Mill 6/27/1862, and believed to have died (NCT 8, 146).

HUFFMAN, Levi L, Co. C, Private (1839–). Catawba farmer, e. 8/13/1861, age 22. Captured at Winchester abt 12/2/1862. Confined at Camp Chase, OH 3/4/1863. Paroled and trans to City Pt. on 4/1/1863 for exchange. Wounded in shoulder in Virginia May 1864. Captured in a Richmond Hospital on 4/3/1864; trans to Newport News 4/23/1865. Released there 6/30/1865 after OOA (NCT 8, 146).

HUFFMAN, Marcus J., Co. C, Private (1844–1862). Catawba resident, e. 3/15/1862, age 18. Captured at Hanover CH on 5/27/1862; confined at Ft. Monroe, then Ft. Columbus. Died in hospital there on 7/1–2/1862 of "febris typhoides" (NCT 8, 146).

HUFFMAN, Nelson C., Co. D, Private. Lived in Catawba, e. at Camp Stokes 10/28/1864. Captured near Petersburg 4/2/1865; confined at Pt. Lookout until released 6/27/1865 after OOA (NCT 8, 157).

HUFFSTETLER, Ephriam M., Co. B, Private (1836–). Gaston resident, e. on 8/6/1861, age 25. Present through war; surrendered at Appomattox CH 4/9/1865 (NCT 8, 132).

HUFFSTETLER, Joshua, Co. B, Private (1831–1864). B. in Gaston, e. there on 3/29/1862, age 31. Captured at Hanover CH on 5/27/1862; confined at Ft. Monroe, then Ft. Columbus. Paroled and sent to Aiken's Landing for exchange on 8/5/1862. Wounded and captured at Gettysburg 7/1–4/1863. Hospitalized at Davids Island 7/17–24/1863, paroled and trans to City Pt. for exchange 9/27/1863. Killed near Petersburg, 6/23/1864 (NCT 8, 132).

HUFFSTETLER, William A., Co. B, Private (1840–1862). Lived, e. in Gaston 3/29/1862, at age 22. Captured at Hanover CH 5/27/1862. Confined at Ft. Monroe, then Ft. Columbus, until paroled and sent to Aiken's Landing for exchange on 8/5/1862. Killed at Fredericksburg, 12/13/1862 (NCT 8, 132).

HUGHES, A.J., Co. H, Private (1841–). Lived, e. in Cleveland 3/17/1862, age 21. No further information (NCT 8, 202).

HUGHES, Berry E., Co. H, Corporal (1841–1863). Lived, e. in Cleveland 8/22/1861, age 20, as a private. Promoted to corporal Nov. 1862–July 1863. Captured at Gettysburg 7/3–4/1863; confined at Ft. Delaware where he died 9/25/1863 (NCT 8, 202).

HUGHES, James E., Co. H, Private (1844–). Lived, e. in Cleveland 12/20/1862, age 18. Wounded in right hand at Chancellorsville 5/1–3/1863. Captured at Spotsylvania CH 5/12/1864; confined at Pt. Lookout, trans to Elmira 7/25/1864. Released 6/27/1865 after OOA (NCT 8, 202).

HULIN, Newton A., Co. D, Private (1841–1863. Stanly resident, e. 7/29/1861, age 20. Captured at Hanover CH 5/27/1862; confined at Ft. Monroe, then Ft. Columbus until paroled and sent to Aiken's Landing for exchange on 8/5/1862. Wounded at Chancellorsville 5/1–4/1863; hospitalized at Richmond, and died 6/5/1863 of a gunshot wound, "a dutiful soldier" (NCT 8, 157).

HULIN, Thomas B., Co. D, Sergeant (1839–1862). Lived, e. in Stanly 7/29/1861, age 22. Mustered in as private, promoted to corporal March–Apr.. 1862. Promoted to sergeant 7/27/1862. Wounded in the abdomen at Fredericksburg 12/13/1862, died in Richmond hospital 12/18/1862 of his wounds (NCT 8, 157).

HUMPHRIES, Perry G., Co. H, Private (1832–). Lived, e. in Cleveland 8/22/1861, age 29. Wounded at Chancellorsville 5/2–3/1863. Hospitalized in Richmond 11/29/1863, reason unspecified. May have served late in Co. C, 15th NCT (NCT 8, 202).

HUNEYCUTT, Henry, Co. D, Private (1837–). Lived, e. in Stanly 7/29/161, age 24. Captured at Hanover CH 5/27/ 1862; confined at Ft. Monroe, then Ft. Columbus. Paroled and trans to Aiken's Landing for exchange 8/5/1862. Wounded in the head and captured at Gettysburg 7/3/1863. Confined at Ft. Delaware, then trans to Pt. Lookout 10/15–18/1863. Paroled at Pt. Lookout; sent to Cox's Wharf for exchange on 2/14–15/1865 (NCT 8, 157).

HUNEYCUTT, John W., Co. D, Private (1835–1863). Lived, e. in Stanly 7/29/1861, age 26. Killed at Chancellorsville 5/3/1863 (NCT 8, 158).

HUNEYCUTT, Joseph, Co. D, Private? NC pension records indicate he served in this company (NCT 8, 158).

HUNEYCUTT, Lindsey L., Co. D, Private (1840–). B., lived, e. in Union, 7/29/1861, age 21. Captured at Hanover CH 5/27/1862; confined at Ft. Monroe, then Ft. Columbus. Trans to Aiken's Landing for exchange on 8/5/1862. Deserted 7/1/1863. Returned. Captured 5/6/1864 at Wilderness. Confined at Pt. Lookout until released 6/25/1864, after joining the U.S. Army. Assigned to Co. C, 1st Reg U.S. Volunteer Infantry (NCT 8, 158).

HUNEYCUTT, Solomon, Co. C, Private (1826–). Lived and e. in Catawba 3/15/1862, age 26. Captured at Hanover CH 5/27/1862; confined at Ft. Monroe, then Ft. Columbus. Trans to Aiken's Landing for exchange on 8/5/1862. Wounded at Chancellorsville abt 5/2/1863. On detail at Richmond Sept.1864–Feb. 1865 due to disability. Surrendered at Appomattox CH 4/9/1865 (NCT 8, 146).

HUNSUCKER, George Henderson, Co. E, Private (1834/35–). Lived and e. in Montgomery 3/4/1862 (or 3/4/1863), age 28. Wounded at Gettysburg 7/1–3/1863. Captured at Williamsport, MD; paroled and trans to City Pt. 8/17/1863 for exchange. On light duty as hospital nurse 7/1/1864–9/30/1864. Rejoined company 10/9/1864. Present through Feb. 1865 (NCT 8, 168–169).

HUNSUCKER, John A., Co. E, Private (1838–1863). Lived, e. in Montgomery 8/1/1861, age 23. Killed at Chancellorsville 5/3/1863 (NCT 8, 169).

HUNT, Richard, Co. F, Private (1833–). E. in Yadkin 6/18/1861, age 28. Deserted 65/1863. Returned to duty. Captured at Wilderness 5/6/1864; confined at Pt. Lookout, then Elmira on 8/10/1864. Released 5/19/1865 after OOA (NCT 8, 179).

HUNTER, Anderson, Co. G, Private (1839–). B, lived, e. in Orange 9/2/1861, age 22. Dis. 12/14/1861 due to "general debility" from "anemia." May later have served in Co. G, 11th Reg NCT (NCT 8, 190).

HUNTER, Richard, Co. G, Private (1827–1862). Lived, e. in Orange 3/5/1862, age 35. Wounded at Hanover CH 5/29/1862 and "left on the field." Died of wounds (NCT 8, 190).

HURLEY, Elias, Co. E, 2nd Lieutenant (1834–). Montgomery resident, e. 8/1/1861, age 27 as a sergeant. Promoted to 1st sergeant 11/9/1861. Rank reduced March–Apr. 1862; elected 2nd lieutenant 11/1/1862. Wounded at Gettysburg 7/1–3/1863. Captured at Wilderness abt 5/6/1864; confined at Ft. Delaware. Trans to Pt. Lookout 10/6/1864; trans to Washington, DC 11/2/1864, then back to Ft. Delaware 12/16/1864. Paroled there and sent to City Pt. 2/27/1865 for exchange (NCT 8, 164).

HURT, Mason A., Co. E, Private (1836–). B., lived, e. in Montgomery 8/1/1861, age 25. Wounded at Chancellorsville 5/2–3/1863. Present through 2/20/1865, when furloughed for 18 days. Paroled at Troy, NC 5/23/1865 (NCT 8, 169).

HUTCHENS, Columbus V., Co. I, Private (1840–). Lived, e. in Yadkin 8/13/1861, age 21. Captured at New Bern 3/14/1862; confined at Ft. Columbus. Paroled, trans to Aiken's Landing for exchange 8/5/1862. Present through Feb. 1863 (NCT 8, 213).

HUTCHENS, Isaac, Co. I, Private (1844–). Lived, e. in Yadkin 3/8/1862, age 18, as a substitute. Present until he surrendered at Appomattox CH 4/9/1865 (NCT 8, 213).

HUTCHENS, Vestol C., Co. I, Private. E. in Yadkin 9/7/1861. Present through Dec. 1861 (NCT 8, 213).

HUTCHINGS (Hutchins/Hutchens), C.B., Co. B, Private. Lived in Yadkin (date and of enlistment unknown). Deserted to the enemy; confined at Louisville, KY, until he took the OOA on 8/9/1864, and released on 8/16/1864 (NCT 8, 132).

HUTCHINS, Richard H., Co. F, Private (1841–). Lived, e. in Yadkin. 6/18/1861, age 20. Absent-wounded Nov.–Dec. 1862. Captured near Gettysburg 7/1–5/1863; confined at Davids Island. Paroled and trans to City Pt. 8/28/1863 for exchange. Absent on detail Sept. 1864–Feb. 1865. Surrendered at Appomattox CH 4/9/1865 (NCT 8, 179).

HUTCHENS, Samuel G., Co. F, Private (1843–). Yadkin resident, e. 6/18/1861, age 18. Furloughed for 20 days 12/7/1862, and did not return (NCT 8, 179).

HUTCHENS, William D., Co. F, Private. B. in Yadkin, e. 11/5/1863. Wounded in breast near Petersburg 6/22/1864; died there 6/23/1864 from wounds (NCT 8/179),

INGLE, Levi, Co. H, Private (1832–1863). Lived in Lincoln, e. at Camp Holmes, 10/2/1862, age 30. Died in Richmond hospital 6/10/1863 of pneumonia (NCT 8, 202).

INGRAM, Andrew, Co. K, Private. E. in Davidson 11/20/1863. Died in Lynchburg hospital 6/1/1864 of "abscessus chron[ic]" (NCT 8, 225).

INGRAM, William B., Co. E, Private. Enlisted at Camp Stokes 11/5/1864. Surrendered at Appomattox CH 4/9/1863 (NCT 8, 169).

ISAACS, Godfrey L., Co. A, Private (1832–1912). E. initially in 1862 and was sent to Camp Holmes for instruction; dis. due to rheumatism. On 10/13/1863, he was conscripted or tried to enlist but was again discharged. E. again at Dobson, Surry, on 11/1/1864. Wounded at Petersburg. Present at the surrender at Appomattox CH 4/9/1865. B. in Surry to Samuel and Nancy Snow Isaacs of the Zephyr community, Godfrey m. in 1854 Pherebee Wiley, and had four children (NCT 8, 119; SCS 98).

ISAACS, N.J., Co. A, Private (1845–). Son of Samuel and Nancy Snow Isaacs, and the brother to Godfrey L. Isaacs. No further information except that he applied for a pension (NCT 8, 119; SCS 98).

JAMES, William C., Co. D, Private. E. at Camp Stokes 10/31/1864. Surrendered at Appomattox CH 4/9/1865 (NCT 8, 158).

JARVIS, Luckett C., Co. I, Private (1837–1863). Lived, e. in Yadkin 3/8/1862, age 25. Captured at Hanover CH 5/27/1862; confined at Ft. Monroe, then Ft. Columbus. Paroled and trans to Aiken's Landing for exchange 8/5/1862. Died in Richmond hospital 6/24/1863 of "febris typhoides." He was the son of Bryant and Peggy Danner Jarvis (NCT 8, 213, CWY 230).

JARVIS, Willie L., Co. I, Private. (1836–). Lived, e. in Yadkin 8/13/1861 as corporal. Rank reduced Nov.–Dec. 1861. Captured at New Bern 3/14/1862; confined at Ft. Columbus. Paroled and trans to Aiken's Landing for exchange on 8/5/1862. Captured near Petersburg 4/2/1865; confined at Ft. Delaware until released 6/19/1865 after OOA (NCT 8, 213).

JAYNES— See JOYNER

JEFFERSON, Zachariah M., Co. I, Private; Co. H, 54th Private (1829–1913). Previously served in Co. H, 54th Reg NCT 8/29/1862. Wounded near Fredericksburg 12/13/1862. Wounded again in finger near Fredericksburg 5/24/1862. Hospitalized at Danville. Deserted 5/25/1863. Trans to Co. I on 10/30/1863. Paroled at Lynchburg 4/15/1865. Bur. Boonville Bapt. Ch. Cem., Boonville, NC (NCT 8, 213; CWY 230).

JENKINS, Andrew Jackson, Co. B, Corporal (1835–). Gaston resident, e. on 7/30/1861, at age 26, as a corporal, but was reduced in rank on 2/28/1862. Captured at Hanover CH 5/27/1862, confined at Ft.

Monroe, then at Ft. Columbus. Paroled and sent to Aiken's Landing for exchange on 8/5/1862. Returned to duty. Detailed as the brigade blacksmith through Feb. 1865. Surrendered at Appomattox CH 4/9/1865 (NCT 8, 132).

JENKINS, Caleb A., Co. B, Private (1843–1861). E. in Gaston on 9/17/1861, at age 18. He died 12/31/1861 (NCT 8, 132).

JENKINS, E.W., Co. B, Private (1837–1862). Lived in Gaston, e. on 7/30/1861, age 24. Died at Wilmington 1/4/1862 (NCT 8, 132).

JENKINS, George W., Co. B, Private (1839–1862). Lived, e. in Gaston 7/30/1861, at age 22. Died at Richmond abt 8/8/1862 (NCT 8, 132).

JENKINS, Linzay G., Co. H, Private (1806–). B. in Chester District, SC, lived, e. in Cleveland 3/17/1862, age 54. Dis. 6/19/1862 due to "advanced age" and physical inability "to do duty" (NCT 8, 202).

JENKINS, Lodewick, Co. I, Private (1803–). B. in Surry, lived, e. in Yadkin 8/13/1861, age 58. Dis. 3/15/1863. Discharge certificate gave age as 60 (NCT 8, 213).

JENKINS, Robert M., Co. I, Private (1840–). Lived, e. in Yadkin 3/8/1862. Wounded at Chancellorsville 5/2–3/1863. Trans to Co. H, 9th Reg NC State Troops (1st Reg NC Cavalry) 10/31/1863. May have served previously in Co. D, 21st Reg NCT (NCT 8, 214). JENKINS, Rufus M., Co. B, Private (1837–). Lived and e. in Gaston 7/30/1861, age 24. Captured at Fredericksburg on 12/13/1862, and paroled abt 12/17/1862. Captured at Gettysburg 7/3/1863. Confined at Ft. Delaware, trans to Pt. Lookout on 10/15–18/1863. Paroled and trans to Cox's Wharf 2/14–15/1865 for exchange (NCT 8, 132).

JENNINGS, David H., Co. I, Private (1840–). Lived, e. in Yadkin 9/3/1861, age 21. Wounded at Frayser's Farm 6/30/1862. AWOL Jan.–Feb. 1863 (NCT 8, 214).

JENNINGS, John W., Co. I, Private (1844–1863). Lived, e. in Yadkin 3/8/1862. Wounded in leg at Chancellorsville 5/2–3/1863. Hospitalized at Richmond where he died 11/24/1863 of wounds (NCT 8, 214).

JENNINGS, S.W., Co. I, Private (1832–1862). Lived, e. in Yadkin 3/8/1862, age 30. Captured at Hanover CH 5/27/1862; confined at Ft. Monroe, then Ft. Columbus. Died at Davids Island 6/28–30/1862 of "fever" (NCT 8, 214).

JERRELL (Jarrell), Rufus A., Co. A, Private (1840–). Surry farmer e. 3/18/1862, age 22, son of Fontain and Fannie Jarrell of Ivy Green near Round Peak. Wounded in left leg at Ox Hill, on 9/1/1862. Absent-wounded through Oct. 1862. Listed as a deserter Jan.–Feb. 1863. Wounded in the left eye and/or both arms at Jericho Mills abt 5/23/1864. Deserted to the enemy abt 2/24/1865; confined at Washington, DC, until released abt 2/27/1865 after OOA. He m. in Surry in 1868 Susan Sandifer. (NCT 8, 119; SCS 99–100).

JOBE, John T., Co. F, Private (1836–). Lived in Alamance, e. at Camp Gregg, age 27, 2/18/1863. Deserted before 11/1/1864 (NCT 8, 179).

JOHN, James P., Co. I, Private. (18__–1862). Date and place of enlistment not reported. Captured at Hanover CH 5/27/1862. Exc at Aiken's Landing 8/5/

1862. Died in Richmond 12/7/1862 of pneumonia (NCT 8, 214).

JOHNSON, James P., Co. G, Private (1831–). Lived, e. in Orange e. 1/1/1862, age 21. Present until he surrendered at Appomattox CH 4/9/1865 (NCT 8, 190).

JOHNSON, Lewis W., Co. I, Corporal (1840–). Lived, e. in Yadkin 8/13/1861, age 21, as corporal. Reduced in rank Jan.–Oct. 1862. Captured at New Bern 3/14/1862; confined at Ft. Columbus. Paroled and trans to Aiken's Landing for exchange 8/5/1862. Returned Jan.–Feb. 1863 after being AWOL for 4 months. Promoted to corporal Mar. 1863–Oct. 1864. Wounded at Gettysburg 7/1–3/1863. Hospitalized at Richmond 5/18/1864 with gunshot wound. Absent-sick Sept. 1864–Feb. 1865. Captured in Richmond hospital 4/3/1865, paroled 4/24/1865 (NCT 8, 214).

JOHNSON, Thomas, Co. A, Private (1825–1863). Surry shoemaker, e., age 35, on 3/18/1862. Dis. 4/4/1863 due to "phthisis pulmonalis." Hospitalized in Richmond and died 4/25/1863 from that disease and/or "smallpox" (NCT 8, 119; SCS 103).

JOHNSON, Thomas, Co. E, Private (1824–). Lived, e. in Montgomery 8/1/1861, age 37. Captured in Richmond hospital 4/3/1865; confined at Newport News until released 6/15/1865 after OOA (NCT 8, 169).

JOHNSTON, Gabriel P., Co. G, Private; Field & Staff, Ordnance Sergeant (1842–) E. in Co. G, 28th Reg in Orange where he lived on 9/2/1861, age 19. Promoted to Ordnance Sergeant on 12/9/1861, and trans to Field & Staff of the 28th. Present until June 1864, when he was absent-sick through Feb.1865 (NCT 8, 112, 190).

JOHNSTON, George Burgwyn, Co. G, Captain; Lane's Brigade, Assistant Adjutant General. Previously served as private, Co. D, 1st Reg NCT. Appointed 1st lieutenant of Co. G 9/2/1861; promoted to captain 5/1/1862. Captured at Hanover CH 5/27/1862; confined at Ft. Monroe, then Ft. Columbus. Trans to Johnson's Island on 6/21/1862, to Vicksburg 9/20/1862, Exc at Aiken's Landing 11/10/1862. Appointed AAG of Lane's Brigade 1/19/1863 and trans (NCT 8, 184–185).

JOLLEY, Benjamin A., Co. H, Private (1831–1862). Lived, e. in Cleveland 8/22/1861. Died in Lynchburg hospital 5/26/1862 of "camp fever" (NCT 8, 202).

JOLLEY, Clingman C., Co. H, Private (1842–1862). Lived in Rutherford, e. in Cleveland 8/22/1861, age 19. Captured at Hanover CH 5/27/1862; confined at Ft. Monroe, then Ft. Columbus. Paroled and trans for exchange Died 8/4/1862 "on a steamboat coming up James River to Richmond" (NCT 8, 202–20).

JOLLEY, James P., Co. H, Private (1828–1862). Lived, e. in Cleveland 3/17/1862, age 34. Wounded near Shepherdstown abt 9/20/1862. Died at Winchester 9/30/18962 of wounds and/or disease (NCT 8, 203).

JOLLEY, Jesse L., Co. H, 1st Sergeant (1833–1863). Lived, e. in Cleveland 8/22/1861, age 28, as a private. Promoted to 1st sergeant 11/14/1862. Killed at Chancellorsville 5/3/1863 (NCT 8, 203).

JOLLEY, Leander O., Co. H, Private (1827–). B. in Cleveland, lived in Rutherford where he farmed before he e. in Cleveland 8/22/1861, age 34. Dis. 12/7/1861 due to "deformity in one of his feet" (NCT 8, 203).

JOLLEY, Meredith M., Co. H, Sergeant (1844–). Lived in Rutherford, e. in Cleveland 3/10/1862, age 18, as private. Promoted to corporal May 1862. Wounded at Gettysburg 7/1–3/1863. Promoted to sergeant Aug. 1863–Oct. 1864. Surrendered at Appomattox CH 4/9/1865 (NCT 8, 203).

JOLLEY, William A., Co. H, Private (1824–1862). Lived, e. in Cleveland 8/22/1861, age 34. Killed at Ox Hill 9/1/1862 (NCT 8, 203).

JONES, Robert, Co. H, Private (1844–1862). Lived, e. in Cleveland 8/22/1861, age 17. Died in Raleigh, NC hospital 9/1/1862 of typhoid fever (NCT 8, 203).

JONES, William J., Co. H, Private (1842–). Lived, e. in Cleveland 3/17/1862, age 20. Present through Feb. 1865 (NCT 8, 203).

JOYCE, Abner R., Co. I, Private (1842–). Lived in Yadkin, e. 10/8/1861 in New Hanover, age 19. Wounded at Chancellorsville 5/3/1863. Wounded at Gettysburg 7/2/1863. Present Sept. 1864–Feb. 1865. Surrendered at Appomattox CH 4/9/1865 (NCT 8, 214).

JOYCE, Robert H., Co. I, Private; Co. B, 38th Reg, 1st Sergeant (1836–1864). Lived, e. Yadkin 9/3/1861, age 25. Captured at Hanover CH abt 5/27/1862; confined at Ft. Columbus. Exc.. Trans to Co. B, 38th Reg NCT 3/25/1863. After trans, promoted to sergeant 10/4/1863, and 1st sergeant 4/7/1864. Killed near Petersburg 6/22/1864 (NCT 8, 214; 10, 26).

JOYNER (Jaynes?), Abraham, Co. I, Private. E. at Camp Holmes 10/14/1863. AWOL Dec 1864 (NCT 8, 214).

JOYNER, David W., Co. F, Corporal (1828–). Lived, e. in Yadkin 6/18/1861, age 23 as a private. Captured at Hanover CH 5/27/1862; confined at Ft. Monroe, then Ft. Columbus. Paroled and trans to Aiken's Landing for exchange 8/5/1862. Promoted to corporal Jan. 1863–Oct. 1864. Captured near Petersburg 4/2/1865; confined at Pt. Lookout until released 6/28/1865 after OOA (NCT 8, 179).

JOYNER, John S., Co. F, Private (1843–1862). Lived, e. in Yadkin 6/18/1861. Died in Richmond hospital 8/6/1862 of typhoid fever (NCT 8, 179).

JOYNER, John T., Co. F, Private (1845–). B., lived, e. in Yadkin 4/23/1862, age 17, as a substitute. Dis. 7/24/1862 due to lung disease (NCT 8, 179).

JOYNER, Timothy, Co. F, Private (1843–1862). Lived, e. in Yadkin 6/18/1861, age 18. Wounded at Ox Hill 9/1/1862; died "at home" abt.6/13/1863 of wounds (NCT 8, 179).

KAYLER, Alfred A., Co. C, Private (1846–). E. in Catawba on 2/12/1864. Wounded in the chin at Jericho Mills 5/23/1864. Retired to Invalid Corps on 12/28/1864 due to disability. Detailed for hospital duty at Danville 1/2/1865 (NCT 8, 146).

KAYLER, George E., Co. C, Sergeant (18__–1863). Catawba resident, e. 8/13/1861 as a corporal. Promoted to sergeant 9/1/1862. Died at Jordan Springs near Winchester abt 7/19/1862, "a gallant soldier" (NCT 8, 146–147).

KELLY, John C., Co. F, Ordnance Sergeant; Field & Staff, Quartermaster Sergeant (1817–). Yadkin school teacher, e. there May 1861, age 44, as ordnance sergeant, promoted to quartermaster sergeant abt 10/9/

1861; trans to Field & Staff. Dis. 6/10/1862 due to "pre-disposition to disease of the lungs, and debility." He m. Sarah A. Baker, lived in East Bend, son of William D. and Elizabeth Creson Kelly. (NCT 8, 112, 179, CWY 234, HYC 451).

KELLY, William D., Co. F, Corporal (1841–1864). B., lived, e. in Yadkin 6/18/1861, age 20, as corporal. Rank reduced Jan.–June 1862. Wounded, captured at Gettysburg 7/3/1863; confined at Ft. Delaware; then Pt. Lookout 10/15–18/1864; died there 3/10/1864 (NCT 8, 179).

KENDALL, William D., Co. K, Private (1829–1864). B., lived and e. in Stanly 9/7/1861, age 32. Killed at Reams' Station 8/25/1864 (NCT 8, 225).

KENNEDY, F. Milton, Field & Staff, Chaplain. B. in South Carolina, lived, e. in Mecklenburg, age 28. Appointed chaplain on 12/6/1862. Trans to Charlotte to become Hospital Chaplain 4/6/1864 (NCT 8, 111).

KENNEDY, John, Co. G, Private (1840–). Lived, e. in Orange 9/2/1861. Present through Feb. 1865 (NCT 8, 190).

KENNEDY, William G., Co. D, Private. E. at Camp Stokes 10/31/1864. Present through Feb. 1865 (NCT 8, 158).

KENT, John, Co. C, 1st Lieutenant (18__–1862). Catawba resident, e. at Camp Fisher 9/9/1861 as a private. Promoted to sergeant 10/17/1861. Elected 2nd lieutenant 2/27/1862, and promoted to 1st lieutenant 4/14/1862. Died at Brook Church near Richmond 7/14/1862 of fever (NCT 8, 139–140).

KENYON— see KINYON

KESTER, Moses M., Co. E, Private. E. in Wake 10/16/1863. Died in Richmond hospital 2/19/1864 of typhoid fever (NCT 8, 169).

KEY, Andrew Jackson, Co. A, Private (1837–). Son of John Andrew and Eleanor Payne Key, Hotel (Elkin) District, of Surry, he e. in Surry, age 17, 10/12/1864. Present at the surrender at Appomattox CH 4/9/1865. Bur. Beulah Methodist Ch. Cemetery (NCT 8, 119; SCS 105).

KEY, James Ransome, Co. A, Private (1836–1862). Surry resident e. 3/18/1862, age 26. Killed at Hanover CH 5/27/1862. Andrew Jackson Key was his brother (NCT 8, 119; SCS 106).

KEY, John A. Key, Co. A, Private (1827–) . Son of Milburn and Elizabeth Mankins Key, Dobson District, Surry, e. on 5/4/1861, age 36. Captured at Petersburg on 4/2/1865, and confined at Ft. Delaware. Released 6/19/1865 after OOA (NCT 8, 119; SCS 107).

KEY, Martin V., Co. A, Corporal (1843–1862). Lived, e. age 18, in Surry 5/4/1861. Promoted to corporal May of 1862. Killed at Hanover CH 5/27/1862. His brother James Ransome killed the same day, same battle (NCT 8, 119; SCS 108).

KEY, Samuel C., Co. A, Private (1837–). Lived, e. in Surry, age 24, 5/4/1861. AWOL abt 2/7/1865. Son of John and Eleanor Key of the Marsh District. Applied for a pension (NCT 8, 119; SCS 108).

KILLIAN, Anthony, Co. H, Private (1828–). B. in Columbus, e. at Camp Vance 9/23/1863. Present through Feb. 1865 (NCT 8, 203).

KILLIAN, Calvin M., Co. C, Private (18__–1862).

Lived, e. in Catawba 8/13/1861. Wounded at Frayser's Farm 6/30/1862. Died 7/1/1862 of wounds (NCT 8, 147).

KILLIAN, Casper E., Co. C Private. E. in Catawba on 2/9/1864. Surrendered at Appomattox CH 4/9/1865 (NCT 8, 147).

KILLIAN, Elijah, Co. C, Private. Catawba blacksmith, e. 8/13/1861. Captured at Gettysburg 7/1–4/1863; confined at Davids Island, trans to City Pt. 9/8/1863 for exchange. Paroled at Lynchburg 4/13/1865 (NCT 8, 147).

KILLIAN, Joseph E., Co. C, Private (1844–1864). B., lived in Catawba, e. 3/15/1862, age 18. Captured at Hanover CH 5/27/1862; confined at Ft. Monroe, then Ft. Columbus. Paroled and trans to Aiken's Landing for exchange 8/5/1862. Wounded at Gettysburg, 7/1–3/1863. Killed at Reams' Station 8/25/1864 (NCT 8, 147).

KIMBALL, William W., Co. D, Private. E. at Camp Stokes 10/31/1864. Hospitalized in Richmond abt 4/2/1865 with unspecified wound. Captured in the hospital 4/3/1865 paroled 4/26/1865 (NCT 8, 158).

KIMERY, Leonard A., Co. K, Private (1832–1862). Lived and e. in Stanly 3/27/1862, age 30. Died in Richmond 7/8/1862 of disease (NCT 8, 225).

KINCAID, David, Co. C, 1st Sergeant. Lived in Lincoln before enlisting at Camp Fisher on 8/26/1861. Promoted to corporal 2/27/1862; promoted to 1st sergeant 4/14/1862. Wounded at Ox Hill 9/1/1862. Wounded at Chancellorsville 5/1–3/1863. Wounded and captured at Gettysburg 7/1–2/1863. Hospitalized at Gettysburg, then at Chester on 7/17/1863. Paroled ans trans to City Pt. on 9/23/1863 for exchange(NCT 8, 147).

KINCAID, James, Co. C, 2nd Lieutenant (18__ –1862). Lincoln resident, e. at Camp Fisher 8/26/1861 as a sergeant. Promoted to 1st sergeant 2/27/1862; appointed 3rd lieutenant 4/14/1862 and 2nd lieutenant abt 7/14/1862. Died at home 12/7/1862 of disease — "a gallant officer" (NCT 8, 140).

KING, Hiram D., Co. E, Private. Lived in Henderson County. Deserted to the enemy abt 3/20/1864. Confined at Knoxville, TN until released abt 10/7/1864 after OOA (NCT 8, 169).

KING, William Duncan, Co. G, Private (1841–). Lived., e. in Orange 9/2/1861, age 20. Captured at Hanover CH 5/27/1862; confined at Ft. Monroe, then Ft. Columbus. Paroled and trans to Aiken's Landing for exchange on 8/5/1862. Dis. 9/21/1862 due to "rigidity of muscles of arm" (NCT 8, 190).

KINYON (KENYON), John Hendricks, Co. F, Captain (1828–1903). A physician, he lived, e. in Yadkin 8/18/1861, age 33, and appointed captain. Resigned 3/28/1862 in order to take a medical position. Appointed Assistant Surgeon of the 66th Reg NCT (NCT 8, 174). After the war, Dr. Kinyoun moved to Missouri (see Joseph Kinyoun Houts, Jr., *A Darkness Ablaze*, 2005).

KIRK, George E., Co. K, Private (1843–1863). Lived and e. in Stanly 9/7/1861. Reported missing and "supposed to have been killed" at Gettysburg 7/3/1863 (NCT 8, 225).

KIRK, James M., Co. F, Private (1842–). Lived, e. in Yadkin 6/18/1861. Captured near Petersburg 4/2/1865; confined at Pt. Lookout until released 6/28/1865 after OOA (NCT 8, 179).

KIRK, John P., Co. F, Private (18___–1864). Lived, e. in Yadkin e. 11/5/1863. Killed at Wilderness 5/5/1864 (NCT 8, 179).

KIRK, John S., Co. D, 1st Sergeant (1823–). B. and lived in Stanly, a carpenter, e. 7/29/1861, age 38, as 1st sergeant. Wounded in elbow near Frayser's Farm abt 6/30/1862. Dis. 2/23/1863 due to disability from wounds (NCT 8, 158).

KIRK, Lewis D. H., Co. K, Private (1842–1862). Lived and e. in Stanly 4/3/1862, age 20. Died in Danville hospital 7/25/1864 of "phthisis pulmonalis" (NCT 8, 225).

KIRK, Parham, Co. K, Private. Lived and e. in Stanley 10/31/1864. Captured near Petersburg 4/2/1865; confined at Pt. Lookout until released 6/28/1865 after OOA. May have served previously on Co. I, 52nd Reg NCT (NCT 8, 225).

KIRK, Thomas F., Co. D, Private (1843–). Lived, e. in Stanly resident 7/29/1861, age 18. Captured at Hanover CH 5/27/1862; confined at Ft. Monroe, then Ft. Columbus. Paroled and trans to Aiken's Landing for exchange 8/5/1862. Wounded at Chancellorsville 5/2–3/1863. AWOL Nov.–Dec. 1864. Captured near Petersburg 4/2/1865; confined at Pt. Lookout until released 6/28/1865 after OOA (NCT 8, 158).

KIRK, William A., Co. K, Private. E. in Stanly 10/31/1864. Surrendered at Appomattox CH 4/9/1865. May have served previously in Co. I, 52nd Reg NCT (NCT 8, 225).

KIRK, William D., Co. K, Private (1835–). Lived and e. in Stanly 9/7/1861, age 26 as a corpora. Rank reduced Jan.–Apr.. 1862. Captured near Hanover CH 5/27/1862; confined at Ft. Monroe, then Ft. Columbus. Exc. and returned. Wounded in leg at Gettysburg 7/3/1863. Captured near Petersburg 4/2/1865; confined at Pt. Lookout until released 6/28/1863 after OOA (NCT 8, 225–226).

KIRK, William G., Co. K, Private (1821–1863). Lived and e. in Stanly 9/7/1861, age 40. Captured at Hanover CH 5/27/1862; confined at Ft. Monroe, then Ft. Columbus. Trans to Aiken's Landing for exc 8/5/1862. Returned. Died "of sunstroke while on the march" in Virginia 6/18/1863 (NCT 8, 226).

KIRKLAND, Samuel D., Co. G, Private (1842–). Lived, e. in Orange 9/17/1861, age 19. Captured near Hanover CH abt 5/28/1862; confined at Ft. Monroe, then Ft. Columbus. Paroled and trans to Aiken's Landing for exchange 8/5/1862. Absent, on light duty in Richmond hospital Sept. 1864–Feb. 1865 (NCT 8, 190).

KISER, Caleb, Co. B, Private (1843–1862). Lived in Gaston, e. 7/30/1862, age 18. Wounded at Gaines' Mill 6/27/1862. Died "at home" 7/28/1862 of wounds and/or disease (NCT 8, 132).

KISER, Henry, Co. B, Private. A Gaston resident, e. at Liberty Mills on 3/15/1864. Captured near Petersburg 4/2/1865. Confined at Pt. Lookout until released 6/28/1865 after OOA (NCT 8, 132).

KISER, Michael, Co. B, Private (1843–). Lived and e. in Gaston, age 18, on 7/20/1862. Bayoneted in right shoulder and captured at Fredericksburg 12/13/1862, and paroled 12/14/1862. Surrendered at Appomattox CH 4/9/1865 (NCT 8, 132).

KITTLE, Costin, Co. F, Musician (1837–1862?). Lived, e. in Yadkin 6/18/1861, age 24, as a musician (Fifer) but reduced in rank July–Oct.1862. Reported missing in action at Frayser's Farm 6/30/1862 (NCT 8, 179).

KITTLE, Eugene, Co. F, Private (1835–). B., lived, e. in Yadkin 6/18/1861, age 26 as a musician (drummer). Rank reduced Jan.–June 1862. Dis. 6/10/1862 due to "chronic diarrhoea & debility" (NCT 8, 179–180).

KITTLE, Joseph, Co. F, Private (1841–) A carpenter, b., lived, e. in Yadkin 4/5/1862, age 21. Dis. 7/7/1862 due to "chronic disease of the lungs or phthisis pulmonalis" (NCT 8, 180).

LADD, Miles W., Co. I, Private (1842–1861). Lived, e. in Yadkin 8/13/1861, age 19. Died near Hamptonville, NC 9/25/1861 of typhoid fever (NCT 8, 214).

LAEL, Abel, Co. C, Private (1845–) B., lived, e. in Catawba 8/12/1863, age 18. Surrendered at Appomattox CH, 4/9/1865 (NCT 8, 147).

LAEL, Cicero, Co. C, Private (1843–1865). Catawba resident, e. 3/15/1862, age 19. Wounded at Ox Hill 9/1/1862. Wounded and captured at Gravel Hill abt 7/28/1864; confined at Pt. Lookout, then trans to Elmira on 8/8/1864. He died at Elmira 1/4/1865 of "pneumonia" (NCT 8, 147).

LAEL, Polycarp, Co. C, Private (1845–). Catawba resident, e. 3/9/1863, age 18. Wounded in the thigh at Spotsylvania CH 5/12/1864. Trans to Co. H, 28th Reg. 2/1/1865. Surrendered at Appomattox CH 4/9/1865 (NCT 8, 147, 203).

LAFFOON, Nathan D., Co. A, 2nd Lieutenant. Lived, e. in Surry, appointed 2nd lieutenant 5/4/1861. Resigned on 9/6/1861. E. as a private on 9/1/1862 in Co. B, 2nd Battalion, NC Infantry; elected 2nd lieutenant 3/3/1863. Wounded at Gettysburg. Captured at Smithburg, PA 7/4/1863; confined at Ft. Delaware, then Johnson's Island 7/18/1863. Paroled and sent to Ft. Monroe for exchange 9/16/1864. Admitted to Richmond, hospital 9/21/1864. Furloughed 10/5/1864. On 2/25/1865, readmitted to hospital with bronchitis; furloughed for 30 days 3/29/1865 (NCT 3, 279, 8, 113).

LAIL, Sidney, Co. H, Private. Lived in Burke, e. 9/20/1863 at Camp Holmes. Hospitalized in Richmond 5/16/1864 with gunshot wound. Captured near Petersburg 4/2/1865; confined at Ft. Delaware until released 6/19/1865 after OOA (NCT 8, 203).

LAMBERT, C. Wiley, Co. K, Private. Previously served in Co. H, 8th Reg NCT. Trans to Co. K 10/1/1864. Captured near Jones' Farm abt 9/30/1864; confined at Pt. Lookout. Trans to Boulware's Wharf 3/19/1865 for exc (NCT 8, 226).

LANDID, J.F., Co. A, Private. Paroled at Farmville on 4/11–21, 1865 (NCT 8, 119).

LANE, James Henry, Field & Staff, Brigadier General (1833–1907). E. as Lt. Colonel, 1st Reg. N. C. Infantry ("Bethel Reg."); appointed colonel of 28th Reg 9/21/1861. Wounded at Frayser's Farm 6/30/1862 and

Malvern Hill 7/1/1862. Assumed command of Branch's Brigade at Sharpsburg (Antietam). Promoted to Brigadier General 11/1/1862. Surrendered at Appomattox with what remained of his brigade. (NCT 8, 110).

LANE, Thomas B., Field & Staff, Surgeon. Virginia resident, appointed assistant surgeon 6/25/1862, then surgeon. Trans to 18th Reg NCT 3/19/1863 (NCT 8, 111).

LANIER, Alexander, Co. B, Private (1838–). Resident of Gaston, e. 7/30/1861, age 23. Dis. abt 10/16/1861 for "cutting off three of his fingers" (NCT 8, 132).

LASSITER, James A., Co. E, Private (1836–). Lived, e. in Montgomery 8/1/1861, age 25. Present through Feb 1865 (NCT 8, 169).

LATON, Christian Green, Co. K, Private (1826–). Lived and e. in Stanly 10/31/1864, age 38. Captured near Petersburg 4/2/1865; confined at Pt. Lookout until released 6/28/1865 after OOA (NCT 8, 226).

LAWING, William A., Co. B, Private (1830–). Gaston farmer, e. 7/31/1861, age 31. Captured at Fredericksburg 12/13/1862, paroled abt 12/17/1862. Wounded in jaw, captured at Gettysburg 7/1–3/1863. Hospitalized at Gettysburg, then Baltimore abt 9/14/1863. Paroled and sent to City Pt. on 9/27/1863 for exchange. Detailed to hospital duty abt 2/25/1864. Dis. 3/28/1864 due to a "gunshot wound of the face causing the loss of right side of the lower jaw" (NCT 8, 132–133).

LAY, Peter, Co. F, Private (1827–). Lived, e. in Alamance 10/1/1862, age 35. Wounded at Chancellorsville 5//1–4/1863. Absent-sick Sept.–Oct. 1864 and 12/14/1864–Feb. 1865. Paroled at Greensboro, NC 5/11/1865 (NCT 8, 180).

LEACH, Alexander M., Co. E, Private (1840–1862). B., lived, e. in Montgomery 8/1/1861, age 21. Died in a Richmond hospital 12/18/1862 of pneumonia (NCT 8, 169).

LEAGANS, Ananias, Co. I, Private (1820–1890). Lived, e. in Yadkin 3/8/1862, age 41. Captured at Hanover CH 5/27/1862; confined at Ft. Monroe, then Ft. Columbus. Paroled and trans to Aiken's Landing for exchange 8/5/1862. Detailed as a shoemaker at Salisbury Feb. 1863. Absent on detail through Feb. 1865. Bur. Deep Creek Bapt. Ch., Yadkin County, NC (NCT 8, 214, CWY 237).

LEAGANS, James M., Co. I, Private. E. 8/13/1861 in Yadkin; captured at Hanover CH 5/27/1862. Confined at Ft. Monroe, and Ft. Columbus, then trans to Aiken's Landing for exchange 8/5/1862. Wounded in neck and shoulder at Fredericksburg 12/13/1862. AWOL 7/1/1863–1/5/1864. Present Nov. 1864–Feb. 1865 (NCT 8, 214).

LEAGANS, Matthew, Co. I, Private (1842–). Lived, e. in Yadkin. 8/13/1861, age 19. Deserted 7/15/1863 (NCT 8, 214).

LEDBETTER, Anonymous, Co. H, Private (1830–1863). Lived, e. in Cleveland 3/17/1862, age 32. Died at Lynchburg abt 1/27/1863 (NCT 8, 203).

LEDBETTER, John A., Co. E, Private (1819–). Lived, e. in Montgomery 8/1/1862, age 43. Surrendered at Appomattox CH 4/9/1865 (NCT 8, 169).

LEE, Drury B., Co. H, Private (1843–). B., lived in Cleveland, e. 3/17/1862. Dis. 4/23/1863 due to "anchylosis of knee joint" (NCT 8, 203).

LEE, John W., Co. H, Private (1842–1863). B. , lived, e. in Cleveland 3/17/1862. Killed at Gettysburg 7/3/1863 (NCT 8, 203).

LEE, Robert B., Co. K, Private. Lived and e. in Stanly 4/20/1863. Deserted 4/25/1863 (NCT 8, 226).

LEE, Walter E., Co. H, Private (1812–1863). Lived, e. in Cleveland 3/17/1862, age 40. Died in Richmond hospital 6/3/1863 of "pluritis" (NCT 8, 203).

LEE, Watson E., Co. H, Private (1839–1863). B., lived, e. in Cleveland 3/17/1862, age 23. Killed at Gettysburg 7/3/1863 (NCT 8, 203).

LEE, William W., Co. H, Private (1841–). Lived, e. in Cleveland 3/17/1862, age 21. Wounded in abdomen and side at Reams' Station 8/25/1864. Recovered and captured at Petersburg 4/3/1865. Confined at Hart's Island until released 6/20/1865 after OOA (NCT 8, 203).

LEFLER, Charles, Co. D, Corporal (1841–1864). B., e. in Stanly 7/29/1861, age 20, as a private. Promoted to corporal 12/1/1862. Died "at home" 9/4/1864 (NCT 8, 158).

LEFLER, Coleman, Co. D, Sergeant (1835–). Stanly resident, e. 7/29/1861, age 23. Captured at Hanover CH 5/27/1862; confined at Ft. Monroe, then Ft. Columbus. Paroled and trans to Aiken's Landing for exchange 8/5/1862. Promoted to corporal 12/1/1862; promoted to sergeant July 1863–Feb. 1864. Wounded in right leg and captured at Petersburg 3/27/1865. Leg amputated. Hospitalized at Pt. Lookout until released abt 6/28/1865 after taking OOA (NCT 8, 158).

LEFLER, Daniel A., Co. D, Private. Stanly resident, e. 2/1/1865. Captured near Petersburg 4/2/1865; confined at Hart's Island until released abt 6/17/1865 after OOA. Hospitalized at New York City 6/19/1865, and "sent south" on 6/22/1865 (NCT 8, 158).

LEFLER, Martin Alexander, Co. D, Private (1836–1862). Lived, e. in Stanly 7/29/1861, age 25. Died in Richmond hospital 7/26–27/1862 from typhoid fever (NCT 8, 158).

LEFLER, Monroe, Co. D, Private. B. and lived in Stanly, e. at Camp Gregg 3/26/1863. Killed at Wilderness 5/5/1864 (NCT 8, 158).

LEMONS, Archibald, Co. E, Private. E. in Wake 11/17/1864. Deserted Feb. 1865. Surrendered at Appomattox CH 4/9/1865 (NCT 8, 169).

LEMONS, Malcolm, Co. E, Private (1828–). Lived, e. in Montgomery 8/1/1861, age 33. Deserted Feb. 1865. Surrendered at Appomattox CH 4/9/1865 (NCT 8, 169).

LEPER, Franklin W., Co. B, Corporal (1831–). Lived in Gaston, e. 3/14/1862. Captured at Fredericksburg 12/13/1862; paroled on 12/17/1862. Wounded in forearm and captured at Gettysburg 7/1–4/1863. Hospitalized at Gettysburg; trans to Davids Island, 7/17–24/1863. Paroled and trans for exchange on 8/31/1863. Promoted to corporal Sept. 1863–Oct. 1864. Surrendered at Appomattox CH 4/9/1865 (NCT 8, 133).

LEWIS, John J., Co. B, Private (1844–). Lived, e. in Gaston 3/29/1862, at age 18. Surrendered at Appomattox CH 4/9/1865 (NCT 8, 133).

LEWIS, James, Co. C, Private. Paroled at Salisbury, NC 5/2/1865 (NCT 8, 147).

LEWIS, W.F., Co. B, Private (1842–1863). Gaston resident, e. on 7/30/1861, age 19. Wounded in the leg and captured at Gettysburg 7/1–5/1863. Hospitalized at Gettysburg where he died on 7/17/1863 of wounds (NCT 8, 133).

LILLY, Armstead, Co. D, Private (1842–). B. and lived in Stanly, e. 7/29/1861, age 19. Dis. 12/14/1861 due to "chronic disease of the lungs" (NCT 8, 158).

LINEBARGER, A.C., Co. B, Corporal (1839–1862). Resident of Gaston, e. 7/30/1861, age 22, as a corporal. Died at Wilmington abt 1/20/1862 of disease (NCT 8, 133).

LINEBARGER, Avery P., Co. C, Private (1844–1864). Lived and e. in Catawba 3/15/1862, age 18. Wounded at Shepherdstown 9/20/1862. Captured near Deep Bottom abt 7/27/1864. Confined at Pt. Lookout until trans to Elmira on 8/16/1864. Died at Elmira on 9/21/1864 of "typhoid fever" (NCT 8, 147).

LINEBARGER, Davis A., Co. B, Corporal (1831–). Lived and e. in Gaston 7/30/1861, age 30, as a corporal, but rank reduced Jan.–April 1862. Captured at Fredericksburg 12/13/1862; paroled 12/17/1862. Wounded in right hand at Gettysburg 7/1–3/1863, and hand amputated. No discharge date given, but pension records indicate he survived the war (NCT 8, 133).

LINEBARGER, Frederick Middleton, Co. C, Private. Catawba resident, e. 10/25/1864. Captured in Richmond hospital 4/3/1865; trans to Newport News 4/23/1865; released 6/30/1864 after OOA. NC pension records indicate he was "slightly wounded once or twice" (NCT 8, 147).

LINEBARGER, Jacob A., Co. C, Private. Previously served in Co. K, 23rd NC Reg. before transferring to this company 3/21/1863. Wounded at Chancellorsville 5/2–3/1863. Wounded at Gettysburg. Died 7/5/1863 of wounds (NCT 8, 147).

LINEBARGER, Levi M., Co. C, 1st Sergeant (1844–) Catawba resident, e. 3/15/1862, age 18, as a private. Promoted to sergeant 1/22/1863; to 1st sergeant May 1863–Oct. 1864. Present through Feb. 1865 (NCT 8, 147).

LINEBARGER, M. Monroe, Co. C, Private. E. in Catawba 11/16/1863. Surrendered at Appomattox CH 4/9/1865 (NCT 8, 147).

LINEBARGER, T. James, Co. C, Captain (1838–). Lived, e. in Catawba resident 8/13/1861, age 23, as a private. Appointed 2nd lieutenant 9/26/1861. Elected 1st lieutenant 2/27/1862, and promoted to captain 4/14/1862. Wounded at Fredericksburg 12/13/1862. Wounded at Chancellorsville 5/2–3/1863. Surrender at Appomattox CH 4/9/1865 (NCT 8, 139).

LINEBARGER, William Alexander, Co. D, Private. Previously served in Co. G, 12th Reg NCT. Trans to this company 2/8/1865. Absent-wounded in Feb. 1865. Paroled at Statesville, NC 5/26/1865 (NCT 8, 158).

LINGERFELT, Jacob, Co. B, Private (1840–). Gaston farmer e. on 7/30/1861, age 21. Captured at Hanover CH 5/28–31/1862; confined at Ft. Delaware, until exc at Aiken's Landing 8/5/1862. Wounded in the abdomen, right hip, and/or foot at Fredericksburg 12/13/1862. Dis. 2/13/1864 due to disability (NCT 8, 133).

LINK, Ephraim M., Co. C, Private. Lived, e. in Catawba resident 3/15/1862. Captured at Hanover CH 5/27/1862; confined at Ft. Monroe, then Ft. Columbus. Trans to Aiken's Landing for exchange 8/5/1862. Wounded at Gettysburg 7/1–3/1863, and "left there." Believed to have died of wounds received at Gettysburg (NCT 8, 147).

LINKER, W. Monroe, Co. K, Private. E. at Camp Stokes 12/19/1864. Hospitalized at Charlotte 3/19/1865 with gunshot wound of the left lower extremity. Paroled at Charlotte May 1865 (NCT 8, 226).

LINVILLE, Berry, Co. A, Private (1837–). Son of Moses and Henrietta White Linville, of the Marsh District, Berry e. at age 24 on 5/4/1861. Trans to Co. B, 2nd Battalion, NC Infantry on 10/23/1862. Hospitalized in Aug. 1864, and absent-sick in October that year. He m. Martha Jane Slaydon in 1855 in Surry. He applied for a pension. (NCT 8, 119; SCS 112).

LIPE, Levi, Co. D, Private. Stanly resident, e. at Camp Stokes 10/31/1864. Captured near Petersburg 4/2/1865; confined at Pt. Lookout until released 6/28/1865 after OOA (NCT 8, 158).

LISK, Joshia T., Co. E., Private (1843–). Lived in Montgomery, e. in Lenoir 3/20/1862, age 19. Surrendered at Appomattox CH 4/9/1865 (NCT 8, 169).

LISK, Washington, Co. E, Private (1816–1862). Lived, e. in Montgomery 8/1/1861, age 45. Died in Richmond hospital 8/3–6/1862 of typhoid fever (NCT 8, 169).

LISK, William T., Co. E, Musician (1832–). Lived, e. in Montgomery 8/1/1861, age 29, as a musician. Surrendered at Appomattox CH 4/9/1865 (NCT 8, 169).

LITTLE, Joshua A., Co. C, Sergeant (1841–1864). B. and lived in Catawba where he e. 8/13/1861 as a corporal. Promoted to sergeant 2/17/1862. Wounded at Ox Hill 9/1/1862. Wounded in the right thigh and captured near Gravel Hill 7/28/1864. Leg amputated, he died in a hospital at City Pt. on 10/9/1864 from his wound (NCT 8, 148).

LITTLE, Junius Pinkney, Co. C, Private; Field & Staff, Ensign (1st Lieutenant) (1835–). Lived and e. in Catawba 8/13/1861, age 16, a private. Wounded at Frayser's Farm 6/30/1862. Wounded at Chancellorsville 5/3/1863 "while gallantly bearing the colors in the charge on the enemy's works." Appointed Ensign (1st Lt) 5/2/1864, trans to Field & Staff. Captured at Spotsylvania CH 5/12/1864; confined at Pt. Lookout, Maryland, trans to Elmira, New York on 8/10/1864. Released on 6/16/1865 after OOA. Praised for his bravery in carrying the regimental colors at Hanover CH, Mechanicsville, Cold Harbor, Frayser's Farm and Fredericksburg (NCT 8, 111, 148).

LITTLE, Olmstead, Co. D, Private (1830–). Stanly farmer, e 3/15/1862, age 32. Wounded in right hand at Chancellorsville 5/2–3/1863. Captured near Petersburg 4/4/1865; confined at Pt. Lookout until released 6/28/1865 after OOA (NCT 8, 158–159).

LLOYD, Bunk, Co. G, Private (1847–1864). Lived and e. in Orange in Jan. 1863, age 16, as a substitute. Captured near Spotsylvania CH 5/10/1864; confined at Pt. Lookout, trans to Elmira. Died there 10/20/1864 of "typhoid fever" (NCT 8, 190).

LLOYD, Green H., Co. G, Private (1813–). Lived, e. in Orange 9/2/1861, age 48. Captured at Frederick, MD 9/12/1862; confined at Ft. Delaware. Paroled and trans to Aiken's Landing, exc 11/10/1862. Dis. Jan. 1863 after providing substitute (NCT 8, 190).

LLOYD, Henry, Co. G, Private (1844–). Lived and e. in Orange 3/5/1862, age 18. Captured at Fredericksburg 12/13/1862; exc abt 12/17/1862. Captured near Spotsylvania CH 5/10–12/1864; confined at Pt. Lookout, trans to Elmira 8/10/1864. Paroled and trans to James River for exchange 3/2/1865. Hospitalized at Richmond with "debilitas" Furloughed for 30 days 3/9/1865 (NCT 8, 190).

LLOYD, Henry W., Co. G, Private. Lived and e. in Orange 3/24/1864. Captured near Spotsylvania CH abt 5/12/1864; confined at Pt. Lookout; trans to Elmira 8/10/1864. Paroled and trans to Venus Pt. 11/15/1864. Returned and was present through Feb. 1865 (NCT 8, 190).

LLOYD, Lucian, Co. G, Private (1840–1863). Lived and e. in Orange 9/2/1861, age 21. Captured at Fredericksburg 12/13/1862; exc abt 12/17/1862. Wounded and captured at Gettysburg 7/3/1863, and died there abt 7/10/863 of wounds (NCT 8, 190).

LLOYD, Lucius J., Co. G, Sergeant (1843–). Lived and e. in Orange 12/20/1861, age 18, as a private. Captured at Fredericksburg 12/13/1862; exc abt 12/17/1862. Promoted to corporal 8/21/1863. Captured at Wilderness 5/12/1864; confined at Pt. Lookout, then Elmira. Paroled and trans to Venus Pt. 11/15/1864 for exchange. Promoted to sergeant 1/1/1865. Surrendered at Appomattox CH 4/9/1865 (NCT 8, 190).

LOGAN, G.M., Co. B, Private (1843–1863). Gaston resident, e. 7/30/1861, age 18. Wounded and captured at Gettysburg 7/1–4/1863, he was hospitalized at Davids Island 7/17–24/1863 and died there on 8/15/1863 of "pneumonia" (NCT 8, 133).

LOGAN, H.A., Co. F, Private (1841–1863). Lived and e. in Yadkin 4/27/1862, age 21. Died "at home" 4/18/1863 (NCT 8, 180).

LOGAN, Richard M., Co. F, Sergeant (1835–). Lived and e. in Yadkin 6/18/1861 as a sergeant; reduced in rank Jan.–June 1862. Promoted to corporal Nov.–Dec. 1862. AWOL 9/1/1863–Feb. 1865 (NCT 8, 180).

LONG, Ellis, Co. I, Private (1841–). Lived and e. in Yadkin 8/13/1861, age 20. Captured at Fredericksburg 12/13/1862; exc abt 12/17/1862. Deserted 7/23/1862. Returned and present from Sept. 1864–Feb. 1865. Captured near Petersburg 4/2/1865; confined at Ft. Delaware, released 6/19/18965 after OOA (NCT 8, 214).

LONG, Francis, Co. I, Private (1843–1862). Lived and e. in Yadkin 8/13/1861, age 18. Died abt 7/20/1862 of diphtheria (NCT 8, 214).

LONG, Frederick, Co. I, 2nd Lieutenant (1840–1862). Son of John and Nancy Davis Long, lived and e. in Yadkin 8/13/1861, appointed 2nd lieutenant. Wounded at Shepherdstown 9/20/1862, and died at Winchester 10/23/1862 of wounds, a "brave and gallant officer." Bur. Stonewall Cem., Winchester VA (NCT 8, 207; CWY 239).

LONG, Nathan, Co. I, Private (1825–). Lived in Yadkin, e. 4/17/1864 at Camp Vance. Hospitalized at

Richmond 4/2/1865 with gunshot wound. Captured in hospital on 4/3/1865; trans to Newport News 4/23/1865 and released 6/30/1865 after OOA (NCT 8, 214, CWY 289).

LONGBOTTOM, Manor, Co. A, Private (1839–). He m. in 1860, Surry, Melissa Chandler, e. 5/4/1861, age 22. Captured near Petersburg on 4/2/1865; confined at Ft. Delaware, until released 6/19/1865 after OOA (NCT 8, 119; SCS 114).

LOTHROP, William H., Co. E, Private (1837–1864). Lived in Union, e. in Wake 10/2/1862, age 25. Captured near Gravel Hill 7/28/1864; confined at Pt. Lookout, then Elmira 8/8/1864. Trans to Baltimore hospital abt 10/13/1864, died 12/19/1864 of "chronic diarrhoea" (NCT 8, 169).

LOVE, John, Co. D, Private (1840–1862). Lived and e. in Stanly 3/15/1862, age 22. Died at Richmond or Chancellorsville 8/23/1862 of disease (NCT 8, 159).

LOVE, Martin, Co. D, Private (1840–1862). Stanly resident, e. 3/15/1862, age 22. Died at Danville 11/27/1862 of "erysipelas" (NCT 8, 159).

LOVE, Samuel Wilson, Co. B, Sergeant (1834–1862). B. in Lincoln, lived, e. in Gaston 7/30/1861, at age 27, as a sergeant. Wounded in the left leg at Gaines' Mill on 6/27/1862; hospitalized at Richmond where he died on 7/25/1862 from his wound (NCT 8, 133).

LOVELACE, James L., Co. H, Private (1844–). Lived and e. in Cleveland 3/17/1862, age 18. Captured at Hanover CH 5/27/1862; confined at Ft. Monroe, then Ft. Columbus. Paroled and trans to Aiken's Landing for exchange 8/5/1862. Captured at Warrenton or at Middleburg 8/25–26/1863; confined at Old Capitol Prison 9/3/1863. Trans to Pt. Lookout 9/26/1863. Exc abt 3/14/1864. Surrendered at Appomattox CH 4/9/1865 (NCT 8, 203).

LOVELL (Lovill), Edward F., Co. A, Captain (1842). E. 5/4/1861, age 19, as a private. Elected 2nd lieutenant 10/4/1864; promoted to captain 4/9/1862. Wounded in the right arm at Gettysburg. Wounded in both thighs at Jones' Farm on 9/10/1864. Absent-wounded until 12/17/1864, when he was reported AWOL. Surrender on 4/9/1865 at Appomattox. The son of William R. and Eliza G. Reeves Lovill of Siloam, he m. Josephine L. Marion in 1866, in Surry (NCT 8, 112; SCS 115).

LOVILL, Henry P., Co. A, 2nd Lieutenant (1839–). Surry farmer, e. 5/4/1861, age 22, as sergeant. Rank reduced before 11/1/1861. Trans, appointed 2nd lieutenant of Co. A, 54th Reg NCT on 3/2/1062. (NCT 8, 119–120; SCS 115).

LOWDER, John M., Co. K, Private (1831–). Lived and e. in Stanly 3/25/1862, age 31. Wounded at Ox Hill 9/1/1862. Returned. Captured at Wilderness 5/6/1864; confined at Pt. Lookout. Trans to Elmira 8/10/1864; released there 6/23/1865 after OOA (NCT 8, 226).

LOWDER, Lee, Co. K, Private (1820–1863). Lived and e. in Stanly 3/20/1862, age 42. Captured at Fredericksburg 12/13/1862; exc abt 12/17/1862. Died in Lynchburg hospital 12/9/1863 of "pneumonia" (NCT 8, 226).

LOWDER, Lindsey, Co. D, 3rd Lieutenant (1835–).

Stanly resident, e. 7/29/1861, as a sergeant, age 26. Elected 3rd lieutenant 7/27/1862. Wounded in left leg at Chancellorsville 5/3/1863. Resigned 4/11/1864 due to disability from wounds received (NCT 8, 153).

LOWDER, Malachai, Co. D, Sergeant (1840–) Lived and e. in Stanly 7/29/1861, age 21, as a private. Promoted to corporal 11/16/1862; promoted to sergeant 12/18/1862. Company records state he was captured 7/3/1863. Federal provost marshal records do not substantiate that (NCT 8, 159).

LOWE, John F., Field & Staff, Sergeant Major (1837–1862). Lived, e. in Mecklenburg 12/1/1862 at age 25, as sergeant major. Killed at Fredericksburg 12/13/1862, "a brave and good man" (NCT 8, 111.

LOWE, Milton A., Co. C, Sergeant; Field & Staff, Sergeant Major (1842–). B. in Lincoln, e. in Catawba 8/13/1861, age 19 years, as a sergeant. Appointed sergeant major 10/17/1861. Trans to Field & Staff of the Reg. and elected 3rd Lt. 8/4/1862. Trans back to Co. C., and promoted to 1st Lt. abt 11/14/1862. Trans to Co. H of the 28th Reg. Captured near Gravel Hill abt 7/28/1864; confined at Old Capitol Prison in Washington, then Ft. Delaware on 8/11/1864, and paroled on 10/6/1864. Exc at Cox's Wharf. Resigned 2/23/1865. No reason was given (NCT 8, 111, 140, 196).

LOWE, Samuel D., Co. C, Captain; Field & Staff, Colonel. Resided in Lincoln, appointed 1st Lt. 8/13/1861, promoted to captain 9/26/1861. Appointed Major 4/12/1862, joined Field & Staff. Captured at Hanover CH 5/27/1862; confined at Ft. Columbus. While a prisoner of war, was promoted to Lt. Col. 6/11/1862. Trans to Johnson's Island on 6/21/1862, then Vicksburg on 9/20/1862 for exchange. Promoted to colonel 11/1/1862. Wounded at Gettysburg 7/1–3/1863; retired to Invalid Corps 7/8/1864 due to general "debility," and "phthisis pulmonalis"(NCT 8, 110, 139).

LOWE, Sidney H., Co. H, Private (1845–). Lived and e. in Lincoln 8/11/1863. Present through Feb. 1865 (NCT 8, 203).

LOWE, Thomas L., Co. C, Lt. Colonel; Field & Staff, Colonel. (1831–1854). A Catawba resident, e. in Co. C, appointed captain 8/13/1861; elected Lt. Col. 9/21/1861. Appointed major 11/1/1862, and joined Field & Staff. Promoted to lieutenant colonel 3/12/1863. Wounded at Chancellorsville 5/2–3/1863. Wounded at Gettysburg 7/1–3/1863. Promoted to colonel 7/9/1864. Wounded in head at Reams' Station 8/25/1864. Hospitalized and died at Petersburg 8/29/1864. He had attended Catawba College, and was writer, speaker, school teacher, surveyor. He m. Anna D. Coulder. (NCT 8, 110, 139, SCS 173).

LOWE, Tullius C., Co. H; Field & Staff, Quartermaster Sergeant. Lived in Lincoln, e. on May 9, 1863, age 19, in Co. H, 28th Reg. Promoted to quartermaster sergeant before 11/1/1864; trans to Field & Staff of the 28th. Present at Appomattox on 4/9/1865 for the surrender (NCT 8, 112, 203).

LUCKEY, Francis N., Field & Staff, Assistant Surgeon. Lived in Rowan, appointed Assistant Surgeon 9/25/1861; trans to Surgeon of the 25th Reg, NCT, abt 3/21/1862 (NCT 8, 111).

LUTHER, Godfrey W. Co. E, Private (1840–) Lived

in either Montgomery or Randolph, e. in Montgomery 8/1/1861, age 21. Wounded in both thighs at Fredericksburg 12/13/1862; hospitalized at Richmond. Furloughed for 90 days 3/26/1863. On light duty at Staunton 3/10/1864 through Feb. 1865. Arrested by the enemy 3/10/1865; confined at Wheeling, WVA abt 3/12/1865 until released abt 3/12/1865 after OOA (NCT 8, 169).

LUTHER, Jesse M., Co. E, Private (1838–). Lived, e. in Montgomery 8/1/1861, age 23. Captured near Gravel Hill 7/28/1864; confined at Pt Lookout, then trans to Elmira 8/8/1864 where he arrived 8/12/1864. Paroled on 3/14/1865 and trans to Boulware's Wharf on 8/18–21 for exchange (NCT 8, 169).

LYERLY, Jacob C., Co. D, Private (1840–1862). Lived, e. in Stanly on 7/29/1861, age 21. Died in a Lovingston hospital abt 8/21/1862 of typhoid fever (NCT 8, 159).

LYERLY, Jacob H., Co. D, Corporal (1839–1863). Lived, e. in Stanly 7/29/1861, age 22, as a private. Promoted to corporal 12/1/1862. Died at Lynchburg 8/10/1863 or 8/31/1863 of typhoid fever (NCT 8, 159).

LYERLY, Jacob H., Co. D, Corporal (1844–). E. 3/15/1862, age 18, as a private; promoted to corporal 12/1/1864. Surrendered at Appomattox CH 4/9/1865 (NCT 8, 159).

LYNCH, Pleasant H., Co. F, Private (1838–). Lived, e. in Yadkin 2/18/1863, age 25. Deserted to the enemy abt 4/1/1863; confined at Ft. Monroe; released after OOA (NCT 8, 180).

MACKIE, Jonas, Co. I, Private. (1844–1863). Lived in Caldwell, e. 4/13/1863, age 19, Killed at Gettysburg 7/3/1863 (NCT 8, 215).

MACKIE, Robert Alexander, Co. I, Private (1839–) Lived in Caldwell, e. 8/28/1862, age 23. Wounded in right thigh, captured at Spotsylvania CH 5/12/1864. Hospitalized at Washington, DC. Trans to Elmira 12/16/1864; released 6/12/1865, after OOA (NCT 8, 215).

MACON, Calvin, Co. E, Private. Previously served in Co. K, 34th Reg NCT. Trans to Co. E on 3/12/1864 in exc for Private Joel G. Henderson. Deserted Feb. 1865, but returned to surrender at Appomattox CH 4/9/1865 (NCT 8, 170).

MACY, Thomas E., Co. I, Private (1942–). Lived, e. in Yadkin 11/12/1861, age 19. AWOL May–Oct. 1862. Returned. Hospitalized at Richmond 5/18/1864 with gunshot wound. On Duty as prison guard at Salisbury Sept. 1863–Feb. 1865 (NCT 8, 215).

MACY, William L., Co. I, Private (1837–). Lived, e. in Yadkin or New Hanover 11/12/1861, age 24. Captured at Hanover CH 5/27/1862; confined at Ft. Monroe, then Ft. Columbus. Paroled and trans to Aiken's Landing for exc 8/5/1862. Hospitalized in Richmond 4/21/1864 with gunshot wound of left thigh. Absent-sick Sept.–Oct.1864. Captured near Petersburg 4/2/1865; confined at Ft. Delaware; released 6/19/1865 after OOA (NCT 8, 215).

MANN, William C., Co. K, Private (1839–). Lived and e. in Stanly 9/7/1861, age 22. Trans to Co. C, 42nd Reg NCT abt 9/10/1862 (NCT 8, 226).

MARBERRY, Archibald C., Co. K, Private. (1838–).

Lived and e. in Stanly 9/7/1861. Wounded in head near Richmond abt 5/9/1864. Returned. Surrendered at Appomattox CH 4/9/1865 (NCT 8, 226–227).

MARBERRY, Thomas F., Co. K, Private (1845–1863). Lived and e. in Stanly 3/2/1863, age 18, Died in Richmond hospital 6/4–5/1863 of typhoid fever (NCT 8, 227).

MARCOM, William W., Co. G, Sergeant. Lived, e. in Orange 9/2/1861 as a private. Captured at Fredericksburg 12/13/1862; exc abt 12/17/1862. Promoted to corporal 4/1/1863. Wounded at Chancellorsville 5/2–3/1863. Promoted to sergeant before 1/24/1864. Captured near Wilderness abt 5/6/1864; confined at Pt. Lookout, trans to Elmira 8/10/1864. Released 6/27/1865 after OOA (NCT 8, 191).

MARION, Azariah, Co. A, Private (1844–). Lived, e. in Surry 3/18/1862, age 18. Hospitalized in Richmond on 7/2/1862 with a gunshot wound to right side. Dis July 1862. Pension records indicate that Marion was wounded in the right hip at Richmond in July of 1863 He m. Sarah Franklin in 1861 and by 1880 they had six living children (NCT 8, 120; SCS 121).

MARION, Jeremiah, Co. A, Private (1836–1861). Son of Adam and Sally Reeves Marion of Siloam, e. 5/13/1861 in Surry, age 25. Died 3 months later on 8/24–25/1861 in High Pt., NC, cause unknown. His family believed he died of exposure. His body is believed to have been brought home for burial (NCT 8, 120; SCS 122).

MARION, Nathan J., Co. A, Private (1842–1861). Lived, e. in Surry, age 19, 5/4/1861. Died in training camp at Garysburg, NC on 8/19/1861 (NCT 8, 120).

MARION, Sidney, Co. A, Private (1839–). Surry resident, e. on 5/3/1861, age 22. He was dis on 9/24/1861 because of disability (NCT 8, 120).

MARKE, A. P., Co. D, Private. Captured in a Richmond hospital 4/3/1865; paroled 4/20/1865 (NCT 8, 159).

MARLER, James N., Co. F, Corporal (1845–). Lived, e. in Yadkin 8/5/1861, age 16 as a private. Promoted to corporal 5/11/1863. Captured near Petersburg 4/2/1865; confined at Pt. Lookout until released 6/15/1865 after OOA (NCT 8, 180).

MARLER, Joseph F. Co. F, Private (1827–1865). Lived, e. in Yadkin 6/18/1861, age 34. Captured at Wilderness or Spotsylvania 5/6–12/1864; confined at Pt. Lookout. Trans to Elmira 7/25/1864; died there 2/25/1865 of "pneumonia" (NCT 8, 180).

MARLER, William A., Co. F, 2nd Lieutenant (1839–). Lived, e. in Yadkin 6/18/1861, appointed 3rd lieutenant. Defeated for reelection 4/12/1862. E. in Co. H. 63rd Reg NCT (5th Reg NC Cavalry) 7/18/1862 with rank of private. Trans back to Co. F in June 1863 and appointed 2nd lieutenant to rank from 4/9/1863. Captured at Gettysburg 7/3/1863; confined at Ft. Delaware, then Johnson's Island 7/18/1863. Paroled, trans to Cox's Wharf 3/22/1865 for exc (NCT 8, 174).

MARSH, John, Co. A, Private (1838–1863). B. in Surry to Minor and Hetty Brown Marsh of the Dobson District. E. at "Wough Hill," age 24, 3/18/1862. Hospitalized in Richmond on 7/2/1862 with a "contused wound." Captured at Fredericksburg 12/13/1862;

exc 12/17/1862. Died in Staunton hospital 7/11/1863 of typhoid fever (NCT 8, 120; SCS 122).

MARSH, William, Co. A, Private (1842–) Son of Minor and Mary Marsh of Surry, e., age 20, on 3/18/1862. Captured at Hanover CH 5/27/1862; sent to Ft. Monroe. Exc. at Aiken's Landing 8/5/1862. Wounded in left shoulder at Gettysburg 7/1/1863. Captured at Jericho Ford 5/23/1864; confined at Elmira. Released, date unspecified (NCT 8, 120; SCS 122).

MARTIN, Abram M., Co. H, Private (1841–). B., lived, e. in Cleveland. 3/17/1862, age 21. Dis 9/27/1862 due to "pulmonary consumption" which destroyed most of his "right lung" (NCT 8, 204).

MARTIN, Alfred W., Co. I, Private (1840–). Lived, e. in Yadkin 8/13/1861, age 21. Deserted 8/5/1862 (NCT 8, 215).

MARTIN, Bennett, Co. F, Private. B., living, e. in Yadkin 2/1/1863, age 29, he was killed At Jericho Mills 5/23/1864 (NCT 8, 180).

MARTIN, Edward A., Co. G, Sergeant (1842–). Lived, e. in Orange 3/5/1862 as a private. Promoted to sergeant 5/1/1862. Captured at Hanover CH 5/27/1862; confined at Ft. Monroe, then Ft. Columbus. Paroled and trans to Aiken's Landing for exc 8/5/1862. Trans to Co. K, 11th Reg NCT 8/1/1863 (NCT 8, 191).

MARTIN, Gilbert, Co. F, Private (1828–). B., lived, e. in Yadkin 6/18/1861, age 33. Dis 11/7/1861 due to "an affection of the spine of some eight years standing & which interferes with the use of his lower limbs" (NCT 8, 180).

MARTIN, James W., Co. C, Private (18__–1862). Lived in Lincoln, e. at Camp Fisher on 9/5/1861. Wounded in thigh at 2nd Manassas 8/27–30/1862. Leg amputated. Hospitalized at Lynchburg, where he died on 9/27/1862 from his wound and/or typhoid fever. Roll of Honor called him "a most gallant soldier" (NCT 8, 148).

MARTIN, John H., Co. F, Private. E. in Yadkin 4/27/1864. AWOL 10/26/1864 (NCT 8, 180).

MARTIN, John H., Jr., Co. I, Private (1843–). Lived, e. in Yadkin 8/13/1861, age 18. Captured at Hanover CH 5/27/1862; confined at Ft. Monroe, then Ft. Columbus. Paroled and trans to Aiken's Landing, exc 8/5/1862. Captured at Wilderness 5/6/1864; confined at Pt. Lookout; trans to Boulware's Wharf 2/20–21/1865 for exc (NCT 8, 215).

MARTIN, John H., Sr., Co. I, Private. Lived in Forsyth, e. at Camp Holmes 10/20/1862. Captured at Fussell's Mill 8/16/1864; confined at Pt. Lookout; released 6/29/1865 after OOA (NCT 8, 215).

MARTIN, Reps, Co. F, Private (1826–). B., lived, e. in Yadkin 6/18/1861, age 35, as sergeant. Rank reduced Jan.–June 1862. Dis 6/10/1862 due to "predisposition to disease of the lungs, accompanied with severe cough of long standing" (NCT 8, 180).

MARTIN, Robert N.M., Co. C, Private (18__–1862). Lived in Lincoln, e. at Camp Fisher on 9/5/1861. Captured at Hanover CH 5/27/1862; confined at Ft. Monroe, then Ft. Columbus where he died 7/16/1862 of typhoid fever (NCT 8, 148).

MARTIN, Weldon H., Co. H, Private (1839–). Lived, e. in Cleveland 3/17/1862, age 23. Present through Feb. 1865 (NCT 8, 204).

MARTIN, William A., Co. C, Private (1836–). Catawba resident, e. 9/5/1861, age 25. Wounded by an "exploding shell from a gunboat" near Frayser's Farm 7/30/1862. In the fighting at Fredericksburg, Martin was said to have "cooly sat on the (railroad) track and called to his comrades to watch the Yankee colors, then fired and down they went." He did this several times. Wounded in left arm and shoulder at Gettysburg 7/3/1863. Wounded in head, pelvis and right leg near Petersburg abt 8/18/1864. Surrendered at Appomattox CH 4/9/1865 (NCT 8, 148).

MARTIN, William Joseph, Co. G, 28th Reg, Captain; 11th Reg, Colonel (1831–). B. in Richmond; e. in Orange where he was a college professor. Appointed captain 9/2/1861; to major 4/28/1862. Trans to 11th Reg NCT to serve as its colonel (NCT 8, 184).

MASK, J.F., Co. E, Private (1844–1862). Lived, e. in Montgomery 3/20/1862, age 18. Died in Lynchburg hospital 6/6/1862 of typhoid fever (NCT 8, 170).

MASON, John T., Co. E, Sergeant (1834–1862). "A cheerful soldier" John lived, e. in Montgomery 8/1/1861, age 27, as sergeant. Killed at Gaines' Mill 6/27–30/1862 (NCT 8, 170).

MATHENEY, John, Co. H, Corporal (1942–1862). Lived in Lincoln, e. 8/22/1861 in Cleveland, age 19, as a private. Promoted to corporal May–Aug. 1862. Died in field hospital near Richmond 8/9/1862, cause not reported (NCT 8, 204).

MATHENEY, Lewis H., Co. H, Sergeant (1832–1864). B. in Cleveland, lived and e. in Lincoln. 8/22/1861, age 29 as a private. Promoted to corporal before 11/1/1861; then sergeant before 5/1/1862. Killed at Wilderness 5/6/1864 (NCT 8, 204).

MATHENY, David, Co. H, Private? NC pension records indicate he served in this company (NCT 8, 204).

MATHERSON, Malcolm D., Co. E, Private. B. in Moore, lived in Montgomery, e. In Wake 11/5/1864. Captured near Petersburg 4/2/1865; confined at Ft. Delaware until released 6/19/1865 after OOA (NCT 8, 170).

MATHESON, John L., Co. E, Corporal (1844–). Montgomery blacksmith e. there 8/1/1861, age 17, as a private. Wounded in thigh at Gaines' Mill 6/27/1862. Promoted to corporal July 1863–Oct. 1864. Captured near Petersburg 4/2/1865; confined at Pt. Lookout until released 6/29/1865 after OOA (NCT 8, 170).

MATTHEWS (Mathews), Henry D., Co. F, Private (1844–1864). B., e. in Yadkin 9/28/1863. Killed At Wilderness 5/5/1864. Son of Absalom and Amitty Poindexter Mathews (NCT 8, 180; 1850 Surry Census).

MATTHEWS, James T. Stokely, Co. F, Private; Co. I, 21st Reg, Private (1849–). E. in Co. I, 21st Reg NCT 11/1/1863. Hospitalized in Danville 7/1/1864 for gunshot wound to right foot. Deserted from hospital 8/19/1864 (NCT VI, 616). NC pension records indicate he served in Co. F, 28th Reg He m. Curlista Jane Martin 12/13/1866, Yadkin (NCT 8, 180; CWY 243).

MATTHEWS, John V., Co. F, Private (1841–1895). Lived, e. in Yadkin 9/28/1863. Captured near Petersburg 4/2/1865; confined at Pt. Lookout until released

6/29/1865 after OOA (NCT 8, 180). Son of Absalom and Amitty Poindexter Matthews, John m. Martha Warden in 1867. Bur. Prospect Meth. Ch. cem., Yadkin (HYC 502; 1850 Surry Census).

MATTHEWS, T.C., Co. F, Private; Co. I, 21st Reg. E. in Yadkin 11/1/1863. Absent-wounded Sept.–Oct. 1864 through Feb 1865 (NCT 6, 616). NC pension records indicate he served in Co. F, 28th Reg (NCT 8, 180).

MAULDIN, Benjamin E., Co. D, Private (1839–). Lived, e. in Stanly resident 7/29/1861, age 22. Wounded in head, captured at Gettysburg 7/1–4/1863. Hospitalized at Davids Island 7/17–24/1863. Paroled and trans to City Pt. on 9/8/1863 for exc. Paroled at Farmville 4/11–21/1865 (NCT 8, 159).

MAULDIN, James, Co. K, Private (1832–1862). Lived and e. in Stanly 3/15/1862, age 30. Killed at Hanover CH 5/27/1862 (NCT 8, 227).

MAULDIN, Thomas, Co. K, Private. E. in Stanly 9/10/1863. Captured in Richmond hospital 4/3/1865. Paroled at Richmond 5/3/1865 (NCT 8, 227).

MAULT, Isaac C., Co. D, Private (1845–1864). Stanly resident, e. at Camp Gregg 4/27/1863, age 18. Died 12/13/1864 (NCT 8, 159).

MAULT, James P., Co. D, Private (1841–). Lived in Stanly or Rowan, e. in Stanly, age 21, 3/15/1862. Wounded in left lung, captured at Gettysburg 7/1–4/1863. Hospitalized at Davids Island, then paroled and trans to City Pt on 9/8/1863 for exc. Detailed for light duty 6/23/1864; absent on detail through Feb. 1865. Paroled at Salisbury 6/14/1865 (NCT 8, 159).

MAUNEY, James E., Co. B, Private. E. 5/1/1864 at Liberty Mills. Hospitalized in Richmond on 6/16/1864 with a gunshot wound. Furloughed for 30 days 7/30/1864, and returned before 11/1/1864. Captured in a Richmond hospital on 4/5/1865 (NCT 8, 134).

MAUNEY, William Andrew, Co. B, Private; Field & Staff, Commissary Sergeant. (1842_) Lived, e. in Gaston. 8/6/1861, as a private. Promoted to commissary sergeant in Oct. 1861; trans to the Field & Staff of the 28th Reg. Captured at Hanover CH 5/17/1862; confined at Ft. Monroe, then Ft. Columbus in New York Harbor. Paroled and trans to Aiken's Landing 7/12/1862 for exc 8/5/1862. Paroled at Charlotte, NC 5/3/1865 (NCT 8, M, 112, 134).

MAYO, M. Lewis, Field & Staff, Assistant Surgeon. A Virginia native, Mayo was appointed to assistant surgeon abt 5/2/1863. Trans to a hospital in Charlotte, NC in January 1865, and was paroled there in May 1865 (NCT 8, 111).

McARVER, Franklin Harper, Co. B, Private (1841–). Gaston resident, e. at Camp Fisher on 8/21/1861, age 20. Captured at Hanover CH 5/27/1862; confined at Ft. Monroe, then Ft. Columbus until sent to Aiken's Landing for exc on 8/5/1862. Surrendered at Appomattox CH 4/9/1865 (NCT 8, 133).

McAULAY, Angus M., Co. E, Corporal (1834–). Lived, e. in Montgomery 8/1/1861, age 27. Mustered in as corporal; reduced in rank March–Apr. 1862. Captured at Hanover CH 5/27/1862; confined at Ft. Monroe, then Ft. Columbus. Paroled and trans to Aiken's Landing for exc 8/5/1862. Hospitalized in Richmond

5/16/1864 with gunshot wound of left thigh. Captured near Petersburg 4/2/1865; confined at Pt. Lookout until released 6/29/1865 after OOA (NCT 8, 169).

McAULAY, H.W., Co. E, Private (1836–1861). Lived, e. in Montgomery 8/1/1861, age 25. Died at Wilmington 12/31/1861 (NCT 8, 170).

McAULAY, John T., Co. E, Private. Previously served as 2nd lieutenant and sergeant in Co. E, 1st Reg, NC Junior Reserves. Trans to Co. E, with rank of private 1/20/1865. Surrendered at Appomattox CH 4/9/1865 (NCT 8, 170).

McAULAY, Martin A., Co. E, Private. E. in Wake 11/5/1864. Captured in Richmond hospital 4/3/1865; trans to Newport News 4/23/1863, died there 1/1865 of chronic diarrhea and/or "rubeola" (NCT 8, 170).

McBRAYER, Samuel C., Co. H, 1st Sergeant (1841–). B in Rutherford, lived, e. in Cleveland 8/22/1861, age 20. Dis 1/30/1862 due to "an attack of typhoid pneumonia producing disease threatening the development of tubercular phthisis" (NCT 8, 203).

McBRIDE, Daniel B., Co. I, Private (1841–1862). Lived, e. in Yadkin 8/13/1861, age 20. Wounded in abdomen at Frayser's Farm or at Malvern Hill 7/30–7/1/1862. Hospitalized at Richmond, died there 7/3/1864 of wound (NCT 8, 214–215).

McBRIDE, John G., Co. I, Sergeant (1836–). Lived, e. in Yadkin 8/13/1861, age 25 as private. Captured at Hanover CH 5/27/1862; confined at Ft. Monroe, then Ft. Columbus. Paroled and trans to Aiken's Landing for exc 8/5/1862. Promoted to sergeant Mar. 1863–June 1864. Absent-sick Sept.–Oct., 1974; AWOL Nov.–Dec. 1864. Returned. Captured near Petersburg 4/2/1865; confined at Ft. Delaware until released 6/19/1865, after OOA (NCT 8, 215).

McCASKILL, James, Co. E, Private (1809–) Lived, e. in Montgomery as a substitute there 3/6/1862, age 53. Captured at Hanover CH 5/27/1862; confined at Ft. Monroe then Ft. Columbus. Paroled and trans to Aiken's Landing for exc on 8/5/1862. Dis 11/21/1863 due to "varicose veins of leg & infirmities of old age" (NCT 8, 170).

McCAULEY, Benjamin, Co. G, Private (1840–1862). Lived, e. in Orange 9/2/1861, age 21. Killed at Frayser's Farm or Malvern Hill 6/30/1862–7/1/1862 (NCT 8, 191).

McCAULEY, George W., Co. G, Captain (1832–). Lived, e. in Orange 9/2/1861 as a sergeant; promoted to 1st sergeant March–Apr. 1862. Appointed 2nd lieutenant 5/1/1862; promoted to 1st lieutenant 1/19/1863. Promoted to captain 7/19/1863. Wounded in right hip and captured near Petersburg 4/2/1865. Hospitalized at Washington; released abt 6/9/1865 after OOA (NCT 8, 185).

McCAULEY, Mathew J. W., Co. G, Private. E. on 10/19/1864 in Orange. Dis 11/27/1864 (NCT 8, 191).

McCAY, Alexander R., Co. B, Private (1821–). Lived, e. in Gaston 7/30/1861, age 40. Detailed teamster from 6/9/1863–Feb. 1865. Captured at Amelia CH 4/5/1865; confined at Pt. Lookout until released on 6/5/1865 after OOA (NCT 8, 133).

McCLARTY, John M., Co. K, Private (1840–). Lived in Cabarrus, e. in New Hanover 2/4/1862, age 22. Cap-

tured near Petersburg 4/2/1865; confined at Hart's Island until released 6/17/1865 after OOA (NCT 8, 226).

McCOLLUM, Charles, Co. G, Private. Lived, e. in Orange 10/19/1864. Captured in Richmond hospital 4/3/1865. Trans to Newport News 4/23/1865. Released 7/3/1865 after OOA (NCT 8, 191).

McCOLLUM, John, Co. F, Private (1845–). E. in Yadkin 10/27/1863. AWOL 8/1/1864 (NCT 8, 180).

McCRAW, Almerein, Co. H, Private (1841–1864). B., lived, e. in Cleveland 8/22/1861, age 20. Killed at Spotsylvania CH 5/12/1864 (NCT 8, 204).

McCURDY, Caleb S., Previously served in Co. A, 20th Reg NCT. E. in Co. K 4/26/1862 in Stanly. Died in Richmond hospital abt 11/25/1863 of phthisis pulmonalis (NCT 8, 226).

McDANIEL, David, Co. D, Private (1824–) Stanly resident, e. 3/15/1862, age 38. Captured near Petersburg; confined at Hart's Island until released 6/17/1865 after OOA (NCT 8, 159).

McDANIEL, John, Co. E, Private (18__–1865). Served first in Junior Reserves; trans to Co. E, 1/20/1865. Captured in Petersburg hospital 4/3/1865; died there 4/7/1865 (NCT 8, 170).

McDONALD, Howell G., Co. E, Private (1840–1865). Lived, e. in Montgomery 8/1/1861, age 21. Captured near Petersburg 6/22/1864; confined at Pt. Lookout, and died there 4/20/1865 of chronic diarrhea (NCT 8, 170).

McGEE, James Lemuel, Co. A, Private (1844–). B. in Virginia, e. in Surry, age 20 on 1/18/1864. He surrendered at Appomattox on 4/9/1865. He m. in Surry in 1868 Nancy Stanley, dau of Garrett and Mimi Stanley of Rockford. James lived to apply for a Confederate pension (NCT 8, 120; SCS 118).

McGINNIS, James L.B., Co. H, Private (1845–1863). Lived in Rutherford, e. 8/22/1861 in Cleveland, age 16. Wounded, captured and hospitalized at Gettysburg 7/3/1863. Trans to Chester 7/14/1863, and died there 9/5/1863 of "hemorrhage" (NCT 8, 204).

McGUFFIN, William A., Co. A, Private (1844–1862). E. at age 18 on 5/16/1861. Killed near Frayser's Farm Virginia, abt 6/30/1862. Son of Robert F. McGuffin and wife Sarah, who were merchants in Dobson, NC in 1860. This family was from Virginia (NCT 8 120; SCS 119).

McINNIS, Evander J., Co. E, Private (1842–1863). B., lived, e. in Montgomery 8/1/1861, age 19. Wounded, captured and hospitalized at Gettysburg 7/3/1863; hospitalized at Chester, and died there 7/12/1863 (NCT 8, 170).

McINTOSH, Isaac L., Co. B, Private (1830–). Gaston resident, e. 7/30/1861, age 31. Captured at Fredericksburg on 12/13/1862; paroled 12/17/1862. Wounded in the foot and captured at Gettysburg 7/1–5/1863. Hospitalized at Davids Island 7/17–24/1863. Paroled and sent to City Pt. on 9/16/1863 for exc. Reported absent-wounded through Feb. 1865, and paroled at Charlotte, NC 5/15/1865 (NCT 8, 133).

McINTYRE, Isaiah, Co. K, Private (1839–). Lived and e. in Stanly 9/7/1861, age 22. Captured at Hanover CH 5/27/1862; confined at Ft. Monroe, then Ft. Columbus. Trans to Aiken's Landing for exc 8/5/1862. Captured at Spotsylvania CH 5/12/1864; confined at

Pt. Lookout. Trans to Elmira 8/10/1864, and released there 7/7/1865 after OOA (NCT 8, 226).

McINTYRE, John F., Co. K, Private (1829–). Lived and e. in Stanly 9/7/1861, age 32. Captured at Hanover CH 5/27/1862; confined at Ft. Monroe, then Ft. Columbus. Trans to Aiken's Landing for exc 8/5/1862. Returned. Hospitalized at Danville 5/18/1864 with gunshot wound of shoulder. Retired to Invalid Corps 11/9/1864, due to disability (NCT 8, 226).

McINTYRE, Stokes, Co. K, Private (1806–). B., lived, and e. in Stanly 9/7/1861, age 56. Dis 3/6/1862 due to "varicose veins of the legs" (NCT 8, 226).

McKAUGHN, B. Temple, Co. I, Private (1844–). Lived, e. in Yadkin 3/8/1862, age 18. Captured; confined at Ft. Monroe 8/26/1862. Paroled and exc abt 9/21/1862. Wounded at Gettysburg 7/1–3/1863 (NCT 8, 215).

McKAY, Robert B., Co. E, Sergeant (1843–). Lived in Montgomery, e. in Guilford 9/25/1861, age 18, as private. Promoted to sergeant Nov. 1862–Oct. 1864. Captured near Petersburg 4/2/1865; confined at Pt. Lookout until released 6/19/1865 after OOA (NCT 8, 170).

McKEE, J.W., Co. B, Private (1823–1862). Gaston resident, e. 7/30/1861, age 38. Wounded at Fredericksburg on 12/13/1862, died there 12/14/1862 from wounds (NCT 8, 133).

McKENZIE, James A., Co. E, Private (1837–). Lived, e. in Montgomery where he e. 8/1/1861, age 24. Surrendered at Appomattox CH 4/9/1865 (NCT 8, 170).

McKINLEY, Steven C., Co. K, Private (1843–1864). B. and lived in Cabarrus, e. in New Hanover 2/4/1862, age 19. Captured near Hanover CH 5/28/1862; confined at Ft. Monroe, then Ft. Delaware. Trans to Aiken's Landing for exc on 8/5/1862. Returned. Hospitalized at Richmond abt 8/26/1864 with gunshot wound of chest. Died "at his home" 11/23/1864 of wounds (NCT 8, 226).

McKINNEY, Joseph D., Co. H, Private (1844–1862). Lived, e. in Cleveland 8/22/1861, age 17. Died at Wilmington NC abt 2/15/1862 (NCT 8, 204).

McKINNIE (McKinney), Jesse, Co. A, Corporal (1841–1863). B. in Surry to Fountain and Martha Moore McKinney, of Dobson. Joined the 74th Reg, 18th Brigade of militia, then Co. A 3/18/1862, age 21. Killed at Chancellorsville 5/3/1863. Jesse m. in 1859, Surry, Phoebe Gillespie. After the war Phoebe and her son, Thomas P., lived with her parents near Dobson (NCT 8, 120; SCS 120).

McLEAN, John, Co. E, Private (1835–1863). Lived, e. in Montgomery 8/1/1861, age 26. Captured at 2nd Manassas 8/28–30/1862; confined at Ft. Monroe. Paroled, trans to Aiken's Landing 9/21/1862 for exc. Died in Richmond hospital 2/18/1863 of "pneumonia" (NCT 8, 170).

McLESTER, Alexander G., Co. D, Private (1840–). Stanly resident, e. 7/19/1861, age 21. Dis in fall of 1863 because of a "fistula." NC pension records state he was wounded at Guinea Station in Nov. 1862 (NCT 8, 159).

McLURE, John J., Co. B, Private (1844–1863). Lived, e. in Gaston 3/29/1862, age 18. Captured at Hanover CH 5/27/1862; confined at Ft. Monroe, then

Ft. Columbus. Paroled and sent to Aiken's Landing for exc 8/5/1862. Died in Richmond hospital abt 1/18/1863 of pneumonia (NCT 8, 133).

McRAE, Duncan A., Co. I, 3rd. Lt; Field & Staff, 1st Lieutenant (1837–). Lived in Montgomery, e. at age 24, and appointed 3rd Lt. 8/1/1861, then Adjutant (1st Lt.) 10/18/1861. Trans to Field & Staff of the 28th. Resigned on 1/6/1863, no reason given. (NCT 8, 110, 164).

McRAE, George W., Co. E, Private (1842–). Lived, e. in Montgomery 8/1/1861, age 19. Wounded in right arm at Reams' Station 8/25/1864. Retired to Invalid Corps 12/21/1864 due to disability (NCT 8, 170).

McRAE, James Lawrence, Co. E, 3rd Lieutenant (1841–). Lived, e. in Montgomery 8/1/1861 as a sergeant. Elected 3rd lieutenant 2/28/1862. Resigned 7/23/1862; continued to serve in Co. E as a private. Wounded at Gettysburg 7/1–3/1863. Captured near Petersburg 4/2/1865; confined at Pt. Lookout until released 6/29/1865 after OOA (NCT 8, 164, 170).

McREE, James Fergus, Field & Staff, Surgeon. Previously surgeon of the 3rd Reg NCT, appointed surgeon of the 28th sometime in 1864. "Relieved" before 10/1/1864 (NCT 8, 111).

McROBERTS, Benjamin, Co. A, Private (1827–). B. in Virginia to John and Bency McRoberts, he e. 3/16/1862, age 30. Deserted May–Oct. 1862. Some censuses list McRoberts as "Roberts." He m. Amy Frances Williams, and had several children by 1880. (NCT 8, 120; SCS 120).

McSWAIN, Benjamin F., Co. H, Private (1818–). Cleveland resident, e. 8/22/1861 there, age 43. Dis 9/23/1864, reason not stated (NCT 8, 204).

McSWAIN, Burrell B., Co. H, Private (1829–). Lived, e. in Cleveland 3/17/1862, age 33. Wounded at Cedar Mt 8/9/1862. Wounded at Chancellorsville 5/1–3/1863. Wounded at Gettysburg. Served as hospital guard 8/19/1864–Feb 1865 (NCT 8, 204).

McSWAIN, C.J., Co. K, Private (1824–1863). Lived and e. in Stanly 9/7/1861, age 37. Deserted 8/26/1863. Apprehended and court-martialed abt 9/17/1863. "Shot by order of court-martial" near Liberty Mills 9/26/1863 (NCT 8, 226).

McSWAIN, David L., Co. H, Private (1840–1862). Lived, e. in Cleveland 3/17/1862, age 22. Captured at Hanover CH; confined at Ft. Monroe, then Ft. Columbus. Paroled and trans to Aiken's Landing for exc 8/5/1862. Died in Richmond 8/29/1862, cause not reported (NCT 8, 204).

McSWAIN, George W., Co. H, Private (1830–1863). Lived, e. in Cleveland 3/17/1862, age 32. Died at home abt 2/11/1863 of "chronic rheumatism and diarrhoea" (NCT 8, 204).

McSWAIN, James, Co. H, Private. E. in Cleveland 8/22/1861. Hospitalized at Wilmington NC abt 2/25/1862; died there from "febris typhoides" 3/3/1862 (NCT 8, 204).

McSWAIN, Robert E., Co. H, Private (1839–1862). Lived, e. in Cleveland 3/17/1862. Wounded at Gaines' Mill abt 6/27/1862. Hospitalized in Raleigh, NC; died there 9/5/1862 of wounds and/or typhoid fever (NCT 8, 204).

McSWAIN, William D., Co. H, Private (1822–1864).

Lived, e. in Cleveland 3/17/1862, age 40. Wounded at Ox Hill 9/1/1862. Returned. Died in Richmond hospital 10/30–/1864 from gunshot wound of hand and amputation of arm (NCT 8, 204).

McWEBB, John, Co. H, Private (1841–). B., lived, e. in Cleveland 3/17/1862, age 21. Dis 9/14/1863 due to "hypertrophy and dilation of left ventricle of heard, attended with great debility [and] chronic diarrhoea" (NCT 8, 204).

MELTON, Richard Greene, Co. I, Private (1827–1862). Lived, e. in Yadkin 3/8/1862; age 35. Died in Richmond hospital 7/27/1862 or 8/9/1862 of chronic diarrhea or "erysipelas" (NCT 8, 215). He was the brother to Zacharia Melton in same company.

MELTON, Zacharia, Co. I, Private (1839–). Lived, e. in Yadkin 3/8/1862, age 23. Captured at Hanover CH 5/27/1862; confined at Ft. Monroe, then Ft. Columbus. Paroled and trans to Aiken's Landing for exc 8/5/1862. AWOL Jan.–Feb. 1863. Returned and trans to Co. G, 52nd Reg NCT on 9/22/1864 (NCT 8, 215).

MENDENHALL, E.B., Co. B, Private (1837–1862). Gaston resident, e.7/30/1861, age 24. Died "on the march" near Smithfield 10/28/1862 of "apoplexy" (NCT 8, 134).

MERRITT, Morris, Co. G, Private (1843–1862). Lived, e. in Orange 9/17/1861, age 18. Died in Richmond hospital 6/29/1862 "of exhaustion in the battle of Cold Harbor [Gaines' Mill]" (NCT 8, 191).

MICHAELS, Nicholas, Co. F, Private (1837–) Lived, e. in Yadkin 6/18/1861. Wounded in left hand and captured near Hanover CH 5/27/1862; confined at Ft. Monroe, then Ft. Columbus. Paroled and trans to Aiken's Landing for exc 8/5/1862. Returned. Deserted 5/27/1864 (NCT 8, 180).

MILLER, A.S., Co. D, Private (1838–). Stanly resident, Miller e. 7/29/1861, age 23, but was "rejected when mustered in service" (NCT 8, 159).

MILLER, Abel A., Co. H, Private. Born in Catawba, e. at Camp Vance 2/24/1864. Died at Richmond or at Lynchburg 5/2–6/1864 of chronic bronchitis (NCT 8, 204).

MILLER, Adam D., Co. D, Private (1843–1862). Stanly resident, e. 3/15/1862, age 19. Died "in the United States" July 1863. (NCT 8, 159).

MILLER, Arthur K., Co. D, Private (1839–). B., lived, in Stanly, a blacksmith when he e. there 7/29/1861, age 22. Captured at Hanover CH 5/17/1862; confined at Ft. Monroe, then Ft. Columbus in New York Harbor. Paroled and trans to Aiken's Landing, on 7/12/1862, and was exc 8/5/1862. Captured at Chancellorsville 5/3/1863; confined at Washington, DC. Paroled and trans to City Pt. 5/13/1863 for exc. Captured again at Gettysburg 7/3/1863; confined at Ft. Delaware, trans to Pt. Lookout 10/15–18/1863. Released 1/25/1864 after OOA and joining the U.S. Army. Assigned to Co. D, 1st Reg U.S. Volunteer Infantry (NCT 8, 159).

MILLER, Caleb, Co. C, Corporal (18__–1862). Catawba resident e. 3/15/1862, promoted to corporal 4/15/1862. Died in Richmond 12/1/1862 of smallpox (NCT 8, 148).

MILLER, David, Co. H, Private. E. 8/22/1863 at Camp Vance. Present through Feb. 1865 (NCT 8, 204).

MILLER, David E., Co. C, Private. Lived, e. in Catawba 3/14/1863. Wounded at Wilderness 5/5/1864. Retired to Invalid Corps 12/18/1864 due to disability (NCT 8, 148).

MILLER, Dennis, Co. B, Private (1836–1862). Lived, e. in Gaston 7/30/1861, age 25. Died in a Richmond hospital 11/19/1862 of typhoid fever (NCT 8, 134).

MILLER, Hiram A., Co. C, Private. Lived, e. in Catawba 3/15/1862. Wounded in the hand at Frayser's Farm 6/30/1862. Wounded at Chancellorsville 5/2–3/1863. Wounded and captured at Gettysburg. Hospitalized at Davids Island 7/17–24/1863. Paroled and trans to City Pt. on 9/16/1863 for exc. Trans to C. S. Navy on 4/3/1864 (NCT 8, 148).

MILLER, Jones M., Co. H, Private. Previously served in Co. E, 12th Reg NCT. Trans to Co. H, 28th Reg Mar–Apr 1864. Surrendered at Appomattox CH 4/9/1865 (NCT 8, 204).

MILLER, Marcus, Co. C, Private (18__–1864). Lived, e. in Catawba 8/13/1861. Killed at Spotsylvania CH 5/12/1864 (NCT 8, 148).

MILLER, Roland C, Co. D, Corporal (1837–). Stanly farmer before he e. on 3/15/1862, age 25, as a private. Promoted to corporal Jan. 1863–June 1864. Wounded in left hand at South Anna bridge in 1863. Reported AWOL abt 11/30/1864; reduced in rank that day. Retired from service 1/4/1865 due to disability of hand (NCT 8, 159).

MILLER, Samuel E., Co. C, Private (18__–1863). B., lived in Catawba, e. at Camp Fisher on 9/9/1861. Died at Lynchburg 1/6/1863 of chronic diarrhea and/or "phthisis pulmonalis" (NCT 8, 148).

MILLER, Thomas A.G., Co. D, Private. E. Camp Stokes 12/13/1864. Present through Feb. 1865 (NCT 8, 159).

MILLER, William A., Co. B, Private (1841–1864). B. in York District, SC, lived and e. in Gaston 7/30/1861, age 20. Wounded at Gaines' Mill 6/27/1862. Died in hospital at Liberty (Mills?) 6/24/1864 of pneumonia (NCT 8, 134).

MILLER, William Henry, Co. F, Private (1820–) Lived, e. in Yadkin 11/5/1863, age 43. Captured in Richmond hospital 4/3/1865; confined at Pt. Lookout until released abt 6/26/1865, after OOA (NCT 8, 180).

MILLER, William J., Co. C, Private. Lived, e. in Catawba 8/13/1861. Killed at Gettysburg 7/3/1863. "A most gallant soldier" (NCT 8, 148).

MILLS, Hiram M., Co. E, Private (1831–1862). Lived, e. in Montgomery 8/1/1861, age 30. Died in Richmond hospital 6/15/1862 of remittent fever (NCT 8, 171).

MILTON, Elisha H, Co. K, Private (1839–). B., lived, he was a wheelwright before he e. in Stanly 9/7/1861, age 22. Captured at Falling Waters 7/14/1863; confined at Ft. McHenry; trans to Pt. Lookout 8/21–22/1863. Released 1/24/1864 after OOA and joining the U.S. Army, Co. B, 1st Reg U.S. Volunteer Infantry (NCT 8, 227).

MILTON, George, Co. K, Private (1844–). Lived and e. in Stanly 3/14/1862, age 18. Captured at Hanover

CH 5/27/1862; confined at Ft. Columbus. Trans to Aiken's Landing for exchange 8/5/1862. Returned. Wounded at Fredericksburg 12/13/1862. Present through Feb. 1865 (NCT 8, 227).

MILTON, J., Co. K, Private. Date and place of enlistment not reported. Surrendered at Appomattox CH 4/9/1865 (NCT 8, 227).

MISENHIMER, John A., Co. K, Private (1842–1862). Lived and e. in Stanly 9/7/1861, age 19. Died in hospital near Lynchburg 6/23/1864 of typhoid fever (NCT 8, 227).

MITCHELL, Hiram, Co. F, Private (1839–1862). B., lived e. in Yadkin 6/18/1861, age 22. Died in Yadkin abt 2/25/1862 (NCT 8, 180).

MOCK, John, Co. I, Private (1824–1862). B. in England, lived and e. in Yadkin 3/8/1862, age 38. Captured at Hanover CH 5/27/1862; confined at Ft. Monroe, then Ft. Columbus. Paroled and trans to Aiken's Landing for exc 8/5/1862. Hospitalized at Richmond 8/7/1862 with "phthisis" and died in a Richmond "horse pittle"[sic] 8/11/1862 (NCT 8, 215; W. A. Tesh letter, 8/13/1862, Duke Univ.).

MONTGOMERY, William James, Co. D; Field & Staff, Major (1835–). Lived, e. in Stanly in Co. D, 28th Reg, age 26. Appointed captain 7/29/1861. Appointed major 6/12/1862, and trans to Field & Staff. Resigned 9/29/1862 due to severe and prolonged diarrhea (NCT 8, 110, 153).

MOODY, Daniel W., Co. K, Private (1843–1864). B. and lived in Cabarrus, e. in New Hanover 2/4/1862, age 19. Wounded in left hand and captured at Gettysburg 7/1–3/1863. Middle finger amputated. Exc before 8/1/1863, when he was hospitalized at Petersburg. Died "at his home" 11/23/1864. Cause not reported (NCT 8, 227).

MOODY, John A., Co. K, Captain (1828–). Lived in Surry, e. and appointed captain 9/7/1861. Resigned 7/1/1863 due to disability fro pneumonia, typhoid fever, chronic diarrhea and rheumatism (NCT 8, 220).

MOODY, Woodson, R., Co. A, Corporal (1840–). E. 5/4/186, age 21, as a private; promoted to corporal in Nov. 1862–Feb. 1863. Present through Feb. 1865. Woodson, b. in Surry, was the son of John R. and Saran Snow Moody, who lived in the Hotel (Elkin) District. He m. in Surry in 1864 Mary Ann Cunningham (NCT 8, 120; SCS 126).

MOORE, David O.H.P., Co. H, Private. E. 10/5/1864 at Camp Vance. Surrendered at Appomattox CH 4/9/1865 (NCT 8, 204–205).

MOORE, Elijah, Co. A, Private (1831–). E. in Surry, age 30, 5/13/1861. Surrendered at Appomattox 4/9/1865. Son of John Moore, Sr., and second wife, Nancy Dezern Moore, of Siloam. Elijah m. in Surry in 1865 Elizabeth Franklin (NCT 8, 120; SCS 127).

MOORE, George M., Jr., Co. H, Private (1847–). E. 1/10/1864 in Cleveland, age 17. Wounded in left foot at Reams' Station 8/25/1864, foot amputated. Absent-wounded through Feb. 1865 (NCT 8, 205).

MOORE, George M., Sr., Co. H, Private. E. 10/9/1864 at Camp Holmes. Surrendered at Appomattox CH 4/9/1865 (NCT 8, 205).

MOORE, Isaac, Co. I, Private (1825). Lived, e. in

Yadkin 3/8/1862, age 37. Captured near Petersburg 4/2/1865; confined at Ft. Delaware; released 6/19/1865 after OOA (NCT 8, 215).

MOORE, James J., Co. G, Private (1843–1862). Lived, e. in Orange 3/5/1862. Died in Orange 11/23/1862 of disease (NCT 8, 191).

MOORE, John A., Co. C, Private (18__–1862). Lived, e. in Catawba 8/13/1861. Wounded at Hanover CH 5/27/1862. Died in Richmond 6/10–11, 1862 of wounds (NCT 8, 148).

MOORE, Lemuel, Co. K, Private. E. in Granville 10/20/1863. Captured near Spotsylvania CH abt 5/12/1864; confined at Pt. Lookout, where he died 7/20/1864 of "dysentery acute" (NCT 8, 227).

MOORE, Thomas H., Jr., Co. A, Private (1840–). B., lived, e. in Surry 5/13/1861, age 21. Captured near Petersburg 4/2/1865; confined at Ft. Delaware until released on 6/19/1865, after OOA. NC pension records indicate he was wounded in the head and left side at Petersburg in 1864. Son of Thomas Moore, Sr., and Mary Phillips Moore (NCT 8, 120; SCS 128).

MOOSE, Alexander F., Co. D, Corporal (1839–1862). Stanly resident, e. 7/29/1861, age 22, as a corporal. Died "at home" 11/5/1862 of disease. "A noble soldier" (NCT 8, 159–160).

MOOSE, Daniel W., Co. K, Private (1842–). Lived and e. in Stanly 3/15/1862, age 20. Captured near Petersburg 4/2/1865; confined at Davids Island abt 7/1/1865 until released 7/12/1865 after OOA (NCT 8, 227).

MOOSE, Edmund, Co. D, Sergeant; Field & Staff, Quartermaster Sergeant (1833–1863). Edmund lived, e. in Stanly in Co. D, 28th Reg on 7/19/1861, age 28, as sergeant; promoted to quartermaster sergeant from May–December 1861. Trans to Field & Staff of the 28th Reg. Appointed 2nd lieutenant on 3/18/1863, he trans back to Co. D, and was promoted to 1st lieutenant 5/2/1863. Wounded and captured at Gettysburg 7/1–5/1863; hospitalized in Baltimore. Trans to Chester hospital 7/20/1863, and died 9/27/1863 of "exhaustion." (NCT 8, 112, 153).

MOOSE, Henry D., Co. D, Private (1842–1862). B., lived, e. in Stanly 7/29/1861, age 19. Died at Wilmington 1/27/1862 (NCT 8, 160).

MOOSE, Jacob A., Co. K, Private. Lived and e. in Stanly 10/31/1864. Captured near Petersburg 4/2/1865; confined at Hart's Island until released 6/17/1865 after OOA (NCT 8, 227).

MORGAN, George H., Co. E, Private (1845–). Lived, e. in Montgomery 3/4/1863, age 18. Captured at Spotsylvania CH 4/12/1864; confined at Pt. Lookout; trans to Elmira 8/10/1864. Released there 6/27/1865 after OOA (NCT 8, 171).

MORRIS, Baxter B., Co. G, Private (1841–1862). Lived, e. in Orange 3/5/1862, age 21. Wounded in knee and/or left thigh and captured at Hanover CH 5/27/1862. Died in hospital at Ft. Monroe abt 6/30/1862 of wounds (NCT 8, 191).

MORRIS, David A., Co. D, Private. Lived, e. in Stanly 3/15/1862, Wounded in the hip at Gaines' Mill 6/27/1862. Dis 2/23/1863 due to disability. Reenlisted in the same company 3/1/1864. Captured near Petersburg 4/2/1865; confined at Pt. Lookout until released 6/29/1865 after OOA (NCT 8, 160).

MORRIS, Doctor M., Co. D, Private (1841–). B., lived, e. in Stanly 7/29/1861. Dis 12/14/1861 due to "rheumatism" (NCT 8, 160).

MORRIS, Green Richardson, Co. E, Private (1834–). Lived, e. in Montgomery 8/1/1861, age 27. Company records indicate he was captured at 2nd Manassas, but Federal provost marshal records do not agree. Trans to Co. B, 14th Reg NCT 4/14/1864 (NCT 8, 171).

MORRIS, Isaac J., Co. G, Private (1838–) Lived, e. in Orange e. 3/5/1862, age 24, as a substitute. Captured near Hanover CH abt 5/27/1862; confined at Ft. Monroe and Ft. Columbus. Paroled and trans to Aiken's Landing for exc 8/5/1862. Wounded in left leg near Kelly's Ford abt 11/7/1863. Hospitalized at Richmond. Furloughed 2/10/1864. Retired to Invalid Corps 11/15/1864. NC pension records state he was wounded in the right knee at Gaines' Mill 6/26/1862, and in the left shoulder at Petersburg 4/26/1865(4?) (NCT 8, 191).

MORRIS, J.F., Co. D, Private (18__–1862). E. in Stanly 3/15/1862; died in Lynchburg hospital 7/25/1862 of "phthisis pulmonalis" (NCT 8, 160).

MORRIS, James C., Co. E, Private (1831–). Lived, e. in Montgomery 8/1/1861, age 30. Dis 12/30/1861 due to "chronic rheumatism" (NCT 8, 171).

MORRIS, John A., Co. G, Private (1843–1863). Lived, e. in Orange 3/5/1862, age 19. Captured near Hanover CH abt 5/27/1862; confined at Ft. Monroe and Ft. Columbus. Paroled and trans to Aiken's Landing for exc 8/5/1862. Captured at Fredericksburg 12/13/1862; exc abt 12/17/1862. Wounded at Chancellorsville 5/2–3/1863. Killed at Gettysburg 7/3/1863 (NCT 8, 191).

MORRIS, John R., Co. G, Private (1844–). Lived, e. in Orange 3/5/1862, age 18. Captured near Hanover CH abt 5/27/1862; confined at Ft. Monroe and Ft. Columbus. Paroled and trans to Aiken's Landing for exc 8/5/1862. Wounded in right leg at Chancellorsville 5/2/1863. Retired to Invalid Corps 9/28/1864 (NCT 8, 191).

MORRIS, Sampson, Co. E, Private (1829–). Lived, e. in Montgomery. 8/1/1861, age 32. Wounded at Gettysburg 7/1–3/1863. Wounded in left knee at Jones' Farm 9/30/1864. AWOL 12/25–1864 through Feb. 1865. Paroled at Troy, NC 5/22/1865 (NCT 8, 171).

MORRIS, Wilson C., Co. D, Private (1838–). Stanly resident, e. 3/15/1862, age 24. Wounded in right foot, captured at Gettysburg 7/1–3/1863; hospitalized at Davids Island until paroled and trans to City Pt. on 8/28/1863 for exc. Hospitalized at Richmond 2/23/1864 with gunshot wound of left hand. Dis 4/18/1864 due to "disease of the heart" (NCT 8, 160).

MORROW, Alexander, Co. C, Private. E. in Lenoir 4/10/1862. Captured near Hanover CH abt 5/27/1862; confined at Ft. Monroe and Ft. Columbus. Paroled and trans to Aiken's Landing for exc 8/5/1862. (NCT 8, 191).

MORROW, Daniel F., Co. G, 1st Lieutenant (1842–). A student, b., lived in Alamance; e. in Orange 9/2/1861, age 19. Promoted to sergeant 3/1/1862. Cap-

tured at Hanover CT 5/27/1862; confined at Ft. Monroe, then Ft. Columbus. Paroled and trans to Aiken's Landing for exc 8/5/1862. Wounded at Chancellorsville 5/2–3/1863. Appointed 2nd lieutenant abt 8/18/1863; then 1st lieutenant 1/28/1865. Surrendered at Appomattox CH 4/9/1865 (NCT 8, 185).

MORROW, Elijah Graham, Co. G, Captain (1833–1863). Lived, e. in Orange 9/2/1861, age 28, and was appointed 2nd lieutenant. Promoted to 1st lieutenant 5/1/1862. Captured at Fredericksburg 12/13/1862; exc 12/17/1862. Promoted to captain 1/19/1863. Wounded at Chancellorsville 5/2–3/1863. Wounded in thigh and captured at Gettysburg. Leg amputated. Died in hospital there 7/19/1863 of wounds (NCT 8, 185).

MORROW, John A., Co. B, Private (1841–). Lived, e. in Gaston 7/30/1861, age 20. Captured at Fredericksburg 12/13/1862; paroled 12/17/1862. Wounded at Chancellorsville 5/2–3/1863. Wounded, captured at Gettysburg, 7/1–5/1863. Hospitalized at Gettysburg, then Chester 7/19/1863. Paroled and sent to City Pt. on 9/23/1863 for exc. Captured at Petersburg 7/29–30/1864; confined at Pt. Lookout, trans to Elmira 8/8/1864. Paroled and sent back to Pt. Lookout 10/11/1864. Trans to Venus Point, Savannah River, GA on 11/15/1864 for exc. Retired to Invalid Corps 1/18/1865 due to debility (NCT 8, 134).

MORROW, Richard A., Co. G, Private (1842–1862). Lived, e. in Orange 3/5/1862, age 20. Captured at Hanover CH 5/27/1862; confined at Ft. Monroe then Ft. Columbus. Paroled and trans to Aiken's Landing for exc 8/5/1862. Wounded at Fredericksburg 12/13/1862 and died 12/14/1862. May have served previously in Co. D, 1st Reg NC Infantry (NCT 8, 191).

MORROW, William J., Co. B, Private. From Gaston, e. at Liberty Mills 3/15/1864. Died at Spotsylvania CH on 5/22/1864 (NCT 8, 134).

MORTON, Edmund D., Co. D, Private (1838–1863). Stanly resident, e. 7/29/1861, age 23. Died at Guinea Station 2/4/1863 of disease (NCT 8, 160).

MORTON, Ezekiel R., Co. K, Private (1840–1862). Lived and e. in Stanly 3/20/1862, age 22. Hospitalized at Richmond 7/2/1862 with gunshot wound of hand. Died in Richmond hospital 8/23/1862 of typhoid fever (NCT 8, 227).

MORTON, James, Co. K, Musician (1830–). Lived and e. in Stanly 3/20/1862, age 22. Hospitalized at Richmond 10/2/1864 with gunshot wound of right arm. Returned. Surrendered at Appomattox CH 4/9/1865 (NCT 8, 227).

MORTON, Jesse A., Jr., Co. K, Private (1842–1862). Lived and e. in Stanly 3/20/1862, age 20. Killed in fighting near Richmond June 1862 (NCT 8, 227).

MORTON, Jesse A., Sr., Co. K, Private (1838–), Lived and e. in Stanly 9/7/1861, age 23. Captured at Hanover CH 5/27/1862; confined at Ft. Monroe, then Ft. Columbus. Trans to Aiken's Landing for exc 8/5/1862. Returned. Captured near Petersburg 4/2/1865; confined at Pt. Lookout until released 6/29/1865 after OOA (NCT 8, 227).

MORTON, Lemuel, Co. K, Private (1840–1863). Lived and e. in Stanly 9/7/1861, age 21. Captured at Hanover CH 5/27/1862; confined at Ft. Monroe, then

Ft. Columbus. Trans to Aiken's Landing for exc 8/5/1862. Returned. Wounded at Chancellorsville 5/1–4/1863. Died at Guinea Station 5/8/1863 of wounds (NCT 8, 227).

MORTON, W.B., Co. D, Private (1834–1862). B., lived in Stanly as a "daguerrean artist;" e. 7/29/1861, age 27. Dis 1/27/1862 due to "a protracted attack of pneumonia followed by a chronic cough and diarrhea." Died 1/30/1862 of disease (NCT 8, 160).

MORTON, William G., Co. K, Private (1841–). Lived and e. in Stanly 3/10/1862, age 21. Captured at Hanover CH 5/27/1862; confined at Ft. Monroe, then Ft. Columbus. Trans to Aiken's Landing for exc 8/5/1862. Returned. Captured near Spotsylvania CH 5/12/1864; confined at Pt. Lookout. Trans to Elmira 8/10/1864, then trans to Boulware's Wharf for exc 3/18–21/1865 (NCT 8, 227–228).

MOSELEY (Mosley), Henry D., Co. A, Private 1820–1896). B. in Surry to Henry and Martha East Mosley, Hotel (Elkin) District of Surry. E. at age 40 on 5/4/1861; Dis 5/2/1862 as overage. Died 2/21/1896, bur. at the Rock Springs Cemetery, Surry (NCT 8, 120; SCS 129).

MOSS, James R., Co. D, Private ? NC pension records indicate he served in this company (NCT 8, 160).

MOTLEY, Thomas, Co. K, Private (1832–). Lived and e. in Stanly 3/17/1862, age 30. Captured at Hanover CH 5/27/1862; confined at Ft. Monroe, then Ft. Columbus. Trans to Aiken's Landing for exc 8/5/1862. Returned. Surrendered at Appomattox CH 4/9/1865 (NCT 8, 228).

MUNN, Martin A., Co. F., Sergeant (1833–1862). Lived, e. in Montgomery 8/1/1861, age 28, as a private; promoted to sergeant 9/8/1862. Wounded at Shepherdstown 9/20/1862, and died at Winchester 9/25/1862 of wounds (NCT 8, 171).

MURPHY, Abraham, Co. F, Private (1833–1863). B., lived, e. in Yadkin 6/18/1861, age 28. Died at Camp Gregg 3/6/1863 of "pneumonia" (NCT 8, 180).

MURPHY, Benjamin, Co. F, Private (1833–). Lived, e. in Yadkin 11/5/1863, age 30. AWOL 3/2/1864–9/10/1864. Returned. Captured near Petersburg 4/2/1865; confined at Pt. Lookout until released 6/29/1865 after OOA (NCT 8, 180–181).

MURPHY, James, Co. D, Private. Catawba resident, e. at Camp Stokes 10/28/1864. Trans to Co. G, 12th Reg NCT on 2/8/1865 (NCT 8, 160).

MURPHY, John F., Co. B, Private (1840–). Gaston farmer, e. 7/30/1861, age 21. Hospitalized in Richmond 7/2/1862 with gunshot wound of hand. Wounded in finger and/or arm at 2nd Manassas 8/27–30/1862. Wounded at Chancellorsville 5/2–3/1863. Wounded and captured at Gettysburg 7/1–5/1863. Hospitalized at Gettysburg, then Davids Island. Trans to City Pt. on 9/8/1863 for exc. Wounded in left leg near Petersburg 9/16/1864. Leg amputated. Absent-wounded 2/15/1865; retired due to disability (NCT 8, 134).

MURPHY, John O., Co. B, Private (1845–). Lived, e. in Lincoln 3/9/1863, age 18. Wounded at Chancellorsville 5/1–3/1863. Wounded at Gettysburg 7/1–3/1863. Wounded "in Virginia" 5/3–14/1864. Captured at Amelia CH 4/3/1865. Confined at Pt. Lookout until released on 6/29/1865 after OOA (NCT 8, 134).

MURRAH (Murray/Murry), Milton, Co. F, Private (1839–1863). Lived in Yadkin, e. 6/18/1861, age 22. Killed at Chancellorsville 5/3/1863 (NCT 8, 181).

MYERS, Frederick A., Co. F, Sergeant (1840–). Lived, e. in Yadkin 6/18/1861 as a private. Promoted to sergeant 5/11/1863. Captured near Petersburg 4/2/1865; confined at Pt. Lookout until released 6/29/1865 after OOA (NCT 8, 181).

MYERS, George D., Co. F, Private (1842–). Lived, e. in Yadkin 6/18/1861, age 19. Wounded in left shoulder at Ox Hill 9/1/1862. Went home on furlough 10/1/1862, and never returned (NCT 8, 181).

MYERS, John, Co. I, Private (1839–1862). Lived and e. in Yadkin 3/8/1862, age 23. Died in Lynchburg hospital abt 12/18/1862 of "pneumonia" (NCT 8, 215).

MYERS, William H., Co. F, Private (1846–). Lived, e. in Yadkin 11/5/1863, age 17. Captured near Petersburg 4/2/1865; confined at Pt. Lookout until released 6/29/1865 after OOA (NCT 8, 181).

NANCE, Joseph W., Co. F, Corporal (1840–1864). Lived, e. in Yadkin 6/18/1861, age 31. Promoted to corporal Jan. 1863–Oct. 1864. Captured near Petersburg 7/29/1864; confined at Pt. Lookout; then Elmira 8/8/1864 and died 10/25/1864 of "pneumonia" (NCT 8, 181).

NANCE, Richard S., Co. A, Private (1839–). B. in what is now Yadkin. In 1850, he was living with his mother, Cisley, and attended school. He e. in Surry 5/4/1861, age 22. Wounded in left arm at Malvern Hill 7/1/1862, last of the Seven Days Battles. Arm amputated; Dis 1/26/1863 due to disability (NCT 8, 120; SCS, 1850 Surry Census).

NASH, Simpson J., Co. K, Private (1843–). Lived and e. in Stanly 9/7/1861, age 18. Wounded, captured at Gettysburg 7/1–3/1863. Hospitalized at Davids Island. Exchanged before 9/28/1863. Retired to Invalid Corps 9/28/1864 due to disability (NCT 8, 228).

NEAGLE, J.L.K., Co. B, Corporal (1839–1862). B. in Mecklenburg, lived and e. in Gaston 7/30/1861, age 22. Promoted to corporal Jan.–April. 1862. Killed at Fredericksburg 12/13/1862 by a gunshot wound near his heart (NCT 8, 134).

NEAL, George W., Co. F, Private (1841–). Lived in Forsyth, e. in Alamance, age 21, 10/1/1862. "Went home on furlough on April 28, 1864, & never returned" (NCT 8, 181).

NEAL, James, Co. H, Private (1834–1862). A Cleveland miller, e. there 3/17/1862, age 28. Died in Lynchburg hospital abt 5/23/1862 of "rubeola" (NCT 8, 205).

NEIL, Christopher, Co. B, Corporal (1841–1864). B. and e. in Gaston 7/30/1861, age 20, as a private. Captured at Hanover CH 5/27/1862; confined at Ft. Monroe, then Ft. Columbus. Paroled and sent to Aiken's Landing for exc 8/5/1862. Captured at Fredericksburg 12/13/1862; paroled 12/17/1862. Promoted to corporal March–Dec. 1863. Wounded at Chancellorsville 5/2–3/1863. Captured at Gettysburg 7/3–51863. Hospitalized at Chester, before being sent 9/22/1863 to City Pt. for exc. Wounded in the left leg near Stoke's Farm abt

5/28/1864. Hospitalized at Richmond where he died abt 9/26/1864 of wounds (NCT 8, 134).

NEIL, Peter, Co. B, Private (1839–). Lived, e. in Gaston age 22. Wounded in the thigh and captured at Gettysburg 7/3/1863. Hospitalized at Chester, then trans to City Pt. for exc on 8/20/1863. Wounded in right thigh and captured near Petersburg 4/2/1865. Hospitalized at Ft. Monroe 4/4/1865; released 6/11/1865 (NCT 8, 135).

NELSON, John, Co. K, Private (1831–1863). Lived in Cabarrus, e. in Stanly 9/27/1862, age 31. Missing in action and "supposed to be killed" at Gettysburg 7/3/1863 (NCT 8, 228).

NEVILL, Jesse, Co. G, Sergeant (1842–1864). Lived, e. in Orange 9/2/1861, age 19 as a private. Captured at Hanover CH 5/27/1862; confined at Ft. Monroe then Ft. Columbus. Paroled and trans to Aiken's Landing for exc 8/5/1862. Captured at Fredericksburg 12/13/1862; exc abt 12/17/1862. Promoted to corporal Jan 1863, and to sergeant April 1863. Killed at Wilderness 5/6/1864 (NCT 8, 191–192).

NEWBY, William, Co. D, Private (1830–). Stanly resident, e. 3/15/1862, age 32. Deserted 9/14/1863. Captured at Wilderness 5/12/1864. Confined at Pt. Lookout until released 5/30/1864 after OOA and joining the U.S. Army (NCT 8, 160).

NICHOLS, Abraham S., Co. B, Private (1843–1865). Lived, e. in Gaston 7/30/1861, age 18. Captured at Hanover CH 5/27/1862; confined at Ft. Monroe, then Ft. Columbus. Paroled and sent to Aiken's Landing for exc 8/5/1862. Captured at Fredericksburg 12/13/1862. Paroled 12/17/1862. Wounded and captured at Gettysburg 7/1–5/1863. Hospitalized at Davids Island 7/17–24/1861. Paroled and sent to City Pt. 8/28/1863. Exc. Died in brigade hospital 1/29/1865 of disease (NCT 8, 135).

NICHOLS, Jesse, Co. I, Private (1838–). Lived and e. in Yadkin 8/13/1861, age 23. Present through Dec. 1861. Discharged after providing a substitute (NCT 8, 216).

NICHOLS, Noah W., Co. E, Private (1843–) Lived, e. in Montgomery 8/1/1861, age 18. Captured near Petersburg 4/2/1865; confined at Pt. Lookout until released 6/29/1865 after OOA (NCT 8, 171).

NICHOLS, William, Co. I, Private. E. in Yadkin 8/13/1861. Killed at Frayser's Farm 6/30/1862 (NCT 8, 216).

NICHOLS, William A., Co. B, Private (1847–). Gaston farmer, e. at Liberty Mills 2/16/1864, Nichols was wounded in the leg and captured at Wilderness abt 5/6/1864. Exc. Present through Feb. 1865 (NCT 8, 135).

NICHOLSON, James C., Co. F, Private (1834–). Lived, e. in Yadkin 6/18/1861, age 27. Captured at Hanover CH 5/29/1862; confined at Ft. Columbus. Exc. and returned to duty. Captured near Petersburg 4/2/1865; confined at Pt. Lookout until released 6/29/1865 after OOA (NCT 8, 181).

NIXON, F.M., Co. A, 3rd Lieutenant (1836–). Son of Nathan and Mary Nixon, owners of Kapp's Mill on the Mitchell River, e., age 25, 5/4/1861. Promoted to sergeant before 11/1/1863. Rank reduced April of 1862.

Wounded at Gaines' Mill 7/27/1862. Promoted to 1st sergeant 7/1/1862; to 3rd lieutenant on 9/21/1862. Wounded at Cold Harbor June 1864. Present through February 1865. (NCT 8, 113; SCS 130).

NIXON, Nathaniel G., Co. A, Private (1841–1864). B. in Surry to Nathan and Mary Nixon of Devotion, e. 3/24/1864, age 21. Killed 2 months later on 5/23/1864 at Jericho Ford, North Anna River, near Hanover Junction (NCT 8, 120; SCS 131).

NIXON, William P., Co. A., Private (1830–). E., age 21, 5/4/1861. Wounded in left shoulder at Fredericksburg 12/13/1862. Surrender 4/9/1865 at Appomattox (NCT 8, 120).

NOBLES, Thomas, Co. D, Private (1835–). Lived, e. in Stanly 7/29/1862, age 26. Wounded in the side and/or right hand at Frayser's Farm 6/30/1862. Dis 2/23/1863 due to disability from wounds (NCT 8, 160).

NORMAN, Ansel P., Co. A., Private (1832–). Surry resident, e. at age 30 on 3/18/1862; deserted 8/1/1862 (NCT 8, 120).

NORMAN, Henry I., Co. F, Private (1844–). Lived, e. in Yadkin 2/18/1863, age 19. Deserted 9/12/1863. Returned to duty. Captured near Petersburg 4/2/1865; confined at Pt. Lookout until released 6/29/1865 after OOA (NCT 8, 181).

NORMAN, Matthew H., Co. A, 2nd Lieutenant (1841–). Lived in Surry, the son of Clement Norman and Anna Wolff Norman, of Union Hill, Matthew taught school before he e. at Dobson 5/4/1861 as a sergeant in the first group from Surry. Promoted to 2nd lieutenant 4/9/1862 at the reorganization. Captured at Liberty Mills, abt 9/22/1863, confined first at Old Capitol Prison; trans to Johnson's Island. His brother, William M. Norman, was also a prisoner there. Released on 6/12/1865 after OOA (NCT 8, 113; SCS 133).

NORMAN, Thomas, Co. I, Private. Previously with Co. A, 44th Reg NCT, trans to Co. I July 1863–May 1864. Captured at Wilderness 5/12/1864; confined at Pt. Lookout; trans 8/10/1864 to Elmira. Released 6/12/1865 after OOA (NCT 8, 216).

NORMAN, Thomas P., Co. A, Private (1842–1864). B. in Surry to Thomas and Mary Baker Norman of Union Hill. Volunteered on 3/18/1862, age 20, and died 8/31/1864 of gunshot wounds and/or asthma in a Gordonsville hospital (NCT 8, 120–121; SCS 134).

NORMAN, William, Co. F, Private (1825–1863). B., lived in Yadkin, e. 6/19/1861, age 36. Died at Camp Gregg 3/24–26/1863 of pneumonia (NCT 8, 181).

NORMAN, William M., Co. A, Captain (10/14/1833– aft 1886). Surry resident, had attended Judge Richmond Pearson's Law School in Yadkin. After the fall of Ft. Sumter, e. 5/5/1861 as a 1st sergeant. Appointed 1st lieutenant 7/8/1862, then captain 9/21/1861. Present until the election in April of 1862. Trans to 2nd Co. A, of the 2nd Reg NCT; appointed lieutenant to rank from 9/9/1863; promoted to captain to rank from 5/22/1863. Captured at Kelly's Ford 11/17/1863; confined at Old Capitol Prison 11/8/1863; trans to Johnson's Island 11/11/1863. released 5/9/1865. Son of Clement and Anna Catherine Wolff Norman, William m. Letitia Holyfield in 1860, had 9 children between

1861 and 1886). After the war, he became a farmer and surveyor. His war experiences have been published as, *A Portion of My Life* (see bibliography) (NCT 3, 382, NCT 8, 112; SCS 134).

NORTON, James S., Co. A, Private (1834–1862). Son of Jesse and Gilley Bledsoe Norton, Dobson District, Surry, e. 3/18/1862, age 28; died 3 months later on 8/26/1862 of an unspecified illness in Richmond hospital (NCT 8, 121; SCS 134).

OLDHAM, William P., Co. G, 3rd Lieutenant (1837–). Lived, e. in Orange 9/2/1861; appointed 3rd lieutenant. Defeated for reelection abt 3/1/1862. Later was captain of Co. K, 44th Reg NCT (NCT 8, 185).

ORMAND, Robert Dixon, Co. B, 2nd Lieutenant (1834–). Gaston resident, e. at Camp Fisher 8/20/1861, age 27. Wounded in shoulder and/or arm at 2nd Manassas 8/28–30/1862. At Chancellorsville 5/1–3/1863, he reported that the enemy "shot a bomb under me ... & blew me up." He was not seriously injured. Appointed 2nd lieutenant 5/11/1863. Wounded at Falling Waters 7/14/1863. Wounded in the side and/or right shoulder at Spotsylvania CH 5/12/1864. Surrendered at Appomattox CH 4/9/1865 (NCT 8, 126).

OWEN, Elias P., Co. H, Private (1822–1862). Lived, e. in Cleveland 3/17/1862, age 40. Died in Lynchburg hospital 7/29/1862 of typhoid fever (NCT 8, 205).

PACK, Reason A., Co. F, Private (1833–). Lived in Forsyth, e. at Camp Fisher, age 28, 9/20/1861. Wounded in left thigh and left hand and captured at Gettysburg 7/1–4/1863. Hospitalized at Davids Island. Paroled and trans to City Pt. 8/28/1863 for exc. AWOL Sept.–Dec. 864. Captured in Richmond hospital 4/3/1865. NC pension records indicate he was wounded at Petersburg (NCT 8, 181).

PADGETT, James C., Co. H. Lived in Rutherford, e. 3/10/1862 in Cleveland. Captured near Petersburg 4/2/1865; confined at Ft. Delaware until released 6/19/1865 after OOA (NCT 8, 205).

PADGETT, John H., Co. H, Private (1838–1862). Lived, e. in Cleveland 3/17/1862, age 24. Wounded at Gaines' Mill abt 6/27/1862. Died in Richmond hospital 7/20/1862 of wounds (NCT 8, 205).

PADGETT, Lorenzo G., Co. H, Private (1832–1863). Lived in Rutherford, e. 3/17/1862 in Cleveland . Died in Charlotte hospital abt 4/13/1863 of "chronic diarrhoea (NCT 8, 205).

PAGE, Henry C., Co. K, Private (1842–). Lived and e. in Stanly 9/7/1861, age 19. Promoted to sergeant May–Dec. 1862. Wounded in scalp, captured at Hanover CH 5/27/1862. Confined at various Federal hospitals until 9/17/1862. Trans to Ft. Monroe for exchange at Aiken's Landing 11/10/1862. Returned. Captured at Spotsylvania CH 5/12/1864; confined at Pt. Lookout. Trans to Elmira 8/8/1864 and held until released 5/17/1865 after OOA (NCT 8, 228).

PALMER, Charles W., Co. H, Private (1943–1863). Lived, e. in Cleveland 3/17/1862, age 19. Killed at Chancellorsville 5/3/1863 (NCT 8, 205).

PALMER, Napoleon B., Co. K, Corporal (1836–1962). Lived and e. in Stanly 9/7/1861, age 25, as a corporal Killed at Cedar Run 8/9/1862 (NCT 8, 228).

PALMER, William A., Co. D, Private (1823–). B.,

lived, e. in Stanly 7/29/1861. Dis as overage 4/30/1862 (NCT 8, 160).

PARKE, Ebenezer, Co. F, Private. Previously served in Co. H, 54th Reg NCT. Trans to Co. F, 28th Reg 2/17/1865; captured near Petersburg 4/2/1865, and confined at Pt. Lookout. Released 6/17/1865 after OOA (NCT 8, 181).

PARKER, Doctor F., Co. K, Sergeant (1835–1861). Lived and e. in Stanly 9/7/1861, age 26, as a sergeant. Died at Wilmington 12/2/1861 of "fever" (NCT 8, 228).

PARKER, Durant A., Co. D, Captain; Field & Staff, Assistant Quartermaster. From Stanley Co., e. in Co. D, 28th Reg, age 33; appointed 1st Lt. 7/29/1861. Promoted to captain 6/12/1862. then Assistant Quartermaster (Captain) on 5/2/1863; trans to Field & Staff. Trans to 1st Reg Confederate Engineering Troops as captain 8/19/1864 (NCT 8, 111, 160).

PARKER, George A., Co. D, Private (1838–1862). Lived, e. in Stanly 3/15/1862, age 24. Died "at home" abt 12/30/1862 of disease (NCT 8, 160).

PARKER, Howell A., Co. D, 1st Lieutenant (1843–). Lived, e. in Stanly 7/29/1861, age 18. Promoted to corporal on 11/16/1862; promoted to sergeant Feb. 1863, and to 1st sergeant 8/1/1863. Elected 2nd lieutenant 6/1/1864, then promoted to 1st lieutenant Jan.–Feb. 1865. Wounded in action after 2/28/1865. Captured in a Richmond hospital on 4/3/1865; paroled 5/11/1865 (NCT 8, 153).

PARKER, James A., Co. D, Corporal (1840–1862). Lived, e. in Stanly e. 7/29/1861, age 21, as a private. Promoted to corporal Nov.–Dec. 1861. Killed near Richmond 7/25/1862 (NCT 8, 160).

PARKER, John C., Co. E, Private (1838–1863). Lived, e. in Montgomery 8/1/1861, age 23. Reported missing and "supposed to be dead" at Gettysburg 7/3/1863 (NCT 8, 171).

PARKER, Wiley, Co. K, Private (1839–). Lived and e. in Stanly 3/20/1862, age 23. Died 7/13/1862 of disease (NCT 8, 228).

PARKS, Britton, Co. K, Private (1831–1865). Lived and e. in Stanly 9/7/1861, age 30. Wounded at Cedar Mt. 8/9/1862. Wounded at Chancellorsville 5/1–4/1863. Captured at Spotsylvania CH 5/12/1864; confined at Pt. Lookout. Trans to Elmira 8/10/1864 and died there 4/1/1865 of chronic valvular disease of the heart (NCT 8, 228).

PARKS, William Calvin, Co. A, Private (1830–aft 1880). E. on 3/18/1862, age 32, and was captured on 5/27/1862 at Hanover CH. Confined at Ft. Monroe, then Ft. Columbus. Trans to Aiken's Landing in July 1862 for exc 8/5/1862. Wounded in the thigh at 2nd Manassas. Left the company and joined the Confederate Navy on 4/3/1864. Parks m. Mary L. Messemore of Rowan, and had several children. In 1880, Parks and family lived in Rockford Township, where he was a carpenter (NCT 8, 121; SCS 136).

PARNELL, H.H., Co. E, Private (1843–). B. in Montgomery, e. 3/10/1862, age 19. Dis 12/15/1863 due to "disease of the heart" (NCT 8, 171).

PARNELL, Larkin N., Co. E, Private (1836–1861). Lived, e. in Montgomery 8/1/1861, age 25. Died at Wilmington 11/19/1861 (NCT 8, 171).

PARSONS, Albert, Co. A, Private. (1840–1862). E. in Surry, age 22, 3/18/1862. Captured at Hanover CH 5/27/1862; confined at Ft. Columbus. Paroled and trans to Aiken's Landing on 7/12/1862 for exc. Died 8/3/1862 of disease. His widow applied for a pension under the name of Nancy Paul (NCT 8, 121; SCS 136).

PARSONS, Daniel C., Co. A, Private (1837–1962). E. in Surry, age 25, 3/18/1862. Reportedly died at home abt 11/19/1862. He was the son of Allen and Edney Parson, farmers in the Haystack section, Surry (NCT 8, 121; SCS 137–138).

PARSONS, Thomas A., Co. E, Private (1840–). Lived, e. in Montgomery e. 8/1/1861, age 21. Deserted Feb. 1865. Surrendered at Appomattox CH 4/9/1865 (NCT 8, 171).

PATTERSON, J.C., Co. F, Private. Lived in Yadkin . Deserted to the enemy on unspecified date. Took OOA at Louisville, KY 8/16/1864 (NCT 8, 181).

PATTERSON, William Henry Harrison, Co. A, Sergeant (1840–1911). B. in TN to William C. (1810–1891) and Caroline Mainard (Maynard) Patterson (1812–1871), who lived at Siloam in 1850, who are bur. in Patterson Family cem, near Pilot Mt. Their son, William, e. on 3/18/1862 in Surry. Captured at Hanover CH; confined at Ft. Monroe, then Ft. Columbus. Exc. 8/5/1862. Promoted to corporal on 6/1/1863. Wounded in right leg 5/5/1864 at Wilderness, and at Spotsylvania CH that same month in the left arm. Promoted to sergeant on 9/1/1864. Pension application stated he was wounded at Petersburg. He m. in 1867 in Surry Sarah Elizabeth Whitaker (1812–1871), dau. of Abram and Lydia Whitaker, and had 8 children between 1867–1883. After the war, William farmed in the Hills Grove Community. Bur. at Copeland Baptist Ch., Copeland, NC (NCT 8, 121; SCS 138). A bronze Confederate plaque marks his grave.

PAYSOUR, David Rufus, Co. B, Private (1838–). Gaston blacksmith, e. in Gaston on 7/30/1861, age 23. Wounded in the right arm at Cedar Mt. 8/9/1862, arm amputated. Dis 2/12/1863 due to disability (NCT 8, 135).

PEAL, D., Co. F, Private. Place/date he e. not reported. Hospitalized at Richmond 3/28/1864 with gunshot wound to right leg. Captured in that hospital 4/3/1865 (NCT 8, 181).

PEARSON, John W., Co. I, Private (1843–). Lived, e. in Yadkin, 8/13/1861, age 18, as 1st sergeant. Rank reduced 10/8/1861. Appointed drillmaster and trans to 31st Reg NCT Dec. 1861. Records of 31st do not support this (NCT 8, 216).

PEDIGO, James, Co. A, Private (1823–). B. in Patrick County, VA, a carpenter, lived in Franklin Township of Surry, e. at Dobson 5/4/1861, age 37. Sent to the training camp at Garysburg and then High Pt. Dis 5/1/1862, overage (NCT 8, 121; SCS 139).

PEEL, Thomas, Co. A, Private (1838–1862). B/. in Surry to Jesse and Elizabeth Freeman Peel, of Ararat, e. 5/4/1861 in the first group to organize in Surry Died in a Middleburg hospital 9/29/1862 from wounds received at 2nd Manassas on 8/27/1862 (NCT 8, 121; SCS 139).

PEGRAM, Edward Larkin, Co. B, 2nd Lieutenant. Lived, e. in Gaston, appointed 2nd lieutenant 7/30/

1861. Defeated for reelection 2/27/1862. Reenlisted in the company with rank of private 4/30/1863. Wounded in face at Gettysburg 7/1–3/1863. Detailed as wagon master 2/25/1864–Feb. 1865. (NCT 8, 126, 135).

PENDERGRASS, John S., Co. G, Private (1840–). B., lived, e. in Orange 9/2/1861, age 21. Captured at Hanover CH 5/27/1862; confined at Ft. Monroe and Ft. Columbus. Paroled and trans to Aiken's Landing for exc 8/5/1862. Dis 1/18/1864 due to "organic disease of the heart" (NCT 8, 192).

PENDERGRASS, Nathaniel, Co. G, Private (1840–). Lived, e. in Orange 9/2/1861, age 21. Wounded in left hand at Chancellorsville 5/2–3/1863. Captured at Spotsylvania CH 5/12/1864; confined at Pt. Lookout, then Elmira. Paroled at Elmira, trans for exc 2/20/1865. NC pension records indicate he was wounded in knee at "Bull Run: and in the right knee at Brandy Station (NCT 8, 192).

PENDRY, J.F., Co. A, 28th ?. NC pension records indicate he served in this company (NCT 8, 121).

PENDRY, Roby, Co. I, Private (1840–1862). Lived, e. in Yadkin 8/13/1861, age 21. Died at Wilmington 2/4/1862 of measles (NCT 8, 216).

PENDRY, Wilson S., Co. I, Private (1838–1861). Lived, e. in Yadkin 8/13/1861, age 23. Died at Wilmington 11/6/1861 of measles (NCT 8, 216).

PENNINGTON, John S., Co. K. Private. Lived and e. in Stanly 10/31/1864. Captured at Petersburg 4/2/1865; confined at Pt. Lookout until released 6/16/1865 after OOA (NCT 8, 228).

PENNINGTON, Nelson C., Co. D, Private (1841–). Lived, e. in Stanly 7/29/1861, age 20. Captured at Hanover CH 5/27/1862; confined at Ft. Monroe, then Ft. Columbus. Tans to Aiken's Landing on 7/12/1862 for exc on 8/5/1862. Wounded in the left shoulder, captured at Gettysburg 7/1–5/1863. Hospitalized at Davids Island 7/17–24/1863. Paroled and trans to City Pt., 9/16/1863 for exc. Detached as hospital guard in Richmond 6/29/1864 through Feb. 1865. Captured in Richmond hospital 4/3/1865. Paroled in Richmond 4/24/1865 (NCT 8, 160).

PEOPLES, Albert. Co. G, Private; Co. I, 28th Reg, Private. E. at Camp Holmes 11/30/1863. Deserted. Returned 9/9/1864. Trans to Co. G 10/31/1864 (NCT 8, 192).

PEOPLES, William, Co. I, Private. E. at Camp Holmes 11/3–/1863. Deserted abt 4/1/1864 (NCT 8, 216).

PERKINS, John, Co. B, Private (1839–). Lived in Gaston He e. 7/30/1861, age 22. Deserted 4/27/1863. Trans to C. S. Navy on 4/3/1864 (NCT 8, 135).

PERKINS, Michael C., Co. B, Private (1835–). Lived in Gaston, e. on 7/30/1861, age 26. Captured at Hanover CH 5/27/1862; Received at Aiken's Landing on 7/12/1862 for exc 8/5/1862. Wounded in right leg at Reams' Station 8/25/1864. Reported absent-wounded through Feb. 1865 (NCT 8, 135).

PERRY, Benjamin, Co. D, Private (1843–1863). Stanly resident, e. 7/29/1861, age 18. Wounded in the hand at 2nd Manassas abt 8/27–30/1862. Wounded and captured at Gettysburg 7/3–5/1863. Confined at Ft. Delaware. Paroled and trans to City Pt. for exc

8/1/1863. Died in Petersburg hospital abt 8/30/1863 of wounds and/or chronic dysentery (NCT 8, 160).

PETERSON, Charles J., Co. D, Private. Lived in Gaston, e. 10/27/1864 at Camp Stokes. Captured near Petersburg 4/2/1865; confined at Pt. Lookout until released 6/16/1865 after OOA (NCT 8, 160–161).

PETERSON, John, Co. D, Private. Lived in Catawba, e. 10/28/1864 at Camp Stokes. Captured near Petersburg 4/2/1865; confined at Pt. Lookout until released 6/16/1865 after OOA (NCT 8, 161).

PETERSON, Peter J., Co. H, Private. B., e. in Catawba, 3/1/1864. Died in Staunton hospital 5/20/1864 of gunshot wound (NCT 8, 205).

PETTITT, William Co. F, Private (1825–1862). B., lived, e. in Yadkin 8/15/1861, age 36. Killed at Ox Hill 9/1/1862 (NCT 8, 181).

PETTY, Elijah, Co. I, Private (1842–). Lived, e. Yadkin, 8/13/1861, age 19. AWOL May–Oct. 1862. Returned. Deserted 8/5/1863. Returned 9/22/1864. Deserted to enemy 11/19/1864. Confined at Washington DC; released abt 11/23/1864, after OOA (NCT 8, 216).

PETTY, Miles, Co. I, Private (1836–). Lived, e. in Yadkin 8/13/1861, age 25. Present through Feb. 1863. Deserted, returned 9/22/1864. Deserted to the enemy 11/19/1864. Confined at Washington, DC; released abt 11/25/1864 after OOA (NCT 8, 216).

PETTYJOHN, James, Co. I, Private (1839–1862). Lived, e. in Yadkin 8/13/1861, age 22. Captured at Hanover CH 5/27/1862; confined at Ft. Monroe, then Ft. Columbus. Exc. Died in Richmond hospital 12/7/1862 of "pneumonia" (NCT 8, 216).

PETTYJOHN, William, Co. I, Private (1839–1862). Lived, e. in Yadkin 8/13/1861, age 22. Captured at Hanover CH 5/27/1862; confined at Ft. Monroe, then Ft. Columbus. Trans to Aiken's Landing for exc 8/5/1862. Returned. Killed at Fredericksburg 12/13/1862 (NCT 8, 216).

PHILLIPS, Abraham, Co. F, Private (1825–1864). B. in Yadkin, e. in Wake 11/15/1863. Killed at Wilderness 5/5/1864. Bur. Kelly Family cem. Yadkin County (NCT 8, 181).

PHILLIPS, Benjamin A., Co. F, Private (1833–1903). B., e. in Yadkin 4/27/1862. Wounded in right arm near Wilderness abt 5/5/1864. Arm amputated; retired 1/11/1865 due to disability. Bur. Baltimore Meth. Ch. Cem., Yadkin County (NCT 8, 181, CWY 251).

PHILLIPS, James, Co. G, Private. E. 3/15/1864 in Orange. Surrendered at Appomattox CH 4/9/1865 (NCT 8, 192).

PHILLIPS, John W., Co. A, Private (18__–1940). John Winston Phillips, b. in Surry to Jesse P., a blacksmith, and Polly Sweat Phillips, residents of the Mt. Airy District, Surry John ran away from home to e. 3/18/1862. Wounded in both knees, captured at Spotsylvania CH on 5/12/1864. Confined at Pt. Lookout; trans to Elmira 8/10/1864. Released there 6/19/1865 after OOA. One of the last 8 Confederate veterans living in Surry, he was featured in the *Mount Airy Times* on 6/23/1939. Died 2/14/1940 at his home near Mt. Airy on Fancy Gap Road. Bur. at Mt. Carmel Ch. cem. (NCT 8, 121; SCS 140–141).

PHILLIPS, W.A., Co. F, Private (1839–). B., e. in Yadkin 4/24/1862, age 23, as a substitute. Dis 6/23/1864 due to "general debility" (NCT 8, 181).

PHILLIPS, William, Co. E, Private (1842–1863). Lived, e. in Montgomery 8/1/1861, age 19. Reported missing and "supposed to be dead" at Gettysburg 7/3/1863 (NCT 8, 171).

PICKARD, William W., Co. G, Private (1841–). Lived, e. in Orange 9/2/1862, age 20. Wounded and captured at Fredericksburg 12/13/1862; exc abt 12/17/1862. Trans to Co. I, 6th Reg NCT 3/18/1863 (NCT 8, 192).

PILCHER, Wiley, Co. I, Private (1839–1862). Lived, e. in Yadkin 9/1/1861, age 22. Died at Wilmington 3/30/1862 or 4/1/1862 of fever (NCT 8, 216).

PINSON, David G., Co. H, Private. E. 8/22/1861 in Cleveland. Died at Wilmington NC 2/8/1862. Cause of death not reported (NCT 8, 205).

PITMAN, John A., Co. E, Private (1839–1863). Lived, e. in Montgomery 8/1/1861, age 22. Died in Richmond hospital abt.6/3/1863 of typhoid fever (NCT 8, 171).

PLOWMAN, Henry, Co. I, Private. E. at Camp Holmes 11/30/1863. Trans to Co. G, 18th Reg NCT 9/1/1864 (NCT 8, 216).

PLOWMAN, James H., Co. I, Private ? NC pension records indicate he served in this company (NCT 8, 216).

PLOWMAN, John W., Co. I, Private (1841–) B., lived, e. in Yadkin 8/13/1861, age 20. Dis 12/24/1861 due to "loss of motion of the left arm" caused by an old fracture of collar bone and rheumatism (NCT 8, 216).

PLOWMAN, William, Co. I, Private. E. at Camp Holmes 11/30/1863. Captured near Gravel Hill abt 7/28/1864; confined at Pt. Lookout, trans to Elmira 8/8/1864. Released there 5/9/1865 after OOA (NCT 8, 216).

PLYLER, Daniel W., Co. D, Corporal (1841–). Lived, e. in Stanly 7/29/1861 there, age 20. Wounded at Ox Hill 9/1/1862. Promoted to corporal Jan. 1863–Oct. 1864. Surrendered at Appomattox CH 4/9/1865 (NCT 8, 161).

PLYLER, Edmond A., Co. D, Private. Probably from Stanly, e. 3/1/1864 at Liberty Mills. Surrendered at Appomattox CH, 4/9/1865 (NCT 8, 161).

PLYLER, Henry D., Co. D, Private (1844–). Lived, e. in Stanly 3/15/1862, age 18. Captured at Hanover CH abt 5/28/1862; confined at Ft. Monroe. Paroled and trans to Aiken's Landing for exc on 8/5/1862. Hospitalized at Petersburg 6/23/1864 with a gunshot wound. Surrendered at Appomattox CH 4/9/1865 (NCT 8, 161).

POE, Nauflet F., Co. G, Private. E. 4/1/1864 in Orange. Captured at Spotsylvania CH 5/12/1864; confined at Elmira. Trans to Pt. Lookout 10/14/1864 for exc; died there 10/30/1864 of "chronic diarrhoea." May have previously served in Co. D, 1st Reg NC Infantry (NCT 8, 192).

POE, Norfleet H., Co. G, Private (1838–1862). Lived, e. in Orange 12/20/1861, age 23. Wounded at Gaines' Mill 6/27/1862. Hospitalized at Richmond, died there abt 7/24/1862 of wounds (NCT 8, 192)

POE, Reuben P., Co. G, Private (1836–). Lived, e. in Orange 12/20/1861, age 25. Captured at Spotsylvania CH 5/12/1864; confined at Pt. Lookout, trans to Elmira 8/10/1864. Paroled and sent to Venus Pt. 11/15/1864 for exc. Returned and surrendered at Appomattox CH 4/9/1865 (NCT 8, 192).

POE, Stephen A., Co. G, Private (1842–). Lived, e. in Orange 12/20/1861, age 19. Captured at Fredericksburg 12/13/1862; exc abt 12/17/1862. Present through Feb. 1865, and surrendered at Appomattox CH 4/9/1865 (NCT 8, 192).

POINDEXTER, A.L., Co. A, Private ?. NC pension records indicate that he served in this company (NCT 8, 121).

POINDEXTER, Alexander Roby, Co. F (1844–1926). NC pension records indicate he served in this company (NCT 8, 181). Son of Denson Asbury and Sarah Jones Poindexter, Alexander m. in 1868 Emma Catherine Ireland. Both are bur. Boonville Bapt. Ch. cem., Boonville, NC (NCT 8, 181; CWY, 253).

POINDEXTER, Charles A., Co. F, Private. Lived, e. in Yadkin 3/12/1864. Captured in Richmond hospital 4/3/1865; trans to Newport News 4/23/1865. Released 6/30/1865 after OOA (NCT 8, 181).

POINDEXTER, Isaac C., Co. F, Sergeant (1838–1916). Lived, e. in Yadkin 6/18/1861, age 23, as a private. Promoted to sergeant Jan.–Apr. 1862. Rank reduced 4/23/1862. Promoted to corporal 2/1/1863, t sergeant March–May 1864. Captured at Wilderness or Spotsylvania May 1864; confined at Pt. Lookout. Trans to Elmira 8/15/1864. Paroled 3/14/1865, sent to Boulware's Wharf 3/18–21/1865 for exc. Captured in Richmond hospital 4/3/1865; confined at Pt. Lookout until released 7/25/1865 after OOA. Bur. Friendship Bapt. Ch. Cem., Yadkin (NCT 8, 182; CWY 253).

POINDEXTER, John H., Co. F, 2nd Lieutenant (1829–). Lived, e. in Yadkin 6/18/1862. Resigned abt 9/5/1861, but continued to serve as a private. Promoted to corporal Jan.–June 1862. Hospitalized in Richmond 7/3/1862 with flesh wound of hand. Promoted to sergeant 7/16/1862. Captured at Burkeville, VA 4/6/1865; confined at Pt. Lookout. Released 6/17/1865 after OOA (NCT 8, 174, 182).

POINDEXTER, Pleasant Henderson, Co. G, Private (1837–1913). Previously served in Co. I, 6th Reg NCT. Trans to Co. G, 28th Reg Mar.–April 1863. Wounded in the back at Gettysburg 7/1–3/1863. Present through Feb. 1865 and surrendered at Appomattox CH 4/9/1865. Bur. Macedonia Meth. Ch., Yadkin (NCT 8, 192; CWY 254).

POINDEXTER, Roby H., Co. G, Private; Co. F, Private (1835–). Lived, e. in Yadkin 9/15/1862, age 27. Trans to Co. F, 28th Reg abt 9/28/1863. Deserted 9/13/1864 (NCT 8, 182, 192).

POINDEXTER, Thomas C. M., Co. F, Sergeant (1831–1862). Lived, e. in Yadkin 6/18/1861 as sergeant. Rank reduced Jan.–June 1862. Died in Richmond hospital 7/10/1862 of typhoid fever (NCT 8, 182).

POINDEXTER, William G. W., Co. G, Private (1835–1863). Previously served in Co. I, 6th Reg NCT, trans to Co. G, 28th Reg 3/18/1863. Wounded and captured at Gettysburg 7/3/1863. Hospitalized at Gettys-

burg, and died 7/5/1863 of wounds. Bur. Macedonia Meth. Ch. cem., Yadkin (NCT 8, 192, CWY 254).

POLK, John, Co. C, body guard. John, a Negro, and probably a slave, served as a body guard to Colonel Samuel Lowe of the 28th Reg (NCT 8, 148).

POLLARD, Hiram, Co. C, Private (1827–). Lived in Catawba but e. at Camp Fisher on 9/9/1861. Wounded in both arms at 2nd Manassas, 8/27–30/1862. Wounded in the arm again "in Virginia" in May 1864. Captured near Petersburg 4/2/1865; confined at Ft. Delaware, until released 6/19/1865 after OOA (NCT 8, 148).

POOL, Henry G., Co. A, Private (1834–1862). B. in Scotland, lived, e. in Surry 5/4/1861, age 27. Captured at Hanover CH on 5/27/1862 and confined at Ft. Monroe then Ft. Columbus. Paroled and Trans to Aiken's Landing for exc on 7/12/1862. Exc on 8/5/1862. Died 11/1/862 in a Petersburg hospital (NCT 8, 121; SCS 142).

POOVEY, A. Levi, Co. C, Private (1845–). Levi lived, e. in Catawba 1/17/1863, age 18. Wounded in the face at Gettysburg 7/1–3/1863. Captured and hospitalized at Davids Island, then trans to City Pt. 9/8/1863 for exc. Paroled at Farmville 4/11–21/1865 (NCT 8, 149).

POOVEY, David A., Co. C, Private (1840–1863). Lived, e. in Catawba 3/15/1862, age 20. Captured at Hanover CH 5/27/1862; confined at Ft. Columbus. Paroled and exc. Wounded at Chancellorsville 5/1–3/1863. Missing, believed to have been killed at Gettysburg 7/1–3/1863 (NCT 8, 149).

POOVEY, Henry F., Co. C, Private. Lived, e. in Catawba 3/14/1863. Killed at Gettysburg 7/3/1863 (NCT 8, 149).

POOVEY, Hiram H., Co. C, Private (1838–). Lived, e. in Catawba 3/15/1862, age 24. Wounded in right arm at Jones' Farm 9/30/1864. Surrendered at Appomattox CH 4/9/1865 (NCT 8, 149).

POOVEY, Joshua A., Sr., Co. C, Private (1843–). Lived, e. in Catawba. 3/15/1862, age 19. Wounded at Gettysburg 7/3/1863. Surrendered at Appomattox CH 4/9/1865 (NCT 8, 149).

POOVEY, Julius A., Co. C, Private (1845–). Catawba resident, e. on 1/17/1863. Wounded in left leg at Chancellorsville 5/1/1863. Wounded in the head at Wilderness abt 5/3/1864. Surrendered at Appomattox CH 4/9/1865 (NCT 8, 149).

POOVEY, Lawson A., Co. C, Private. E. in Catawba on 5/6/1864. Surrendered at Appomattox CH 4/9/1865 (NCT 8, 149).

POOVEY, Taylor, Co. C, Private. E. in Catawba on 9/1/1864. Surrendered at Appomattox CH 4/9/1865 (NCT 8, 149).

POOVEY, William F., Co. C, Private (1827–1862). Lived, e. in Catawba 9/1/1862, age 35. He died in a Lynchburg hospital abt 12/6/1862 of typhoid fever (NCT 8, 149).

POOVEY, William H.H., Co. C, Private (1841–). Lived, e. in Catawba resident 8/13/1861, age 20. Wounded at Shepherdstown 9/20/1862. Surrendered at Appomattox CH 4/9/1865 (NCT 8, 149).

POPLIN, David, Co. K, Private. E. at Liberty Mills 4/1/1864. Surrendered at Appomattox CH 4/9/1865 (NCT 8, 228).

POPLIN, Nathan, Co. K, Private (1843–). B., lived, and e. in Stanly 9/7/1861, age 18. Dis 8/9/1862 due to "phthisis pulmonalis" (NCT 8, 228).

PORTIS, John, Co. A, Private (1839–). Lived, e. in Surry 5/4/1861, age 22. Captured in September 1862, and confined in Washington, DC. Paroled and trans to Aiken's Landing abt 9/27/1862 for exc on 11/10/1862. Portis deserted prior to 3/1/1863. He m. in 1865 Frances McKinney, widow of William McKinney. (NCT 8, 121; SCS 142–143).

POTTS, John H., Co. I, Musician (1836–). Lived, e. in Yadkin 3/8/1862, age 26. Promoted to musician before 11/1/1862. Rank reduced before 3/1/1863. Deserted 7/23/1863 (NCT 8, 216).

POTTS, Nicholas H., Co. F, Private (1844–). Lived, e. in Yadkin 6/20/1863, age 19. Hospitalized at Richmond 6/3/1864 for gunshot wound. Furloughed 6/30/1864; reported AWOL 8/28/1864 (NCT 8, 182).

POWEL, Manley B., Co. G, Private (1840–1862). B., lived, e. in Orange 3/5/1862, age 22. Died in Richmond hospital abt 6/29/1862 of "phthisis pulmonalis" (NCT 8, 192).

POWELL, Marcus D., Co. H, Private (1831–1862). Lived, e. in Cleveland 8/22/1861, age 30 as a corporal. Rank reduced after 4/20/1862. Killed at 2nd Manassas 8/28–29, 1862 (NCT 8, 205).

POWELL, William H., Co. G, Private (1843–). B., lived, e. in Orange 9/17/1861, age 18. Hospitalized at Richmond 2/26/1863 with gunshot wound of head. Returned. Deserted May 1863, but returned. Captured at Spotsylvania CH abt 5/12/1864; confined at Pt. Lookout. Released 5/30/1864 after joining the U.S. Army, assigned to Co. I, 1st Reg U.S. Volunteer Infantry (NCT 8, 192).

PRITCHARD, Starling, Co. D, Private (1826–1863). Stanly resident e. 7/29/1861, age 35. Died in Richmond hospital 5/19/1863 of typhoid pneumonia — "a good soldier" (NCT 8, 161).

PROPST, Alfred, Co. C, Private. Lived, e. in Catawba resident 8/13/1861. Died in Lynchburg hospital 1/29/1863 of typhoid pneumonia — "a brave boy" (NCT 8, 149).

PRUETT, James C., Sr., Co. H, Private (1839–). Lived, e. in Cleveland 3/17/1862, age 23. Present until he surrendered at Appomattox CH 4/9/1865 (NCT 8, 205).

PRUETT, John, Co. H, Private. E. at Camp Holmes 9/25/1864. Surrendered at Appomattox CH 4/9/1865 (NCT 8, 205).

PRUETT, Thomas J., Co. H, Private (1838–1863). Lived and e. in Cleveland 3/17/1862, age 24. Died at Camp Gregg or Guinea Station 1/5/1863 (NCT 8, 205).

PRUETT, William T., Co. H, Private (1745–). Lived, e. in Cleveland 3/17/1862, age 17. Wounded in right leg at Gettysburg 7/1–3/1863. Absent-wounded through 1/28/1864. Served as hospital guard at Charlotte Sept. 1864–Feb. 1865. Paroled at Charlotte, NC May 1865 (NCT 8, 205).

PRUITT, Jacob, Co. D, Private. E. at Liberty Mills 3/1/1864. Wounded in left knee at Wilderness 5/5–6/1864. Surrendered at Appomattox CH 4/9/1865 (NCT 8, 161).

PRYOR, David, Co. C, Private. Lived in Lincoln, e.

at Camp Fisher 8/26/1861. Captured at Hanover CH on 5/27/1862; confined at Ft. Monroe, then Ft. Columbus. Paroled and trans to Aiken's Landing for exc 8/5/1862. Reported missing, believed killed at Gettysburg 7/3/1863 (NCT 8, 149).

PRYOR, Samuel, Co. C, Private. A Lincoln resident, he e. at Camp Fisher 8/26/1861. Captured at Hanover CH on 5/27/1862; confined at Ft. Monroe, then Ft. Columbus. Paroled and trans to Aiken's Landing for exc 8/5/1862. Wounded and captured at Gettysburg 7/1–4/1863. Hospitalized at Davids Island, paroled and trans to City Pt. 9/16/1863 for exc. Captured at the Appomattox River 4/3/1865. Confined at Hart's Island 4/11/1865. Trans to Davids Island 7/1/1865 and released 7/11/1865 after OOA (NCT 8, 149).

PRYOR, Sidney, Co. C, Private (1844–). Lived, e. in Catawba on 3/15/1862, age 18. Dis 6/15/1862 due to "anemia accompanied with general debility" (NCT 8, 149).

PUCKET (Puckett), James M., Co. A, Private (1834–1863). E., age 28, on 3/18/1862. Captured at Hanover CH on 5/27/1862. Confined at Ft. Monroe; paroled and trans to Aiken's Landing on 9/1/1862 for exc on 11/10/1862. Reported absent-sick Jan.–Feb. 1863. Died in a Danville hospital abt 3/15/1863 of "dyspepsia" (NCT 8, 121; SCS 144).

PUCKETT, Hugh, Co. A, Private (1842–). Son of Isham and Mary Puckett, of Stuart's Creek, Hugh e. 3/18/1862, age 20, along with his brother James. Wounded in right leg at Hanover CH on 5/27/1862, and captured. Leg amputated. Confined in several Federal hospitals before being exc at Aiken's Landing on 9/1/1862. Dis 1862 due to his disability. Hugh m. Elizabeth Golding, and had several children (NCT 8, 121; SCS 143–144).

PUNCH, Joseph L., Co. C, Private (1843–). Lived, e. in Catawba 8/13/1861. Dis 6/15/1862 due to "general muscular debility." Dis certificate gave his age as 19. May have served later in Co. A, 23rd NC Reg (NCT 8, 149).

PUNCH, Robert W., Co. C, Private (18__–1862). Lived in Catawba, e. at Camp Fisher on 9/9/1861. Wounded at Hanover CH 5/27/1862. Wounded in the abdomen at Fredericksburg 12/13/1862. Died in Richmond hospital 12/16/1862 of wounds—"a good soldier" (NCT 8, 149).

PUNCH, William S., Co. C, Private (18__1863). Catawba resident, e. at Camp Fisher 9/9/1861. Captured at Hanover CH 5/27/1862; confined at Ft. Monroe, then Ft. Columbus. Paroled, trans to Aiken's Landing for exc 8/5/1862. Died "at home" 7/15/1863 of disease (NCT 8, 149–150).

QUAKENBUSH, Frederick S., Co. G, Sergeant (1839–). Lived, e. in Orange 3/5/1862, age 23 as a private. Captured at Fredericksburg 12/13/1862; exc abt 12/17/1862. Wounded at Chancellorsville 5/2–3/1863. Captured at Spotsylvania CH 5/12/1864; confined at Pt. Lookout, then trans to Elmira 8/14/1864. Promoted to sergeant before 2/28/1865 while still a POW. Released at Elmira 6/27/1865, after OOA (NCT 8, 192–193).

QUINN, Isaac, Co. A, Private (1843–1862). Son of William and Mahala Linville Quinn, he lived, e. in Surry, age 18, 5/4/1861. Died at Wilmington abt 7/21/1862 of disease. (NCT 8, 122; SCS 144).

RADER, Jonas Monroe, Co. H, Private (1848–). E. 3/1/1864 at Camp Vance, age 16. Wounded in left leg at Spotsylvania CH abt 5/12/1864. Retired to Invalid Corps 1/14/1865 (NCT 8, 205).

RADER, William Pinkney, Co. C, Private. Lived, e. in Catawba 8/13/1861. Captured at Hanover CH 5/27/1862; confined at Ft. Monroe, then Ft. Columbus. Paroled and trans to Aiken's Landing for exc 8/5/1862. Surrendered at Appomattox CH 4/9/1865 (NCT 8, 150).

RAMSEY, Gilliam O., Co. D, 2nd Lieutenant (1839–), Stanly resident e., age 22; appointed 3rd lieutenant 7/29/1861. Promoted to 2nd lieutenant 7/12/1862. Resigned 12/28/1862 due to "chronic rheumatism" (NCT 8, 154).

RANDALL, Isaac J., Co. K, Private (1838–1864). B., lived, e. in Stanly 9/7/1861, age 23. Killed at Spotsylvania CH 5/12/1864 (NCT 8, 228).

RANDLE, John W., Co. D, Captain (1838–1863). Lived, e. in Stanly 7/29/1861, age 23, and appointed 2nd lieutenant. Promoted to 1st lieutenant 6/12/1862, then to captain 5/2/1863. Wounded at Gettysburg 7/1–3/1863, and died 7/10/1863 of wounds (NCT 8, 153).

RANDLEMAN, Augustus T., Co. F, Sergeant (1841–1863). B., lived, e. in Forsyth 6/18/1861, age 20. Promoted to corporal Nov.–Dec. 1862; then sergeant 5/11/1863. Wounded and captured at Gettysburg 7/1–4/1863. Hospitalized at Davids Island where he died 7/23/1864 of hemorrhage in lungs (NCT 8, 182).

RANKIN, William Rufus, Co. B, 28th, Sergeant-Major; Field and Staff, Sergeant Major. Rankin e. in Wake on 4/7/1863 in Co. B, 28th Reg. Previously served as a major of the 37th Reg NCT. Promoted to sergeant major 4/29/1863, he trans to Field & Staff of the 28th Reg. Wounded at Gettysburg in 1863. With the 28th Reg 4/9/1865 at Appomattox CH (NCT 8, 112, 135).

RANKIN, William Washington, Co. B, Private (1845–). E. at Liberty Mills on 2/15/1864. Surrendered at Appomattox CH 4/9/1865. Probably a Gaston resident (NCT 8, 135).

RASH, Richard M., Co. F, Private (1840–). B., lived, e. in Yadkin 6/18/1861, age 21. Captured near Fussell's Mill abt 8/16/1864; confined at Pt. Lookout until released 10/14–17/1864 after OOA and joining the U.S. Army, assigned to Co. B, 4th Reg U.S. Volunteer Infantry (NCT 8, 1862).,

RASH, Robert, Co. F, Private (1842–1862). Lived, e. in Yadkin 6/18/1861. Died In Wilmington hospital 3/6/1862 of typhoid fever and/or chronic dysentery (NCT 8, 182).

RATCHFORD, J.H., Co. B, Private (1835–1862). Lived, e. in Gaston 7/30/1861, age 26. Wounded at Gaines' Mill 6/27/1862. Died at Richmond on 7/20/1862 of wounds (NCT 8, 135).

RATCHFORD, John G., Co. B, Private (1838–1864). B., e. in Gaston 3/17/1864, age 24. Wounded in the left

hip and captured at Fredericksburg 12/13/1862. Hospitalized in Washington, DC. Paroled and trans to City Pt. for exc on 3/29/1863. Wounded in the face at Reams' Station 8/25/1864; hospitalized at Petersburg, and died there 8/30/1864 of wounds (NCT 8, 135).

REAVES (Reavis), James Washington, Co. I, Private (1843–). Lived, e. in Yadkin 3/8/1862, age 19. AWOL 2/8/1865 (NCT 8, 216).

REAVIS, Nathan, Co. I, Private (1838–1864). B., lived, e. in Yadkin 3/8/1862, age 24. Died "at home" 11/17/1864, cause not reported (NCT 8, 216).

REDEN, James A., Co. E, Private. Previously served in Co. F, 44th Reg NCT. Enlisted in Co. E "without a transfer" March–May 1862. Captured at Hanover CH 5/27/1862; confined at Ft. Monroe, then Ft. Columbus. Paroled and trans to Aiken's Landing for exc 8/5/1862. Captured at Gettysburg 7/3/1863; confined at Ft. Delaware. Released 5/3/1865 after OOA (NCT 8, 171).

REECE, Asburn H., Co. I, Private (1841–1863). Lived, e. in Yadkin 9/10/1862, age 21. Died in hospital at Montgomery White Sulphur Springs, VA abt 3/9/1863 of "smallpox" (NCT 8, 217).

REECE, Evan H., Co. I, Private (1843–). Lived, e. in Yadkin 3/8/1862, age 19. Captured at Hanover CH 5/27/1862; confined at Ft. Monroe, then Ft. Columbus. Paroled, trans to Aiken's Landing for exc 8/5/1862. Returned. Wounded at Gettysburg 7/1–3/1863. Surrendered at Appomattox CH 4/9/1865 (NCT 8, 217).

REEVES, John W., Co. G, Private (1843–). B., lived in Orange, was a tailor. E. 9/17/1861, age 18. Dis 12/26/1861 due to "general debility following an attack of measles" (NCT 8, 193).

REEVES, Richard Elwell, Co. A, Major; Field and Staff, Major (1825–) Surry resident, Reeves organized the first group of Surry volunteers at Dobson (Co. A, 28th Reg) and e. 5/4/1861, age 40. Elected Major 9/21/1861, trans to Field & Staff. According to William M. Norman's memoirs, Reeves was injured in a train wreck when the Reg was sent from High Pt. to Wilmington on 9/30/1861(see Norman, *A Portion of My Life*, p. 131). Reeves was defeated for re-election at the reorganization 4/12/1962. He m. Louise Galloway (1848–1908), and had 2 daus (NCT 8, 110, 112; SCS 146).

REID, Irvin, Co. A, Sergeant (1839–). B/. to Jacob and Tabitha Linville Reid, e. with his brother Isaac on 5/4/1861; promoted to sergeant in April 1862. Irvin was wounded at Chancellorsville on 5/2/1863. Captured at Petersburg on 4/2/1865; released 6/17/1865 after OOA. M., 1863, Martha E. Atkerson, and had several children (NCT 8, 122; SCS 144).

REID, Isaac, Co. A, Private (1840–1863). Isaac e. 3/18/1862, age 22, and deserted 8/1/1862. Died in a Richmond hospital on 5/30/1863 of "febris typhoid." Before 1860, Isaac m. Charlotte Dezern and they had two daus (NCT 8, 122, 147).

REID, Jacob F., Co. A, Private (1833–1870). B. in Surry to Isaac and Elizabeth McGlaughlin Reid of Siloam, he e. Dobson on 5/4/1861. Returned home sick on 4/30/1863 and remained through Feb. 1865. Jacob

m. Nancy Whitaker in Surry in 1860. He and his wife died of fever in 1870 along with several other family embers (NCT 8, 122; SCS 147).

REID, John, Co. A, Private (1838–). B.. in Surry to Jacob and Telitha (Tabitha) Reid of Siloam. E., age 24, 3/18/1862. Captured at Hanover CH on 5/27/1862. Sent to Aiken's Landing, exc 8/5/1862. Captured again on 5/12/1864 at Spotsylvania CH, and confined first to Pt. Lookout, then to Elmira 8/10/1864; released 5/29/1865 after OOA (NCT 8, 122; SCS 147).

REYNOLDS, F. Harvey, Co. C, Private (18__–1862). Catawba resident e. there 3/15/1862. Died in hospital at Liberty 11/19/1862 of disease (NCT 8, 150).

REYNOLDS, George T., Co. I, Private (1844–). Lived, e. in Yadkin 3/8/1862, age 18. Captured at Hanover CH 5/27/1862; confined at Ft. Monroe, then Ft. Columbus. Paroled, trans to Aiken's Landing for exc 8/5/1862. Returned. Reported missing at Gettysburg 7/1–3/1863 (NCT 8, 217).

REYNOLDS, James A, Co. C, Private (18__–1863). Catawba resident, e. at Camp Fisher on 9/2/1861. Captured at Hanover CH on 5/27/1862; confined at Ft. Monroe, then Ft. Columbus before paroled and trans to Aiken's Landing, exc 8/5/1862. Reported missing and presumed k. at Gettysburg 7/3/1863 (NCT 8, 150).

RHYNE, Alexander A., Co. B, Private (1834–) Resident of Gaston, e. there on 7/30/1861, age 27. Captured at Hanover CH 5/27/1862; confined at Ft. Monroe, then Ft. Columbus. Paroled and sent to Aiken's Landing for exc on 8/5/1862. Wounded and captured at Gettysburg 7/1–5/1863. Hospitalized in Chester; paroled and sent to City Pt. on 9/17/1863 for exc. Returned. Captured in a Richmond hospital 4/3/1865. Confined at Newport News 4/24/1865, until released 6/30/1865 after OOA (NCT 8, 135).

RHYNE, Alfred M., Co. B, Corporal (1843–). Lived, e. in Gaston 7/30/1861, age 18, as a private. Captured near Sharpsburg abt 9/17/1862; confined at Ft. McHenry, then at Ft. Columbus, before trans to Aiken's Landing on 10/22/1862 for exc on 11/20/1862. Promoted to corporal 10/1/1864. Surrendered at Appomattox CH 4/9/1865 (NCT 8, 136).

RHYNE, Ambrose, Co. B, Private (1837–). Lived, e. in Gaston 8/5/1861, age 24. Wounded in the forehead near Richmond June of 1862. Captured at Fredericksburg 12/13/1862; paroled abt 12/17/1862. Surrendered at Appomattox CH 4/9/1865 (NCT 8, 136).

RHYNE, George C., Co. B, Private (1830–). Lived in Gaston, e. 8/6/1861, age 31. Captured at Hanover CH 5/27/1862; confined at Ft. Monroe, then Ft. Columbus. Paroled and sent to Aiken's Landing for exc on 8/5/1862. Wounded in the elbow and captured at Spotsylvania CH 5/12/1864. Confined in various Federal hospitals before being sent to Old Capitol Prison 9/24/1864. Trans to Elmira 10/27/1864; paroled 2/9/1865 and sent to Boulware's Wharf 2/20–21/1865 for exc (NCT 8, 136).

RHYNE, Robert D., Co. B, Captain (1841–). E. in his home county of Gaston, age 20, 7/30/1861 as a private. Elected 3rd lieutenant 2/27/1862; to 2nd lieutenant 12/14/1862, and 1st lieutenant 4/16/1863. Wounded at Chancellorsville 5/2–3/1863. Wounded

again at Reams' Station 8/25/1864. Promoted to captain same day. Absent-wounded through Feb. 1865 (NCT 8, 125).

RICHARDSON, John T. Co. E, Private (1835–1861). A resident of Montgomery, e. 8/1/1861, age 26. Died at Wilmington 12/30/1861 of disease (NCT 8, 171).

RICHEY, Eben, Co. K, Private (1844–1862). Lived and e. in Stanly 3/10/1862, age 18. Died in Staunton hospital abt 11/17/1862 of typhoid fever (NCT 8, 228).

RICHIE, John, Co. D, Private (1831–). Lived, e. in Stanly 3/15/1862 , age 21. Captured near Petersburg 4/2/1865; confined at Pt. Lookout; l released 6/17/1865 after OOA (NCT 8, 161).

RICK, John, Co. C, Private. John e. in Catawba 10/17/1864. Present through Feb. 1865 (NCT 8, 150).

RIDENHOUR, Franklin A., Co. D, Private (1827–). Lived, e. in Stanly 7/29/1861, age 34. Hospitalized at Petersburg 6/23/1864 with gunshot wound. Captured near Petersburg 4/2/1865; confined at Pt. Lookout until released 6/17/1865 after OOA. NC pension records indicate he was wounded in the right leg at Petersburg, date not given (NCT 8, 161).

RIDENHOUR, William, Co. D, Private (1841–1862). Lived, e. in Stanly 7/29/1861, age 20. Wounded near Sharpsburg abt 9/16/1862. Died at Shepherdstown 9/30/1862 of wounds. "A good soldier" (NCT 8, 161).

RIGGAN, Joseph M., Co. A, Private (1833–1861). Lived, e. in Surry., age 28, 5/4/1861. Died at training camp in Garysburg of disease on 8/8/1861. He m. Mary Hodges, Surry, and had 2 children (NCT 8, 122; SCS 150).

RIGGS, Christopher C., Co. A, Sergeant (1839–). Son of Jesse and Lydia Hodges Riggs, Christopher Riggs, he lived near the Fisher River; e., age 22, 5/4/1861. Hospitalized in Richmond on 5/24/1864 gunshot wound. Promoted to sergeant on 9/1/1864. Wounded in left arm near Jones' Farm. Arm amputated, and he retired 2/4/1865 (NCT 8, 122; SCS 150).

RIGGS, George W., Co. A, Private (1842–1862). E. in Surry on 5/4/1861. Died at 2nd Manassas on 8/29/1862. Son of Daniel and Deborah Haynes Riggs, who lived near Fisher River, Surry (NCT 8, 122; SCS 150).

RIGGS, Thomas J., Co. A, Private (1845–1889). The brother of George W. Riggs (above). Thomas e. 2/18/1864. Wounded, he was sent to a Richmond hospital on 6/6/1864. Captured near Petersburg on 4/1/1865; confined at Pt. Lookout. Released after OOA on 6/17/1865. Returned home to operate a store in Dobson. He m. Mattie Norman and had two children. Bur. in the Dobson Cemetery (NCT 8, 122; SCS 150).

RILEY, John W., Co. G, Private (1841–). Born in SC, lived in Orange, where he e. 9/2/1861, age 20. Captured at Fredericksburg 12/13/1862; exc abt 12/17/1862. Hospitalized in Richmond 12/31/1862 with gunshot wound of head. Returned and present through Sept. 1864–Feb. 1865 (NCT 8, 193).

RING, Adam, Co. A, Private (1842–). E. in Surry 3/18/1862, age 20. Son of Martin and Rachel Ring of Siloam, he was hospitalized in Charlottesville on 9/12/1862 with a gunshot wound. Captured near Petersburg 4/2/1865; confined at Ft. Delaware until released on 6/19/1865 after OOA. NC pension records indicate he was wounded by a "falling limb at Manassas," no date was given. Adam m. in 1868 Mary Matilda Shore (NCT 8, 122; SCS 151).

RING, Stephen, Co. A, Private (1844–1864). Son of Martin and Rachel Ring of Siloam, and the brother of Adam Ring, Stephen entered the army on 12/30/1863. Killed at Jericho Ford 5/23/1864 (NCT 8, 122; SCS 152).

RING, William, Co. A, Private (1824–1861). William, the son of William and Elizabeth, was a millwright at Siloam. He volunteered on 5/4/1861, age 37, in the first group to leave Surry. His company began their training at Garysburg, NC, where he died of an unknown illness on 8/6/1861. His widow, Rebecca, applied for a pension (NCT 8, 122; SCS 152).

RINK, Henry, Co. C, Private (1840–1862). Lived, e. in Catawba 3/15/1862. Wounded in the forearm and captured at Hanover CH 5/27/1862. Hospitalized at Ft. Monroe, where he died 7/6/1862 of wounds. Federal provost marshal records gave his age as 32 in 1862 (NCT 8, 150).

RITCHIE, Marvel, Co. D, Sergeant (1845–). Lived, e. in Stanly 7/29/1861, age 16, as a private. Wounded in the right heel and left thigh near Richmond in June 1862. Promoted to corporal 11/16/1862; promoted to sergeant Jan. 1863–Oct 1864. Wounded in left side at Gettysburg 7/1–3/1863. Wounded near Petersburg. Surrendered at Appomattox CH 4/9/1865 (NCT 8, 161).

RIVERVILLE, J. J., Co. G, Private. His name appears on a list of Federal prisoners paroled at Farmville, VA 4/11–21/1865. No more information (NCT 8, 163).

ROBERSON, Haston M., Co. G, Private (1837–1862). Lived, e. in Orange 9/2/1861, age 24, as a corporal. Rank reduced Mar.–Apr.1862. Killed at Hanover CH 5/27/1862 (NCT 8, 163).

ROBERSON, John A., Co. G, Private (1842–1864). Lived, e. in Orange 12/20/1861, age 19. Captured at Hanover CH 5/27/1862; confined at Ft. Monroe, then Ft. Columbus. Paroled and trans to Aiken's Landing for exc 8/5/1862. Killed at Spotsylvania CH 5/18/1864 (NCT 8, 193).

ROBERSON, Thomas C., Co. D, Private. He previously served in Co. E, 1st Reg Junior Reserves. Trans to Co. E 1/20/1865. Surrendered at Appomattox CH 4/9/1865 (NCT 8, 171).

ROBERSON, Thomas H., Co. G, Private (18__–1862). E. in Orange 9/2/1861. Killed at Shepherdstown 9/20/1862 (NCT 8, 193).

ROBERSON, Thomas J., Co. G, Private (1939–). Lived, e. in Orange 9/2/1861, age 22. On light duty as a guard at Charlotte Dec. 1862–Feb. 1865 (NCT 8, 193).

ROBERTS, A.W., Co. F, Private (1837–). Lived, e. in Yadkin 10/1/1862, age 25. Deserted in March 1863 (NCT 8, 182).

ROBERTS, Pleasant H., Co. A, Private (1842–1862). B. in Surry to S. C. and Melinda Roberts of the Dobson District, he e. 5/4/1861, age 19. Wounded in the thigh and captured at Hanover CH 5/27/1862. Exc.

Died from wounds abt 6/2/1862 at Gaines' Mill (NCT 8, 122; SCS 152).

ROBERTSON, Alfred G., Co. G, Private (1840–). Lived, e. in Orange 9/2/1861, age 21, as a sergeant. Rank reduced Mar.–Apr. 1862. On detail as enrolling and enlisting officer 2/10/1864–Feb. 1865 (NCT 8, 193).

ROBERTSON, Henry F., Co. G, Private (1832–1862). Lived, e. in Orange 9/2/1861. Killed at Shepherdstown 9/20/1862 (NCT 8, 193).

ROBERTSON, Henry H., Co. G, Private (1845–). Lived, e. in Orange 9/1/1863, age 18. Surrendered at Appomattox CH 4/9/1865 (NCT 8, 193).

ROBESON, William R., Co. H, Private (1833–1862). Lived, e. in Cleveland 3/17/1862, age 29. Died in Richmond hospital 9/4/1862 of "dyspepsia" (NCT 8, 205).

ROBINSON, John L., Co. E, Private (1842–). B. in Montgomery, e. 8/1/1861, age 19. Dis 2/25/1862 due to an "inguinal hernia of the right side." NC pension records indicate he was wounded in face near Petersburg 6/30/1862 (NCT 8, 171).

ROBINSON, Livingston, Co. E, Private (1828–1861). Lived, e. in Montgomery 8/1/1861, age 33. Killed at Fredericksburg 12/13/1862 (NCT 8, 171).

ROGERS, Aaron, Co. K, Private (1825–). Lived and e. in Stanly 3/27/1862, age 37. Captured at Hanover CH 5/27/1862; confined at Ft. Monroe, then Ft. Columbus. Trans to Aiken's Landing for exc 8/5/1862. Wounded in elbow and captured at Fredericksburg 12/13/1862; exc 12/17/1862. Paroled at Farmville 4/11–21/1865 (NCT 8, 228).

ROGERS, David W., Co. K, Private (1836–). A cabinetmaker, b., lived, and e. in Stanly 9/7/1861, age 25. Wounded at Gettysburg 7/1–3/1863. Hospitalized at Richmond 5/18/1864 with gunshot wound of right leg, place not reported. Returned. Paroled at Lynchburg 4/15/1865 (NCT 8, 228–229).

ROGERS, John W., Co. K, Sergeant (1838–1863). Lived, e. in Stanly 9/7/1861, age 23, as sergeant. Captured at Hanover CH 5/27/1862; confined at Ft. Monroe, then Ft. Columbus. Trans to Aiken's Landing for exc 8/5/1862. Captured at Fredericksburg 12/13/1862; exc abt 12/17/1862. Died in Richmond hospital 6/8–9/1863 of typhoid fever (NCT 8, 229).

ROGERS, Madison M., Co. D, Private. Stanly resident, e. 2/1/1865. Captured near Petersburg 4/2/1865; confined at Pt. Lookout until released 6/19/1865 after OOA (NCT 8, 161).

ROLEN, John, Co. I, Private. (1810–). Lived in Wilkes, and was a farmer before he e. In Yadkin, age 52 9/20/1862, as a substitute. Present through Feb. 1865 (NCT 8, 217).

ROLLINS, Doctor O., Co. H, Private 1834–). Born and living in Cleveland where he e. 8/22/1861, age 27. Trans to Co. I, 34th Reg NCT Sep.–Oct. 1864 (NCT 8, 205).

ROLLINS, Drury D., Co. H, 2nd Lieutenant (1823–). Lived, e. in Cleveland 8/22/1861, age 38. Appointed 2nd lieutenant; defeated for reelection when regiment was reorganized 4/7/1862. He may have later served in Co. I, 34th Reg NCT (NCT 8, 196).

ROLLINS, James J., Co. H, Sergeant (1834–1863). Lived, e. in Cleveland 8/22/1861 as a corporal, age 27. Promoted to sergeant May–Oct. 1862. Wounded in left leg and right shoulder and captured at Gettysburg 7/1–3/1863. Died in Federal field hospital at Gettysburg 7/22/1863 from wounds (NCT 8, 205).

ROLLINS, Noah J., Co. H, Private (1836–). Lived, e. in Cleveland 8/22/1861, age 25. Wounded in left hip at Ox Hill. On guard detail Nov.–Dec. 1864. Retired to Invalid Corps 12/28/1864 (NCT 8, 205).

ROPER, John W., Co. E, Private (1840–1863). Lived, e. in Montgomery 8/1/1861, age 21. Hospitalized in Richmond 12/16/1862 with gunshot wound. Died in Richmond hospital 3/18/1864 of "varioloid" and gangrene (NCT 8, 1871).

ROSE, Isaac W., Co. I, Musician (1839–) Lived, e. in Yadkin 8/13/1861, age 22, as a musician. Rank reduced Jan.–Oct. 1862. Captured at Hanover CH 5/27/1862; confined at Ft. Monroe, then Ft. Columbus. Paroled, trans to Aiken's Landing for exc 8/5/1862. Returned. Deserted 6/20/1863. Returned, but was AWOL 9/22/1864 (NCT 8, 217).

ROSE, Thomas A., Co. I, Private. E. at Camp Holmes 10/14/1862. AWOL 10/17/1864(2?) (NCT 8, 217).

ROSS, Doctor M., Co. K, Sergeant (1836–). Lived, e. in Stanly 9/7/1861, age 25. Promoted to sergeant May–Dec. 1862. Captured at Hanover CH 5/27/1862; confined at Ft. Monroe, then Ft. Columbus. Paroled, trans to Aiken's Landing for exc 8/5/1862. Returned. Wounded in right hip at Gettysburg 7/3/1863. Returned. Surrendered at Appomattox CH 4/9/1865 (NCT 8, 229).

ROSS, George P., Co. K, Private (1830–). Lived, e. in Stanly 3/27/1862, age 32. Captured at Hanover CH 5/27/1862; confined at Ft. Monroe, then Ft. Columbus. Paroled, trans to Aiken's Landing for exc 8/5/1862. Returned. Wounded in left hip and captured at Gettysburg 7/1–4/1863. Hospitalized at Davids Island; trans to City Pt. 10/28/1863 for exc. Returned. Surrendered at Appomattox CH 4/9/1865 (NCT 8, 229).

ROSS, William J., Co. K, Sergeant (1840–). Lived, e. in Stanly 9/7/1861, age 21 as sergeant. Wounded in right arm at Gettysburg 7/3/1863. Returned. Surrendered at Appomattox CH 4/9/1865 (NCT 8, 229).

ROUGHTON, James I, Co. I, Private (1838–). Lived, e. in Yadkin 8/13/1861, age 23. Wounded in right shoulder near Richmond 6/25/1862–7/1/1862. Returned. Captured by enemy. Paroled and trans to Aiken's Landing for exc 9/21/1862. AWOL, but returned before 3/1/1863. Deserted 6/20/1863 (NCT 8, 217).

ROWLAND, Columbus W., Co. D, Private (1839–). Lived in Stanly, e. 3/15/1862, age 23. Wounded near Richmond, date not reported. Absent on detached service at Charlotte, NC Sept.–Oct. 1864 through Feb. 1865 (NCT 8, 161).

ROWLAND, Mathias, Co. D, Private (1809–) Lived and e. in Stanly 7/29/1861, age 52. Dis 6/19/1862 due to "general debility and advanced age" (NCT 8, 161).

ROYAL, Willie D., Co. I, Musician (1942–). Lived, e. in Yadkin 8/13/1861, age 19. Promoted to musician (drummer) Jan.–Oct. 1862. Captured at Hanover CH

5/27/1862; confined at Ft. Monroe, then Ft. Columbus. Paroled, trans to Aiken's Landing for exc 8/5/1862. Returned. Captured at Amelia CH 4/6/1865; confined at Pt. Lookout. Released 6/19/1865 after OOA (NCT 8, 217).

RUDASILL, John, Co. D, Private. E. 10/28/1864 at Camp Stokes. Surrendered at Appomattox CH 4/9/1865 (NCT 8, 1861).

RUSSELL, Alexander, Co. K, Private ? NC pension records indicate he served in this company (NCT 8, 229).

RUSSELL, Gabriel, Co. K, Private (1844–) Lived, e. in Stanly 3/18/1862, age 18. Wounded at Gettysburg 7/3/1863. Company records indicate he was missing and presumed captured at Gettysburg, but Federal provost marshal records do not report his capture (NCT 8, 2329).

RUSSELL, Henry, Co. K, Private (1829–). Lived, e. in Stanly 9/7/1861, age 32. Blinded in left eye from wound received at Harpers Ferry abt 6/1/1863. Returned. Present Sept. 1864–Feb. 1865. Captured near Petersburg 4/2/19865; confined at Pt. Lookout until released 6/19/1865 after OOA (NCT 8, 229).

RUSSELL, Jason, Co. E, Private (1823–1863). Lived, e. in Montgomery 3/4/1863, age 40. Died in Salisbury, NC 7/18/1863 (NCT 8, 172).

RUSSELL, Joseph C., Co. E, Private (1832–1863). Lived, e. in Montgomery 3/10/1862, age 30. Captured at Hanover CH 5/27/1862; confined at Ft. Monroe, then Ft. Columbus. Paroled and trans to Aiken's Landing for exc 8/5/1862. Died in Lynchburg hospital 4/9/1863 of chronic diarrhea (NCT 8, 172).

RUSSELL, William H., Co. K, Private (1844–). Lived, e. in Stanly 9/7/1861, age 17. Wounded in right leg at Chancellorsville 5/1–4/1863. Absent-sick in Salisbury hospital Aug. 1864–Feb. 1865. Paroled at Salisbury 5/2/1865. Took OOA at Salisbury 6/14/1865 (NCT 8/229).

RUTLEDGE, Ruburtus Gamwell, Co. B, Private. Previously served in Co. H, 27th Reg NCT before enlisting in Co. B, 28th Reg at Liberty Mills 3/15/1864. Hospitalized at Petersburg 8/26/1864 with a gunshot wound of the right thigh. Present through Feb. 1865 (NCT 8, 136).

RYAN, Samuel G., Co. G, Sergeant (1843–). Lived, e. in Orange 3/5/1862, age 19, as a private. Captured at Hanover CH 5/27/1862; confined at Ft. Monroe. Trans to Aiken's Landing for exc 8/5/1862. Wounded at Gettysburg 7/1–3/1863. Promoted to sergeant 9/1/1863. Detailed as provost guard at Raleigh 12/19/1863–Feb. 1865 (NCT 8, 193).

SAFLEY, William W., Co. D, Private (1841–). B. in Stanly, e. 7/29/1861, age 20. Wounded in left leg and right hip at Gaines' Mill 6/27/1862. Leg amputated. Dis 2/23/1863 due to disability (NCT 8, 161).

SANDERS, Thomas L., Co. B, Private (1843–). Gaston resident, e. there 7/30/1861, age 18. Captured at Hanover CH 5/27/186; confined at Ft. Monroe; then Ft. Columbus until paroled. Sent to Aiken's Landing for exc 8/5/1862. Surrendered at Appomattox CH 4/9;/1865 (NCT 8, 136).

SARVIS, Alexander, Co. B, Private. E. at Liberty

Mills 4/1/1864. Wounded somewhere in "Virginia" in May 1864. Absent-wounded through Feb. 1865 (NCT 8, 136).

SARVIS, F.A., Co. B, Private (1845–). E. in Feb. 1864, age 19. Wounded at Wilderness abt 5/5/1864. NC pension records indicate he survived the war (NCT 8, 136).

SARVIS, John R., Co. B, Private (1844–) Lived, e. in Gaston 3/29/1862, age 18. Captured at Hanover CH 5/27/1862; confined at Ft. Monroe, then Ft. Columbus until paroled, and trans to Aiken's Landing for exc 8/5/1862. Wounded in right eye at Gettysburg 7/1–3/1863. Wounded in left hip at Reams' Station 8/25/1864. Recovered and was present Jan.–Feb.1865. Captured in Richmond hospital 4/3/1865; confined at Newport News 4–24–1865. Released on 6/30/1865 after OOA (NCT 8, 136).

SAWYER, Edwin, Co. F, Private? NC pension records indicate that this Negro served in this company (NCT 8, 182).

SCARBOROUGH, Benjamin F., Co. E, Private. E. at Liberty Mills 2/15/1864. Wounded in the hip at Jones' Farm, 9/30/1864 (NCT 8, 172).

SCOTT, B. Franklin, Co. K, Private. Lived in Stanly, place/date of enlistment not reported. First listed on records Jan.–Feb. 1865. Captured near Petersburg 4/2/1865; confined at Pt Lookout until released 6/20/1865 after OOA (NCT 8, 229).

SCOTT, Calvin, Co. G, 3rd Lieutenant (1832–). Lived, e. in Orange 9/2/1861, age 29, as a 1st sergeant; appointed 3rd lieutenant 3/1/1862. Wounded and captured at Hanover CH 5/27/1862; confined at Ft. Monroe, then Ft. Columbus. Trans to Johnson's Island 6/21/1862; trans to Vicksburg 9/20/1862; exc at Aiken's Landing on 11/10/1862. Resigned 1/5/1863 due to "bronchial affection" (NCT 8, 185).

SCOTT, Thomas G., Co. I, Private (1843–). B. to Robert and Martha Scott, lived, e. in Yadkin, age 19, 3/8/1862. Present at the surrender at Appomattox CH 4/9/1865. Returned to Yadkin, m. Alice Harding, and had a dau, Cora (NCT 8, 217; CWY 260).

SCRUGGS, Lorenzo B., Co. H, Private (1833–). A Cleveland farmer, he e. 8/22/1861, age 28. Wounded in left hand at 2nd Manassas 8/28–30/1862. Deserted near Chancellorsville. Returned. Captured at Spotsylvania CH 5/12/1864; confined at Pt. Lookout. Trans to Elmira 8/10/1864; trans to Venus Pt. for exc 11/15/1864 (NCT 8, 205–206).

SEABOCH, George W., Co. C, Private (1828–). Catawba resident e. at Camp Fisher, age 33, 9/9/1861. Captured at Hanover CH 5/27/1862; confined at Ft. Monroe, then Ft. Columbus until paroled and trans to Aiken's Landing. Exc. there 8/5/1862. Present through Feb. 1865 (NCT 8, 150).

SEABOCH, John Pinkney, Co. C, Private (1841–1862). Catawba resident e. at Camp Fisher on 9/9/1861, age 20. Killed at Gaines' Mill 6/27/1862 (NCT 8, 150).

SEABOCH, William H., Co. C, Private (1844–1864). Lived, e. in Catawba 3/15/1862, age 18. Captured at Hanover CH 5/27/1862; confined at Ft. Monroe, then Ft. Columbus until paroled and trans to Aiken's Landing for exc 8/5/1862. Killed at Jones' Farm 9/30/1864 (NCT 8, 150).

SEDBERRY, John A., Co. E, Private (1830–1863). Lived, e. in Montgomery 8/1/1861, age 31. Wounded near Frayser's Farm abt 6/30/1862. Captured at Gettysburg 7/3/1863; confined at Ft. Delaware, trans to Pt. Lookout 10/15–18/1863. Died there 12/27/1863 (NCT 8, 172).

SEITZ, Laban M., Co. C, Private. Lived, e. in Catawba 3/15/1862. Wounded in right hand at Sharpsburg 9/17/1862. Two fingers amputated. Dis _/1863 due to disability (NCT 8, 150).

SEITZ, Marcus, Co. C, Private. Lived, e. in Catawba 3/15/1862. Hospitalized at Richmond on 9/27/1862 with a gunshot wound. Wounded and died at Chancellorsville 5/3/1863 (NCT 8, 150).

SEITZER, Franklin, Co. C, Private. Lived, e. in Catawba 8/13/1861 as sergeant. Rank reduced abt 2/28/1862. Captured at Hanover CH 5/27/1862; confined at Ft. Monroe, then Ft. Columbus. Paroled and trans to Aiken's Landing for exc 8/5/1862. Present through Feb. 1865 (NCT 8, 150).

SELL, J.P., Co. D, Private (1829–). B. in Stanly, e. there 3/15/1862, age 32. Dis 2/23/1863 due to "prolapsis ani of seven months standing" (NCT 8, 161).

SELL, John E., Co. D, Private (1836–). Stanly resident, e. 5/6/1862, age 26. Reported missing at Gettysburg 7/3/1863. No further information (NCT 8, 161).

SELL, Richmond, Co. D, Private (1819–). B. in Rowan, lived, e. in Stanly 7/29/1861, age 42. Dis 7/16/1862 due to disability (NCT 8, 161–162).

SELL, Samuel, Co. D, Private (1841–). Stanly resident who worked as a "minor," Sell e. 3/15/1862, age 21. Paroled at Salisbury, NC 5/20/1865 (NCT 8, 162).

SHARPLIN (Choplin?), J., Co. A, Private. Hospitalized in Richmond on 3/28/1865 with a gunshot wound to his right leg. Captured while in the hospital on 4/3/1865 (NCT 8, 122; SCS 156, CWY 200).

SHEPARD, George W., Co. F, Private (1839–1864). B, in Franklin, lived, e. in Yadkin 6/18/1861, age 22 Captured at Fredericksburg 12/13/1862, exc 12/17/1862. AWOL, but returned. Deserted again 6/23/1863. Hospitalized at Richmond 6/20/1864. Died "at home" 9/7/1864 or 10/1/1864 of disease (NCT 8, 182).

SHIELDS, Isaac Wilson, Co. B, Private (1839–). Lived, e. in Gaston 7/30/1861, age 22. Captured at Hanover CH 5/27/1862; confined at Ft. Monroe then Ft. Columbus until paroled and trans to Aiken's Landing for exc 8/5/1862. Wounded in right leg, captured at Gettysburg 7/3–5/1863. Hospitalized on Davids Island 7/17–24/1863. Paroled and sent to City Pt. 9/16/1863 for exc. Surrendered 4/9/1865 at Appomattox CH (NCT 8, 136).

SHIELDS, James D. C., Co. C, Musician (1845–) Lived in Gaston, e. in Iredell on 2/25/1863, age 18. Mustered in as a private, and promoted to Musician Nov.–Dec. 1864. Reduced in rank before 2/28/1865. Surrendered at Appomattox CH 4/9/1865 (NCT 8, 136).

SHIPWASH, George W., Co. F, Private (1837–). Lived, e. in Yadkin 6/18/1861, age 24. Deserted 6/30/1862. Returned, deserted again 7/19/1863. Captured by the enemy at Culpeper 12/4/1863; confined at Old Capitol Prison. Released 3/19/1864 after OOA.

Roll of Honor indicates he deserted 3 times (NCT 8, 182).

SHOE, Redding, Co. K, Private. E. at Liberty Mills 3/1/1864. Surrendered at Appomattox 4/9/1865 (NCT 8, 229).

SHORES (Shore), Alexander F., Co. I, Corporal (1840–1862). Lived, e. in Yadkin 8/13/1861. Promoted to captain Jan.–Oct. 1862. Captured at Hanover CH 5/27/1862; confined at Ft. Monroe, then Ft. Columbus. Paroled, trans to Aiken's Landing for exc 8/5/1862. Returned. Wounded at 2nd Manassas; died 9/11/1862 of wounds (NCT 8, 217).

SHORES, Anderson, Co. I, Private (1839–1862). Lived, e. in Yadkin 8/13/1861, age 22. Killed at 2nd Manassas 8/28–30/1862 (NCT 8, 217).

SHORES, David, Co. I, Private (1839–). Lived, e. in Yadkin 8/13/1861, age 19. May have served later in Co. A, 21st Reg (NCT 8, 217).

SHORES, Henry, Co. I, Private (1840). B. in Surry, e. in Yadkin 8/13/1861, age 21. Dis 4/14/1862 due to "scrotal hernia" (NCT 8, 217).

SHORES (Shore), John, Co. F, Private (1822–). Born in Yadkin where he was a farmer before he e. 11/11/1863. Dis 12/21/1863 due to "double inguinal hernia" (NCT 8, 182).

SHORES, Lewis W., Co. I, Private (1843–). Lived and e. in Yadkin 8/13/1861, age 18. Wounded at Chancellorsville 5/2–3/1863. Trans to Co. H, 54th Reg before 11/1/1863 (NCT 8, 217).

SHORT, John, Co. C, Private (1843–1862). Lived in Catawba, but e. at Camp Fisher 9/2/1861, age 18. Captured at Hanover CH 5/27–28/1862; confined at Ft. Monroe, then Ft. Columbus, where he died 7/30/1862 (NCT 8, 150).

SHOTTLE, Christopher, Co. K, Private (1843–) Lived, e. in Stanly 9/7/1861, age 18. Company records indicate he was captured at Spotsylvania CH, but Federal provost records do not agree (NCT 8, 229).

SHOUSE, Frederick, Co. A, Private (1828–1862). Lived in Forsyth, e. in Davidson, age 33, 9/17/1861. Killed at Frayser's Farm 6/30/1862 (NCT 8, 122).

SHREVE, Robert J., Co. A, Private (1837–1862). E. in Surry, age 24, 5/13/1861. Died in a Richmond hospital sometime between June–Oct. 1862 (NCT 8, 122)

SHROPSHIRE, Jeremiah, Co. A, Private (1839–). E., age 22, 5/2/1861. Wounded in right leg near Petersburg, on 3/27/1865. Hospitalized in Richmond, where he was captured on 4/3/1865. Trans to Pt. Lookout 5/12/1865; released abt 6/28/1865 after OOA (NCT 8, 122).

SHRUM, John A., Co. B, Private (1841–). E., age 20, 7/30/1861. Surrendered 4/9/1865 at Appomattox CH 4/9/1865 (NCT 8, 136).

SIDES, Alexander, Jr., Co. D, Private (1841–). B., lived in Stanly, e. 7/29/1861, age 20. Present through Feb. 1865 (NCT 8, 162).

SIDES, Alexander, Sr., Co. D, Private (1819–). Stanly resident, Alexander, Sr., e. 7/29/1861, age 42. Captured and paroled at Warrenton, VA 9/29/1862. Captured at Gettysburg 7/3/1863; confined at Ft. Delaware, then trans to Pt. Lookout 10/15–18/1863 . Paroled, sent to Boulware's Wharf 2/18/1865 for exc.

Captured near Petersburg, 4/2/1865; confined at Pt. Lookout until released 6/20/1865 after OOA (NCT 8, 162).

SIDES, Calvin T., Co. E, Private. Previously served in Co. B, 14th Reg NCT. Trans to Co. E, 28th Reg 4/14/1864. Captured at Fussell's Mill 8/16/1864; confined at Pt. Lookout. Paroled, trans to Boulware's Wharf on 3/16/1865 for exc (NCT 8, 172).

SIDES, Charles W., Co. D, Private (1843–). Lived, e. in Stanly 3/15/1862, age 19. Captured at Fredericksburg 12/13/1863; exc abt 12/17/1862. Wounded in the thigh and captured at Gettysburg 7/1–4/1863. Hospitalized at Davids Island; paroled and trans to City Pt. on 9/27/1863 for exc. Reported absent-sick Sept.–Oct. 1864. Captured near Petersburg 4/2/1865. Confined at Pt. Lookout until released 6/30/1865 after OOA (NCT 8, 162).

SIDES, Green H., Co. D, Private. Stanly resident e. at Liberty Mills 2/1/1864. Wounded at Wilderness 5/5/1864. Captured in Richmond hospital 4/3/1865; trans to Newport News 4/23/1865. Released 6/14/1865 after OOA (NCT 8, 162).

SIDES, Henry C., Co. D, Private (1832–1862). Stanly resident e. there 7/29/1861, age 29. Roll of Honor indicates he was k. at the battle of 2nd Manassas 8/29/1862. *Raleigh Register*, 9/24/1862, reported he was wounded in the finger at Ox Hill 9/1/1862. Company muster rolls for 6/30/1862–10/31/1862 states he died 9/17/1862 of wounds received in an unspecified engagement (NCT 8, 162).

SIDES, Henry W., Co. D, Private. E. 10/22/1864 at Camp Holmes in NC. Present through Feb. 1865. May have previously served in Co. A, 4th Reg NC State Troops (NCT 8, 162).

SIDES, Jacob, Co. D, Private (1830–1862). Stanly resident e. there 3/15/1862. Killed at or near Gaines' Mill abt 6/28/1862 (NCT 8, 162).

SIDES, James A., Co. D, Private (1841–). E. 7/29/1861 in Stanly where he lived. Present through Feb. 1865 (NCT 8, 162).

SIDES, Joseph, Co. D, Private (1832–). Lived, e. in Stanly 7/29/1861, age 29. Wounded in left side near Richmond, date not stated. Captured at/near Gettysburg abt, 7/3/1863; confined at Ft. Delaware; trans to Pt. Lookout 10/15–18/1863. Paroled there 2/18/1865 and trans to Boulware's Wharf for exc abt 2/20/1865 (NCT 8, 162).

SIDES, William W., Co. D, Private (1843–). Lived, e. in Stanly 9/18/1861, age 18. Captured at Fredericksburg 12/13/1862; exc 12/17/1862. Deserted 9/14/1863. Captured near Spotsylvania CH. Confined at Pt. Lookout until released 5/30/1864 after joining the U.S. Army. (NCT 8, 162).

SIFFORD, Daniel M., Co. B, Private (1830–). Gaston resident, Daniel e. in Lenoir, age 32, 4/8/1862. Captured at Hanover CH 5/27/1862; confined at Ft. Monroe, then Ft. Columbus. Exc. before 7/31/1862. Captured at Fredericksburg 12/13/186; paroled 12/17/1862. Detailed as brigade blacksmith 2/1/1863–Feb. 1865. Surrendered at Appomattox CH 4/9/1865 (NCT 8, 136–137).

SIGMAN, Alfred P., Co. C, Private. Lived at "Hickory Station," e. in Catawba 4/14/1864. Captured at Spotsylvania CH 5/12/1864; confined at Pt. Lookout; trans to Elmira 8/10/1864. Released from Elmira 6/27/1865 after OOA (NCT 8, 150).

SIGMAN, Isaiah, Co. C, Private. E. in Catawba where he lived on 3/15/1862. Died at Charlottesville 5/29/1862 of "typhoid pneumonia" (NCT 8, 150).

SIGMAN, Jesse A. Co. H, Private. E. in Catawba 2/1/1865 . Present through Feb. 1865 (NCT 8, 206).

SIGMAN, Martin M., Co. C, Private (18__–1864). Lived, e. in Catawba 3/15/1862. Wounded at Cedar Mt. 8/9/1862. Captured at Spotsylvania CH 5/12/1864; confined at Pt. Lookout, then trans to Elmira 8/10/1864; died there 11/14/1864 of chronic diarrhea (NCT 8, 150–151)

SIGMAN, Maxwell A., Co. C, Corporal. Catawba resident, e. 8/13/1861 as a private. Captured at Hanover CH 5/17/1862; confined at Ft. Monroe, then Ft. Columbus. Trans to Aiken's Landing for exc 8/5/1862. Promoted to corporal 3/15/1863. Wounded in left leg and captured at Gettysburg 7/3–5/1863. Hospitalized at Davids Island 7/17–24/1863. Paroled and trans 10/28/1863 to City Pt. for exc. Retired to Invalid Corps 4/15/1864 (NCT 8, 151).

SIMMONS, Noah, Co. C, Private (18__–1865). Catawba resident e. 3/14/1863. Captured at Wilderness 5/12/1864; confined at Pt. Lookout, then trans to Elmira 8/10/1864. Died at Elmira 4/10/1865 of chronic diarrhea (NCT 8, 151).

SIMMONS, Stephen A., Co. H, 3rd Lieutenant (18__–1863) Lived, e. in Cleveland 8/22/1861, age 18 as a private. Promoted to 1st sergeant 4/7/1862; appointed 3rd lieutenant 11/14/1862. Killed at Gettysburg 7/3/1863 (NCT 8, 196).

SIMPSON, Allison, Co. H, Private (1837–1863). Lived, e. in Wilkes 10/2/1862, age 25. Died in hospital at Guinea Station 1/30/1863 or 7/30/1863 (NCT 8, 206).

SIMPSON, Andrew, Co. F, Private (1841–). B. in Union, lived, e. in Forsyth 10/1/1862, age 21. Dis 1/17/1863 due to "imbecility of mind" (NCT 8, 182).

SIPE, David, Co. C, Private (18__–1863). Lived, e. in Catawba 8/13/1861. Killed at Gettysburg 7/3/1863 (NCT 8, 151).

SIMPSON, Isaac, Co. K, Private (1814–1863). Lived, e. in Stanly 9/7/1861, age 47. Died in Richmond hospital abt 1/7/1863 of chronic bronchitis (NCT 8, 229).

SIZEMORE, John E., Co. C, Private (1840–1862). Lived, e. in Catawba 8/13/1861. Wounded and captured at Hanover CH 5/27/1862; confined at Ft. Monroe, and died abt.6/30/1862 of wounds. Federal provost marshal records give his age as 32 in 1862 (NCT 8, 151).

SMART, E.M., Co. E, Private (1837–1862). Lived, e. in Montgomery 3/10/1862, age 25. Died in Richmond hospital 6/22/1862 of disease (NCT 8, 172).

SMART, G.H., Co. E, Private (1839–1862). Lived, e. in Montgomery 3/10/1862, age 23. Died at Winchester 11/30/1862 (NCT 8, 172).

SMART, Joseph A., Co. E, Corporal (1831–). Lived, e. in Montgomery 8/1/1861, age 30, as a private. Captured at Hanover CH 5/27/1862; confined at Ft. Mon-roe, then Ft. Columbus. Paroled, trans to Aiken's Landing for exc 8/5/1862. Promoted to corporal July 1863–May 1864. Captured at Spotsylvania CH 5/12/1864; confined at Pt. Lookout. Trans to Cox's Wharf abt 2/14/1865 for exc. Paroled at Troy, NC 5/22/1865 (NCT 8, 1865).

SMITH, Benjamin F., Co. K, Private. (1833–). Lived, e. in Stanly 9/7/1861, age 28. Wounded in both knees and captured at Gettysburg 7/3/1863. Confined at various Federal hospitals. Trans to City Pt. 11/17/1863 for exc. Dis abt 9/4/1864 due to disability (NCT 8, 229).

SMITH, Charles, Co. F, Private (1804–1863). B., lived, e. in Forsyth 8/20/1862, age 58, as a substitute. Died at Camp Gregg 4/5/1863 (NCT 8, 182).

SMITH, David B., Co. C, Private; Field & Staff, Sergeant Major (1836–). E. in Co. C, in Gaston, age 25. Appointed 3rd Lt. 7/30/1861, but defeated for reelection at reorganization on 2/27/1862. Reenlisted as a private in Co. C 12/13/1862. Promoted to sergeant major in Jan. 1863. Trans to Field & Staff, 28th Reg. Elected 2nd Lieutenant of Co. H, 28th Reg 4/6/1863 and trans to that unit. Resigned 9/28/1864 because his company was "small having only abt fifteen (15) enlisted men for duty and having a full number of officers and being a profession a mechanic I feel that I can be of far greater service to my country in such a capacity than as a commissioned officer over a handful of men...." (NCT 8, 111, 126, 137, 196).

SMITH, David D., Co. K, Private (1838–). Lived, e. in Stanly 9/7/1861. Present through 4/9/1865 (NCT 8, 229).

SMITH, David P., Co. A, Private (1841–1863). Son of David and Martha Smith of the Dobson District, e. at Dobson on 5/13/1861. Wounded in arm at 2nd Manassas, 8/27–30/1862. Killed at Gettysburg 7/3/1863 (NCT 8, 123; SCS 159).

SMITH, Doctor E., Co. E, Private (1843–1863). Smith lived in Stanly where he e. 7/29/1861, age 18. Wounded, captured at Gettysburg 7/3/1863. Hospitalized at Chester where he died 8/21/1862 of "pyaemia" (NCT 8, 162).

SMITH, Edmund R., Co. K, Private (1842–). Lived, e. in Stanly 9/7/1861, age 19. Captured near Richmond 6/28/1862; confined at Ft. Columbus. Trans to Ft. Delaware 7/9/1862. Trans to Aiken's Landing for exchange 8/5/1862. Captured at Spotsylvania CH 5/12/1864; confined at Pt. Lookout; trans to Elmira abt 8/10/1864. Released there 5/29/1865 after OOA (NCT 8, 229–230).

SMITH, Evan, Co. K, Private (1831–1865). Lived, e. in Stanly 9/7/1861, age 30. Captured at Hanover CH 5/27/1862; confined at Ft. Monroe, then Ft. Columbus. Trans to Aiken's Landing for exc 8/5/1862. Returned. Captured at Spotsylvania CH 5/12/1864; confined at Pt. Lookout. Trans to Elmira 8/10/1864 and died there 4/2/1865 of chronic diarrhea (NCT 8, 230).

SMITH, Freeman S., Co. A, Private (1819–1865). Lived in Dobson District, Surry , e., age 47, 3/18/1862. Captured 5/12/1864 at Spotsylvania CH; confined at Pt. Lookout, then Elmira, where he died of chronic diarrhoea on 2/22/1865. He had two children by his first wife. He m. 2nd Lucy Jane Dezern in 1849 and they had 5 children. His widow applied for a pension (NCT 8, 123; SCS 159–160).

SMITH, George, Co. G, Private (1840–1864). Lived, e. in Orange 9/2/1861, age 21. Captured at Hanover CH 5/27/1862; confined at Ft. Monroe, then Ft. Columbus. Paroled and trans to Aiken's Landing for exc 8/5/1862. Captured near Wilderness abt 5/6/1864; confined at Pt. Lookout, then trans to Elmira 8/10/1864. Died there 10/25/1864 of "chronic diarrhoea" (NCT 8, 193).

SMITH, George C., Co. K, Private (1828–). B., lived, e. in Stanly 9/7/1861, age 33, as a corporal Promoted to sergeant Jan.–Apr.. 1862. Rank reduced Jan. 1863–Oct. 1864. Surrendered at Appomattox CH 4/9/1865 (NCT 8, 230).

SMITH, George L., Co. K, Private. (1838–1862). Lived, e. in Stanly 3/12/1862, age 24. Died in Lovingston hospital 8/16/1862 of typhoid fever (NCT 8, 230).

SMITH, Green, Co. E, Private (1839–1863). B., lived, e. in Montgomery 8/1/1861, age 22. Wounded in right arm at Fredericksburg 12/13/1862. Dis 12/25/1863 due to disability (NCT 8, 172).

SMITH, James L., Co. G, Private (1942–). Lived, e. in Orange 9/2/1861, age 19. AWOL Aug. 1864–Feb. 1865 (NCT 8, 193).

SMITH, John, Co. I, Private (1844–1864). Lived, e. in Yadkin 1/6/1862, age 18. Died in Lynchburg hospital 2/5/1864 of self-administered overdose of morphine (NCT 8, 217).

SMITH, John, Co. F, Private. E. in Yadkin 5/8/1862. Died in Richmond hospital 8/9/1863 of typhoid fever (NCT 8, 182).

SMITH, John D., Co. K, Corporal (1842–1862). Lived, e. in Stanly 9/7/1861, age 19. Promoted to corporal Jan.–Apr.. 1862. Wounded in battle near Richmond. Hospitalized at Richmond where he died 8/10/1862 of wounds and/or disease (NCT 8, 230).

SMITH, John M., Co. K, Private. E. in Stanly 10/15/1863. Captured at Spotsylvania CH 5/12/1864; confined at Pt. Lookout. Trans to Elmira 8/10/1864, and died there abt 4/9/1865 of "hospital gangrene" (NCT 8, 230).

SMITH, John R., Co. E, Private (1838–1862). Lived, e. in Montgomery 8/1/1861, age 22. Hospitalized in Richmond 7/1/1862 with gunshot wound of hand. Died at Guinea Station 1/17–19/1863 (NCT 8, 172).

SMITH, Josiah, Co. D, Private (1837–). Stanly resident e. there 7/29/1861, age 24. Trans to Co. H, 42nd Reg NCT abt 5/12/1862. Trans back to Co. D, 28th Reg 5/1/1863. Captured at Spotsylvania CH 5/12/1864. Reported confined at Elmira 9/30/1864. Roll of Honor indicates that he "deserted twice." No further information (NCT 8, 162).

SMITH, Lawson M., Co. B, Private (1840–). Lived, e. in Gaston 7/30/1861, age 21. Captured near Spotsylvania CH abt 5/12/1864; confined at Pt. Lookout until trans to Elmira 8/10/1864. Released there 6/19/1865 after OOA (NCT 8, 137).

SMITH, Mitchell, Co. G, Private (1831–). Lived, e. in Orange 9/2/1861, age 30. Captured at Hanover CH 5/27/1862; confined at Ft. Monroe, then Colum-

bus. Paroled and trans to Aiken's Landing for exc 8/5/1862. Wounded in foot, captured at Gettysburg 7/1–4/1863; confined at Ft. Delaware. Trans to Pt. Lookout 10/15–18/1863; paroled and trans to Boulware's Wharf 2/20–21/1865 for exc. Paroled at Greensboro, NC 5/10/1865 (NCT 8, 193).

SMITH, Noah, Co. B, Private (1843–). Lived, e. in Gaston 7/30/1861, age 18. Captured at Hanover CH 5/27/1862; confined at Ft. Monroe, then Ft. Columbus until paroled and trans to Aiken's Landing. Exc. 8/5/1862. Deserted but returned 9/27/1864. Present through Feb. 1865 (NCT 8, 137).

SMITH, P.H., Co. B, Private (1829–). Gaston mechanic e. 7/30/1861 in Gaston, age 29. Captured at Hanover CH, 5/27/1862; confined at Ft. Monroe, then Ft. Columbus. Sent to Aiken's Landing and exc 8/5/1862. Killed "instantly" at Fredericksburg 12/13/1862 (NCT 8, 137).

SMITH, Reuben, Co. E, Private (1833–1862). Lived, e. in Montgomery 3/10/1862, age 29. Died in Lynchburg hospital 9/2/1862 of typhoid fever (NCT 8, 172).

SMITH, Tapley, A., Co. I, Private (1840–). Lived, e. in Yadkin 8/13/1861. Absent-wounded May–Oct. 1862. Returned, present through Feb. 1865. NC pension records indicate he was wounded in forehead at Cedar Mt., 5/1/1864. Roll of Honor indicates he was wounded several times (NCT, 8, 217–218).

SMITH, Thomas R., Co. E, Private (1828–1864). Lived, e. in Montgomery 8/1/1861, age 33. Killed at Spotsylvania CH 5/12/1864 (NCT 8, 172).

SMITH, Thomas T., Co. B, Captain (1832–1864). Lived, e. in Gaston, age 29, on 7/30/1861, as a sergeant. Promoted to 2nd lieutenant 2/27/1862, to 1st lieutenant 12/14/1862, to captain 4/16/1863. Wounded in left thigh at Gettysburg 7/3/1863. Killed at Reams' Station, 8/25/1864 (NCT 8, 125).

SMITH, W.A., Co. E, Private (1830–1863). Lived in Montgomery, e. in New Hanover, age 32, 3/12/1862. Wounded and captured at Gettysburg 7/1–3/1863. Died there 7/11/1863 of wounds (NCT 8, 172).

SMITH, William A., Co. B, Private (1843–) E. on 7/30/1861, age 18. Surrender at Appomattox CH on 4/9/1865 (NCT 8, 137).

SMITH, William D., Co. E, Private (1843–). Lived, e. in Montgomery. 3/10/1862, age 19. Wounded in chest at Fredericksburg 12/13/1862. Wounded at Chancellorsville. Deserted in Feb. 1865, but returned to duty. Surrendered at Appomattox CH 4/9/1865 (NCT 8, 172).

SMYER, Jones S., Co. C, Musician (1836–1863). Lived, e. in Catawba 9/2/1861, as a private. Promoted to musician Jan.–Apr. 1862. Wounded, captured at Chancellorsville 5/1–4/1863. Died at Governor's Island of wounds, date not reported.(NCT 8, 151).

SNIPES, Calvin P., Co. G, Private (1841–). Lived, e. in Orange 9/2/1861, age 20. Captured at Hatcher's Run 4/2/1865; confined at Pt. Lookout until released 6/19/1865, after OOA (NCT 8, 193).

SNIPES, Jesse B., Co. G, Private (1837–1863). Lived in Orange where he e. 9/2/1861, age 24. Captured at Hanover CH 5/27/1862; confined at Ft. Monroe, then Ft. Columbus. Paroled and trans to Aiken's Landing for exc 8/5/1862. Died in Richmond hospital abt 6/6/1863 of "febris typhoides" (NCT 8, 194).

SNIPES, John B., Co. G, Corporal (1836–1862). Lived, e. in Orange. 9/2/1862, age 25 as a corporal. Died at Goldsboro 3/21/1862 of disease (NCT 8, 194).

SNIPES, John W., Co. G, Private (1845–1864). B. and e. in Orange 9/2/1863, age 18. Captured, date not specified. Confined at Pt. Lookout, and died 6/27/1864 of disease (NCT 8, 194).

SNIPES, Thomas E., Co. G, Private (1840–). Lived, e. in Orange 3/5/1862, age 22 as a private. Promoted to corporal 3/14/1862. Wounded at Gaines' Mill 6/27/1862. Trans to Co. G, 63rd Reg NCT 8/18/1863 (NCT 8, 194).

SNOW, Frost, Jr., Co. A, Corporal (1843–). E. in Surry 5/4/1861, age 18. Promoted to corporal on 10/4/1861. Rank reduced 4/9/1862; promoted to corporal on 8/10/1862. Wounded in arm, captured at Spotsylvania 5/12/1864. Confined in Old Capitol Prison; trans to Ft. Delaware 6/15/1864, and released on 6/19/1865 after OOA. Son of Birdie and Eliza Harris Snow, of Snow Creek, Surry, Frost m. in 1866 Mary Golding and had 5 children before 1880 (NCT 8, 123; SCS 161–162).

SNOW, James Smith. Co. A, 3rd Lieutenant (1826–). James and his twin brother lived in Surry, the sons of Dick and Sally Tucker Snow, of Pine Ridge. A constable in the Dobson District before the war, James volunteered 5/4/1861 in Surry as a corporal; promoted to 3rd lieutenant 4/9/1862. Resigned 6/15/1862 due to his age (over 35). Left the service 8/20/1862, to serve as a Home Guard captain. He m. Matilda Snow in Surry, and had 7 children (NCT 8, 113; SCS 163).

SNOW, Jordan H., Jr., Co. I, 1st Lieutenant (1832–). Lived, e. in Yadkin 8/13/1861 as a private, age 29. Elected 3rd lieutenant 1/3/1863; promoted to 1st lieutenant 6/20/1863. Wounded in right thigh at Gettysburg 7/3/1863. Captured near Pickett's Farm abt 7/21/1864; confined at Pt. Lookout 7/28/1864. Trans to Old Capitol Prison 8/4/1864, then to Ft. Delaware 8/11/1864. Released 6/17/1865, after OOA (NCT 8, 207).

SNOW, Shadrick, Co. A, Private (1844–1862). A bound boy in the home of Hannah Thompson in the Dobson District in 1860, he e., age 18, 3/18/1862. Died 4 months later in a Lynchburg hospital of an unknown "febris" (fever) (NCT 8, 123; SCS 163).

SOLOMON, James A., Co. K, Private (1841–). Lived and e. in Stanly 9/7/1861, age 20. Court-martialed and "drummed out of camp" on 11/24/1861 for conduct "unbecoming a soldier or a gentleman" (NCT 8, 230).

SOUTHARD, Levi, Co. A, Private (1827–1864). Son of Job and Morning Southard, Dobson District, Surry. Levi was a miller in the Hotel (Elkin) District, Surry, when he e. 3/18/1862, age 35. Captured at Gravel Hill 7/28/1864; imprisoned at Pt. Lookout, then Elmira on 8/8/1864, where he died 4/6/1865 of pneumonia. He m. Sarah L. Isaacs in Surry, and had three children by 1860 (NCT 8, 123; SCS 164).

SPAINHOWER, John W., Co. F, Private. Lived in Stokes, e. 10/19/1864 in Forsyth . Captured near Petersburg 4/2/1865; confined at Pt. Lookout until released 6/20/1865 after OOA (NCT 8, 1862).

SPARROW, James T., Co. G, Private (1942–). Lived, e. in Orange 12/20/1861, age 19. Captured at Petersburg 6/22–30/1864; confined at Pt. Lookout, then trans to Varina on 9/22/1864 for exc. Absent-sick through Feb. 1865 (NCT 8, 194).

SPARROW, Sidney, B., Co. G, Private (1846–). Lived, e. in Orange 4/15/1864. Retired from service 3/8/1865 due to "ascites & organic disease of the heart." Retirement papers list his age as 19 (NCT 8, 194).

SPEAS, William H., Co. F, Corporal (1839–1863). Lived, e. in Yadkin 6/18/1861, age 22. Promoted to corporal 7/10/1862. Died In hospital at or near Richmond abt 1/7/1863 (NCT 183).

SPEER, Alex, Co. F, Private (1843–1865). Lived, e. in Yadkin 4/5/1862, age 19. Captured near Petersburg 4/2/1865; confined at Pt. Lookout. Died there 5/8/1865 of "diphtheria" (NCT 8, 183).

SPEER, James D., Co. F, Private. Lived, e. in Yadkin 11/5/1863. Captured near Petersburg 4/2/1865; confined at Pt. Lookout until released 6/20/1865 after OOA (NCT 8, 183).

SPEER, Lewis H., Co. F, Private. B., e. in Yadkin. 6/18/1861. Hospitalized at Richmond 7/2/1862 with gunshot wound of right shoulder. Captured near Fussell's Mill 8/16/1864; confined at Pt. Lookout until released 10/16/1864 after OOA and joining the U.S. Army, assigned to Co. C, 4th Reg U.S. Volunteer Infantry (NCT 8, 183).

SPEER, William A., Co. F, Private (1845–). B., lived, e. in Yadkin. 4/10/1862, age 17. Deserted 8/7/1862. Captured near Fussell's Mill abt 8/16/1864. Confined at Pt. Lookout until released 10/16/1864, after joining the U.S. Army, assigned to Co. E, 4th Reg U.S. Volunteer Infantry (NCT 8, 183).

SPEER, William H. Asbury, Co. I, Captain; Field & Staff, Colonel. (1826–1864). Lived, e. 8/13/1861, appointed captain. Captured at Hanover CH 5/27/1862; confined at Ft. Monroe, Ft. Columbus, and Johnson's Island. Paroled and trans to Vicksburg, MS for release Appointed major 11/1/1862, trans to Field & Staff. Promoted to lieutenant colonel on 3/1/2/1863. Wounded at Chancellorsville 5/2–3/1863. Wounded at Gettysburg. Promoted to colonel 7/9/1864. Fatally wounded in head at Reams' Station. Died 8/29/1864. Bur. Speer family cemetery, Yadkin (NCT 8, 110; CWY 267; *Voices from Cemetery Hill;* Harding Family Papers*)*.

SPENCER, Eli, Co. C, Private. Lived, e. in Catawba 8/13/1861. Wounded at Cedar Mt. 8/9/1862. Present through 11/30/1863 (NCT 8, 151).

SPENCER, J. Pinkney, Co. C, Private. Lived, e. in Catawba 8/13/1861. Spencer was wounded in the hand at Gaines' Mill 6/27/1862. Surrendered at Appomattox CH 4/9/1865. NC pension records state he was wounded at Turkey Ridge near Richmond(NCT 8, 151).

SPENCER, Sidney E., Co. C, Private. Catawba resident, e. on 2/17/1864. Surrendered at Appomattox CH 4/9/1865 (NCT 8, 151).

SPILLMAN, Matthew D., Co. F, Private (1845–). Lived, e. in Yadkin 2/11/1863. Wounded and captured at Spotsylvania 5/12/1864; confined at Old Capitol Prison 5/19/1864. Trans to Ft. Delaware 6/15/1864. Released 6/19/1865 after OOA (NCT 8, 183).

SPILLMAN, William, Co. F, Corporal (1841–). Lived, e. in Yadkin 6/18/1861 as a private. Absent-wounded July–Oct 1862. Promoted to corporal 5/11/1863. Retired to Invalid Corps 11/19/1864 due to unspecified disability (NCT 8, 183).

SPILLMAN, William H., Co. F, Private (1841–). Lived, e. in Yadkin 4/28/1862. Captured at Wilderness 5/12/1864; confined at Pt. Lookout; trans to Elmira 8/10/1864. Released 6/21/1865 after OOA (NCT 8, 183).

SPRINKLE, Clem C., Co. F, Private (1840–) Yadkin resident, e. 4/30/1862, age 22. Captured in Richmond hospital 4/3/1865; confined at Pt. Lookout until released abt 6/28/1865 after OOA (NCT 8, 183).

SPRINKLE, John S., Co. I, Private. In Yadkin, place, date of enlistment not reported. First listed in company records Mar.1864. Killed at Wilderness 5/5/1864 (NCT 8, 218).

SPRINKLE, John T., Co. F, Private. Lived, e. in Yadkin 4/28/1862. Died at Richmond abt.7/11/1862 of wounds and/or disease (NCT 8, 183).

SPRINKLE, Thomas A., Co. A, Private (1836–). Lived in Dobson District, Surry, e. there, age 26, on 3/18/1862. Captured at Gettysburg on 7/3/1863; confined at Ft. Delaware. Trans to Pt. Lookout in Oct. 1863, the sent to City Pt., on 4/30/1864 for exc. Reported absent-sick Sept.–Oct. 1864 until 1/18/1865. Feb. 1865 reported absent-sick. Sprinkle m. in 1860 in Surry Martha Jane Moore (NCT 8, 123; SCS 167).

STAFFORD, J.A., Co. E, Private (1837–1862). Lived in Montgomery or Randolph, e. in Lenoir 3/20/1862, age 21. Captured at Gettysburg 7/1–3/1863; confined at Ft. Delaware, then Pt. Lookout 10/15–18/1863. Released at Pt. Lookout 6/20/1865 after OOA (NCT 8, 172).

STAFFORD, John M., Co. E, Private (1841–). Lived in Montgomery or Randolph, e. in Lenoir, age 21, 3/20/1862. Captured at Gettysburg 7/1–3/1863; confined at Ft. Delaware; trans to Pt. Lookout 10/15–18/1863. Released at Pt. Lookout 6/20/1865 after OOA (NCT 8, 172).

STANFORD, William G., Co. G, Private (1942–). Lived, e. in Orange 9/2/1861, age 19. Wounded and captured at Hanover CH abt 5/27/1862; confined at Ft. Monroe, then Ft. Columbus. Paroled and trans to Aiken's Landing for exc 8/5/1862. Absent on light duty in Richmond hospital April 1864–Feb 1865. Captured in Richmond hospital 4/3/1865, and paroled 4/18/1865 (NCT 8, 194).

STANLEY, Henderson ("Luke") D., Co. A, Private (18__–1919). B. in Surry to Jesse Stanley, Jr., and Sally Wilmoth. Lived in Rockingham, e. at Camp Mangum near Raleigh on 4/29/1862 in Co. G, 45th Reg. Wounded 7/13/1864 at Washington, DC. Trans to Co. A, 28th Reg. Left arm amputated after he was wounded 4/2/1865 at Petersburg. Captured 4/3/1865; trans to hospital at Ft. Monroe on 5/17/1865. Released 6/21/1865. After the war, Henderson moved to SC where he sold tobacco out of a covered wagon. He m. in Colleton, SC, abt 1866 Mary Elizabeth Carter and had 9 children. He died 9/30/1919 and was bur. beside his wife in family cem. near Lodge, SC (NCT 8, 123; SCS 167–168).

STANLEY, James, Co. A, Private (1838–). Son of William and Nancy Kyle Stanley, a farming family of Rockford, Surry, James was a constable before he e. 5/4/1861, age 23. Dis on 1/18/1862 due to "chronic rheumatism" (NCT 8, 123; SCS 168).

STANLEY, John H., Co. A, Private (1839–1863). Son of William and Nancy Kyle Stanley, and brother of James and Joseph (both in Co. A), e. age 22, 5/4/1861. Killed at Chancellorsville on 5/3/1863 (NCT 8, 123; SCS 168).

STANLEY, Joseph M., Co. A, Private (1840–1861). B. in Surry to William and Nancy Stanley of Rockford, he e. on 5/4/1861, age 21, and was one of several soldiers who died of an unknown illness in the training camp at High Point, NC on 8/15/1861 (NCT 8, 123; SCS 168).

STANLEY, Oliver, Co. A, Private (1839–1915). Son of Jesse Stanley, Jr., and Sarah Wilmoth Stanley, of Bear Creek, e. 3/18/1862, age 22. Wounded in the right hip at Petersburg on 4/1/1865. Captured in Farmington hospital. Released in April 1865. Bur. in family cemetery near Dobson on Rockford Road, has a Confederate marker (NCT 8, 123; SCS 168).

STANLEY, Solomon, Co. A, Sergeant (1840–1862). Third son of Jesse and Sally W. Stanley to serve in the Confederate Army, he e., age 21, on 5/13/1861. Promoted to sergeant 4/10/1862, died 9/9/1862 in Richmond hospital of jaundice (NCT 8, 123; SCS 169).

STANTLIFF, Oliver, Co. A, Private (1827–). B. in Virginia, lived in Haystack community, Surry, unmarried in 1860. Entered the army 3/18/1862, age 35. Captured at Hanover CH on 5/27/1862; confined at Ft. Columbus. Paroled and sent to Aiken's Landing 5/12/1862; exc 8/5/1862 (NCT 8, 123; SCS 169).

STARLING, James M., Co. F, 3rd Lieutenant (1839–). Lived, e. in Yadkin 6/18/1861 as a private. Promoted to sergeant Jan.–June 1862. Rank reduced to corporal; promoted to sergeant 9/26//1862. Absent-wounded Nov.–Dec. 1862. Appointed 3rd lieutenant 5/11/1863. Present through Feb. 1865 (NCT 8, 174).

STARR, Edmund Jones, Co. C, Private (18__–1864). B. in Catawba, e. in Rowan 2/2/1864. Hospitalized at Richmond 6/16/1864 with a gunshot wound. Died there on 7/5/1864 of wounds and/or disease (NCT 8, 151).

STARR, Elon M., Co. C, Private. Lived, e. in Catawba 3/14/1863. Captured in a Richmond hospital 4/3/1865, he was paroled about 4/25/1865 (NCT 8, 151).

STARR, J. Abel, Co. C, Private. Lived, e. in Catawba 3/14/1863. Surrendered at Appomattox CH 4/9/1865 (NCT 8, 151).

STARR, Jacob S.D., Co. C, Private. Catawba resident e. in Rowan on 2/2/1864. Captured on the South Side Railroad near Petersburg 4/2/1865; confined at Hart's Island until released 6/17/1865 after OOA (NCT 8, 151).

STEELMAN, William, Co. B, Private? NC pension records indicate he served in this company (NCT 8 137).

STEPHENS, John, Co. G, Private. E. 4/15/1864 in Orange. Captured at Spotsylvania CH 5/12/1864; confined at Pt. Lookout, trans to Elmira 8/10/1864. Paroled and sent to Boulware's Wharf 3/15/1865 for exc (NCT 8, 194).

STEPHENS, Robert H., Co. G, Private (1839–). Lived, e. in Orange 9/2/1861, age 22. Present through Feb. 1865 (NCT 8, 194).

STINSON, Abraham, Co. I, Private. E. in Yadkin 11//1/1862. Wounded in head and leg at the Petersburg & Weldon Railroad, near Petersburg 6/22/1864. Returned. Wounded in right leg, captured near Petersburg 4/2/1865. Leg amputated. Reported in hospital at Ft. Monroe through 6/21/1865 (NCT 8, 218).

STINSON, Elias, Co. I, Private (1842–1864). B., lived, e. In Yadkin 8/13/1861, age 19. Present through Feb.1863. Died before 12/17/1864. No more information (NCT 8, 218).

STOKER, Evan A., Co. K, Private (1820–1861). Lived and e. in Stanly 9/7/1861, age 41. Promoted to commissary before 11/1/1861, but rank reduced before 12/19/1861. Died in Wilmington 12/29/1861 of disease (NCT 8, 230).

STOKER, Robert, Co. D, Private (1825–1863). B., lived, e. in Stanly. 7/29/1861, age 39. Wounded at Fredericksburg 12/13/1862. Captured near Gettysburg 7/4/1863; confined at Ft. Delaware. Trans to Pt. Lookout 10/15–18/1863, and died there 12/23/1863 (NCT 8, 162).

STOKER, Thomas A., Co. A, Private (1842–1862). Son of William and Louisa Stoker of the Nixon District, Surry, e. at Judsville on 3/18/1862, age 20. Died at home from unknown illness 11/19/1862 (NCT 8, 123; SCS 170).

STOKES, James, Co. I, Private (1843–). B. in Yadkin, e. in New Hanover, 1/1/1862. AWOL May–Oct. 1862. Listed as a deserter 5/27/1863 (NCT 8, 218).

STONE, Adam Whitmon, Co. I, Captain (1835–). Lived, e. in Surry 9/7/1861, age 31. Appointed 3rd lieutenant 9/7/1861; promoted to 2nd lieutenant 4/12/1862. Wounded at Gettysburg 7/1–3/1863. Promoted to 1st lieutenant 7/8/1863. Hospitalized at Chancellorsville 5/12/1864 with gunshot wound of chest. Trans to Salisbury 6/5/1864. Promoted to captain 6/24/1864. Returned Jan.–Feb. 1865, and surrendered at Appomattox CH 4/9/1865 (NCT 8, 220).

STONE, Robert B., Co. B, Private (1838–). Lived, e., age 23, in Gaston 7/30/1861. Captured at Falling Waters abt 7/14/1863; confined at Old Capitol Prison until sent to Pt. Lookout 8/8/1863. Paroled there 3/16/1864, and sent to City Pt. for exc. Surrendered at Appomattox CH 4/9/1865 (NCT 8, 137).

STOWE, Beverly F., Co. B, Private (1824–1862). Gaston resident, e. at age 37 on 7/30/1861. Captured at Hanover CH 5/27/1862; confined at Ft. Monroe then Ft. Columbus. Paroled and sent to Aiken's Landing for exc 8/5/1862. Died at Petersburg 8/5/1862 of disease (NCT 8, 137).

STOWE, Samuel N., Co. B, Captain; Major, 28th, Field & Staff (1823–). Lived, e. in Gaston, age 38. Appointed 1st Lt. 7/30/1861; elected captain 2/27/1862. Captured at Hanover CH 5/17/1862. Confined at Ft. Monroe and Ft. Columbus; trans to Johnson's Island 6/21/1862. Paroled and sent to Vicksburg 9/20/1862. Exc at Aiken's Landing 12/13/1862. Promoted to major on 4/16/1863 for "gallant conduct at Fredericksburg," and trans to Field & Staff. Wounded at Gettysburg

July 1863. Retired to Invalid Corps 12/13/1864 due to disability. (NCT 8, 110, 125).

STOWE, T.B., Co. B, Private (1830–1864). Lived and e. in Gaston 7/30/1861, age 31. Captured at Hanover CH 5/27/1862; confined at Ft. Monroe, then Ft. Columbus. Paroled and sent to Aiken's Landing for exc 8/5/1862. Killed at Spotsylvania CH 5/12/1864 (NCT 8, 137).

STRANGE, John R., Jr., Co. A, Private (1848–). Son of John R. and Mary Bledsoe Strange, NC pension records indicate he served in this company (NCT 8, 123; SCS 170).

STRAUGHAN, George W., Co. G, Private (1831–). Lived, e. in Orange 9/2/1861, age 30. Captured at Fredericksburg 12/13/1862; exc abt 12/17/1862. Wounded at Wilderness May 1864. Captured near Petersburg 4/2/1865; confined at Pt. Lookout until released 6/19/1865 after OOA (NCT 8, 194).

STRAUGHAN, Julian R., Co. G, Corporal (1830–1862). Lived, e. in Orange 9/2/1861, age 31 as a private. Promoted to corporal Mar.–Apr.. 1862. Killed at Gaines' Mill 6/27/1862 (NCT 8, 194).

STRAUGHAN, Nathan R., Co. G, Private (1842–). Lived, e. in Orange 9/2/1861, age 19. Captured at Fredericksburg 12/13/1862; exc abt 12/17/1862. Captured at Chancellorsville 5/3/1863. Exc. at City Pt. abt 5/13/1863. Wounded at Gettysburg 7/1–3/1863. Captured near Petersburg 4/2/1865; confined at Pt. Lookout until released 6/19/1865, after OOA (NCT 8, 194).

STRAUGHAN, Wiley H., Co. G, Private. Lived, e. in Orange 10/19/1864. Captured near Petersburg 4/2/1865; confined at Pt. Lookout until released 6/19/1865 after OOA (NCT 8, 194).

STRICKLAND, Carson C., Co. F, Private (1840–). Lived, e. in Nash 10/1/1862, age 22. Absent-wounded Nov.–Dec. 1862. Wounded in thigh near Petersburg 6/22/1864. Captured at Hatcher's Run 4/2/1865; confined at Pt Lookout until released 6/19/1865 after OOA (NCT 8, 143).

STRICKLAND, Stephen B., Co. F, Private (1842–1863). B. in Yadkin, lived in Alamance, and e. there 10/1/1862, age 20. Killed at Gettysburg 7/3/1863 (NCT 8, 183).

STRICKLAND, William S., Co. I, Private. B. in Yadkin, e. at Liberty Mills 12/17/1863. Killed in battle at the Petersburg &Weldon Railroad, Petersburg, 6/22/1864 (NCT 8, 218).

STROUD, John B., Co. G, Private 1836–). B. in Orange, e. 9/2/1861, age 25. Captured at Fredericksburg 12/1/3/1862; exc abt 12/17/1862. Dis 3/28/1864 due to "general debility and disease of the heart." Paroled at Raleigh 5/12/1865 (NCT 8, 194).

STRUPE, Joseph H., Co. B, Private (1831–). Lived in Gaston, e. 7/30/1861, age 30, and was captured at Spotsylvania CH 5/12/1864. Confined at Pt. Lookout, he was sent to Elmira on 8/8/1864. Paroled at Elmira 10/11/1864; trans to Venus Point for exc 11/15/1864. Captured in a Richmond hospital on 4/3/1865, then confined at Newport News 4/23/1865, until released on 6/30/1865 after OOA (NCT 8, 137).

STRUPE, Moses, Co. B, Private (1839–) Lived in Gaston, e., age 22, 7/30/1861. Captured at Hanover

CH 5/27/1862; confined at Ft. Monroe, then Ft. Columbus. Paroled and sent to Aiken's Landing for exc on 8/5/1862. Captured at Fredericksburg 12/13/1862; paroled 12/17/1862. Wounded in right foot and captured at Gettysburg 7/1–5/1863. Hospitalized at Chester, then sent to City Pt. 9/23/1863 for exc. Captured at Spotsylvania CH. Confined at Pt. Lookout until trans to Elmira 8/8/1864. Released from there 6/19/1865 after OOA (NCT 8, 137).

STUBBINS, John, Co. G, Private (1942–1861). Lived, e. in Orange e. 9/2/1861. Died at Wilmington 12/26/1861 of "typhoid pneumonia" (NCT 8, 194).

STUTTS, Matthew H., Co. E, Corporal (1841–). Lived, e. in Montgomery . 8/1/1861, age 20, as a private. Promoted to corporal Nov. 1862–Oct. 1864. Deserted 2/2/1865. Surrendered at Appomattox CH 4/9/1865 (NCT 8, 173).

SUGGS, L.L., Co. B, Corporal (1832–). B., e. in Gaston 7/30/1861, age 19, as a private. Promoted to corporal Nov. 1862–Feb. 1863. Wounded in right arm at Chancellorsville 5/3/1863. Dis 1/16/1864 due to disability (NCT 8, 138).

SUMMIT, Heglar P., Co. C, Private (1840–1864). Catawba resident e. at Camp Fisher on 9/2/1861, age 21. Captured in an unspecified engagement; confined to a Federal prison 9/14/1862. Paroled and trans to Aiken's Landing for exc 11/10/1862. Captured at Spotsylvania CH 5/12/1864; confined at Pt. Lookout, then trans to Elmira 8/10/1864. Died at Elmira 11/16/1864 of chronic diarrhea (NCT 8, 151).

SWAIM, Little M., Co. I, Corporal (1843–). Lived, e. in Yadkin 8/13/1861, age 18. Hospitalized at Richmond 9/27/1862 with gunshot wound to shoulder and hip. Returned. Promoted to Corporal 12/1/1864. Captured near Petersburg 4/2/1865; confined at Ft. Delaware 6/19/1865 after OOA (NCT 8, 218).

SWAIM, Milas G., Co. I, Privae (1844–). B., lived, e. in Yadkin 3/8/1862, age 18. Trans to Co. G, 44th Reg NCT Mar.–Dec. 1863. Trans back to Co. I 10/1/1864. Present through Feb. 1865 (NCT 8, 218).

SWAIM, Solomon D., Co. I, Private (1830–1865). Lived, e. in Yadkin 4/17/1862, age 32, Co. H, 54th Reg NCT. AWOL June 1862, returned. Deserted 12/18/1862. Trans to Co. I, 28th Reg 10/19/1863. Records of Co. I state he e. 7/19/1862, then trans to Co. G, 44th Reg Mar.–Dec. 1863. Records of Co. G, 44th indicate he "Gave himself up voluntarily to the Union pickets near Spotsylvania Court House 5/18–21/1864. Confined at Pt. Lookout 5/10/1864, trans to Elmira 7/25/1864, where he died 2/21/1865 of "pneumonia" (NCT 8, 218; NCT 10, 463; NCT 13, 3258).

SWAIM, William, Co. I, Private (1825–). B. in Surry, lived and e. in Yadkin, e. 9/1/1861, age 37. Dis 6/23/1862 due to heart condition following pneumonia (NCT 8, 218).

SWARINGEN, Henry C., Co. K, Private (1844–1863). Lived in Cabarrus, e. in New Hanover 2/4/1862, age 18. Captured at Fredericksburg 12/13/1862; exc abt 12/17/1862. Returned. Killed at Gettysburg 7/3/1863 (NCT 8, 230).

SWARINGEN, John, Co. K, Private (1843–). Lived

and e. in Stanly 9/7/1861, age 18. Disc before 10/1/1861, reason not reported (NCT 8, 230).

SYKES, Henry C., Co. G, Private (1841–). Lived , e. in Orange 9/2/1861, age 20. Captured at Fredericksburg 12/13/182; exc abt 12/17/1862. Captured at Falling Waters 7/14/1863; confined at Pt. Lookout, trans to Elmira 8/16/1864. Paroled and trans to Boulware's Wharf 3/15/1865 for exc (NCT 8, 194–195).

SYKES, Jasper J., Co. G, Private (1844–). E. in Orange 10/19/1864, age 20. Surrendered at Appomattox CH 4/9/1865 (NCT 8, 195).

SYKES, John A., Co. G, Private (1942–1862). Lived, e. in Orange e. 9/2/1861, age 19. Captured at Winchester abt 12/3/1862; paroled there 12/4/1862. Died in Winchester hospital 12/7/1862 of typhoid pneumonia (NCT 8, 195).

SYKES, Johnson C., Co. G, Private (1842–) Lived, e. in Orange. 9/2/1861, age 19. Captured at Hanover CH 5/27/1862; confined at Ft. Monroe, then Ft. Columbus. Paroled and trans to Aiken's Landing for exc on 8/5/1862. Hospitalized at Petersburg 8/26/1864 with gunshot wound of left foot. Present through Feb. 1865 (NCT 8, 195).

TACKETT, B. Frank, Co. F, Private (1745–1863). B., lived, e. in Yadkin 4/5/1862, age 17. AWOL Nov.–Dec 1862. Returned and died at Camp Gregg 4/19/1863 of "pneumonia" (NCT 8, 183).

TACKETT, James W., Co. F, Private (1841–). Lived, e. in Yadkin 4/26/1862, age 21. Wounded and captured at Gettysburg 7/1–5/1863. Hospitalized at Davids Island. Paroled and trans to City Pt. 8/28/1863 for exc. AWOL 6/1/1864–8/13/864. Captured near Petersburg 4/2/1865; confined at Pt. Lookout, released abt 6/21/1865 after OOA (NCT 8, 183).

TACKETT, John W., Co. F, Private (1841–). Lived, e. in Yadkin 6/18/1861, age 20. Captured at Gettysburg 7/3–4/1863; confined at Ft. Delaware. Trans to Pt. Lookout, then to City Pt on 3/20/1864 for exc. AWOL 4/20/1864–8/28/1864. Captured at Petersburg 4/2/1865; confined at Pt. Lookout until released 6/20/1865, after OOA (NCT 8, 183).

TACKETT, Thomas E., Co. F, Private (1844–). Lived, e. in Yadkin 4/29/1862, age 18. Wounded in left thigh at Bethesda Church, VA 5/31/1864. Captured near Petersburg 4/2/1865; confined at Pt. Lookout until released 6/21/1865, after OOA (NCT 8, 183).

TALLY, C.A., Co. F, Private (1831–1864). Lived in Cabarrus, e. in Mecklenburg 10/1/1862, age 31. Missing at Gettysburg 7/1–3/1863 (NCT 8, 184).

TALLY, Francis W., Co. D, Sergeant (1840–) Lived, e. in Stanly 7/29/1861, age 21. Mustered in as private, promoted to corporal 8/15/1863, then to sergeant Sept. 1863–Oct. 1864. Surrendered at Appomattox CH 4/9/1865 (NCT 8, 163).

TALLY, Martin V.B., Co. D, Private (1841–1862). Lived, e. in Stanly 7/29/1861, age 20. Captured at Hanover CH 5/27/1862; confined at Ft. Monroe, then Ft. Columbus. Paroled and sent to Aiken's Landing for exc on 8/5/1862. Died in Richmond hospital abt 10/19/1862 of "febris typhoid" (typhoid fever) (NCT 8, 163).

TATE, James, Co. A, Private (1822–). Surry resident

e., age 39, 5/4/1861. Captured near Liberty Mills on 9/22/1863; confined at Old Capitol Prison. Trans to Pt. Lookout 9/26/1862, then to Elmira 8/16/1864. Paroled at Elmira, trans to Boulware's Wharf in March 1865 for exc. In 1850, James lived in Rockford and worked as a cabinet maker. He m. in Surry in 1845 to Rebecca Wilmoth. They had several children (NCT 8, 123; SCS 172).

TATE, Kinchen T., Co. H, Private (1844–). Lived in Cleveland where he e. 3/17/1862, age 18. Dis Nov. 1862. Later served in Co. C, 15th Reg NCT(NCT 8, 206).

TATE, Lewis F., Co. I, Private. E. at Camp Holmes 10/8/1863. Deserted, returned on 9/22/1864. Absent-wounded Sept. 1864–Feb. 1865 (NCT 8, 218).

TAYLOR, Francis W., Co. F, Private (1840–1864). B., lived, e. in Yadkin. 6/18/1861. Died in Richmond Hospital abt 7/25/1864 of disease (NCT 8, 184).

TAYLOR, William Columbus, Co. F, Private (1846). Lived, e. in Yadkin 4/21/1862, age 16, as a substitute. Hospitalized at Danville abt 8/13/162 with pneumonia. Deserted from hospital 10/6/1862. NC pension records indicate he was wounded at Richmond June 1862 (NCT 8, 184).

TEAL, Thomas Frank, Co. E, Private (1835–1862). Lived, e. in Montgomery 8/1/1861, age 26. Wounded near Gaines' Mill abt 6/27/1862. Died in Richmond hospital 7/1–2/1862 of wounds (NCT 173).

TEASH— see TESH

TENNEY, Oregon Burns, Co. G, Private (1843–). Lived, e. in Orange 12/20/1861, age 18. Wounded in both hands at Cedar Mt. 8/9/1862. Returned and surrendered at Appomattox CH 4/9/1865 (NCT 8, 195).

TESH, William Addison, Co. I, Corporal (1844–1864). B., lived, e. in Yadkin 3/8/1862, age 18. Promoted to corporal Nov. 1862–Feb./ 1863. Died "at home" or at Lynchburg 5/4/1864. Many letters to his parents, Moses and Mary Mock Tesh, during this period are at Duke University (NCT 8, 218; CWY 273).

THOMAS, John F., Co. B, Private (1845–). Lived in Gaston, e. in Mecklenburg on 8/18/1863, age 18. Surrendered at Appomattox CH 4/9/1865 (NCT 8, 138).

THOMAS, William R., Co. B, Private (1843–). Lived, e. in Gaston 3/29/1862. Captured at Hanover CH 5/27/1862; confined at Ft. Monroe, then Ft. Columbus. Paroled and sent to Aiken's Landing for exc on 8/5/1862. Captured at Fredericksburg 12/13/1862, paroled 12/17/1862. Surrendered at Appomattox CH 4/9/1865 (NCT 8, 138).

THOMPSON, Alfred R., Co. I, Private (1845–). Lived, e. in Lincoln 8/14/1863, age 18. Absent-wounded Sept.–Oct. 1864. Returned, present through Feb. 1865 (NCT 8, 218),

THOMPSON, Calvin C., Co. K, Private (1840–1865). Lived and e. in Stanly 9/7/1861, age 21. Captured at Hanover CH 5/27/1862; confined at Ft. Monroe, then Ft. Columbus. Paroled and sent to Aiken's Landing for exc on 8/5/1862. Returned. Died "at his home" 1/13/1865, cause of death not reported (NCT 8, 230).

THOMPSON, Charles T., Co. A, Sergeant (1835–1864) . Son of Jesse Killed Thompson and wife Elizabeth Tucker, Dobson District, Surry, e. at age 25 on

5/4/1861. Promoted to sergeant on 1/12/1862. Died in Richmond hospital of "febris typhoid" on 6/3/1864. Charles m. in 1853, Surry, Mary A. Altizer; 2 children by 1860 (NCT 8, 113; SCS 173).

THOMPSON, Daniel G., Co. I, Private. Previously served as sergeant, Co. G, 52nd Reg NCT. Trans to Co. I 11/1/1864 as a private. Paroled at Greensboro 5/1/1865 (NCT 8, 218).

THOMPSON, Edmund R., Co. K, Private (1830–1862). Lived, e. in Stanly 9/7/1861, age 31. Captured at Hanover CH 5/27/1862; confined at Ft. Monroe, then Ft. Columbus. Paroled and sent to Aiken's Landing for exc on 8/5/1862. Returned. Killed at Fredericksburg 12/1/3861 (NCT 8, 230).

THOMPSON, Elijah T., Co. A, 1st Lieutenant (1835–). Son of Elijah and Martha Thompson, Elijah e. in Surry 5/4/1861, age 26, as sergeant; promoted to 1st sergeant 1/12/1862; promoted to 1st lieutenant 4/9/1862 at the reorganization. Wounded at 2nd Manassas on 8/28/1862. Wounded in the thigh, captured at Gettysburg 7/1–3/1863. Sent to Johnson's Island, 8/31/1863. Trans to Ft. Delaware, then to Aiken's Landing for exc. Retired to Invalid Corps 1/31/1865. Thompson m. in Surry Rebecca Hodges and had a dau. (NCT 8, p. 113; SCS 174).

THOMPSON, Francis Wilburn, Co. C, Private (1833–). B. in Lincoln, lived in Gaston, e. in New Hanover, age 29. Captured at Hanover CH 5/27/1862; confined at Ft. Monroe, then Ft. Columbus. Paroled and sent to Aiken's Landing for exc 8/5/1862. Wounded, captured at Gettysburg 7/3–4/1863. Confined at Ft. Delaware, then Pt. Lookout 10/15–18/1863. Trans to Aiken's Landing 5/8/1864 for exc. Absent on detail 11/10/1864 through Feb. 1865 (NCT 8, 138).

THOMPSON, George S., Co. C; Field & Staff, Brigade Quartermaster (Major) (1839–). Lived, e. in Orange 9/2/1861, age 22. Appointed Assistant Quartermaster (Captain) 10/18/1861, and trans to Field & Staff. Promoted to Brigade Quartermaster (Major) 1/23/1863; trans to Brigade staff. (NCT 8, 111, 195)

THOMPSON, George W., Co. A, Private (1844–). Son of Stephen and Mary Marsh Thompson who lived in the Devotion area, Surry, e. 5/4/1862 at Dobson, age 18. Deserted 8/1/1862 (NCT 8, 123–124; SCS 174).

THOMPSON, James, Co. E, Private. B. in Montgomery, e. In Wake 11/26/1863. Died in a Gordonsville hospital 3/27/1864 of pneumonia (NCT 8, 173).

THOMPSON, James O., Co. G, Sergeant (1835–). B. in Alamance, e. in Orange 9/17/1861, age 26 as a private. Promoted to sergeant 3/1/1862. Dis 12/25/1863 due to "general debility of long standing" (NCT 8, 195).

THOMPSON, James Sidney, Co. G, Private (1840–1864). Lived in Alamance, e. 9/2/1865 in Orange, age 21. Wounded in the arm and thigh at Wilderness 5/5–7/1864. Died at Lynchburg 5/31/1864 of wound (NCT 8, 195).

THOMPSON, Reece, Co. F, Private (1827–1862). Lived, e. in Forsyth 3/17/1862. Died at Churchville, VA 12/4/1862 of disease (NCT 8, 184).

THOMPSON, Samuel Tunstall, Co. I, 2nd Lieutenant. Previously served as 1st sergeant in Co. K, 23rd

Reg NCT. Trans to Co. I, 28th Reg Sep.–Oct. 1863; appointed 2nd lieutenant to rank from 4/11/1863. Surrendered at Appomattox CH 4/9/1865 (NCT 8, 207).

THOMPSON, Thomas H., Co. G, Private (1845–). E. 10/19/1864 in Orange . Surrendered at Appomattox CH 4/9/1865 (NCT 195).

THORNBURG, Jacob L., Co. B, Private (1842–). Lived, e. in Gaston 3/29/1862, age 20. Surrendered at Appomattox CH, 4/9/1865 (NCT 8, 138).

THRONEBURG, Jonathan S., Co. C, Private. Lived in Catawba, e. at Camp Stokes on 10/24/1864. Captured in hospital at Richmond 4/3/1865. Trans to Newport News 4/23/1865, and released 6/30/1865 after OOA (NCT 8, 151).

THRONEBURG, Marcus Augustus, Co. C, 1st Lieutenant. Lived, e. in Catawba 8/13/1861 as a 1st sergeant; appointed 2nd lieutenant 2/27/1862. Captured at Hanover CH 5/27/1862; confined at Ft. Monroe, then Ft. Columbus. Trans to Ft. Delaware 7/16/1862. Exc. 7/10/1862. Promoted to 1st lieutenant abt 7/15/1862. Wounded in head and/or left hip at Reams' Station 8/25/1864. Absent-wounded through Dec. 1864; present but sick Jan.–Feb. 1865 (NCT 8, 140).

THRONEBURG, Mathias Miller, Co. C, 2nd Lieutenant (1838–). Lived, e. in Catawba 8/13/1861, age 23. Promoted to sergeant 2/27/1862. Wounded in the neck at Gaines' Mill 6/27/1862. Promoted to 2nd lieutenant 7/3/1863. Surrendered at Appomattox CH 4/9/1865 (NCT 8, 140).

TILLEY, James L., Co. A, Private (1846–). Son of John M. and C. L. Tilley, Dobson District, e., age 16, 3/18/1862. Wounded in right leg at Gaines' Mill on 6/27/1862. AWOL from July 1, 1863–Feb. 1865. By 1880 he and his wife were farming in Bryan Township, Surry with their 6 children (NCT 8, 124; SCS 175).

TIPPET, William, Co. E, Corporal (1831–). B. in England, lived, e. in Montgomery 8/1/1861, age 30. Promoted to corporal March–Apr. 1862. Captured at Hanover CH 5/27/1862; confined at Ft. Monroe then Ft. Columbus. Paroled and trans to Aiken's Landing for exc 8/5/1862. Hospitalized at Richmond 12/19/1863 with unspecified complaints (NCT 8, 173).

TODD, Leander Alonzo, Co. I, 3rd Lieutenant (1838–1870). Son of Thomas and Mary Zachary Todd, lived, e. in Yadkin 3/8/1862 as a private. Elected 3rd lieutenant 10/20/1863. Surrendered at Appomattox CH 4/9/1865. He married Eunice Folger and had 2 daus. Leander and wife died at Dobson, Surry (NCT 8, 207; Marti S. Utter).

TOLBERT, Harrison F., Co. D, Private (1841–). B. in Stanly, e. 7/29/1861, age 20. Captured abt 9/1/1862; confined at Ft. Monroe. Paroled and trans to Aiken's Landing 9/7/12862 for exc. Captured at Spotsylvania CH 5/12/1864; confined at Pt. Lookout until released 5/20/1864 after OOA, and joining the U.S. Army. Assigned to Co. I, 1st Reg U.S. Volunteer Infantry (NCT 8, 163).

TOLBERT, Josiah P., Co. K, Private (1835–). Lived and e. in Stanly 9/7/1861, age 26. Captured at Hanover CH 5/27/1862; confined at Ft. Monroe, then Ft. Columbus. Trans to Aiken's Landing for exchange on 8/5/1862. Returned. Captured near Gravel Hill abt 7/28/1864; confined at Pt. Lookout. Trans to Elmira 8/8/1864; released 7/3/1865 after OOA (NCT 8, 230).

TOLBERT, Pinkney T., Co. E, Private (1826–). Lived, e. in Montgomery. 8/1/1861, age 35. Deserted 8/15/1863. Captured near Petersburg 4/2/1865; confined at Pt. Lookout until released 6/20/1865 after OOA (NCT 8, 173).

TORRENCE, Hugh A., Co. B, Sergeant (1840–) Lived, e. in Gaston 7/30/1861, age 21. He mustered in as sergeant. Wounded at Frayser's Farm 6/30/1862. Wounded in left eye, captured at Gettysburg 7/1–5/1863. Hospitalized at Gettysburg until trans to Davids Island 7/17–24/1863. Paroled and trans to City Pt. 8/28/2863 for exc. Reported absent-wounded until detailed for light duty as hospital guard abt 4/6/1864. Rejoined company 8/9/1864. Present through Feb. 1865. Wounded in head and captured. Hospitalized at Ft. Monroe until released 6/18/1865 (NCT 8, 138).

TOWNSEND, Benjamin J., Co. E, Sergeant (1840–1862). Lived in Richmond, e. In Montgomery 8/1/1861, age 21, as a sergeant. Killed at Cedar Mt. 8/9/1862 (NCT 8, 173).

TOWNSEND, Solomon Richardson, Co. E., 1st Lieutenant (1835–). Lived in Richmond resident, e. in Montgomery 8/1/1861, age 26. Appointed 2nd lieutenant 8/1/1861; promoted to 1st lieutenant 4/9/1862. Resigned 8/17/1862 due to "rheumatism" and an "attack of a low form of fever" (NCT 8, 164).

TOWNSON, Aaron Elijah, Co. C, Private (1845–). B., lived, e. in Catawba., age 17, 3/15/1862. Captured at Hanover CH 5/27/1862; confined at Ft. Monroe, then Ft. Columbus. Paroled and trans to Aiken's Landing for exc 8/5/1862. Surrendered at Appomattox CH 4/9/1865 (NCT 8, 151).

TOWNSON, Solomon, Co. C, Private (1837–1862). Catawba resident e., age 25, 3/15/1862. Captured at Hanover CH 5/27/1862; confined at Ft. Monroe, then Ft. Columbus. Paroled and trans to Aiken's Landing for exc on 8/5/1862. Died in a Virginia hospital 8/10/1862 of typhoid fever (NCT 8, 152).

TREECE, Peter, Co. D, Private (1830–1865). B., lived, e. in Stanly 3/15/1862. Wounded in the middle finger of his right hand at Sharpsburg 9/17/1862. Deserted from Danville hospital 1/23/1863. Reported absent-sick Sept.–Oct. 1864. Retired from service 3/1/1865 due to chronic bronchitis and "organic disease of the heart" (NCT 8, 163).

TRULOVE, John George, Co. F, 1st Lieutenant (1832–1864). Yadkin resident, e. 6/18/1861, age 29, as a private. Appointed 2nd lieutenant 4/12/1862. Promoted to 1st lieutenant 4/27/1863. Wounded in the neck at Gettysburg 7/1–3/1863. Wounded in abdomen near Petersburg 6/22/1864. Hospitalized at Richmond. Furloughed 8/11/1864. Wounded again at Jones' Farm 9/30/1864. Died 10/11/1864 of wounds (NCT 8, 174–175).

TUCKER, G. B., Co. B, Private? NC pension records indicate he served in this company (NCT 8, 138).

TURBYFILL, Elam A., Co. C, Private (1843–1862). Lived, e. in Catawba 3/15/1862, age 19. Died in a Richmond hospital 6/5–12/1862 (NCT 8, 152).

TURBYFILL, Elkana, Co. C, Corporal (1829–1864).

Lived, e. in Catawba, age 32, on 3/15/1862. Promoted to corporal 9/1/1862. Wounded at Chancellorsville 5/2–3/1863. Died "at home" 6/28/1864 (NCT 8, 15 2).

TURBYFILL, John L., Co. C, Musician (1840–). Lived in Catawba, e. at Camp Fisher, age 21, on 9/10/1861, as a private. Wounded at Mechanicsville 6/26/1862. Promoted to musician May 1863–Oct. 1864. Surrendered at Appomattox CH 4/9/1865 (NCT 8, 152).

TURBYFILL, Jonas A., Co. C, Private (1836–). Lived, e. in Catawba 8/13/1861, age 25. Present through April 1862 (NCT 8, 152).

TURNER, David H., Co. C, Private (18__–1865). E. at Camp Stokes 10/31/1864. Present through Feb. 1865. NC pension records indicate he was "presumed dead on retreat from Petersburg, Virginia" (NCT 8, 152).

TURNER, Enoch, Co. K, Private (1835–). Lived and e. in Stanly 9/7/1861, age 26. Captured at Hanover CH, 5/27/1862; confined at Ft. Monroe, then Ft. Columbus. Trans to Aiken's Landing for exc 8/5/1862. Died in Richmond hospital 12/13/1862 from typhoid fever (NCT 8, 231).

TURNER, Ferdinand G., Co. D, Private (1841–). Stanly resident e. 7/29/1861, age 20. Captured at Hanover CH 5/27/1862; confined at Ft. Monroe, then Ft. Columbus. Paroled and trans to Aiken's Landing for exc on 8/5/1862. Retired to Invalid Corps 4/15/1864. Rejoined Co. D 9/15/1864. Captured near Petersburg 4/2/1865; confined at Pt. Lookout until released 6/20/1865 after OOA (NCT 8, 163).

TURNER, George L., Co. C, Private (1840–1863). B., lived, e. in Catawba, 8/13/1861, age 21. Died in Lynchburg hospital 6/14/1863 of pneumonia (NCT 8, 152).

TURNER, Henry Clay, Co. K, 2nd Lieutenant. Previously served as sergeant major of 52nd Reg NCT. Trans to Co. K 1/19/1865 upon election as 2nd lieutenant. Surrendered at Appomattox CH 4/9/1865 (NCT 8, 220).

TURNER, James E., Co. D, Private (1840–). Lived, e. in Stanly 3/15/1862, age 22. Deserted to the enemy abt 4/1/1865. Took the OOA at Washington, DC about 4/6/1865 (NCT 8, 163).

TURNER, John, Co. C, Private. B., e. in Catawba 8/6/1864. Died in a Richmond hospital 10/27/1864 of typhoid fever (NCT 8, 152).

TURNER, Laban Cicero, Co. C, Private (1844–). A civil engineer living in Catawba, e. there 3/15/1862. Present through Feb. 1865 (NCT 8, 152).

TURNER, Preston H., Co. K, 1st Lieutenant. Previously served as sergeant major 14th Reg NCT. Trans to Co. K upon election as 2nd lieutenant about 10/15/1863. Captured near Spotsylvania CH abt 5/12/1864; confined at Ft. Delaware. Promoted to 1st lieutenant 6/24/1864, while a prisoner. Confined at Ft. Delaware until released 6/14/1865 after OOA (NCT 8, 220).

TURNER, Samuel H., Co. A, Private (1834–1861). B. in Virginia, lived at Dobson, and was a cabinet maker. Volunteered, age 27, 5/4/1861. Two months later he died of some unknown illness in the training camp at Garysburg, NC. He was the first man from Dobson to die in the war, and the first bur. in the Dobson Cem. on land donated to the Dobson Community

by S. Davis, a friend, in Turner's honor (NCT 8, 124; SCS 176).

UNDERWOOD, John Hubbert, Co. D, Private (1846–). E at Camp Stokes 10/28/1864, age 18. Surrendered at Appomattox CH 4/9/1865 (NCT 8, 163).

USERY, James, Co. E, Private (1842–). Lived, e. in Montgomery 8/1/1861, age 19. Wounded at Gaines' Mill 6/27/1862. Deserted Feb. 1865, but returned to duty. Surrendered at Appomattox CH 4/9/1865 (NCT 8, 173).

USHER, John B., Co. E, Private (1839–). Lived, e. in Montgomery 4/10/1862, age 23. Dis 3/13/1863 due to "physical disability" (NCT 8, 173).

VANCE, John, Co. G, Private (1841–). E. 12/20/1861 in Orange, age 20. In Richmond hospital June–July 1863, and in Nov. 1863 (NCT 8, 195).

VANHOY, Amos, Co. K, Private (1843–). Lived and e. in Stanly 9/7/1861, age 18. Present until he surrendered at Appomattox CH 4/9/1865 (NCT 8, 231).

VANHOY, John A. Co. D, Private ? NC pension records indicate he served in this company (NCT 8, 163).

VENABLE, Joseph, Co. A, Private (1822–). Surry resident, Joseph e. at age 39 on 5/4/1861. Dis abt 5/1/1862 because he was overage (NCT 8, 124).

VENABLE, Joshua, Co. A, Private (1825–). E. on 11/1/1864. Present through Feb. 1865. Son of John and Nancy Venable, a Rockford family, Joshua farmed in the Copeland community, Surry . He m. Elizabeth Snow in 1849, and had 3 children. He and wife Elizabeth believed bur. at Doshier Venable home place, Copeland community (NCT 8, 124; SCS 178).

VESTAL, J.M., Co. I, Private (1837–). Lived in Yadkin, e. 8/13/1861, age 24. Disc. Due to disability, date unknown (NCT 8, 218).

VESTAL, John B., Co. I, Private (1834–). B., lived in Yadkin, e. in New Hanover 10/8/1861, age 27. Trans to Co. B, 38th Reg NCT before 4/1/1862 (NCT 8, 218).

VESTAL, Larkin Henry, Co. F, Private. E. at Liberty Mills 3/30/1864. Trans to Co. H, 54th Reg NCT 2/17/1865 (NCT 8, 184).

VESTAL, Martin V. B., Co. I, Private (1838–). Lived, e. in Yadkin 3/8/1862, age 24. Captured at Fredericksburg 12/13/1862, exc abt 12/17/1862. Returned. Company records indicate he was captured at Spotsylvania 5/12/1864; Federal provost marshal records do not substantiate that (NCT 8, 218).

VESTAL, Miles J., Co. I, Sergeant (1838–). B. in Surry, e. In New Hanover 10/8/19861 as sergeant. Dis 2/14/1862 due to "scrotal hernia of both sides" (NCT 8, 218).

VICKERS, Joseph G., Co. G, Corporal (1842–). Lived, e. in Orange. 9/2/186. Captured at Hanover CH 5/27/1862; confined at Ft. Monroe. Paroled, trans to Aiken's Landing for exc 8/5/1862. Promoted to corporal Nov. 1862–May 1864. Captured at Spotsylvania CH 5/12/1864; confined at Pt. Lookout. Trans to Elmira 8/10/1864; released 6/14/1865 after OOA (NCT 8, 195).

WADE, Edwin P., Co. E, Private (1840–1862). Lived, e. in Montgomery. 8/1/1861, age 21. Wounded in the lungs at Cedar Mt. 8/9/1862. Died in Charlottesville hospital abt 9/1/1862 of wounds (NCT 8, 173).

WADE, James W., Co. E, Private (1843–). Lived in Montgomery, e. In Lenoir 3/20/1862, age 19. Wounded in the arm, captured at Gettysburg 7/1–4/1863. Hospitalized there, then at Davids Island. Paroled, trans to City Pt. where he arrived 10/28/1864 for exc. Absent- wounded until retired to Invalid Corps 10/13/1864 or 12/21/1864 due to disability (NCT 8, 173).

WAESNER, G.W., Co. E, Private (1835–1863). Lived, e. in Montgomery 3/10/1862, age 27. Died in Lynchburg hospital 6/22/1863 of pneumonia (NCT 8, 173).

WAESNER, Solomon E, Co. E, Private (1837–1863). Lived, e. in Montgomery 5/23/1862, age 25. Wounded in right hip, captured at Gettysburg 7/1–3/1863. Died in hospital there 8/18/1863 (NCT 8, 173).

WAGGONER, Calvin, Co. I, Private. (1840–). Lived, e. in Yadkin 8/13/1861, age 21. Deserted 7/1/1863. Returned. Wounded in right elbow near Reams' Station abt 8/25/1864. Absent-wounded until 12/1/1864, then AWOL (NCT 8, 218).

WAGGONER, Jacob M., Co. I, Private (1842–). Lived, e. in Yadkin 8/13/1861, age 19. Captured, confined to Ft. Monroe. Trans to Aiken's Landing for exchange 9/21/1862. AWOL through Feb. 1863. Returned. Captured 7/21/1864, Federal provost records do not agree. NC pension records indicate he was wounded in hip at Wilderness, 10/16/1863, and survived the war (NCT 8, 219).

WAGGONER, John W., Co. I, Private (1842–). Lived in Yadkin, e. in Orange, age 21, 9/20/1863. Surrendered at Appomattox CH 4/9/1865 (NCT 8, 219).

WAGNER, Benjamin, Co. C, Private (18__–1863). Lived, e. in Catawba 3/14/1863. Killed at Chancellorsville 5/3/1863 (NCT 8, 152).

WAGNER, Noah P., Co. C, Private (1842–1864). B., lived, e. in Catawba e. on 3/15/1862, age 20. Captured at Hanover CH 5/27/1862; confined at Ft. Monroe, then Ft. Columbus. Paroled and trans to Aiken's Landing for exc 8/5/1862. Died at Richmond 6/27/1864 of disease (NCT 8, 152).

WAGNER, Thomas J., Co. C, Private (1839–). Captured at Hanover CH 5/27/1862; confined at Ft. Monroe, then Ft. Columbus. Paroled and trans to Aiken's Landing for exc on 8/5/1862. Wounded at Gravel Hill 7/28/1864. Absent-wounded through Feb. 1865. Captured in a Richmond hospital 4/3/1865; trans to Newport News on 4/23/1865. Released 6/14/1865 after OOA (NCT 8, 152).

WAISNER, David W., Co. E, Private (1840–) Lived in Montgomery, e. in Lenoir 3/20/1862, age 22. Captured at Hanover CH 5/27/1862; confined at Ft. Monroe then Ft. Columbus. Paroled and trans to Aiken's Landing for trans 8/5/1862. Captured at Gettysburg 7/3/1863, hospitalized at Chester 7/17/1863. Trans to City Pt. for exc 8/20/1863. Wounded and captured at Gravel Hill 7/28/1864; confined at Pt. Lookout abt 12.3.1864. Paroled and trans to Boulware's Wharf on 3/18/1865 for exc (NCT 8, 173).

WAISNER, Wilson D., Co. D, Private (1833–1862). Lived, e. in Stanly 7/29/1861, age 28. Killed at Fredericksburg 12/13/1862 (NCT 8, 163).

WAITT, George N., Co. G, Private (1843–). Lived, e. in Orange 9/2/1861, age 18. Present until the surrender at Appomattox CH 4/9/1865 (NCT 8, 195).

WALKER, Elisha, Co. A, Private (1841–1862). Lived, e. in Surry, age 21, 3/18/1862. Died in camp at Richmond 7/3/1862 of an unknown disease. Son of E. W. And Sarah Walker of the Dobson District. (NCT 8, 124; SCS 179).

WALKER, Joseph Harrison, Co. A, Private (1840–). E., age 22, 3/18/1862 Deserted on 8/1/1862; returned 10/13/1862. Wounded 8/16/1864 near Winchester. Present through Feb. 1865 (NCT 8, 124; SCS 179).

WALLACE, George, Co. D, Private (1843–1862). Lived, e. in Stanly 7/29/1861. Killed at the battle of 2nd Manassas 8/27–30/1862 (NCT 8, 163).

WALLACE, John, Co. D, Private (1843–1862). Lived, e. in Stanly 9/10/1861, age 18. Killed at Gaines' Mill 6/27/1862.

WARD, John R., Co. G, Private. E. in Orange 10/19/1864. Trans to Co. G, 63rd Reg NCT 3/8/1865 (NCT 8, 195).

WARD, S. Brown, Co. F, Private (1832–1863). Lived, e. in Alamance 10/1862. Hospitalized at Richmond 5/30/1863 and died there 7/2/1863 from typhoid fever (NCT 8, 184).

WARD, William J., Co. G, Private (1835–1864). B., lived, e. in Orange 12/20/1861, age 26. Captured at Hanover CT 5/27/1862; confined at Ft. Monroe, then Ft. Columbus. Paroled and trans to Aiken's Landing for exc 8/5/1862. Captured near Spotsylvania CH 5/12/1864; confined at Pt. Lookout. Trans to Elmira 8/10/1864 where he died 10/6/1864 of "chronic diarrhoea" (NCT 8, 195).

WARDEN, Cary W., Jr., Co. I, Private. (1840–). Lived, e. in Yadkin 8/13/1861, age 21. Present until trans to Co. B, 38th Reg NCT (NCT 8, 219).

WARNER, James A, Co. E, Private (1838–). Lived, e. in Montgomery 8/1/1861, age 23. Dis 11/13/1861 or 2/27/1862 due to "variocele of both sides" (NCT 8, 173).

WARNER, John, Co. I, Private ? Place and date of enlistment not reported. Deserted to enemy abt 2/1/1865. Confined at Beverly, WVA 4/19/1865; released after OOA (NCT 8, 219).

WARNER, William G., Co. E, Musician (1834–1863). William lived in Montgomery where he e. 8/1/1861, age 27. Mustered in as a musician. Died in hospital at Montgomery White Sulphur Springs, VA 2/6/1863 of chronic diarrhea (NCT 8, 173).

WARREN, J.T., Co. B, Private (1841–). Lived in Gaston, e. 3/29/1862, age 21. Wounded in the left leg at Cedar Mt. 8/9/1862. Dis 9/25/1862 due to contractions and atrophy of left leg (NCT 8, 138).

WATTS, Rufus, Co. C, Private (1829–). Lived in Catawba, e. at Camp Fisher on 9/2/1861, age 32. Dis 4/25/1862 for "dyspepsia" (NCT 8, 152).

WEATHERMAN, Bartholomew W., Co. I, Private (1841–1864). Lived, e. in Yadkin 8/13/1861, age 20. Captured near Gravel Hill abt 7/28/1864; confined at Pt. Lookout. Trans to Elmira 8/8/1864, and died there 12/12/1864 of "pneumonia" (NCT 8, 219).

WEATHERMAN, Robert W., Co. I, 1st Sergeant (1840–1863). Lived, e. in Yadkin 8/13/1861, age 21. Promoted to sergeant Nov.–Dec. 1861; to 1st sergeant Jan.–Oct.1862. Captured at Hanover CH 5/27/1862; confined at Ft. Monroe, then Ft. Columbus. Trans to Aiken's Landing for exc 8/5/1862. Returned. Died in Richmond hospital abt 7/19/1863 of chronic diarrhea (NCT 8, 219).

WEAVER, James M., Co. I, Private (1838–). Lived, e. in Yadkin 8/13/1861, age 23. Captured at Hanover CH 5/27/1862; confined at Ft. Monroe, then Ft. Columbus. Trans to Aiken's Landing for exc 8/5/1862. Returned, and present through Feb. 1863. NC pension records indicate he was wounded at Fredericksburg, and at Wilmington, but he survived the war (NCT 8, 219).

WEAVER, John Thomas, Co. G, Private (1840–). Lived, e. in Orange 9/2/1861, age 21. Captured at Gravel Hill 7/28/1864; confined at Pt. Lookout, trans to Elmira 8/8/1864. Released there 6/19/1864 after OOA (NCT 8, 195).

WEBB, Benjamin R., Co. E, Private (1838–1862). Lived in Richmond, e. in Montgomery 8/1/1861, age 23. Died at Berryville, VA 11/6/1862 of disease (NCT 8, 173).

WEBB, Charles E., Co. H, Private (1833–). Lived, e. in Cleveland 8/22/1861, age 28. Hospitalized at Richmond 5/25/1864 with gunshot wound of left hand. Absent-wounded Jan–Feb 1865. NC pension records indicate he survived war (NCT 8, 206).

WEBB, George, Co. B, Private (1841–1862). Lived in Gaston, e. on 3/29/1862, age 21. Wounded at 2nd Manassas on 8/29/1862; died the same day at Richmond of wounds (NCT 8, 138).

WEBB, John Mc., Co. H, Private? NC pension records indicate he served in this company. (NCT 8, 206).

WEBB, Lorenzo Dow, Co. H, 2nd Lieutenant (1842–). Lived, e. in Cleveland 3/17/1862, age 20, as a private. Appointed 2nd lieutenant 4/7/1862. Wounded in right ankle at Gaines' Mill 6/27/1862. Resigned 1/8/1863 due to disability from wounds (NCT 8, 196–197).

WEBB, Thomas P., Co. F, Private (1842–). Lived, e. in Yadkin 6/18/1861. Present until 1/10/1865 when listed AWOL (NCT 8, 143).

WEBB, Willis J., Co. H, Private (1842–). Lived, e. in Cleveland 3/17/1862, age 20. Wounded in left hand at Wilderness 5/6/1864. Captured in Richmond hospital 4/3/1865; trans to Newport News 4/23/1865, and released 6/30/1865 after OOA (NCT 8, 206).

WEIR, M. S., Co. H, Private. Date/place of enlistment not reported. Paroled at Charlotte NC May 1865 (NCT 8, 206).

WELCH, John J., Co. E, Private. E. in 'Guilford 10/16/1863. Captured near Petersburg 4/2/1865; confined at Pt. Lookout until released 6/21/1865 after OOA (NCT 8, 173–174).

WELCH, W.W., Co. F, Private (1828–). Lived, e. in Forsyth 10/1/1862, age 34. Wounded at Chancellorsville 5/2–3/1863. Deserted from hospital June 1863 (NCT 8, 184).

WELLS, George, Co. B, Private (18__–1862). E. in Gaston 3/29/1862, and was killed at 2nd Manassas on 8/29/1862 (NCT 8, 138).

WHITAKER, Andrew Jackson, Co. A, Private (1827–1888). E., age 34, 3/18/1862 when Capt. E. F. Lovill was sent to Surry to recruit more men for Co. A. Wounded at Ox Hill 9/1/1862. Present through Feb. 1865. Son of Edmond and Dicey Safeley Whitaker, Pine Hill-Siloam area, Surry. He m. Hannah Bass in Surry on 10/8/1846, and had 13 or 14 children, 70 grandchildren. Widow applied for a pension. He is bur. at Pine Hill Community Ch. cem., Pilot Mt., NC (NCT VII 124; SCS 185; Anne Whitaker McCracken).

WHITAKER, David, Co. A, Private (1832–). E., age 30, 3/18/1862, in Surry. Dis 7/21/1862 due to "weak lungs and chronic cough. Son of Jesse and Mary Campbell Walker, farmers in Surry and Wilkes (NCT 8, 124; SCS 185).

WHITAKER, James A., Co. D, Private (1838–). B. , lived, e. in Stanly 7/29/1861, age 23. Wounded at Cedar Mt. 8/9/1862. Wounded in right thigh, captured at Gettysburg 7/3/1863. Hospitalized at Chester. Paroled and trans to City Pt. 9/23/1863 for exc. Dis 3/21/1864 due to wounds he received at Gettysburg (NCT 8, 163).

WHITAKER, Lewis, Co. A, Private (1841–). Lived, e. in Surry, age 21, on 3/18/1862. Dis 7/7/1862 due to "chronic affection of the lungs." Son of Elisha and Nancy Williamson Whitaker, after the war, Lewis moved to Ohio (NCT 8, 124; SCS 188).

WHITAKER, Thomas J., Co. A, Private (1845–1862). Lived, e. in Surry, age 17, 3/18/1862. Died in Danville hospital 8/14/1862 of "febris typhoides." Son of Abraham and Lydia Whitaker of Siloam (NCT 8, 124; SCS 189).

WHITE, Charles Malone, Co. K, Corporal (1844–). Lived in Cabarrus, e. in New Hanover 2/4/1862, age 18. Promoted to corporal 9/5/1864. Captured near Petersburg 4/2/1865; confined at Pt. Lookout, until released 6/21/1865 after OOA (NCT 8, 231).

WHITE, E.M., Co. B, Private (1839–1863). Lived, e. in Gaston on 7/30/1861, age 22. Captured at Hanover CH 5/27/1862; confined at Ft. Monroe, then Ft. Columbus. Paroled and trans to Aiken's Landing for exc on 8/5/1862. Captured at Fredericksburg 12/13/1862; paroled abt 12/17/1862. Died in Richmond hospital on 1/16/1863 of "erysipelas" (NCT 8, 138).

WHITE, Hewel L., Co. A, Private (1845–1863). Son of Robert and Nancy Snow White of Fairview, he e. at Dobson, Surry, 5/4/1861, age 22. Died on 11/25/1863 of "chronic diarrhoea" in Lynchburg hospital (NCT 8, 124; SCS 189).

WHITE, James P., Co. A, Private (1834–1862). Son of Joseph and Temperance White, Dobson district, Surry, he e. at Dobson on 5/4/1861, age 27. Died of typhoid fever 8/12/1862 in Lynchburg hospital (NCT 8, 124; SCS 189).

WHITE, John E., Co. B, Sergeant (1832–1863). Lived in Gaston, e., age 29, 7/30/1861. Promoted to sergeant 2/27/1862. Wounded in head at Gaines' Mill 6/27/1862. Captured at Gettysburg 7/4/1863; confined at Ft. Delaware; trans to Pt. Lookout 10/15–18/1863 where he died in hospital there abt 11/3/1863 of "chronic diarrhoea" (NCT 8, 138).

WHITE, Richard C., Co. A, Private (1837–). Son of

Robert and Nancy Snow White, Fairview community, Surry. He e. on 3/18/1862, age 24; Dis on 6/3/1862 due to an "abscess of the chest" (NCT 8, 124; SCS 189).

WHITE, Robert Adam, Co. B, 1st Lieutenant (1841–). B., lived, e. in Gaston 7/30/1861, age 20, as a sergeant. Promoted to 1st sergeant 2/27/1862. Reduced in rank on 11/12/1862. Promoted to sergeant Mar.–Oct. 1864. Wounded in the leg at Jericho Mills, 5/23/1864. Elected 2nd lieutenant 1/12/1865; promoted to 1st lieutenant 1/23/1865. Surrendered at Appomattox CH 4/9/1865 (NCT 8, 126).

WHITE, Robert, Jr., Co. A, Sergeant (1831–). B. in Surry to John and Sally White, Marsh district, Surry. A miller all his life, Robert e. 5/4/1861 at age 30. Promoted to corporal on 11/1/1861, then sergeant in Dec. 1861. Rank reduced corporal 1/25/1862, and reduced May–Oct. 1862. Captured on 4/2/1865 at Petersburg; confined at Ft. Delaware; released after OOA on 6/19/1865. NC pension records indicate he was wounded in right leg at Williamsport in July 1863. Robert m. first Elizabeth White and had 8 children. He then m. Mary Adkins. She applied for a widow's pension (NCT 8, 124; SCS 190).

WHITE, Swan (Snow), Co. A, Private (1845–1864). B. in Surry to John and Sally White of the Marsh district, conscripted 1/15/1864 at age 19. Captured on 5/12/1864 at Spotsylvania CH. Died 6 months later of acute dysentery while a POW at Pt. Lookout. (NCT 8, 124; SCS 190).

WHITE, William J., Co. A, Private (1835–). B. in Surry, e. at Dobson 5/4/1861. Wounded in the abdomen at Gettysburg in July 1863. Captured, paroled and exc. Wounded again in the left side and back, date unspecified, taken to a Richmond hospital on 10/2/1864. Surrendered 4/9/1865 at Appomattox CH. Pension application indicates he was wounded in the right leg at Petersburg in 1864. He m. in 1861, Surry, Sarah White (NCT 8, 124; SCS 190).

WHITEHEAD, Calvin, Co. I, Private. E. at Camp Holmes 5/4/1864. Deserted 1/11/1865 (NCT 8, 219).

WHITEHEAD, Henry W., Co. I, Private (1839–). Lived, e. in Yadkin 3/8/1862, age 23. Wounded near Gravel Hill 7/28/1864. Captured near Petersburg 4/2/1865; confined at Ft. Delaware. Released 6/19/1865 after OOA (NCT 8, 219).

WHITEHEAD, James S., Co. I, Private (1841–1863). Lived, e. in Yadkin 8/13/1861, age 20. Captured at Hanover CH 5/27/1862; confined at Ft. Monroe, then Ft. Columbus. Trans to Aiken's Landing for exc 8/5/1862. Returned, and died in Richmond hospital abt 6/27/1863 of gunshot wound and/or fever (NCT 8, 219).

WHITEHEAD, John, Co. I, Private? NC pension records indicate he served in this company (NCT 8, 219).

WHITLEY, George, Co. K, 1st Sergeant (1816–). B., lived and e. in Stanly 9/7/1861, age 45. Captured at Hanover CH 5/27/1862; confined at Ft. Monroe, then Ft. Columbus. Trans to Aiken's Landing for exc 8/5/1862. Returned. Promoted to 1st sergeant. Dis 9/23/186, overage. Paroled at Salisbury 5/19/1865 (NCT 8, 231).

WHITLEY, Jesse J., Co. K, Private. Lived, e. in Stanly 11/17/1863. Captured near Petersburg 4/2/1865; confined at Pt. Lookout until released 6/21/1865 after OOA (NCT 8, 231).

WHITLEY, Monroe, Co. K, Private. E. at Liberty Mills 4/1/1864. Surrendered at Appomattox CH 4/9/1865 (NCT 8, 231).

WHITLEY, Thomas W., Co. K, Private. (1835–). Lived and e. in Stanly 3/20/1862, age 27. Wounded at Chancellorsville 5/2–3/1863. Hospitalized at Richmond 7/20/1864 with gunshot wound. Absent on furlough Nov.–Dec. 1864. Surrendered at Appomattox CH 4/9/1865 (NCT 8, 231).

WHITESIDE, M.G., Co. B, Private. Gaston resident, e. on 7/30/1861. Dis 2/15/1862 due to disability (NCT 8, 248).

WHITESIDES, E.L., Co. B, Sergeant (1834–1864). Lived, e. in Gaston, age 27, on 7/30/186. Promoted to corporal 2/27/1862; to sergeant Jan. 1863. Killed at Spotsylvania CH 5/12/1864 (NCT 8, 138).

WHITESIDES, William E., Co. B, Private (1838–). Lived, e. in Gaston 7/30/1861, age 23. Surrendered at Appomattox on 4/9/1865 (NCT 8, 138–139).

WILES, Margamin, Co. D, Private (1819–1862). Lived in Stanly, e. 3/15/1862, age 43. Died 10/9–10/1862 of disease (NCT 8, 163).

WILES, William, Co. D, Private (1839–). Lived, e. in Stanly 3/15/1862, age 23. Wounded in the finger at 2nd Manassas 8/27–30/1862. Hospitalized in Richmond 6/5/1864 with a gunshot wound. Paroled at Salisbury, NC abt 7/10/1865 (NCT 8, 163).

WILLIAMS, George D., Co. F, Sergeant (1827–). Lived, e. in Yadkin, 6/18/1861, age 34 as a sergeant. Rank reduced 4/15/1862. Captured at Hanover CH 5/27/1862; confined at Ft. Monroe, then Ft. Columbus. Paroled and trans to Aiken's Landing for exc. 8/5/1862. Dis 9/18/1862 (NCT 8, 184).

WILLIAMS, Isaac, Co. E, 2nd Lieutenant (1837–). Lived in either Montgomery or Chatham. E. in Montgomery 8/1/1861, age 24, as Ensign (Private); promoted to corporal Jan.–Feb. 1862. Promoted to 1st sergeant March–Apr. 1862. Captured at Hanover CH 5/27/1862; confined at Ft. Monroe, then Ft. Columbus. Trans to Aiken's Landing for exc 8/5/1862. Elected 2nd lieutenant 12/20/1863. Captured at Gravel Hill 7/28/1864; confined at Old Capitol Prison. Trans to Ft. Delaware 8/12/1864 (NCT 8, 164).

WILLIAMS, James W., Co. H, Private (1832–). B. in Rutherford, lived, e. in Cleveland 8/22/1861, age 29. Dis 11/8/1861 due to "scrotal hernia of the right side" (NCT 8, 206).

WILLIAMS, John I., Co. F, Private. Lived, e. in Yadkin 10/27/1863. Furloughed 2/21/1864, Deserted, went over to enemy, took OOA at Louisville, KY 8/16/1864 (NCT 8, 184).

WILLIAMS, John W., Co. A, Private (1847–). B. in Surry to Jackson and Caroline Williams who farmed near Rockford. He entered the army at age 18 on 2/18/1865. Captured on 5/12/1864 near Spotsylvania CH; confined at Pt. Lookout. Trans to Elmira on 8/10/1864, and released on 11/5/1864 (NCT 8, 124; SCS 193).

WILLIAMS, John Wesley, Co. C, 2nd Lieutenant. Lived and e. in Catawba 8/13/1861. Promoted to corporal 11/25/1862; o sergeant 4/1/1863. Appointed 2nd lieutenant 9/14/1863. Surrendered at Appomattox CH 4/9/1865 (NCT 8, 140).

WILLIAMS, Lewis A., Co. I, Corporal (1842–1861). Lived and e. in Yadkin 8/13/1861, age 19, as a corporal. Died in Wilmington hospital abt 12/7/1861 of "measles" (NCT 8, 219).

WILLIAMS, Randolph S., Co. E, Private. E. in Wake 11/17/1864. Surrendered at Appomattox CH 4/9/1865 (NCT 8, 174).

WILLIS, Martin V.B., Co. B, Private (1840–). Gaston resident, e. on 7/30/1861, age 21. Deserted 4/29/1863. Reported in confinement through Dec. 1864. Released, returned to duty, and surrendered at Appomattox CH on 4/9/1865. NC pension records indicate he was wounded in right shoulder at Malvern Hill 4/1/1862 (NCT 8, 139).

WILMOTH, Ambrose, Co. A, Private (1827–). E. in Surry, age 35, 3/18/1862. Present through Feb. 1865. He m. in 1856, Surry, Lucinda Whitaker of the Little Richmond area, Surry (NCT 8, 124; SCS 194).

WILSON, Albert C., Co. H, Private (1844–1862). Lived in Cleveland, e. 5/10/1862, age 18. Died in Charlottesville hospital 5/31/1862 from pneumonia (NCT 8, 206).

WILSON, Benjamin F., Co. C, Private. Catawba resident, e. at Camp Fisher 9/10/1861. Died in Lynchburg hospital on 5/30/1862 of chronic diarrhea (NCT 8, 152).

WILSON, David P., Co. H, Private. E. at Camp Vance 8/1/1864. Present through Feb. 1865 (NCT 8, 206).

WILSON, George W., Co. H, Private (1840–1862). Lived in SC, e. in Cleveland 3/17/1862, age 22. Captured at Hanover CH 5/27/1862; confined at Ft. Monroe, then Ft. Columbus. Paroled and trans to Aiken's Landing for exc 8/5/1862. Killed at Fredericksburg 12/13/1862 (NCT 8, 206).

WILSON, H., Co. C, Private. Captured near Petersburg 4/2/1865; confined at Ft. Delaware, 4/4/1865. No further information (NCT 8, 152).

WILSON, James T., Co. H, Private (1840–). Lived, e. in Cleveland 8/22/1861, age 21. Wounded in face and neck and captured at Gettysburg 7/1–4/1863. Hospitalized there; trans to Davids Island 7/17–24/1863. Paroled and trans to City Pt. for exc 9/8/1863. Wounded at Fussell's Mill 8/16/1864. Paroled at Farmville 4/11–12/1865 (NCT 8, 206).

WILSON, John, Co. E, Private. E. in Wake 10/3/1863. Present through Feb. 1865 (NCT 8, 174).

WILSON, Leroy L., Co. B, Private (1842–). Lived, e. in Gaston 3/29/1862, age 20. Captured at Fredericksburg 12/13/1862; paroled 12/17/1862. Absent, in hospital through Feb. 1863. Captured at Falling Waters abt 7/14/1863. Paroled at Baltimore 8/23/1863, trans to City Pt. for exc 8/24/1863. On detached service at Charlotte, NC 12/20/1863 through Dec. 1864. Rejoined company Jan.–Feb. 1865; surrendered at Appomattox CH 4/9/1865. He married Margaret Eliza Baity, dau of Pleasant and Harriet Baity in 1864 in Yadkin, and they had a daughter (NCT 8, 139).

WISHON, James Thomas, Co. I, Private (1841–1864). B., lived, e. in Yadkin 8/13/1861, age 19. Captured at New Bern 3/14/1862; confined at Ft. Columbus. Trans to Aiken's Landing for exc on 8/5/1862. Returned. Hospitalized at Danville 6/16/1864 with gunshot wound of neck. Returned before 10/1/1864, and killed in action near Jones' Farm (NCT 8, 219).

WISHON, Samuel A., Co. I, Private (1835–). Lived, e. in Yadkin 3/8/1862, age 27. Captured at Hanover CH 5/27/1862; confined at Ft. Monroe, then Ft. Columbus. Trans to Aiken's Landing for exc 8/5/1862. Returned. Deserted 7/15/1863. Returned. Wounded in left side and captured near Gravel Hill 7/28/164. Hospitalized at City Pt., trans to Pt. Lookout 12/5/1864. Trans to Boulware's Wharf 3/18/1865 for exc. Paroled at Salisbury April–May 1865 (NCT 8, 219–220).

WOMACK, Allen M., Co. F, Private (1839–1862). Lived in Yadkin and e. at Camp Enon 8/20/1861, age 22. Wounded at Gaines' Mill 6/27/1862; hospitalized at Richmond and died there 7/3–6/1862 of wounds (NCT 8, 184).

WOOD, Dempson, Co. A, Private (1842–). Son of Andrew and Lucinda Holyfield Wood of Siloam, Surry, e. on 5/4/1861, age 19. Captured at Petersburg 4/2/1865; confined at Ft. Delaware. Released 6/19/1865 after OOA. Wood and his wife Emiline, farmed at Eldora. By 1880 they had 5 children (NCT 8, 124–125; SCS 197).

WOOD, Joshua, Co. K, Private (1830–). B., lived, e. in Stanly 3/15/1862, age 32. Dis 8/23/1862 due to "deafness in both ears, chronic rheumatism and general debility" (NCT 8, 231).

WOOD, Ransom, Co. A, Private (1833–aft 1880). Surry resident, e., age 29, 3/18/1862, son of Michael and Cindy Wood of Stuart's Creek. Wounded in right hand and right shoulder, captured at Gettysburg 7/1–3/1863. Hospitalized at Davids Island; trans to Ft. Delaware 9/14/1864. Trans to Varina on 9/22/1864 for exc. Retired to Invalid Corps 12/21/1864 due to injuries. He and wife Debby were living at Dobson in 1880 with their children. Widow applied for pension (NCT 8, 125; SCS 198).

WOOD, Silas W., Co. A, Private (1839–). Son of James and Nancy Wood, Dobson district, Surry, he e. at Dobson 5/4/1861, age 22. Captured at Harrison's Landing 6/28–30/1862; confined at Ft. Columbus, then Ft. Delaware. Trans to Aiken's Landing for exc 8/5/1862. Present through Feb. 1865. Silas m. Mary Strange in 1866 in Surry In 1880 they were living in Marsh Township with their 4 children. He applied for a pension (NCT 8, 125; SCS 198–199).

WOODHOUSE, Francis M., Co. I, Private (1843–1862). Lived and e. in Yadkin 3/8/1862, age 18. Died in camp near Richmond 8/4/1862 of "fever" (NCT 8, 220).

WOOTEN, Thomas H., Co. F, Private (1842–). A Yadkin resident, he e. there 6/18/1861. Wounded in left thigh, captured at Gettysburg 7/3/1863. Hospitalized at Chester. Paroled and trans to City Pt. 9/23/1863 for exc. AWOL 9/22/1864–Feb. 1865 (NCT 8, 184).

WORKMAN, Gaston B., Co. G, Private. E. 12/16/

1863 in Orange. Surrendered at Appomattox CH 4/9/1865 (NCT 8, 195).

WORKMAN, Henry N., Co. G, Private (1817). B., e. in Orange 3/5/1862. Died at Chapel Hill, NC 8/12/1864 of disease (NCT 8, 195).

WORKMAN, Sidney M., Co. G, Private (1843–). Lived, e. in Orange 9/17/1861, age 18. Captured at Frederick MD 9/12/1862; confined at Ft. Delaware. Paroled and trans to Aiken's Landing on 10/2/1862 for exc on 11/10/1862. Captured at Spotsylvania CH abt 5/12/1864; confined at Pt. Lookout. Trans to Elmira 8/10/1864, died there 2/1/1865 of "variola" (NCT 8, 195–196).

WRIGHT, Abner B., Co. H, Private (1835–). Lived, e. in Cleveland 8/22/1861, age 26 as a sergeant. Rank reduced. Trans to Co. E, 12th Reg NCT 4/24/1863 (NCT 8, 206).

WRIGHT, Samuel, Co. C, Private (1834–) Lived, e. in Catawba 3/15/1862, age 28. Wounded at Chancellorsville 5/2–3/1863. Deserted, but returned 9/23/1863. Wounded at Spotsylvania CH 5/21/1864. Captured near Petersburg 4/2/1865; confined at Ft. Delaware, until released 6/19/1865 after OOA (NCT 8, 152).

WRIGHT, William W., Co. H, Captain. Previously served as 1st sergeant, Co. E, 12th Reg NCT. Appointed captain of Co. H, 28th Reg 8/22/1861. Defeated for re-election 4/7/1862 (NCT 8, 196).

WYATT, Wyley A., Co. B, Private (1840–). Gaston resident, e. there 7/30/1861, age 21. Captured at Hanover CH 5/27/1862; confined at Ft. Monroe, then Ft. Columbus. Trans to Aiken's Landing for exc 8/5/1862. Returned to duty, captured at Fredericksburg 12/13/1862; paroled 12/17/1862. Trans to C. S. Navy 4/3/1864 (NCT 8, 139).

YARBORO, Lewis H., Co. H, Private (1839–). Lived, e. in Cleveland 3/17/1862, age 23. Wounded in left hand near Wilderness abt 5/3/1864. Wounded in left wrist at Petersburg 4/2/1865. Captured in Richmond hospital 4/3/1865; paroled 4/23/1865 (NCT 8/206).

YARBOROUGH, Thomas, Co. E, Private. (1832–1864). Lived, e. in Montgomery 3/18/1862, age 30. Hospitalized in Richmond 2/22/1864 with "variola" and died 3/7/1864 (NCT 8, 174).

YARBROUGH, Andrew J., Co. F, Private (1842–). Lived, e. in Yadkin 6/18/1861, age 19. Captured near Petersburg 4/2/1865; confined at Pt. Lookout, released 6/6/1865 (NCT 8, 184).

YORK, Little C., Co. A, Private (1848–). Lived in

Surry, e. at age 14 on 3/18/1862. Wounded in forehead and thigh and captured at Gettysburg 7/3–5/1863. Confined at Ft. McHenry, then at Ft. Delaware. Paroled and trans to City Pt. on 8/1/1863 for exc. Surrendered at Appomattox CH on 4/9/1865 (NCT 8, 125).

YOUNG, Solomon, Co. I, Private? NC pension records indicate he served in this company (NCT 8, 220).

YOUNG, Woodson S., Co. I, Private (1841–). Lived in Yadkin, e. there 3/8/1862, age 21. Deserted 8/1/1862 (NCT 8, 220).

YOUNT, Abel M., Co. C, Private. Catawba resident, e. there 8/13/1861. Surrendered at Appomattox CH 4/9/1865 (NCT 8, 152).

YOUNT, Daniel P., Co. C, Private (1843–). B., lived, e. in Catawba 3/25/1862; Dis 6/15/1862 due to "general debility and want of physical ability for active service." He later served in Co. E, 12th Reg NCT (NCT 8, 152–153).

YOUNT, David, Co. C, Private (1820–). B., lived, e. in Catawba 8/13/1861, age 41. Dis 5/1/1862 due to Conscription Act. Later served in Co. E, 12th Reg NCT (NCT 8, 153).

YOUNT, Laban A., Co. C, Private (18__–1863). Catawba resident, e. at Camp Fisher 9/9/1861. Killed at Chancellorsville 5/3/1863, "a most gallant soldier" (NCT 8, 153).

YOUNT, Lawson M., Co. C, Private (1831–). B., lived, e. in Catawba 8/13/1861. Wounded in head at Gaines' Mill 6/27/1862. Dis 12/5/1862 due to "general debility and rheumatism" (NCT 8, 153).

YOUNT, Noah, Co. C, Private. Catawba resident, e. there 3/14/1863. Wounded at Chancellorsville 5/2–3/1863. On detail as wagon sergeant 7/1/1864 through Feb. 1865. Surrendered at Appomattox CH 4/9/1865 (NCT 8, 153).

YOW, Timothy, Co. D, Private (1837–). Lived, e. in Stanly. 3/15/1862, age 25. Wounded near Richmond, date unknown. Retired from service 10/20/1864. NC pension records indicate he was wounded at Ox Hill 6/26/1863 (NCT 8, 163).

YOW, William C., Co. D, Private (1840–). Lived, e. in Stanly 7/29/1861, age 21. Wounded in right thigh and/or right side at Spotsylvania CH abt 5/12/1864. Captured near Petersburg 4/2/1865; confined at Pt. Lookout until released 6/22/1865 after OOA. NC pension records indicate he suffered a bayonet wound in right side at Seven Pines (NCT 8, 163).

Notes

Introduction

1. Michael C. Hardy, *The Battle of Hanover Court House* (Jefferson, NC: McFarland, 2006), p. 2 and pp. 153–177.

Chapter 1

1. Hugh T. Lefler and Albert R. Newsome, *North Carolina: The History of a Southern State*, 3rd ed. (Chapel Hill, NC: University of North Carolina Press, 1973), p. 450; Noble J. Tolbert, ed. *The Papers of John Willis Ellis*, Vol. II (Raleigh, NC: North Carolina Department of Archives and History, 1964), pp. 621–622.
2. John G. Barrett, *The Civil War in North Carolina* (Chapel Hill, NC: The University of North Carolina Press, 1963), p. 3.
3. Boatner, *The Civil War Dictionary*, pp. 729–730.
4. Lefler and Newsome, p. 449.
5. Election Returns of Yadkin County, North Carolina, State Department of Archives and History, Raleigh, North Carolina.
6. Lefler and Newsome, p. 397.
7. *Ibid.*, p. 715.
8. *Ibid.*, p. 400.
9. *Ibid.*, p. 448.
10. *Ibid.*, p. 450.
11. Tolbert, ed. *The Papers of John Willis Ellis*, Vol. II, pp. 621–622.
12. Lefler and Newsome, p. 450.
13. *Ibid.*
14. Salem, N.C., *People's Press*, June 21, 1861.
15. Lefler and Newsome, p. 451.
16. "The North Carolina State Flag," online http://www.confederateflags.org/states/FOTCncarolina.htm.
17. "Confederate Flags of the Old South," online http://www.infoplease.com/spot/confederate3.html.
18. "Naming the American Civil War," Wikipedia, online http://en.wikipedia.org/wiki/Naming_the_American_Civil_War.
19. *Ibid.*

Chapter 2

1. The song is generally credited to Daniel Decatur Emmett. It is known as "Dixie" and also as "Dixie's Land" and "I Wish I Was in Dixie." Wikipedia, "Dixie" (song), online at http://en.wikipedia.org/wiki/Dixie_(song).
2. Weymouth T. Jordan, Jr., *North Carolina Troops, 1861–1865: A Roster*, Vol. 8 (Raleigh, NC: Division of Archives and History, 1981), pp. 112–125. Hereafter cited as *North Carolina Troops*.
3. Kinyoun Genealogical Records, Notebook of Dr. John Hendricks Kinyoun, Captain Company F, 28th North Carolina Infantry Regiment, 1861–1862, courtesy of Joseph K.

Houts, Jr., St. Joseph, Missouri. Hereinafter cited as Kinyoun notebook.
4. Boatner, pp. 611–613; "North Carolina and the Civil War: Organization and Rank," online http://www.ncmuseum ofhistory.org/exhibits/civilwar/resources_section2.html.
5. Reminiscences of John B. Carson, Box 70–, Folder 29, Military Collection, North Carolina Department of Archives and History, Raleigh, North Carolina, cited in William McKinley McDaid, "'Four years of arduous service': The History of the Branch-Lane Brigade in the Civil War" (Ph.D. dissertation, Michigan State University, 1987), p. 11.
6. Kinyoun notebook.
7. Brigadier General J.H. Lane, "Twenty-Eighth Regiment," in Walter C. Clark, *The Histories of the Several Regiments and Battalions from North Carolina in the Great War, 1861–1865, Written by Members of the Respective Commands*, Vol. 4 (Goldsboro, NC: Nash Bros., 1901), p. 465. Hereinafter cited as Clark, *North Carolina Regiments.*
8. Nicholas Biddle Gibbon, "Diary of Nicholas Biddle Gibbon, 28th Regt. North Carolina Volunteers, 1861–1863," typescript, University of North Carolina at Charlotte, p. 9. Hereinafter cited as Gibbon, Diary.
9. Kinyoun notebook.
10. Jordan, *North Carolina Troops*, Vol. 8, p. 168.
11. *Ibid*, Vol. 8, p. 132.
12. McDaid, p. 14.
13. Boatner, p. 471.
14. George B. Johnston to James H. Lane, September 21, 1861, Folder 48, James H. Lane Papers, Auburn University archives, Auburn University, cited in McDaid, p. 14.
15. McDaid, p. 15; Boatner, pp. 63, 471.
16. John Thomas Conrad to Sallie Conrad, October 15, 1861, in Julia Harris O'Daniel and Laura Conrad Patton, *Kinfolk of Jacob Conrad* (Privately published, 1970), p. 285. The original letters from John Thomas Conrad to his family are housed in the John Thomas Conrad Papers, North Carolina Department of Archives and History, Raleigh, NC.
17. William M. Norman, *A Portion of My Life* (Winston-Salem, NC: John F. Blair, 1959), pp. 131–132.
18. Jordan, *North Carolina Troops*, Vol. 8, p. 99.
19. Norman, p. 131.
20. John Thomas Conrad, Wilmington, October 15, 1861, in O'Daniel, p. 285.
21. James H. Lane to J.G. Martin, October 18, 1861, Governor Henry Clark to James H. Lane, October 24, 1861, Governor's Letter Book 155, pp. 175–176, North Carolina Department of Archives and History; John Thomas Conrad to Sallie Conrad, Conrad Papers, North Carolina Department of Archives and History; Henry Clark to J.R. Anderson, October 25, 1861, Governor's Letter Book 155, p. 177, North Carolina Department of Archives and History.
22. R.C. Gatlin to Brig. Gen. J.R. Anderson, Goldsboro, November 13, 1862, *The War of the Rebellion: A Compilation of the Official Records of the War of Union and Confederate Armies*, Ser. I, Vol. 51, Pt. II, pp. 367–377. Hereafter cited as O.R.

23. Gibbon, Diary, p. 9.

24. *Ibid.*

25. Jordan, *North Carolina Troops*, Vol. 8, p. 99; J.H. Lane, "Twenty-Eighth Regiment," in Clark, *North Carolina Regiments*, Vol. 2, p. 467.

26. Lane, "Twenty-Eighth Regiment," in Jordan, *North Carolina Troops*, Vol. 2, pp. 465–466.

27. Gibbon, Diary, p. 9.

28. Jordan, *North Carolina Troops*, Vol. 8, pp. 112–125.

29. Gettysburg National Military Park Kidzpage, "Civil War Flags," online http://www.nps.gov/gett/gettkidz/flag.htm.

30. Gibbon, Diary, p. 9.

31. Lane, "Twenty-Eighth Regiment," in Clark, *North Carolina Regiments*, Vol. 2, p. 467.

32. *Ibid.*, p. 467.

33. John Hendricks Kinyoun to wife, October 13, 1861. John Hendricks Kinyoun Papers, Duke University, Durham, North Carolina.

34. John Thomas Conrad to Sallie Conrad, October 15, 1861, John Thomas Conrad Papers, North Carolina Department of History, Raleigh, North Carolina.

35. Lane, "Twenty-Eighth Regiment," in Clark, *North Carolina Regiments*, Vol. 2, p. 467.

36. Jordan, *North Carolina Troops*, Vol. 8, p. 99; Lane, "Twenty-Eighth Regiment," in Clark, *North Carolina Regiments*, Vol. 2, p. 467.

37. Kinyoun notebook.

38. *Ordinances and Resolutions Passed by the State Convention of North Carolina, 1861–1862* (February 19, 1862), (Raleigh, NC: John W. Syme, 1862).

39. Norman, pp. 134–135.

40. Lane, "Twenty-Eighth Regiment," in Clark, *North Carolina Regiments*, Vol. 2, p. 468.

41. Norman, pp. 134–135.

42. Lane, "Twenty-Eighth Regiment," in Clark, *North Carolina Regiments*, Vol. 2, p. 468.

43. John Hendricks Kinyoun to wife, March 28, 1862; April 2, 1862; April 4, 1862; John Hendricks Kinyoun Papers, Duke University, cited in McDaid, pp. 51–52.

44. Numbers complied from Manarin and Jordan, *North Carolina Troops*, Vol. 6, pp. 305–423; Vol. 8, pp. 110–231, and Vol. 9, pp. 468–604, and cited in McDaid, p. 53.

45. Brigadier General James H. Lane, "The Branch-Lane Brigade," in Clark, *North Carolina Regiments*, Vol. 4, p. 465.

46. *Dictionary of American Biography*, II (New York: Scribner's, 1919), pp. 597–598, cited in McDaid, p. 17.

47. Boatner p. 80.

48. Extracted from Richard Dobbins, American Civil War Research Database, extracted and e-mailed to me July 9, 2006 by Jim Pierce, Sons of the Confederate Veterans Genealogy Committee chairman. For more information see http://www.civilwardata.com; Boatner, *Civil War Dictionary;* and CWSAC Battle Summaries.

49. Jordan, *North Carolina Troops*, Vol. 8, pp. 99–110.

50. Extracted from the database of Richard Dobbins, and sent to me by Jim Pierce, Sons of Confederate Veterans, International Genealogists-in-Chief by e-mail 7/9/2006.

51. D.S. Freeman, *Lee's Lieutenants: A Study in Command*, Vol. 3, xxix, cited in Boatner, p. 400.

52. McDaid, pp. 67–68.

53. Boatner, p. 400.

Chapter 3

1. William Tecumseh Sherman is reported to have made that statement in a speech he gave at the Ohio State Fair in 1880. Online "William Tecumseh Sherman," http://www.military-quotes.com/william-sherman.htm; "War is Hell," http://www.mi5th.org/warishell.htm.

2. Lane, "Twenty-Eighth Regiment," in Clark, *North Carolina Regiments*, Vol. 2, p. 470.

3. Boatner, p. 340.

4. Gibbon, Diary, p. 24.

5. "Life in a Civil War Army Camp," extracted from The Civil War Society, *Encyclopedia of the Civil War* (New York: Wings Books, 1997), online http://www.civilwarhome.com/camplife.htm.

6. Boatner, p. 760.

7. "Civil War Soldier Vocabulary," online http://www.nps.gov/archive/gett/getteducation/cwsvocab.htm.

8. "Life in a Civil War Army Camp," *Encyclopedia of the Civil War.*

9. John Thomas Conrad, Wilmington, October 23, 1861, in O'Daniel, *Kinfolk of Jacob Conrad* (Privately printed, 1970), p. 287.

10. Calvin Holcomb to Respected Brother, March the 10 [1862], in Casstevens, *Heritage of Yadkin County*, Vol. 1, p. 144.

11. John Thomas Conrad, May 4, 1862, Gordonsville, Virginia, in O'Daniel, *Kinfolk of Jacob Conrad* (Privately printed, 1970), p. 295.

12. James M. Collins to brother, Ambrose Collins, June 9, 1862, Richmond, VA, in Hester Bartlett Jackson, ed., *Surry County Soldiers in the Civil War* (Charlotte, NC: Delmar Printing, 1992), p. 290.

13. G.B. Harding to Father & Mother, November 25, 1863, Camp near Orange Court House, Virginia, Harding Family Papers.

14. Samuel S. Harding to Father, Wilmington, January 23, 1862, Harding Family Papers..

15. John Thomas Conrad, Wilmington, April 17, 1862, in O'Daniel, *Kinfolk of Jacob Conrad* (Privately printed, 1970), p. 293.

16. John Thomas Conrad, Camp near Winchester, Virginia, November 21, 1862, in O'Daniel, p. 317.

17. S.S. Harding to Father, January 24, 1863, Camp Gregg, VA, Harding Family Papers.

18. G.B. Harding to Father & Mother, November 25, 1863, Camp near Orange Court House, Virginia, Harding Family Papers.

19. John Thomas Conrad, Orange County, May 8, 1862, in O'Daniel, p. 298.

20. Boatner, *Civil War Dictionary*, p. 681.

21. Mrs. Hale Houts, "Presents for the Yadkin Boys," *Journal of North Carolina Genealogy*, Vol. 9, No. 2 (Summer 1963): pp. 1133–1135.

22. John Thomas Conrad, Wilmington, October 23, 1861, in O'Daniel, p. 287.

23. William A. Tesh to Father, Richmond, VA, June 4, 1862, William A. Tesh Papers, Duke University, Durham, NC.

24. Garry Fisher, *Rebel Cornbread and Yankee Coffee: Authentic Civil War Cooking and Camaraderie* (Birmingham, AL: Crane Hill Publishers, 2001), pp. 24–25.

25. John Thomas Conrad, Wilmington, October 23, 1861, in O'Daniel, p. 287.

26. John Thomas Conrad, Lynchburg, Virginia, October 12, 1862, in O'Daniel, pp. 314–315.

27. John Thomas Conrad, Wilmington, October 15, 1861, in O'Daniel, p. 285.

28. S.S. Harding to Father, January 24, 1863, Camp Gregg, VA, Harding Family Papers.

29. John Thomas Conrad, Nov. 21, 1861, in O'Daniel, p. 291.

30. *Ibid.*

31. Artha Bray, Jr., to King Hiram Bray, December 20, 1862, Fredericksburg, VA, in Jackson, *Surry County Soldiers in the Civil War*, p. 269.

32. John Thomas Conrad, Orange County, May 8, 1862, in O'Daniel, p. 302.

33. James Collins to Ambrose Collins, May 9, 1862, Rapidan Station, in Jackson, *Surry County Soldiers in the Civil War*, p. 289.

34. John Thomas Conrad, Camp near Berryville, Virginia, November 3, 1862, in O'Daniel, p. 316.

35. John Thomas Conrad, June 24, 1862, in O'Daniel, p. 305.

36. John Thomas Conrad, Camp near Berryville, Virginia, November 3, 1862, in O'Daniel, p. 316.

37. John Thomas Conrad, Camp 28th Regt., N.C., Volunteers, December 28, 1862, in O'Daniel, pp. 319–320.

38. *Ibid.*, p. 320.

39. John Thomas Conrad, 1st N.C., Cav. Camp near Balfield, Va., January 20, 1865, in O'Daniel, p. 324.

40. Caleb S. McCurdy to S.M. McCurdy, Richmond, VA, February 11, 1863, McCurdy Papers, courtesy of Duke University, Durham, North Carolina.

41. G.B. Harding to Father & Mother, November 25, 1863, camp near Orange Court House, VA, Harding Family Papers.

42. John S. Bowman, ed. *Who Was Who in the Civil War* (1998, rpt. North Dighton, MA: World Publications, 2002), p. 99.

43. William Joseph Hardee, *Rifle and Infantry Tactics* (Raleigh, NC: J. Spelman, 1862), online Drill Network, http://home.att.net/%7EMrsMajor/1862.htm.

44. John Thomas Conrad, Wilmington, November 21, 1861, in O'Daniel, p. 290.

45. John Thomas Conrad, Orange County, May 8, 1862, in O'Daniel, p. 302.

46. John Thomas Conrad, April 17, 1862, Kinston, North Carolina, in O'Daniel, p. 293.

47. Samuel Speer Harding to father, William Harding, Wilmington, January 23, 1862, Harding Family papers.

48. Gibbon, Diary, p. 10.

49. John Thomas Conrad, June 24, 1862, in O'Daniel, p. 305.

50. Calvin Holcomb to Brother, February 19, 1862, in Casstevens, *Heritage of Yadkin County*, Vol. 1, p. 143.

51. Samuel S. Harding to Father, Wilmington, January 23, 1862, in Frances H. Casstevens, *The Civil War and Yadkin County, North Carolina* (Jefferson, NC: McFarland, 1997), pp. 128–129.

52. John Thomas Conrad, Wilmington, October 23, 1861, in O'Daniel, p. 287.

53. Jordan, *North Carolina Troops*, Vol. 8, p. 174.

54. Joseph Kinyoun Houts, Jr., *A Darkness Ablaze* (St. Joseph, MO: Platte Purchase Publishers, 2005), pp.140–315.

55. H.W. and Jas. Collins to Father, Mother, Brothers and Sisters, November 3, 1861, Wilmington, NC, in Jackson, *Surry County Soldiers in the Civil War*, p. 288.

56. William A. Tesh to Father and Mother, Kinston, NC April 25, 1862, William A. Tesh Papers, Special Collections, Duke University, Durham, NC. Hereafter cited at Tesh Papers.

57. John Thomas Conrad, Wilmington, October 23, 1861, in O'Daniel, p. 287.

58. John Hendricks Kinyoun to wife, October 13, and 20, 1861; November 7 and 18, 1861; January 1 and 12, 1862, John Hendricks Kinyoun Papers, Duke University, cited in McDaid, p. 27.

59. John Thomas Conrad, Wilmington, November 8, 1861, in O'Daniel, p. 290.

60. *Ibid.*, November 18, 1861, cited in McDaid, p. 27.

61. Samuel S. Harding to Father, Wilmington, January 23, 1862, in Casstevens, *The Civil War and Yadkin County*, pp. 128–129.

62. Gibbon, Diary, p. 20.

63. Jordan, *North Carolina Troops*, Vol. 8, p. 217.

64. Calvin Holcomb to Dear Brother, July 7, 1864, in Casstevens, *Heritage of Yadkin County*, Vol. 1, p. 144.

65. John Thomas Conrad, Gordonsville, Virginia, May 18, 1862, in O'Daniel, p. 298.

66. Calvin Holcomb to Respected Brother, March the 10 [1862], in Casstevens, *Heritage of Yadkin County*, Vol. 1, p. 144.

67. Muster rolls for Company I, 28th Regiment, in Jordan, *North Carolina Troops*, Vol. 8, pp. 206–220.

68. John Thomas Conrad, Lynchburg, Virginia, September 6, 1862, in O'Daniel, pp. 312–313.

69. Artha Bray, Jr., to Brother, September 25, 1862, Danville, VA, in Jackson, *Surry County Soldiers in the Civil War*, p. 268.

70. T.M. Bellamy to Mrs. M.M. McCurdy, Richmond, VA, November 28, 1863, in Caleb S. McCurdy Papers, courtesy of Duke University.

71. Thomas P. Lowry, *The Story the Soldiers Wouldn't Tell: Sex in the Civil War* (Mechanicsburg, PA: Stackpole Books, 1994), p. 104.

72. Joseph K. Barnes, Joseph Janvier Woodward, and Charles Smart, eds. *Medical and Surgical History of the War of the Rebellion*, Vol. 2, Pt. III, 3rd Medical Volume (Washington, DC: Government Printing Office, 1888), p. 891.

73. "Life in a Civil War Army," *Encyclopedia of the Civil War*.

74. Artha Bray, Jr. to Mother, December 18, 1861, Camp of the 28th Regiment, Wilmington, NC, in Jackson, *Surry County Soldiers in the Civil War*, p. 266.

75. Artha Bray, Jr. to Mother, September 25, 1862, Danville, VA, in Jackson, *Surry County Soldiers in the Civil War*, p. 268.

76. Jordan, *North Carolina Troops*, Vol. 9, p. 227.

77. John Thomas Conrad, Camp Lee, near Winchester, Virginia, November 21, 1862, in O'Daniel, p. 318.

78. Thomas G. Scott to William Harding, Petersburg, Virginia, August 27, 1864, in Casstevens, *The Civil War and Yadkin County*, pp. 128–129.

79. Harding family tradition.

80. Carl C. Hoots, *Cemeteries of Yadkin County, North Carolina* (Spartanburg, SC: The Reprint Co., 1985).

81. Information from Miss Eugenia Poindexter, cited in Casstevens, *The Civil War and Yadkin County*, p. 66.

82. John Thomas Conrad, 1st North Carolina Cavalry Camp near Balfield, Virginia, January 20, 1865 [1863?], O'Daniel, p. 323.

83. John Thomas Conrad, Wilmington, October 23, 1861, in O'Daniel, p. 287.

84. John Thomas Conrad, Wilmington, October 15, 1861, in O'Daniel, p. 285.

85. Calvin Holcomb to Respected Brother, March the 10 [1862], in Casstevens, *Heritage of Yadkin County*, Vol. 1, p. 144.

86. A picture of such cross-written letter can be seen in O'Daniel, p. 306.

87. Casstevens, *The Civil War and Yadkin County*, p. 224; Jordan, *North Carolina Troops* Vol. 8, pp. 212–213.

88. Calvin Holcomb to My Dear Brother, College Hospital, Lynchburg, VA, July 7, 1864, in Casstevens, *Heritage of Yadkin County*, Vol. 1, p. 144.

89. Casstevens, *The Civil War and Yadkin County*, p. 224; Jordan, *North Carolina Troops*, Vol. 8, p. 212.

90. William M. Norman to his wife, Letitia, January 1, 1865, Johnson's Island, Ohio, in Jackson, *Surry County Soldiers in the Civil War*, p. 255.

91. John L.(T.) Holcomb to Dear Brother, July 26, 1863, in Casstevens, *Heritage of Yadkin County*, Vol. 1, p. 144.

92. James Collins to brother Ambrose Collins, May 9, 1862, Rapidan Station, Culpeper County, VA, in Jackson, *Surry County Soldiers in the Civil War*, p. 289.

93. John Thomas Conrad, Wilmington, October 15, 1861, in O'Daniel, pp. 285, 291–292. See copy of furlough, signed by John H. Kinyoun, Captain of Company F, 28th Regiment, on page 292 of above book.

94. John Thomas Conrad, April 26, 1862, Kinston, NC, in O'Daniel, p. 294.

95. John Thomas Conrad, May 8, 1862, Orange County, Virginia, in O'Daniel, p. 298.

96. C.M. Holcomb to My Dear Brother [Bloom Holcomb], July 23, 1864, College Hospital, Lynchburg, VA, in Casstevens, *Heritage of Yadkin County*, Vol. 1, p. 144.

97. Gibbon, Diary, p. 30.

Chapter 4

1. Allen Paul Speer, *Voices from Cemetery Hill* (Johnson City, TN: Overmountain Press, 1997), pp. 54–55.

2. Samuel S. Harding to Father, Wilmington, January 23, 1862, in Harding Family Letters.

3. Jordan, *North Carolina Troops,* Vol. 8, p. 99.

4. Civil War Sites Advisory Commission Report on the Nation's Civil War Battlefields (CWSAC), "New Bern," NC003, online www.cr.nps.gov/hps/abpp/battles/tvii.htm. Henceforth cited as CWSAC plus the reference number.

5. Gibbon, Diary, p. 10.

6. Gibbon, Diary, p. 10.

7. "Record of the War Service of W.F. Swaringen, Confederate Veteran," *Confederate Veteran* Papers, Duke University, cited in McDaid, p. 40.

8. Gibbon, Diary, p. 10.

9. *Ibid.*

10. William Groves Morris, Company H, 37th Regiment, Kinston, North Carolina, March 17, 1862, in Hazel Morris Ritch Lawing, *The Life and Letters of Colonel William G. Morris (1825–1918),* (Privately published typescript, 1935–1937), p. 30.

11. Glenn Dedmondt, *The Flags of Civil War North Carolina* (Gretna, LA: Pelican Publishing, 2003), p. 121.

12. Report of Brig. Gen. L. O'B. Branch, March 26, 1862, O.R. Ser. I, Vol. 9, pp. 242–243.

13. James H. Lane, "History of Lane's North Carolina Brigade," *Southern Historical Society Papers,* Vol. 7 (1879): p. 513. Hereinafter cited as Lane, "History of Brigade," SHP.

14. Jordan, *North Carolina Troops,* Vol. 8, p. 99.

15. Special Orders, No. 224, November 16, 1861, and Special Orders, No. 272, December 21, 1861, O.R., Ser. I, Vol. 4, pp. 700, 715.

16. McDaid, p. 30.

17. North Carolina *Standard,* November 23, 1861.

18. Gibbon, Diary, p. 11; Jordan, *North Carolina Troops,* Vol. 8, p. 111.

19. Lane, "The Twenty-Eighth North Carolina," in Clark, *North Carolina Regiments,* Vol. 2, p.469.

20. Gibbon, Diary, p. 11; Jordan, *North Carolina Troops,* Vol. 8, p. 111.

21. Gibbon, Diary, p. 11.

22. William A. Tesh to Father, Hanover Station, VA, May 23, 1862, Tesh Papers, Duke Univ.

23. Gibbon, Diary, p. 11; George Burgwin Johnston Diary, North Carolina Department of Archives and History; McDaid, p. 57.

24. C.S. McCurdy to A. Boger, Hanover County, VA, May 24, 1862, Caleb Shive McCurdy Papers, Perkins Library, Duke University, Durham, North Carolina.

25. William A. Tesh to Father, Hanover Court House, May 25, 1862, Tesh Papers, Duke Univ.

26. *Ibid.*

27. Boatner, p. 373.

28. CWSAC #VA013.

29. McDaid, p. 58.

30. L. O'B. Branch to Major Richard C. Morgan, May 29, 1862, in Hardy, *The Battle at Hanover Court House,* p. 149.

31. Lawrence O'B. Branch to Joseph E. Johnston, May 23 and 24, 1862, Lawrence O'B. Branch Letter Book, Duke University, Durham, North Carolina, cited in McDaid, p. 59.

32. McDaid, p. 58.

33. Alexander S. Webb, *The Peninsula* (New York: Scribner's, 1881), p. 93, cited in McDaid, p. 58.

34. Lane, "History of Brigade, No. 4, SHP, No. 3, Vol. 8 (March 1880): p. 103.

35. Jordan, *North Carolina Troops* Vol. 8, 113.

36. Gibbon, Diary, p. 11.

37. Calvin D. Cowles, comp. *Atlas to Accompany the Official Records of the Union and Confederate Armies* (Washington: Government Printing Office, 1891–1895; reprint as *The Official Military Atlas of the Civil War* New York: The Fairfax Press, 1983), Plate XXI, No. 9. Hereafter cited as Cowles, OMA.

38. Hardy, p. 53.

39. Report of Colonel James H. Lane, Twenty-eighth North Carolina Infantry, of engagement May 27, O.R., Ser, I, Vol. 11, Pt. I, pp. 743–745, quoted in Boatner, pp. 99–100.

40. Lane, O.R., Ser, I, Vol. 11, Pt. I, pp. 743–745.

41. *Ibid.*

42. *Ibid.*

43. George Burgwin Johnston Diary, North Carolina Department of Archives and History;
Colonel James H. Lane, report of action, O.R., Ser. I, Vol. 11, Pt. 1, pp. 743–744, cited in McDaid, p.59.

44. William G. Morris to Dear Companion, 3 miles from Richmond, May 30, 1862, in Lawing, p. 49.

45. Lane, O.R. Series I, Vol. 11, Pt.1, pp. 743–745, quoted in Boatner, pp. 99–100.

46. Lane, O.R. Series I, Vol. 11, Pt.1, pp. 743–745.

47. *Ibid.*

48. *Ibid.*

49. *Ibid.*

50. *Ibid.*

51. Gibbon, Diary, p. 12.

52. Speer, pp. 46–58.

53. *Ibid.*

54. Gibbon, Diary, p. 12.

55. Speer, pp. 49–50.

56. Gibbon, Diary, p. 12.

57. Speer, pp. 50, 52.

58. *Ibid.,* pp. 52–53.

59. *Ibid.,* p. 53.

60. *Ibid.,* pp. 53–54.

61. *Ibid.,* p. 54.

62. *Ibid.*

63. *Ibid.,* pp. 54–55.

64. *Ibid.,* pp. 56–57.

65. *Ibid.*

66. Gibbon, Diary, p. 14.

67. *Ibid.,* pp. 14–15.

68. William G. Morris to Dear Companion, 3 miles from Richmond, May 30, 1862, in Lawing, p. 49.

69. Gibbon, Diary, p. 15.

70. Speer, pp. 58–59.

71. *Ibid.,* pp. 59–60.

72. *Ibid,* p. 60.

73. *Ibid.,* pp. 60–61.

74. *Ibid.,* pp. 61–62.

75. *Ibid.,* pp. 64–65.

76. For more information on where the captive soldiers of the 28th North Carolina and other North Carolina regiments were sent, see various volumes of Manarin and Jordan's *North Carolina Troops, 1861–1865: A Roster.*

77. George B. McClellan, to Brig. Gen. L. Thomas, June 10, 1862, O.R., Ser. II, Vol. 3, p. 670.

78. *Ibid.*

79. William G. Morris to Dear Companion, May 30, 1862, in Lawing, p. 49.

80. Jordan, *North Carolina Troops,* Vol. 8, p. 100.

81. Boatner, p. 373.

82. Jordan, *North Carolina Troops,* Vol. 8, p. 100.

83. Casualty figures for the 18th and the 28th can be found in Box 158, Governor Henry T. Clark's Papers. Casualties for the 37th Regiment are in Box 78 of the Miscellaneous Records of the Adjutant General's Office. Both collections are in the North Carolina Department of Archives and History, Raleigh, North Carolina. These figures were cited in McDaid, p. 62.

84. The Branch Brigade casualties were determined by adding those reported in O.R., Ser. I, Vol. 11, Pt. 1, p. 742 to the losses of the 28th Regiment found in Box 158, of the Governor's Papers, North Carolina Department of Archives and History, and compiled by McDaid, p. 62.

85. Boatner, p. 373.

86. Jordan, *North Carolina Troops,* Vol. 8, pp. 110–231.

87. *Ibid.,* p. 100.

88. John Thomas Conrad, June 6, 1862, in O'Daniel, pp. 302–303.

89. *Ibid.*

90. John Thomas Conrad, June 24, 1862, in O'Daniel, pp. 305–306

91. William G. Morris to wife, May 30, 1862, William Groves Morris Papers, UNC Chapel Hill, cited in Hardy, p. 129.

92. Richmond *Examiner,* quoted in the North Carolina *Standard,* June 4, 1862.

93. Hardy, p. 129.

94. Branch to Morgan, cited in Hardy, p. 151.

95. Boatner, p. 373.

96. Hardy, p. 129.

97. R.E. Lee to Brig. Gen. L. O'B. Branch, June 3, 1862, O.R., Ser. I, Vol. 11, Pt. 1, p. 743.

98. Lawrence O'B. Branch to Henry T. Clark, June 6, 1862, Governor Clark's Papers, Box 158, North Carolina Department of Archives and History, cited in McDaid, p. 65.

99. Wilmington *Daily Journal,* June 17, 1862, cited in Mc-Daid, p. 64.

100. McDaid, pp. 64–65.

Chapter 5

1. John Thomas Conrad, June 24, 1862, in O'Daniel, pp. 308–309.

2. William A. Tesh to Father, Richmond, VA, June 4, 1862, Tesh Papers, Duke Univ.

3. William A. Tesh to Father, Richmond, VA, June 8, 1862, Tesh Papers, Duke Univ.

4. Boatner, pp. 731–732.

5. "Seven Days' Battles," O.R., Ser. I, Vol. 11, Pt. 2, p. 487.

6. CWSAC, #VA015.

7. James H. Lane, O.R., Series I, Vol. 11, Pt. II, p. 892; Jordan, *North Carolina Troops,* Vol. 8, p. 100.

8. James H. Lane, O.R., Series I, Vol. 11, Pt. II, p. 892; Jordan, *North Carolina Troops,* Vol. 8, p. 100.

9. "Extracts from General A.P. Hill's Report," in Lane, "History of Brigade," SHP Vol. 8 (March 1880): p. 100.

10. CWSAC, #VA016.

11. James H. Lane, O.R., Series I, Vol. 11, Pt. II, p. 892; Jordan, *North Carolina Troops,* Vol. 8, p. 100.

12. Boatner, p. 321; CWSAC, #VA016.

13. CWSAC, #VA016.

14. Boatner, p. 321.

15. "Extracts from General Lee's Report," in Lane, "History of Brigade," SHP Vol. 8 (March 1880): p. 101.

16. *Ibid.,* pp. 101–02.

17. McDaid, p. 74.

18. "Extracts from General A.P. Hill's Report," in Lane, "History of Brigade," SHP Vol. 8 (March 1880): p. 102.

19. James H. Lane, O.R., Series I, Vol. 11, Pt. II, p. 892–93; Jordan, *North Carolina Troops,* Vol. 8, pp. 100–101.

20. *Ibid.*

21. See Appendix II.

22. Jordan, *North Carolina Troops,* Vol. 8, p. 210.

23. W.A. Tesh to Father, July 4, 1862, Tesh Papers, Duke Univ.

24. John Thomas Conrad, June 24, 1862, in O'Daniel, pp. 308–309.

25. *Ibid.*

26. *Ibid.,* p. 309.

27. *Ibid.,* pp. 310–311.

28. *Ibid.*

29. *Ibid.*

30. Reminiscences of Noah Collins, pp. 24–25, in Isaac Spencer London Collection, North Carolina Department of Archives and History, cited in McDaid, p. 77.

31. *Ibid.*

32. Boatner, p. 501.

33. McDaid, p. 77.

34. CWSAC, #VA020a.

35. Boatner, pp. 915–916.

36. McDaid, p. 78.

37. CWSAC, #VA020a, #VA020b.

38. Boatner, pp. 915–916.

39. CWSAC, #VA020a, #VA020b.

40. Boatner, pp. 915–916.

41. "Extracts from General A.P. Hill's Report," in Lane, "History of Brigade," SHP Vol. 8 (March 1880): p. 101.

42. James H. Lane, O.R., Ser. I, Vol. 11, Pt. II, p. 893; Jordan, *North Carolina Troops,* Vol. 8, p. 101.

43. James H. Lane, "History of Brigade," SHP Vol. 8 (March 1880): p. 99.

44. Hezekiah Collins to brother A.R. Collins, July 3, 1862, Brigade Camp 28th Reg. N.C. Troops, near Richmond, in Jackson, *Surry County Soldiers in the Civil War,* p. 291.

45. McDaid, p. 80.

46. "Extracts from General Lee's Report," in Lane, "History of Brigade," SHP Vol. 8 (March 1880): p. 101.

47. Boatner, p. 507.

48. CWSAC, #VA021.

49. "Extracts from General A.P. Hill's Report," in Lane, "History of Brigade," SHP Vol. 8 (March 1880): p. 101.

50. McDaid, p. 80.

51. Jordan, *North Carolina Troops,* Vol. 8, p. 101.

52. *Ibid.*

53. William F. Fox, *Regimental Losses in the America Civil War* (1898; reprint Dayton, Ohio: Morningside Bookshop, 1985), p. 564; Jordan, *North Carolina Troops,* Vol. 8, p. 101.

54. James H. Lane, "Report of Col. James H. Lane, Twenty-Eighty North Carolina Infantry of the Battles of Mechanicsville, Gaines' Mill, Frazier's Farm (Nelson's Farm, or Glendale) and Malvern Hill, O.R., Ser. I, Vol. 11, Pt. II, pp. 892–893; William M. Barbour, "Report of Col. William M. Barbour, Thirty-Seventh Infantry of the Battles of Mechanicsville, Gaines' Mill, Frazier's Farm (Nelson's Farm, or Glendale) and Malvern Hill," O.R., Ser. I, Vol. 11, Pt. 2, p. 896; "Return of Casualties in the Confederate Forces During the Seven-Days' Battles, June 25–July 1, 1862," O.R., Ser. I, Vol. 11, Pt. II, p. 982; Clark, *North Carolina Regiments,* Vol. I, p. 369.

55. James H. Lane, O.R., Ser. I, Vol. 11, Pt. II, p. 894.

56. Jordan, *North Carolina Troops,* Vol. 8, p. 112.

57. James H. Lane, O.R., Ser. I, Vol. 11, Pt. II, p. 894; Lane, "History of Brigade," SHP, Vol. 8 (March 1880): p. 99.

58. L. O'B. Branch, "Report of Brigadier General Branch," SHP Vol. 8 (January 1880): p. 6.

59. Jordan, *North Carolina Troops,* Vol. 8, p. 101.

60. "Organization of the Army of Northern Virginia, July 23, 1862," O.R., Ser. I, Vol. 2, Pt. III, pp. 648–649.

61. McDaid, p. 80.

62. *Ibid.,* pp. 80–81.

63. "List of Casualties in the Army of Northern Virginia in the fights before Richmond commencing June 26, 1862, and ending July 1, 1862," O.R., Ser. I, Vol. 11, Pt. II, p. 503.

64. "Return of Casualties in the Confederate forces during Seven-Days' Battles, June 25–July 1, 1862," O.R., Ser. I, Vol. 11, Pt. II, p. 982.

65. James H. Lane, "History of Brigade," SHP Vol. 8 (March 1880), pp. 99–100.

66. "Returns of Casualties in the Confederate forces during Seven-Days' Battles, June 25–July 1, 1862," O.R., Ser. I, Vol. 11, Pt. II, pp. 973–984.

67. Little, "Co. C," p. 166.

68. W.A. Tesh to Father, July 4, 1862, Tesh Papers, Duke Univ.

69. Joseph Saunders to Laura L. Saunders, July 13, 1862, Leonidas C. Glenn Collection, SHC.

70. Lane, "History of Brigade," SHP, Vol. 8 (March 1880): p. 104.

71. L. O'B Branch, "General Order No. 6," July 20, 1862, in Lane, "History of Brigade," SHP Vol. 8 (March 1880): pp. 102–104.

Chapter 6

1. George W. Hahn, ed., *The Catawba Soldier in the Civil War* (Hickory, NC: Clay Printing, 1911), pp. 167.
2. CWSAC #VA022.
3. "Report of Brig. Gen. James H. Lane, C.S. Army, commanding Fourth Brigade," O.R., Ser. I, Vol. 12, Pt. II, p. 220.
4. *Ibid.,* p. 220.
5. R.E. Lee, "Battle of Cedar Run," O.R., Ser. I, Vol. 12, Pt. II, pp. 177–179.
6. Hahn, p. 167.
7. R.E. Lee, "Battle of Cedar Run," O.R., Ser. I, Vol. 12, Pt. II, p. 179.
8. "Report of Brig. Gen. L. O'B. Branch," August 18, 1862, O.R. Ser. I, Vol. 12, Pt. 22, p. 222.
9. "Report of Surg. Lafayette Guild, C.S. Army, Medical Director, of the killed and wounded," O.R., Ser. I, Vol. 12, Pt. II, pp. 179–180.
10. "Report of Brig. Gen. L. O'B. Branch," August 18, 1862, O.R. Ser. I, Vol. 12, Pt. 22, p. 222.
11. "Extracts from General Branch's journal, covering period August 6–13 [1862], O.R., Ser. I, Vol. 12, Pt. II, p. 223; McDaid, p. 95.
12. James H. Lane, "History of the 28th North Carolina Infantry, SHP, Vol. 24 (1896), p. 330.
13. "Extracts from General Branch's journal, covering period August 6–13 [1862], O.R., Ser. I, Vol. 12, Pt. II, p. 223.
14. McDaid, p. 98.
15. *Ibid.,* pp. 98–99.
16. *Ibid.,* p. 99.
17. CWSAC #VA024.
18. Boatner, p. 103.
19. Clarence Allen C. Redwood, "Jackson's 'Foot-Cavalry' at Second Bull Run," in Robert U. Johnson and Clarence C. Buel, eds., *Battles and Leaders of the Civil War,* Vol. II (New York: Thomas Yoseloff, 1956), p. 532; Clark, *North Carolina Regiments,* Vol. 2, p. 665.
20. James H. Lane, "History of Lane's North Carolina Brigade," SHP, Vol. 8, No. 6 (June 1880): p. 248; James Sidney Harris, *Historical Sketches of the Seventh Regiment North Carolina Troops* (Mooresville, NC: Mooresville Printing, 1893), p. 18, cited in McDaid, p. 101.
21. Jordan, *North Carolina Troops,* Vol. I, p. 102.
22. John F. Shaffner Speech, Vol. 7, Fries–Shaffner Papers, Southern Historical Collection University of North Carolina at Chapel Hill; cited in McDaid, pp. 101–102.
23. *Ibid.*
24. CWSAC #VA026.
25. Brigadier General J.H. Lane, "Twenty-Eighth Regiment," in Clark, *NC Regiments,* Vol. II, p. 473.
26. Boatner, p. 103.
27. "Report of Brig. Gen. James H. Lane, C.S. Army, commanding Branch's Brigade, of operations August 24–Sept 2" [1862], O.R., Ser. I, Vol. 12, Pt. II, pp. 675–677; Jordan, *North Carolina Troops,* Vol. 8, p. 201–103; Brigadier General James H. Lane, "History of Lane's North Carolina Brigade," SHP, Vol. 8, No. 4 (April 1880): pp. 152–154.
28. *Ibid.*
29. Lane, O.R., Ser. I, Vol. 12, Pt. II, p. 676.
30. Lane, "History of Lane's North Carolina Brigade," SHP Vol. 8, No. 4 (April 1880): p. 153.
31. Lane, "History of Lane's Brigade, SHP, Vol. 10 No. 6 (June): p. 242; O.R., Ser. I, Vol. 12, Pt. II, p. 681.
32. Lane, O.R., Ser. I, Vol. 12, Pt. II, p. 676.
33. *Ibid.*
34. McDaid, p. 106.
35. Lane, O.R., Ser. I, Vol. 12, Pt. II, p. 676.

36. John F. Shaffner to Carrie Fries, Sept. 7, 1862, Fries–Shaffner Papers, SHC, cited in McDaid, p. 107.
37. Lane, O.R., Ser. I, Vol. 12, Pt. II, p. 677; Jordan, *North Carolina Troops,* Vol. 8, pp. 102–103.
38. J.P. Little, "Company C, 28th Regiment Volunteers," in Hahn, *The Catawba Soldier of the Civil War,* p. 167. Hereinafter cited as Little, "Co. C."
39. Lane, "Twenty-Eighth Regiment," in Clark, *North Carolina Regiments,* Vol. 2, p. 473; Jordan, *North Carolina Troops,* Vol. 8, p. 103.
40. Lane, O.R., Ser. I, Vol. 12, Pt. II, p. 677.
41. "Report of Surg. Lafayette Guild, C.S. Army, Medical Director," O.R., Ser. I, Vol. 12, Pt. II, p. 562.
42. Harris, *Historical Sketches,* p. 20, cited in McDaid, p. 108.
43. R.E. Lee., "Reports of General Robert E. Lee, of operations August 13–September 2 [1862], O. R., Ser. I, Vol. 12, Pt. 2, p. 556.
44. Lane, Summer Campaign of 1862 — Extract from General Jackson's report, in "History of Lane's North Carolina Brigade," SHP, Vol. 8, Nos. 6 and 7 (June, July 1880): p. 242.
45. Harris, *Historical Sketches,* p. 21, cited in McDaid, p. 109.
46. CWSAC, #VA027.
47. Lane, O.R., Ser. I, Vol. 12, Pt. II, p. 677; Jordan, *North Carolina Troops,* Vol. 8, p. 103.
48. *Ibid;* Lane, "Twenty-Eighth regiment," in Clark, *North Carolina Regiments,* Vol. 2, p. 473.
49. *Ibid.*
50. *Ibid.*
51. Gibbon, Diary, p. 18.
52. Lane, "History of Lane's Brigade," SHP, Vol. 10, No. 6 (June 1882): p. 242.
53. Jordan, *North Carolina Troops,* Vol. 8, p. 103.

Chapter 7

1. "Report of Brig. Gen. James H. Lane, C.S. Army, commanding Branch's Brigade, of operations September 2–20," O.R., Ser. I, Vol. 19, Pt. I, pp. 985–986.
2. Dennis E. Frye, "Stonewall's Brilliant Victory: The Siege & Capture of Harpers Ferry," online www.nps.gov/hafe/jackson.htm; "Harpers Ferry History," online www.nps.gov/hafe/history.htm.
3. *Ibid.*
4. *Ibid.*
5. Jordan, *North Carolina Troops,* Vol. 8, p. 103.
6. Boatner, p. 17.
7. CWSAC #WV010.
8. McDaid, p. 113.
9. Jordan, *North Carolina Troops,* Vol. 8, p. 103.
10. Gibbon, Diary, p. 18.
11. *Ibid.*
12. Jordan, *North Carolina Troops,* Vol. 8, p. 103.
13. Lane, "History of Brigade," SHP, Vol. 8 (May 1880): p. 193.
14. Jordan, *North Carolina Troops,* Vol. 8, p. 103.
15. "Extracts from General A.P. Hill's Report," in Lane, "History of Brigade," SHP, Vol. 8 (May 1880): p. 200.
16. *Ibid.*
17. Jordan, *North Carolina Troops,* Vol. 8, p. 103.
18. Lane, "History of Brigade," SHP, Vol. 8 (May 1880): p. 193.
19. Gibbon, Diary, p. 19.
20. Dennis E. Frye, "Stonewall's Brilliant Victory: The Siege & Capture of Harpers Ferry," online www.nps.gov/hafe/jackson.htm.
21. William Groves Morris to Dear Companion and family, Frederick City, Maryland, September 23, 1862, in Lawing, p. 64.
22. Little, "Co. C.," p. 167.
23. Dennis E. Frye, "Stonewall's Brilliant Victory: The

Siege & Capture of Harpers Ferry," online www.nps.gov/hafe/jackson.htm

24. "Report of Brig. Gen. James H. Lane, commanding Branch's Brigade, of operations September 2–20," November 14, 1862, O.R., Ser. I, Vol. 19, Pt. I, p. 985.

25. Jordan, *North Carolina Troops,* Vol. 8, p. 103.

26. CWSAC #MD003.

27. "Extracts from General A.P. Hill's Report," in Lane, "History of Brigade," SHP, Vol. 8 (May 1880): p. 200.

28. A.P. Mason, Special Orders, No. 234, by Robert E. Lee, November 6, 1862, O.R., Ser. I, Vol. 19, Pt. II, pp. 698–699.

29. Clark, *North Carolina Regiments,* Vol. 2, p. 33.

30. "Extracts from General A.P. Hill's Report," in Lane, "History of Brigade," SHP, Vol. 8 (May 1880): p. 200.

31. Gibbon, Diary, p. 19.

32. Clark, *North Carolina Regiments,* Vol. 2, pp. 553–554.

33. James Henry Lane, O.R., Ser. I, Vol. 19, Pt. I, pp. 985–986.

34. Lane, "History of Brigade," SHP, Vol. 8 (May 1880): p. 194; James Henry Lane, O.R., Ser. I, Vol. 19, Pt. I, pp. 985–986.

35. William Groves Morris to Dear Companion and family, Frederick City, Maryland, September 23, 1862, in Lawing, p. 64.

36. "Extracts from General A.P. Hill's Report," in Lane, "History of Brigade," SHP, Vol. 8 (May 1880): pp. 200–201.

37. Thomas L. Livermore, *Numbers and Losses in the Civil War in America 1861–65* (Boston: Houghton Mifflin, 1901), pp. 92–93, cited in Boatner, *The Civil War Dictionary,* p. 21.

38. Lane, O.R., Ser. I, Vol. 19, Pt. I, p. 986; Lane, "History of Lane's North Carolina Brigade," SHP, Vol. 8 (May 1880): p. 247.

39. A.P. Mason, Special Orders, No. 234, by Robert E. Lee, November 6, 1862, O.R., Ser. I, Vol. 19, Pt. II, pp. 698–699.

40. Boatner, p. 471.

41. *Ibid.*

42. CWSAC, #WV016.

43. Jordan, *North Carolina Troops,* Vol. 8, pp. 103–104.

44. Andrew J. Profitt to William Profitt, September 22, 1862, Profitt Family Papers, SHC, UNC-CH.

45. "Extract from Brigadier General Archer's Report," in Lane, "History of Brigade," SHP, Vol. 8 (May 1880): p. 196.

46. John F. Shaffner Speech, Vol. 7, Fries–Shaffner Papers, SHC, UNC-CH

47. Lane, O.R., Ser. I, Vol. 19, Pt. I, p. 986; Lane, "History of Brigade," SHP, Vol. 8 (May 1880): p. 195.

48. Little, "Co. C," pp. 167–168.

49. Lane, O.R., Ser. I, Vol. 19, Pt. I, p. 986.

50. Jordan, *North Carolina Troops,* Vol. 8, pp. 103–104.

51. CWSAC, #WV016.

52. Gibbon, Diary, p. 20

53. *Ibid.*

54. Little, "Co. C," p. 168.

55. Gibbon, Diary, p. 20.

56. Lane, "Twenty-Eighth Regiment," in Clark, *North Carolina Regiments,* Vol. 2, pp. 474–475.

57. W.A. Tesh to Father and Mother, Camp near Fredericksburg, VA, December 6, 1862, Tesh Papers, Duke Univ.

58. "Casualties from Cedar Run to Shepherdstown," in Lane, "History of Brigade," SHP (June and July 1880): p. 247.

59. Gibbon, Diary, p. 20.

60. CWSAC #VA028.

61. Jordan, *North Carolina Troops,* Vol. 8, pp. 103–104.

62. Boatner, diagram, page 312.

63. "Report of Maj. Gen. Ambrose P. Hill, C.S. Army, commanding A.P. Hill's division, January 1, 1863," O.R., Ser. I, Vol. 21, p. 645.

64. Troop positions map in Speer, *Voices form Cemetery Hill,* p. 87.

65. "Report of Maj. Gen. Ambrose P. Hill, C.S. Army, commanding A.P. Hill's division," O.R., Ser. I, Vol. 21, p. 645.

66. James H. Lane, Ser. I, Vol. 21, pp. 653–654.

67. Clark, *North Carolina Regiments,* Vol. 2, p. 556.

68. James H. Lane, "Incidents of Individual Gallantry," Military Collection, North Carolina Department of Archives and History, Raleigh, North Carolina, cited by McDaid, p. 154; Jordan, *North Carolina Troops* Vol. 8, p. 148.

69. "Report of Brig. Gen. James H. Lane," O.R., Ser. I, Vol. 21, pp. 653–655. Also quoted in Jordan, *North Carolina Troops,* Vol. 8, pp. 104–105.

70. "Report of Maj. Gen. Ambrose P. Hill, C.S. Army, commanding A.P. Hill's division," O.R., Ser. I, Vol. 21, p. 646.

71. "Report of Maj. Gen. Ambrose P. Hill, C.S. Army, commanding A.P. Hill's division," O.R., Ser. I, Vol. 21, O.R., Ser. I, Vol. 21, p. 646.

72. McDaid, p. 156.

73. "Report of Maj. Gen. Ambrose P. Hill, C.S. Army, commanding A.P. Hill's division," O.R., Ser. I, Vol. 21, p. 646.

74. McDaid, footnote 18, p. 362. McDaid cites James Fritz James Caldwell, *History of a Brigade of South Carolinians* (Philadelphia, PA: King & Baird Printers, 1866), p. 59; Branch Spalding, "Jackson's Fredericksburg Tactics," *Military Analysis of the Civil War* (Millwood, NY: Kraus–Thompson Organization Ltd., 1977), pp. 67–70; and Jackson's report in O.R., Ser. I, Vol. 21, p. 632.

75. Jordan, *North Carolina Troops,* Vol. 8, p. 105.

76. Boatner, *The Civil War Dictionary,* diagram, page 313.

77. "Report of Maj. Gen. Ambrose P. Hill, C.S. Army, commanding A.P. Hill's division," O.R., Ser. I, Vol. 21, p. 648.

78. L. Guild, Surgeon and Medical Director, Army of Northern Virginia, "List of killed and wounded in the battle of Fredericksburg, transmitted by Medical Director L. Guild, January 19, 1863," O.R., Ser. I, Vol. 21, pp. 558–562.

79. Jordan, *North Carolina Troops,* Vol. 8, p. 105.

80. Norman, *A Portion of My Life,* p. 160.

81. Artha Bray, Jr. to Brother, December 20, 1862, Fredericksburg, VA, in Jackson, *Surry County Soldiers in the Civil War,* p. 269.

82. Little, "Co. C," p. 168.

83. R.E. Lee, O.R., Ser. I, Vol. 21, p. 562.

84. Little, "Co. C," p. 168.

85. "Report of Brig. Gen. James H. Lane," O.R., Ser. I, Vol. 21, pp. 655–656.

86. Lane, "Twenty-Eighth Regiment," in Clark, *North Carolina Regiments,* Vol. 2, p. 475.

87. Speer, *Voices from Cemetery Hill,* p. 86.

88. Clark, *History of the Several Regiments,* Vol. II, p. 475.

89. Gibbon, Diary, p. 20.

90. Norman, *A Portion of My Life,* p. 160.

91. *Ibid.,* pp. 158–159.

92. *Ibid.,* p. 159.

93. Gibbon, Diary, p. 20.

94. Jordan, *North Carolina Troops,* Vol. 8, p. 105.

95. John Thomas Conrad, Camp 28th North Carolina Volunteers, January 11, 1863, in O'Daniel, *Kinfolk of Jacob Conrad,* p. 322.

96. S.S. Harding to Mother, from Camp Gregg, VA, January 24, 1863, Harding Family Papers.

97. *Ibid.*

98. "List of Casualties in Lane's Brigade, in Campaign of 1861," in Lane, "History of Brigade," SHP (June and July, 1880): p .403.

99. Gibbon, Diary, pp. 20–21.

100. James H. Lane, "Campaign of 1863," in Lane, "History of Brigade," SHP, Vol. 8 (June and July 1880): p. 489.

Chapter 8

1. Lane, "The Branch-Lane Brigade," in Clark, *North Carolina Regiments,* Vol. 4, p. 471; McDaid, p. 1.

2. W. A. Tesh to Mother and Father, Camp near Port Royal, January 6, 1863, Tesh Papers, Duke Univ.

3. *Ibid.*

4. CWSAC #VA032.

5. "The Chancellorsville Campaign," O. R., Ser. I, Vol. 21, p. 791.

6. Jordan, *North Carolina Troops*, Vol. 8, p. 105; Report of Col. Samuel D. Lowe, Twenty-eighth North Carolina Infantry, May 8, 1863, O. R., Ser. I, Vol. 25, Pt. 1, pp. 920–921.

7. James H. Lane, "Campaign 1863," in Lane, "History of Brigade," SHP (June and July 1880), p. 489.

8. Speer, pp. 98–100.

9. Jordan, *North Carolina Troops*, Vol. 8, p. 105; Lowe, O. R., Ser. I, Vol. 25, Pt. I, pp. 920–921.

10. Lane, "Campaign 1863," in Lane, "History of Brigade," SHP (June and July 1880), p. 489

11. Octavius A. Wiggins, speech on the Battle of Chancellorsville delivered to the Daughters of the Confederacy, 1895, Box 75, Folder 1, Military Collection, North Carolina Department of Archives and History, cited in McDaid, p. 711–173.

12. Jordan, *North Carolina Troops*, Vol. 8, p. 105; Lowe, O. R., Ser. I, Vol. 25, Pt. 1, pp. 920–921.

13. Lane, "History of Brigade," SHP (June and July 1880), p. 489

14. Boatner, p. 370; James H. Lane to Col. Wm. G. Morris, Auburn, Ala., Dec. 14, 1894, in Lawing, p. 129.

15. "Lane's Account of Chancellorsville to Augustus C. Hamlin, 1892," in James H. Lane papers, Auburn Univ., online at http://www.lib.auburn.edu/archive/find-aid/501/ff109.htm; "How Stonewall Jackson Met His Death: An Interesting and Authentic Statement from General James H. Lane," *Richmond Dispatch*, January 1, 1873, in Lane, "History of Brigade," SHP, Vol. 8 (1880), pp. 493–496.

16. Major General. Henry W. Slocum, XII Army Corps, May 17, 1863, O.R., Ser. I, Vol. 25, Pt. I, p.670.

17. *Ibid.*

18. *Ibid.*

19. Lane, "History of Brigade," SHP, Vol. 8 (1880), p. 495; Lowe, O. R., Ser. I, Vol. 25, Pt. 1, 922.

20. Frank Vanndiver, *Mighty Stonewall* (New York: McGraw-Hill, 1957), pp. 477–478.

21. Clark, *North Carolina Regiments*, Vol. 2, p. 100.

22. Clark, *North Carolina Regiments*, Vol. 5, p. 95; Freeman, *Lee's Lieutenants*, Vol. II, p. 567.

23. Clark, *North Carolina Regiments*, Vol. 2, p. 100.

24. Dr. Hunter McGuire, Medical Director of Jackson's Corps, "The Death of Stonewall Jackson," SHP, Vol.14 (January–December 1886), pp. 156–157.

25. Clark, *North Carolina Regiments*, Vol. 2, p. 38.

26. McDaid, p. 179.

27. Lane, "History of Brigade," SHP Vol. 8 (1880), pp. 490–491.

28. "How Stonewall Jackson Met His Death: An Interesting and Authentic Statement from General James H. Lane," *Richmond Dispatch*, January 1, 1873, in Lane, "History of Brigade," SHP, Vol. 8 (1880), pp. 493–496.

29. "Lane's Account of Chancellorsville to Augustus C. Hamlin, 1892," in James H. Lane papers, Auburn University archives, Auburn, AL, online at http://www.lib.auburn.edu/archive/find-aid/501/ff109.htm.

30. *Ibid.*, cited in McDaid, p. 179–180.

31. "Report of Brig. Gen. James H. Lane," May 11, 1863, O. R., Ser. I, Vol. 25, Pt. I, pp. 916; "Report of Capt. Joseph H. Saunders, Thirty-third North Carolina Infantry, May 9, 1863, O.R., Ser. I, Vol. 25, Pt. 1, 922–923.

32. Brigadier General David R. Birney, Commanding, 1st Division, U. S. Army, May 9, 1863, O. R., Series I, Vol. 25, Pt. I, p. 409; Report of Brig. Gen. J. H. Hobart Ward, Second Brigade, Fist Division, Third Army Corps, May 9, 1863, O. R., Series I, Vol. 25, Pt. I, p. 429.

33. Lane, "History of Brigade," SHP Vol. 8 (1880), pp. 490–491.

34. *Ibid.*; Lowe, O.R., Ser. I, Vol. 25, Pt. 1, p. 921.

35. "How Stonewall Jackson Met His Death: An Interesting and Authentic Statement from General James H. Lane,"

Richmond Dispatch, January 1, 1873, in Lane, "History of Brigade," SHP, Vol. 8 (1880), p. 495.

36. Report of Col. Samuel B. Hayman, Thirty-Seventh New York Infantry, commanding Third Brigade, May 8, 1863, O.R., Ser. I, Vol. 25, Pt. 1, p. 433; Col. Byron R. Pierce, Third Michigan Infantry, May 7, 1863, O.R., Ser. I, Vol. 25, Pt. 1, p. 437.

37. Maj. Gen. Henry W. Slocum, Twelfth Army Corps, May 17, 1863, O.R., Ser. I, Vol. 25, Pt. 1, p. 670; Reports of Brig. Gen. Henry Heth, commanding brigade and Ambrose P. Hill's divisions, respectively, May 17, 1863, O.R., Ser. I, Vol. 25, Pt. 1, p. 890.

38. McDaid, p. 182.

39. Lowe, O. R., Ser. I, Vol. 25, Pt. 1, pp. 920–921.

40. Lane, "History of Brigade," SHP (June and July 1880), p. 489

41. *Ibid.*

42. Wiggins, Speech on the Battle of Chancellorsville, North Carolina Department of Archives and History, cited in McDaid, p. 183.

43. Lowe, O. R., Ser. I, Vol. 25, Pt. 1, p. 921.

44. *Ibid.*

45. James H. Lane, "Reminiscences of Gallant Men in the Brigade," Box 71, Folder 49, Military Collection, North Carolina Department of Archives and History, cited. McDaid, p. 184.

46. Harris, *Historical Sketches*, p. 29; O. R., Ser. I, Vol. 25, Pt. I, pp. 893–894

47. Lowe, O. R., Ser. I, Vol. 25, Pt. 1, p. 921.

48. *Ibid.*, pp. 920–921.

49. Report of Col. Robert M. Mayo, Forty-seventh Virginia Infantry, May 14,1863, O. R., Ser. I, Vol. 25, Pt. I, p. 897.

50. William Groves Morris to James H. Lane, January 3, 1895, Folder 113, James H. Lane Papers, Auburn University, cited in McDaid, p. 186.

51. Jordan, *North Carolina Troops*, Vol. 8, p. 106.

52. Gibbon, Diary, p. 21.

53. John Macdonald, *Great Battles of the Civil War* (New York: Macmillan, 1988), p. 99.

54. James H. Lane, May 10, 1863, O. R., Ser., I, Vol. 25, Pt. I, p. 918; North Carolina *Standard*, May 20, 1863.

55. Lane, "History of Brigade," SHP, Vol. 8 (1880), p. 493.

56. Jordan, *North Carolina Troops*, Vol. 8, p. 106.

57. Lowe, O. R., Ser. I, Vol. 25, Pt. 1, pp. 920–922.

58. Lane, O. R., Ser., I, Vol. 25, Pt. I, p. 918; North Carolina *Standard*, May 20, 1863.

59. *Ibid.*

60. Francis M. Kennedy Diary, May 6, 1863, SHC, UNC-CH.

61. Speer, pp. 98–100.

62. *Ibid.*, p. 100.

63. Lane, "The Branch-Lane Brigade," in Clark, *North Carolina Regiments*, Vol. 4, p. 467.

64. Report of Surg. L. Guild, C. S. Army, Medical Director, of the killed and wounded" [in the Chancellorsville campaign], O.R., Ser. I, Vol. 25, Pt. I, p. 807.

65. "Thomas Jonathan Jackson (1824–1863)," online www.civilwarhome.com/jackbio.htm.

66. For the position of the brigades of the Light Division at the time of Lane's move across the Plank Road, see man in John Bigelow, *The Campaign of Chancellorsville* (New Haven, CT: Yale University Press, 1910), p. 22.

67. McDaid, p. 179.

68. Lane, O. R., Ser., I, Vol. 25, Pt. I, p. 917.

69. H. Heth to A. S. Pendleton, Headquarters Light Division, May 21, 1863, O.R. Ser. I, Vol. 25, Pt. 1, pp. 892–893; Lowe, Ser. I, Vol. 25, Pt. 1, pp. 920–921

70. "Lane's Account of Chancellorsville to Augustus C. Hamlin, 1892," in James H. Lane papers, Auburn Univ., online at http://www.lib.auburn.edu/archive/find-aid/501/ff109.htm.

71. Lane, "The Branch-Lane Brigade," in Clark, *North Carolina Regiments*, Vol. 4, p. 471.

72. Lane, "History of Brigade, SHP, Vol. I (1880), p. 492.

73. Lane, "History of Brigade, SHP, Vol. I (1880), p. 492.

74. Gibbon, Diary, p. 21.

75. Colonel Will M. Barbour, May 9, 1863, O. R., Ser. I, Vol. 25, Pt. I, p. 924.

76. "Report of Brig. Gen. James H. Lane, C. S. Army, Commanding brigade, Aug. 13, 1863, O. R., Ser. I, Vol. 27, Pt. 2, pp. 664–665.

77. Jordan, *North Carolina Troops*, Vol. 8, p. 106.

78. Bowman, p. 159.

79. Note by Lane at end of the article, "How Stonewall Jackson Met His Death: An Interesting and Authentic Statement from General James H. Lane," *Richmond Dispatch,* January 1, 1873, in Lane, "History of Brigade," SHP, Vol. 8 (1880), p. 496.

Chapter 9

1. Macdonald, *Great Battles of the Civil War,* p. 109.

2. "Report of Brig. Gen. James H. Lane, C.S. Army, Commanding brigade, Aug. 13, 1863, O.R., Ser. I, Vol. 27, Pt. II, pp. 664–665.

3. *Ibid.*

4. 28. CWSAC #PA002.

5. Lt. Gen. Ambrose P. Hill, November 1863, O.R., Ser. I, Vol. 28, Pt. II, p.607.

6. "The Gettysburg Campaign," O.R., Ser. I, Vol. 27, Pt. II, pp. 289–290.

7. "Report of Maj. Joseph A. Englehard, Assistant Adjutant-General, C.S. Army, of operations of Pender's Division," O.R., Ser. I, Vol. 28, Pt. II, p. 656.

8. Lane, "The Branch-Lane Brigade," in Clark, *North Carolina Regiments*, Vol. 4, pp. 467–468.

9. Boatner, p. 23.

10. "Report of Brig. Gen. James H. Lane, August 13, 1863," O.R., Ser. I, Vol. 27, Pt. II, pp. 664–665, quoted in Jordan, *North Carolina Troops*, Vol. 8, p. 106.

11. *Ibid.*

12. *Ibid.*

13. *Ibid.*

14. "Report of Maj. Joseph A. Englehard, Assistant Adjutant-General, C.S. Army, of operations of Pender's Division," November 14, 1863, O.R., Ser. I, Vol. 27, Pt. II, pp. 656–657; Brig. Gen. John Buford to Lt. Col. C. Ross Smith, August 27, 1863, O.R., Ser. I, Vol. 27, Pt. I, p. 927; Col. William Gamble, First Brigade, First Division, to Capt. T.C. Bacon, A.A.G., First Cavalry Division, August 24, 1863, O.R., Ser. I, Vol. 27, Pt. I, 934; Johnson and Buel, *Battles and Leaders of the Civil War,* Vol. 3, p. 285; Edward G. Longacre, *The Cavalry at Gettysburg: A Tactical Study of Mounted Operations during the Civil War's Pivotal Campaign, 9 June–14 July, 1863* (Rutherford, NJ: Associated University Presses, 1986), pp. 191–192.

15. Lane, O.R., Ser. I, Vol. 27, Pt. II, pp. 664–665; also quoted in Jordan, *North Carolina Troops*, Vol. VIII, p. 106.

16. Boatner, p. 694.

17. Milledge Louis Bonham, ed. "A Little More Light on Gettysburg," *Mississippi Valley Historical Review 24* (1980): p. 520; Lane, O.R., Ser. I, Vol. 27, Pt. II, p. 665; Lt. Gen. Ambrose P. Hill, November 1863, O.R., Ser. I, Vol. 27, Pt. II, p. 607.

18. Faust, p. 358.

19. Lane, "The Branch-Lane Brigade," in Clark, *North Carolina Regiments*, Vol. 4, pp. 467–468.

20. Lane, O.R., Ser. I, Vol. 27, Pt. II, p. 665, quoted in Jordan, *North Carolina Troops*, Vol. 8, p. 107.

21. *Ibid.*; Boatner, p. 631.

22. Jordan, *North Carolina Troops*, Vol. 8, p. 107; O.R., Ser. I, Vol. 27, Pt. II, pp. 666–667.

23. Englehard to Palmer, O.R., Ser. I, Vol. 27, Pt. II, p. 659; Lane to Englehard, O.R., Ser. I, Vol. 27, Pt. II, p. 666.

24. Macdonald, p. 109.

25. Lane, "The Branch-Lane Brigade," in Clark, *North Carolina Regiments*, Vol. 4, pp. 467–468.

26. I.R. Trimble to S.D. Pool, October 15, 1875, in Lane, "History of Brigade," Vol. 9 (1881): pp. 30–31.

27. Englehard to Palmer, O.R., Ser. I, Vol. 27, Pt. II, p. 659; Lane to Englehard, O.R., Ser. I, Vol. 27, Pt. II, p. 666; Harris, *Historical Sketches*, p. 35.

28. Lane, "History of Brigade," SHP, Vol. 9 (1881): p. 33.

29. McDaid, pp. 216–217.

30. *Ibid.*

31. Trimble to Pool, in Lane, "History of Brigade," Vol. 9 (1881): p. 33.

32. William G. Morris to Col. W. Saunders, Dallas, North Carolina, October 1, 1877, in Lawing, p. 128.

33. McDaid, p. 217.

34. William G. Morris to Col. W. Saunders, Dallas, North Carolina, October 1, 1877, in Lawing, p. 128.

35. Boatner, pp. 331, 337.

36. Lane, O.R., Ser. I, Vol. 27, Pt. II, p. 666.

37. Clark, *North Carolina Regiments*, Vol. 5, pp. 144–146; John McLeod Turner to Editors, Raleigh *Observer*, November 29, 1877, cited in McDaid, p. 281.

38. Clark, *North Carolina Regiments*, Vol. 5, p. 147; Trimble to Pool, in Lane, "History of Brigade," Vol. 9 (1881): p. 33.

39. North Carolina *Standard*, July 29, 1863, cited in McDaid, p. 219.

40. Clark, *North Carolina Regiments*, Vol. 5, pp. 144–146; John McLeod Turner to Editors, Raleigh *Observer*, November 29, 1877.

41. Clark, *North Carolina Regiments*, Vol. 5, p. 147; Harris, *Historical Sketches*, p. 37.

42. Clark, *North Carolina Regiments*, Vol. 2, p. 564; Trimble to Pool, in Lane, "History of Brigade," Vol. 9 (1881): pp. 33–34.

43. Boatner, p. 849.

44. Joseph Saunders to Editors, Raleigh *Observer*, November 29, 1877; Clark, *North Carolina* Regiments, Vol. 5, p. 155; James H. Lane to Editors, Richmond *Times*, April 11, 1867, quoted in Raleigh *Observer*, August 30, 1877; Clark, *North Carolina Regiments*, Vol. 2, p. 478, cited in McDaid, p. 220.

45. Trimble to Pool, in Lane, "History of Brigade," Vol. 9 (1881): p. 35.

46. Lane, O.R., Ser. I, Vol. 27, Pt. II, pp. 666–667, quoted in Jordan, *North Carolina Troops*, Vol. 8, p. 107.

47. William G. Morris to Col. W. Saunders, Dallas, North Carolina, October 1, 1877, in Lawing, p. 128.

48. Lane, O.R., Ser. I, Vol. 27, Pt. II, pp. 666–667; Jordan, *North Carolina Troops*, Vol. 8, p. 107.

49. William G. Morris to Col. W. Saunders, Dallas, North Carolina, October 1, 1877, in Lawing, p. 128.

50. *Ibid.*

51. *Ibid.*

52. North Carolina *Standard*, July 29, 1863.

53. "Return of Casualties in the Army of Northern Virginia, at the battle of Gettysburg, July 1–3 [1863]," O.R., Ser. I, Vol. 27, Pt. II, p. 346.

54. *Ibid.*, p. 345.

55. *Ibid.*, p. 344.

56. Fox, *Regimental Losses in the American Civil War*, p. 558.

57. Lane, O.R., Ser. I, Vol. 27, Pt. 2, p. 667, quoted in Jordan, *North Carolina Troops*, Vol. 8, p. 107.

58. "The 28th N.C. Regiment Remembered," online at http://dldunncsa.tripod.com.

59. "History of the 28th North Carolina Regiment, C.S.A. 1861–1865," online www.dixiedave.homestead.com/28thNCT ~ns4.html; see also 28th NC Infantry Flag, online www.nps.gov/gett/gettkidz/flagnc.htm.

60. Don Harvey, "Battle Flag of the 28th North Carolina," online http://users.aol.com/michflags/28nc.htm.

61. Dedmondt, p. 122.

62. Speer, to Father and, Mother, Brothers and Aunt, July 10, 1863, Hagerstown, MD, in Speer, *Voices from Cemetery Hill,* pp. 105–107.

63. *Ibid.*

64. *Ibid.,* p. 107.

65. *Ibid.,* pp. 105–109.

66. *Ibid.*

67. Jordan, *North Carolina Troops,* Vol. 8, p. 226.

68. Lane, O.R., Ser. I, Vol. 27, Pt. II, p. 667.

69. CWSAC #MD004.

70. Lane, O.R., Ser. I, Vol. 27, Pt. II, p. 667; McDaid, p. 223.

71. Harris, *Historical Sketches,* pp. 38–39, cited in McDaid, p. 224.

72. Lane, O.R., Ser. I, Vol. 27, Pt. II, p. 667, quoted in Jordan, *North Carolina Troops,* Vol. 8, p. 107.

73. *Ibid.*

74. Lane, "The Branch-Lane Brigade," in Clark, *North Carolina Regiments,* Vol. 4, p. 468.

75. Boatner, pp. 273–274.

76. Boatner, p. 649.

77. Lane, O.R., Ser. I, Vol. 27, Pt. II, pp. 664–667; Clark, *North Carolina Regiments,* Vol. 2, p. 568.

78. Lane, "History of Brigade," SHP, Vol. 9, p. 73.

79. Dedmondt, p. 124.

80. W.A. Tesh to Father and Mother, Camp near Orange Court House, August 25, 1863, Tesh Papers, Duke Univ.

Chapter 10

1. S.S. Harding to Dear Father, November 25, 1863, Harding Family Papers. See Appendix VII for full text of letter.

2. Douglas Southall Freeman, *Lee's Dispatches* (New York: Putnam's, 1957), pp. 115–116.

3. Jordan, *North Carolina Troops,* Vol. 8, p. 107.

4. Bowman, p. 217; Boatner, pp. 918–919.

5. *Ibid.*

6. R.H. Chilton, for R.E. Lee, July 26, 1863, O.R., Ser. I, Vol. 27, Pt. III, p. 1040.

7. R.E. Lee to Jefferson Davis, July 27, 1863, O.R., Ser. I, Vol. 27, Pt. III, p. 1040.

8. General Orders No. 109, August 11, 1863, O.R., Ser. I, Vol. 29, Pt. II, pp. 641–642.

9. R.E. Lee to S. Cooper, August 14, 1863, O.R., Ser. I, Vol. 29, Pt. II, p. 647.

10. R.E. Lee to Jefferson Davis, August 17, 1863, O.R., Ser. I, Vol. 29, Pt. II, pp. 649–650.

11. *Ibid.,* p. 650. McDaid, p. 234.

12. Harris, *Historical Sketches,* p. 41; S.D. Davis to Jinnie, September 19, 1863, Patterson–Cavin Family Letters, Duke University; Francis M. Kennedy Diary, September 14, 1863, Southern Historical Collection, University of North Carolina, hereafter cited as SHC.

13. General Orders No. 88, September 10, 1863, National Archives Microfilm Publication M921, Roll l, cited in McDaid, p. 235.

14. General Orders No. 88, September 10, 1863, National Archives Microfilm Publication M921, Roll l; Spencer Glasgow Welch, *A Confederate Surgeon's Letters to His Wife* (New York: Neale Publishing, 1911), p. 79; Iredell *Express,* quoted in the Salisbury *Watchman,* October 12, 1863, cited in McDaid, p. 236.

15. Clark Avery to Zebulon B. Vance, October 24, 1863, and Petition to Vance by officers of Thirty-Third North Carolina, October 28, 1863, in Zebulon B. Vance Papers, North Carolina Department of Archives and History. See also Zebulon B. Vance to James A. Seddon, December 11, 1863, O.R., Ser. I, Vol. 29, Pt. II, pp. 866–867.

16. R.E. Lee, O.R., Ser. I, Vol. 29, Pt. II, pp. 867–869.

17. Gibbon, Diary, p. 21.

18. CWSAC #VA040.

19. Harris, *Historical Sketches,* p. 42. Francis M. Kennedy Diary, October 9, 1863, SHC; George A. Williams to Mary Williams, October 23, 1863, Williams–Womble Papers, North Carolina Department of Archives and History.

20. Francis M. Kennedy Diary, October 13, 1863, SHC; Richmond *Dispatch,* quoted in the Charlotte *Western Democrat,* November 10, 1863; Raleigh *Progress,* cited in the Charlotte *Western Democrat,* November 17, 1863, all cited in McDaid, p. 241.

21. Jordan, *North Carolina Troops,* Vol. 8, p. 108.

22. *Ibid.*

23. Harris, *Historical Sketches,* p. 42, George Williams to Mary Williams, October 23, 1863, Williams–Womble Papers, North Carolina Department of Archives and History, cited in McDaid, p. 242.

24. R.E. Lee to Secretary of War, October 13, 1863, O.R., Ser. I, Vol. 29, Pt. I, p. 406.

25. *Ibid.*

26. R.E. Lee, O.R., Ser. I, Vol. 29, Pt. I, pp. 406–408; R.E. Lee, April 27, 1864, O.R., Ser. I, Vol. 29, Pt. I, pp. 830, 832.

27. Gibbon, Diary, p. 22.

28. "Report of Maj. Thomas W. Baird, Eighty-second New York Infantry, Blackburn's Ford, Va., October 15, 1863," O.R., Sec. I, Vol. 29, Pt. I, pp. 282–283.

29. Francis M. Kennedy Diary, October 16, 1863, SHC; McDaid, p. 243.

30. L. Guild, "Return of Casualties in the Confederate forces, October 26–November 8, 1863," O.R., Ser. I, Vol. 29, Pt. I, pp. 616–617.

31. Boatner, 681.

32. Lane, "History of Brigade," SHP, Vol. 9 (1881): p. 72; Frances M. Kennedy Diary, November 9, 1863, SHC.

33. Maj. Gen. Cadmus M. Wilcox, November 12, 1863, O.R., Ser. I, Vol. 29, Pt. I, pp. 636–637.

34. S.S. Harding to Dear Father, November 25, 1863, Harding Family Papers. See Appendix VII for full text of letter.

35. Gibbon, Diary, p. 22.

36. CWSAC #VA044.

37. Boatner, p. 552.

38. Lane, "History of Brigade," SHP, Vol. 9 (1881): p. 72; Francis M. Kennedy Diary, November 9, 1863, SHC.

39. Clark, *North Carolina Regiments,* Vol. I, p. 393; Lane, "History of Brigade," SHP, Vol. 9 (July–December, 1881): p. 72; Francis M. Kennedy Diary, November 30, 1863, SHC.

40. Francis M. Kennedy Diary, December 2–3, 1863, SHC.

41. W.A. Tesh to Father and Mother, Camp Orange Court House, December 5, 1863, Tesh Papers, Duke Univ.

42. "Close of the Campaign of 1863," in Lane, "History of Brigade," SHP, Vol. 9 (January–December 1881): p. 71.

43. Boatner, p. 552.

44. Gibbon, Diary, p. 22.

45. "Abstract from field return of the Army of Northern Virginia, General Robert E. Lee, C.S. Army, commanding, December 10, 1863," O.R., Ser. I, Vol. 29, Pt. II, p. 866.

46. "List of Casualties in Lane's Brigade — Campaign 1863," in Lane, "History of Brigade," SHP, Vol. 9 (January–December, 1881): p. 73.

47. Jordan, *North Carolina Troops,* Vol. 8, p. 108.

48. W.A. Tesh to Father and Mother, Camp near Orange Court House, November 24, 1863, Tesh Papers, Duke Univ.

49. S.S. Harding to father and mother, November 25, 1863, Harding family papers.

50. G.B. Harding to Father and Mother, Camp near Orange Court House, Virginia, November 25, 1863, Co. I, Harding family papers.

51. *Ibid.*

52. Letter to Mr. J.M. McCurdy from a friend of Caleb McCurdy, December 20, 1863, Camp Liberty Mills, VA, Caleb S. McCurdy Papers, courtesy of Perkins Library, Duke University, Durham, NC.

53. SHP, Vol. 18, p. 307, cited in McDaid, p. 248.

54. Lane, "History of Brigade," SHP, Vol. 9 (1881): p. 358.

55. W.A. Tesh to Father, Camp near Orange Court House, February 8, 1864, Tesh Papers, Duke Univ.

56. Lane, "History of Brigade," SHP, Vol. 9, (1881): pp. 360–361.

57. Francis M. Kennedy Diary, February 4, 1864; Noah Collins Reminiscences, Isaac Spencer London Collection, North Carolina Department of Archives and History.

58. Fayetteville *Observer*, February 25, 1864, cited in Mc-Daid, p. 250.

Chapter 11

1. Little, "Co. C," p. 170.

2. Several articles have examined the peace movement in North Carolina. See A. Sellow Roberts, "The Peace Movement in North Carolina," *Mississippi Valley Historical Review* 9 (1924): p. 195; Richard Yates, "Governor Vance and the Peace Movement," *North Carolina Historical Review* 27 (1940): p. 5; and Horace Raper, "William W. Holden and the Peace Movement in North Carolina, in *North Carolina Historical Review* 31 (1954), pp. 501–502, cited in McDaid, p. 230, and footnote 6, p. 372.

3. Raleigh *Register*, August 26, 1863.

4. *Ibid.*

5. Wilmington *Journal*, September 3, 1863.

6. "Campaign 1865," in Lane, "History of the Brigade," SHP, Vol. 9 (1881): pp. 489–490.

7. *Ibid.*

8. *Ibid.*, pp. 491–493.

9. Lane, "Glimpses of Army Life in 1864," SHP, Vol. 18 (1890): p. 407.

10. *Ibid.*, p. 411.

11. Gibbon, Diary, p. 22.

12. CWSAC #VA046.

13. John Macdonald, *Great Battles of the Civil War* (New York: Macmillan, 1988), p. 136.

14. Macdonald, p. 136.

15 Jordan, *North Carolina Troops*, Vol. 8, p. 108.

16. Cadmus M. Wilcox Manuscript Report of 1864–1865 Campaign, Robert E. Lee Headquarters Collection, p. 29, Virginia Historical Society, Richmond, Virginia, cited in McDaid, p. 255.

17. W.H.A. Speer to Capt. E.J. Hale, Jr., Headquarters 28th NCT, July 19, 1864, in James H. Lane Papers, RG 501, ff73, Auburn University Archives, online http://www.lib.auburn.edu/archive/find-aid/501/ff73.htm.

18. *Ibid.*

19. Lane, "Report of the Battle of the Wilderness," *Southern Historical Society Papers*, Vol. 9, p. 124.

20. Speer to Hale, July 19, 1864, in James H. Lane Papers, RG 501, ff73, Auburn University Archives, online http://www.lib.auburn.edu/archive/find-aid/501/ff73.htm.

21. Jordan, *North Carolina Troops*, Vol. 8, p. 108.

22. Wilcox, Manuscript Report, p. 31.

23. Jordan, *North Carolina Troops*, Vol. 8, p. 108.

24. *Ibid.*

25. Lane, "Report of the Battle of the Wilderness," SHP, Vol. 9, p. 125.

26. Report of James S. Harris for Seventh North Carolina, July 19, 1864, Folder 73, James H. Lane Papers, Auburn Univ.

27. Speer, July 19, 1864, James H. Lane Papers, Auburn Univ.

28. "Lane's Report, Sept. 8, 1864–Wilderness (May 5, 1864)," James H. Lane Papers, Auburn Univ., online http://www.lib.auburn.edu/archive/find-aid/501/ff78.htm.

29. *Ibid.*

30. Lane, "Report of the Battle of the Wilderness," SHP, Vol. 9, p. 125; Report of William H.A. Speer for Twenty-Eighth North Carolina, July 19, 1864, Folder 73, James H. Lane Papers, Auburn Univ.

31. "Lane's Report, Sept. 8, 1864–Wilderness (May 5, 1864)," James H. Lane Papers, Auburn Univ., online http://www.lib.auburn.edu/archive/find-aid/501/ff78.htm.

32. Jordan, *North Carolina Troops*, Vol. 8, p. 108.

33. Lane, Wilderness Report, SHP, Vol. 9, p. 125.

34. "Lane's Report, Sept. 8, 1864–Wilderness (May 5, 1864)," James H. Lane Papers, Auburn Univ., online http://www.lib.auburn.edu/archive/find-aid/501/ff78.htm.

35. Edward Steere, *The Wilderness Campaign* (New York: Bonanza Books, 1960), p. 240.

36. Lane, "Wilderness Report," SHP, Vol. 9, p. 125.

37. Jordan, *North Carolina Troops*, Vol. 8, p. 108.

38. Speer to Hale, July 19, 1864, in James H. Lane Papers, RG 501, ff73, Auburn Univ., online http://www.lib.auburn.edu/archive/find-aid/501/ff73.htm.

39. "Lane's Report, Sept. 8, 1864–Wilderness (May 5, 1864)," James H. Lane Papers, Auburn Univ., online http://www.lib.auburn.edu/archive/find-aid/501/ff78.htm.

40. *Ibid.*

41. *Ibid.*

42. *Ibid.*

43. Speer to Hale, July 19, 1864, in James H. Lane Papers, RG 501, ff73, Auburn Univ., online http://www.lib.auburn.edu/archive/find-aid/501/ff73.htm.

44. Jordan, *North Carolina Troops*, Vol. 8, p.180; correspondence from descendant Richard C. Poindexter on 7/11/2006.

45. Little, "Co. C," p. 169.

46. Macdonald, p. 143.

47. Jordan, *North Carolina Troops*, Vol. 8, p. 108.

48. "Battle of the Wilderness, Lane's Report," Sept. 8, 1864, in Lane, "History of Brigade," SHP, Vol. 9 (January–December 1881): p. 128.

49. *Ibid.*

50. *Ibid.*, pp. 128–129.

51. "Lane's Report, Sept. 8, 1864–Wilderness (May 5, 1864)," James H. Lane Papers, Auburn Univ., online http://www.lib.auburn.edu/archive/find-aid/501/ff78.htm.

52. Mcdonald, p. 139.

53. Lane, Wilderness Report, SHP, Vol. 9, p. 128.

54. G.B. Harding Letter, May 20, 1863, Harding Family Papers.

55. CWSAC #VA048.

56. Jordan, *North Carolina Troops*, Vol. 8, p. 108.

57. "Lane's Report, Sept. 16, 1864–Spotsylvania (May 8–20, 1864)," in James H. Lane Papers, RG 501, ff79, Auburn Univ., online http://www.lib.auburn.edu/archive/find-aid/501/ff79.htm.

58. Speer to Hale, July 19, 1864, in James H. Lane Papers, RG 501, ff73, Auburn Univ., online http://www.lib.auburn.edu/archive/find-aid/501/ff73.htm.

59. "Lane's Report, Sept. 16, 1864–Spotsylvania (May 8–20, 1864)," in James H. Lane Papers, RG 501, ff79, Auburn Univ., online http://www.lib.auburn.edu/archive/find-aid/501/ff79.htm.

60. "Lane's Report, Sept. 8, 1864–Wilderness (May 5, 1864)," James H. Lane Papers, Auburn Univ., online http://www.lib.auburn.edu/archive/find-aid/501/ff78.htm.

61. Speer to Hale, July 19, 1864, in James H. Lane Papers, RG 501, ff73, Auburn Univ., online http://www.lib.auburn.edu/archive/find-aid/501/ff73.htm.

62. *Ibid.*

63. "Battle of Spotsylvania Court-House–Report of General Lane," in Lane, "History of Brigade," SHP, Vol. 9 (April 1881): p 146; "Lane's Report, Sept. 16, 1864–Spotsylvania (May 8–20, 1864)," in James H. Lane Papers, RG 501, ff79, Auburn Univ., online http://www.lib.auburn.edu/archive/find-aid/501/ff79.htm.

64. Speer to Hale, July 19, 1864, in James H. Lane Papers, RG 501, ff73, Auburn Univ., online http://www.lib.auburn.edu/archive/find-aid/501/ff73.htm.

65. "Battle of Spotsylvania Court-House–Report of Gen-

eral Lane," in Lane, "History of Brigade," SHP, Vol. 9 (April 1881): p 146; "Lane's Report, Sept. 16, 1864–Spotsylvania (May 8–20, 1864)," in James H. Lane Papers, RG 501, ff79, Auburn Univ., online http://www.lib.auburn.edu/archive/find-aid/501/ff79.htm.

66. Speer to Hale, July 19, 1864, in James H. Lane Papers, RG 501, ff73, Auburn Univ., online http://www.lib.auburn.edu/archive/find-aid/501/ff73.htm.

67. Jordan, *North Carolina Troops,* Vol. 8, p. 108.

68. Speer to Hale, July 19, 1864, in James H. Lane Papers, RG 501, ff73, Auburn Univ., online http://www.lib.auburn.edu/archive/find-aid/501/ff73.htm.

69. *Ibid.*

70. "Lane's Report, Sept. 16, 1864–Spotsylvania (May 8–20, 1864)," in James H. Lane Papers, RG 501, ff79, Auburn Univ., online http://www.lib.auburn.edu/archive/find-aid/501/ff79.htm.

71. Lane, "The Branch-Lane Brigade," in Clark, *North Carolina Troops,* Vol. 4, pp. 468–469.

72. "Lane's Report, Sept. 16, 1864–Spotsylvania (May 8–20, 1864)," in James H. Lane Papers, RG 501, ff79, Auburn Univ., online http://www.lib.auburn.edu/archive/find-aid/501/ff79.htm.

73. *Ibid.*

74. Little, "Co. C," p. 170.

75. G.B. Harding to family, undated letter written from the battlefield at Spotsylvania, probably about May 20, 1863, Harding family papers.

76. *Ibid.*

77. *Ibid.*

78. Gibbon, Diary, p. 22.

79. Little, "Co. C," p. 170.

80. *Ibid.*

81. "Battle of Spotsylvania Court-House–Report of General Lane," in Lane, "History of Brigade," SHP, Vol. 9, pp. 151–152.

82. "What General Early says about Lane's Brigade at Spotsylvania Courthouse, on the 12th May," in Lane, "History of Brigade," SHP, Vol. 9, p. 155.

83. "Battle of Spotsylvania Court-House–Report of General Lane," in Lane, "History of Brigade," SHP, Vol. 9, pp. 151–152.

84. *Ibid.*, pp. 149–150.

85. *Ibid.*, pp. 157–158.

86. Jordan, *North Carolina Troops,* Vol. 8, p. 207; Casstevens, *The Civil War and Yadkin County,* p. 189; Yadkin County, North Carolina, Marriage Register.

87. "Battle of Spotsylvania Court-House–Report of General Lane," in Lane, "History of Brigade," SHP, Vol. 9 (April 1881): pp. 149–150.

88. *Ibid.*, p. 153.

89. *Ibid.*, pp. 153–154.

90. "General Lee Compliments the Sharp-Shooters of Lane's Brigade," in Lane, "History of Brigade," SHP, Vol. 9 (April 1881): p. 156.

91. T. James Linebarger to Family, May 15, 1864, Ann L. Snuggs Papers, Southern Historical Collection, University of North Carolina; McDaid, pp. 282–283.

92. CWSAC #VA055.

93. Boatner, p. 597.

94. Speer to Hale, July 19, 1864, in James H. Lane Papers, RG 501, ff73, Auburn Univ., online http://www.lib.auburn.edu/archive/find-aid/501/ff73.htm.

95. "Lane's Report, Sept. 29, 1864–Campaign (May 21–June 2, 1864)," in James H. Lane Papers, RG 501, ff80, Auburn Univ., online http://www.auburn.edu/archive/find-a/501/ff80.htm.

96. Jordan, *North Carolina Troops,* Vol. 8, p. 108.

97. "Lane's Report, Sept. 29, 1864–Campaign (May 21–June 2, 1864)," in James H. Lane Papers, RG 501, ff80, Auburn Univ., online http://www.auburn.edu/archive/find-aid/501/ff80.htm.

98. *Ibid.*

99. *Ibid.*

100. Speer to Hale, July 19, 1864, in James H. Lane Papers, RG 501, ff73, Auburn Univ., online http://www.lib.auburn.edu/archive/find-aid/501/ff73.htm.

101. "Lane's Report, Sept. 29, 1864–Campaign (May 21–June 2, 1864)," in James H. Lane Papers, RG 501, ff80, Auburn Univ., online http://www.auburn.edu/archive/find-aid/501/ff80.htm.

102. Boatner, p. 598.

103. Jordan, *North Carolina Troops,* Vol. 8, p. 108.

104. "Battle of Jericho Ford–Report of General Lane," in Lane, "History of Brigade," SHP, Vol. 9, (June 1881): pp. 241–242; see also "Lane's Report, Sept. 29, 1864–Campaign (May 21–June 2, 1864)," in James H. Lane Papers, RG 501, ff80, Auburn Univ., online http://www.auburn.edu/archive/find-aid/501/ff80.htm.

105. Lane, "The Branch-Lane Brigade," in Clark, *North Carolina Troops,* Vol. IV, p. 469.

106. Jedidiah Hotchkiss, *Confederate Military History,* Vol. 3 (reprint, New York: Thomas Yoseloff, 1962), p. 460.

107. Speer to Hale, July 19, 1864, in James H. Lane Papers, RG 501, ff73, Auburn Univ., online http://www.lib.auburn.edu/archive/find-aid/501/ff73.htm.

108. "Lane's Report, Sept. 29, 1864–Campaign (May 21–June 2, 1864)," in James H. Lane Papers, RG 501, ff80, Auburn Univ., online http://www.auburn.edu/archive/find-aid/501/ff80.htm.

109. Boatner, p. 598.

Chapter 12

1. Ulysses S. Grant, *Ulysses S. Grant: Memoirs and Selected Letters 1839–1865* (New York: Library of America, 1990), p. 588.

2. CWSAC #VA062.

3. Daniel H. Hill, "Lee's Attacks North of the Chickahominy," in Robert U. Buel and Clarence C. Johnson, eds., *Battles and Leaders of the Civil War,* Vol. 2 (1887, rpt. Secaucus, NJ: Castle, 1982,) p. 354.

4. G. Moxley Sorrell, *Recollections of a Confederate Staff Officer* (1905, rpt. Nashville: Mclowat-Mercer Press, 1958), p. 249; cited in Frances H. Casstevens, *Clingman's Brigade in the Confederacy, 1862–1865* (Jefferson, NC: McFarland, 2002), p. 66.

5. Colonel George H. Sharp to Major General Humphreys, June 3, 1864, O.R., Ser. I, Vol. 36, Pt. III, pp. 527–528.

6. R. Ernest Dupuy and Trevor N. Dupuy, *Compact History of the Civil War* (New York: Hawthorn Books, 1960), p. 304.

7. Francis Trevelyan Miller and Robert S. Lanier, "Cold Harbor," in *Photographic History of the Civil War: The Decisive Battles,* Vol. III (1911, rpt. New York: Castle Books, 1957), p. 82; Hill, *Confederate Military History: North Carolina,* Vol. 4, p. 251.

8. Captain W.H.A. Speer to Captain E.J. Hale, Jr., Headquarters, 28th NCT, July 19, 1864, in James H. Lane Papers, RG 501, ff73, Auburn Univ., online http://www.lib.auburn.edu/archive/find-aid/501/ff73.htm.

9. Jordan, *North Carolina Troops,* Vol. 8, p. 109.

10. Speer to Hale, July 19, 1864, in James H. Lane Papers, RG 501, ff73, Auburn Univ., online http://www.lib.auburn.edu/archive/find-aid/501/ff73.htm.

11. McDaid, p. 289.

12. Boatner, p. 163.

13. Jordan, *North Carolina Troops,* Vol. 8, p. 109.

14. Clement Evans, *A History of the Southern Confederacy* (New York: The MacMillan Co., 1982), p. 286.

15. Grant, *Ulysses S. Grant: Memoirs and Selected Letters 1839–1865,* p. 588.

16. Speer to Halem July 19, 1864, in James H. Lane Papers,

RG 501, ff73, Auburn Univ., online http://www.lib.auburn.edu/archive/find-aid/501/ff73.htm.

17. *Fayetteville Observer,* June 16, 1864, cited in McDaid, p. 289.

18. W.F. Fox, *Fox's Regimental Losses* (1888, rpt. Dayton, OH: Morningside Book Shop, 1985), pp. 449, 450, 541, 542.

19. North Carolina *Standard,* June 10, 1864; T.J. Linebarger to E. Ann Linebarger, June 7, 1864, in Ann L. Snuggs Papers, SHC.

20. A.L. Long, *Memoirs of Robert E. Lee,* pp. 349–350.

21. Speer to Hale, July 19, 1864, in James H. Lane Papers, RG 501, ff73, Auburn Univ., online http://www.lib.auburn.edu/archive/find-aid/501/ff73.htm.

22. Wilcox, Manuscript Report, pp. 50–51, Virginia Historical Society, cited in McDaid, p. 291.

23. Speer to Hale, July 19, 1864, in James H. Lane Papers, RG 501, ff73, Auburn Univ., online http://www.lib.auburn.edu/archive/find-aid/501/ff73.htm.

24. Long, p. 372.

25. Boatner, p. 646.

26. Jordan, *North Carolina Troops,* Vol. 8, p. 109.

27. Boatner, p. 646.

28. Speer to Hale, July 19, 1864, in James H. Lane Papers, RG 501, ff73, Auburn Univ., online http://www.lib.auburn.edu/archive/find-aid/501/ff73.htm.

29. Harris, *Historical Sketches,* p. 51; Caldwell, *History of a Brigade of South Carolinians,* p. 162, cited in McDaid, p. 292.

30. Speer to Hale, July 19, 1864, in James H. Lane Papers, RG 501, ff73, Auburn Univ., online http://www.lib.auburn.edu/archive/find-aid/501/ff73.htm.

31. Lane, "The Branch-Lane Brigade," in Clark, *North Carolina Regiments,* Vol. 4, p. 469.

32. CWSAC #VA065.

33. Jordan, *North Carolina Troops,* Vol. 8, p. 109.

34. See maps of the engagement at the Jerusalem Plank Road prepared by the National Park Service, http://www.nps.gov/archive/oete/mahan/eduhistbtlup.html; and http://www.nps.gov/archive/oete/mahan/eduhistJPRB.html.

35. Speer to Hale, July 19, 1864, in James H. Lane Papers, RG 501, ff73, Auburn Univ., online http://www.lib.auburn.edu/archive/find-aid/501/ff73.htm.

36. *Ibid.*

37. *Ibid.*

38. *Ibid.*

39. *Ibid.*

40. James Fitz James Caldwell, *The History of a Brigade of South Carolinians* (Philadelphia, PA: King & Baird Printers, 1866), p. 163; Harris, *Historical Sketches,* p. 52, cited in McDaid, p. 300.

41. Speer to Hale, July 19, 1864, in James H. Lane Papers, RG 501, ff73, Auburn Univ., online http://www.lib.auburn.edu/archive/find-aid/501/ff73.htm.

42. Boatner, p. 229.

43. Wilcox, Manuscript Report, p. 44, Virginia Historical Society, cited in McDaid, p. 301.

44. CWSAC #VA069; eHistory, "Deep Bottom I (1864), online http://ehistory.osu.edu/world/BattleView.Cfm?BID=743.

45. James H. Lane, Report of Brigade for 21 May–3 June, 1864, Cadmus Wilcox Papers, Library of Congress; Clipping Scrapbook, pp. 172–173, Cadmus Wilcox Papers, Library of Congress, cited in McDaid, p. 301.

46. Boatner, p. 171.

47. Harris, *Historical Sketches,* p. 53.

48. Report of James S. Harris for Seventh Regiment, July 29, 1864; Report of William H.A. Speer for Twenty-Eighth Regiment, July 31, 1864, both in Folder 74, James H. Lane Papers, Auburn University, cited in McDaid, p. 302.

49. Report of J.M. Bost for Thirty-Seventh Regiment, August 3, 1864; Caldwell, *History of a Brigade of South Carolinians,* p. 170, cited in McDaid, p. 302.

50. Report of James S. Harris for Seventh Regiment, July 29, 1864; Report of W.J. Callais for Thirty-Third Regiment,

in Folder 74, James H. Lane Papers, Auburn University, cited in McDaid, p. 302.

51. Report of William H.A. Speer, July 31, 1864; Report of J.M. Bost, August 3, 1864, both in Folder 74, James H. Lane Papers, Auburn University; Caldwell, *History of a Brigade of South Carolinians,* pp. 172–173; Casualty figures from Folder 94, James H. Lane Papers, Auburn University, cited in McDaid, pp. 302–303.

52. W.H.A. Speer to Hale, Capt. E.J. Hale, Jr., July 28, 1864, "Lane's Brigade Battle Reports, July 28, 1864," in Gen. James H. Lane Papers, Auburn University Archives & Manuscripts Department, Auburn, AL, online www.lib.auburn.edu/archive/find-aid/501/ff77.htm.

53. Boatner, pp. 229–230.

54. Jordan, *North Carolina Troops,* Vol. 8, p. 109.

55. Jordan, *North Carolina Troops,* Vol. 8, p. 212. *The Civil War and Yadkin County,* p. 219; Casstevens, *The Heritage of Yadkin County, North Carolina,* Vol. I, p. 384; and the William Harding Family Bible.

56. Boatner, pp. 647–648.

57. Boatner, pp. 648–649.

58. Fox, p. 547.

59. Boatner, p. 649.

60. *Ibid.*

61. Little, "Co. C," p. 172.

62. Lane, "The Branch-Lane Brigade," in Clark, *North Carolina Regiments,* Vol. 4, p. 469.

Chapter 13

1. Little, "Co. C," p. 171.

2. Special Orders, Number 189, August 11, 1864, O.R., Ser. I, Vol. 42, Pt. II, p. 1171.

3. James H. Lane, "The Branch-Lane Brigade," in Clark, *North Carolina Regiments,* Vol. 4, p. 469.

4. Harris, *Historical Sketches,* p. 54.

5. Samuel Speer Harding to Mother, August 11, 1864, Harding Family Papers. See Appendix VIII for entire text.

6. Samuel Speer Harding to Mother, August 11, 1864, Harding Family Papers. See Appendix VIII for entire text.

7. *Ibid.*

8. A.A. Humphreys, *The Virginia Campaign of '63 and '65* (New York: Scribner's, 1883), cited in McDaid, p. 303.

9. CWSAC #VA071.

10. Longacre, 13.

11. Harris, *Historical Sketches,* p. 94; "Narrative of Major-General C.W. Fields," SHP, Vol. 14, pp. 553–554; Wilcox, Manuscript report, p. 54; Fayetteville *Observer,* August 29, 1864.

12. *Ibid.*

13. Longacre, p. 13.

14. Clark, *North Carolina Regiments,* Vol. 2, p. 57.

15. "List of Casualties in Lane's Brigade from May 5, 1864, to October 1, 1864," SHP, Vol. 9 (1881): p. 357.

16. Jordan, *North Carolina Troops,* Vol. 8, p. 178.

17. *Ibid.,* p. 109.

18. CWSAC #VA073.

19. Boatner, p. 780; National Park Service, "Reams' Station: Prelude," online http://www.nps.gov/pete/mahan/eduhistbtlrs.html.

20. Longacre, pp. 13–14.

21. *Ibid.,* p. 14.

22. *Ibid.,* pp. 14–15.

23. *Ibid.,* p. 15.

24. *Ibid.*

25. Cadmus Wilcox, Report of the Battle of Reams' Station, Cadmus Wilcox Papers, Library of Congress, Washington, D.C.

26. Longacre, p. 16.

27. *Ibid.,* pp. 16–17.

28. Clark, *North Carolina Regiment,* Vol. 4, pp. 565–566; Fayetteville *Observer,* September 8, 1864.

29. Major S.N. Stowe, August 28, 1864, in "Battle Reports, Reams' Station, Lane's Brigade (Aug. 25, 1864)," in Gen. James H. Lane Papers, Auburn University Archives & Manuscripts Department, Auburn, AL, online www.lib.auburn.edu/archive/find-aid/501/ff77.htm.

30. Longacre, p. 16.

31. Stowe, August 28, 1864, in Gen. James H. Lane Papers, Auburn Univ., online www.lib.auburn.edu/archive/find-aid/501/ff77.htm.

32. Longacre, pp. 16–17.

33. *Ibid.*, p. 17.

34. John Horn, *The Destruction of the Weldon Railroad: Deep Bottom, Globe Tavern, and Reams' Station, August 14–25, 1864* (Lynchburg, VA: H.E. Howard, 1991), p. 159; Clark, *North Carolina Regiments,* Vol. 4, pp. 565–566; Fayetteville *Observer,* September 8, 1864; Lane, "History of Brigade," SHP, Vol. 9 (1881): pp. 353–354.

35. Lane, "History of Brigade," SHP, Vol. 9 (1881): p. 358.

36. Jordan, *North Carolina Troops,* Vol. 8, p. 196.

37. Ashe, *History of North Carolina.* Vol. 2, p. 922.

38. A.P. Hill to Col. W.H. Taylor, August 31, 1864, O.R., Ser. I, Vol. 42. Pt. I, p, 940; Report of Samuel N. Stowe, August 28, 1864, Folder 77, James H. Lane Papers, Auburn Univ.

39. Horn, p. 173.

40. Longacre, p. 17.

41. Horn, p. 173.

42. Walton Rawls, ed., *Great Civil War Heroes and Their Battles* New York: Abbeville Press, 1985), p. 78.

43. *Ibid.*

44. Longacre, p. 13.

45. Horn, p. 171.

46. Clark, *History of the Several Regiments,* Vol. 2, p. 480, cited in Horn, p. 171.

47. McDaid, p. 308.

48. Jordan, *North Carolina Troops,* Vol. 8, p. 109.

49. Lane, "History of Brigade," SHP, Vol. 9 (1881): p. 357; Record Group 109, National Archives; the *Augusta Chronicle and Sentinel,* September 9, 1864; and the *Raleigh Daily Confederate,* September 28, 1864, cited in Horn, footnote 171, p. 239.

50. Horn, footnote 171, p. 240; *Lee's Lieutenants,* Vol. 1, p. 258, note 86.

51. Report of Major S.N. Stone, August 28, 1864, in James H. Lane Papers, Auburn Univ., cited in Horn, p. 159, footnote 63.

52. Ashe, p. 922.

53. Catherine D. Edmondston, *Journal of a Secesh Lady,* Beth Crabtree and James W. Patton, eds. (Raleigh, NC: Department of Archives and History, 1979), p. 609; R.E. Lee to James A. Seddon, August 26, 1864, O.R., Vol. 42, Pt. I, p. 851.

54. Edmondston, p. 612.

55. A.P. Hill to Col. W.H. Taylor, August 31, 1864, O.R., Ser. I, Vol. 42, Pt. I, p. 940.

56. Edmondston, p. 613.

57. Petersburg, VA, *The Daily Register,* August 27, 1864.

58. Report of Maj. S.N. Stowe, August 28, 1864, in Battle Reports, Reams' Station, Lane's Brigade (Aug. 25, 1864), General James H. Lane Papers, Auburn Univ. Online http://www.lib.auburn.edu/archive/find-aid/501/ff77.htm. See also, Speer, *Voices from Cemetery Hill,* p. 148.

59. Speer, *Voices from Cemetery Hill,* pp. 149–150.

60. T.G. Scott to William Harding, Petersburg, VA, August 27, 1864, cited in Speer, *Voices from Cemetery Hill,* pp. 148–149. See also footnote 46 on p. 148. Complete letter reproduced in Appendix VIII of this work.

61. Casstevens, *The Civil War and Yadkin County,* p. 219; Jordan, *North Carolina Troops,* Vol. 8, p. 212.

62. T.G. Scott to William Harding, Petersburg, VA, August 27, 1864, cited in Speer, *Voices from Cemetery Hill,* pp. 148–149. See also footnote 46, p.148.

63. Jordan, *North Carolina Troops,* Vol. 8, p. 175; Casstevens, *The Civil War and Yadkin County,* pp. 188–189.

64. R.E. Lee to Z.B. Vance, August 29, 1864, O.R., Ser. I,

Vol. 42, Pt. II, p. 1207; Lane, "The Branch Lane Brigade," in Clark, *North Carolina Troops,* Vol. 4, pp. 469–470.

65. Ashe, pp. 922–923.

66. R.E. Lee to Z.B. Vance, August 29, 1864, O.R., Ser. I, Vol. 42, Pt. II, p. 1207. See also same letter in the *Southern Historical Society Papers,* Vol. 19 (1891): pp. 119–120.

67. Ashe, p. 923.

68. Little, "Co. C," p. 171.

69. R.E. Lee, Special Order No. 205, August 29, 1864, O.R., Ser. I, Vol. 42, Pt. 2, p. 1207.

70. Jordan, *North Carolina Troops,* Vol. 8, p. 110.

71. Correspondence via e-mail from Tom Myrick, April 11, 1999, who is a regular visitor to the battlefield site.

72. Lane, "History of Brigade," SHP, Vol. 9 (June 1881): p. 354; Harris, *Historical Sketches,* pp. 56–57.

73. Lane, "Glimpses of Army Life," in SHP, Vol. 9 (1881): p. 412.

74. Lane, "History of Brigade," SHP, Vol. 9 (June 1881): p. 354.

75. G.G. Holland, Capt. Commanding Regiment, to Capt. E.A.T. Nicholson, October 2, 1864, "Battle Reports–Lane's Brigade–Petersburg (Sept. 20–Oct. 1, 1864), in Lane Papers, Auburn University Archives and Manuscript Department, Auburn, AL. Online http://www.lib.auburn.edu/archive/find-aid/501/ff77.htm.

76. Report of Thomas J. Wooten for Lane's Brigade Sharpshooters, October 7, 1864, Folder 82, James H. Lane Papers, Auburn University; Lane, "History of Brigade," SHP Vol. 9, pp. 354–355; Harris, *Historical Sketches,* p. 57, cited in McDaid, p. 310.

77. Lane, "History of Brigade," SHP, Vol. 9 (1881): p. 356; Harris, *Historical Sketches,* p. 57, cited in McDaid, p. 314.

78. Lane, "History of Brigade," SHP, Vol. 9 (1881).

79. McDaid, p. 112.

80. G.G. Holland, Capt. Commanding Regiment, to Capt. E.A.T. Nicholson, October 2, 1864, "Battle Reports–Lane's Brigade–Petersburg (Sept. 20–Oct. 1, 1864), in Lane Papers, Auburn University Archives and Manuscript Department, Auburn, AL. Online http://www.lib.auburn.edu/archive/find-aid/501/ff77.htm.

81. Report of Gold Holland for the Twenty-Eighth Regiment, October 2, 1864; Report of J.H. Bost for the Thirty-Seventh Regiment, October 6, 1864; Report of John McGill for the Eighteenth Regiment, October 6, 1864, all in Folder 82, James H. Lane Papers, Auburn University, cited in McDaid, pp. 312.

82. G.G. Holland, Capt. Commanding Regiment, to Capt. E.A.T. Nicholson, October 2, 1864, "Battle Reports–Lane's Brigade–Petersburg (Sept. 20–Oct. 1, 1864)," in Lane Papers, Auburn University Archives and Manuscript Department, Auburn, AL. Online http://www.lib.auburn.edu/archive/find-aid/501/ff77.htm.

83. "List of Casualties in Lane's Brigade from May 5, 1864, to October 1, 1864," Lane, "History of Brigade," SHP, Vol. 9 (1881): p. 357.

84. James H. Lane, "Glimpses of Army Life," in SHP, Vol. 9 (1881): p. 412.

85. G.G. Holland, Capt. Commanding Regiment, to Capt. E.A.T. Nicholson, October 2, 1864, "Battle Reports–Lane's Brigade–Petersburg (Sept. 20–Oct. 1, 1864)," in Lane Papers, Auburn University Archives and Manuscript Department, Auburn, AL. Online http://www.lib.auburn.edu/archive/find-aid/501/ff77.htm.

86. Lane, "History of Brigade," SHP, Vol. 9 (1881): p. 356.

87. Lane, "Glimpses of Army Life," in SHP, Vol. 9 (1881): p. 413; Jordan, *North Carolina Troops,* Vol. 9, p. 468; General Orders No. 112, December 31, 1862, Orders and Circulars Issued by the Army of the Potomac and the Army and Department of Northern Virginia, National Archives Microfilm Publication 921, Roll. 1, cited in McDaid, p. 312–313.

88. Lane, "History of Brigade," SHP, Vol. 9 (1881): p. 356.

89. McDaid, p. 313.

90. Report of Thomas J. Wooten for Lane's Brigade Sharp-shooters, October 7, 1864, Folder 82, James H. Lane Papers, Auburn University; James H. Lane, "Glimpses of Army Life," in SHP, Vol. 9 (1881): p. 412.

91. Lane, "Campaign of 1864," in Lane, "History of Brigade," SHP, Vol. 9 (June 1881): p. 356; Harris, *Historical Sketches*, p. 57.

92. Lane, "History of Brigade," SHP Vol. 9 (1881): p. 356.

93. Richard J. Sommers, *Richmond Redeemed* (New York: Doubleday, 1981), pp. 333–336.

94. Lane, "History of Brigade," SHP Vol. 9 (1881): p. 356.

95. Lane, "History of Brigade," SHP Vol. 9 (1881): p. 357.

96. Lane, "Glimpses of Army Life in 1864, Near Peters-burg, VA, October 14, 1864," SHP, Vol. 18 (1890): p. 415.

97. "List of Casualties in Lane's Brigade from May 5, 1864, to October 1, 1864," Lane, "History of Brigade," SHP, Vol. 9 (1881): p. 357.

98. Lane, "History of Brigade," SHP Vol. 9 (1881): p. 357.

Chapter 14

1. Little, "Co. C," p. 172.

2. Gibbon, Diary, p. 23.

3. Harris, *Historical Sketches*, p. 58.

4. Jordan, *North Carolina Troops*, 8, p. 109.

5. Lane, "Campaign 1865," in Lane, "History of Brigade," SHP, Vol. 9 (1881): p. 489.

6. *Ibid.*

7. Clark, *North Carolina Regiments*, Vol. 2, p. 59; "Glimpses of Army Life in 1864: Extracts from Letters writ-ten by Brigadier-General J.H. Lane," in SHP, Vol. 18 (1890): pp. 416–417; Harris, *Historical Sketches*, p. 59; William D. Alexander Diary, December 9–12, 1864, SHC.

8. Jordan, *North Carolina Troops*, 8, p. 109.

9. Lane, "Glimpses of Army Life, Near Petersburg, De-cember 13, 1864," SHP, Vol. 18 (1890): pp. 416–417.

10. Lane, "Glimpses of Army Life, December 18, 1864," SHP, Vol. 18 (1890): p. 419.

11. *Ibid.*, p. 420.

12. Alfred N. Profitt to R.L. Profitt, January 1, 1865, Profitt Family Papers, SHC, cited in McDaid, pp. 316–317.

13. Lane, "History of Brigade," SHP, Vol. 9 (1881): p. 357.

14. McDaid, pp. 317–318.

15. Freeman, *R.E. Lee: A Biography*, Vol. 3 (New York: Scribner's, 1939), pp. 498–499.

16. H.M. Wagstaff, ed. *The James A. Graham Papers, 1861–1864* (Chapel Hill, NC: University of North Carolina Press, 1928), p. 128.

17. Figures from McDaid, calculated from the Roster of the 18th Regiment in Manarin and Jordan, *North Carolina Troops*, Vol. 6, pp. 305–423, cited in McDaid, p. 318.

18. R.E. Lee to President Jefferson Davis, near Appomat-tox Court House, Va., April 12, 1865, O.R., Ser. I, Vol. 46, Pt. 2, pp. 1265; W.H. Taylor, "Report of desertions for ten days ending March 8, 1865," O.R. Ser. I, Vol. 46, Pt. 2, pp. 1292–1293; also see Manarin and Jordan, *North Carolina Troops*, rosters of the regiments in Lane's Brigade.

19. Alfred N. Profitt to R.L. Profitt, March 4, 1865, Profitt Family Papers, SHC; A.P. Hill to Lt. Col. C.S. Venable, Jan-uary 22, 1865, O.R., Ser. I, Vol. 41, Pt. 2, p. 1145.

20. "Abstract from return of Wilcox's division, Ambrose P. Hill's corps, Maj. Gen. Cadmus M. Wilcox commanding, for September 30, 1864," O.R., Ser. I, Vol. 42, Pt. II, pp. 1307–1308.

21. "Strength of the Army of Northern Virginia, General Robert E. Lee commanding, November 30, 1864, as shown by inspection reports," O.R., Ser. I, Vol. 42, Pt. III, p. 1237.

22. Jordan, *North Carolina Troops*, 8, p. 117; personal com-munication from descendant, Esther Draughn Johnson.

23. Gibbon, Diary, p. 23.

24. Jordan, *North Carolina Troops*, Vol. 8, p. 109.

25. "Organization of the Infantry and Cavalry of the Army of Northern Virginia, General R.E. Lee Commanding, Feb-ruary 28, 1865," O.R., Ser. I, Vol. 46, Pt. II, p. 1272.

26. Jordan, *North Carolina Troops*, Vol. 8, p. 109.

27. CWSAC #VA084.

28. Humphreys, *The Virginia Campaign of '64 and '65*, p. 324–325, cited in McDaid, p. 326.

29. Fox, *Regimental Losses*, p. 548, also cited in Boatner, p. 299.

30. Freeman, *R.E. Lee*, Vol. 4, pp. 14–17; Lane, "History of Brigade," SHP, Vol. 9 (1881): p. 494.

31. Fox, *Regimental Losses*, p. 548.

32. *Ibid.*

33. Freeman, *R.E. Lee*, Vol. 4, pp. 14–17.

34. *Ibid.*; Lane, "History of Brigade," SHP, Vol. 9 (1881): pp. 494–495

35. Michael C. Hardy, "America's Civil War: Assault at Pe-tersburg," The History Net, online http://www.historynet. com/wars-conflicts.america_civil_war/3033781.html.

36. Lane, "History of Brigade," SHP, Vol. 9 (1881): p. 495; Clark, *North Carolina Regiments*, Vol. II, pp. 60–61, 670.

37. McDaid, p. 326; C.M. Wilcox, "Defence of Batteries Gregg and Whitworth, and the Evacuation of Petersburg," SHP, Vol. 4, pp. 20–21, 23; "Report of Brig. Gen. James H. Lane," Appomattox Court House, April 10,1865, O.R. Ser. I, Vol. 46, Pt. I, p. 1285.

38. "Report of Brig. Gen. James H. Lane," Appomattox Court House, April 10, 1865, O.R., Ser. I, Vol. 46, Pt. 1, pp. 1285–1286, cited in Jordan, *North Carolina Troops*, Vol. 8, p. 109.

39. *Ibid.*

40. *Ibid.*

41. Lane, "The Branch-Lane Brigade," in Clark, *North Carolina Troops*, Vol. 4, pp. 470–471.

42. *Ibid.*, p. 470.

43. Michael C. Hardy, "America's Civil War: Assault at Petersburg," The History Net, online http://www.history net.com/wars-conflicts. america_civil_war/ 3033781.html.

44. CWSAC #VA089.

45. Hardy, "America's Civil War: Assault at Petersburg," The History Net, online http://www.historynet.com/wars-conflicts.america_civil_war/3033781.html.

46. *Ibid.*

47. General Cadmus Wilcox, "Defence of Battery Gregg and Evacuation of Petersburg," SHP, Vol. 4, pp. 20–21, 23; "Report of Brig. Gen. James H. Lane," Appomattox Court House, April 10, 1865, O.R., Ser. I, Vol. 46, Pt. 1, p. 1285.

48. Hardy, "America's Civil War: Assault at Petersburg," The History Net, online http://www.historynet.com/wars-conflicts.america_civil_war/3033781.html.

49. *Ibid.*

50. "Report of Brig. Gen. James H. Lane," Appomattox Court House, April 10, 1865, O.R., Ser. I, Vol. 46, Pt. I, pp. 1285–1286; Jordan, *North Carolina Troops*, Vol. 8, pp. 109–110.

51. Lane, "History of Brigade," SHP, Vol. 9 (1881): pp. 104–105; "Report of Brig. Gen. James H. Lane," Appomattox Court House, April 10, 1865, O.R., Ser. I, Vol. 46, Pt. I, p. 1285.

52. James H. Lane, "Defence of Fort Gregg," SHP, Vol. 3, pp. 22; Cadmus Wilcox, "Defence of Battery Greg and evac-uation of Petersburg," SHP, Vol. 4, p. 28.

53. "The Defence of Battery Gregg–General Lane's Reply to General Harris," SHP, Vol. 9, p. 106; E.J. Hale to James H. Lane, June 13, 1884, Folder 105, May 20, 1867, Folder 95, James H. Lane Papers, Auburn Univ..

54. "Report of Brig. Gen. James H. Lane," Appomattox Court House, April 10, 1865, O.R., Ser. I, Vol. 46, Pt. I, pp. 1285–1286; Jordan, *North Carolina Troops*, Vol. 8, pp. 109–110.

55. General Cadmus Wilcox, "Defence of Battery Gregg and Evacuation of Petersburg," SHP, Vol. 4 (July 1877): p. 29.

56. Freeman, *Lee's Lieutenants*, Vol. 3, pp. 682–863.

57. Michael C. Hardy, "America's Civil War: Assault at Pe-tersburg," The History Net, online http://www.historynet. com/wars-conflicts.america_civil_war/3033781.html.

58. The number of prisoners lost at Petersburg was calculated from the regimental troop rosters in Manarin and Jordan's series of *North Carolina Troops, 1861–1865: A Roster*, cited in McDaid, footnote 17, p. 385.

59. CWSAC #VA089.

60. Clark, *North Carolina Regiments*, Vol. II, p. 61; E.J. Hale to James H. Lane, June 13, 1834, Folder 105, James H. Lane Papers, Auburn Univ., cited in McDaid, p.327.

61. C.M. Wilcox, "Battery Gregg–Reply to General N.H. Harris," SHP, Vol. 3, p. 170.

62. Clark, *North Carolina Regiments*, Vol. 2, p. 76; Reminiscences of R.M. Gaston, Box 70 Folder 52, Military Collection, North Carolina Department of Archives and History.

63. Jordan, *North Carolina Troops*, 8, p. 111.

64. Little, "Co. C," p. 172.

65. Wilcox, Manuscript Report, pp. 78–79; Freeman, *R.E. Lee*, Vol. 4, pp. 66–71, cited in McDaid pp. 331–332.

66. *Ibid.*

67. CWSAC #VA091.

68. Boatner, pp. 10–11.

69. CWSAC #VA094.

70. Clark, *North Carolina Regiments*, Vol. II, p. 762; Wilcox Manuscript Report, pp. 79–83.

71. "Report of Brig. Gen. James H. Lane," Appomattox Court House, April 10, 1865, O.R., Ser. I, Vol. 46, Pt. 1, pp. 1285–1286; Jordan, *North Carolina Troops*, Vol. 8, p. 110.

72. O. Latrobe to Maj. Gen. C.M. Wilcox, April 6, 1865, O.R., Ser. I, Vol. 41, Pt. III, p. 1386.

73. Wilcox, Manuscript Report, pp. 82–83, cited in McDaid, p. 333.

74. Freeman, *R.E. Lee*, Vol. 4, pp. 114–115.

75. Wilcox, Manuscript Report, p. 83; Clark, *North Carolina Regiments*, Vol. II, pp. 62–63; "Report of Brig. Gen. James H. Lane," Appomattox Court House, April 10, 1865, O.R., Ser. I, Vol. 46, Pt. 1, pp. 1285–1286, cited in Jordan, *North Carolina Troops*, Vol. 8, p. 110.

76. R.E. Lee to President Jefferson Davis, near Appomattox Court House, Va., April 12, 1865, O.R., Ser. I, Vol. 46, Pt. 1, pp. 1265–1267.

77. CWSAC #VA097.

78. R.E. Lee to President Jefferson Davis, near Appomattox Court House, Va., April 12, 1865, O.R., Ser. I, Vol. 46, Pt. 1, p.1267.

79. *Ibid.*

80. George Petrie, *General James Henry Lane 1833–1907* (Auburn, AL: Auburn Printing, 1946), pp. 6–7.

81. Lane, "The Branch-Lane Brigade," in Clark, *North Carolina Regiments*, Vol. 4, p. 471.

82. "Tabular statement of officers and men of the Confederate Army paroled at Appomattox Court House," O.R., Ser. I, Vol. 46, Pt. I, pp. 1277–1279.

83. "List of Officers and Men of Lane's Brigade Present on April 9, 1865 at Appomattox Court House," transcribed by Terri Stout-Stevens, Pfafftown, NC, 1997–1998, online http://www.lib.auburn.edu/archive/find-aid/501/ff85.htm.

84. Petrie, pp. 6–7.

85. Jordan, *North Carolina Troops*, Vol. 8, p. 110.

86. R.A. Brock, *The Appomattox Roster* (New York: Antiquarian Press, Ltd., 1962), pp. 361–364.

87. Harris, *Historical Sketches*, p. 63, cited in McDaid, p. 336.

88. Jordan, *North Carolina Troops*, Vol. 8, p. 207.

Chapter 15

1. Little, "Co. C," p. 172.

2. Frances H. Casstevens, "The Yankee Invasion — Stoneman's Raid," *Yadkin County and the Civil War*, p. 99.

3. *Ibid.*

4. *Ibid.*

5. *Ibid.*, p. 100.

6. *Ibid.*

7. *Ibid.*

8. Boatner, p. 441.

9. Barrett, *The Civil War in North Carolina*, p. 391.

10. *Ibid.*

11. "The Last Battle of the Civil War," http://freepages.history.rootsweb.com/~bellware/; see also Daniel A. Bellware, "The Last Battle. Period. Really," *Civil War Times* (April 2003): pp. 48–56.

12. CWSAC #AL006.

13. CWSAC #TX005; Sanford L. Davis, "Palmito Ranch, The Last Battle of the Civil War: A Gentlemen's Agreement Broken," online http://www.buffalosoldier.net/PalmitoRanch, LastBattleoftheCivilWar.htm.

14. Boatner, p. 838; Missouri Society Military Order of the Stars & Bars, online www.rulen.com/momosb/thompson.htm. copied 5/3/2004

15. Boatner, p. 770.

16. *Ibid.*, p. 894.

17. *Ibid.*, p. 739.

18. Lefler and Newsome, pp. 456–457.

19. Jordan, *North Carolina Troops*, Vol. 8, p. 181.

20. Jackson, *Surry County Soldiers in the Civil War*, p. 134; Norman, *A Portion of My Life*, pp. v–vi.

21. Jordan, *North Carolina Troops*, Vol. 8, pp. 212–213.

22. Artha [Arthur] Bray, Jr. to King Hiram Bray, July 14, 1862, Richmond, VA, in Jackson, *Surry County Soldiers in the Civil War*, p. 267.

23. Lefler and Newsome, p. 456.

24. *Ibid.*

25. Fox, p. 553.

26. Fox, p. 554; Lefler and Newsome, p. 457.

27. Lefler and Newsome, p. 457.

28. McDaid, "'Four years of arduous service': The History of the Branch-Lane Brigade in the Civil War," p. 1.

29. Lane, "The Branch-Lane Brigade," in Clark, *North Carolina Regiments*, Vol. 4, p. 471.

30. *Ibid.*, p. 469.

31. *Ibid.*, p. 471.

32. *Ibid.*, p. 465.

33. *Ibid.*, p. 466.

34. *Ibid.*, p .467.

35. *Ibid.*, p. 468.

36. *Ibid.*

37. Jim Pierce, Sons of the Confederate Veterans Genealogy Committee Chairman, N.C. Division Historian and Genealogists, Drexel, North Carolina, has compiled these numbers from Manarin and Jordan's *North Carolina Troops, 1861–1865: A Roster*; Frederick H. Dyer, *A Compendium of the War of the Rebellion*; Clement A. Evans, ed., *Confederate Military History*; William A. Fox, *Regimental Losses in the American Civil War 1861–1865*; and the National Archives, *Index to Compiled Service Record*, in addition to the *Official Records of the War of the Rebellion*.

38. Jordan, *North Carolina Troops*, Vol. 8, p. 110.

39. "Confederate Pension Records," online www.archives.gov/genealogy/military/civil-war/confederate/pension.html.

40. R. Ernest Dupuy, *Men of West Point* (New York: William Sloane Associates, 1951), pp. 111–112.

41. Boatner, p. 432.

42. *Ibid.*, p. 400.

43. *Ibid.*, p. 631.

44. *Ibid.*, p. 918.

45. *Ibid.*, p. 80.

46. *Ibid.*, p. 471.

47. Special Orders, Numbers 189, August 11, 1864, O. R., Ser. I, Vol. 42, Pt. II, p. 1171.

48. Jordan, *North Carolina Troops*, Vol. 6, pp. 306, 400.

49. *Ibid.*

50. Boatner, p. 471.

51. Jordan, *North Carolina Troops*, Vol. 8, p. 110.

52. *Ibid.*

53. Brock, *The Appomattox Roster*, p. 361.

54. Jordan, *North Carolina Troops,* Vol. 8, p. 112.

55. James H. Lane to Col. Wm. G. Morris, Auburn, Alabama, December 14, 1894, in Lawing, *The Life and Letters of Colonel William G. Morris,* p. 129.

56. *Ibid.*

57. *Ibid.*

58. "Civil War flags," online http://www.nps.gov/gett/gettkidz/flagnc.htm.

59. "Register of Captured Flags, 1861–1865," Records of the Adjutant-General's Office, Record Group No. 94, National Archives, Washington, D.C.

60. Tom Belton, Curator of Military History, North Carolina Museum of History, Raleigh, North Carolina, e-mail dated July 28, 2006. War Department Capture #149, courtesy North Carolina Museum of History, Reference #1914.252.29.

61. Tom Belton, Curator of Military History, North Carolina Museum of History, Raleigh, North Carolina, e-mail dated July 28, 2006; see also O.R., Ser. I, Vol. 36, Pt. I, pp. 348, 1020.

62. Tom Belton, Curator of Military History, North Carolina Museum of History, Raleigh, North Carolina, e-mail dated July 28, 2006. War Department Capture #149, courtesy North Carolina Museum of History, Reference #1914.252.30.

63. Richard Manning, "Unit Designation: 28 Regiment North Carolina Volunteer Infantry, C.S.A.," in Jackson, *Surry County Soldiers in the Civil War,* p. 370.

64. Tom Belton, Curator of Military History, North Carolina Museum of History, Raleigh, North Carolina, e-mail dated July 28, 2006; courtesy North Carolina Museum of History, Reference #1914.252.17.

65. Richard Manning, "Unit Designation: 28 Regiment North Carolina Volunteer Infantry, C.S.A.," in Jackson, *Surry County Soldiers in the Civil War,* p. 370.

66. Little, "Co. C," p. 172.

67. *Ibid.*

68. *Ibid.*

69. Danny Casstevens, "Reams' Station," a CD recording of the title cut, an original, and other Civil War–era songs.

Appendix I

1. Weymouth T. Jordan, Jr., *North Carolina Troops, 1861–1865: A Roster,* Vol. VIII, pp. 99–110.

Appendix II

1. Jordan, *North Carolina Troops,* Vol. VIII, p. 212.

2. List written on an envelope, found in the family papers in possession of Libby Harding Carter of Winston-Salem, and transcribed on August 24, 2004 by Frances H. Casstevens.

3. Written by Flora Harding Robinson, professor at Mars Hill, June 2, 1933.

Appendix III

1. Walter Clark, *Histories of the Several Regiments and Battalions,* Vol. II, pp. 465–484; Jordan, *North Carolina Troops, 1861–1865,* Vol. VIII, pp 110–231; John W. Moore, ed., *Roster of North Carolina Troops in the War Between the States,* Vol. II (Raleigh, NC: Ashe and Gatling, 1882.), pp. 429–471.

Appendix IV

1. Mrs. Hale Houts, "Yadkin Boys," *Journal of North Carolina Genealogy,* Vol. IX, No. 2 (Summer 1963), pp. 1131–1135.

Appendix V

1. "List of Casualties in Lane's Brigade from May 5, 1864 to October 1, 1864," James H. Lane Papers, RG 501, Auburn University Special Collections and Archives Department, Auburn, AL, online www.lib.auburn.edu/archive/find-aid/501.htm.

Appendix VI

1. "Letter, E.J. Hale, Jr. to General Lane, and Reports of Wartime Casualties, May–October 1864," in James H. Lane Papers, RG 501, File 94, Auburn University Special Collections & Archives, Auburn University, Auburn, AL, online http://ww.lib.auburn.edu/archive/find-aid/501/ff94.htm.

Appendix VII

1. Lane, "Twenty-Eighth Regiment," in Clark, *North Carolina Troops,* Vol. II, p. 475. Lane did not state how many officers were killed or wounded in his account.

2. *Ibid.,* p. 478.

3. "Lane's Report, Sept. 8, 1864–Wilderness (May 5, 1864)," in General James H. Lane Papers, Auburn University Archives & Manuscripts Department, Auburn, AL, online www.lib.auburn.edu/archive/find-aid/501/ff78.htm.

4. "Lane's Report, Sept. 16, 1864–Spotsylvania (May 8–20,1864)," in General James H. Lane Papers, Auburn University Archives & Manuscripts Department, Auburn, AL, online www.lib.auburn.edu/archive/find-aid/501/ff78.htm.

5. *Ibid.*

6. *Ibid.*

7. "Lane's Report, Sept. 29, 1864–Campaign (May 21–June 2,1864)," in General James H. Lane Papers, Auburn University Archives & Manuscripts Department, Auburn, AL, online www.lib.auburn.edu/archive/find-aid/501/ff78.htm.

8. *Ibid.*

9. Report of Lt. Col. W.H.A. Speer, "Lane's Brigade Battle Reports, Wilderness Campaign–(May 5–July 27, 1864)," in General James H. Lane Papers, Auburn University Archives & Manuscripts Department, Auburn, AL, online www.lib.auburn.edu/archive/find-aid/501/ff78.htm.

10. *Ibid.*

11. Jordan, *North Carolina Troops,* Vol. VIII, p. 109; Lt. Col. W.H.A. Speer to Cap. E.J. Hale, Jr., July 31, 1864; "Lane's Brigade Battle Reports, July 28, 1864," in James H. Lane Papers, Auburn University Archives & Manuscripts Department, Auburn, AL, online www.lib.auburn.edu/archive/find-aid/501/ff74.htm.

12. Report of Capt. G.G. Holland, Battle Reports–Lane's Brigade–Petersburg (Sept.20–Oct. 1, 1864), in General James H. Lane Papers, Auburn University Archives & Manuscripts Department, Auburn, AL, online www.lib.auburn.edu/archive/find-aid/501/ff78.htm.

Appendix VIII

1. "Officers and Men Captured, 28 NC Rgt. (April 9, 1865)," original list by T.J. Linebarger, Captain, commanding the regiment, transcribed by Terri Stout-Stevens, Pfafftown, 1997, 1998, edited by Marty Olliff, Assistant Archivist, Auburn University, in Papers of General James H. Lane, RG 501, ff86, Auburn University Archives and Manuscript Department, Auburn, AL.

2. R.A. Brock, *The Appomattox Roster* (Richmond, VA: The Society, 1887; rpt. New York: Antiquarian Press, 1962), pp. 358–359, 361–364.

Appendix IX

1. Casstevens, *The Civil War in Yadkin County, North Carolina*, p. 219; Jordan, *North Carolina Troops*, Vol. VIII, p. 212.

2. *Ibid.*

3. Lewis S. Brumfield, ed. *Historical Architecture of Yadkin County, North Carolina* (Winston-Salem, NC: Winston Printing Co., 1987), p. 84.

4. Frances H. Casstevens, "Huntsville," in Frances H. Casstevens, ed. *Heritage of Yadkin County, North Carolina*, Vol. I (Winston-Salem, NC: Hunter Publishing, 1981), pp. 23–26.

5. 1860 Federal Census, Yadkin County North Carolina, enumerated July 24, 1860, house 118, Family 116.

6. William Wade Hinshaw, *Encyclopedia of American Quaker Genealogy*, Vol. I (1936, rpt. Baltimore, MD: Genealogical Publishing, 1969), pp. 971–1000.

Bibliography

Primary Sources

Newspapers

Petersburg [Virginia] *The Daily Register*
Raleigh [North Carolina] *Standard*
Richmond [Virginia] *Examiner*
Salisbury [North Carolina] *Watchman*
Wilmington [North Carolina] *Daily Journal*

Published Public and Official Records

Barnes, Joseph K., Joseph Janvier Woodward, and Charles Smart, eds. *Medical and Surgical History of the War of the Rebellion*. 3 vols. Washington, DC: Government Printing Office, 1870–1888.

Cowles, Calvin D., comp. *Atlas to Accompany the Official Records of the Union and Confederate Armies*. Washington, DC: Government Printing Office, 1891–1895; reprint as *The Official Military Atlas of the Civil War*. New York: Fairfax Press, 1983.

Ordinances and Resolutions Passed by the State Convention of North Carolina, 1861–1862. Raleigh, NC: John W. Syme, 1862.

The War of the Rebellion: A Compilation of the Official Records of the War of Union and Confederate Armies. 70 vols. 130 parts. Washington, DC: United States Government Printing Office, 1880–1905.

Unpublished Diaries, Letters and Manuscripts

Alexander, William D. Diary. Southern Historical Collection, University of North Carolina, Chapel Hill, NC.

Branch, Lawrence O'B. Letter Book. Duke University, Durham, NC.

Clark, Henry T. Governor Henry T. Clark's Papers, North Carolina Department of Archives and History, Raleigh, NC.

Collins, Noah. "Reminiscences of Noah Collins." Isaac Spencer London Collection, North Carolina Department of Archives and History, Raleigh, NC.

Conrad, John Thomas. Papers, North Carolina Department of Archives and History, Raleigh, NC.

Fries–Shaffner Papers. Southern Historical Collection, University of North Carolina, Chapel Hill, NC.

Gibbon, Nicholas Biddle. Diary of Nicholas Biddle Gibbon, 28th Regt. North Carolina Volunteers, 1861–1863. University of North Carolina at Charlotte, NC.

Glenn, Leonidas C. Collection. Southern Historical Collection, University of North Carolina at Chapel Hill, NC.

Harding, Greenberry. Family Papers. Libby Harding Carter, Winston-Salem, NC.

Harding, Samuel Speer, and Greenberry Harding. Letters in Harding Family Papers, Frances H. Casstevens, Yadkinville, NC.

Johnston, George Burgwin, Diary. North Carolina Department of Archives and History, Raleigh, NC.

Kennedy, Francis M. Diary. Southern Historical Collection, University of North Carolina, Chapel Hill, NC.

Kinyoun Genealogical Records. Notebook of Dr. John Hendricks Kinyoun, Captain Company F, 28th North Carolina Infantry Regiment, 1861–1862. Courtesy of Joseph K. Houts, Jr., St. Joseph, MO.

Kinyoun, John Hendricks Papers. Duke University, Durham, NC.

Lane, James H. "Incidents of Individual Gallantry." Military Collection, North Carolina Department of Archives and History, Raleigh, NC.

_____. James H. Lane Papers, Auburn University Archives, Auburn, AL.

Lee, Robert E. Headquarters Collection. Cadmus M. Wilcox Manuscript Report for the 1864-65 Campaign. Virginia Historical Society, Richmond, VA.

London, Isaac Spencer, Collection. North Carolina Department of Archives and History, Raleigh, NC.

McCurdy, Caleb Shrive. Caleb Shrive McCurdy Papers, 1852–1866. Duke University, Durham, NC.

Profitt, Andrew J. Profitt Family Papers. Southern Historical Collection, University of North Carolina at Chapel Hill, Chapel Hill, NC.

Vance, Zebulon B., Papers. North Carolina Department of Archives and History, Raleigh, NC.

Wilcox, Cadmus M. Manuscript Report of 1864–1865 Campaign. Robert E. Lee Headquarters Collection, Virginia Historical Society, Richmond, VA.

Williams–Womble Papers. North Carolina Department of Archives and History, Raleigh, NC.

Published Diaries and Letters

Edmondston, Catherine D. *Journal of a Secesh Lady*. Beth G. Crabtree and James W. Patton, eds. Raleigh, NC: Department of Archives and History, 1979.

Graham, James A. *The James A. Graham Papers, 1861–1864*. H.M. Wagstaff, ed. Chapel Hill, NC: University of North Carolina Press, 1928.

Harding, Samuel Speer. Letter from Samuel Speer Harding to Father, and letter from T.G. Scott to William Harding, in Frances H. Casstevens, *The Civil War and Yadkin County, North Carolina*. Jefferson, NC: McFarland, 1997.

Holcomb Brothers' Letters, in Frances H. Casstevens, *Heritage of Yadkin County, North Carolina*. Winston-Salem, NC: Hunter Publishing, 1981.

Morris, William G. *The Life and Letters of Colonel William G. Morris (1825–1918)*. Hazel Morris Ritch Lawing, transcriber and compiler. Privately published typescript, 1935–1937.

Norman, William M. *A Portion of My Life*. Winston-Salem, NC: John F. Blair, 1959.

Speer, William H. Asbury. The Letters of Colonel William H. Asbury Speer, in Allen Paul Speer, *Voices from Cemetery Hill*. Johnson City, TN: Overmountain Press, 1997.

Welch, Spencer Glasgow. *A Confederate Surgeon's Letters to His Wife*. New York: Neale Publishing, 1911.

Memoirs

Buel, Robert U., and Clarence C. Johnson, eds. *Battles and Leaders of the Civil War*. 4 vols. 1887, rpt. Secaucus, NJ: Castle, 1982.

Grant, U.S. *Personal Memoirs of U.S. Grant*. 2 vols. New York: Charles L. Webster, 1892.

Harris, James Sidney. *Historical Sketches of the Seventh Regiment North Carolina Troops*. Mooresville, NC: Mooresville Printing, 1893.

Hill, D.H., Jr. "North Carolina." In Clement A. Evans, ed. *A Confederate Military History*. 12 vols. Atlanta, GA: Confederate Publishing, 1899.

Long, A.L., ed. *Memoirs of Robert E. Lee: His Military and Personal History Embracing a Large Amount of Information Hitherto Unpublished*. New York: J.M. Stoddart, 1886.

Sorrell, G. Moxley. *Recollections of a Confederate Staff Officer*. 1905, rpt. Nashville: Mclowat-Mercer Press, 1958.

Unpublished Public Records

"Register of Captured Flags, 1861–1865." Records of the Adjutant-General's Office, Record Group No. 94, National Archives, Washington, DC.

Secondary Sources

Books

Ashe, Samuel A'Court. *History of North Carolina*, 2 vols. Raleigh, NC: Edwards and Broughton Printing Co., 1925; reprinted Spartanburg, SC: Reprint Co., 1971.

Barrett, John G. *The Civil War in North Carolina*. Chapel Hill, NC: The University of North Carolina Press, 1963.

Bigelow, John. *The Campaign of Chancellorsville*. New Haven, CT: Yale University Press, 1910.

Boatner, Mark M., III. *The Civil War Dictionary*, rev. ed. New York: Vintage Books, 1991.

Bowman, John S., ed. *Who Was Who in the Civil War*. North Dighton, MA: J.G. Press, World Publications, 1998, reprint 2002.

Brock, R.A. *The Appomattox Roster*. Richmond, VA: The Society, 1887; rpt. New York: Antiquarian Press, 1962.

Brock, R.A., and Douglas Southall Freeman. *Southern Historical Society Papers*, 52 vols. Richmond, VA: Virginia Historical Society, 1876–1910.

Caldwell, James Fitz James. *The History of a Brigade of South Carolinians*. Philadelphia, PA: King & Baird Printers, 1866.

Casstevens, Frances H. *The Civil War and Yadkin County, North Carolina*. Jefferson, NC: McFarland, 1997.

_____. *Clingman's Brigade in the Confederacy, 1862–1865*. Jefferson, NC: McFarland, 2002.

_____. *The Heritage of Yadkin County, North Carolina*. Vol. 1. Winston-Salem, NC: Hunter Publishing, 1981.

Civil War Society. *Encyclopedia of the Civil War*. New York: Wings Books, 1997.

Clark, Walter, ed. *Histories of the Several Regiments and Battalions in the Great War, 1861–1865, Written by Members of the Respective Commands*. 5 vols. Goldsboro, NC: Nash Brothers, 1901.

Dedmondt, Glenn. *The Flags of Civil War North Carolina*. Gretna, LA: Pelican, 2003.

DePriest, Virginia Greene. *Cleveland and Rutherford Counties, N.C., Confederate Soldiers and Pension Rolls 1861–1865*. Shelby, NC: Privately published, 1986.

Dictionary of American Biography. 20 vols. New York: Scribner's, 1928.

Dupuy, R. Ernest, and Trevor N. Dupuy. *Compact History of the Civil War*. New York: Hawthorn Books, 1960.

Evans, Clement. *A History of the Southern Confederacy*. New York: The MacMillan Co., 1982.

Fisher, Garry Fisher. *Rebel Cornbread and Yankee Coffee: Authentic Civil War Cooking and Camaraderie*. Birmingham, AL: Crane Hill Publishers, 2001.

Fox, William F. *Regimental Losses in the America Civil War*. 1898; reprint Dayton, OH: Morningside Bookshop, 1985.

Freeman, Douglas Southall. *Lee's Dispatches*. New York: Putnam's, 1957.

_____. *Lee's Lieutenants: A Study in Command*. 3 vols. New York: Scribner's, 1943–1944.

_____. *R.E. Lee: A Biography*. 4 vols. New York: Scribner's, 1937–1940.

Hahn, George W., ed. *The Catawba Soldier of the Civil War*. Hickory, NC: Clay Printing, 1911.

Hardy, Michael C. *The Battle of Hanover Court House*. Jefferson, NC: McFarland, 2006.

Hinshaw, William Wade. *Encyclopedia of American Quaker Genealogy*, 7 vols. 1936, rpt. Baltimore, MD: Genealogical Publishing, 1969.

Hoots, Carl C., comp. *Cemeteries of Yadkin County, North Carolina*. Spartanburg, SC: Reprint Co., 1985.

Horn, John. *The Destruction of the Weldon Railroad: Deep Bottom, Globe Tavern, and Reams' Station, August 14–25, 1864.* Lynchburg, VA: H.E. Howard, 1991.

Houts, Joseph Kinyoun, Jr. *A Darkness Ablaze.* St. Joseph, MO: Platte Purchase Publishers, 2005.

Jackson, Hester Bartlett, ed. *Surry County Soldiers in the Civil War.* Charlotte, NC: Delmar Printing, 1992.

Lefler, Hugh T., and Albert Ray Newsome. *North Carolina: The History of a Southern State.* 3rd. ed. Chapel Hill, NC: University of North Carolina Press, 1973.

Livermore, Thomas L. *Numbers and Losses in the Civil War in America 1861–65* Boston: Houghton Mifflin, 1901.

Longacre, Edward G. *The Cavalry at Gettysburg: A Tactical Study of Mounted Operations during the Civil War's Pivotal Campaign, 9 June–14 July, 1863.* Rutherford, NJ: Associated University Presses, 1986.

Lowry, Thomas P. *The Story the Soldiers Wouldn't Tell: Sex in the Civil War.* Mechanicsburg, PA: Stackpole Books, 1994.

Macdonald, John. *Great Battles of the Civil War.* New York: Macmillan, 1988.

Manarin, Louis H., and Weymouth T. Jordan, Jr., comp. *North Carolina Troops, 1861–1865: A Roster.* Raleigh, NC: North Carolina Department of Archives and History, 1966–1998.

Miller, Francis Trevelyan, and Robert S. Lanier. *The Photographic History of the Civil War.* 10 vols. 1911; rpt. New York: Castle Books, 1975.

Moore, John W., ed. *Roster of North Carolina Troops in the War Between the States.* 4 vols. Raleigh, NC: Ashe and Gatling, 1882.

O'Daniel, Julia Harris, and Laura Conrad Patton. *Kinfolk of Jacob Conrad.* Privately printed, 1970.

Petrie, George. *General James Henry Lane 1833–1907.* Auburn, AL: Auburn Printing, 1946.

Pleasants, Henry, Jr., and George H. Straley. *Inferno at Petersburg.* Philadelphia, PA: Chilton, 1961.

Rawls, Walton, ed. *Great Civil War Heroes and Their Battles.* New York: Abbeville Press, 1985.

Sommers, Richard J. *Richmond Redeemed.* New York: Doubleday, 1981.

Speer, Allen Paul. *Voices from Cemetery Hill.* Johnson City, TN: Overmountain Press, 1997.

Steere, Edward. *The Wilderness Campaign.* New York: Bonanza Books, 1960.

Tolbert, Noble J., ed. *The Papers of John Willis Ellis,* 2 vols. Raleigh, NC: North Carolina Department of Archives and History, 1964.

Webb, Alexander S. *The Peninsula.* New York: Scribner's, 1881.

Vandiver, Frank. *Mighty Stonewall.* New York: McGraw-Hill, 1957.

Journal Articles

Bellware, Daniel A. "The Last Battle. Period. Really." *Civil War Times,* Vol. 42, No. 1 (April 2003): pp. 48–56.

Bonham, Milledge Louis, ed. "A Little More Light on Gettysburg." *Mississippi Valley Historical Review,* Vol. 24 (1983).

Harris, N.H. "Defence of Battery Gregg." *Southern Historical Society Papers,* Vol. 8, Nos. 6 & 87 (June–July, 1880): pp. 475–488.

Houts, Mrs. Hale. "Yadkin Boys." *Journal of North Carolina Genealogy,* Vol. 9, No. 2 (Summer 1963): pp. 1131–1135.

Lane, James H. "History of Lane's North Carolina Brigade." *Southern Historical Society Papers,* Vol. 7 (1879): pp. 513–522; Vol. 8 (1880): pp. 1–8, 67–75, 97–104, 145–154, 193–202, 241–248, 396–403, 489–496; Vol. 9 (1881): pp. 29–35, 71–129, 145–156, 241–246, 353–361, 489–496.

_____. "The Defence of Battery Gregg — General Lane's Reply to General Harris." *Southern Historical Society Papers,* Vol. 9 (1881): pp. 102–107.

Longacre, Edward G. "The Blackest of All Days." *Civil War Times Illustrated* (March 1986), pp. 13–19.

Wilcox, C.M. "Battery Gregg — Reply to General N. H. Harris," *Southern Historical Society Papers,* Vol. 9 (1881): pp. 168–178.

Theses

McDaid, William Kelsey. "'Four Years of Arduous Service': The History of the Branch–Lane Brigade in the Civil War." Ph.D. dissertation, Michigan State University, 1987.

Phillips, Kenneth E. "James Henry Lane and the War for Southern Independence." M.A. Thesis, Auburn University, 1982.

Microfilm

"Index to Moore's Roster of North Carolina Troops." 15 reels. Raleigh, NC: Mann Film Laboratories, 1958.

Primary Online Sources

Civil War Sites Advisory Commission Report on the Nation's Civil War Battlefields (CWSAC), online www.cr.nps.gov/hps/abpp/battles/tvii.htm.

Index